Advanced German Course

Revised Edition

A. RUSSON and L. J. RUSSON M.A.

LONGMAN

By A. RUSSON and L. J. RUSSON
Simpler German Course for First Examinations
A First German Reader
A Second German Reader

By L. J. RUSSON
Complete German Course for First Examinations

LONGMAN GROUP LIMITED
Longman House,
Burnt Mill, Harlow, Essex CM20 2JE, England
and Associated Companies throughout the World.

First published 1965
Second edition 1978
Sixth impression 1986

ISBN 0 582 35245 2

Produced by Longman Group (FE) Ltd
Printed in Hong Kong

Contents

Foreword

This volume is designed to meet the needs of those who are preparing for the German papers set by the various University Boards at A and S level and by Universities for their Entrance and Scholarship candidates.

The material offered here has been tried out on many generations of pupils who have unwittingly contributed a great deal to the book. It ranges in difficulty from work that can be tackled, with the help given, by the pupil who has just taken O level in German to work that will extend the pupil who is just about to attempt a University Scholarship Examination.

Part One (Grammar and Syntax) is primarily meant to give help with the syntactical, semantic and stylistic problems that arise in translating from English into German. It also includes, however, a good deal of idiomatic material, as well as the sort of information that will help a student to grasp the meaning and function of prefixes and suffixes and thus enable him to enlarge considerably his vocabulary. It further contains all the basic grammar that those beginning to specialise have sometimes forgotten.

The sentences and other exercises in Part Two will be found to give the student ample opportunity to practise and consolidate the basic grammatical constructions given in Part One.

Part Three consists of English passages, graded in difficulty and length, for translation into German. The passages chosen come mainly from twentieth-century authors and include a number that have been set by the various Boards at A and S level and by University Scholarship examiners. Prose composition is a difficult skill and we have been concerned to give considerable help with the earlier passages, since those beginning to specialise in German will probably be translating 'undoctored' English for the first time. In the earlier passages numerous references are given to Part One, and we have not hesitated on occasion to suggest a re-phrasing of the original English when this will lead to a more idiomatic German rendering. Later on the principle adopted is that of only giving anything more than very occasional help in every alternative passage.

Part Four (Free Composition) offers a wide variety of subjects for free composition ranging from comparatively simple narrative to philosophical themes. It has proved impracticable in a work of this kind to give help in the way of specific vocabularies.

The German prose passages for translation in Part Five are drawn mainly from twentieth-century authors and cover a wide range of subjects. They have been graded according to length and difficulty.

Part Six consists of German prose passages for comment and appreciation. We have deliberately refrained from setting questions on the texts. Teachers vary considerably in their approach to 'practical criticism' and might well feel irked by the presence of 'leading' or 'misleading' questions. We have chosen instead to offer our own literary analyses of two passages. We hope that, despite all their shortcomings, they will at least give some idea of what can reasonably be expected of candidates attempting questions of this type. The passages selected for this part have been grouped according to the subject matter, and within each group according to their length. The names of the authors have been withheld. This is the practice in many examinations and it has the advantage, in our experience, of compelling the student to study the text more closely and of not tempting him to seek dangerous short cuts.

Quite a number of passages in Part Five lend themselves also to comment and appreciation and all those in Part Six to unseen translation.

Practice varies from Examination Board to Examination Board and from University to University in the matter of setting verse passages for translation. We realise that no completely adequate translation of poetry into another tongue is possible, but provided we are under no illusion as to what we are doing this need not be a fruitless exercise. Some indeed would consider translation of verse an important ancillary test since one meets in verse syntax and vocabulary not encountered in prose. However, those teachers who disapprove of this practice could equally well use most of the poems and verse passages given in Part Seven for comment and appreciation.

The verse passages for comment and appreciation offered in Part Eight are preceded by a brief account of German versification and by two commentaries of our own. In this section, too, we have omitted the names of the poets.

The German-English vocabulary contains (i) the words occurring in Part Five (Prose Passages for Translation) and in Part Seven (Verse Passages for Translation) and (ii) the more difficult German words occurring in Part One (Grammar and Syntax) that are not translated. No *ad hoc* vocabulary has been compiled for Parts Six and Eight.

The English-German vocabulary contains (i) the words occurring in Part Two that are not given in the corresponding sections of the Grammar and Syntax; (ii) the words occurring in the first ninety English prose passages (Part Three). It must however be realised that very often several translations will be offered for a given English word, simply because the same 'word' occurring in different contexts may well have different meanings. In such cases a dictionary or dictionaries should be consulted (see Select Bibliography, p. xiii). For the last thirty English prose passages dictionaries must be consulted. How to use a dictionary sensibly has to be learnt like other things; and some opportunity to acquire this somewhat difficult art should, we think, be given to those specialising in languages at school.

It should perhaps be stressed that this course is primarily concerned with the literary and not with the colloquial language; and the examples given in Part One are drawn mainly from the prose writings of modern authors of repute. We have, however, made occasional reference to colloquial usage, and we have given a certain number of conversational passages for translation into German.

We take this opportunity to thank Mr. K. B. Kettle for his helpful criticism, and we owe a special debt of gratitude to Mr. J. R. Surry who has given us much valuable help with several parts of this volume, particularly with Part One.

Many friends here and in Germany have helped us to prepare a Key of suggested translations of the English Prose Passages, together with a number of variants. The Key is obtainable from the publishers. The Key also contains the names of the authors of the passages of prose and verse for comment and appreciation. A separate list of these is also obtainable from the publishers.

A.R.

L.J.R.

Winchester, 1964

Foreword to the Second Edition

The major change in the second edition of the *Advanced German Course* is the deletion of Part Seven of the first edition, making possible the addition of a new section to Part Five. If practice in translating German verse into English is required there is still plenty of material for this given in the new Part Seven (formerly Part Eight).

The new section of Part Five consists for the most part of non-literary passages and includes a wide variety of registers. Most of the new extracts are culled from newspapers and deal with topical, but by no means ephemeral, problems. They will also serve as useful starting-points for discussion and as a basis for essay-writing.

In Part Four fifteen more essay subjects have been added to Section VI, many of these linking up with the new passages now included in Part Five.

The German-English vocabulary has been re-written. In order to make a meaningful enlargement of Part Five possible, words whose meaning can easily be guessed, as well as those words that can reasonably be considered basic, have been omitted; and the more difficult new words occurring in the new extracts have been incorporated.

Apart from these changes, and in order to keep down costs as much as possible, passages 101–120 of Part Three, passages 41–45 of Part Five and passages 41–46 of Part Six of the first edition have also been omitted in this new edition.

We have again much profited from the advice given us by Mr. J. R. Surry, as well as from that given us by Mrs. Gisela Beckett, for which we offer them both our grateful thanks.

A.R.

L.J.R.

Chandler's Ford, 1977

Acknowledgments

We are grateful to the following for permission to reproduce copyright material:

George Allen & Unwin Ltd. for material from *The Magic Flute* by G. Lowes Dickinson, and *In Praise of Idleness* by Bertrand Russell; George Allen & Unwin Ltd. and Simon and Schuster Inc. for material from *History of Western Philosophy* by Bertrand Russell; Verlag der Arche-Peter Schifferli for 'Dann' by Gottfried Benn; Edward Arnold (Publishers) Ltd. and Harcourt Brace & World Inc. for material from *A Passage to India* by E. M. Forster; Edward Arnold (Publishers) Ltd. and Alfred A. Knopf Inc. for material from *The Longest Journey* by E. M. Forster; Atlantis Verlag for material from *Goethe* by Emil Staiger; C. H. Beck'sche Verlagsbuchhandlung for material from *Stilkunst* by Ludwig Reiners, *Kultur-geschichte der Neuzeit* by Egon Friedell, and *Aus meiner Kindheit und Jugendzeit* by Albert Schweitzer; Ernest Benn Ltd. for material from *The Evolution of Modern Germany* by W. H. Dawson; Ernest Benn Ltd. and The Macmillan Company of New York for material from *Aims of Education* by A. N. Whitehead; Biederstein Verlag, München, for material from *Die Strudlhofstiege* by Heimito von Doderer; The Bodley Head Ltd. for material from *Why Was I Killed?* by Rex Warner; Bowes & Bowes Publishers Ltd. and Farrar, Straus & Company Inc. for material from *The Disinherited Mind* by Erich Heller; F. A. Brockhaus, Wiesbaden, for material from *Die deutsche Katastrophe* by Friedrich Meinecke; Cambridge University Press for material from *Goethe and the Greeks* by H. Trevelyan; Cambridge University Press and Her Majesty's Stationery Office for material from *A Short History of Germany* 1815–1945 by E. G. Passant; Jonathan Cape Ltd. for material from *The Thirty Years War* by C. V. Wedgwood; Jonathan Cape Ltd. and Alfred A. Knopf Inc. for material from *The Death of the Heart* by Elizabeth Bowen; Chatto and Windus Ltd. and Harper & Row, Publishers, for material from *On the Margin* by Aldous Huxley; Chatto and Windus Ltd. and The Viking Press Inc. for material from *Under the Net* by Iris Murdoch; the author's agents and Jonathan Cape Ltd. for material from *The Window* by Alasdair Clayre; Claassen Verlag, Hamburg, for material from *Marie Curie* by Elizabeth Langgässer, and for 'Die Ewigkeit' and 'Die Wolke' from *Gedichte* (1947) by Marie Luise Kaschnitz; The Clarendon Press for material from *A Study of Goethe* by Barker Fairley; Miss D. E. Collins, Cassell & Co. Ltd. and Dodd, Mead & Company for material from 'The Sins of Prince Saradine' from *The Innocence of Father Brown* by G. K. Chesterton; Constable & Co. for material from *Peacemaking 1919* by Harold Nicolson; Constable & Co. Ltd. and Charles Scribner's Sons for material from *The Last Puritan* by George Santayana, Copyright 1936 Charles Scribner's Sons; renewal copyright © 1964 Old Colony Trust Co. and *Soliloquies in England* by George Santayana; the Trustees of the Joseph Conrad Estate and J. M. Dent & Sons Ltd. for material from *Lord Jim*, *Nostromo* and *The Shadow Line* by Joseph Conrad; Curtis Brown Ltd. on behalf of the Estate of Joyce Cary and Harper & Row, Publishers, for material from *The Horse's Mouth* by Joyce Cary; Curtis Brown Ltd. on behalf of the Estate of Kenneth Grahame and Dodd, Mead & Company for material from *The Golden Age* from *The Kenneth Grahame Book*; the author's agents and Victor Gollancz Ltd. for material from *Elders and Betters* by I. Compton Burnett; Verlag Kurt Desch, München, for material from *Wälder und Menschen* by Ernst Wiechert; Eugen Diederichs Verlag for 'Am Morgen' by Karl Bröger, and 'Lokomotive' by Gerrit Engelke; Franz Ehrenwirth Verlag KG, München, for material from *Die Verfemte* by Gertrud von le Fort © 1960 by Franz Ehrenwirth Verlag KG; Verlag Heinrich Ellermann, München, for 'Mit den fahrenden Schiffen' from *Gesammelte Gedichte* by Georg Heym; the author for material from *Franz Kafka*, and *Die Literatur-Revolution und die moderne Gesellschaft* by Professor Dr. Wilhelm Emrich; Eyre & Spottiswoode (Publishers) Ltd. and The Viking Press Inc. for material from *The Riders in the Chariot* by Patrick White; Faber & Faber Ltd. and Putnam's & Coward-McCann for material from *Lord of the Flies* by William Golding; S. Fischer Verlag for material from *Die Schnecke* by Manfred Hausmann from *Einer muss wachen*, published in Gesammelte Schriften in Einzelausgaben, Copyright 1950 by S. Fischer Verlag, Frankfurt am Main; *Königliche Hoheit* and *Lotte in Weimar* by Thomas Mann. Copyright 1909 by S. Fischer Verlag, Berlin, and 1939 by Bermann-Fischer Verlag AB, Stockholm, respectively; *Die Welt von gestern* by Stefan Zweig, Copyright 1944 by Bermann-Fischer Verlag AB, Stockholm; *Der veruntreute Himmel* by Franz Werfel, Copyright 1939 by Alma Mahler-Werfel; 'Der Mensch ist stumm' from *Gedichte aus dreissig*

Jahren by Franz Werfel, Copyright 1939 by Bermann-Fischer Verlag A-B, Stockholm; 'Über einer Todesnachricht' from *Aber im Winde das Wort* by Albrecht Goes, Copyright G. B. Fischer und Co. Frankfurt am Main 1963; 'Spät im Jahre' from *Gedichte* by Albrecht Goes, Copyright 1950 by S. Fischer Verlag GmbH, Frankfurt am Main; *Auf der Galerie* by Franz Kafka, *Herr und Hund, Buddenbrooks*, and *Mario und der Zauberer* by Thomas Mann, *Salwàre oder die Magdalena von Bozen* by Carl Zuckmayer, and *Triumph und Tragik des Erasmus von Rotterdam* by Stefan Zweig; Francke Verlag for material from *Der Dichter und die Zeit* by Fritz Strich; the author for material from *Germany* by G. P. Gooch; the Trustees to the Granville-Barker Estates for material by Harley Granville-Barker; the author's agents, William Heinemann Ltd. and The Viking Press, Inc. for material from *The Quiet American* by Graham Greene, Copyright © 1955 by Graham Greene; Hamish Hamilton Ltd. for material from *The Habsburg Monarchy* by A. J. P. Taylor; Hamish Hamilton and Alfred A. Knopf Inc. for material from *Bismarck* by A. J. P. Taylor; Carl Hanser Verlag, München, for material from *Am Pass Nascondo* by Gerd Gaiser (1960), and *Grüne Zweige* by Friedrich Georg Jünger (1951); the Trustees of the Hardy Estate and Macmillan & Co. Ltd. for material from *The Return of the Native* by Thomas Hardy; Harvard University Press for material from *Three Philosophical Poets: Goethe's Faust* by George Santayana; Jakob Hegner Verlag, Köln, for material from *Der Gouverneur* by Edzard Schaper; William Heinemann Ltd. and Charles Scribner's Sons for material from *The Forsyte Saga* by John Galsworthy, and *Father and Son* by Edmund Gosse, Copyright 1907 Charles Scribner's Sons, renewal copyright 1935 Philip Gosse; the Executors of the Ernest Hemingway Estate and Charles Scribner's Sons for material from Ernest Hemingway's *A Farewell to Arms*, Copyright 1929 Charles Scribner's Sons, renewal copyright 1957 Ernest Hemingway, and *For Whom the Bell Tolls*, Copyright 1940 Ernest Hemingway; Verlag Herder, Freiburg, for material from *Liebe zum deutschen Gedicht* and *Ehrfurcht vor dem deutschen Wort* by Wilhelm Schneider; Hoffman & Campe Verlag for 'An den antiken Vers' and 'Notturno' from *Dokumente des Herzens* by Josef Weinheber; Insel-Verlag for material from *Geheimnisse des reifen Lebens* by Hans Carossa and *Aufzeichnungen des Malte Laurids Brigge* by Rainer Maria Rilke, and for 'Sturmlied' by Ricarda Huch from *Liebesgedichte*, 'Corrida', 'Das Karussell' and 'Abschied' from *Sämtliche Werke* by Rainer Maria Rilke, 'Reiselied', 'Ballade des äusseren Lebens', 'Weltgeheimnis' and 'Was ist die Welt?' by Hugo von Hofmannsthal, and 'Wo sind nun Rosen' by Hans Carossa; the author's agents for material from *Washington Square* by Henry James; the author's agents and Paul R. Reynolds Inc. for material from *A Little Tour of France*, Copyright 1885 by Henry James; the author for material from *Darmstädter Rede* by Marie Luise Kaschnitz; Verlag Kiepenheuer & Witsch, Köln, for material from *Und sagte kein einziges Wort* by Heinrich Böll; Ernst Klett Verlag, Stuttgart, for material from *Auf den Marmorklippen* by Ernst Jünger, and 'Mit einem Strauss aus dem botanischen Garten' by Rudolf Borchardt from *Gesammelte Werke, Gedichte* (1957); Vittorio Klostermann, Frankfurt am Main, for 'Wintermorgen' by F. G. Jünger and for material from *Das abenteuerliche Herz* by Ernst Jünger and *Perfektion der Technik* by F. G. Jünger; Kosel-Verlag, München, for 'Traum vom Fliegen' and 'Nächtliche Stunde' by Karl Kraus, and 'Weltende' by Else Lasker-Schüler; Verlag Helmut Kossodo for material from *Der Gehülfe* by Robert Walser; Verlag Helmut Küpper for 'Fenster wo ich einst mit dir'; the Executors of the T. E. Lawrence Estate, Jonathan Cape Ltd. and Doubleday & Co. Inc. for material from *Seven Pillars of Wisdom* by T. E. Lawrence, Copyright 1926, 1935 by Doubleday & Co. Inc.; the author's agents and Thomas Y. Crowell Co. for material from *The Habit of Loving* by Doris Lessing; Lothar Blanvalet Verlag for 'Die Wächter' from *Moabiter Sonette* by Albrecht Haushofer; Hermann Luchterhànd Verlag GmbH for 'Heringe' by Günter Grass and for material from *Die Blechtrommel* by Günter Grass; Macdonald & Co. (Publishers) Ltd. for material from *Rich Relatives* by Sir Compton Mackenzie; the owners of the copyright of the late George Moore for material from *Esther Waters* by George Moore; Otto Müller Verlag for 'Vorstadt im Föhn' by Georg Trakl from *Die Dichtungen*; the Executors of the L. H. Myers' Estate, Jonathan Cape Ltd. and Harcourt, Brace & World Inc. for material from *The Near and the Far* by L. H. Myers; Mr. Nigel Nicolson for material from *All Passion Spent* by V. Sackville-West; Nymphenburger Verlagshandlung, München, for material from 'Der Eisläufer' by Georg Britting from *Gesamtwerk, Band V, Erzählungen 1941–1960*, 'Der Hahn' by Georg Britting from *Gesamtwerk, Gedichte 1919–1939*, and 'Die Ratten' by Georg Britting from *Der unverstörte*

viii

Select Bibliography

Dictionaries

SPRINGER, O., *Langenscheidt's Encyclopaedic Dictionary. Part I, English-German*. Berlin-Schöneberg, Langenscheidt, and London, Methuen. 2 vols., 1962–3. *Part II*, German-English, 2 vols. 1975.

JONES, T., *Harrap's Standard German and English Dictionary. Part I, German-English*. London, Harrap. Vol. 1, 1964. Vol. 2, 1967. Vol. 3, 1974.
Cassell. 12th ed. 1968.

MOTEKAT, E. AND BOURKE, J., *Brockhaus Illustrated Dictionary, German-English, English-German*. London, Pitman and Wiesbaden. 1961.

DER SPRACH-BROCKHAUS, *Deutsches Bildwörterbuch für jedermann*. Wiesbaden, 7th rev. ed. 1956.

DUDEN *Stilwörterbuch der deutschen Sprache*. Mannheim, Bibliographisches Institut. 6th ed. 1971.

DUDEN *Rechtschreibung*. Mannheim, Bibliographisches Institut. 16th ed. 1967.

FARRELL, R. B., *A Dictionary of German Synonyms*. Cambridge. Corrected reprint 1955, paperback ed. 1963.

EGGELING, H. F., *A Dictionary of Modern German Prose Usage*. Oxford. 1961.

Grammars

STOPP, F. J., *A Manual of Modern German*. London, University Tutorial Press. 2nd ed. 1960.

DUDEN, *Die Grammatik der deutschen Gegenwartssprache*. Mannheim, Bibliographisches Institut. 2nd ed. 1966.

KOLISKO, G. AND YUILL, W. E., *Practice in German Prose*, London, Macmillan. 1959.

Versification

ATKINSON, H. G., *A History of German Versification*. London, Methuen. 1923.

KAYSER, W., *Kleine deutsche Versschule*. München, Lehnen Verlag. 4th ed. 1954.

PAUL, O. AND GLIER, I., *Deutsche Metrik*. München, Max Huebner Verlag. 1961.

Literary Criticism

KAYSER, W., *Das sprachliche Kunstwerk*. Bern, A Francke. 6th rev. ed. 1960.

WELLEK, R. AND WARREN, A., *Theory of Literature*. London, Cape. 1963. 3rd (paperback) ed. Peregrine. 1963.

PRAWER, S. S., *German Lyric Poetry*. London, Routledge and Kegan Paul. 1952.

GURREY, P., *The Appreciation of Poetry*. Oxford. 1935.

REEVES, J., *The Critical Sense*. London, Heinemann. 1956.

SCHNEIDER, W., *Stilistische deutsche Grammatik*. Freiburg, Herder. 1959.

Abbreviations and Signs Used

A	accusative; governs accusative
AD	governs accusative and dative
adj.	adjective
adv.	adverb
AG	governs accusative and genitive
cf.	compare
D	dative; governs dative
e.g.	for example
etc.	etcetera
F.	familiar
f.	feminine
fig.	figurative meaning
G	genitive; governs genitive
i.e.	that is
imp.	impersonal
intr.	intransitive
irr.	irregular verb
Lit.	literary
m.	masculine
N	nominative
n.	neuter
o.s.	oneself
pl.	plural
s.	strong verb
s.b.	somebody
sing.	singular
s.th.	something
tr.	transitive
*	conjugated with *sein*
(*)	conjugated with *sein* or *haben* according to the meaning
⁄	indicates that the syllable so marked is stressed
×	indicates that the syllable so marked is unstressed
-	inserted between the prefix and verb indicates that the verb is separable

Part One

Grammar and syntax

1 Word Order in Main Clauses

(a) In the **main clause** (statements) the finite verb is, with very few exceptions (see (d), (e) and (f) below), always the **second** idea. Unless there are other considerations such as special emphasis, emotional intensity, etc., the past participle, the infinitive(s), the separable verbal prefix (but see 6(g)ii) and the verbal complement will come last.

1	2			
Er	hat	ihr	einige Zeit zum Besinnen	gelassen.
Wir	werden	also	zusammen	arbeiten.
Du	kannst	sie	eine halbe Stunde draußen	spazierenfahren.
Ich	will	sie	alle um mich	haben.
Sie	marschieren	oft	an meinem Fenster	vorbei.
Sie	hatten	ihn	eine Woche lang	zu Besuch.

(b) The finite verb may be preceded by any **one** of the following: the subject (noun, pronoun or noun clause or phrase), the introductory *es*, the object (noun, pronoun (except *es*) or noun clause or phrase), an adverb or adverbial phrase or adverbial clause, a present or past participle or participial phrase, an infinitive, a predicative adjective or a separable verbal prefix.

It does not, however, follow that any word order will do, provided the finite verb is the second idea. The placing of any word(s) except the noun or pronoun subject before the verb tends to give it (or them) special emphasis or sometimes emotional intensity, which in every case must be justified by the context.

The noun or pronoun subject preceding the verb normally carries no particular stress. If it is desired to give the noun subject more weight a position last in the clause is sometimes a very effective way of doing this.

1	2			
Der Zug	kam	pünktlich	in Hannover	an.
Daß er da ist,	muß	ein Geheimnis		bleiben.
So etwas zu behaupten	ist			unerhört.
Es	ist	niemand		da.

1	2			
Meinen Bruder	habe	ich	dort	getroffen.
Den	kenne	ich		nicht.
Daß er krank war,	wußte	ich		schon.
„Ja",	sagte	er		zu ihm.
„Ich kann nicht kommen",	sagte	sie		traurig.
Gern	hätte	ich	ihm	geholfen.
Am nächsten Morgen	fühlte	er	sich	krank.
Als er zurückkam,	fand	er	niemand	zu Hause.
Suchend	blickte	er	sich	um.
Bestraft	muß	er		werden!
Auf die Folter gespannt,	gestand er			alles.
Gewinnen	müssen	wir		unbedingt.
Arbeiten	tut	er		nie.
Still	war	es		ringsum.
Fort	ging	er!		
Außerordentlich förderlich für das Aussagevermögen einer Sprache	ist	neben dem Wortvorrat die freie Wortstellung (W. SCHNEIDER).		

(c) The first element of the main clause, provided it remains a single entity, can be amplified at will. This can be done, if the clause begins with a noun or pronoun, by means of appositional or attributive phrases or clauses, or by relative clauses; and also by adverbs, adverbial phrases or adverbial clauses or relative clauses if the clause begins with an adverbial expression

1	2	
Das anhaltend gellende Klingeln, das Zeichen zum Beginn der Montagsandacht,	schlug	an sein Ohr (T. MANN).
Ich als ältester Sohn	habe	allein das Recht darauf.
Der Mann, seines Lebens nicht sicher,	suchte	bei Freunden seine Zuflucht.
Onkel Justus, galant wie er war,	schritt	ihr entgegen (T. MANN).
Kinder, solange sie schweigen,	mag	ich gern leiden.
Der Zug, den ich nehmen wollte,	kam	pünktlich an.
Der Koffer da	gehört	mir.
Am nächsten Morgen, als er aufwachte,	fühlte	er sich schon besser.
Durch den Anblick des lieben Gottes, der doch eine Weile alles in bleichen Schrecken versetzte,		

1	2
indem er mit fürchterlichem Brummen nach verschiedenen Richtungen auf das Butterbrot- papier zeigte, das hie und da auf den Fliesen lag,	war Kai in vorzügliche Laune geraten (T. MANN).

(d) In questions introduced by an interrogative (*wo? wer?* etc.) and in the 3rd person imperative the finite verb is the second idea; in questions not introduced by an interrogative and in first and second person imperative forms the finite verb comes **first**.

> Was **hat** er gesagt?   Man **nehme** sechs Eier!
> *But* **Hat** er schon geantwortet?   **Gehen** wir! **Gehen** Sie nach Hause!

(e) In main clauses expressing a wish the finite verb comes **first**.

> **Wären** wir doch zu Hause!

(f) In exclamations introduced by *wie, was für, welcher*, etc., the verb most commonly comes **last** (see *82*).

> Wie blaß du **aussiehst**!   Was für ein Mann das **war**!

(g) Interjections, *ja* and *nein*, and words and phrases that are separated by a comma from the beginning of the German sentence like *nun, im Gegenteil, kurz, kurzum, mit einem Wort* and, occasionally also, *gewiß, freilich, allerdings* and *immerhin* are treated as being outside the main clause and as therefore not affecting the word order.

> Ach! das **ist** wahr. Nein, das **glaube** ich nicht.
> Im Gegenteil, ich **bin** gefahren. Mit einem Wort, du **bist** verrückt.
> Freilich, da **kann** man nichts sagen.

(h) In the Volkslied and in poetry akin to it in spirit the finite verb often comes first. The finite verb is also to be found in poetry coming at the end of the main clause.

> Liegt eine Stadt im Tale (DEHMEL).
> Am Fenster ich einsam stand (EICHENDORFF).
> Ein Schweigen in schwarzen Wipfeln wohnt (TRAKL).

2 Word Order in Compound Sentences

In a compound sentence, i.e. a sentence consisting of two or more main clauses, the finite verb is the **second** idea in each of the clauses. The main clauses may be (and usually are, if there are only two) linked by co-ordinating conjunctions (7).

1	2		1	2		
Er	legte sich hin	und	(er)	schlief	bald	ein.
Er	legte sich hin,	und	bald	schlief	er	ein.
Er	legte sich hin,	denn	er	war	müde.	

1	2		1	2		1	2	
Er	zog sich aus,	(er)	legte sich hin	und	(er)	schlief ein.		

NOTE: The subject, if it is the same as in the first clause, may be omitted after *und, aber* and *sondern* in the subsequent clause(s), provided no other word precedes the verb.

3 Word Order in Subordinate Clauses

(a) In subordinate clauses which begin either with a subordinating conjunction (*8 (a)*), an interrogative (*8 (b)*) or a relative pronoun (*46*) the finite verb normally comes **last** in the subordinate clause (i). If the verb is a separable verb its prefix immediately precedes it and is attached to it (ii). The past participle or infinitive immediately precedes the finite verb (iii).

i Während er so in seinem Buch **las**, ...
ii Obgleich sie gar nicht so häßlich **aus**sah, ...
iii Der Mann, der zuerst ins Zimmer **getreten** war, ...
Sie fragte, wie er **geschlafen** habe.
Da er endlich ins Zimmer **kommen** mußte, ...

(b) *Exceptions:*

i When there are two or more infinitives in the clause the finite auxiliary verb (*haben* or *werden*) normally immediately precedes them.

Der Tag wird kommen, an dem sie das **werden** tun müssen.
Das Buch, das er **hatte** drucken lassen, ...
Wenn er das **hätte** wissen können, ...

ii When a verb in the main clause introduces direct speech the finite verb comes second in the subordinate clause.

Er sagte: „Ich **gehe** jetzt nach Hause."

iii When a verb in the main clause introduces indirect speech without *daß* the finite verb comes second in the subordinate clause.

Er sagte, er **sei** sehr müde.
Er sagte, sie **solle** sofort zu Bett gehen.
But Er sagte, daß er sehr müde sei.

iv When *wenn* is omitted in conditional clauses the finite verb comes first.

Hätte er den Brief gelesen, so... (*if he had read*).

v When *ob* or *wenn* are omitted in *als ob* or *als wenn* clauses the finite verb immediately follows *als*.

Er tat, als **wüßte** er nichts davon.
But Er tat, als ob er nichts davon wüßte.

4 Word Order in Complex Sentences

(a) In complex sentences (i.e. in sentences consisting of one or more main clauses and one or more subordinate clauses) the main clause may (i) precede the subordinate clause(s); (ii) follow the subordinate clause(s); (iii) enclose the subordinate clause(s). The subordinate clause may itself (iv) enclose one or more subordinate clauses.

i   Er sagte sofort, daß er es tun würde, wenn er Zeit hätte.
ii Nachdem er sich hingelegt hatte und eingeschlafen war, klopfte es.
iii Er wollte den Brief, der eben gekommen war und den er schnell gelesen hatte, sofort beantworten.
iv Er sagte sofort, daß, wenn er Zeit hätte, er es tun würde.

(b) It is often stylistically preferable to complete one clause before starting the next, especially when the sentence would otherwise end haltingly or become too involved.

Er las den Brief **durch**, der eben gekommen war und auf den er so lange und sehnsüchtig gewartet hatte.
Ich werde ihm das Buch **geben**, das ich ihm versprochen habe.
Er sagte, daß er ein Haus **gekauft habe**, das mitten in einem Wald stehe.

5 Word Order in Concessive Clauses

After a concessive clause introduced by conjunctions such as *was ... auch*, *welcher ... auch, wie/so ... auch* and also by *ob ... ob/oder, sei es (daß) ... sei es (daß)* there is usually no inversion of the subject and verb in the main clause.

Welche Talente er auch besitzen mochte, er konnte ... (*whatever talents*). In welcher Richtung man auch reisen mag, man ... (*in whichever direction*).
Wie/so schön sie auch sein mag, sie ist ... (*beautiful though she is*).
Ob es regnet oder nicht, ich gehe jeden Tag spazieren.

NOTE: One occasionally meets the same construction after a *wenn*-clause Students are, however, not advised to adopt this practice.

Wenn mich die Welt so fragen wird, es wird schwer sein ... (KAFKA).

6 Word Order within the Clause

(a) In a main clause the weakest element tends to come immediately after the finite verb, in a subordinate clause immediately after the introductory word. The stronger the element, the closer it will tend to come to the end of both main and subordinate clause.

In the following sections dealing with word order within the clause this principle should always be borne in mind; for if a word or phrase normally spoken without stress is given particular significance it will then tend to come later in the clause than it would otherwise have done.

(b) Direct and Indirect Objects

If there are two noun objects in a clause the indirect (dative) normally precedes the direct (accusative). If there are two personal pronoun objects, the direct normally precedes the indirect. But any pronoun object will normally precede a noun object. (Note that the second of the two objects has the greater stress.)

> Er gab dem Mann das **Buch.**
> Er gab es **ihm.** Geben Sie es **mir!**
> Er gab ihm das **Buch.** Er gab es dem **Mann.** Er hat das meinem **Freund** gesagt.

However, emphasis would require one to say:

> Er hat mir **das** gesagt. Ich bringe dir **ihn** (= den Koffer).
> Er gab den Apfel seiner **Schwester** (und nicht seinem Bruder).
> Er zieht das Land der **Stadt** vor.

(c) The Prepositional Object

The prepositional object normally follows other objects.

> Er schrieb den Brief an meinen Bruder.

(d) The Reflexive Pronoun and the Personal Pronoun Object

i In the main clause the reflexive pronoun or the personal pronoun object immediately follows the finite verb except when there is inversion of verb and pronoun subject.

> Er setzte sich/ihn auf den Stuhl.
> Er hat sich/ihn auf den Stuhl gesetzt.
> Dann setzte sich mein Vater. Dann setzte sie mein Vater auf einen Stuhl. Dann gab ihr mein Vater einen Trunk Wasser.

But Dann setzte er sich. Dann setzte er sie auf einen Stuhl.

ii In a subordinate clause it is considered more correct for the reflexive pronoun or personal pronoun object to come immediately before the noun subject of the clause, though many modern writers place it after the noun subject. If the subject of the clause is a pronoun the pronoun object or reflexive pronoun comes immediately after it.

6

Da sich mein Bruder jetzt erholt hat, ...
Wenn mich die Welt so fragen wird, ...
But Da er sich jetzt erholt hat, ... Wenn er mir so antwortet, ...

iii *Es* (accusative) precedes the dative reflexive pronoun, unless it is contracted to *'s*, when it is attached to it.

Stell es dir vor! Stellen Sie es sich vor!
But Stell dir's vor! Stellen Sie sich's vor!

(e) Nicht

i In a negative main clause *nicht* immediately precedes the past participle, infinitive(s), separable prefix, predicative adjective or noun, or adverb or adverbial phrase of place, manner or degree. If none of these is present *nicht* is the last word.

Ich habe ihn nicht gesehen.
Du kannst ihn heute nicht sehen.
Du brauchst nicht zu kommen.
Du hättest es nicht sagen sollen.
Sehen Sie sich jetzt nicht um!
Es ist heute nicht kalt.
Das ist nicht mein Mann.
Er ist heute nicht in der Schule.
Ich bin nicht zu Fuß gekommen.
Ich mag ihn nicht sehr.
Ich sehe ihn nicht. Vergessen Sie mich nicht!
Ohne diese Erkenntnis hilft aller gute Wille nicht.

ii In a negative subordinate clause *nicht* precedes the finite verb. If there is a past participle, one or more infinitives, a predicative adjective or noun, or an adverb or adverbial phrase of place, manner or degree in the clause *nicht* precedes these.

Wenn ich es nicht tue, ...
Wenn ich es nicht getan hätte, ...
Wenn Sie nicht kommen können, ...
Wenn Sie nicht hätten kommen können, ...
Wenn es heute nicht kalt wäre, ...
Da er nicht mein Sohn ist, ...
Obgleich er noch nicht da ist, ...
Da ich nicht zu Fuß gekommen bin, ...
Da er heute nicht genug gearbeitet hat, ...

iii If a particular word in the clause is to be negatived *nicht* immediately precedes that word.

Ich mag sie sehen, aber nicht **ihn**.
Ich habe nicht **ihn** gesehen, sondern seinen Bruder.
Komm nicht **heute**, komm lieber morgen!

7

(f) Adverbs and Adverbial Phrases

i The order of adverbs or adverbial phrases within the clause tends to be as follows: (1) cause, (2) time, (3) manner, (4) place, (5) purpose or result, (6) degree. The underlying principle, which generally accounts for this order, as well as for deviations from it, is that the more intimately an adverbial expression is linked with the finite verb, the further away it stands from it in the main clause (and the closer to it in the subordinate clause).

Er trat|heute morgen|ganz unerwartet|ins Zimmer.
Als er|heute morgen|ganz unerwartet|ins Zimmer|trat, ...
Sie marschierten|oft|mit Fahnen und Musik und Gesang|an meinem Fenster|vorbei (DÖBLIN).
Wir mußten|wegen des weiten Weges|sofort|nach Hause|zur Klavierstunde|gehen.
Ich habe|heute nachmittag|im Garten|nur wenig|geschafft.

ii It is often possible to avoid too many adverbial expressions coming together by beginning the sentence with the one or other of them that is not intimately linked with the verb.

Heute morgen trat er ganz unerwartet ins Zimmer.
Ganz unerwartet trat er heute morgen ins Zimmer.

iii If there are several adverbial expressions of time or of place the more general tends to come first.

Er kommt jeden Morgen um 9 Uhr.
Der Hund liegt draußen im Garten vor der Tür.

iv Two or more place adverbs or two or more time adverbs coming at the beginning of the sentence may be looked upon as constituting one idea only (cf. *1(c)*).

Eines Abends, Ende Mai, klopfte es wieder an ihrer Tür (RINSER).
Draußen im Garten vor dem Haus liegt der Hund.

v The adverb(ial expression), unless it comes first in the sentence, is preceded by all direct and indirect pronoun objects (cf. *6(a)*), but usually stands between two noun objects, and comes before a prepositional object, a single noun object and a predicative adjective.

Gestern hat er sich sehr amüsiert.
Er hat sich gestern sehr amüsiert.
Ich habe es ihm gestern gegeben.
But Ich habe meiner Schwester gestern das Buch gegeben.
Ich habe gestern mit ihr gesprochen.
Ich habe gestern meinen Freund getroffen.
Ich habe es gestern meinem Freund gesagt.
Sie sah gestern sehr blaß aus.

(g) The Prefix of Separable Verbs (cf. 60 (*f-k*))

i   In the present and imperfect tenses of main clauses and in the imperative the prefix of separable verbs comes last.

Er geht um 8 Uhr **aus**. Er ging um 8 Uhr **aus**.
Geh doch **aus**!

NOTE: Occasionally, and then usually in poetry (but see *I(b)*), the separable prefix precedes the verb (and is sometimes attached to it) in the simple tenses of main clauses.

Auf tat sich das Licht (GOETHE).
Aufflattern weiße Vögel (TRAKL).

ii   Separable verbs are in all other cases written as one word, the prefix coming first.

Als er gestern **ausging**, ... Er ist schon **ausgegangen**.
Er wollte **ausgehen**. Er wagte nicht **auszugehen**.

(h) Deviations from Normal Word Order

i   In comparisons the incomplete clause dependent on *als* or *wie* usually follows the clause with which it is compared.

Gestern hat es weniger geregnet als heute.
Gestern hat es nicht so viel geschneit wie heute.
Da er viel älter ist als ich, ... Da er ebenso alt ist wie ich, ...

ii   Both in main clauses and in subordinate clauses a phrase that would normally precede the verb will sometimes be found to follow it. This occurs quite often in conversation; but it is also met with in careful writing when the sentence is deliberately dislocated in order to point a meaning more clearly, or sometimes to avoid too remote an antecedent of a relative clause.

Es kann **bedeuten** Begriff oder Vorstellung oder Gedanke oder Einfall (W. SCHNEIDER).
Dichtung hat nur dem etwas zu schenken, der empfangbereit **ist** für ihre Gaben (W. SCHNEIDER).
Er tat es nicht, weil er einen Brief bekommen **hatte** von seiner Mutter, die ihm davon abriet (DRACH).

(i) Parenthetical Clauses

There is inversion of verb and subject only in the short parenthetical clause.

Er ist, glaube ich, höchst intelligent.
Eine Dame, heißt es, könne ...
But Er ist – ich habe es mehr als einmal gesagt – höchst intelligent.

(j) For the position of the present and past participles in participial phrases, see *64(b)*.

7 Co-ordinating Conjunctions

(a) All six co-ordinating conjunctions – *und, oder, sondern, aber, denn, allein* (= *but*, in literary use only) – link clauses without affecting the word order.

> Er kann heute nicht kommen, denn er ist viel zu müde.
> Als er ins Zimmer trat und mich sah, wurde er blaß.

(b) The first three – *und, oder* and *sondern* – also link nouns, pronouns, adjectives, etc., with one another; and *aber* can be used to link adjectives.

> Du und ich; ihr Bruder oder ihre Schwester; nicht schön, sondern häßlich; er ist klug, aber faul.

8 Subordinating Conjunctions and Interrogatives

Subordinating conjunctions and subordinating interrogatives send the finite verb to the end of the clause.

(a) Subordinating Conjunctions

als	*when, as, than*	falls	
als ob; als wenn	*as if, as though*	für den Fall daß	*in case, if*
angenommen, daß	*supposing that*	im Falle, daß	
(an-)statt daß	*instead of* (+ *gerund*)	indem	*while, as, by* (+ *gerund*)
auch wenn	*even if*		
auf daß	*so that* (*purpose*)	indes(-sen)	*while, as*
ausgenommen, daß	*except that*	in dem Maße, wie	(*in proportion*) *as*
außer daß		in gleichem Maße, wie	*to the same extent as*
ausgenommen, wenn	*unless, except when*	insofern insoweit	*in so far as, according as*
außer wenn			
außer im Falle, daß	*except when, unless*	insofern ..., als	*in so far ... as*
bevor; ehe	*before*	je nachdem (wie)	*according as*
bis	*until, by the time that*	jedesmal, wenn	*whenever*
da	*as, since* (*causal*)	kaum daß	(*preceding main clause*) *no sooner ... than, hardly ... when*
dadurch, daß	*by* (+ *gerund*)		
damit	*so that* (*purpose*)		
damit ... nicht	*unless, lest*		
daß	*that*		(*following main clause*)
es sei denn, daß	*unless*		
erst als	*not until, only when*		*hardly* (*result*)
erst wenn			

10

nachdem	*after*	wann ... (auch) immer	*whenever*
nicht eher, (als) bis	*not until*	was ... auch (immer)	*whatever (= pronoun)*
nun (,da)	*now that*	was für ... auch	*whatever (+ noun)*
ob ..., ob/oder	*whether ... or*	weil	*because*
obgleich obschon obwohl obzwar	*although*	welcher ... auch	*whichever*
		wenn	*if, when (-ever)*
ohne daß	*without (+ gerund)*	wenn ... auch	*even if*
		wenn ... (erst) einmal	*once*
sei es, daß ...	*whether ... or*	wenn ... nicht	*unless*
sei es, daß ...	*(whether)*	wenngleich wennschon	*although*
seit(-dem)	*since (temporal)*		
so ... auch (immer)	*however (+ adjective or adverb)*	wer ... auch (immer)	*whoever*
		wie	*as (manner, time), how, when*
sobald; sowie	*as soon as*		
so daß	*so that (result)*	wie ... auch (immer)	*however (+ adj. or adv.)*
sofern; soweit	*as/so far as*		
sofern nur	*if only, as long as*	wie sehr ... auch (immer)	*however (+ verb)*
solange	*as long as*		
sooft	*whenever*	wiewohl	*although*
so sehr ... auch (immer)	*however much (+ verb)*	wo ... auch (immer)	*wherever*
		wohin ... auch (immer)	*wherever, in whatever direction*
soviel	*as far as*		
trotzdem	*despite the fact that, although*	wogegen wohingegen	*whereas*
um so (+ comparative) als	*all the (+ comparative) because*	zu ..., als daß	*too (+ adjective or adverb) for (+ gerund)*
ungeachtet (daß)	*although*	zumal (,da)	*especially as*
unter der Bedingung, daß	*on condition that*		
vorausgesetzt, daß	*provided that*		
während	*while, whereas*		

NOTE 1: *Auf daß, indes(-sen), ungeachtet* are literary or archaic as conjunctions.
NOTE 2: In older German *obgleich, obschon, obwohl, obzwar, wenngleich* and *wennschon* were often separated by the subject.

   Ob er gleich krank war, ...

NOTE 3: Only *obgleich, obschon,* etc., *wenn (auch), ob ... ob/oder* and *weil* can be used in phrases without a verb.

   Obgleich arm, führt er ein volles Leben.
   Ob jung oder alt, man gibt nie die Hoffnung auf.
   Seine persönliche Gestalt ist, weil schwer faßbar ..., stark verschattet worden (S.ZWEIG).

Interrogative Adverbs, Pronouns and Adjectives introducing Indirect Questions

ob	*whether, if*	welcher	*which*
wann	*when*	wer	*who*
warum, weshalb	*why*	wo	*where*
wie	*how, what ... like*	woher	*where from*
wieviel	*how much, how many*	wohin	*where to*
		womit	*with what*
wie viele	*how many*	worein	*into what*
wie lange	*how long*	worin	*in what*
was	*what*	wozu	*for what purpose*
was für	*what (sort of), which*	etc.	

9 Some difficult Conjunctions

(a) **as**:

Während (= *while*) er sich setzte, half ich ihm.

Da (= *since*) er krank ist, liegt er im Bett.

Als/wie (= *when*) er hereinkommt, stolpert er. (*Historic present*)

Als (= *when*) er hereinkam, stolperte er.

Wie (= *when*) er hereinkam, stolperte er. (*More colloquial*)

Wie (= *just as*) sie langsam auf mich zukam, ging ich ihr einen Schritt entgegen.

Er schreibt, wie (= *in the same way as*) er spricht.

Er zählte das Geld, wie (= *at the same time as*) er es aus den Taschen kramte.

In dem Maße wie (= *in proportion as*) das Hochwasser anwuchs, vergrößerte sich die allgemeine Unruhe.

Wie (= *in the way*) es manchmal geschieht, hörten wir die Vögel ganz deutlich.

Wie (= *as*, i.e. *which fact*) du weißt, bin ich jetzt allein.

Das Wetter verschlechterte sich, je weiter (= *the further*) sie nach Norden fuhren.

Genau so wie (= *just as*) der Fluß sich windet, genau so läuft der Weg daneben.

Indem er das sagte (= *saying that*), drehte er sich um.

(b) **but**:

Es ist nicht kalt, aber (= *however*) ich friere.

Sie ist nicht mehr jung, sondern (= *but on the contrary*) alt.

Er ist nicht nur reich, sondern steinreich.

Dort war nichts (weiter/anderes) als (= *except*) Unkraut.

Das ist alles andere als (= *anything but*) wahr.

Er ist nichts weniger als/alles andere als (= *anything but*) höflich.

(c) **since**:

Da (= *as*) er noch jung ist, benimmt er sich schlecht.

Seit(-dem) (= *now that he is*) er wieder gesund ist, geht er jeden Tag schwimmen.

Zwanzig Jahre war(en) es nun, daß (*or* seit) (=*since the time*) sie dort lebten.

(d) **so that**:

Wechsele deinen Platz, damit (= *in order that*) ich besser sehen kann.

Ich wechselte meinen Platz, so daß (= *with the result that*) ich ihn jetzt sehen konnte.

Er ist sehr beschäftigt, kaum daß man (= *so that one hardly*) ihn jetzt sieht.

(e) **when**:

Wenn er kommt, könnt ihr gehen.   ⎱ (*Reference to future*
Wenn es geklingelt hat, könnt ihr gehen. ⎰ *event*.)

Wenn (= *whenever*) er vorbeigeht, grüßt er mich immer.

Als/wie (= *when, historic present*) er endlich vorbeigeht, grüßt er mich.

Wenn (= *whenever*) er vorbeiging, grüßte er mich immer.

Jedesmal wenn/sooft (= *whenever*) er daran dachte, lächelte er.

Als/wie (= *when, on one occasion*) er vorbeiging, grüßte er mich.

Als/nachdem/sobald (= *after, as soon as*) er seine Rede beendet hatte, setzte er sich.

Wann (= *when, direct question*) kommt er?

Wir wissen nicht, wann (= *when, indirect question*) er kommt.

Kaum war er aufgestanden, als man anfing, ihn auszupfeifen.

Kaum war er aufgestanden, so/da fing man an, ihn auszupfeifen.

Kaum daß er aufgestanden war, so/da fing man an, ihn auszupfeifen.

Der Tag kam, an dem (*or* wo *or* da (= *literary style*)) sie das Haus verlassen mußten.

Der Augenblick kam, in dem (*or* wo *or* da (= *literary style*)) sie es ihm sagen mußte.

(f) **while**:

Während (= *all the time during which*) er in Berlin lebte, ging er oft ins Theater.

Während (= *at one moment while*) er mit mir sprach, kam seine Frau auf uns zu.

Er blieb stehen, während (= *whereas*) ich einen Schritt weiter ging.

Indem er sich leicht verbeugte (= *bowing*), küßte er ihr die Hand. (*Same subject in both clauses*.)

10 Adverbial Conjunctions

also; so; daher; darum	*therefore, and so*	deswegen deshalb	*that is (the reason) why*

auch	*also, too, and*	folglich	⎫
auch … nicht	*nor, neither, not either*	infolgedessen	⎬ *consequently*
		indes(-sen)	⎫
außerdem	⎫	unterdessen	⎬ *meanwhile*
ferner	⎪ *besides, moreover,*	kaum	*hardly, scarcely*
überdies	⎬ *in addition,*	nichtsdesto-	*nevertheless*
übrigens	⎪ *further*	weniger	
zudem	⎭	sonst	*otherwise, or else*
besonders	⎱ *especially, particu-*	(so-)wie auch	*as well as*
namentlich	⎰ *larly*	sowieso	*anyhow, as it is*
da	*then, so*	trotzdem	*in spite of that, all the same*
dennoch	⎫		
(je-)doch	⎬ *yet, nevertheless*	und zwar	*in fact, to be precise*
gleichwohl	⎭		

Examples:

Auch wußte er nichts davon. Ich auch nicht (*nor did I*). Sie malt Bilder, und zwar Landschaftsbilder. Obgleich er jedoch nichts davon wußte, … (*However, although* …)

NOTE: When adverbial conjunctions begin a sentence, inversion of subject and verb is usual; after *doch* there is inversion normally only in literary style.

Außerdem bin ich zu müde. Deshalb haben wir nicht angerufen.
But Doch es geht mich nichts an (P. WEISS).

11 Correlative Conjunctions

etwas anderes … etwas anderes ⎱	
ein anderes/eines … ein anderes ⎰	*one thing … another thing*
bald … bald	*now … now*
ebenso … wie	*just as much … as*
einerseits … and(e)rerseits	*on the one hand … on the other*
entweder … oder	*either … or*
(genau) wie … (genau) so	*as … so*
gerade so wie … so	*as … so*
in gleichem Maße wie … so	*as … so*
je (+ comparative) … desto/um so	*the … the*
nicht … noch	*not … nor*
nicht genug (*or* nur wenig *or* kaum) … geschweige denn	*not enough* (or *few* or *hardly*) … *let alone*
sei es … sei es	*whether … or*
sowohl … als/wie auch	*both … and*
teils … teils	*partly … partly*
weder … noch	*neither … nor*
zwar … aber/(je-)doch	*it is true … but/yet*

Examples:

Etwas anderes/ein anderes/eines ist es, in einem Land zu reisen, **etwas anderes/ein anderes** (ist es), Land und Leute wirklich kennenzulernen.
Er wird sich **ebenso** gelangweilt haben, **wie** ich mich gelangweilt habe.
Entweder du gehst (gehst du *is less emphatic*) zu ihm, **oder** er kommt zu dir. **Entweder** er wird **oder** ich werde ihn sehen. **Entweder** sein Vater **oder** seine Mutter **wird** kommen.
Er hat es **nicht** getan, **noch** weiß er, wer es getan hat.
Es gibt sehr **wenig** Lehrer, **geschweige denn** Mathematiklehrer.
Je weiter wir vorwärts kamen, **desto** öder wurde die Landschaft.
Weder er hat geschrieben, **noch** sie hat von sich hören lassen. (*Different subjects in the two clauses.*) **Weder** hat er geschrieben, **noch** ist er zu uns gekommen. (*Same subject in both clauses*) **Weder** er **noch** ich **haben** ihn gesehen. **Weder** von ihm **noch** von seiner Mutter habe ich etwas gehört.
Ich habe nichts gehört, **weder** von ihm **noch** von seiner Mutter (*either ... or*).
Wie's kommt, **so** wird's gegessen.

12 The Definite and Indefinite Articles

(a) For declension, see *87, 88.*

(b) Examples of deviation from English usage:

i Where English omits the article:

Der Mensch ist sterblich; die Zeit vergeht schnell (i.e. *in generalising statements*).
Der junge Karl; das protestantische Deutschland.
Der Bodensee (*Lake Constance*); der Mont Blanc; in der Schillerstraße; auf dem Humboldtplatz.
Im Sommer, im Mai, am Mittwoch, nach dem Frühstück.
Die Schweiz, die Türkei, die Tschechoslowakei, die Bretagne (*i.e. with feminine names of countries and provinces*); *but also:* der Harz, der Breisgau, das Elsaß. (*But* Elsaß-Lothringen (*Alsace-Lorraine*).)
In der Schule, in der Stadt, im Bett, aus dem Bett; zur Schule, zur Kirche, zur Arbeit gehen; mit der Post/Bahn, mit dem Auto/Zug/Schiff/Flugzeug kommen (*by post, etc.*).
An den Masern (*measles*), Windpocken (*chicken-pox*), am Mumps erkranken; an der Schwindsucht (*consumption*), am Krebs (*cancer*), an den Pocken (*small-pox*) sterben.

ii Where German omits the definite article:

Nach Verlauf mehrerer Stunden; zu Anfang/Beginn des Jahres; gegen Ende des Monats; seit Beendigung des Kriegs; Anfang Juni (*at the beginning of June*); Mitte Juli; Ende August.

Nach Norden; gegen Süden.
Wir waren bei Beneckes (*at the Benecke's*).
Folgende Zitate; aus obigem Grunde.

iii   Where German omits the indefinite article:

Er ist Engländer, sie ist Ausländerin; er will Ingenieur werden; er war nie Minister gewesen. (*But:* Er ist ein reicher Engländer.)
Ich als alter Arzt; er diente als Lehrer; er war als Bauer verkleidet (*disguised as a*).
Er hat guten Appetit; er hat Fieber (*a temperature*); er hat Kopfschmerzen, Halsschmerzen; wir haben Besuch (*a visitor/visitors*); er hat große/keine Eile (*is in a great/in no hurry*).
Er spricht mit leiser, lauter Stimme; er ist (in) guter, schlechter Laune/Stimmung; er ist anderer Meinung/Ansicht; es kam zu Ende.

iv   Where German omits the partitive (*some, any*):

Hast du Butter? Ja, ich habe Butter. Ich esse nie Butter.
Er ißt vom (*some of the*) Brot, er trinkt vom Wein.

v   Where English uses the indefinite article, German the definite:

2 Mark das Kilo, 3 Schilling das Pfund, 10 Pfennig das Stück (*apiece, each*).
Er verdient 100 DM in der Woche, 400 DM im Monat, 5000 DM im Jahr. Er fuhr 80 Meilen in der Stunde.
Er kommt zweimal am Tage, in der Woche, im Monat. Er kommt zweimal die Woche.
Im Nu (*in a moment*); zum Spaß (*for a joke*); zur Abwechslung (*for a change*); im Trab/Galopp (*at a trot/gallop*); zur Not (*at a pinch*).

vi   Where English uses the possessive adjective, German the definite article:

Ich reichte ihm die (*my*) Hand. Er stand da, den Hut auf dem Kopf und die Hände in den Taschen.
Ich habe mich in die (*my*) Hand geschnitten. Er hat mir das Leben gerettet. Wasch dir die Hände!

13 The Gender of Nouns [1]

It is very often not possible to tell the gender of a noun from its meaning or form. The following rules, however, should be borne in mind:

(a) Generally speaking, nouns referring to males are masculine, to females, feminine, to their young (when the word exists), neuter, e.g. der Mann, die Frau, das Kind; der Stier, die Kuh, das Kalb; das Lamm, das Fohlen (*foal*); das Junge (*young of animals*).

[1] For the declension of nouns, see *101*

16

Note however the following exceptions:

der Backfisch (*flapper*), der Junge (*boy*), der Teenager.

die Ordonnanz (*orderly*), die Person, die Wache (*sentry*), die Waise (*orphan*).

das Frauenzimmer (*female*), das Fräulein, das Genie (*genius*), das Opfer (*victim*), das Weib (*woman, wife, derogatory now except in set phrases*, e.g. mit Weib und Kind), das Mädchen.

(b) Other parts of speech (except cardinal numerals) are nearly always neuter when used as nouns, e.g. das Schweigen, das Können, das Nichts, das Ja und Nein, das Für und Wider, das Auf und Ab, ,,Die Philosophie des Als Ob" (*title of book*).
But: die Fünf, die Sechs, unsere Elf.

(c) Suffixes usually indicating **masculine** nouns:

Native words: **-er** (*persons only*), **-ich, -ig, -ling, -s.**
Foreign words: **-ant, -ar** (*persons only*), **-är** (*persons only*), **-ast, -eur,**
-ier (*persons only*), **-iker, -ismus, -ist, -loge, -or.**

Exception: **-ig**: das Reisig (*twigs*).
(d) Suffixes usually indicating **feminine** nouns:

Native words: **-e** (*not animate objects*), **-ei, -heit, -in** (*persons only*), **-keit,**
-schaft, -ung.
Foreign words: **-ade, -age, -ance, -anz, -enz, -ette, -ie, -ik, -ille -ine,**
-ion, -isse, -itis, -ive, -ose, -sis, -tät, -ur, -üre.

Exceptions: **-e**: der Buchstabe, Friede, Funke, Gedanke, Glaube,
Haufe, Name, Wille, Käse, Kaffee, Tee.
das Auge, Ende, Erbe (*inheritance*), Knie, Gebäude,
Gemüse.
Collectives in *Ge-* (mostly neuter, but see *15 1(e).*))

(e) Suffixes usually indicating neuter nouns:

Native words: **-chen, -icht, -lein, -nis, -tel** (= -teil), **-tum.**
Foreign words: **-ett** (*not persons*), **-in** (*not persons*), **-ma, -ment, -um.**

Exceptions: **-icht**: der Habicht (*hawk*).
-nis: die Erlaubnis, Erkenntnis (*knowledge, realisation*),
Finsternis, Verdamnis (*damnation*), Wildnis.
-tum: der Irrtum, der Reichtum.
-ment: der Moment (*moment*), der Zement.

(f) The nouns with the suffix **-sal** are sometimes feminine, sometimes neuter, sometimes both:

die Mühsal (*trouble*), Trübsal (*affliction*).
das Drangsal (*distress, also f.*), Scheusal (*monster*), Wirrsal (*confusion*).

14 Nouns whose Meaning Changes according to Gender

der Band (⸚e)	*volume*	das Band (⸚er)	*ribbon*
		das Band (-e)	*bond*
der Bord (-e)	*board (ship-)*	das Bord (-e)	*shelf*
der Bund (⸚e)	*league, covenant*	das Bund (-e)	*bundle, bunch (of keys)*
der Erbe (-n, -n)	*heir*	das Erbe (Erb-schaften)	*inheritance*
der Flur (-e)	*hall, vestibule*	die Flur (-en)	*meadow*
der Gefallen (-)	*favour*	das Gefallen [1]	*pleasure*
der Gehalt (-e)	*content*	das Gehalt (⸚er)	*salary*
der Heide (-n, -n)	*heathen*	die Heide (-n)	*heather, moor*
der Hut (⸚e)	*hat*	die Hut	*guard*
der Junge (-n, -n)	*boy*	das Junge (see 29)	*young of animals*
der Kiefer (-)	*jaw*	die Kiefer (-n)	*spruce fir*
der Kunde (-n, -n)	*customer*	die Kunde (-n)	*news, tidings*
der Leiter (-)	*manager*	die Leiter (-n)	*ladder*
das Mark	*marrow (of bone)*	die Mark (-en)	*marches*
		die Mark (-)	*mark (coin)*
der Messer (-)	*surveyor*	das Messer (-)	*knife*
der Moment (-e)	*moment*	das Moment (-e)	*motive, factor*
der Reis	*rice*	das Reis (-er)	*shoot, twig*
der Schild (-e)	*shield*	das Schild (-er)	*sign-board, label, name-plate*
der See (-n)	*lake*	die See	*sea*
das Steuer (-)	*rudder, helm, steering-wheel*	die Steuer (-n)	*tax*
der Tau	*dew*	das Tau (-e)	*rope*
der Taube (see 29)	*deaf man*	die Taube (-n)	*dove, pigeon*
der Tor (-en, -en)	*fool*	das Tor (-e)	*gate*
der Verdienst (-e)	*earnings*	das Verdienst (-e)	*merit, services*
das Wehr (-e)	*weir*	die Wehr (-en)	*defence, resistance*
der Weise (see 29)	*sage, wise man*	die Weise (-n)	*manner, way, melody, tune*

15 The Formation of Nouns

I Nouns can be formed by **derivation**

(a) From verbs:

i By adding the masculine suffix **-er** to the stem or contracted stem of the infinitive, sometimes modifying the stem vowel, to denote agents, e.g. der Diener, Dichter, Maler, Heuchler (*hypocrite*), Käufer, Händler.

---

[1] Also masculine in this sense

18

ii By adding the feminine suffix **-ung** to the stem or contracted stem of the infinitive, e.g. die Dichtung, Handlung, Bedeutung, Einladung.

iii By the omission of the last letter of the infinitive (all feminine), e.g. die Rede, Ausrede (*excuse*), Regel, Klingel.

iv By adding the feminine suffix **-erei** to the stem of the infinitive (**-ei** if the stem ends in *-el* or *-er*), e.g. die Raserei (*frenzy*), Zauberei, Heuchelei.

v By substantivising the infinitive (all neuter), e.g. das Lesen, Versprechen, Lächeln.

(b) From adjectives or past participles:

i By adding **-e** to adjectives not ending in *-bar*, *-haft*, *-ig*, *-isch*, *-lich*, *-los* or *-sam* and modifying the vowel if possible (all feminine), e.g. die Ebene, Größe, Nähe, Wärme.

ii By adding the feminine suffixes **-heit**, **-schaft** to past pasticiples, and to adjectives not ending in *-bar*, *-haft*, *-ig*, *-isch*, *-lich*, *-los* or *-sam*, e.g. die Schönheit, Vergangenheit, Eigenschaft, Gefangenschaft.

iii By adding the feminine suffix **-keit** to adjectives ending in *-bar*, *-ig*, *-lich* and *-sam*, e.g. die Dankbarkeit, Häufigkeit (*frequency*), Ähnlichkeit, Langsamkeit.

iv By adding the feminine suffix **-igkeit** to adjectives ending in *-haft* and *-los* and to a few others, e.g. die Mangelhaftigkeit, Machtlosigkeit, Müdigkeit, Kleinigkeit.

(c) From nouns or verbal nouns:

i By adding the feminine suffixes **-heit**, **-schaft**, e.g. die Christenheit (*Christendom*), Kindheit, Mannschaft, Leidenschaft.

ii By adding the feminine suffix **-ei**, e.g. die Bäckerei, Abtei (*abbey*, *abbacy*).

iii By adding the feminine suffix **-erei**, e.g. die Schurkerei, Schweinerei, die Kinderei.

iv By adding the neuter suffix **-tum**, (but see *13(e)*), e.g. das Christentum (*Christianity*), Judentum (*Jewry*).

(d) From nouns to form collectives by modification of the vowel usually and by adding the prefix **Ge-** and the suffix **-e** (the latter frequently omitted, especially after *-el* and *-er*), e.g. das Gelände, das Gebirge, das Gestirn, das Gemäuer.

(e) From verbs to form collectives as in (d) above, e.g. das Getriebe, das Gespräch. Often derogatory, e.g. das Getue, das Geplapper.

NOTE: Though most nouns beginning with *Ge-* are neuter there are a number of common exceptions, e.g.

(masculine): der Gedanke, Gebrauch, Gefallen (*favour*), Gehalt (*contents*), Geschmack, Genuß, Gesang, Gewinn

(feminine): die Gebärde (*gesture*), Gebühr (*fee*, *due*), Geburt, Geduld, Gefahr, Gemeinde (*congregation*), Geschichte, Gestalt

(f) From nouns by adding the particle **Un-** meaning (i) negation: das Unglück, die Ungeduld, die Unlust, der Unsinn, die Unruhe; (ii) 'a bad sort of': der Unmensch, die Unnatur, der Unstern, die Untat, das Untier; (iii) 'an excessive amount': die Unmenge, die Unsumme.

(g) From nouns by adding the particle **Ur-** meaning 'very old' or 'original': der Urvater, die Urwelt, der Urwald, die Ursprache, die Urform.

(h) From nouns to form diminutives (all neuter) by adding the suffixes **-chen** or **-lein** and usually modifying the vowel if possible, e.g. das Brötchen *roll*), das Fräulein. *But:* Frauchen (*little wife;* (*dog's, etc.*) *mistress*).

II The other method of noun formation is by **composition**. Note that:

(a) The gender and declension (see *101*) of a compound noun is always that of its last component: **der** Hausherr (-n, -en); **die** Kuhglocke (-n); **das** Flußufer (-); **die** Kiefernholzwand (÷e).

(b) Compounds consisting of two or more nouns are formed in the following ways:

i   By simple juxtaposition of two or more nouns (forming so-called 'true' compounds), e.g. der Hausschlüssel, der Hauptstaat, das Fischerboot, der Lastautofahrer.

ii By adding **-s** or **-es** to the first noun (including feminine nouns!) before compounding. This is always done with *Armut* and with feminine nouns ending in *-heit, -keit, -schaft, -ung, -ion* and *-tät*; with masculine and neuter nouns ending in *-tum*; with infinitive-nouns; with strong masculine and neuter nouns that do not form 'true' compounds; and, generally, with nouns that are already compounded, e.g. die Sicherheitsnadel, der Wirklichkeitssinn, der Landschaftsmaler, die Überredungskunst, das Armutszeugnis (*certificate of poverty*), der Stationsvorsteher, der Universitätsprofessor; die Altertumskunde (*archaeology*); die Schaffenskraft; der Ortswechsel, die Geisteskraft, das Glückskind; das Weihnachtslied, das Geburtstagsgeschenk.

iii By adding **-n** or **-en** to the first noun before compounding. This is normally done with feminine nouns that have none of the suffixes in (ii) above, as well as with masculine and neuter nouns of weak or mixed declension, e.g. der Ulmenast, der Sonnenschein; der Hirtenknabe, der Löwenanteil, der Augenblick.

iv By omitting the final **-e** of the first noun (nearly always feminine) before compounding, e.g. die Erdoberfläche.

v   By simple juxtaposition, the first noun being plural, e.g. das Wörterbuch, die Bretterbude (*shanty*).

NOTE: Der Landmann (*farmer, countryman*), der Landsmann (*fellow-countryman, compatriot*); das Geschichtsbuch (*history book*), das Geschichtenbuch (*story-book*).

(c) Compounds are also formed consisting of a noun preceded by some other part of speech, e.g.

i   verb + noun: der Heizkörper, das Lesebuch, die Fahrkarte.

ii adjective or past participle + noun: die Hochzeit, der Gebraucht-wagen (*used car*).

iii numeral + noun: das Einhorn (*unicorn*), das Doppelsegel, die Erstge-burt, die Halbinsel (*peninsula*).

iv pronoun + noun: die Ichsucht (*selfishness*), die Selbstzucht (*self-discipline*).

v   preposition or adverb + noun: die Mehrzahl (*majority*), der Nebenfluß (*tributary*), der Rückweg, die Umwelt.

16 Nouns: Singular in German, Plural in English

(a) die Asche (*ashes*), die Brille (*spectacles*), der Dank, der Gram (*sorrows*), das Hauptquartier (*headquarters*), die Kaserne (*barracks*), der Lohn (*wages*), das Mittelalter (*Middle Ages*), die Schere (*scissors*), das Spielzeug (*toy(s)*), die Treppe (*stairs*), die Umgebung (*surroundings*); *and* die Ethik (*ethics*), die Physik, die Politik, die Statistik, etc.

(b) Some of these words have a plural, e.g. die Löhne, die Statistiken, die Brillen (*pairs of spectacles*), die Scheren (*pairs of scissors*), die Treppen (*flights of stairs*); er wohnt vier Treppen hoch (*on the fourth floor*).

17 Proper Nouns and Adjectives derived therefrom

(a) Afrika, Amerika, Asien, Australien, Europa; das Britische Weltreich; Ägypten, Belgien, Bulgarien, Celebes, China, Dänemark, England, Frankreich, Griechenland, Großbritannien (*UK* or *Great Britain*), Indien, Irland, Italien, Japan, Jugoslawien, Kanada, Litauen (*Lithuania*), Neuseeland, die Niederlande (*pl.*), Norwegen, Österreich, Polen, Portugal, Rumänien, Rußland, UdSSR (= *USSR*), Schottland, Schweden, die Schweiz, Spanien, die Tschechoslowakei, die Türkei, Ungarn, die Vereinigten Staaten (*USA*), Wales.

(b) Bayern (*Bavaria*), Brandenburg, das Elsaß, Hessen, Kärnten (*Carinthia*), Lothringen (*Lorraine*), Mittelengland (*the Midlands*), das Oberammergauerland, Ostpreußen, Pommern (*Pomerania*), Preußen, die Provence, das Rheinland, Sachsen, die Steiermark (*Styria*), Tirol, West-falen.

(c) Bern, Braunschweig (*Brunswick*), Brüssel, Florenz, Frankfurt am Main, Hannover, Lissabon, Luzern, Mandalay, Moskau, München, Nürnberg, Rom, Triest, Tripoli, Tschandrapur (*Chandrapore*), Venedig, Warschau.

(d) die Donau (*Danube*), die Elbe, die Isar, das Isartal, der Main, die Mosel, die Oder, der Rhein, die Seine, die Themse (*Thames*), die Weser; das Tote Meer; die/der Pont du Gard.

(e) der Afrikaner (-), der Amerikaner (-), der Araber (-), der Asiat (-en, -en), der Australier (-), der Bayer (-n, -n), der Bur (-en, -en) (*Boer*), der Belgier (-), der Chinese (-n, -n), der Däne (-n, -n), der Deutsche (*29*), der Engländer (-), der Franzose (-n, -n), der Grieche (-n, -n), der Holländer (-), der Inder (-), der Irländer (-) *or* Ire (-n, -n), der Italiener (-), der Japaner (-), der Kanadier (-), der Neuseeländer (-), der Norweger (-), der Österreicher (-), der Pole (-n, -n), der Portugiese (-n, -n), der Preuße (-n, -n), der Russe (-n, -n), der Sachse (-n, -n), der Schotte (-n, -n), der Schwede (-n, -n), der Spanier (-), der Südafrikaner (-), der Tscheche (-n, -n), der Türke (-n, -n), der Ungar (-n, -n), der Waliser (-).

(f) afrikanisch, amerikanisch, asiatisch, australisch, bayrisch, chinesisch, deutsch, englisch, eurasisch (*Eurasian*), europäisch, französisch, griechisch, holländisch, irisch, italienisch, kanadisch, polnisch, preußisch, römisch, russisch, walisisch, westindisch.

(g) Christus (*Christ*), der Jude (-n, -n), Kain, der Levit (-en, -en), der Samariter (*Samaritan*);
Königin Anne, Franz Josef (*Francis Joseph*), Johanna (*Joan*), Leibniz (*Leibnitz*), Königin Viktoria.

(h) die Aufklärung (*Enlightenment*), der Burenkrieg (*Boer War*), der Dreißigjährige Krieg, die Gegenreformation (*Counter Reformation*), der Siebenjährige Krieg, der Sturm und Drang, der Westfälische Friede (*Peace of Westphalia*), die Weimarer Klassik;
der Bolschewik/Bolschewist (-en, -en), der Faschist (-en, -en), die Habsburger (*pl.*), der Quäker (-), die Schwarz-Gelben (*Black and Tans*).

(i) bolschewistisch, elisabethanisch, habsburgisch, hegelsch (*Hegelian*), viktorianisch.

NOTE: The names of towns and of most countries are neuter.

18 The Declension of Proper Nouns

(a) Christian names (masculine and feminine) and surnames normally take -*s* in the genitive. If the name ends in *s*, *ß*, *x*, *z*, *tz* possession is shown by adding an apostrophe or by a preceding *von*.

Karls Mutter, Elisabeths Schwester, Goethes Werke (*or* die Werke Goethes), Fritz' Hut (*or* der Hut von Fritz).

(b) With two or more names in combination only the last shows the genitive. With a surname including *von* if the name following *von* clearly refers to a place, only the last name preceding *von* shows the genitive ending.

Ricarda Huchs Romane; die Werke Friedrich von Schillers; unter der Regierung Friedrich Wilhelms des Zweiten von Preußen.

(c) If a title without article precedes a name, the name shows the genitive ending; if the title has the article, the title is inflected. *Herr* is always inflected in the oblique cases.

Onkel Herberts Wagen; der Wagen Onkel Herberts; der Wagen des Onkels Herbert; Professor Dr. Franks Sprechstunde; die Siege des Königs Friedrich des Zweiten; an Herrn Professor Lütgen.

(d) Surnames usually add -*s* to form the plural.

„Buddenbrooks". Wir gehen zu Schmidts. Das sind Dürers (*pictures by Dürer*).

(e) Place names are uninflected except in the masculine and neuter genitive and occasionally in the plural. When an article and adjective precedes, the genitive ending -*s* is now usually omitted.

Preußens Siege; die Erhebung Deutschlands; die Ufer des Rheins; die zwei Deutschland(s); des alten China.

(f) With geographical names ending in a sibilant possession is shown by *von* or by the addition of a preceding appositional noun.

die Landschaft von Wales; die Landschaft der Halbinsel Wales; die Theater der Hauptstadt Paris.

(g) The titles of books, plays, etc., remain unchanged if preceded by an appositional noun. If preceded by the author's name the article (if part of the title) is omitted; otherwise the full title is declined, leaving the article outside the inverted commas.

in dem Schauspiel „Die Räuber"; in Schillers „Räubern"; in den „Räubern".

(h) The months of the year are sometimes written with -*s* in the genitive, sometimes without. When preceded by a noun the months are uninflected. With the days of the week the genitive ending -*s* is still considered more correct.

die ersten Tage des August(s); Anfang Mai; Ende Juli; Mitte Juni; des Monats Mai; am Morgen des folgenden Montags.

19 The Nominative

The nominative is used to denote:

(a) The subject of the sentence: Der Tisch ist rund.

(b) The complement of the verbs *sein, bleiben, verbleiben, werden* and *heißen*: Ich bin und bleibe dein Freund. Er wurde mein zweiter Vater. Mit besten Grüßen verbleibe ich dein Freund. Er heißt Herr Schmidt.

20 The Accusative

The accusative is used:

(a) To denote the direct object of a transitive verb: Sie liebt ihren Vater.

(b) To denote duration of time and distance covered: Er blieb eine Weile, einen Monat (lang), einen Augenblick nur. Er ging einen Schritt weiter.

(c) To express measurements: Das Holz ist einen Finger dick/einen Zoll breit. Das Kind ist erst einen Monat alt. Sie sitzt drei Reihen weiter.

(d) In distributive expression (cf. *12(b)v*): Es kostet 3 Mark die Flasche/ das Stück/das Pfund.

(e) To denote 'definite time when' unless a preposition (*an, in*) is used: Er kommt nächsten Mittwoch, nächstes Jahr, jeden Tag; er kam voriges Jahr.

(f) To denote direction up or down: Er ging den Berg hinauf, die Treppe hinunter.

(g) In absolute constructions: Er saß da, den Kopf in die Hände gestützt.

(h) With certain adjectives: Ich bin/wurde ihn endlich los. Ich bin diese Arbeit gewohnt. Ich bin (*or* habe) diese Arbeit satt. Ich bin ihn überdrüssig (*sick of him*).

(i) In certain elliptic phrases: Vielen Dank! Guten Tag! Guten Abend! Herzliche Grüße! Herzliche Glückwünsche! (*Congratulations!*)

(j) After certain prepositions, see *52, 55*.

21 The Genitive

The genitive is used:

(a) To denote possession: der Wagen meines Vaters; Goethes Werke.

NOTE: Except in the case of names and of close relatives, and in a few fixed phrases, a preceding genitive is now literary or archaic.

(b) To denote 'indefinite time when': Eines Tages (*one day*), eines schönen Apriltages, eines Abends, eines Nachts(!) verschwand er.

(c) To denote manner: Er fährt nur erster Klasse. Sei guten Mutes! Er sah mich unverwandten Blickes an. Wir gingen unseres Weges.

(d) With certain adjectives: bar (*devoid of*), bewußt (*aware of*), eingedenk (*mindful of*), entkleidet (*stripped of*), gewärtig (*prepared for*), gewiß (*certain of*), kundig (*thoroughly acquainted with*), ledig (*devoid, free of*), sicher (*sure of*), ungewohnt (*unused to*), unkundig (*ignorant of*), würdig (*worthy of*), e.g.

Ich bin mir dessen bewußt. Er ist des Erfolgs sicher.

NOTE: Other adjectives like *fähig* (capable of), *müde, schuldig, überdrüssig, voll, wert* are also used with the genitive, but other constructions are possible, e.g. Er ist dieser Tat fähig; er ist zu allem fähig. Sie war voll weiblichen Charmes; der Saal war voll von (*or* mit) Menschen, war voll Menschen.

(e) In certain expressions: Ich bin der Meinung (*or* Ansicht). Es ist der Mühe wert. Es lohnt der (*or* die) Mühe (nicht). Wir sahen ihn dieser Tage (*the other day*). Sie wurde seiner ansichtig (*caught sight of him*). Sie werden auch der Segnungen der Zivilisation teilhaftig (*share in the blessings*). Die Stadt ist ihrer Vorrechte verlustig gegangen (*lost*).

(f) After certain prepositions, see 53.

(g) After certain verbs, see 76, 77.

22 The Dative

The dative is used:

(a) To denote the indirect object: Er gab mir das Buch.

(b) To denote interest or advantage: Kauf mir ein Buch! Ich habe mir eine Zigarette angezündet (*lit myself a ...*).

(c) To denote possession (restricted almost exclusively to parts of the body): Es flog ihm ins Gesicht (*into his face*). Er rettete mir das Leben (*my*).

(d) With certain adjectives, which tend mostly to follow the noun or pronoun they govern: abhold (*averse from/to*), abgeneigt (*averse from/to*), ähnlich (*similar to, like*), (un)begreiflich ((*in)comprehensible to*), (un)bekannt, dankbar, ebenbürtig (*equal to, rivalling*), eigen (*peculiar to*), ergeben (*devoted to*), fern, fremd (*alien to*), gemäß (*appropriate, conformable(y) to*), gemeinsam (*common to*), gewachsen (*a match for, up to*),

25

gleich (*like, the same for*), gleichgültig, langweilig, lästig (*a nuisance to*), nach-
teilig, nahe, am nächsten (*nearest to*), nützlich, schädlich, (un)sympathisch
((*un*)*congenial to*), treu (*loyal to*), überlegen (*superior to*), untergeordnet
(*subordinate to*), unterworfen (*subject to*), (un)verständlich,((*in*)*comprehensible to*), vertraut (*familiar to*), zuwider (*repugnant to*), e.g.

> Er ist seiner Mutter ganz ähnlich. Er ist jeder Arbeit abgeneigt. Er
> ist ihm nicht gewachsen. Dieser Instinkt ist allen Menschen gemein-
> sam. Er ist mir sympathisch (*I like him*). Das ist mir gleich.

(e) In certain idiomatic phrases: Das Kleid ist mir zu lang. Mir ist zu
kalt, mir ist warm. Mir ist schlecht/gut/wohl zumute. Er tat es mir
zuliebe (*for my sake*). Ich stehe ihm zu Diensten (*at his service*). Das
gereicht ihm zur Ehre (*does him honour*). Das kam ihm zugute (*was for his
advantage*). Das wurde mir zuteil (*allotted to*). Wie dem auch sei (*however
that may be*); dem ist so (*that is the case*); wenn dem so ist (*if that is so*). Ich
stelle dir den Wagen zur Verfügung (*I place my car at your disposal*). Der
Wagen steht dir zur Verfügung (*is at your disposal*). Es steht uns frei, zu. . .
(*we are free to . . .*). Das Buch ist mir abhanden gekommen (*I have lost*).

(f) After certain prepositions, see 54, 55.

(g) After certain verbs, see 74, 75.

23 Apposition

(a) The noun in apposition is normally in the same case as the noun or
pronoun with which it stands in apposition. Note:

i   Mein Lehrer, ein großer Gelehrter; von ihm, einem großen Gelehrten,
    hätte ich das nicht erwartet; der Nachfolger Wilhelms des Eroberers;
    ein Paar Handschuhe; am Freitag, dem (*or* den) 17. April; die
    Universität Göttingen (*of G.*); die Hochhäuser der Stadt Berlin; in
    der Stadt Berlin; im Monat Mai.
ii Ein Dutzend Eier; mit einem Dutzend Eiern; der Preis einer Flasche
    Rotweins. *But:* der Preis eines Stückes Rindfleisch (*to avoid double
    strong genitive*).
iii Ein Paar schwarze (*or* schwarzer (G.)) Schuhe; mit einem Dutzend
    frischen Eiern (*or* frischer Eier (G.)).

(b) Note the similar construction after **als** (*as, as a*) and **wie** (*like*):

i   Ich als ältester Sohn; mir als jüngstem Bruder; die Kunst als solche;
    Tolstois Beschimpfung der Ärzte als nichtsnutziger Schufte (T. MANN).
    Ich kenne mich aus mit Menschen wie Ihnen (ANDERSCH).
ii Er wurde als ehrenhafter Mann betrachtet. Sie erkannte ihn als ihren
    Sohn wieder. Er sieht wie ein ganz gesunder Mensch aus.
But Er betrachtet sich als großer Dichter (*accusative now obsolete*).

24 The Formation of Adjectives

(a) A large number of adjectives are formed by means of the following suffixes and prefixes:

i   From nouns by adding the adjective-suffixes **-reich** (*rich in*), **-voll** (*full of*), **-los** (*lacking in*), **-wert** and **-würdig** (*-worthy*), **-fertig** (*ready to*), **-dicht** (*proof against*), **-fest** (*resisting, firm as*), **-sicher** (*safe against*), **-frei** (*free of*), **-artig** (*resembling*), **-mäßig** (*like*):

aufschlußreich (*revealing*), hoffnungsreich, kinderreich; liebevoll sorgenvoll; erfolglos, hoffnungslos, kinderlos; lesenswert, lobenswert, liebenswürdig; reisefertig; wasserdicht; feuerfest, felsenfest; bombensicher; zollfrei; eigenartig; regelmäßig

ii From nouns by adding the suffixes **-ig** (= *1. possession; 2. nature; 3. similarity*), **-isch** (= *1. origin* (*derived from proper names*); *2. qualities* (*mostly bad*); *3. -ic and -ical*) and **-(e)n** or **-ern** (= *made of*):

geduldig, sandig, silberig, jetzig; russisch, Kölnisch Wasser; kindisch; historisch, musikalisch; seiden, bleiern, steinern

iii From nouns, adjectives and verbs by adding the suffix **-lich** or **-erlich** (= *1. similarity; 2. possession; 3. approximation*):

kindlich, männlich, herzlich, täglich, rötlich, kränklich, fraglich, zerbrechlich, unbeschreiblich; lächerlich, fürchterlich

iv From nouns of towns by adding the suffix **-er**. Such adjectives are written with a capital and do not inflect.

im Kölner Dom; die Münchener Zeitungen

v   From adjectives, verb-stems or nouns by adding the suffix **-bar** (= *1. bearing; 2. -able, -ible*), **-haft** (= *1. subject to; 2. characteristic of*) and **-sam** (= *capacity or tendency*):

fruchtbar, offenbar, eßbar, unverkennbar; krankhaft, nahrhaft, mädchenhaft; langsam, sparsam, friedsam

vi From adjectives by adding the prefixes **un-** (= *in-, im-, dis-, un-*) and **ur-** (= *very*):

unmenschlich, unmöglich, unzufrieden, ungesund; uralt, urplötzlich

(b) Foreign suffixes are numerous but are only very rarely used with native words:

rent*abel*, nation*al*, hum*an*, mond*än*, risk*ant*, interstell*ar*, revolution*är*, priv*at*, tradition*ell*, intellig*ent*, grot*esk*, kompl*ett*, flex*ibel*, hybr*id*, stab*il*, mass*iv*, dubi*os*, nerv*ös*

(c) Compound adjectives are formed by the juxtaposition of (i) two adjectives: *hellblau, dunkelrot*; (ii) of noun and adjective: *aschblond, schneeweiß, zimmerrein*; (iii) of numeral or numeral pronoun and adjective or adjectival

suffix: *dreieckig, vierstöckig, mehrstöckig, zweistündig, dreitägig, vierjährig*;
(iv) of adverb or noun and present participle: *vielversprechend, weitreichend, atemberaubend haarsträubend.*

(d) Note the following compound (intensified) adjectives which are the equivalent of similes:

> blitzschnell, federleicht, hellwach, lammfromm, mäuschenstill, mausetot, pechdunkel, rabenschwarz, saugrob, schnurgerade, steinhart, steinreich (*enormously rich*), stockdürr, stocktaub, todmüde

25 The Predicative Adjective

(a) The adjective used predicatively, i.e. after the verbs *sein, werden, bleiben, scheinen* has no case or gender inflection.

> Er ist alt. Sie wird immer jünger. Er scheint jünger, als er ist. Bleib gesund!

(b) A small number of adjectives are used only predicatively, of which the most common are: allein, barfuß, gar (*properly cooked, done*), quitt (*quits*), schuld (*to blame*), unpaß (*unwell*); gang und gäbe (*customary*).

26 The Attributive Adjective

(a) See *91–93* for paradigms of declension.

(b) Note the following points:
   i   The attributive adjective is declined weak (see *86(b)*) when preceded by the definite article or any word similarly declined strong. Otherwise the adjective is declined strong (see *93*).
   ii Two or more ordinary attributive adjectives preceding the noun have each the same inflection (but see *28(c)*).
   iii The inflection of the possessive adjective (see *89*) immediately following *all(er), dieser, jener* is unaffected by them:

> mit all(er) **meiner** Kraft; mit diesem **meinem** Wort; all(e) **meine** Freunde.

   iv The inflection of *dieser* and *jener* immediately following *all(er)* is unaffected by it:

> die Straßen all(er) **dieser** Städte.

   v   The adjective after the personal pronoun should by the rule given above ((*b*)*i*) be declined strong. In the feminine dative singular and nominative plural however it is now usually declined weak (cf. *37(p)iv*):

ich armer Mann, ihm altem/alten Mann, uns Deutsche (*acc.*); *but* ihr arm**en** Frau, wir/ihr Deutsch**en**, wir arm**en** Leute.

vi   After the genitive of the relative pronoun and of *zwei*, *drei* the adjective is declined strong.

die Mutter, deren ältest**er** Sohn ...; der Mann, mit dessen ältest**em** Sohn ...
die Freundschaft zweier/dreier groß**er** Völker.

27 Indeclinable Adjectives

(a) Adjectives ending in -*er* derived from the names of towns (see *24(a)iv*)

(b) A few adjectives of foreign origin denoting colours, e.g. *beige, creme, lila, oliv, orange, rosa* (often inflected, however, in conversation), and the words *prima* (first rate) and *uni* (plain, of one colour):

ein **rosa**/rosa(n)es Band, ein **orange**/orangenes Kleid; **prima** Tee *But* ein rosafarbiges/rosafarbenes Kleid, ein olivgrüner Rock

28 Uninflected Adjectives

(a) Adjectives in apposition following or preceding a noun or pronoun:

Ein Edelmann ganz und gar auch er, **unabhängig** und **stolz**... (E. MARCKS)
Vulkanisch und **gütig** und im Innersten **fromm**, er steht unter ihnen... (E. MARCKS)

(b) In a very few stereotyped expressions, e.g. auf **gut** Glück, ein **halb** Dutzend, ein **gut** Stück des Weges; sie sind wieder **gut** Freund.

(c) The first of two attributive colour adjectives, e.g. viele **weiß** und schwarze Kühe.

(d) In poetry and in proverbial expressions, before neuter singular nouns and after nouns of any gender or number:

Unrecht Gut gedeiht nicht. (*Ill-gotten gains seldom prosper*).
Röslein **rot**. O Täler **weit**!

29 The Adjective-Noun

(a) Adjective-nouns can refer to persons or to things and are usually written with a capital.

der Kranke; die Kranke; die Kranken (*pl.*); das Schöne, das Innere (*interior*); das Böse (*evil*).

(b) They are declined for the most part according to the usual rules applying to adjectives (see *91–93*):

ein Kranker; mit dem Kranken; einige Kranke; Junge und Alte; des Schönen. *But:* dir als gut**em** Bekannt**en**.

(c) Certain former noun-adjectives have now become weak nouns (see *101*), e.g. der Junge (*boy*), (*but not* das Junge (*young of animals*)), der Invalide (*disabled soldier*).

(d) After *etwas, viel, soviel, wenig, nichts* and *allerlei* the adjective-noun is declined strong.

Nom., acc. etwas Gutes; *gen.* (*rare*) etwas Guten; *dat.* etwas Gutem.

(e) After *alles, vieles, weniges* the adjective-noun is declined weak.

Nom., acc. alles Gute; *gen.* alles Guten; *dat.* allem Guten.

NOTE: Certain adjectives in (a), (d) and (e) above are written with small letters, e.g. etwas anderes, alles mögliche alles übrige, das einzige.

(f) The neuter adjective-noun is widely used in German and will often be found to offer a neat translation of abstract nouns preceded by the indefinite article, or of English expressions involving such words as 'thing(s)', 'course', 'quality', 'phenomenon', 'element(s)', 'touch', 'what is', 'much that is'.

etwas Bezauberndes (*a fascination*), das erste (*the first thing*), das einzige (*the only thing*), das Allernötigste (*the very most necessary thing*), viel Liebes (*lots of nice things*), das Verrückte daran (*the crazy thing about it*), Wichtiges und Wertvolles (*things/lessons of importance and value*), das Sicherste (*the safest course*), das Wahnsinnige (*the frantic quality/mad thing*), das Auffallendste (*the most striking phenomenon*), etwas Katzenartiges (*a feline element*), das Gegensätzliche (*conflicting elements*), das Gedachte und Gesagte (*what is thought and said*), viel Dramatisches (*much that is dramatic*).

30 Adjectives in Titles

Such adjectives are attributive although they follow the noun. They are declined weak and are written with a capital.

Friedrichs des Großen; Elisabeths der Zweiten

31 The Comparison of Adjectives

(a) Predicative:

Der Fluß ist breit, breiter, hier am breitesten.

(b) Attributive:

Das ist ein breiter, ein breiterer, der breiteste Fluß.

NOTE: Most adjectives of one syllable modify the vowels **a**, **o** or **u** (but not **au**) in the comparative and superlative. Common exceptions are: bunt, falsch, flach, froh, hohl, kahl, klar, rasch, rund, satt, stumpf (*blunt*), voll, wahr. None of these modify.

(c) Irregular forms of comparison:

groß	größer	am größten/der größte
gut	besser	am besten/der beste
hoch	höher	am höchsten/der höchste
nah	näher	am nächsten/der nächste
viel	mehr[1]	am meisten/das meiste
wenig	{ weniger[1]	am wenigsten/das wenigste
	{ minder	am mindesten/das mindeste

(d) Examples of comparison of adjectives:

i   Er ist (eben) so alt, nicht so alt, bei weitem nicht so alt wie ich. Es ist ebenso gefährlich wie kostbar. Wir sind gleich alt (*both the same age*).

ii Er ist reicher, viel reicher, noch (*even*) reicher, bei weitem reicher, weniger reich als ich.
Er wird immer reicher (*richer and richer*). Er ist mehr fleißig als klug.
Er ist nichts weniger als klug (*anything but clever*).
Mehr oder minder gut. Um so (*or* desto) besser.
Es ist um so wichtiger, als ... (*all/so much the more ... because*).

iii Ein älterer (*elderly*) Herr; ein längerer (*prolonged*) Aufenthalt; die neuere (*modern*) Geschichte.
Helga und Irma sehen sich ähnlich, doch hat erstere (*the former*) schwarze, letztere (*the latter*) blonde Haare.
Es wäre besser, wenn wir jetzt gingen (*we had better go now*).

iv Er ist der klügste von allen. Das ist das schönste aller Kleider/von, unter allen Kleidern. Er ist mit der klügste (*one of the cleverest*) in der Klasse.
Das allerbeste; die weitaus gebildetsten (*by far the most cultured*).
Die meiste Zeit, die meisten Leute, die meisten von uns.
Es ist am besten, wenn wir gehen. Es wäre das beste, nichts zu sagen.
Ich halte es für das beste, du schweigst.

32 The Formation of Adverbs

(a) The predicative adjective and the past and present participle may generally be used as an adverb:

Er arbeitet fleißig. Er kam unerwartet/überraschend schnell.

[1] Indeclinable

(b) Some adverbs are formed from other parts of speech by adding such suffixes as: **-erweise, -weise, -s, -lich,** (bekanntlich), **-lings** (blindlings), **-wärts** (heimwärts), **-e** (lange), **-(e)ns** (namens, höchstens), **-maßen, -heim** (daheim), **-halber** (gesundheitshalber).

(c) Some adverbs are underived words like: hier, dort, da, dann, irgend, nie, je, etc.

33 Adverbs of Manner

NOTE:
(a) The very common suffix **-weise** (= *-wise,* (*bit*) *by* (*bit*), *by way of*) added to nouns: stückweise, teilweise, schrittweise, beispielsweise, ausnahmsweise, bissenweise (*in mouthfuls*).

(b) The common suffix **-erweise** (= *it is . . . ly the case that, . . .ly enough*) changes the meaning of an existing adverb:

> Sie ist erstaunlich jung. Erstaunlicherweise wußte er nichts davon.

(c) The suffix **-maßen** (= *in ... measure, to ... extent*) added to the genitive plural of adjectives and pronouns:

> einigermaßen, gewissermaßen, unverdientermaßen.

(d) The common modal adverbs:

> anders (*different*), fast/beinahe (*almost*), eigentlich (*strictly speaking, actually, as a matter of fact*), ungefähr/etwa (*approximately*), leider (*unfortunately*), natürlich (*of course*), sogar/selbst (*even*), umsonst/ vergebens (*in vain*), vielleicht, ziemlich (*rather*), zufällig (*by chance*).

34 Adverbs of Time

NOTE:
(a) Adverbs formed by the suffix **-s** to mean 'of a (morning)', 'during the (morning)', 'every (morning)': morgens, vormittags, mittags, nachmittags, abends, nachts, sonntags, wochentags, winters, etc.

(b) Adverbs formed by the suffix **-lang** added to the plural of nouns to mean 'for ...', 'for ... on end': sekundenlang, minutenlang, stunden-lang, tagelang, wochenlang, monatelang, jahrelang, jahrhundertelang.

(c) The adverbial use of **lang** in time phrases like: einen Augenblick lang ((*for*) *a moment*), mehrere Tage lang, etc.

(d) Immer wieder (*again and again*).

35 Adverbs of Place

(a) Place where (**wo**?): da, dort, hier, draußen (*out(-side)*), drinnen (*inside, within*), oben (*at the/on top*), unten (*at the bottom*), vorn, hinten, rechts, links, drüben (*over there*), überall, irgendwo, nirgendwo/nirgends, woanders/anderswo, unterwegs (*on the way*).

(b) Place where to (**wohin**?): dahin, dorthin, hierhin, hinaus, hinein, hinauf/nach oben, hinunter/nach unten, nach vorn, nach hinten, nach rechts, nach links, nach drüben, überallhin, irgendwohin, nirgendwohin, anderswohin.

(c) Place from where (**woher**?): daher/von da, hierher/von hier, von dort, von draußen, von drinnen, von oben, von unten, von vorn, von hinten, von rechts, von links, von drüben, (von) überallher, (von) irgendwoher, (von) nirgendwoher, (von) anderswoher.

(d) Motion away from the speaker = **hin**; towards the speaker = **her**. Therefore:

> Ich gehe hin, hinaus, hinein, hinauf, hinunter, hinab, hinan, hinüber.
> Er kommt her, heraus, herein, herauf, herunter, herab, heran, herüber.
> Ich ging den Berg/die Treppe hinauf.
> Er kam den Berg/die Treppe herunter.

(e) Note the double forms (i) two adverbs; (ii) preposition + adverb; (iii) adverbial compound + adverb:

i   Er ging **auf** und **ab** (*up and down*), **hin** und **her** (*hither and thither, to and fro, this way and that*). Wir gehen **ab** und **zu/hin** und **wieder/dann** und **wann** (*now and again*) ins Kino.

ii   Er ging **am** Fluß **entlang** (*along*), **am** Dom **vorbei** (*past*), **auf** sie **zu** (*up to, towards*), **durch** die Lücke **hindurch** (*through the gap*), **hinter/neben/vor** ihr **her** (*along behind/next/in front of her*), **ins** Dorf **hinab/hinunter** (*down into*), **in** das Zimmer **hinein** (*into*), **nach** dem Wald **zu** (*towards*). Er kam **zu** mir **herüber** (*across*).
Er sah **nach/zu** mir **hin** (*towards me, in my direction*), **vor** sich **hin** (*straight in front*); es kam **von oben/unten her** (*from above/below*); sie standen **um** mich **her/herum** (*round about me*).
Es läuft **auf** dasselbe **hinaus** (*amounts to the same thing*); die Fenster gehen **nach** dem Garten **hinaus** (*look out on to*); er wohnt **nach hinten hinaus** (*at the back*); das Zimmer **nach hinten hinaus** (*the back room*); er sah **zum** Fenster **hinaus/heraus** (*out of*); das Wasser floß **über** die Steine **hinweg** (*flowed over*).
Auf die Gefahr **hin** (*at the risk*), **auf** meinen Rat **hin** (*on my advice*); **aus** einer natürlichen Abneigung **heraus** (*from*), **aus** unserem eigenen Empfinden **heraus**, **aus** dem Verlangen **heraus**; **nach außen hin**

(*outwardly*), **nach oben hin** (*towards the top*); **über** das Ziel **hinaus** (*beyond*), **über** den Tod **hinaus** (*after*); **aus** der Erde **hervor** (*from under*); **von** dem Tage **an** (*from that day onwards*), **von** Anfang **an**; **von** klein **an/auf** (*from childhood*); **von** dort **aus, vom** Fenster **aus, von** Natur **aus** (*by nature*), **von** mir **aus** (*as far as I am concerned*).

iii Er sah nicht weiter **darüber hinaus** (*beyond it, further*); das Wasser floß **darüber hinweg** (*over it*); er geht **darüber hinweg** (*ignores, disregards it*); er kommt **darüber hinweg** (*gets over it*); er sieht **darüber hinweg** (*overlooks it*).

36 The Comparison of Adverbs

(a) Adverbs have the same comparison as predicative adjectives (*31(a)*). Note however the following irregularities:

bald	eher/früher	am ehesten/am frühesten
gern	lieber	am liebsten
gut/wohl	besser	am besten
viel/sehr	mehr	am meisten
wenig	weniger/minder	am wenigsten/am mindesten

Komm so schnell du kannst (*as quickly as you can*)!
Er stürzte hinaus, so schnell er konnte (*as fast as he could*).
Er verdient weniger als ich. Dieser Zug fährt am schnellsten.
Sie fahren am besten mit dem Frühzug.
Er sorgt für mich mehr als Koch denn als Vater (*as ... than*).

(b) Adverbs have in addition an absolute superlative: aufs wärmste, aufs beste, aufs schönste, etc.
Compare: Er begrüßte sie **am herzlichsten** (*most cordially*, i.e. *more cordially than the others, than on other occasions*).
Er begrüßte sie **aufs herzlichste** (*most*, i.e. *exceedingly cordially*).

(c) Note the following forms of the superlative:
i erstens, letztens (*in the first, last place*); frühestens, höchstens, spätestens (*at the earliest, most, latest*); meist/meistens (*mostly*) strengstens (*strictly*); wenigstens/mindestens (*at least*); nicht im mindesten (*not in the least*); nicht zum wenigsten/mindesten im Sommer (*not least in summer*); nächster Tage (*in the course of the next few days*); nächstens/demnächst (*shortly, in the near future*).
Wollen Sie gütigst Platz nehmen (*please be seated*)! Es geht ihm bestens (*very well*). Ich lasse ihm bestens danken (*send him my best thanks*).
ii höchst (*most*) dumm; äußerst (*extremely*) klug; das meist aufgeführte Stück (*the most performed play*).
Komm möglichst schnell (*as quickly as possible*)!

34

37 Cardinal Numbers

Note the following points of spelling and usage:

(a) Sechzehn, siebzehn, sechzig, siebzig, hundert (*one hundred*), tausend; (im Jahre) neunzehnhundertvierundsechzig (*in 1964*).

(b) Eins (*when not followed by its dependent noun*), hunderteins, hundertzwei, tausendeins; einmal eins ist eins; eins Komma null sechs (= *1·06*); zehn nach eins (=zehn Minuten nach ein Uhr).

(c) Um ein Uhr, vor ein oder zwei Tagen, mit ein wenig/bißchen Geduld, mit ein paar Freunden, von hundertein Städten (*or* von hundertundeiner Stadt), in ein und derselben Straße, er ist mein ein und alles.

(d) Der Mann, dessen einer Sohn/eines Kind (*whose one ...*); diese eine Frau, sein eines Glas Wasser.

(e) Noch ein (*another*) Brötchen, noch zwei Glas Bier.

(f) In telephoning *zwo* is used for *zwei*: zwo acht—sieben sechs—null drei (287603).

(g) Die Freundschaft zweier/dreier großer Völker; er ging auf allen vieren; wir sind/gehen/sitzen zu zweien/zu zweit, zu dreien/zu dritt, zu vieren/zu viert. (Zu vieren = *in groups of four*; zu viert = *four in a group*.)

(h) Die Null, die Eins, die Zwei etc. (= *the figures 0, 1, 2, etc.*).

(i) Er bekam eine Eins, eine Vier (*or* einen Einser, einen Vierer) (= *school marks or gradings*); die Elf gewann das Spiel (mit) acht zu vier.

(j) Wir fahren mit der Fünfzehn (= *tram or bus*).

(k) Er ist ein Mann Mitte Fünfzig, über Fünfzig, um die mittleren Vierzig, in den Fünfzigern (*in his fifties*).

(l) Es geschah in den zwanziger/dreißiger Jahren (*in the 'twenties/'thirties*).

(m) Ein Achter (*a rowing 'eight'*); ein Achtziger/eine Achtzigerin (*octogenarian*). Ich habe nur einen Zwanziger/Hunderter (= *20/100 mark note*). Er ist in den Achtzigern (*in his eighties*).

(n) Hunderte/Tausende von Menschen; Tausende und Abertausende (*thousands and thousands*); einige Hunderte/Tausende; zu Hunderten und Tausenden; einige hundert/tausend Menschen (*a few hundred/thousand*); ein paar hundert/tausend Schritt(e).

(o) Zwei Dutzend Eier, ein halbes Dutzend Nägel.

(p) Beid- (*both, the two*)

i   Beide Brüder, die beiden Brüder, meine beiden Brüder.

ii Keine der beiden Parteien (*neither of the (two) parties*); ich mag beide nicht (*I don't like either of them = persons*).

iii Die ersten beiden (= *the first and second*); die beiden ersten (= *the two who are first*).

iv Wir beide, ihr beide, sie beide; wir beiden Deutschen; ihr beiden andern (*you other two*). Wir kamen beide früh an.

v   Beides (= *either of two things*) ist möglich. Ich mag beides nicht. Keines von beidem (*neither*).

38 Ordinal Numbers

Note the following points of spelling and usage:

(a) Der erste, der dritte, der sieb(en)te, der achte.

(b) Das erste beste Hotel (= *the first hotel (you come to)*); der zweitbeste, der drittbeste Roman; der vorletzte/zweitletzte (*last but one*), der drittletzte; der zweithöchste, der dritthöchste.

(c) Erstklassig, zweitklassig; erstrangig, zweitrangig.

(d) Er war der erste, der das sagte (*the first to say that*).

(e) Das erstemal, zum erstenmal; das erste Mal, zum ersten Mal.

(f) Der erste April, den zweiten Mai, am dritten Juni; der Erste des Monats.

(g) Er ist der Erste der Klasse; er kam als erster an (*was the first to arrive*).

(h) Friedrich der Zweite, Ludwig der Vierzehnte, Erste Hilfe.

39 Fractions

(a) (ein) halb, in halb Europa, eine halbe Stunde, das halbe Jahr, ein halbes Dutzend, auf halbem (Wege (*half way*), alle halbe Stunde (*every half hour*); die Hälfte meines Vermögens (*half my fortune*); wir kennen ihn nur zur Hälfte.

(b) eineinhalb/anderthalb Stunden ($1\frac{1}{2}$ hours), zweieinhalb, dreieinhalb, etc. (The forms *dritt(e)halb* ($2\frac{1}{2}$), *viert(e)halb* ($3\frac{1}{2}$), etc., are now obsolete.)

(c) ein Drittel, ein Viertel, das Sechstel meines Vermögens; zwei Drittel, sieben Zwanzigstel, ein Hundertstel, drei Hunderteintel, drei Hundert-zweitel etc.

(d) eine Viertelstunde, zwei Viertelstunden, in (einer) dreiviertel Stunde (*or* in drei viertel Stunden) (= *45 minutes*) ein, drei achtel Liter, eine hundertstel Sekunde.

40 Other Numeral Expressions

(a) einmal (*once*), zweimal, dreimal, etc.; vier mal vier ist sechzehn; kein einziges Mal (*not once*); nicht einmal (*not even!*).

(b) einfach (*simple*), zweifach (*twofold*), dreifach, etc.; mehrfach, vielfach, mannigfach/mannigfaltig (*manifold*); einfältig (*simple-minded!*).

(c) doppelt (*double*), ein doppeltes Vergnügen, doppelt so groß wie; um das Doppelte größer.

(d) einerlei (*of one kind*), zweierlei, dreierlei, etc.; zweierlei Arbeit; Sagen und Tun sind zweierlei (*two different things*); Kinder beiderlei Geschlechts; keinerlei Unterschied (*no distinction of any kind*); vielerlei Leute, allerlei Bücher; mir war das ganz einerlei (*all the same*).

(e) einzig (*sole, only, single, solitary*), sein einziges Kind, eine einzige Ausnahme, das einzige, was … (*the only thing that*); einzigartig (*unique*).

(f) einzeln (*separate(ly), singly, individual*), sie kamen einzeln an, die Bände werden einzeln (*singly*) verkauft; ins einzelne gehen (*go into details*), der Einzelne (*the individual*) ist machtlos; vereinzelt (= *occasional*).

(g) einsam (*lonely*), eine einsame Straße.

(h) erstens (*first, in the first place*), zweitens, drittens … letztens.

41 Measurements

Masculine and neuter nouns denoting measurements do not inflect in the plural; feminine nouns, however, (except *Mark*) do inflect in the plural.

10 Pfund, 4 Fuß breit, 100 Schritt (*100 yards*), 6 Meter zu (*by*) 3 Meter, 2000 m hoch. 8 Meter im Quadrat (*8 metres square*), 20 Qua-dratmeter groß (*20 square metres in size*), drei Paar Strümpfe, mit drei Paar Strümpfen; sie bekamen je (*they each got*) 20 Mark.
But zwei Tassen Tee, drei Flaschen Rotwein, drei Meilen.

42 Time

(a) By the clock:

i   Wieviel Uhr ist es? Wie spät ist es?
Es ist ein Uhr/eins, fünf (Minuten) nach eins/ein Uhr fünf, Viertel
nach eins/Viertel zwei, halb zwei, Viertel vor zwei/dreiviertel zwei,
zehn (Minuten) vor zwei.
Es ist zwölf Uhr, es ist Mittag, Mitternacht, es ist halb zwölf.
Es ist 3 Uhr nachts, 6 Uhr morgens, 10 Uhr vormittags, 3 Uhr
nachmittags, 6 Uhr abends, 11 Uhr nachts.
ii Um (*at*) wieviel Uhr? Um 7 Uhr, gegen (*about*) 8 Uhr, um (*round
about*) Mittag/Mitternacht. Ich komme Punkt 5 Uhr an.
iii Die Uhr geht vor, geht nach, geht richtig.
iv Es ist ein Uhr (*it is one o'clock*); es ist eine Uhr (*it is a clock*); eine
Stunde (*an, one hour, a lesson*).

(b) Date and age

i   Der wievielte ist heute? Heute ist der zweite April.
ii Wann kommt er? Er kommt nächsten Mittwoch, nächste Woche,
nächstes Jahr, in den nächsten Tagen, nächster Tage, Dienstag,
Dienstag abend, am Mittwoch, am Sonntagmorgen, am Montag-
abend, am zweiten April, im September; er kommt am Freitag, dem/
den 18. Februar.
Wann war die Schlacht bei Belle Alliance (*what was the date of the
battle of Waterloo?*)?
Wann bist du geboren? Ich bin/wurde (=*formal*) (im Jahre) 1950
geboren. Wann wurde Goethe geboren? Er wurde (im Jahre) 1749
geboren (wurde . . . geboren *used of deceased persons*). Er war damals
noch nicht geboren (worden) (*had not yet been born*).
iii Er ist sechs (Jahre alt); mit sechs Jahren ging ich zur Schule (*at the
age of 6*). In reiferen Jahren (*at a riper age*) denkt man anders. Er ist
in den besten Jahren (*in his prime*). Er ist schon bei Jahren (*getting on in
years*). Im Jahre 1000 vor Christi Geburt (*B.C.*), nach Christi Geburt
(*A.D.*).
iv Er steht in meinem Alter (*is my age*), im besten Mannesalter (*in the
prime of life*). Er starb im Alter von 60 Jahren. In ihrem Alter (*at her
age*) war ich viel größer. Er ist ein Mann mittleren Alters (*middle-
aged*), in mittlerem Alter (*in middle life*).

NOTE: Im Mittelalter (= *in the Middle Ages*); mittelalterlich (= *medieval*).

v   Weihnachten/Ostern/Pfingsten (*Christmas/Easter/Whitsun*) kommt
bald. Wir wünschen Ihnen fröhliche Weihnachten/Ostern, ein
fröhliches Weihnachtsfest, ein gesegnetes Osterfest. Er kam zu
Weihnachten/Silvester (*New Year's Eve*)/Neujahr/Ostern/Pfingsten/zu
den Ferien (*for the holidays*) nach Hause. Er kommt am Weihnachts-

abend (*Christmas Eve*) am ersten Weihnachtstag (*Christmas Day*) am zweiten Weihnachtstag (*Boxing Day*).

(c) Idiomatic expressions of time

i heute abend (*tonight, i.e. before bed-time*), heute nacht/diese Nacht (*tonight, i.e. after bed-time; last night, i.e. during the night*), morgen früh (*tomorrow morning*), gestern abend (*last night*), vorgestern, übermorgen.

ii acht Tage (*a week*), vierzehn Tage (*fortnight*), vor acht Tagen, heute vor acht Tagen (*a week ago today*), in vierzehn Tagen (*in a fortnight's time*), morgen in 14 Tagen/über 14 Tage.

iii Er kam am Morgen, am Abend, am vorigen Abend, am Vorabend (*eve*) der Hochzeit, am andern Tag (*the following day*), am nächsten Morgen, voriges Jahr, in einem anderen Jahr (*another year*), in der vorigen Woche, vorigen/letzten Dienstag. An **dem** Abend (*that night*).

43 Personal Pronouns

(a) See *98* for declension.

(b) *Du* (sing.) and *ihr* (pl.) are the familiar forms of address used with relatives, close friends, children and animals. *Sie* (sing. and pl.) is the polite form of address.

NOTE 1: *Du, ihr, dein, euer,* etc., are always written with capitals in letters.
NOTE 2: *Sie* is modern and should be replaced by *Ihr* (sing. and pl.) in older contexts and by *du* (sing.) or *ihr* (pl.) in biblical contexts.
NOTE 3: The reader, formerly addressed by the author as *du,* is now addressed as *Sie.*

(c) Remember that 'it' will be rendered by *er, sie* or *es*, etc., according to the gender of the noun 'it' refers to.

(d) The third person personal pronoun object is added after *wie* to render the English 'such as' in sentences like the following:

Sie trug Kleider, wie **sie** ihre Großmutter getragen hatte.
Er trug einen Hut, wie **ihn** sein Vater getragen hatte.

(e) The demonstrative pronoun *dessen* (m. and n. sing. gen.) and *deren* (f. sing. gen., and pl. gen.) usually replace *seiner* and *ihrer*, the genitive of *er, es* and *sie*, when things are referred to.

Er ist **ihrer** (*of her*) nicht würdig. Er schämt sich **dessen** (*of it*). Er sank auf **dessen** Armlehne (*the arm of it*).

(f) The genitive forms of *derselbe* are normally used to render the third person pronoun (referring to things or concepts) when preceded by a preposition governing the genitive, e.g. außerhalb derselben (= Familie).

(g) Note the following 'genitive' forms:

meinerseits, deinerseits, unserseits, etc. (*for my part, etc.*); meinetwegen (*for my sake; (certainly) for all I care, I don't mind*), deinetwegen (*for your sake*), etc.; (um) meinetwillen (*for my sake*) (um) unsertwillen, etc.; unsereins/unsereiner (*people like us*) darf es sagen.

(h) With most prepositions *da(r)-* is usually used instead of the accusative and/or dative of the personal pronoun when referring to things:

dafür (*for it, for them*), dahinter, darüber, darunter, (dicht) daneben (*close to it*), obendrauf (*on the top of it*)

NOTE 1: Such compounds are not possible with the prepositions *außer, entlang, gegenüber, ohne* and *seit*.

NOTE 2: In addition to their literal meanings some of these compounds have acquired other quite distinctive meanings, e.g. **dabei** (*in doing so, at the same time, while*), **dafür** (*in return*), **dagegen** (*on/to the contrary, on the other hand*), **nichts dagegen** (*nothing in comparison*), **nichts dagegen haben** (*have no objection*), **darauf** (*thereupon*), **obendrein** (*into the bargain*), **darum** (*therefore*), **dazu** (*in addition*).

NOTE 3: **Deswegen** (*on account of it, for that reason, that is why*), **demgegenüber** (*compared to this*) **dessenungeachtet** (*despite that*):

(i) Note the following uses of *es*:

i   As the object or complement of the verb or standing for an adjective already mentioned where English usually omits 'it' altogether.

Ich habe es nie versucht. Wie er es schon so oft getan hatte. Ich liebe es, hasse es, ziehe (es) vor, dorthin zu gehen. Die Rolle des Willens ist es, sich zu entscheiden (*the function of the will is to decide*). Sie ist so schön, wie es ihre Mutter einmal war. In der Tanzstunde war er nicht ein einziges Mal aufgeregt gewesen. Aber jetzt war er es (M. HAUSMANN).

ii Where *es* is the real subject which is retained even when it is not the first word in the clause.

Es regnet. Gestern hat es geschneit.
Es geht mir gut. Mir geht es schlecht. Wie geht's Ihnen?
Es sind meine Freunde. Wahrscheinlich sind es meine Freunde.
Weißt du, daß es meine Freunde sind?
Es gibt einen Gott. Leute gibt es heute noch, die das behaupten. Hier gibt es viel Obst. Weißt du, was es zum Essen gibt? Ihn gibt es nicht mehr (*he no longer exists*).
Es gibt nichts mehr zu tun. Es gab einen Streit.

iii Where *es* is a purely anticipatory grammatical subject which is omitted unless it comes first in the clause. Note that the number, singular or plural, of the verb will depend not on *es* but on the real subject of the clause.

Es ist kein Mensch da. Es sind keine Menschen da. Keine Menschen sind da. Weißt du, daß kein Mensch da ist?

Es scheint die Sonne. Die Sonne scheint.

Es gehört Mut dazu, das zu behaupten, Das zu behaupten, dazu gehört Mut.

Es wurde lange getanzt. Bei uns wurde lange getanzt.

NOTE: **Es gibt** (*there is*, *there are*) followed by the accusative insists on the existence of a thing or person. **Es ist** (*there is*) and **es sind** (*there are*) followed by the nominative merely assert the presence of a thing or person. **Es gibt** also has the meaning of 'happens', 'occurs', 'comes about'.

iv The phrase: es war einmal (ein König) (*there was once upon a time ...*) always begins with the anticipatory *es*.

v With personal pronouns *es* never introduces the clause but follows the verb which agrees with the personal pronoun.

Du bist es (*it is you*). Sind Sie es? Er ist es, der das gesagt hat.

vi The common English construction: 'it is ... that ...' is not a normal construction in German and is omitted.

Thus:

'It is with regret that I must decline this offer' becomes in German simply: Mit Bedauern muß ich dieses Angebot abschlagen.

NOTE: *Es* as a direct object (unlike other pronouns) cannot be stressed by beginning the main clause with it. Where stress is required it is replaced by *das*. e.g. **Das** weiß ich nicht.

44 Possessive Adjectives and Pronouns

(a) For declension, see *89, 100*.

(b) Note that 'his' = *sein*, 'her' = *ihr* irrespective of the gender of the following noun. Thus: *seine Mutter*, *ihr Vater*.

(c) The expression 'of my, your, etc., own' can often be neatly rendered by *ein eigen(er) ...* Thus:

Ich habe einen eigenen Wagen/ein eigenes Rad.
Wir haben ein eigenes Haus (*a house of our own*).

(d) The possessive pronoun (of which there are three related forms: *meiner, der meine, der meinige*) agrees in gender and number with the noun to which it refers. In conversation *meiner*, etc., is more usual.

Deine Ausgabe ist teurer als meine/die meine/die meinige. Mit meinem (e.g. Wagen) fährt es sich schneller als mit deinem. Deiner (e.g. Hut) gefällt mir besser als ihrer. Dies ist mein Buch, das ist deines und das sind ihre (i.e. Bücher). Hier ist ihr Buch, wo ist seines.

(e) The genitive rarely occurs, being generally replaced by the construction *von*+dative:

Das ist eins von meinen (*one of mine*); ein Freund von mir (*a friend of mine*).

(f) Except when, as in (d) above, the subject is *es*, *das* or *dies* the possessive pronouns *mein, dein, sein, unser, euer* (but not *ihr* or *Ihr*) used predicatively are still occasionally, in elevated language, left uninflected.

> Das Buch/der Hut/die Handtasche ist dein. Du bist mein.

(g) Die Sein(ig)en (*his people/family*), das Sein(ig)e (*his property*); du mußt das Dein(ig)e tun (*your share/bit*).

45 Reflexive Pronouns

(a) For declension, see 99.

(b) *Selbst* strengthens the reflexive pronoun and must be added after the third person genitive.

> Er hat sich selbst verletzt. Er spottet seiner **selbst**.
> Du traust dir selbst nicht. Jeder ist sich selbst der Nächste. Er lacht über sich selbst.

(c) The reflexive pronoun generally refers to the subject of the sentence. It can, however, sometimes correctly refer to the object of the sentence.

> Er sah einen Turm vor sich (*in front of him*). Der Turm erhob sich vor ihm (*in front of him*). Er hörte sie zu ihm sprechen. *But:* Er hörte sie zu sich sprechen (*to herself*). Er überließ die beiden sich selbst (*to themselves*).

(d) Das ist ein Problem für sich (*a separate problem*). Er dachte bei sich (*to himself*). An sich (*essentially*) ist es ganz leicht. Das Ding an sich (*in itself*); an und für sich betrachtet (*regarded by itself*).

(e) The dative reflexive pronoun is also used to indicate the possessor when parts of the body and (sometimes) clothing are mentioned:

> Ich wusch mir die Hände, putzte mir die Zähne. Sie zog sich die Jacke/die Schuhe/die Strümpfe an.

46 Reciprocal Pronouns

(a) Wir lieben uns/einander; wir sind uns/einander heute morgen schon begegnet (*one another*); sie lasen sich/einander vor (*to one another*).

(b) Sie denken aneinander; sie sprechen miteinander.

(c) Die Arme einer um des andern Schulter, durchschritten sie den Saal (*their arms round one another's shoulders*) (DIE ZEIT).

47 Interrogative Adjectives and Pronouns

(a) **Welcher** (declension, see 90)

Welchen (*which*) Roman hast du gelesen? Welches ist der höchste Berg. Welches sind die höchsten Berge?
Welche Berge sind die höchsten?

(b) **Was für einer/was für welche; was für (ein)**

Was für einer (*what sort of one*) ist das? Was für welche sind das? Was für ein (*what sort of a*) Roman ist das? Was für Romane sind das? Was für Wein ist das?
Mit was für einem Bleistift schreiben Sie?

(c) **Wer** (declension, see 96)

Wer ist das? Wer sind Sie? Wer sind diese Leute? Wer kommt? (*who is coming ?*) Wer kommt alles ? (*who are coming ?*) Wen traf er ? Wessen (*whose*) Handtasche ist das ? Wem gehört diese Handtasche ? An wen schreibst du ?

(d) **Was** (declension, see 96)

Was ist er? Was sind diese Leute? Was sind das für Leute? Das sind Handwerker. Was meinst du? Wessen (*of what*) ist er schuldig? Woran (an was = *colloquial*) denkst du? Womit (mit was! = *colloquial*) schreibst du? Worin (*in what*) besteht der Unterschied? Worein (wohin *is more usual*) (*into what*) hast du es geworfen? Was (= warum, *colloquial use*) weint sie denn ?

NOTE: *Welches/wer/was* with *sein* are complements, not subjects. Hence the person and number of the verb will depend not on them but on the following noun or pronoun. (Cf. 49(c) NOTE.)

48 Relative Pronouns, Adverbs and Clauses

(a) Relative clauses (with the finite verb coming last!) are introduced by the relative pronouns *der, welcher, so* (obsolete, poetical and indeclinable), *wer, was* (declension, see 95, 96) or by relative adverbs e.g. *wo, da, worüber, womit, um dessentwillen* (m. and n. sing.), *um derentwillen* (f. sing. and m. f. n. pl.), *dessentwegen*, etc., and, in elevated speech, *darin* etc.

(b) The relative pronoun, never omitted in German, agrees with its antecedent in gender and number.

(c) After the genitive of the relative pronoun (*dessen, deren*) the noun immediately following never has the definite article. (Cf. 'whose' in English.)

43

(d) The pronominal adverb forms *womit*, *worauf*, etc., are used with indefinite antecedents. They must never be used with an animate object antecedent, and with definite inanimate object antecedents the full form of the relative tends now to be preferred.

(e) The relative pronoun *welcher* is rarely used in spoken German. Its chief use is for the avoidance of ugly repetitions and as an 'elegant variation'.

(f) Examples of use:

i   Der Mann, **der** gekommen **war**, hieß Hille.
Das ist der Junge, **den** ich heute morgen **traf**.
Das Mädchen, **dessen** Schwester krank **ist**, wohnt jetzt hier.
Frau Meßner, bei **deren** Eltern wir **wohnen**, kam gestern.
Die Kinder, mit **denen** wir gestern **spielten**, waren sehr nett.
Das Messer, mit **dem** (*rather than:* womit) ich mich **schnitt**, ...
Eine Stille, **darin** das Leben ... bemerkbar **ward** (G. HAUPTMANN).
Mein Bruder, **um dessentwillen** (*for whose sake*) sie ihre Stelle aufgegeben **hat**, ...
Die Kleider, **derentwegen** (*because of which*) sie heute **vorbeikam**, ...
Der Grund, **weswegen/dessentwegen/warum/weshalb** er nicht gekommen **ist**, ...
Worte, **die** zu verstehen ich mir keine Mühe **gab**, ... (*which I did not try to understand*).
Pläne, von **denen** er **weiß**, daß er sie nicht wird ausführen können, ... (*which he knows he will not be able to*).

ii Du, **der du** (*you who*) das **sagst**, lügst.
Wir, **die wir** das nicht **glauben**, ...
But Er, **der** (*he, e.g. Karl, who*) das **sagt**, ...
Ich bin es, **der** angerufen **hat** (*It is I who* ...).

iii Das, was; dasjenige, was; dasselbe, was; das wenige, was; alles, was; vieles, was; manches, was; einiges, was; nichts, was; allerlei (mancherlei, vielerlei), was; etwas, was/das.

iv Das Beste, was (*the best thing*); das einzige, was (*the only thing*); das erste, was (*the first thing*).

v   Das ist es/alles, woran ich mich erinnern kann.
(Das,) worum es sich handelt, weiß ich nicht mehr.
Nicht das, um was man kämpfte, ...
(Das,) worauf es ankam, habe ich jetzt vergessen.

vi Tue, was du kannst.
Er erinnerte sich an das (*not:* daran), was ich gesagt hatte.

vii Er behauptet, was (= *a thing which*) ich nicht glaube, daß sie verheiratet ist.

viii Wer wagt, gewinnt. Wem nicht zu raten ist, dem ist auch nicht zu helfen. Wer sie aufmerksam las, kann nicht zweifeln, daß ... (*Nobody who ... can doubt*).

ix Dort, wo der Mann steht, ... Überall, wo ...
Zur Zeit, da (*or* wo) ...

49 Demonstrative Adjectives and Pronouns

(a) **Dieser, jener** (declension, see *90*).

Jener (in conversation usually replaced by *der da/dort*) is used chiefly in opposition to *dieser* and 'that' is otherwise rendered by, e.g. the demonstrative *der* or *dieser* followed later by *da/dort*.

Dieser Hut ist eleganter als jener/als der da. Mit diesem Auto fährt man schneller als mit jenem/als mit dem dort.
Helga und Irma sehen sich ähnlich, doch hat diese (*the latter*) blonde und jene (*the former*) schwarze Haare. (Cf. *31(d)iii.*)
Dies(es) und jenes (*this and that*); wir sprachen von diesem und jenem.
In jener schrecklichen Nacht, in der ... (*On that terrible night when ...*).
But Die/diese Schale dort (*that bowl*) möchte ich haben.

(b) **Solcher** (declension, see *90*); **so ein(er)** (sing. only); **derlei, derart, dergleichen** (all indecl.)

Solcher is declined strong (see *86(a)*), except when preceded by *ein*, when it is declined as in *92*. It is uninflected when followed by *ein*, and may remain uninflected when followed by an adjective.

Ich habe solchen (so einen) Durst, solche Kopfschmerzen.
Sie hatte solche Angst. Wir haben solches schlechte/solch schlechtes Wetter gehabt.
Mit solcher Anmut; mit solchem Ernst.
Ein solcher Mann, solch ein Mann, so ein (*such a*) Mann, solch junge Leute, solche jungen Leute.
Solche, die ... (*those who ....*).
So einer kann es nicht verstehen.
Derlei Überlegungen; derart Briefe; dergleichen Leute.

(c) **Der, die, das** (declension, see *97*); **dies** (indecl.)

Der (*he*) hat es getan. Die (*her*) kenne ich gut. Das ist deins, dies ist meins. Das (*those*) sind deine, dies (*these*) sind meine. Das/der/die bin ich. Ich bin dessen ganz sicher. Dem kann ich nicht widerstehen.

NOTE: *Der/die/das/dies* used with *sein* are complements, not subjects. Hence the person and number of the verb will depend not on them but on the subject. (Cf. *43(i)iii.*)

Der, der das behauptet ... (*he, the person, who*); die, die das behaupten, ... (*those (people) who*). Der (Mann) war es, der ... (*He it was (it was that man) who*). Viele **derer**, die ... (*many of those who*); unter denen, die ... (*among those who*); mit denen anderer Länder.
Dein Wagen fährt schneller als der deines Bruders (*your brother's*).
Mit deinem Wagen fährt es sich bequemer als mit dem deines Bruders.

45

Mein Bruder und dessen (*his*) Freund; ihre Schwester und deren (*her*, i.e. *the sister's*) Freundin.

Der einzige Grund dafür ist der, daß er nicht ausgehen will. Seine einzige Absicht ist die, kein Geld auszugeben.

(d) **Derjenige** (declension, see 94)

Derjenige, der ... (*he, the person, the man, who*); diejenige, die ... (*she who*); diejenigen, die ... (*those, the people, who*); diejenigen Bücher, die ... (*those books that*); mit allen denjenigen, deren ... (*those whose*).

(e) **Derselbe** (declension, see 94); **der gleiche**

Der gleiche means both 'identical' and 'similar', *dasselbe* only means 'identical'. When mere similarity needs to be shown *der gleiche* should be used.

Sie hatte denselben Hut auf wie gestern. Sie hatte den gleichen Hut auf wie ihre Schwester.

An demselben/am selben Tage *or* an dem gleichen Tage.

Es läuft/kommt auf dasselbe/das gleiche hinaus (*amounts to the same thing*).

(f) **Selbst, selber** (indeclinable)

Except in the phrase *von selbst* (of its own accord) *selbst* must be preceded by a noun or pronoun. *Selber* is more colloquial.

Ich selbst, wir selbst, Gott selbst.

Er ist nicht er selbst. Er denkt nur an sich selbst (selber).

Die Tür schließt sich von selbst.

50 Indefinite Pronouns

(a) **Man**

Like *on* in French, *man* (nominative only) is used where English has 'one', 'you', 'we', 'somebody', 'people', etc., or a passive construction. There is no genitive; the accusative is supplied by *einen*, the dative by *einem*.

Man ißt. Man kommt. Man sagt, daß ... (*it is said that*).

Hier verkauft man Zigaretten (*are sold*).

Was man/einer sagt, kann man nicht immer glauben.

Man hat seinen (*one's*) Stolz. Sie sollten einen in Ruhe lassen. Das steht einem ganz frei.

NOTE: *Man* is not interchangeable with *er*, *Sie*, *du*, etc. If you have started using *man*, go on using it consistently.

(b) **Einer; keiner** (declined strong, see *86(a)*, *100(a)*)

Eine(r) von euch muß gehen. Ich weiß eines (*one thing*). Der Titel eines (*of one*) der Bücher. In einem der Bücher. Ich habe es von einem/einer von euch. Keine(r) (*not one*) von euch darf ein Wort sagen.

Gar keiner (*nobody at all*) wollte kommen. In keinem der Bücher. Sie ist meine Nina, keines sonst (*nobody else's*) (RINSER).

NOTE: *One(s)* is not translated when it occurs in English after an adjective: Die große Schale dort, die rote (*the red one*); die großen Schalen dort, die roten (*the red ones*). Dein Leben ist ein sehr volles (*a full one*).

(c) **Jemand; niemand**

Jemand (*somebody*) ist da. Kennst du jemand(en), der ... (*anybody who*). Das ist jemands Hut. Er spricht mit jemand(em).

Ist sonst noch jemand (*anybody in addition*) gekommen?

Jemand anders (*somebody else*, i.e. *different*) ist da.

Er spricht mit jemand(em) anders.

Niemand ist gebildet, der ... Niemand anders als (*other than*).

Der Krieg ist niemands Schuld (HESSE).

(d) **Jeder, jedweder, jeglicher** (declined strong, *90*); **jedermann**

Jedweder is more emphatic than *jeder* and means 'every single' (*jeder einzelne*). It belongs to the literary language only. *Jeglicher* is becoming archaic and is used now only in elevated style. All except *jedermann* can be used adjectivally. *Jedermann* inflects only in the genitive.

Jeder/jedermann weiß das. Er nimmt jeden (*anybody*) an. Jedermanns Sache (*everybody's business*). Wir meinten jeder, daß ... (*we each of us thought ...*). Wie jeder andere (*like everybody/anybody else, any other*); jede beliebige Person (*any person whatever*).

Jede(!) Ferien (*every holidays*).

(e) **Welcher** (declined strong, see *90*)

Er hat keinen Tabak. Hast du welchen (*any*)? Er hat keine Milch. Hast du welche? Er hat kein Geld. Gib ihm welches (*some*)! Er hat keine Zigaretten. Hast du welche?

51 Indefinite Numeral Adjective-Pronouns

a) **Alles** (*everything, all*) ist umsonst. Dies/das alles (*all this/that*) ist falsch. Dies/das alles (*all these/those*) sind triftige (*cogent*) Gründe. Ohne allen (*any*) Grund; trotz alles/allen Lärms; allen Ernstes (*in all seriousness*); mit aller Kraft. Trotz alledem (*despite all that*).

Alle (*everybody, all*) sind gekommen. Sie sind alle gekommen.

Alle anderen sind stehengeblieben. Alle diejenigen, die ... (*all (of) those who*).

All(e) diese Leute, all(e) meine Bücher.
Alle zwei Wochen (*every second week, every two weeks*).
Der Wein, die Milch, das Brot ist **alle** (*all gone, finished*).

(b) Ich will dir **etwas** (*or* **was**: *colloquial*) sagen. So etwas (*that sort of thing*) ist nur zu wahrscheinlich. So etwas Ähnliches (*something of that sort*); bei so etwas (*in that sort of matter*). Sonst etwas gefällig? (*is there anything else you would like?*) Er hat etwas anderes (*something else*) gekauft. Sprechen wir von etwas anderem.
Ich habe **nichts** gesagt.

(c) Gib mir **etwas** Brot, **ein bißchen** Brot, **ein wenig** Brot, **mehr** Brot, **weniger** Brot! Gib mir etwas, etwas mehr, ein bißchen mehr, ein bißchen weniger! Das ist **lauter** (*sheer*) Unsinn.

(d) **Viel(es)**, **nur wenig(es)**, **manches** (*quite a lot*), **einiges** war mir bekannt. Ich habe viel(es), zuviel, nur wenig(es), manches, einiges erlebt. Er hat viel (wenig) Humor, Zeit, Geld. Vie**len** Dank (= *only exception in the acc. masc.*). Er hat einigen Humor, einige Erfahrung. Er hat einiges Verständnis dafür. Mit wenig, viel Mühe, mit viel(er) Anstrengung, viel(em) Fleiß, mit wenig Eifer, mit einiger Anstrengung, mit einigem Fleiß; trotz der vielen Arbeit; wieviel Bücher?

(e) **Viele**, **zu viele**, **wenige**, **einige/etliche** (*some*), **mehrere** (*several*), **manche** (*quite a number*), **sämtliche**, **andere** junge Leute; die Stimmen vieler, weniger, einiger/etlicher, mehrerer, mancher, sämtlicher, anderer junger Leute; einige wenige Leute; wie viele Bücher?

(f) Sein **ganzes** Vermögen (*the whole of his fortune*); in dem **ganzen** Dorf; in **ganz** Berlin, Deutschland, Europa.

(g) **Die einen ... die anderen** (*some ... others*); mit den einen ... mit den anderen. **Nur die wenigen** wissen davon.

52 Prepositions governing the Accusative

(a) **ausgenommen** (*except*)
Alle rauchten, ihn ausgenommen.

NOTE: This word can also be used as a conjunction, e.g. alle rauchten, ausgenommen er; keinem hat er etwas angeboten, ausgenommen mir.

(b) **bis** (*till, by, to, as far as, right up to*)
Er bleibt bis nächsten Montag. Bis (*by*) nächsten Sonntag bin ich zurück. Bis morgen! (*see you tomorrow*). Zwei bis drei Stunden; von

Montag bis Mittwoch. Wir gingen bis zur Stelle, bis zum Ufer (*up to*). Bis zu diesem Tag, bis ans Ende der Welt, bis zum Ende des Reichs, bis (nach) Stuttgart. Alle kamen bis auf einen (*except one*).

(c) **durch** (*through, by*)

Er ging durch den Wald. Er wurde durch das Signal gewarnt.

(d) **entlang** (*along*)

Er ging die Straße entlang (*along, up, down the street*).

(e) **für** (*for, in relation to, for the benefit of, to the value of, by*)

Das ist genug für heute. Er ist kräftig für sein Alter. Er arbeitet für sie. Er kaufte für 2 Mark Äpfel (*worth of*). Schritt für Schritt; Tag für Tag (*by, after*). Er geht für (*colloquial*) vierzehn Tage nach Paris.

(f) **gegen** (*against, towards, approximately, about, compared to*); **wider** (*against; literary, except in a few phrases*).

Das war gegen (wider) meine Absicht, gegen (wider) meinen ausdrücklichen Befehl. Er tat es wider Willen (*reluctantly*). Er kam wider Erwarten (*against all expectation*). Wir fahren gegen Osten, Süden, Westen, Norden. Gegen 4 Uhr, gegen Ende des Monats, gegen 50 Verunglückte (*about*). Er ist nichts gegen Sie (*compared to you*).

(g) **ohne** (*without*)

Er tat es ohne mein Wissen.

(h) **um** (*round, exactly at, about, approximately at, by, for*)

Sie sitzen um den Tisch. Um 4 Uhr (*at*); um diese Zeit (*about*); um 1910 herum; Jahr um Jahr, ein Jahr ums andere (*by, after*). Er ist um einen Kopf größer als sie. Er ist um nichts gebessert. Um alles in der Welt nicht (*not for anything in*). Sie liefen um die Wette miteinander (*raced against one another*).

53 Prepositions governing the Genitive

(a)

abseits *off/away from*	diesseits *on this side of*
angesichts *in view of*	einschließlich *including*
anhand *with the aid of*	gelegentlich *on the occasion of*
anläßlich *on the occasion of*	halber *for the sake of*
(an)statt *instead of*	hinsichtlich *with regard to*
anstelle *in place of*	infolge *owing to, as a result of*
aufgrund *on the basis of*	inmitten *among, in the midst of*
ausschließlich *excluding*	innerhalb *inside, within*
außerhalb *outside*	jenseits *on the other side of*
bezüglich *with regard to*	kraft *by virtue of*

längsseits *alongside*
laut *according to*
(ver)mittels *by means of, with*
nördlich *to the north of*
ob *on account of*
oberhalb *above, higher up*
seitens *on the part of*
trotz[1] *in spite of*
um ... willen *because/for the sake of*
unbeschadet *without detriment to*
ungeachtet *in spite of*

ungerechnet *not including*
unterhalb *below, lower than*
unweit *not far from*
vermöge *by virtue/dint of*
von ... wegen *by the authority of*
während *during*
wegen *because of*
zeit *during*
zugunsten *on behalf of, in favour of*
zwecks *for the purpose of*

(b) *Examples:*

Außerhalb der Stadt, innerhalb der Stadt, oberhalb des Dorfs, unterhalb des Dorfs, der Brücke; innerhalb eines Monats.

Bezüglich derer, die ...; einschließlich der Kosten; der Ehre halber; inmitten der Häuser; kraft seines Amtes; laut seines Briefes; mitten während der Mahlzeit (*in the midst of*); zeit ihres Lebens; zugunsten der neuen Grundsätze. Nördlich/östlich/südlich/westlich des Flusses.

Um Gottes/Himmels willen; von Staats wegen; von Rechts wegen (*by right*).

Um meinetwillen/deinetwillen, etc.; meinetwegen, deinetwegen, etc. *or* (*colloquially*) wegen mir(!), *but not* wegen meiner.

Infolge des Krieges litten viele an Hunger.

But Wegen des Vaters habe ich nichts gesagt.

Er hat es statt meiner gemacht.

But Er hat es mir statt (*conjunction*) meinem Bruder gegeben.

Trotz des schlechten Wetters, *but:* trotzdem, trotz allem, trotz alledem.

54 Prepositions governing the Dative

(a) **aus** (*out of, from, of*)

Er ging aus dem Haus. Er ist aus der Schweiz. Er stammt aus guter Familie. Ich weiß es aus Erfahrung. Themen aus (*from*) Klopstocks Oden.

Es ist aus Leder, Glas, Eisen, etc. Aus (*for what*) welchem Grunde? Er tat es aus (*for*) Liebe, aus (*from*) Interesse, Vaterlandsliebe, aus Versehen (*by mistake, accident*), aus Gründen, die ... (*on grounds*), aus (*for*) Mangel, aus Furcht angetrieben (*actuated by fear*).

(b) **bei** (*at* (*the house of*), *near, with, among(st), in* (*the works of*), *by, on*)

Er wohnt bei seinem Vater. Die Schlacht bei (*of*) Leipzig; Potsdam bei Berlin.

---

[1] Also with dative

Er ist immer bei der (*at his*) Arbeit. Bei den Franzosen; bei Goethe.
Bei (*by*) elektrischem Licht; bei (*in*) schlechtem Wetter.
Bei (*on*) meiner Ankunft, Rückkehr; bei näherer Prüfung (*on closer
examination*); bei so etwas (*on this sort of matter*); bei der Veröffent-
lichung (*on publication*), bei dieser Gelegenheit (*on this occasion*); er
hat kein Geld bei (*on*) sich. Beim ersten Anblick (*at the first glance*); bei
ihrem Anblick (*at the sight of her*); bei (*at*) jedem Schritt, jedem dritten
Wort; bei (*at*) Tagesanbruch, Sonnenuntergang; beim Aussteigen (*on/
while getting out*); bei der Durchsicht (*on perusing, in his perusal*).

(c) **binnen** (*within*, of time)

Binnen einem Jahr, zwei Tagen, kurzem.

(d) **dank** (*thanks to*: also with the genitive)

Dank meinem Fleiße; dank dieser Maßnahmen (C. STERNHEIM).

(e) **entgegen** (*contrary to, against, towards*)

Er tat es entgegen meinen Wünschen/meinen Wünschen entgegen;
entgegen allem Anschein (*contrary to (all) appearances*). Der Wind war
ihnen entgegen. Dem Toten Meer entgegen.

(f) **entlang** (cf. *52(d)*) (*along*: rarely follows noun)

Entlang dem Ufer, dem Ufer entlang waren ...

(g) **gegenüber** (*opposite; towards*, in figurative sense; *compared with*)

Er wohnt mir gegenüber, der Kirche gegenüber/gegenüber der Kirche.
Mir gegenüber hat er sich immer anständig benommen.
Er hatte mir gegenüber viel bessere Chancen gehabt.

(h) **gemäß** (*in accordance, conformity with*)

Deinem Wunsch gemäß, seinem Stande gemäß, den Gesetzen gemäß.

(i) **gleich** (*like*: also regarded as an adjective governing the dative, see *22(d)*)

Gleich mir hat er nichts gegessen.

(j) **längs** (*along*: also with the genitive)

Längs dem Wege (*or*: des Weges) stehen Bäume.

(k) **mit** (*with, in*)

Sie kam mit ihm. Sie winkte mit der Hand, mit dem Taschentuch
(*waved*). Er fuhr mit der Hand (*passed his hand*) über die Stirn. Er
fuhr mit der Hand (*put his hand*) in die Tasche. Er stieß ihn mit dem
Fuß/dem Ellenbogen/der Faust (*kicked/nudged/punched*) Er schrieb

mit (*in*) Tinte, mit Bleistift. Mit Gewalt (*by force*), mit Absicht (*on purpose*), mit der Zeit (*in* (*the course of*) *time*), mit einmal (*all at once*), mit einem Schlag (*at one blow*), mit der Überzeugung (*under the conviction*); mit lauter Stimme (*in a*); mit anderen Worten.

(l) **nach** (*to* (*place*), *after, according to, to judge by*)

Er fuhr nach der Stadt, nach Bonn, nach Italien, nach Amerika, nach Hause (*home*).

Er kam nach (*after*) mir, nach einer Stunde; nach Christi Geburt (*A.D.*).

Nach meiner Ansicht, Meinung/meiner Ansicht, Meinung nach (*in my opinion*), nach Verdienst (*according to merit*), allem Anschein nach (*to all appearance*), der Reihe nach, (*in turn, in rotation*), seinen Jahren nach (*to judge by*); je nach dem Wetter/den Umständen (*depending on/ according to, the weather/circumstances*). Ich kenne ihn dem Namen nach (*by name*). Er malt nach der Natur (*from nature*).

(m) **nächst, zunächst** (*next to*)

Es steht (zu-)nächst dem Bahnhof, dem Bahnhof zunächst; (*with pronouns*) nächst ihm, ihm zunächst.

(n) **nahe** (*near:* also regarded as an adjective governing the dative, see 22(*d*))

Sie stand nahe seinem Hause. Nahe der Erdoberfläche.

(o) **nebst, samt, mitsamt** (*together with*)

Die Mutter kam nebst/(mit-)samt ihren Kindern.

(p) **seit** (*since, for* (*length of time*))

Seit dem Krieg, seit seiner Abreise. Seit (*for*) einem Jahr wohnt sie bei uns.

(q) **von** (*from, of, by, out of*)

Er ist von Berlin nach Hannover gereist. Von Haus zu Haus, von Zeit zu Zeit. Die Königin von England. Ein Mann von 40 Jahren; ein Mann von Ehre; ein Mann von großer, kleiner Statur/Gestalt (*a tall, short man*).

Südlich, nördlich, westlich, östlich von (*to the south, etc., of*) Paris.

Ein Bild von (*by*) Dürer. Er wurde von ihm geschlagen.

Er ist von Geburt (*by birth*) ein Engländer. Ich kenne ihn von Ansehen (*by sight*), von Person (*personally*).

Eine Ausnahme von der Regel (*exception to*). Neun von zehn (*nine out of ten*).

(r) **zu** (*to, in, at*)

Er ging zu ihnen, zum Arzt (*doctor* or *doctor's*), zum Bahnhof, zur Post, zur Brücke, zum Dorf, zum Markt(-platz).
Er ging zu Bett. Bitte, zu Tisch! Er kam heute zu Hause an.
Er kam zu Fuß, zu Pferd, zu Rad, zu Schiff.
Er ißt bei uns zu Mittag, zu Abend.
10 Briefmarken zu (*at*) 20 Pfennig.
Zu unseren Lebzeiten (*in our lifetime*), zu (*in*) unserer Zeit, zu einer Zeit (*at one time, epoch*), zu Anbeginn (*at the very beginning*), zur rechten Zeit (*in time, punctually*), zu (*at*) Ostern, zu Weihnachten, zu Pfingsten.
Zu (*on*) beiden Seiten; zu meiner Rechten/Linken.
Zu unserem Schaden (*to our cost/loss*), zum Wohl (*for the good*) des Volkes, zum Unterschied von (*as distinct from, in contra-distinction to*), zur Not (*if need be*), zum Glück (*fortunately*), zum Beispiel, zur Frau geben/nehmen (*give/take in marriage*), zur Frau haben (*have as a wife*), zum Dichter geboren (*born to be*).
Das Wirtshaus zum Roten Adler (*The Red Eagle Inn*).

N O T E: '**To** a person' (motion) is nearly always *zu*.

(s) **zufolge** (*in accordance with, according to*)

Ihrem Brief zufolge habe ich ...

(t) **zuwider** (*contrary to, against*)

Das ist dem Gesetz, Ihrem Versprechen zuwider.

N O T E: Er ist mir zuwider (= *adverb*) (*he is repugnant to me, I find him loathsome*)

55 Prepositions governing the Accusative or Dative

(a) *An, auf, außer, hinter, in, neben, über, unter, vor, zwischen* govern the accusative to indicate movement **to** a place, the dative to indicate rest or movement **at** a place, e.g.

Er setzte sich (*sat down*) auf **die** Bank; er saß (*was sitting*) auf **einer** Bank.
Das Flugzeug flog über (*flew across*) **die** Stadt; das Flugzeug kreiste über (*circled above*) **der** Stadt.

(b) When used idiomatically the same rule applies if the distinction can still be felt; otherwise the accusative is used after *auf, über*, the dative after *an, in, unter, vor, zwischen*.

The following are common idiomatic expressions:

(c) **an + accusative** (*on, to*)

Er ging ans Meer (*to the seaside*), an die Front; er setzte sich ans Feuer (*by the fire*). Sie kommen an die Reihe (*it is your turn*).

(d) **an** + **dative** (*at, on, by, along, in*)

Am nächsten Tag/Morgen/Abend ((*the*) *next* ...); an diesem Nachmittag (*that afternoon*); am Ende der Woche, am Wochenende.
Wir sind am Meer (*at the seaside*), nahe an (*near*) der Küste, am
Kamin (*by the fireplace*); die Häuser am Ufer (*along the bank, on the
shore*); an der Themse, der Mosel (*by/on the Thames, Mosel(le)*); an
der Seite des Berges; am (*on, along*) Horizont; an dieser Stelle (*in, on,
at this spot*); an deiner Stelle (*in your place, if I were you*); an meiner
Seite (*at*); an meiner Linken, Rechten (*on*); was hast du an (*on*)
der Schulter? Die Sterne am (*in*) Himmel; ein Professor an (*at*) der
Universität.
Die Reihe/es ist an ihm (*it is his turn*); es ist an mir, es zu tun (*it is for
me to* ...); es ist an der Zeit, daß ... (*it is time that*); alles, was sie an
Seele besaß (*possessed in the way of soul*); das Schrecklichste an der
Sache (*the most terrible thing about the matter*).

(e) **auf** + **accusative** (*on to, to, into*)

Er ging auf (*to*) die Post/Bank/Universität/den Markt, auf (*into*)
die Straße.
Er ging auf die Jagd (*hunting*); er ging aufs Land (*into the country*);
er zog aufs Land (*moved into*); er zog sich auf sein Gut zurück (*retired
to his estate*).
Er ging auf (*for*) zehn Tage an die See; auf die Dauer (*in the long run*)
ist das unmöglich.
Auf diese Weise (*in this way*), auf andere Weise, auf jeden Fall (*in any
case*), auf Glück oder Unglück (*for better or worse*), er tat/versuchte es
auf gut Glück (*he risked it*); er tat es auf eigene Kosten (*at his own
cost*); auf den ersten Blick (*at first sight*).
Sage es auf (*in*) deutsch, englisch, französisch!

(f) **auf** + **dative** (*on, at, in*)

Er war auf (*at*) dem Markt, dem Bahnhof, auf (*in*) der Straße, auf
dem Meer (*at sea, on/in the sea*), auf (*at*) der Post, der Bank. Er ist auf
dem Lande (*in the country*).
Auf (*on*) seiner Reise, dem Rückweg, der anderen Seite.
Er wurde auf frischer Tat ertappt (*caught in the act*).

(g) **außer** + **accusative** (*beside, out of*)

Ich geriet außer mich vor Wut (*got beside myself*). Das setzt es außer
allen Zweifel (*puts beyond all doubt*). Die Fabrik ist außer Betrieb
gesetzt worden (*has been closed down*).

(h) **außer** + **dative** (*except for, out of, beside*)

Außer dir (*apart from, except for*) habe ich niemand.
Wir essen montags außer dem Haus (*eat out*). Er ist außer (*aller*)

Gefahr. Er ist außer Atem.
Ich war außer mir vor Freude, Wut, etc. (*beside myself with*).

(i) **hinter + accusative** (*behind*)

Er hat ihn hinters Licht geführt (*deceived, taken him in*).

(j) **hinter + dative** (*behind, beyond*)

Die Sonne verschwand hinter den Wolken. Er versteckte sich hinter einem Baum. Er kam hinter dem Schrank hervor (*came out from behind*).
Das liegt hinter (*beyond*) Osnabrück.

(k) **in + accusative** (*into, to*)

Er kam in die Nähe (*near*), ging ins Freie (*into the open*), reiste ins Ausland (*went abroad*), fuhr in die Schweiz (*went to Switzerland*), flog in die Vereinigten Staaten (*flew to the United States*). Er ging ins (*to*) Theater, ins Kino, ins Konzert, in die Oper, ins Büro. Er brachte es wieder in Ordnung (*put it right*). Ich schnitt mich in den Finger (*cut my finger*).

(l) **in + dative** (*in, on*)

Er ist in der Nähe (*nearby*), im Freien (*in the open, out of doors*); er lebt im Ausland (*abroad*); in der Schule (*at school*); im Radio/ Fernsehen (*on*); im Grunde (genommen) (*basically*); ich bin im Bilde (*I see, I am in the picture*); ich ging im Haus ein und aus.
In dem Augenblick (*at that moment*), im nächsten Augenblick (*the next moment*), im letzten Augenblick (*at*), in den Tagen der Verzweiflung, in einem anderen Jahr (*another year*), in (*on*) diesem Punkt, in einem Abstand/einer Entfernung von (*at an interval/distance of*), in regelmäßigen Abständen, in den Straßen Londons (*not auf*), im Gegensatz zu (*in contrast to, unlike*), im Durchschnitt, (*on the average*), im Dienst (*on duty*), im Schritt/Trott/Galopp (*at a walking pace, at a trot/gallop*), im leichten Galopp (*at a canter*), im wilden Galopp (*galloping madly*).

(m) **über + accusative** (*over, across*)

Er fuhr über (*via*) Ostende nach Köln. Er blieb über Nacht (*overnight*) bei uns. Das Jahr über (*throughout the year*); tagsüber; heute übers Jahr (*a year today*). Tränen liefen ihr über (*down*) die Wangen.
Kinder über 8 Jahre; eine Rechnung über (*for*) 10 Mark.

(n) **über + dative** (*during; because of*, also with accusative)

Er schlief über dem Lesen ein; er vergaß den Dichter über dem/ den Menschen; er erwachte über dem Lärm.

(o) **unter** + **dative** (*among, between, under*)

Unter (*among*) den Leuten, meinen Papieren; unter anderem (*among other things*); unter uns gesagt (*between ourselves*).

Unter dieser Bedingung (*on this condition*), unter der Regierung (*in the reign*) Wilhelms II., unter diesen Umständen (*in/under these circumstances*), unter dem Vorwand (*pretext*), unter dem Namen K. bekannt (*known as K., by the name of K.*).

Unter (*during*) der Woche, der Predigt.

(p) **vor** + **dative** (*in front of, ago, outside*)

Vor (*ago*) vielen Jahren, vor langer Zeit, heute vor einem Jahr.

Vor allem/vor allen Dingen (*above all*).

Vor der Stadt (*just outside*); das liegt vor (*this side of*) Osnabrück.

Er lachte, weinte vor Freude (*for joy*). Sie zitterte vor Angst (*trembled with fear*), strahlte vor Freude (*beamed with, was radiant with*).

Er sieht den Wald vor (*for*) lauter Bäumen nicht.

(q) **zwischen** + **dative** (*between*)

Zwischen seinen eigenen vier Wänden (*within*).

56 Nouns and Adjectives with Prepositional Objects *(cf. 79)*

(a) Many nouns and adjectives take a prepositional object, i.e. either a noun or pronoun preceded by a preposition, or an adverbial compound;

der Glaube an Gott (*belief in God*); seine Abneigung gegen Arbeit, dagegen (*his dislike of work, of it*).

Er ist stolz auf ihn (*proud of him*); er ist zu allem bereit (*ready for anything*).

NOTE: The noun and adjective usually have the same prepositional constructions, but not invariably.

(b) See 79(a)ii, iv and 79(v) for clauses or gerunds as prepositional objects of nouns and adjectives.

The following list gives some of the most common examples where usage often differs from English:

(c) **an** + **accusative** (*to, of, in, on*)

die Anpassung (*adaptation*), der Anspruch (*claim/demand on s.b.*), die Bitte, der Brief, die Erinnerung, die Forderung (*demand on*), der Gedanke, der Glaube.

gewöhnt (*accustomed*).

56

(d) **an + dative** (*of, in, at, for, about*)

der Anteil (*share in*), die Anteilnahme (*regard, concern, sympathy for s.th.*), die Arbeit, der Bedarf (*need, requirements; stock*), die Freude (*joy, pleasure*), das Gefallen/Vergnügen (*pleasure*), das Höchstmaß (*maximum*), das Interesse, der Mangel (*lack*), das Mindestmaß (*minimum*), die Rache (*revenge*), die Teilnahme (*participation*), das Übermaß (*excess*), die Verheißung (*promise*), die Verzweiflung (*despair at*), der Vorrat (*supply of*), der Zweifel.

arm, ebenbürtig (*rivalling*), gewachsen (*a match for s.b. in*), (un)interessiert, jung, krank (*ill with*), reich, schuld (*to blame*), überlegen (*superior to s.b. in*).

(e) **auf + accusative** (*to, of, for, on, in*)

die Anspielung (*allusion to*), die Aussicht (*prospect of*), der Anspruch (*claim, pretension to*), die Antwort, die Anwendung (*application to*), der Blick (*view of*), die Eifersucht (*jealousy*), der Einfluß (*influence on*), die Hoffnung, die Jagd (*hunt, pursuit*), der Neid (*envy*), die Rücksicht (*consideration, thought for, of*), der Stolz, der Verlaß (*reliance*), das Vertrauen (*trust in*), der Verzicht (*renunciation*), die Vorbereitung, die Wirkung (*effect on*), die Zuversicht (*confidence*).

angewiesen (*dependent on, reduced to*), anwendbar (*applicable to*), aufmerksam (*attentive*), bedacht (*intent on*), böse (*angry with*), eifersüchtig, eingebildet (*conceited*), eitel (*vain*), erpicht (*keen*), gefaßt (*ready for*), neidisch, stolz, versessen (*mad about*), vorbereitet (*prepared for*), zornig (*angry with*).

(f) **auf + dative** (*in*)

blind, taub (*deaf*).

(g) **aus + dative** (*from, of*)

die Folgerung (*deduction*), die Mischung (*mixture*), die Übersetzung.

(h) **bei + dative** (*with, at, to*)

die Beliebtheit (*popularity*), der Besuch, die Hilfe, anwesend (*present*), beliebt.

(i) **für + accusative** (*for, in favour of, of, in, to*)

das Beispiel, die Berechtigung (*excuse*), der Beweis, der Dank, die Entscheidung (*decision*), die Erklärung (*explanation of*), die Gefahr (*to*), der Grund, das Interesse, der Maßstab (*measure*), der Rat(-schlag) (*advice to*), die Sorge (*concern*), die Voreingenommenheit (*prejudice*), die Vorliebe (*predilection*), das Vorzeichen (*omen*), der Wunsch.

begabt (*good at*), bezeichnend (*characteristic*), empfänglich (*susceptible, receptive*), geeignet (*appropriate*), gefährlich, passend (*suitable*).

(j) gegen + accusative (*against, from, of, for, to*)

die Abneigung (*disinclination, distaste, dislike*), die Auflehnung (*revolt from*), die Einwendung (*objection*), die Entscheidung (*decision against*), die Feindseligkeit (*hostility*), das Gefeitsein (*immunity*), die Gleichgültigkeit (*insensitiveness, indifference*), die Grausamkeit (*cruelty*), die Güte (*kindness*), der Haß, das Heilmittel (*remedy*), die Klage (*complaint*), das Mißtrauen (*mistrust*), der Protest, die Unempfindlichkeit (*insensitiveness*), der Zorn.

allergisch, (un)empfindlich ((*in*)*sensitive*), feindselig, frech (*insolent*), gefeit (*proof against, immune to*), gefühllos (*insensitive*), gleichgültig, grausam, hart, (un)höflich, immun, mißtrauisch, nachsichtig (*indulgent*), streng, taub (*deaf to*), (vor)eingenommen (*prejudiced*).

(k) gegenüber + dative (*to, towards, with regard to*)

das Benehmen (*behaviour*), die Feindseligkeit (*hostility to*), das Geständnis (*confession*), die Haltung (*attitude*), die Pflicht (*duty*), die Unfreundlichkeit (*unpleasantness*), das Verhältnis (*relation*).

befangen (*ill at ease*), feindlich (*hostile*), schüchtern (*shy*).

(l) in + accusative (*in, into*)

der Einfall (*invasion of*), die Einmischung (*interference with*), die Einsicht (*insight*), Einweihung (*initiation*), die Ergebung (*resignation to*), der Rückfall (*relapse*), die Verwandlung (*transformation*).

eingehüllt (*wrapped*), eingeweiht (*initiated*), eingewickelt (*wrapped, of parcel*), gekleidet, vergraben (*buried*), verliebt (*in love with*), versunken (*sunk*), vertieft (*deep*), verwickelt (*involved in*).

(m) in + dative (*in, at, of*)

die Ankunft, die Bewandertheit (*knowledge*), die Kenntnisse (*pl.*).

beschlagen (*well up in*), bewandert (*versed*), geschickt (*skilled*), gewandt (*skilled*), gut, schwach, tüchtig (*efficient*).

(n) mit + dative (*with, in, for, to*)

die Ähnlichkeit (*likeness*), die Beschäftigung (*concern, occupation*), die Geduld (*patience*), die Freundschaft, das Mitleid (*sympathy, pity*), die Nachsicht (*allowance for, indulgence*), die Verbindung, der Vergleich (*comparison*).

bekannt (*acquainted*), einverstanden (*in agreement*), fertig (*finished, done*), (un)geduldig, streng, vergleichbar, verglichen (*compared to*), verlobt (*engaged to*), verheiratet, (un)verträglich ((*in*)*compatible*), vertraut (*familiar*), verwandt (*related*), zufrieden.

(o) **nach** + **dative** (*after, for, of, about*)

die Erkundigung (*enquiry*), die Frage, die Jagd (*pursuit* (*fig.*)), die Nachfrage (*demand*), die Sehnsucht (*longing*), das Streben (*aspiration*), die Suche (*search*), das Verlangen (*desire*), der Wunsch.

durstig, gierig (*avid*), habgierig (*covetous*), hungrig, sehnsüchtig.

(p) **über** + **accusative** (*about, as to, of, at, on*)

die Ansicht, die Bemerkung (*remark*), der Blick (*view over*), die Entrüstung (*indignation*), die Enttäuschung, die Freude (*joy*), der Gegenstand (*subject*), die Herrschaft (*mastery*), die Klage (*complaint*), die Meinung, die Neugierde (*curiosity*), der Rat(-schlag) (*advice as to*), die Rechnung (*bill for*), der Streit (*dispute, argument*), die Theorie, der Traum, der Überblick (*survey*), das Urteil (*verdict, judgment*), die Verhandlung (*negotiation*), der Vortrag (*lecture*), der Zweifel (*doubt*).

ärgerlich (*annoyed*), aufgebracht (*incensed*), bekümmert (*worried about s.th.*), bestürzt (*dismayed*), entrüstet, enttäuscht (*disappointed with, in*), erhaben (*above s.th., superior*), erstaunt, froh, neugierig, traurig, verlegen (*embarrassed at*).

(q) **um** + **accusative** (*for, on behalf of, about*)

die Bemühung (*exertion, effort*), die Bitte, der Kampf, die Sorge (*concern*), der Streit (*struggle, contest*).

bekümmert (*worried about s.b.*), besorgt (*worried, concerned*), verlegen (*at a loss for*).

(r) **unter** + **accusative** (*to*)

die Unterwerfung (*submission*).

(s) **von** + **dative** (*of, on, by, from*)

die Abhängigkeit (*dependence*), der Aufwand (*expenditure*), die Meinung, die Überzeugung (*conviction as to*), die Unabhängigkeit.

(un)abhängig, berührt (*affected*), entfernt (*far*), ergriffen (*moved, stirred*), frei, gerötet (*flushed*), müde, überzeugt (*convinced*), voll.

(t) **vor** + **dative** (*from, for, against, with*)

die Achtung (*respect*), die Angst, die Ehrfurcht (*reverence, veneration*), der Ekel (*loathing for*), die Furcht, die Hochachtung (*esteem*), der Respekt, der Schutz (*protection*), der Vorrang (*precedence over*), die Warnung.

blaß (*pale*), erschöpft, rot, sicher (*safe from*).

(u) **wegen** + **genitive** (*at, because of, by, for*)

bekannt (*known for*), berühmt (*famous for*), verlegen (*embarrassed by*).

C*

(v) **zu** + **dative** (*to, for, of, (up)on*)

der Anlaß (*occasion*), der Beitrag (*contribution*), die Bereitwilligkeit (*readiness*), die Beziehung (*relation*), die Freundlichkeit, der Gegensatz (*contrast*), die Idee, die Liebe, die Lust (*desire, inclination*), der Mut, die Neigung (*tendency, inclination*), die Notwendigkeit, das Verhältnis (*relation*), die Vorbedingung, (*condition, prerequisite*), die Zeit, die Zuneigung (*affection, devotion*), der Zwang (*compulsion towards*).

ausgerüstet (*equipped*), berechtigt (*entitled*), bereit, entschlossen, freundlich, geeignet (*suitable*), geneigt (*inclined*), gut (*good to*), nötig.

57 Notes on *haben, sein, werden*

(a) Note the following irregular forms:

du hast, er hat; ich hatte, etc.

ich bin, du bist, er ist, wir sind, ihr seid, sie (Sie) sind; sei! seien Sie! seid!; ich sei, er sei; ich war, er war; ich bin gewesen.

du wirst, er wird; werde!; ich wurde, etc. (poetical forms: ich ward, du wardst, er ward); ich bin geworden.

(b) **Haben** is used to form the perfect tenses of all transitive and reflexive verbs and the modal auxiliaries. Exceptions are only apparent, being cognate or adverbial accusatives, old genitives, etc. (Cf. also (*d*) below.)

Er hat das Buch gelesen. Er hat sich gesetzt. Ich habe mir die Hände gewaschen. Er hat nicht kommen können.

But Er **ist** den Berg hinaufgegangen. Er **ist** die Wette eingegangen (*taken on the bet*). Er **ist** Gefahr gelaufen. Ich **bin** es losgeworden.

(c) **Sein** is used to form the perfect tenses of all intransitive verbs expressing the idea of movement to or from a place or of a change of state.

Er ist zum Bahnhof gegangen. Wir sind uns begegnet (*we met one another*). Er ist gestorben. Er ist krank geworden.

(d) **Haben** is used, with few exceptions, e.g. *sein, bleiben, geschehen, gelingen,* to form the perfect tenses of all intransitive verbs other than those excluded under (c) above.

Er hat geschlafen. Es hat geregnet.

But Es **ist** gewesen, geblieben, geschehen, gelungen.

(e) Some verbs can be used both transitively or intransitively or express different kinds of intransitivity. They are conjugated with *sein* if, when used intransitively, they fall under the rule given under (c) above.

Er **hat** den Wagen gefahren. *But:* Er **ist** mit dem Wagen gefahren. Er **hat** viel getanzt. *But:* Das erste Paar **ist** ins Eßzimmer getanzt.

(f) There is a tendency to extend rule (c) above to include many intransitive verbs that express any form of movement, not just movement to or from a place.

> Er **ist** den ganzen Tag geschwommen, geritten, gesegelt, gerudert, etc., *instead of:* er **hat** den ganzen Tag geschwommen, etc.

(g) Both *haben* and *sein* are occasionally omitted after the past participle in subordinate clauses.

> ... aus seiner Heimat, der er Ruhm geschenkt (S. ZWEIG).

(h) **Werden** is used with the infinitive to form the future tenses, with the past participle to form the passive voice. (Cf. 69.)

> Er **wird/würde** das Lied **singen** (*will/would sing*).
> Das Lied **wird/wurde** überall **gesungen** (*is/was sung*).

58 Notes on the Conjugation of Weak and Strong Verbs

(a) General:

i Strong verbs (see *102*) change their stem vowel, and the past participle ends in **-en**.

liegen: liegt, lag, gelegen.

ii Weak verbs do not change their stem vowel but add **-t** to the stem to form the imperfect, and the past participle ends in **-t**.

sagen: sagt, sagte, gesagt.

iii All verbs not stressed on the first syllable, i.e. the weak verbs ending in **-ieren** (a large number) and **-eien** (very few) and verbs compounded with inseparable prefixes (see *60(a)*) have no **ge-** in the past participle.

er hat studiert; sie hat prophezeit; wir haben versucht.

iv Verbs whose stem ends in **-t** or **-d** (except (*b*)*v* below), in **-chn**, **-ckn**, **-dn**, **-fn**, **-gn**, or **-tm** retain the **-e** of the 1st pers. sing. pres. indic. throughout the conjugation.

wartest, reitet, badet, rechnete, trocknete, ordnet, öffnetet, geregnet, atmet.

v A few verbs – *brennen, bringen, denken, kennen, nennen, rennen* and their compounds, and, but not always, *senden* and *wenden* with their compounds – are of mixed conjugation, i.e. though the stem vowel changes in the imperfect indicative and past participle to **a**, the imperfect has the weak imperfect endings and the past participle ends in **-t**.

brennen: brennt, brannte, gebrannt.
denken: denkt, dachte, gedacht.

vi There are very few irregular weak or strong verbs. The modal auxiliaries are given in 67 and the other irregular verbs in 102. Note *wissen*:

pres. indic.: weiß, weißt, weiß, wissen, wißt, wissen;
impf. indic.: wußte, etc.; *past part.*: gewußt.

(b) The Present Tense:
i The present tense indicative endings of both strong and weak regular verbs are:

-e, -st, -t, -en, -t, -en.

ii With verbs whose stem ends in **-s, -ss, -ß, -z** or **-tz** the ending **-st** is either, and more usually, contracted to **-t** or is lengthened to **-est**.

du sitzt/sitzest; du liest/liesest.

iii Verbs ending in **-ern** and **-eln** (all weak) have the following present indicative endings:

-(e)re, -erst, -ert, -ern; -(e)le, -elst, -elt, -eln.

iv If the stem vowel of the infinitive of regular strong verbs is **a, e, o** or **au** it usually changes in the 2nd and 3rd pers. sing. pres. indic. to **ä, i/ie, ö** or **äu** respectively.

tragen: trägst, trägt; geben: gibst, gibt; lesen: liest; stoßen: stößt; laufen; läufst, läuft.

v Verbs so changing whose stem ends in **-d** or **-t** have the contracted endings **-st** and **-t** for the first type, **-st** and **-** for the second.

läd-st, läd-t; rät-st, rät.

(c) The Imperfect Tense:
i The imperfect indicative endings of strong regular verbs are:

-, -st, -, -en, -t, -en.

ii The imperfect indicative endings of weak regular verbs are:

-te, -test, -te, -ten, -tet, -ten.

(d) For the imperative forms see 65; for the subjunctive forms see 70.

59 Notes on the Tenses.

In general the tenses in German correspond to the English. There are however some important differences.

(a) **The Present**
i Since German has only one form of the present tense it is sometimes necessary to add an adverb or to recast the sentence in order to convey the exact English meaning.

Jeden Tag geht er zur Stadt (*goes*). Sie pflegt spät aufzustehen (*gets up*). Er geht jetzt zur Stadt (*is going*). Er ist dabei, den Brief zu schreiben (*is writing*). Er ist beim Rasieren (*is shaving*). Es ist am Regnen (*it is raining*). Das Haus ist im Bau begriffen (*is being built*). Ich hoffe doch sehr, daß ... (*I do hope*). Selbst wenn wir arbeiten (*when we do work*). Er liebt mich tatsächlich/wirklich (*he does love me*).

ii With *seit* or *schon* the present expresses what has been going on and is still going on. Here English normally uses the perfect continuous. But the perfect is used (as in English) in negative sentences.

Er **arbeitet** seit heute morgen, seit acht Stunden (*has been working*). Ich **warte** schon eine Stunde (*have been waiting*).
But Er hat seit Montag nicht gearbeitet.

iii The present is often used in German where English generally uses the future, especially when the idea of futurity is already indicated by some other means.

Morgen kaufe ich (*I shall buy*) welche. Ich schreibe (*I'll be writing*) dir bald.

iv The present tense is often used with a past meaning to give greater vividness. English normally prefers the past tense.

Noch immer stand er auf dem Gang. Er blickte zur Tür hinüber ... Er lugt durch den Spalt ins Zimmer ... Er horcht auf ... öffnet die Tür leicht und tritt mit seinen nackten Füßen völlig geräuschlos ins Zimmer (A. SCHNITZLER).

v Note also: Es ist höchste Zeit/an der Zeit, daß er **kommt** (*he came*); es ist das erstemal, daß ich Sie hier **sehe** (*I have seen you*).

(b) The Imperfect

i Jeden Tag ging er zur Stadt (*he went, used to go, would go*). Er pflegte früh zu Bett zu gehen (*would go, used to go*). Er las die Zeitung, als ... (*he was reading*). Er war schon dabei, den Brief zu schreiben (*was already writing*). Er war beim Rasieren (*was shaving*).
Selbst wenn wir arbeiteten (*even when we did work*).
Wir hofften doch sehr, daß ... (*we did hope*). In der Tat hatte er Erfolg (*he did succeed*).
Er war im Begriff auszugehen, als ... (*he was on the point of*).

NOTE: The construction with *pflegte* should be used with discretion. It is not necessary to use it when an adverb or adverbial expression (e.g. *manchmal, oft, jeden Tag*) already indicates iteration. When there is a series of iterative verbs, once the German has made it clear, e.g. with the construction with *pflegte*, that the verbs are to be understood as having iterative meaning, the simple imperfect is normally adequate subsequently.

ii The imperfect is the normal tense of narrative.

Er stand auf, wusch sich schnell, kleidete sich hastig an und ging ohne zu frühstücken zum Bahnhof.

iii The imperfect with *seit* or *schon* expresses what had been going on and was still going on.

Er **arbeitete** schon seit acht Stunden (*had been working*).
Ich **wartete** schon eine Stunde (*had been waiting for*).

(c) The Perfect

i The perfect is used for isolated acts in the recent past where English often uses the simple past.

Ich habe heute angerufen (*I rang up*). Ich bin gestern gekommen (*I came*). Er ist eben nach Hause gekommen (*has just come*).

ii The perfect is used to express an event whose effect is still felt today.

Die Bundesrepublik ist 1954 ein souveräner Staat geworden (*became*).

iii In colloquial German, especially in South Germany, the perfect is the tense of narrative.

iv The perfect expresses a future perfect when the idea of futurity is already indicated by some other means. (Cf. (*a*)*iii* above.)

Ich habe das Buch bald zu Ende gelesen (*shall soon have finished*).

(d) The Pluperfect

The German pluperfect is used as in English except as shown in (*b*)*iii* above. Sometimes however it will render the English imperfect, e.g.

Früher war er Buchmacher gewesen (*he used to be*).

(e) The Future

i Der Arzt wird kommen müssen (*will have to*).
ii Aber müde wirst du sein (HESSE). (*But I expect you are tired*).
iii Note the following equivalents to the future and compare also (*a*)*iii* above:

Die Sonne will eben untergehen (*is just about to*).
Er ist im Begriff, nach Paris abzureisen (*on the point of*).

iv Note that when 'will' expresses determination or desire the present of *wollen* is used.

Er **will** nicht kommen (*he won't = refuses to*). **Willst** du auch kommen?

(f) The Future Perfect

Er wird das wohl gesagt haben (*I expect he said that*).

(g) The Conditional; the Future in the Past

i Er würde kommen, wenn er könnte (*would come = conditional*).
ii Ich wußte, daß er kommen würde (*would come = future in the past*).
   (N.B. For (i) and not for (ii) *käme* may be substituted.)

iii Note that when 'would' expresses determination the imperfect of *wollen* is used; when it indicates habitual action, the imperfect of the main verb alone is used.

Er **wollte** nicht kommen (*he would not come = refused to come*).
Er **kam** jeden Abend um sechs nach Hause (*he would come = used to come*).

(h) The Conditional Perfect

This cumbrous form is usually replaced by the pluperfect subjunctive. Thus:

Ich hätte es gemacht *instead of*: ich würde es gemacht haben.
Er hätte es tun können *instead of*: er würde es haben tun können.

60 Compound Verbs

(a) All compound verbs are separable except (i) those compounded with the inseparable prefixes **be-**, **emp-**, **ent-**, **er-**, **ge-**, **miß-**, **ver-** and **zer-**, and (ii), with certain meanings only, those compounded with **durch-**, **hinter-**, **über-**, **um-**, **unter-**, **voll-**, **wider-** and **wieder-** (only in the one word *wiederholen* = repeat).

(b) The inseparable prefixes are never stressed, there is no *ge-* in the past participle and the *zu* of the infinitive construction is not inserted between the prefix and the verb.

er hat bezáhlt; er hat gewónnen (*from* gewinnen);
er hat übertríeben; es ist zu bezáhlen.

(c) The prefix *miß-* is sometimes treated as a separable prefix in the past participle and in the infinitive with *zu*.

míßgeachtet/mißáchtet; míßzuachten/zu mißáchten.

(d) Common examples of inseparable verbs belonging to (*a*)*ii* above are:

durchzíehen (*traverse a country*)	umgéhen *evade*
hintergéhen *deceive*	unterbréchen *interrupt*
hinterlássen *bequeath*	unterhálten *entertain, maintain*
überfáhren *run over s.b.*	unternéhmen *undertake*
überhólen *outstrip; overhaul*	unterríchten *instruct, teach*
überréden *persuade*	unterschéiden *distinguish*
überráschen *surprise*	untersuchen *investigate*
übersétzen *translate*	vollénden *complete*
übertréiben *exaggerate*	vollführen *carry out*
überwínden *overcome*	widerlégen *refute*
überzéugen *convince*	widerspréchen (D) *contradict*
umármen *embrace*	widerstéhen (D) *resist*
umfássen *comprise*	wiederhólen *repeat*
umgében *surround*	

(e) Meaning and function of the inseparable prefixes ((a)i)

i **be-** makes intransitive verbs transitive and transitive verbs perfective in meaning: steigen – besteigen; decken – bedecken (*cover all over*);

from nouns forms verbs with the meaning 'provide with', 'endow with', 'give': Freund – befreunden; Glück – beglücken; Glückwunsch – beglückwünschen (*congratulate*);

from adjectives forms verbs with factitive meaning: lustig – belustigen (*make s.b. merry*).

ii **ent-** from nouns, adjectives or other verbs forms verbs expressing the idea of deprivation, separation, escape (cf. English 'de-', 'dis-', 'des-', 'un-', and 'away'): Kleid – entkleiden; mutig – entmutigen; decken – entdecken; kommen – entkommen;

from other verbs forms verbs with inchoative meanings: springen – entspringen ((*a*)*rise*).

iii **er-** from other verbs forms verbs with inchoative meaning or expressing successful completion or conclusion (sometimes with death as a consequence!): wachen – erwachen (*awake*); werben (*sue for, woo*) – erwerben (*acquire*); schießen – erschießen (*shoot dead*);

from adjectives forms verbs with inchoative or factitive meaning: blaß – erblassen (*turn pale*); frisch – erfrischen (*refresh*).

iv **ge-** from other verbs forms verbs with perfective or intensified meaning: brauchen (*need*) – gebrauchen (*use*); reuen – gereuen. (N.B. *ge-* is no longer a productive prefix.)

v **miß-** corresponds to English 'mis-', 'dis-': verstehen – mißverstehen; trauen – mißtrauen.

vi **ver-** from other verbs forms verbs with perfective or intensified meaning: treiben – vertreiben (*drive away s.b.*); schließen – verschließen (*lock up*); zweifeln (*doubt*) – verzweifeln (*despair*); sprechen – versprechen (*promise*);

from other verbs forms verbs expressing the idea of progress to completion or destruction: arbeiten – verarbeiten (*elaborate*); hungern – verhungern (*starve to death*); hallen (*echo*) – verhallen (*die away*);

from other verbs to form verbs with opposite meaning: achten (*esteem*) – verachten (*despise*); kaufen – verkaufen; mieten – vermieten;

from other verbs forms verbs expressing various ways time is spent: bringen – verbringen; schlafen – verschlafen; trinken – vertrinken;

from other verbs forms reflexive verbs implying one has bungled something: laufen – sich verlaufen (*lose one's way*); rechnen –

sich verrechnen (*miscalculate*); sprechen – sich versprechen (*make a slip of the tongue*);

forms transitive from intransitive verbs: folgen – verfolgen (*pursue*); lachen – verlachen;

from adjectives (including comparatives) forms verbs with inchoative or factitive meaning: alt – veralten; dünn – verdünnen (*thin down*); größer – vergrößern;

from nouns forms verbs with the meaning of 'provide with' or 'turn into': Silber – versilbern (*silver plate*); Film – verfilmen.

vii **zer-** expresses the English 'into pieces' and forms verbs chiefly from other verbs and from a few nouns and adjectives: reißen – zerreißen; Trümmer – zertrümmern (*reduce to ruins*); klein – zerkleinern;

from other verbs forms verbs with intensified meaning: knittern – zerknittern (*crease all over*).

(f) All prefixes other than those given in (a) above are separable and stressed.

(g) Most separable prefixes are simple or compound adverbs: *ab-, hinab-*. Some are adjectives as in the verbs *festbinden, freimachen, geringschätzen, hochachten, loslassen, totschlagen, vollaufen, wahrnehmen* (perceive), *weiterfragen*. The remainder are nouns as in the verbs *achtgeben, danksagen, fehlschießen, haltmachen, heimfahren, hohnlachen, maschineschreiben* (type), *preisgeben* (expose), *radfahren, skilaufen, standhalten, stattfinden, teilnehmen*.

(h) Note the most frequent meanings of some of the adverbial prefixes (see also *35(d)*):

ab (*off, away/down*)	Er schnitt es ab. Der Berg fiel steil ab.
an (*on, at*)	Er zieht es an. Er schaltet es an (*switches on*). Er sah ihn an.
auf (*up, open*)	Er steht auf. Er sah zu ihm auf. Er macht die Tür auf.
aus (*out, off, up*)	Er geht aus. Er zieht es aus. Er füllte das Formular aus (*filled up*).
ein (*in*)	Er steigt ein. Er trat ein.
empor (*up(-wards)*)	Er blickte empor. Er strebt empor. Er hob die Hände empor.
fort (*away, on*)	Er geht fort. Er lebt fort.
entgegen (*to meet*)	Er ging ihr entgegen.
nieder (*down*)	Er fiel nieder.
vor (*forward*)	Er trat vor.
voran/voraus (*on ahead*)	Er geht voran/voraus.
vorbei/vorüber (*past*)	Er geht vorbei/vorüber.
zu (*to, shut*)	Er rief mir zu. Er machte die Tür zu.

(i) For word order with separable compound verbs see 6(g).

(j) Compound verbs with double prefixes, the second being inseparable, have no ge- in the past participle, e.g.

Er erkennt an (*acknowledges*); er hat anerkannt; er wünscht anzuerkennen.

Likewise: anvertrauen (*entrust*); auferlegen (*impose*); vorbehalten (*make reservations*); vorenthalten (*withhold*).

(k) Other compound verbs with double prefixes are treated as inseparable, e.g.

Er überanstrengt sich (*over exerts himself*); er hat sich überanstrengt; ohne sich zu überanstrengen.

61 Reflexive Verbs

(a) The reflexive pronoun (see *45* and *99*) is rarely used except in the accusative or dative. Only the first and second person singular show the difference.

Ich wasche **mich**. Ich wasche **mir** die Hände.
Stell **dich** vor (*introduce yourself*)! Stell **dir** mal vor (*just imagine*)!
But Stellt **euch** (D) mal vor! Erkältet **euch** (A) nicht!

(b) The German reflexive verb has often to be used where English uses an intransitive verb.

Die Tür öffnete sich (*opened*). Sie trafen sich (*met*). Die Tür schließt sich von selbst (*shuts*). Er drehte sich um (*turned round*). Er wusch sich (*washed*). Er setzte sich (*sat down*). Er zog sich an (*dressed*). Er zog sich aus (*undressed*). Er zog sich um (*changed*). Sie irren sich (*you are wrong*). Er fühlte sich beleidigt (*felt insulted*).

(c) The English passive is sometimes rendered by a German reflexive verb (see *69*(*h*)*i*)

Solche Bilder verkaufen sich schnell (*are sold*).

(d) Note the common German idiom in which the reflexive verb is used in impersonal constructions like the following:

Es fährt sich bequem in diesem Wagen (*it is pleasant driving in*).
Es schreibt sich schlecht mit Kreide (*chalk is difficult to write with*).

62 Impersonal Verbs

(a) Es blitzt, dämmert, donnert, dunkelt, friert, hagelt, regnet, schneit, klärt sich auf (*is clearing up*), taut (*is thawing; dew is falling*).

(b) So gut es geht (*as well as one can*); es geht (nicht) (*it will (won't) do*); es gibt; es heißt, daß (*it is said that*); es klingelt; es klopft; es handelt sich um (*it is a matter of*); es kommt darauf an (*it depends; that is what matters*); es lohnt (sich) kaum (*it is hardly worth while*); es macht/schadet nichts (*it does not matter*); es zieht (*there is a draught*).

(c) Mir fehlt es an nichts (*I lack nothing*); mir gefällt es dort (*I like being there*); mir geht es gut, schlecht, ausgezeichnet, etc.; mir gelingt es, das zu tun (*I succeed in, manage to*); dir geschieht es recht (*it serves you right*); dir steht es frei, das zu tun (*you are free to*); mir tut es leid (*I am sorry*). *Or:* Es fehlt mir an nichts, *etc.*

(d) Mir ekelt('s) vor ihm (*I loathe him*); mir/mich schaudert('s) vor dir, mir graut('s) vor dir (*I shudder to look at you*); mich/mir juckt('s) am Arm, am Finger, im Ohr (*my arm, etc., itches*); mich friert('s) an den Füßen; mich fröstelt('s).
Or: Es ekelt mir vor ihm, *etc.*

(e) Mich dürstet nach (*I thirst for*); mir fällt ein, daß (*it occurs to me that*); mir ist, als ob (*I feel as if*); mir fehlt nichts (*I am quite well, I want, need, am short of nothing*); mich hungert; mir ist kalt, warm, übel, schlecht; mir ist bange, wohl, etc. zumute (*I feel apprehensive, in good spirits*); mir ist übel (*I feel sick*); mich verlangt nach (*I feel drawn towards*); mich wundert (*I am astonished*).
But: Es dürstet mich nach, es fällt mir ein, daß, *etc.*

63 The Infinitive with and without *zu*

(a) The simple infinitive stands

i after the modal auxiliaries:

Er kann es tun (*is able to*). Er mußte sich setzen (*had to*). Er wollte schreiben (*wanted to*). Er möchte kommen (*would like to*).

ii after *bleiben, fühlen, gehen, heißen* (bid), *hören, lassen* (cf. 68), *machen* and *sehen*:

Er blieb dort stehen. Er fühlte sich erröten. Sie ging tanzen. Er hieß ihn kommen. Ich hörte/sah ihn kommen. Er läßt alles herumliegen. Er machte sie erröten.

iii after *lernen, lehren* and *helfen* when these follow their dependent infinitive; and in simple short sentences even when these precede.

Sie hat kochen gelernt, mich kochen gelehrt. Um den Krieg gewinnen zu helfen, hat er ...
Sie half uns aufräumen.

iv after *haben* in such expressions as:

Man sollte keine Spiegel herumhängen haben, keine Stühle herum-
stehen haben, keine Papiere herumliegen haben (*have hanging,
standing, lying around*).
Du hast gut lachen/reden (*it's all very well for you to laugh/talk*).

v when used as a predicative accusative:

Das nenne ich Eulen nach Athen tragen (= *carrying coals to Newcastle*).

vi in abbreviated questions, direct or indirect, with modal verb usually
understood:

Was jetzt anfangen? Er wußte nicht, wohin gehen.

(b) The infinitive with *zu* is used

i after *lernen, lehren* and *helfen* when these precede their dependent
infinitive:

Er hat endlich gelernt, sich gut zu benehmen.

ii after all verbs and verbal expressions not excluded under (a) above:

Er wünschte, länger zu bleiben. Er vermochte nicht, sie zu überzeugen
(*was unable to*). Es ist ganz unnütz, darüber zu streiten (*quite useless
to*). Ich habe viel zu tun. Er scheint unglücklich zu sein.

iii after *ohne, (an)statt* and *weit (davon) entfernt*:

Ohne aufzublicken; statt zuzuhören; weit davon entfernt, ihn zu
hassen, liebt sie ihn (*far from hating*).

(c) Usage fluctuates in the following cases:

i With the infinitive used as the subject of a sentence:

Ihn allein lassen, das wäre das Klügste (SCHNITZLER).
Euch zu helfen ist mein größter Wunsch (DUDEN).

ii after *nichts (weiter, mehr) als*:

Wir konnten nichts tun als auseinandergehen (HESSE).
So habe man ihr denn nichts mehr antun können, als eben ihr Bild
aus dem Rahmen zu nehmen (LE FORT).

iii after *brauchen*:

Du brauchst nicht (zu) schreiben.

(d) *um ... zu* with the infinitive is used:

i to express purpose (*in order to, so as to*), though *um* is often omitted
with *kommen*:

Er tat es nur, um mich zu ärgern. Er kam zum Bahnhof, (um) mich
abzuholen.

ii after *zu* + adjective and usually after *genug* (+ adjective), *genügen,
ausreichen, brauchen, bedürfen*:

Er war zu gut erzogen, um sie zu unterbrechen (LE FORT).

Ich war nicht schnell genug, um die Chance zu ergreifen (ANDERSCH).

iii   to render 'enough to make' (cf. *80(c)*):

Es war um sich die Haare auszuraufen, um aus der Haut zu fahren (*jump out of one's skin*), um verrückt zu werden.

(e) For the translation of such phrases as 'there was nobody, etc., to ...', 'it was too wet for us to ...' see *73(b)ii*.

64 The Participles

(a) Present and past participles are used attributively in German as extensively as in English.

Er bekam einen tröstenden Brief. Gebranntes Kind scheut das Feuer.

(b) Present and past participles are used predicatively in German much as in English though a good deal less extensively. Normally the participle comes at the end of its construction.

i   Der Junge, vor Freude strahlend, bedankte sich.

Suchend blickte ich mich um (GRASS).

Die Arme verschränkend, stellte sie sich vor mir auf (BROCH).

... stampfte ich taktgebend die vier Treppen hoch (GRASS).

Meine Mutter, die Hölle fürchtend, wollte dort nicht einziehen (GRASS).

Bier, Blutwurst mit Zwiebel bestellend, breiteten wir die Aufnahmen aus (GRASS).

ii   Da ruhte, eingeschmiegt in das Weiß, das schneedachige Oberdorf (BROCH).

Den beiden anderen zugewendet, wiederholte er ... (BROCH).

Obgleich innerlich entrüstet, erklärte er es ihm ruhig.

So betrachtet, sieht die Sachlage anders aus.

Unten auf der Landstraße angekommen, machte Joseph halt (R. WALSER).

(c) Present and past participles can be used in adjectival adjunct constructions where English uses either a following participle, a relative clause or adjectival construction. This construction is sometimes very convenient, but it should be used with discretion.

Wir sind jetzt in einer 200 000 Bände umfassenden Bibliothek (*library containing*).

Er betrachtete die neben ihren Pferden abgesessenen Reiter (*troopers who had dismounted*) (SCHAPER).

(d) The present participle of transitive verbs when preceded by *zu* and declined has modal and passive force. This construction should also be used with discretion.

> Die immer wieder an allen Schweizer Straßen **zu finden** le Mahnung (*that is to be found*) ...
> Er bereitete sich auf das nun nicht mehr **zu umgehende** Geständnis vor (*that could no longer be evaded*) (HEIMERAN).

(e) After *kommen* the German past participle corresponds to the English present participle after 'come'.

> Er kam gelaufen (*running*), galoppiert (*galloping*).

(f) The past participle, but not normally a present participle, may introduce a noun clause in German, i.e. 'disappointed that ...' but not: 'remembering that'. Note however that *gesetzt* (*daß*) and *angenommen* (*daß*) translate the English present participle 'supposing'.

> Enttäuscht, daß sie nicht gekommen war, ging er wieder nach Hause.
> Gesetzt, er käme heute. Angenommen, daß es sich so verhält.

(g) See *32(a)* for the adverbial use of the participles.

(h) See *81* for further ways of translating the English present participle.

65 The Imperative

(a) Sag(e)! sagt! sagen Sie!; komm(e)!, kommt! kommen Sie!

(b) Du schläfst – schlaf(e)!; du stößt – stoß(e)!; du läufst – lauf(e)! *etc. But* du gibst – gib!; du liest – lies! *etc.*

(c) Zitt(e)re nicht! hand(e)le! reinige!

(d) Geh du/geht ihr voran! (Cf. English imperative: *you* go on ahead.)

(e) 'Let us go' = gehen wir! wir wollen gehen! laß, laßt, lassen Sie uns gehen!

(f) Aufstehen! (*get up*). Ausgehalten! (*stick it out*). Wirst du still sein! (*be quiet*).

(g) Note the effect on imperatives of such words as *doch* (urging), *ja* (reminding), *mal* (emphasising), *nur* (persuasive, reassuring, sometimes threatening):

Kauf sie doch! (*Go ahead and buy.*) Hör doch! (*Do listen.*) Iß ja nicht zu viel! (*Mind you don't eat too much.*) Hör mal (zu)! (*Now just listen.*) Komm nur! (*Come on.*)

(h) Note that the imperative is generally followed by an exclamation mark.

66 The Interrogative

(a) Kennst du ihn? Wo hast du ihn kennengelernt?

(b) Du kennst ihn, nicht wahr (*don't you?*)? Du bist krank, nicht wahr (*aren't you?*)? Du hast schon gehört, nicht wahr (*haven't you?*)? Du wirst kommen, nicht wahr (*won't you?*)?

(c) Du kennst ihn schon, ja/nicht/gelt? (= *colloquial forms*).

(d) Du hast doch nicht gewartet? Doch (*yes I did*)!

67 The Auxiliary Verbs of Mood

(a) Er hat es gedurft, gekonnt, gemocht, gemußt, gesollt, gewollt
But Er hat kommen **dürfen, können, mögen, müssen, sollen, wollen.**

(b) **dürfen** (darf, darfst, darf, dürfen, etc.; durfte, etc.)
Er darf jetzt wieder rauchen (*may, is allowed to*).
Er darf nicht rauchen (*must not, is not allowed to, may not*).
Darf ich rauchen? – Du darfst.
Sie dürfen es nur sagen (*you need only say so*).
Er durfte alles machen (*he was allowed to do anything*).
Er durfte jahrelang nicht schwimmen (*was not allowed to swim*).
Das dürfte alles sein (*that, I think, is everything*).
Welcher Mensch dürfte den Zeitpunkt bestimmen (*should be allowed to*)?
Es dürfte ein Leichtes sein (*should be an easy matter*).
Es dürfte zwischen ihnen kaum Differenzen gegeben haben (*there can hardly have been*).
Es dürfte wohl wahr sein (*it may well be true*).
Er hat nicht kommen dürfen (*has not been, was not allowed to come*).
Er hätte kommen dürfen (*would have been allowed, entitled to come*).
Er hätte das Haus nicht verlassen dürfen (*should not have left, should not have disobeyed orders and left*).
Er wird wohl kommen dürfen (*he will be allowed to come all right*).

(c) **können** (kann, kannst, kann, können, etc.; konnte, etc.)

Ich kann schon lesen (*can, am able to*).
Kannst du es beweisen? Ja, ich kann (es) (*I can*).
Du kannst bleiben (*can, may*).
Es kann sein (*it may be*).
Er kann (kein) Deutsch, Französisch, Italienisch, Russisch (*knows*).
Ich kann nicht mehr (*I can't go on any more, I'm finished*).
Ich kann nichts dafür (*I cannot help it*).
Ich kann nicht umhin zu lachen (*cannot help laughing*).
Du kannst das unmöglich sagen (*you cannot possibly*).
Er kann es getan haben (*he may have done it*).

Ich konnte nicht kommen (*could not, was unable to*).
Ich konnte nicht anders als lachen (*could not help*).
Ich konnte es ja getan haben (*I might have done it, it was possible after all that I did it*).

Er könnte wohl finden, daß ... (*might find that ...*).
Ich könnte es dort (vielleicht) kaufen (*could, might be able to*).
Du könntest es schon mitnehmen (*you might as well take it*).
Er könnte es getan haben (*he might have done it for all one knows*).

Er hat nicht kommen können (*has not been able, could not*).

Du hättest ebensogut kommen können (*you might as well have come*).
Er hätte kommen können, wenn ... (*could/might have come if ...*)
Du hättest es mir doch sagen können (*you might have told me = a reproach*).

Sie werden nicht kommen können (*they will not be able to come*).

(d) **mögen** (mag, magst, mag, mögen, etc.; mochte, etc.)

Er mag es vielleicht wissen (*he may perhaps know it*).
Er mag kommen (*may*). Das mag wohl sein (*may*).
Man mag sie vielleicht nicht leiden (*one may not like them*).
Was er auch tun mag (*no matter what he does*).
Mag man sie als Atome oder anders bezeichnen (*whether ... or*).
Er mag 2 Jahre alt gewesen sein (*may have been*).
Er mag gern kommen (*likes coming*).
Er mag nicht abreisen (*does not like*).
Ich mag sie nicht (*I don't care about them*).

Möge er lange gedeihen (*long may he flourish*)!

Was mochte er von mir halten (*what might he think of me*)?
Welche Talente er auch haben mochte (*might have had*).
Es mochte schon 11 Uhr sein (*may have been*).
Er mochte es wohl bemerkt haben (*might well have noticed*).
Er mochte gern zu uns kommen (*liked coming*).

Das ist mehr, als man zuerst annehmen möchte (*might suppose*).
Ich möchte länger bleiben (*should like to*).

Ich habe ihn später auch nicht gemocht (*did not like*).

Sie hätte schreien mögen (*would like to have screamed*).
Das hätte ich nicht sehen mögen (*should not have liked to*).
Er hätte glauben mögen, daß ... (*would have felt inclined to*).

(e) **müssen** (muß, mußt, muß, müssen etc.; mußte, etc.)

Er muß gehorchen (*must, has to*).
Kinder müssen gehorchen (*ought to in the nature of things*).
„Muß man hier Wein trinken?“ – „Sie müssen nicht, aber Sie können.“ (*You don't have to*).
Er muß es noch nicht wissen, sonst ... (*he cannot know it yet, otherwise ...*).
Er muß hier gewesen sein (*must have been, no doubt he was here*).

Wir mußten gehorchen (*had to obey*).
Wir mußten lachen (*could not help laughing*).
Gerade *er* mußte kommen (*as bad luck would have it it was he who came*).
Diese Frage mußte kommen (*was bound to come*).
Sie mußte in der Nacht geschlafen haben (*must have slept, no doubt she had slept*).

Man müßte sich erkundigen, um ... (*would have to inquire*).
Das **müßtest** du doch wissen (*you really ought to know that*).

Er **hat** gehorchen müssen (*he has had to, he had to obey*).

Er hätte das Haus nicht verlassen müssen (*should not have, for he need not have*).
Beim ersten Anblick hätte es ihn verraten müssen (*could not have failed to betray him*).

(f) **sollen** (soll, sollst, soll, sollen, etc.; sollte, etc.)

Er soll alles haben (*shall*). Du sollst nicht stehlen (*shalt*).
Was soll ich tun (*shall*)? Soll ich auch kommen (*shall*).
Sollen wir nach Hause gehen (*shall, i.e. oughtn't we perhaps to*)?
Ich soll hier bleiben (*am to, am supposed to, am expected to*).
Was soll ich tun (*what am I to do*)?
Was soll ich dir vorlesen (*what would you like me to read to you*)?
Du sollst da bleiben (*I want you to stay there*).
Er soll gleich kommen (*tell him to come at once*).
Er soll es tun (*make him do it*).
Was soll das (heißen) (*what is the meaning of that, e.g. behaviour*)?
Was soll man da sagen (*can*)?
Kinder sollen ihren Eltern gehorchen (*should = are expected to*).
Soll er so ins Haus fallen (*is it to be tolerated that*)?
Es soll zum Kloster gehören (*is said to belong*).
Es soll zum Kloster gehört haben (*is said to have belonged*).

Was sollte er anfangen (*was he to do*)?
Er sollte das erst später erfahren (*was to, was destined to*).
Es sollte zum Kloster gehört haben (*was said to have*).

Er sollte (*subj.*) eilen (*ought to*).
Sollte (*subj.*) das wahr sein (*can it be true*)?
Wenn er mich sehen sollte (*subj.*) (*were he to/should he*).
Sollte (*subj.*) er kommen, so ... (*were he to/should he*).

Wie hätte ich das ahnen sollen (*should I have suspected*)?
Er hätte das Haus nicht verlassen sollen (*should not have, ought not to have, i.e. it was his duty not to*).

(g) **wollen** (will, willst, will, wollen, etc.; wollte, etc.)

Er will alles sehen (*wants to*).
Willst du mitkommen (*will*)?
Er will heute früher nach Hause kommen (*intends, wants to*).
Er will durchaus, daß ich komme (*insists on my coming*).
Ich will ihn nicht beleidigen (*don't mean to*).
Er will nicht arbeiten (*will not, refuses to*).
Willst du Weißwein, oder willst du lieber Rotwein (*will you have . . . do you prefer*)?
Wollen wir ins Theater (gehen) (*shall we go*)?
Wir wollen ins Theater (gehen) (*let us go*)!
Wir wollen eben ausgehen (*are just going out*).
Die Arbeit will kein Ende nehmen (*shows no signs of*).
So etwas will gelernt sein (*needs to be*).
Er will alles besser wissen (*claims to know*).
Er will sie gesehen haben (*claims, asserts that*).
Ich will nichts gesagt haben (*I take back what I've said*).

Er wollte alles sehen (*wanted to, meant to, intended to*).
Er wollte nicht arbeiten (*would not, refused to*).
Die Sonne wollte eben untergehen (*was just about to*).
Er wollte sie gesehen haben (*claimed he had*).
Die Arbeit wollte kein Ende nehmen (*showed no signs of*).

Er hat nicht kommen wollen (*did not want to*).

Er hatte kommen wollen (*had intended to*).

Er hätte kommen wollen (*would have liked to*).

Er würde es schon tun wollen, wenn er nur könnte (*he would want to, like to*).

(h) Combinations of modals that are quite possible in English have sometimes to be rendered in other ways in German.

Er hätte das nicht einmal wollen können (R. HUCH).
Warum sollen wir das nicht auch dürfen (H. MANN).

But Er wird vielleicht früher abreisen müssen (*may have to*).
Er wird vielleicht früher abreisen wollen (*may want to*).
Du wirst doch kommen wollen (*you must want to come*)!

(i) The verb *gehen* or *fahren*, etc., is often understood but left unexpressed with modals, e.g. Ich muß/soll/will jetzt nach Hause (gehen). Darf ich jetzt nach Hause (gehen).

68 Lassen

(a) (= *leave*) Ich habe es zu Hause gelassen. Ich habe es auf dem Tisch liegen lassen, in der Ecke stehen lassen. Laß mich allein!

(b) (= *make*) Er hat mich warten lassen. Er läßt seine Schüler zu viel auswendig lernen. Das läßt mich glauben/annehmen/vermuten, daß ...

(c) (= *get s.b. to do s.th.*) Ich ließ die Kinder für mich abwaschen. Ich ließ ihn es mir ausführlich erzählen. Ich ließ ihn den Plan ausführen.

(d) (= *get, have s.th. done (for oneself)*) Ich ließ es sofort bringen. Ich habe mir die Haare schneiden lassen, mir einen Anzug machen lassen.

(e) (= *let*) Laß mich kommen! Das läßt mich hoffen, daß er ... Er ließ sie nicht gehen, ohne ...

(f) (= *can be*) Das läßt sich nur schwer sagen. Das läßt sich nicht leugnen (*denied*).

(g) (*Idioms*) Er hat ihn kommen lassen (*sent for him*). Er läßt Ihnen sagen, daß ... (*he wants me to tell you that* ...). Das lasse ich mir nicht gefallen (*I'll not put up with that*). Er läßt deine Mutter (herzlich) grüßen (*he sends his (kindest) regards to your mother*). Wir wollen es dabei lassen (*we'll leave it at that*).

69 The Passive Voice

(a) Er wird getragen (*is carried, is being carried*), wurde getragen (*was carried, was being carried*), ist getragen worden (*has been carried*), war getragen worden (*had been carried*), wird getragen werden (*will be carried*), sei gegrüßt/umarmt! (*hail!/a hug*)! – the passive imperative is restricted to one or two expressions only.

(b) Es muß aufgegessen werden (*must be eaten up*), mußte aufgegessen werden (*had to be*), hat aufgegessen werden müssen (*has had to be*),

77

hätte aufgegessen werden müssen (*should have been*), wird aufgegessen werden müssen (*will have to be*).

Es muß (mußte) aufgegessen **worden** sein (*must have been eaten up*); damit wir gerettet werden könnten (*so that we could be rescued*); sie hätten nicht geschrieben zu werden brauchen (*might as well have not been written*, i.e. *for all the use ...*).

(c) *By* is translated by *von* (agent), *durch* (means), *mit* (instrument).

Die Tür wurde **von** einem Diener geöffnet.
Durch seine Hilfe wurde es möglich gemacht.
Er wurde **mit** einem Messer erstochen (*stabbed*).

(d) The subject of the passive is the direct object of the active. Indirect objects remain indirect in the passive.

Er wurde freigelassen.
Ihm wurde **ein schöner Wagen** gegeben (*he was given a ...*).
Er wurde seines Amtes enthoben (*he was removed from ...*).

(e) An impersonal passive construction (introduced by *es* – in the main, but never in the subordinate clause – only if this is the first word) has to be used when the verb is intransitive.

Es wurde lange getanzt *or* Lange wurde getanzt (*dancing went on for a long time*).
But Obgleich lange getanzt wurde, ...
Mir wurde versichert, daß ... (*I was assured ...*).
Ihnen muß beigebracht werden, wie ... (*they must be taught how*).
An Ihrem Mut ist nie gezweifelt worden (*your courage has never been doubted*).

(f) The infinitive + *zu* preceded by *sein, bleiben, stehen* and, without *zu*, *lassen* (with reflexive verb) has modal and passive force.

Das ist leicht zu erraten (*can easily be guessed, is easy to guess*).
Nichts war zu finden (*nothing could be, was to be found*).
Das Haus ist zu vermieten (*to (be) let*). Dem ist nicht zu helfen.
Der Erfolg bleibt abzuwarten (*remains to be seen*).
Das steht zu erwarten (*is to be expected*).
Diese Beispiele ließen sich leicht vervielfachen (*could easily be multiplied*).
Das läßt sich leicht sagen (*is easily said*).
Sie ließen sich hineinziehen (*let themselves be drawn in*).

(g) The statal passive (*sein* + past participle) must be distinguished from the actional passive (*werden* + past participle). Compare:

Die Tür **war** schon geschlossen (*was already shut*).
Die Tür **wurde** eben geschlossen (*was just being shut*), **wurde** jeden Abend um 6 Uhr geschlossen (i.e. *habitually*).

Note the following common statal passives:

> Er war entschlossen/geneigt/gezwungen, es zu tun (*resolved/inclined/ compelled*); es war gefüllt/erfüllt mit/von (*filled with*), versehen mit (*provided with*); es war durchdrungen von (*filled with, steeped in*), umgeben von/mit (*surrounded by/with*); sie war in Weiß gekleidet (*dressed in*), in einen dicken Mantel eingehüllt (*wrapped in*).

(h) Note the following alternative ways of expressing the English passive:

i By reflexive verbs: sich befassen mit (*be concerned with*); sich erheben (*be raised*); sich erneuen (*be renewed*); sich (er)öffen (*be opened*); sich spiegeln (*be mirrored*); sich verdichten (*be consolidated*). Es stellte sich heraus, daß sie ... enthielt (*it was found to contain*).

ii By a verb in the active: entstammen (*be derived*); erlöschen (*be extinguished*); erschrecken (*be frightened*); ertrinken (*be drowned*); fußen auf (*be founded on*); heißen (*be called*); ruhen auf (*be based on*); er hatte es ihr angetan (*she was fascinated by him*); sie pflegten zu sagen (*were accustomed to*); er trug einen Anzug (*was dressed in*); sie stimmten darin überein, daß ... (*it was agreed among them that ...*); er geriet in Versuchung (*was tempted*).

iii By *dürfen, sollen, lassen*: er darf es tun (*is allowed to*); er soll es getan haben (*is said to*); mit denen es sich befassen soll (*which it is called upon to deal with*); er sollte sich einmischen (*was expected to*); es sollte ausdrücken (*was meant to*); ich würde sie nicht ertränken lassen (*would not have them, cause them to be, drowned*).

iv By *man*: man fragte ihn (*he was asked*); man hat es erreicht (*it was reached*); sie erwarten, daß man sie verschönert (*they expect to be idealised*); ... das man nennen könnte (*that could be called*).

v By constructions like: es heißt (*we are told*); er zeigte sich wohl überlegen (*he may be said to have shown himself superior*); etwas anderes ist notwendig (*is needed*), ist erforderlich (*is required*).

vi By a present participle construction (cf. *64(d)*): ein nie zu vergessendes Erlebnis (*an experience never to be forgotten*).

70 The Formation of the Subjunctive

(a) The endings of the present and imperfect subjunctive are the same for all verbs, except the 1st and 3rd sing. pres. of *sein*.

> -e, -est, -e, -en, -et, -en.

(b) The present subjunctive (nowadays, however, used only in the third person singular except in the case of *sein* and the first person singular of the modal auxiliaries) is formed by adding these endings to the stem of the infinitive:

> er sag-**e** er geh-**e**, er hab-**e**, er werd-**e**, ich/er könn-**e**.
> *But* ich sei, du sei(**e**)st, er sei, wir sei**en**, ihr sei**et** (*rarely used*), sie (Sie) sei**en**.

(c) The imperfect subjunctive is formed by adding these endings to the past stem of weak and strong verbs. Strong verbs modify the stem vowel if possible, as do also *haben*, *wissen* and *werden*.

ich macht-**e**, er ging-**e**, ihr gäb-**et**, sie wär-**en**; er hätt-**e**, ich wüßt-**e**, sie würd-**en**.

(d) The perfect and pluperfect subjunctive are formed by the present and imperfect subjunctive of *haben* or *sein* together with the past participle. The perfect subjunctive when conjugated with *haben* is now only used in the third person singular.

er habe gesagt, er habe gegeben, ich sei gekommen; ich hätte gesagt, wir hätten gegeben, sie wären gekommen.

(e) Some verbs have older alternative forms of the imperfect subjunctive; *sterben*, *verderben*, *werben* and *werfen* have no alternative modern forms.

beföhle, begönne, empföhle, hülfe, schölte, schwömme, spönne; stürbe, verdürbe, würbe, würfe:

(f) Imperfect subjunctive of irregular weak verbs:

brennte, kennte, nennte, rennte, sendete, wendete and their compounds; brächte, dächte and their compounds; sollte, wollte.

71 The Subjunctive in Indirect Speech

(a) In turning direct speech – statements and questions – into indirect speech the following changes in the mood and tense of the verbs take place:

DIRECT SPEECH		INDIRECT SPEECH
Present Indicative	becomes	Present (or Imperfect) Subjunctive
Imperfect Indicative ⎫ Perfect Indicative ⎬ (= Past) become Pluperfect Indicative ⎭		Perfect (or Pluperfect) Subjunctive
Future Indicative ⎫ Conditional ⎬ (= Future) become		Future Subjunctive or Conditional

  i Er sagt, sie sei (wäre) unglücklich (*she is*), sie sei (wäre) unglücklich gewesen (*has been, was*), sie wolle (wollte) kommen (*wants*), sie habe (hätte) immer kommen wollen (*wanted, has wanted, had wanted*), sie habe (hätte) nicht geschlafen (*has not slept, did not sleep*), sie komme (käme) erst später (*is coming, will be coming*).

    Er sagte, sie sei (wäre) sehr unglücklich (*she was*), sie wolle (wollte) kommen (*wanted*), sie habe (hätte) nicht geschlafen (*had not slept*), sie komme (käme) erst später (*was coming, i.e. would be coming*).

Er sagte,   wenn sie sofort komme (käme), tue (täte) er es.

Er sagte,   es sei die Tochter der Frau, bei der … er wohne (ANDERSCH).

Er sagte, daß sie sehr unglücklich sei (wäre), daß sie nicht kommen wolle (wollte), etc.

ii Er fragte sie, ob sie Zeit habe (hätte) (*if she had*), ob sie gut geschlafen habe (hätte) (*had slept*), wann sie kommen könne (könnte) (*could come*), wann sie komme (käme) (*was coming*, i.e. *would be coming*).

Er fragte,   was der Mann wolle, der eben gekommen sei.

iii Er sagte ihr, sie solle (sollte) sofort kommen (*told her to come*), sie möchte alles liegen lassen (*told her to leave everything*).

(b) If in indirect speech the present, perfect or future subjunctive forms are indistinguishable from the corresponding indicative forms, the imperfect subjunctive, pluperfect subjunctive or conditional **must** be used. Otherwise, modern usage tends to prefer the pluperfect subjunctive and conditional, but, except in N. Germany, not the imperfect subjunctive. In any case, all possible consistency in the use of tenses should be aimed at.

Er sagte mir, sie machten (*not* machen) alles verkehrt, sie hätten (*not* haben) alles verkehrt gemacht, sie würden (*not* werden) alles verkehrt machen, sie würden bald gehen (*not* sie gehen *or* gingen) (*were going*, i.e. *would be going*).

(c) In a passage of indirect speech *daß* is usually omitted.

(d) The subjunctive does not necessarily have to be used in indirect speech. It is normally used in indirect speech either (i) when the writer does not wish to vouch for the truth of what is reported or (ii) when he wishes to convey that what is reported is not true or that he does not agree with it. If on the other hand the writer is certain of his facts and wishes to convey this certainty he will use the indicative. Compare the following examples taken from modern German authors:

Ich sage immer, daß ich nichts davon weiß (= *what I in fact always say*).

Ich sage, ich hätte mich verlaufen (= *I'll say what is not true*).

Ich glaube, sie ist schon zu Hause.

Ich glaube fast, daß Sie der Mann wären, mich zu verstehen.

Ich habe schon geglaubt, du seist nach Hause gegangen (*but now I see I am wrong*).

Sie können nicht wissen, wie meine Worte gemeint sind (*but I know*).

Ohne recht zu wissen, wo er sei …

Plötzlich wußte ich, wer Sie sind.

Sie wußte, sie könne mir nicht helfen.

Er vermutete, daß es sie war.

72 Conditional Sentences and the Use of the Subjunctive

(a) **Indicative** in both clauses

Wenn ich Zeit habe, hole ich dich ab (*if I have time I'll fetch you*).
Wenn du Arbeit willst, können wir zu meinen Leuten fahren.
Ich komme am Montag, wenn ich es einrichten kann.
Ich werde es tun, wenn ich es einrichten kann.

(b) **Conditional** (*or* **subjunctive**) in the **main** clause, **subjunctive** in **subordinate** clause

Wenn ich Zeit hätte, würde ich dich abholen (*or* holte ich dich ab) (*if I had time I would fetch you*).
Wenn er kommen sollte, würden wir uns freuen (*if he were to*).
Wenn du Arbeit wolltest, könnten wir zu meinen Leuten fahren.
Ich würde am Montag kommen (*or* ich käme am Montag), wenn ich es einrichten könnte.

NOTE: The conditional in the subordinate clause, though met with in good authors and though very common in colloquial German is apt to be stylistically clumsy and should be used with discretion in German prose composition, restricted rather to the conversational passages.

Wenn sie ihn lieben würde, würde sie es sofort sagen (MUSIL).
Wenn sie eine Möglichkeit finden würde, ... (KAFKA).
Wenn du sie kennen würdest, dann wüßtest du, daß ... (RINSER).

(c) **Subjunctive** in **both** clauses

Wenn ich Zeit gehabt hätte, hätte ich dich abgeholt (*if I had had time I would have fetched you*).
Wenn du Arbeit gewollt hättest, hätten wir zu meinen Leuten fahren können.
Ich wäre am Montag gekommen, wenn ich es hätte einrichten können (*if I could have managed it*).

(d) Omission of *wenn*

Kommt er, so/dann können wir die Sache besprechen (*if he comes*).
Käme er bald (*or* sollte er bald kommen), so würden wir uns sehr freuen (*were he to*).
Wäre er gekommen, so hätten wir uns gefreut (*had he come*).
Hätte ich das Große Los gewonnen, so ... (*had I won*).

(e) Since *wenn* with the present indicative may also mean 'when' or 'whenever' *falls* ('in case', 'if') or *sollte* should be used when ambiguity must be avoided.

Falls er anruft, sag ihm ... **Sollte** er anrufen, so ...

(f) When either of the clauses states a fact the indicative must be used in both clauses.

Wenn er böse war, so waren wir es noch viel mehr (*if he was angry we were much more so*).

Wenn ihn der Bruder für einen Dieb hielt, so konnte ja jeder Fremde dasselbe oder Besseres leisten als er (SCHNITZLER).

Wenn seine Hand gezittert hat und er nicht völlig Herr seiner selbst war, so geschah es, weil ... (T. MANN).

73 Other Uses of the Subjunctive

(a) In main clauses:
i Man nehme ein Pfund Butter! Es lebe die Freiheit!
Gehen wir! Es koste, was es wolle.
Möge Gott mich totschlagen!
ii Käme er doch bald (*if only he would come soon*)!
Hätte ich nur fleißiger gearbeitet!
Beinahe hätte ich dich nicht erkannt (*I nearly didn't recognise you*).
Er wäre beinahe/fast gestorben (*he almost died*).
iii Nun wären wir zu Hause (*well, home at last*)!
Wäre das möglich (*is it really possible*)?

(b) In subordinate clauses:
i Purpose:
Er wollte, daß wir sofort kämen (*wanted us to*).
Ich wünschte, ich könnte (*I wish I could*).
Sie möchte, daß ich die Sirenen und die Flieger ganz vergäße (LEFORT)
Er wartete, daß sie käme (*for her to come*).
But Er **will**, daß sie sofort **kommt**.
Er tat alles, damit seine Familie zu essen hätte/hatte.
But Er **tut** alles, damit seine Familie zu essen **hat**.
ii Negation, restriction or denial:
Ich kenne niemand, der so dumm wäre (*who is*).
Niemand, der mein wächsernes Gesicht gewärmt hätte (*who warmed, nobody to warm*)! (AICHINGER)
Ein Orchester, das nur aus Pauken, Trommeln, Kastagnetten und Schlag- und Geräuschinstrumenten bestände, wäre ein Unmögliches (W. SCHNEIDER).
Nicht daß er ein Musterschüler geworden wäre (*has become*).
Er leugnete ab, daß es so etwas überhaupt gäbe.
Die Entfernung war zu groß, als daß er das Haus hätte erkennen können (*for him to be able to*) (ANDERSCH).
Kein Tag verging, ohne daß ich daran gedacht hätte/hatte (*without my thinking of it*).

But Kein Tag vergeht, ohne daß er daran **denkt**.

Anstatt daß er zu ihnen gegangen wäre/war, mußte seine Mutter zu ihnen gehen (*instead of his going*).

But Anstatt daß er zu ihnen **geht**, muß seine Mutter zu ihnen gehen.

iii Er sieht aus, als ob er krank sei/wäre, als sei/wäre er krank (*he looks as if he is/were ill*).

Er tat (so), als ob er schliefe (*pretended to be asleep*).

NOTE: The *als ob/als* construction can only be used with a finite verb. With the participles and the infinitive *wie* is used:

> Es sah aus wie aus Gold gemacht (*as if made of*).
> Er lachte wie verrückt (*as if mad, like one mad*).
> Er streckte die Hand aus, wie um sie zu liebkosen (*as though to caress her*).

74 Verbs governing the Dative

WEAK

angehören *belong to (s.th)*
antworten *answer (s.b.)*
*begegnen *meet*
beiwohnen *attend, be present at*
danken *thank*
dienen *serve*
drohen *threaten*
*entstammen *be derived from*
fehlen *be missing; be wrong with*
(*)folgen *follow; obey*
gehorchen *obey*
gehören *belong to (s.b.)*
genügen *suffice*
glauben *believe (s.b.)*
gratulieren *congratulate*
imponieren *impress*
mißtrauen *mistrust*
sich nähern *approach*
nützen *be of use to*
passen *suit*
*passieren *happen to*
schaden *harm*
schmecken *like (taste of)*
schmeicheln *flatter*
trotzen *defy*
vertrauen *trust*
sich widmen *devote o.s. to*
zuhören *listen to*
zulächeln *smile at*

STRONG (see *102*)

*auffallen *strike one's attention, notice*
*einfallen *occur to*
*entfliehen *escape from*
*entgehen *elude, avoid, escape from*
*entkommen *get away, escape (from)*
entsprechen *suit, correspond to*
*entspringen *arise, proceed from, be an outcome of*
*erliegen *succumb to*
gefallen *please, like*
*gelingen *succeed, manage*
gelten *be intended for, matter to*
*geschehen *happen to*
gleichen *resemble*
helfen *help*
leid tun *be sorry (for)*
*mißlingen *fail*
*nachlaufen *run after*
nachsehen *follow with one's eyes*
*vorangehen *precede, go on ahead*
*vorausgehen *precede, go on ahead*
*vorkommen *seem to; (refl.) feel, think o.s.*
*weichen *yield to*
weh tun *hurt, ache*
widersprechen *contradict*
widerstehen *resist*
zusehen *watch*
*zustoßen *befall, happen to*

Ich gratuliere Ihnen. Es gelang mir, der Gefahr zu entkommen. Er tut mir leid (*I am sorry for him*). Es wird Ihnen dort gefallen (*you'll like it there*). Das kommt mir komisch vor (*it seems odd to me*). Ich kam mir dumm vor (*I felt stupid*).

75 Verbs governing the Accusative and Dative

WEAK

anvertrauen *entrust*
auferlegen *impose, inflict on*
beibringen (*irr.*) *teach*
berichten *report*
besorgen *get s.th. for s.b.*
bringen (*irr.*) *bring, take*
einbringen (*irr.*) *bring in, yield*
einflößen *inspire with*
einräumen *concede, give up to*
einschärfen *impress/inculcate on*
erklären *explain; declare*
erlauben *allow, permit*
ersparen *save s.b. s.th.*
erzählen *tell, relate*
gewähren *grant, accord*
gönnen *not begrudge*
hinzufügen *add*
klagen *complain of*
liefern *deliver, furnish, supply*
melden *announce*
mitteilen *impart, inform of*
reichen *hand, pass, reach*
sagen *say, tell*
schenken *give, present*
schicken *send*
senden (*irr.*) *send*
verdanken *owe to*
verkaufen *sell*
verschaffen *get, procure for*
verweigern *refuse s.b. s.th.*
vorspielen *play to*
vorstellen *introduce*
wünschen *wish*
zahlen *pay*
zeigen *show, point out*
zumuten *expect of, demand of*

STRONG (see *102*)

anbieten *offer*
aufgeben *assign, set* (e.g. *a task*)
befehlen *order*
beschreiben *describe*
beweisen *prove*
bieten *bid, offer*
empfehlen *recommend*
entreißen *seize from*
entziehen *deprive of, withdraw from*
geben *give*
gebieten *command*
hinterlassen *bequeath*
leihen *lend*
nachsehen *overlook* (e.g. *fault*)
raten *advise*
schreiben *write*
überlassen *leave to (s.b. else)*
verbergen *conceal from*
verbieten *forbid*
vergeben *forgive*
verleihen *grant, bestow on, confer, endow with*
verraten *betray*
verschreiben *prescribe* (e.g. *medicine*)
versprechen *promise*
verzeihen *pardon*
vorenthalten *withhold from*
vorlesen *read aloud*
vorschlagen *suggest*
vorwerfen *reproach with*
vorziehen *prefer*
weisen *show*
zurückgeben *return*
zurufen *call out to*
es einem antun *fascinate s.b.*

Er flößte ihnen Mut ein. Das kann ich ihnen nicht zumuten. Das verdanke ich Ihnen allein.

76 Verbs governing the Genitive

WEAK
sich bedienen *use*
bedürfen (*irr.*) *need*
sich bemächtigen *seize, take possession of, usurp*
sich entledigen *get rid of, acquit o.s. of, fulfil*
sich erbarmen *have mercy on, take pity on*
sich erfreuen *enjoy*
sich erinnern *remember*
sich erwehren *restrain, ward off*
gedenken (*irr.*) *bear in mind, remember*
sich rühmen *boast of*
sich schämen *be ashamed of*
sich vergewissern *assure o.s. of*
sich versichern *assure o.s. of*

STRONG (see *102*)
sich annehmen *take charge, care of*
sich begeben *waive, renounce*
sich enthalten *refrain, abstain from*
entraten *dispense with*
sich entschlagen *part with, get rid of*
sich entsinnen *remember*
sich verschließen *shut one's eyes to*
sich versehen *expect s.th. confidently*

Es bedurfte nur eines Wortes. Er konnte sich des Lachens nicht enthalten
Er rühmte sich dessen, niemals zu spät gekommen zu sein.

77 Verbs governing the Accusative and Genitive

WEAK
anklagen *accuse of*
berauben *rob of*
beschuldigen *accuse of*
bezichtigen *accuse of*
entkleiden *deprive of, strip*
entwöhnen *break of (habit)*
verdächtigen *suspect of*
würdigen *deem worthy of*

STRONG (see *102*)
entbinden *release, absolve from* (e.g. *duty*)
entheben *remove from, relieve of* (e.g. *office*)
zeihen *accuse of*

Sie wollte mich keines Blickes würdigen. Er wurde seines Amtes enthoben.

78 Verbs governing a Double Accusative

WEAK
kosten *cost*
lehren *teach*
nennen (*irr.*) *call, name*

STRONG (see *102*)
heißen *call*
schelten *call s.b. (s.th. derogatory)*

86

79 Verbs followed by a Prepositional Object

(a) General remarks:

i   Many verbs take a prepositional object, i.e. a noun or pronoun preceded by a preposition or adverbial compound:

Ich verlasse mich auf meinen Freund, auf ihn.
Ich verlasse mich auf mein Glück, darauf (*rely on it*).

ii The prepositional object of a number of such verbs can be a clause or an infinitive phrase. Such clauses or infinitive phrases are normally preceded by the appropriate adverbial compound – *daran, darauf, damit*, etc. If two persons are involved a clause must be used introduced by *daß* or an interrogative; otherwise an infinitive construction is possible and usually preferable. The English translation is often a gerund. (But see *48(f) vi* for construction with relative clauses).

Ich verlasse mich darauf, daß du kommst (*I rely on your coming*).
Sie erinnerte sich daran, wie er ausgesehen hatte.
Es hängt davon ab, wann Sie abreisen wollen.
Ich denke nicht daran, mich darüber zu beklagen (*of complaining*).

iii Those verbs in the following lists that are capable of the above construction (ii) are marked by a dagger †.

iv Some of the nouns and adjectives listed in 56 as well as a few other expressions are also capable of this construction. See (*v*) below.

WEAK	STRONG (see *102*)
(b) an + accusative	
†denken (*irr.*) *think of*	binden *tie to*
†erinnern *remind*	*festbinden *tie up, tether to*
†sich erinnern *remember*	†*gehen *proceed to*
†gewöhnen *accustom to*	sich halten *stick, adhere to* (e.g.
†sich gewöhnen *get used to*	rules)
†glauben *believe in*	*herangehen *go up to, tackle* (e.g.
sich klammern *cling to, clutch at*	problem)
sich lehnen *lean against*	*herankommen *come up to*
†sich machen *proceed to*	schreiben *write to*
stecken *pin to*	verraten *betray to*
sich wenden (*irr.*) *turn, apply to*	verweisen *refer s.b. to s.b.*

Er verriet ihn an seine Feinde. Er hat sich daran gewöhnt, ohne Schlafmittel zu schlafen.

(c) an + dative

arbeiten *work at*	abnehmen *decrease in*
sich beteiligen *take part in*	gewinnen *gain in*
†erkennen (*irr.*) *recognise by*	hängen *care about, be attached to*

WEAK	STRONG (see *102*)
*erkranken *be taken ill with*	leiden *suffer from, be liable to*
fehlen *be lacking in*	liegen *rest with, be up to; be one's*
sich freuen *take pleasure in*	*fault; matter to; be due to*
†hindern *prevent from*	*sterben *die of (illness)*
sich orientieren *take one's bearings*	teilnehmen *partake of,*
by	*participate in*
sich rächen *avenge o.s. on*	tragen *be weighed down by* (e.g. *guilt*)
teilhaben (*irr.*) *participate in*	verlieren *lose in*
†verhindern *prevent from*	* vorbeigehen *go past*
sich versuchen *try one's hand at*	* vorbeikommen *come, get past*
sich versündigen *sin against*	* vorbeilaufen *run past*
verzweifeln *despair of*	ziehen *pull on, at*
sich weiden *feast one's eyes on*	zunehmen *increase in*
zweifeln *doubt*	

Es fehlt ihm an Mut. Er hinderte sie daran, mit seinem Freund zu sprechen.
Es liegt an mir, ob er kommt oder nicht (*it rests with me, it's up to me,
whether* ...). Mir liegt viel/wenig/nichts daran (*it matters much* ...).

(d) auf + accusative

†achten *heed, look after*	es abgesehen haben *have designs on*
†anspielen *.allude to*	†*ankommen *depend on,*
antworten *answer s.th.*	*be concerned to*
anwenden (*irr.*) *apply s.th. to s.th.*	es darauf ankommen *lassen risk,*
sich aufbauen *be based/founded on*	*chance it*
†aufmerksam machen *call attention*	†*ausgehen *be bent on*
to	†*aussein *be out for s.th.*
aufpassen *keep an eye on*	sich belaufen *amount to* (e.g. *bills*)
beschränken *limit, confine to,*	sich besinnen *remember*
cut down to	sich beziehen *refer to*
blicken *look, gaze at*	†dringen *press for s.th.*
fluchen *swear at*	*eingehen *agree to; go into details*
*folgen *follow upon*	sich einlassen *let o.s get involved in*
sich freuen *look forward to*	*gehen *look out on to*
sich gründen *be based on*	*hinauslaufen *amount,*
hinarbeiten *work for* (*an object*)	*be tantamount to*
†hindeuten *indicate, intimate*	†hinweisen *point, refer to, indicate*
†hoffen *hope for*	*kommen *hit upon*
hören *listen, pay attention to*	schießen *shoot at*
*klettern *climb up* (e.g. *tree*)	sehen *look, glance at*
sich konzentrieren *concentrate on,*	sinnen *scheme, plot s.th.*
centre on	*stoßen *come upon, run into s.b.*
passen *watch for, fit* (*on, into*)	trinken *drink to, toast*
†rechnen *count on*	†sich verlassen *rely on*
trauen *trust in*	verschieben *postpone to*

WEAK

vertrauen *trust in*
verwenden *apply s.th. to,*
  bring to bear on
†verzichten *do without, renounce*
†sich vorbereiten *prepare for*
warten *wait for*
zeigen *point to, at*
†zurückführen *attribute,*
  trace back to

STRONG (see *102*)

sich verstehen *be skilled in,*
  expert at
verweisen *refer s.b. to s.th.*
weisen *point to, at*
*zugehen *go up to*
*zukommen *come up to*
*zulaufen *run up to*
zutreffen *apply to, be true of*

Alles ist auf seinen Mangel an Mut zurückzuführen. Er machte mich darauf aufmerksam. Es läuft auf dasselbe hinaus. Es kommt darauf an, wie man es versteht (*it depends on the way*). Ihnen kam es darauf an, zu gewinnen (*they were concerned to*).

(e) auf + dative

†beharren, *stick, adhere to*
  (e.g. *opinion*)
beruhen *be based on, rest on*
fußen *be founded on*

†bestehen *insist on*

Das beruht auf einem Irrtum. Er besteht darauf, daß wir kommen.

(f) aus + dative

erhellen *be evident from*
†*folgen *follow from*
†folgern *infer from*
lernen *learn from*
machen *make s.th. of/from*
resultieren *result from*
übersetzen *translate from*

bestehen *consist of*
*entkommen *escape out of*
*entspringen *escape out of*
*entstehen *originate in, arise*
†sich ergeben *result, follow from*
†ersehen *see from*
†schließen *conclude from*
*werden *become of*

Der Verbrecher entsprang aus dem Zug, aus dem Gefängnis. Daraus ergibt sich, daß kein wahres Wort daran ist.

(g) bei + dative

sich bedanken *thank*
†beharren *stick to* (e.g. *opinion*)
sich beklagen *complain to*
sich entschuldigen *apologise to*
hindern *obstruct*
wohnen *live with*

*bleiben *stay with; stick to*
ergreifen *seize by* (e.g. *hand*)
halten *hold by* (e.g. *hand*)
helfen *help with*
nehmen *take* (e.g. *by hand*)
vorsprechen *call on*

Er bedankte sich bei mir. Er half uns bei der Arbeit. Sie hielt ihn bei der Hand.

WEAK

STRONG (see *102*)

(h) für + accusative

WEAK	STRONG
bestimmen *destine, mean for*	†*eintreten *plead for s.th./s.b.*
†danken *thank for*	†sich entscheiden *decide for, in favour of*
sich einsetzen *champion s.th./s.b.*	
sich interessieren *be interested in*	†gelten *be considered; be true for*
kämpfen *fight for*	halten *consider, deem, think, take for/to be*
schwärmen *enthuse about*	
†sorgen *see to, look after*	nehmen *take*
stimmen *vote for*	zutreffen *be true of*

Nimm es nicht für ungut (*don't take it amiss*)! Er interessiert sich für alles. Er sorgte dafür, daß die Kinder gut erzogen wurden.

(i) gegen + accusative

WEAK	STRONG
†einwenden *object to, have objection to*	abstechen *stand out clearly against*
†etwas/nichts haben *have some/no objection to*	sich aussprechen *make objections to s.th.*
kämpfen *fight against*	*einschreiten *take action against*
†protestieren *protest against*	†sich entscheiden *decide against*
stimmen *vote against*	sich erheben *rise up against*
sich sträuben *boggle at, oppose*	†sprechen *speak against*
sich wehren *oppose*	verstoßen *offend against*

Was haben Sie dagegen? Ich habe nichts dagegen. Er wendete dagegen ein, daß er an dem Tag nicht frei war.

(j) in + accusative

WEAK	STRONG
sich einmischen *interfere in, mix o.s. up in*	*ausbrechen *burst out into*
einweihen *initiate into*	dringen *urge upon, press s.b.*
einwilligen *consent, agree to*	*einbiegen *turn into* (e.g. *road*)
sich fügen *acquiesce in, submit to*	*einbrechen *break into, burgle*
(sich) kleiden *dress (o.s.) in*	*eindringen *force one's way in*
sich mischen *interfere in*	*einfallen *invade*
übersetzen *translate into*	einlassen *let s.b./s.th. in(to)*
sich verlieben *fall in love with*	sich einlassen *let o.s get involved in*
versetzen *place in(to)*	einschließen *confine within, shut in*
verwandeln *transform, change into*	*einsteigen *mount, get in, board* (*vehicle*)
sich verwandeln *turn, be transformed into*	*eintreten *enter*
verwickeln *involve in*	sich ergeben *resign o.s. to*
sich verwickeln *be involved in*	*geraten *get into* (e.g. *difficulties*)

Er übersetzte das Buch aus dem Englischen ins Deutsche. Er hat sich ins Unvermeidliche fügen müssen.

WEAK   STRONG (see *102*)

(k) in + dative

WEAK	STRONG (see *102*)
sich irren *be mistaken, wrong about*	*ankommen *arrive at, in*
*einkehren *put up (at inn)*	†bestehen *consist in*
sich spiegeln *be mirrored in*	*erscheinen *appear at, in*
†übereinstimmen *agree about, in*	†liegen *reside/consist in*
	sich verfangen *catch* (intr.) *in*
	*verschwinden *disappear in*

Ihr Fingernagel verfing sich in ihrem Kleid. Wir stimmten darin überein, daß Karl fort mußte (*we agreed that*).

(l) mit + dative

WEAK	STRONG
aufhören *stop s.th.*	†sich abfinden *accept, acquiesce in, compound with*
sich befassen *deal, be concerned with, handle*	†anfangen *begin by*
†sich beschäftigen *occupy o.s. with*	†beginnen *begin by*
handeln *trade in*	fortfahren *go on with, continue*
nicken *nod (the head)*	sprechen *speak to, with*
prahlen *boast of*	*umgehen *handle, entertain* (e.g. *idea*), *associate with*
†rechnen *count on, expect*	verbinden *connect, join*
übereinstimmen *agree with s.b., square with s.th.*	versehen *provide with*
†verbringen (*irr.*) *spend (doing s.th.)*	*zusammenstoßen *collide with*
sich verschmelzen *melt into*	
verwechseln *confuse with*	
wedeln *wag*	
winken *wave, beckon*	
†zubringen (*irr.*) *spend (doing s.th.)*	

Das stimmt nicht damit überein. Sie winkte mit der Hand. Du mußt dich damit abfinden, daß es nicht anders geht.

(m) nach + dative

WEAK	STRONG
*abreisen *set off for*	aussehen *look like*
angeln *fish for*	graben *dig for*
†sich erkundigen *enquire about s.b.*	greifen *clutch at, catch hold of*
forschen *search after*	riechen *smell of*
†fragen *enquire about s.b./s.th.*	schreien *shout for*
schicken *send for*	sehen *look after*
schmecken *taste of*	sich umsehen *look round for*
†sich sehnen *long for*	
streben *strive after /for*	
suchen *search for*	
†urteilen *judge by*	

Sie schickte nach dem Arzt. Er konnte nur nach dem urteilen, was er gesehen hatte. Ich sehne mich danach, ins Bett zu gehen.

WEAK	STRONG (see *102*)
(n) über + accusative	
†sich beklagen *complain of*	sich aussprechen *discuss*
†berichten *report, impart*	†beraten *give advice about*
†*erstaunen *be surprised at*	entscheiden *decide upon*
†sich freuen *be glad about,*	erfahren *learn about, of*
pleased with	gebieten *have control over, have*
sich hermachen *fall upon, attack*	*at one's command*
herrschen *rule over*	*gehen *exceed, surpass* (e.g.
†klagen *complain of*	*expectations*)
†lachen *laugh at, about*	*kommen *fall on, overwhelm*
†nachdenken *think about, of, over*	lesen *lecture on*
†reden *talk about*	†schreiben *write about*
regieren *govern*	sinnen *meditate, reflect (up)on*
†schimpfen *grumble about*	†sprechen *speak about s.th.*
†spotten *mock at, deride*	streiten *argue, dispute about*
sich täuschen *be mistaken about*	sich streiten *quarrel about*
urteilen *pass judgment on, judge*	† sich unterhalten *converse about*
verfügen *possess, have at one's*	
disposal	
wachen *watch over*	
weinen *weep over, about*	
†sich wundern *be surprised at*	

Er verfügt über überraschende Eigenschaften. Er beklagte sich darüber,
daß sie nicht gekommen war.

(o) um + accusative	
sich bemühen *try to help*	sich bewerben *apply for* (e.g. *post*)
†beneiden *envy*	†bitten *ask for*
bringen (*irr.*) *deprive of, cheat out*	*gehen, *be a matter of, be at*
of	*stake*
†sich drehen *turn, hinge on*	*herumkommen *get round* (e.g.
flehen *implore for*	*difficulty*)
fragen *ask for* (e.g. *advice*)	*kommen *lose*
†sich handeln *be a question,*	ringen *struggle for*
matter of	streiten *contend with s.b. for*
kämpfen *fight, struggle for*	wissen *know about*
sich (be-)kümmern *concern o.s.,*	
worry about	

Er beneidet seinen Bruder um seinen Reichtum. Darum können wir nicht
herumkommen. Es handelt sich darum, ob er noch lebt.

(p) unter + accusative	
gehören *fall under, pertain to*	*geraten *fall among, in with*

Das gehört unter diese Rubrik. Er geriet unter Räuber.

WEAK   STRONG (see *102*)

(q) unter + dative

†leiden *suffer emotionally under,*
          in consequence of

Er litt darunter, daß man nicht mit ihm verkehren wollte.

(r) von + dative

benachrichtigen *inform of*   †abhalten *prevent, keep from*
denken (*irr.*) *think* (e.g. *well*) *of*   †abhängen *depend on*
sich erholen *recover from*   sich abheben *be silhouetted/*
†erzählen *relate about*   *outlined, stand out against*
heilen *cure of*   abziehen *deduct from*
leben *live on*   gelten *be true of*
sagen *tell about*   halten *think* (e.g. *well*) *of*
††träumen *dream of*   lossprechen *acquit of, absolve from*
überzeugen *convince of*   †sprechen *speak of*
wimmeln *teem with*   verstehen *know, understand about*
wissen (*irr.*) *know about*   *weichen *budge from*

Was hielt ihn davon ab? Wovon lebt er?

(s) vor + dative

†Angst haben *be afraid of*   †*erschrecken *be startled at*
†bewahren *preserve from*   *fliehen *flee from*
†sich fürchten *be afraid of*   sich in acht nehmen, *be careful of,*
†sich hüten *beware of*   *mind*
schützen *protect from*   *sterben *die* (e.g. *of boredom*)
verstecken *hide from*   verbergen *conceal from*
†warnen *warn against*   *weichen *give way to*
weinen *weep* (e.g. *for joy*)

Nimm dich in acht davor! Hüten Sie sich (davor), es ihm zu sagen!

(t) wegen + genitive

loben *praise for*   schelten *scold, rebuke for*
sich schämen *be ashamed because*
   of
tadeln *blame for*

Ich schalt ihn wegen seines Betragens.

(u) zu + dative

†auffordern *invite to, call upon to* †antreten *walk up to*
beglückwünschen *congratulate on*   *anwachsen *increase to*
†berechtigen *entitle to*   sich aufschwingen *rise to, bring o.s.*
†bestimmen *destine for*   *to*

WEAK

brauchen *need for*
†bringen (*irr.*) *provoke to, make*
†dienen *serve to, for*
sich entwickeln *develop into*
ernennen (*irr.*) *appoint*
führen *lead to*
gebrauchen *use for*
gehören *belong, pertain to, be one of, be (integral) part of, be required for*
*gelangen *get to*
gratulieren *congratulate on*
machen *make*
†neigen *incline, tend to*
passen *go with, match*
†provozieren *provoke to*
steigern *intensify to*
taugen *be fit for, be worth*
†verdammen *condemn to*
†verurteilen *sentence to*
verweichen *soften into*
wählen *elect*
sich wenden (*irr.*) *turn to*
sich umwenden (*irr.*) *turn round to*

STRONG (see *102*)

†beitragen *contribute to*
†bewegen *induce, persuade to*
bitten *invite, ask s.b. to*
einladen *invite to*
†sich entschließen *decide to*
erziehen *educate, bring up to be s.th.*
greifen *reach for*
†*kommen *come to*
†raten (D) *advise to (do s.th.)*
*schmelzen *melt into*
sprechen *speak to*
†treiben *drive to*
†verhelfen (D) *help to*
*werden *become*
†zwingen *force, compel to*

Die Krawatte paßt zu deinem Anzug. Das hat sicher zum Erfolg beigetragen. Dazu gehört Zeit. Wir brachten ihn zum Lachen (*made him laugh*). Wie sollte ich sie dazu bringen, mir alles zu erzählen?

(v) Clauses or infinitive phrases as prepositional object of (i) nouns and (ii) adjectives or past participles:

i   Das ist der Dank **dafür**, **daß** ich dich jahrelang gepflegt habe (*thanks for my having*).
Er machte keine ernsten Einwendungen **dagegen**, **daß** ich kommen sollte (*objections to my coming*).
Sie hatte große Angst **davor**, allein im Hause bleiben zu müssen (*fear of having to*).
Sie geben Ratschläge **darüber**, was für Befehle erteilt werden sollen (*advice as to what*).

ii Er war schuld **daran**, **daß** sie so elendiglich starb (*to blame for her having*).
Er war **damit** einverstanden, **daß** wir gehen sollten (*agreed that*).
Er war aufgebracht, ärgerlich, bestürzt, entrüstet, froh, traurig **darüber**, **daß** ich das gesagt hatte (*at my having said*).

Unabhängig **davon**, **daß** wir das wollten, beschloß auch er, hinzu-
gehen (*independently of the fact that*).
Ich bin weit **davon** entfernt, Ihre Meinung zu teilen (*far from sharing*).
Abgesehen **davon**, **daß** du zu jung bist, kennen wir den jungen Mann
noch nicht (*apart from the fact that*).
Was er sagt, ist nicht **danach** angetan, mir zu imponieren (*is not
calculated to impress me*).

80 The Infinitive-Noun

(a) Equivalent to the English gerund:

i Das Reisen ist jetzt sehr beliebt geworden. Das Schreiben muß
gelernt werden. Dies Abgeschnittensein (*being cut off*) von Nina ist
nicht zu ertragen (RINSER). Ich war des Wartens müde. Sie verfiel
dem Weinen (*lapsed into weeping*) (GRASS).

ii Vor dem Einschlafen (*before falling asleep*), während des langen
Wachens (*while remaining long awake*), nach dem Einschlafen (*after
falling asleep*).
Es geriet ins Wanken (*started wobbling*). Sie verlegten sich aufs Beten
(*turned to praying*). Er hinderte mich beim Essen (*prevented from eating*). Er munterte mich durch Kopfnicken auf (*encouraged by nodding*).
Die Unruhe äußerte sich im Zerreißen eines kleinen Zettels (*in the
action of tearing up*) (KAFKA). Beim Ein- und Aussteigen muß man
aufpassen (*when getting on and off*). Er war betäubt von dem plötz-
lichen Gewecktwerden aus tiefem Schlaf (*by being woken up*) (KAFKA).
Wir haben nur wenig Zeit zum Ausruhen (*for resting*). Sie wollte zum
Tanzen gehen (*go dancing*). Ist das kein Grund zum Lächeln (*for
smiling*)?

(b) Equivalent to the English infinitive:

Was gibt es zum Essen (*to eat*)? Er war bereit zum Weggehen (*to
go away*). Ich habe kein Geld zum Verschwenden (*to waste*). Er half
mir beim Suchen (*to look*). Das brachte ihn zum Lachen, Weinen,
Schreien, Reden, Schweigen (*made him laugh, cry, scream, talk, stop
talking*).

(c) Equivalent to the English 'enough to (make)' , (cf. *63(d)iii*):

Es ist zum Rasendwerden (*enough to drive one mad*), voll zum Zer-
springen (*to bursting point*).

(d) Compound Infinitive-Nouns

Compound infinitive-nouns are not uncommon in German, ranging from
fairly simple ones like *das Vergessenwerden, das Sichgehenlassen, das Inein-
andergreifen* ('interlocking') to complicated ones like *das So-und-nicht-*

anders-sein (GUNDOLF) and *das Aufeinanderangewiesen- und abgestimmtsein der einzelnen Bauteile* ('the mutual interdependence and balancing of the separate parts of the structure') (W. SCHNEIDER).

Good examples of the use of compound infinitive-nouns are provided by the following passages:

> Auch fiel mir auf, daß Tätigkeiten wie Daumendrehen, Stirnrunzeln, Köpfchensenken, Händeschütteln, Falschgeldprägen, Lichtausknipsen, Zähneputzen, Totschießen und Trockenlegen überall ... geübt wurden (GRASS).

> Und endlich ... entsprang der Tanz ... Das war ein Wellenschlagen in den Sälen, ein Sich-Begegnen und ein Sich-Vermählen, ein Abschiednehmen und ein Wiederfinden, ein Glanzgenießen und ein Lichterblinden und ein Sich-Wiegen in den Sommerwinden, die in den Kleidern warmer Frauen sind (RILKE).

81 The Translation of the English Present Participle and Gerund

The following are common ways in which the English present participle and gerund may be translated. Compare also *63(a)(b)*, *64(a)(b)i*, *(c)(e)*, *79*, *80(a)(b)*.

(a) The infinitive with *zu* when there is no change of subject:

> Es ist wunderschön, hier zu sein (*being*).
> Ich gedenke/habe vor/beabsichtige/habe die Absicht, sie zu besuchen (*I intend visiting*).
> Es gelang ihm, rechtzeitig zu Hause anzukommen (*succeeded in arriving*).
> Ich hasse es/liebe es/ziehe es vor, zu Hause zu bleiben (*hate, love, prefer staying*).
> Er saß da, ohne ein Wort zu sagen (*without saying*).
> Er blieb sitzen, (an)statt aufzustehen (*instead of getting up*).
> Menschen haben die Fähigkeit zu sprechen (*faculty of speaking*).

(b) A dependent clause introduced by *indem; dadurch, daß; ohne daß; (an)statt daß*:

> Ich versuche abzunehmen, indem ich kein Brot esse (*by eating*).
> Dadurch, daß du dich so benimmst, verdirbst du alles (*by behaving like that*). Man kann dadurch alles besser verstehen, daß man die Umstände in Betracht zieht (*by taking into account*).
> Das Haus stand schon vor uns, ohne daß wir es erkannten (*without our recognising it*).
> Anstatt daß er zu mir kommt, muß ich zu ihm gehen (*instead of his coming*).

(c) A dependent clause introduced by the causal conjunction *da* or by the temporal conjunctions *als, nachdem, bevor, ehe, wenn, wobei*:

Da er durstig war, trank er vier Tassen Tee (*being thirsty*).
Als er sich erholt hatte, ... (*having recovered*).
Nachdem er den Brief geschrieben hatte, ... (*after writing*).
Bevor ich einschlafe, ... (*before going to sleep*).
Indem er das sagte, lächelte er (*saying that, he smiled*).
Wenn man einen Brief schreibt, muß man mit dem Datum anfangen (*when/in writing a letter*).
Alle sahen zum Fenster hinaus, wobei sie unverständliche Gesten machten (*making*).

(d) A dependent simple infinitive after *hören* and *sehen*:

Ich hörte sie über die Brücke gehen (*heard them going*).
Sie sah ihn/ihren Mann sich entfernen (*saw him/her husband going away*).

(e) A dependent clause introduced by *wie* after *hören* and *sehen* and after other verbs of perception:

Er sah, wie sie über die Brücke ging (*saw her walking*).
Ich hörte, wie er die Treppe hinunterlief (*heard him running*).
Er sah zu/beobachtete, wie sie dort spielten (*watched them playing*).
Ich hörte ihr zu, wie sie Mozart spielte (*listened to her playing*).

(f) A relative clause:

Der Baum, der in der Ecke steht, ist ein Apfelbaum (*the tree standing*).
Ich bemerkte einen Mann, der neben meiner Frau saß (*sitting*).

(g) A main clause introduced by *und*:

Ich stand da und sah ihnen zu (*stood watching them*).

(h) An infinitive-noun construction introduced by *beim*:

Beim Einsteigen (*when/on/while getting in*) stolperte er.
Beim Erwachen (*on waking up*) bemerkte er sie.
Beim Überholen (*when overtaking*) muß man sehr aufpassen.

(i) The finite verb together with *gern, lieber, am liebsten*:

Ich bleibe gern zu Hause (*like staying*).
Ich tanze lieber (*prefer dancing*).
Ich gehe am liebsten ins Kino (*like best going*).

82 Exclamations

In exclamations the transposed order, with the verb coming at the end, is probably the most common; but both inverted order, with the subject following the verb, and interrogative order, where English asks a negative question, are frequently met with.

(a) Transposed order:

Wie die Zeit vergeht! Wie weit das ist! Wie viele Leute da sind! Wie nett das ist! Wie schön du das gemacht hast! Wie lange das her ist (*what a long time ago that is*)! Was für Geschichten sie erzählen konnte! Was für ein Mann das war! Was du nicht sagst (*you don't say so*)!

(b) Inverted order:

Wie ist das nett! Wie schön hast du das gemacht! Wie lange ist das her! Was für Geschichten konnte sie erzählen! Was haben wir gelacht (*how we laughed*)!

(c) Interrogative order:

Ist das schön (*isn't that lovely*)! Ach, bin ich froh (*aren't I glad*)!

(d) Without verbs:

Was für schlechtes Wetter! Was für eine schöne Überraschung! Welche große Auswahl! Welch ein guter Mann!

83 Some difficult German Words

(a) **auch**

Er kommt auch (*too, also, as well*). Sowohl er als auch ich (*both he and I*). Ich bin hungrig. – Ich auch (*so am I*). Ich habe es nicht gesehen. – Ich auch nicht (*nor have I*). Ohne auch nur mit der Wimper zu zucken (*without even batting an eyelid*). Wie dem auch sei (*however that may be*). So schön sie auch ist (*beautiful as she is*). Kann ich mich aber auch darauf verlassen (*can I really*)? Wenn auch (*so what!*)! Zum Donnerwetter auch (*confound it, no!*)!

(b) **denn**

Wo ist er denn (*then*)? Warum denn (*Why should I?*)? Warum denn nicht (*Why ever not?*)? Warum denn war ... (*So why was ...?*)? Was machen Sie denn da (*What on earth are you doing?*)? Er tut nichts, denn er ist faul (*for he is*). Er sorgte für mich mehr als Koch denn als Vater (*than as*). Ich werde nicht antworten, geschweige denn (*let alone*) Geld schicken.

(c) **doch**

Du bist doch nicht krank? – Doch (*You surely aren't ill, are you? – Yes I am*). Hilf mir doch (*Do help me*)! Sie hassen sich doch wirklich (*do really hate*). Du hast es doch gesagt (*after all, nevertheless*). Das müßtest du doch wissen ~~(You~~ *jolly well ought* ...). Wenn er doch käme (*if only*)! Er kommt doch (*He is coming, isn't he?*)? Er war müde, doch glücklich (*but*). Ungern erinnere ich mich dieser Sammlersonntage: unternahm ich doch an solch einem Tag ... (GRASS) (*for I undertook*).

(d) etwa

Etwa 20 Meilen weit (*about*). Könntest du es etwa morgen tun (*perhaps*)? Hat er es dir etwa angeboten (*by any chance*)? Haben Sie den Zug etwa auch verpaßt (*do you mean to say that* ...)? Sollte er Sie etwa danach fragen ... (*should he happen to*). Nicht etwa, daß ich etwas gegen ihn habe (*not that I really*). Er hat es nicht etwa mir zuliebe getan (*not exactly*).

(e) immer

Er kommt immer um diese Zeit (*always*). Lebe wohl auf immer (*for ever*)! Immer wenn er dabei war (*whenever*). Bleib so lange, wie immer du kannst (*as you possibly can*)! Er ist immer noch krank (*still*). Wo er auch immer ist (*wherever he*). Sie werden immer reicher (*richer and richer*). Immer wieder hat er das behauptet (*again and again*). Wann auch immer (*whenever*) du willst, ich komme.

(f) irgend

Wenn du irgend kannst (*possibly can*). Wenn es irgend möglich ist (*at all possible*). Irgendein/irgendwelches Buch (*any, some or other*); aus irgendeinem beliebigen Grund (*for any or every reason*); irgendeiner/irgend jemand (*somebody (or other)*)); irgendwann (*some time or other*); irgendwie (*somehow or other, in a way, in any way*); irgendwo (*somewhere, anywhere*); irgendwo anders (*anywhere else*); irgend etwas/irgendwas (*something or other, anything*).

(g) ja

Ja freilich (*why, to be sure*)! Sie ist ja ganz jung (*quite young, you know*). Du siehst ja ganz blaß aus (*you do look*). Du bist ja schon dagewesen (*Don't you remember, you* ...). Komm ja bald wieder (*be sure to*)! Ja so, ich ... (*Oh well, oh yes, I* ...). Die Idee ist alarmierend, ja schokkierend (*even*). Warum ißt du nicht? Ich esse ja (*But I am eating*).

(h) mal

Jetzt hör aber mal zu (*now just listen*)! Sie müssen mal kommen (*some day*). Hören Sie mal (*look here*)!

(i) noch

Er ist noch im Bett (*still*). Er ist noch nicht da (*not yet*). Er ist noch nie zu spät gekommen (*never before*). Er ist noch lange nicht gesund (*far from being*). Das ist noch billiger (*even cheaper*). Sie ist weder klug noch schön (*neither ... nor*). Nur noch ein Wort (*just one more*)! Ich habe ihn noch vor drei Tagen getroffen (*only 3 days ago*). Ich werde das noch heute tun (*this very day*).

(j) **nun** (**na** = colloquial form)

Nun, wie du willst (*Oh well ...*). Nun also (*now then, well then*). Nun ja, manchmal (*well*). Nun gut, ich bleibe (*all right*). Nun, los (*now, off you/we go!*)! Nun, nun (*steady! gently!*)! Nun (,da) er gekommen war, konnten wir ... (*now that*). Na, so was (*well, I never*)!

(k) **nur**

Nur noch eins (*just one other thing*). Warte nur (*Just you wait*)! Laß nur (*Please don't bother*)! Komm nur (*Come on*)! Nimm soviel du nur willst (*simply as much, whatever*)! Ich habe nur noch 2 Mark (*only 2 marks left*). Was sollen wir nur tun (*What on earth shall ...*)? Er tut nur so (*he's only pretending*). Wenn er nur käme (*if only*)!

(l) **recht**

An meiner rechten Seite (*right-hand*); auf der rechten Spur sein (*right*); es ist eine rechte Freude (*real*). Recht bald (*quite soon*); recht schönes Wetter (*quite nice*). Ich weiß nicht recht, ob ... (*quite*). Er tut mir recht leid (*truly sorry*). Wenn es dir recht ist ... (*if it suits you*). Das ist alles recht schön, aber ... (*all very well but ...*). Nun weint sie erst recht (*now ... all the more*). Du hast recht (*you are right*).

(m) **schon**

Ist die Post schon da (*already*)? Schon der Gedanke (*the very thought*). Schon an dem Nachmittag ... (*that very afternoon*). Das ist schon wahr, aber ... (*that is true enough, but*). Wir werden das schon schaffen (*we'll manage all right*). Er muß schon da sein (*by now*). Er hat schon genug Geld dafür ausgegeben (*enough as it is*). Schon gut (*all right, very well*)! Wenn schon (*so what!*)!

(n) **so**

Sie ist so schön (*so*). Sie ist genau/nicht so schön wie ihre Schwester (*just/not as*). So ungern ich es auch tat, ich mußte lächeln (*however unwillingly I*). Kommt er früh genug, so trifft er mich zu Hause (*then – or omit in translation*). So sind die Männer (*like that*). „Ich wollte nichts sagen.“ – „So?“ (*Is that so? Really?*). So Gott will (*if it please God, God willing*). Der Ritter, so aus der Burg hervor/Vom Hange trabte in aller Früh (*the knight who*) (DROSTE-HÜLSHOFF).

(o) **wohl**

Mir ist (nicht) wohl ((*un-*)*well*). Leb wohl (*farewell*)! Wohl oder übel (*willy-nilly*). Sie sind wohl K. (*I suppose you ...*)? Es ist wohl an der

Zeit (*surely it*). Sie wird wohl keine Zeit haben (*I expect she*). Ob er wohl noch da ist (*I wonder whether* ...). Heute nicht, wohl aber morgen (*but perhaps*). Es hat wohl Zeit (*it is true*). Es ist wohl möglich, daß ... (*quite possible*). Er zeigte sich wohl ... (*he may be said to have shown himself*).

84 Synonyms

The following list deals exclusively with words occurring in the prose passages for translation and aims only at giving the fundamental distinctions.

TO ACCEPT: **annehmen** (general word); **akzeptieren** (find a person acceptable: *sie haben ihn nie akzeptiert*); **hinnehmen** (accept s.th. submissively); **sich abfinden mit** (accept a given situation, be reconciled to: *wir müssen uns damit abfinden*).

APPEARANCE: **das Aussehen** (external appearance of person); **das Äußere** (external appearance of person or thing); **der Schein** (appearance as opposed to reality: *der Schein trügt*, appearances are deceptive); **der Anschein** (outward show, semblance: *allem Anschein nach*, to all appearances); **das Erscheinen** (appearance of e.g. ghost, book, of person in court); **die Erscheinung** (1. appearance, presence: *sie ist eine stattliche Erscheinung*, a stately figure of a woman; 2. apparition, vision: *sie hatte Erscheinungen*; 3. phenomenon of nature); **die Gegenwart** (presence of somebody in a place).

ARM: **der Arm** (part of body); **die Armlehne** (of chair); **die Waffe** (weapon).

TO ASK: **fragen** (question: *er fragte mich, ob* ...; *er fragte mich nach dem Weg*); **stellen** (put: *er stellte mir eine Frage*); **bitten** (request: *er bat mich um Geld*; *er bat mich, um 2 Uhr da zu sein*); **einladen** (invite: *er lud mich zum Tee ein*); **verlangen/fordern** (demand: *das ist zu viel verlangt/gefordert*); **auffordern** (call upon to do s.th., request, summon: *eine Dame zum Tanz auffordern*; *man forderte ihn auf, den Saal zu verlassen*).

TO BE: **sein** (be: *er ist jung; es sind viele da*); **es gibt** (there is/are: *es gibt Leute, die; was gibt's zum Essen?*); **sich befinden** (find o.s., be situated: *das Haus befindet sich an der Ecke*); **liegen** (lie: *das Buch liegt auf dem Tisch*); **stehen** (stand; *der Weg steht offen; der Fluß stand hoch*); **entstehen** (arise, occur: *es entstand eine Pause*); **sich verhalten** (be the case: *die Sache verhält sich anders*).

N.B. German prefers a more specific word to render 'to be' wherever possible.

TO BEHAVE: **sich benehmen** (refers to the good or bad manners of individuals: *er benahm sich gut/schlecht*); **sich betragen** (refers to conduct, the observance of codes of behaviour: *er hat sich unfreundlich* *gegen uns betragen*); **sich verhalten** (refers to the way things react, or to the psychological attitude of individuals or peoples: *man muß sich in solchen Umständen vorsichtig verhalten*).

BEHAVIOUR, CONDUCT, MANNERS: **das Benehmen** (manners, good or bad); **das Betragen** (conduct, e.g. in school); **das Verhalten** (reaction of things, attitude of individuals and peoples).

TO BELONG: **gehören** (D) (be rightful possession of: *das Buch gehört mir*); **gehören zu** (be part of, be connected with: *alles, was zum Leben gehört; er gehört zur Familie*); **angehören** (to be a property or attribute of; be a member of a community: *das gehört dem Geist an; er gehört dem deutschen Staat an*)..

BOX, CASE: **der Kasten** (solid, well-made, cf. *der Briefkasten*); **die Kiste** (wooden chest for despatching goods, cf. *die Teekiste*); **der Koffer** (suit-case); **der Reisekoffer** (travelling-trunk); **die Truhe** (article of furniture, e.g. rug-chest); **die Schachtel** (flimsy box, often of cardboard, cf. *die Hutschachtel, eine Schachtel Streichhölzer*, a box of matches); **das Kästchen** (casket, e.g. for jewels); **das Etui** (case, e.g. for cigarettes); **der Fall** (instance: *in dem Fall kann ich nicht kommen*).

TO CATCH: **fangen** (general word: *er fing den Ball, den Vogel, den Verbrecher*); **auffangen** (catch s.th. rapidly moving, intercept, e.g. light, glance, words); **erreichen** (reach in time: *sie erreichte gerade noch den Zug*); **nehmen** (take, e.g. a train regularly: *sie nimmt jeden Tag den 8-Uhr-Zug*); **erhaschen** (just manage to catch: *er konnte nur einen Blick von ihr erhaschen*); **gefangennehmen** (capture, take prisoner); **erblicken** (catch sight of); **flüchtig sehen** (catch a glimpse of); **sich erkälten** (catch cold); **sich verfangen** (get caught in: *ihre Hand verfing sich in dem Stoff ihres Kleides*).

TO COMMAND: *see* TO ORDER

TO GET: **werden** (become); **haben** (have); **bekommen** (acquire); **geraten in** (A) (get into, e.g. difficulties); **geraten unter** (A) (get among); **geraten zu** (get to a place); **einsteigen in** (A) (get into, e.g. train); **aufstehen** (get up); **heruntergehen** (get off, e.g. table); **hinübergehen** (get across); **gelangen zu** (come to); **zurückkommen** (get back); **nach Hause kommen** (get home); **kommen zu** (get away to); **auskommen** (get along, manage); **gut auskommen mit** (get on with s.b.).

INTERVAL: **der Abstand** (distance away from: *in regelmäßigen Abständen*); **die Pause** (period between lessons, acts of play, etc.); **die Zwischenzeit** (intervening period).

JEWEL(RY), GEM: **der Schmuck** (jewelry – general word); **das Juwel** (very precious jewel: *die Kronjuwelen*); **der Edelstein** (precious stone); **das Kleinod (-ien)** (gem).

TO KNOW: **kennen** (know persons or things); **kennenlernen** (get to know); **wissen** (know facts through having learnt them: *ich weiß, daß ich nichts weiß; er weiß das Gedicht auswendig; er weiß zu schweigen,* knows how to hold his tongue); **Bescheid wissen** (be well informed: *er weiß gut Bescheid in seinem Fach,* he knows his subject); **können** (know a language: *er kann (kein) Deutsch*); **bekannt sein** (be (well-) known).

KNOWLEDGE: **die Kenntnis** (a good acquaintance with s.th.: *seine Kenntnis der Kunst; seine Kenntnisse in der Mathematik*); **das Wissen** (knowledge that s.th. is the case, also general organised knowledge: *ohne mein Wissen; er hat ein gründliches Wissen*); **die Wissenschaft** (scholarship, learning).

TO LEAVE: **lassen** (leave s.th. or s.o. somewhere or in a certain state: *sie ließen ihn dort liegen*); **verlassen** (1. leave a place: *er hat das Haus, die Schule, Paris verlassen;* 2. leave a person behind, abandon s.o.: *er hat seine Frau verlassen*); **im Stich lassen** (leave in the lurch, abandon: *er mußte seine Arbeit im Stich lassen*); **überlassen** (leave s.th. to s.b. else: *überlassen Sie es mir!*); **hinterlassen** (bequeath: *er hat ihr sein ganzes Vermögen hinterlassen*).

TO LOOK: **aussehen** (look like, have the look of: *Sie sehen ganz wie ein Professor aus*); **(von oben bis unten) mustern** (look s.b. up and down); **ansehen** (look at for some space of time: *er sah uns freundlich an*); **sehen auf** (A) (glance at: *er sah auf die Uhr*); **sich** (D) **ansehen** (have a good look at: *er sah sich (D) die Stadt an*); **aufblicken/ emporblicken/aufsehen/emporsehen** (look up: *er blickte/sah zu ihr auf*); **herabblicken** (look down); **suchen (nach)** (look for: *er hat es überall gesucht; er suchte nach einer Ausrede*); **auf der Suche sein nach** (look for, be on the look-out for: *wir waren auf der Suche nach einer Furt* (ford)); **pflegen** (look after, tend: *sie pflegte den Kranken*).

MATTER: **die Materie/der Stoff** (philosophical term, 'matter' as opposed to 'mind': *die Philosophie stellt Geist und Materie/Stoff einander gegenüber*); **der Stoff** (material for s.th.: *Stoff zum Lesen,* reading matter); **die Sache** (unimportant matter or affair; *das ist Ansichtssache,* matter of opinion; also=(good) cause: *die gute Sache*); **die Angelegenheit** (a matter of some weight: *wichtige Angelegenheiten*); **das Ding** (thing: *wie die Dinge liegen,* as matters stand; *naturwissenschaftliche Dinge*); **der Gegenstand** (subject-matter).
Note also: **tatsächlich** (as a matter of fact); **nüchtern** (matter-of-fact: *ein nüchterner Mensch*); **es handelt sich um** (A)/**es ist eine Frage** + (G) (it is a matter of); **was hast du?** (what is the matter with you?); **das ist etwas anderes** (that is another matter).

MAN, MEN, PEOPLE, PERSON, PERSONAGE: **man** (one, people in general: *man sagt, daß ...*); **jemand** (a man, somebody); **einer, der...** (a man who ...); **derjenige, der ...** (the man who ...); **Leute** (people:

eine Menge Leute; es gibt Leute, die ...); **die (-jenigen), die** ... (people who, the persons who); **der Mensch** (human being: *andere Menschen,* other persons; *so sind die Menschen,* people are like that; *der Mensch ist frei geschaffen,* man is created free); **der Mann** (man, as opposed to woman); **das Volk** (people = nation; *das englische Volk; die Völker der Welt*); **die Person** (1. person, individual: *jede Person zahlt eine Mark; ein Tisch für zwei Personen; die Familie besteht aus sechs Personen;* 2. personage: *königliche Personen,* royal personages; 3. character in a play: *die handelnden Personen,* dramatis personae; *die Hauptpersonen,* leading characters; *die Nebenpersonen,* minor characters).

TO NEED: **brauchen** (need to, want s.th. or s.b.: *Sie brauchen nicht zu kommen; ich brauche Ruhe*); **benötigen** (require, need for some purpose: *er benötigt Zeit, meine Hilfe*); **erfordern** (of things, demand: *die Situation erfordert Takt, Vorstellungskraft*); **bedürfen** (be in need of: *wir bedürfen der Ruhe; es bedarf nur eines Wortes,* only one word is needed); **genügen** (need but: *ein Blick genügte, um ...,* it needed but one glance); **notwendig sein** (be needed: *nur eines ist notwendig,* only one thing is needed).

NEED: **die Not** (distress, need: *in Not/Nöten sein*); **die Notwendigkeit** (necessity to do s.th.: *eine Notwendigkeit erkennen*); **der Bedarf** (*re*-quirements: *Bedarf an Menschen und Materialien*); **es ist nicht notwendig, zu** ... (there is no need to ...); **das Bedürfnis** (need of/for).

TO ORDER, COMMAND: **befehlen** (to command: *er befahl mir zu schweigen*); **gebieten** (enjoin, command – a more lofty term); **heißen** (bid, a command given orally: *er hieß mich hereinkommen*); **bestellen** (order goods: *wir bestellten zwei Glas Bier*).

ORDER, COMMAND, COMMANDMENT: **der Befehl** (order, command: *Befehle erteilen/geben; Befehle ausführen*); **das Gebot** (commandment: *die zehn Gebote*); **die Bestellung** (order for goods: *eine Bestellung auf/für 10 Pfund Zucker*); **das Kommando** (command, authority: *das seinem Kommando zu übergebende Schiff*); **die Beherrschung** (command of a subject or emotion: *seine Beherrschung der Gemütsregungen*).

PLAY: **das Spiel** (game; also play, e.g. of light); **der Spielraum** (play = scope: *wir haben nicht genug Spielraum gehabt*); **der Scherz** (jest: *im Scherz,* in play).

TO PUT: **legen** (put in lying position); **stellen** (put in upright or standing position); **setzen** (put in sitting position: *setz das Kind auf den Stuhl*); **stecken** (put, e.g. into a pocket); **drücken** (put, e.g. into s.o.'s hand: *er drückte ihm ein Geldstück in die Hand*); **anziehen** (put on clothes); **aufsetzen** (put on hat, spectacles); **umschnallen** (put on belt); **ins Bett bringen** (put into bed); **entrücken** (D) (put beyond, e.g. reach: *der Tod hat ihn allen Sorgen entrückt*).

RATHER: **ziemlich** (fairly: *ziemlich spät, weit*); **recht** (quite: *sie ist recht hübsch*); **etwas** (somewhat: *eine etwas melodische Stimme*);

irgendwie (somehow or other: *irgendwie rührend*); **lieber** (preferably: *ich komme lieber später*); **mehr** (more: *mehr aus Furcht als aus Liebe*); **eher** (more correctly: *eher ehrenswert als intelligent*).

TO REALISE: **begreifen** (grasp, understand: *ich fange an zu begreifen, warum ...*); **sich bewußt sein** (be aware of: *ich bin mir der Wichtigkeit des Problems bewußt*); **einem klar werden** (become clear to one: *es wurde mir endlich klar, daß ...*); **sich vergegenwärtigen** (*bring vividly before one's mind: man muß sich vergegenwärtigen, was die Folgen sein werden*).

REALLY: **eigentlich** (strictly speaking, as a matter of fact; *eigentlich hätte ich nicht kommen sollen*); **wirklich** (undoubtedly: *es ist wirklich wahr*); **endlich einmal** (positively, indeed: *der Regen muß endlich einmal aufhören*).

TO SEE: **sehen** (general word); **erblicken** (catch sight of); **ansehen** (look at); **sich** (D) **ansehen** (see for oneself: *sehen Sie es sich mal an*); **halten für** (see as, consider as: *sie hielten ihn für unfreundlich*); **sorgen für** (see to s.th.: *er sorgt dafür, daß sie alles hat*); **einsehen** (understand: *er hat eingesehen, daß ich das nicht machen kann*); **ach so** (*oh I see*); **ja, ich verstehe schon** (*yes, I see*); **siehst du?** (*you see*).

SO: **so** (so: *ich bin so müde*); **deshalb** (therefore, and so: *deshalb habe ich angerufen*); **auch** (also: *Er ist müde. – Ich auch*, so am I); **es** (it: *ich sagte es dir*, I told you so).

TO TAKE: **nehmen** (general word); **mitnehmen** (take with one); **ergreifen** (seize, take up, e.g. arms); **sich beteiligen an** (D) (take part in); **irreführen/hinters Licht führen** (take in, deceive); **entnehmen** (D) (take from: *er hat es diesem Buch entnommen*); **annehmen** (take on, assume, e.g. an appearance); **abnehmen** (take off, e.g. hat); **ausziehen** (take off, e.g. clothes); **zurücktreten** (take (a step) back); **antreten** (enter upon: *ein Amt antreten*); **vertreten** (adopt: *einen Standpunkt vertreten*, take a stand); **halten für** (take for: *ich hielt ihn für ein Genie*); **ansehen als** (take as: *ich sehe es als Kompliment an*); **brauchen** (need: *er brauchte lange Zeit, um es zu tun*). Note also: **Maßnahmen treffen** (take steps); **stattfinden** (take place).

TO THINK: **denken** (general word); **denken an** (A) (think of: *woran denken Sie?*); **denken/halten von** (have opinion of; *was denken/halten Sie von ihm?*); **nachdenken über** (A) (reflect, think over: *wir müssen zuerst darüber nachdenken*); **glauben** (believe: *ich glaube nicht, daß er kommt*); **sich vorstellen** (imagine, conceive: *ich kann mir nicht vorstellen, was sie damit meint*); **meinen** (be of the opinion).

THOUGHT: **der Gedanke** (idea); **das Denken** (thinking)

VERY: **sehr** (very: *es ist sehr spät*); **schon** (already: *schon an dem Nachmittag*, that very afternoon; *schon ihre Grenzen*, its very boundaries); **genau** (exactly: *genau in der Mitte*, in the very middle); **aller-** (of all:

das allergrößte Glück, the very greatest good fortune); **äußerst**
(extreme: *am äußersten Rande*, at the very edge).

WELL: **wohl** (well: *ihm ist wohl; leben Sie wohl!*; *du weißt wohl, daß* ...,
you know quite well that ...); **gut** (well: *schlafen Sie gut!; so gut man
kann*); **gesund** (healthy: *er ist gesund*); **sowohl** (as well: *er sowohl wie/
als ich; sowohl er als ich*, he as well as I); **ebensogut** (just as well:
du kannst ebensogut morgen kommen) ; **nun** (well: *nun, was meinen Sie?*
well, what do you think?); **nun gut** (well, all right); **ja schon** (well yes,
i.e. with some reservations; *Magst du ihn? – Ja schon*); **ja** (well, perhaps, i.e. embarrassed or impatient: *Willst du das haben? – Ja, ich weiß
nicht*).

85 Punctuation, Hyphenation and the Character ß

Indications as to punctuation are only given when German usage differs
from English.

(a) The comma (*das Komma/der Beistrich*) is used in German:

i Before *aber, sondern, und zwar, und das* and *und* preceding another
   conjunction:

   Du bist schön, aber hart. Nicht nur du, sondern auch er. Ich werde
   schreiben, und zwar bald. Er lehnte ab, und das mit Würde. Er war
   viel zu lange dort geblieben, und weil er es jetzt eilig hatte, mußte er
   sehr schnell fahren.

ii Between main clauses, even when these are linked by *und* or *oder*,
    except when the clauses are very short or where the (same) subject
    is not repeated:

    Er stand auf, er ging zur Tür, und er öffnete sie.
    Ihr müßt arbeiten, oder ihr fallt durch.

But Er setzte sich und er las. Er pfiff oder er sang. Er ging zur Tür und
öffnete sie.

iii Between a subordinate clause and a main clause:

    Da es spät war, mußte er sich beeilen.
    Er wußte, daß es spät war.

iv Before the simple infinitive with *zu* when it is the complement of the
    subject of the clause, when *zu* is the equivalent of *um zu*, or when the
    infinitive is itself followed by another infinitive with *zu*:

    Seine Hoffnung war, durchzukommen. Er kommt, zu helfen.
    Er wurde nicht müde, zu lesen und zu lernen.

But Er war immer bereit zu helfen. Er wünschte zu kommen.
Es begann zu regnen. Es hat zu regnen begonnen. Er befahl ihm zu
gehen.

v To separate an extended participle or infinitive (but not a simple participle or infinitive) from the clause:

An der Tür lehnend, rauchte er seine Zigarre. Er arbeitete zwei Stunden lang, ohne aufzuhören. Er arbeitete schwer, um durchzukommen. Er versuchte, ins Haus zu kommen.

But Schweigend arbeitete er weiter. Er versuchte zu antworten.

vi Before the extended infinitive after the verbs *haben, hoffen, pflegen* and *glauben* when these verbs are in some way qualified, but not otherwise:

Er hoffte sehr/doch, sie am nächsten Morgen zu sehen.
Er pflegte damals, sie zu besuchen. Ich glaube bestimmt, das gehört zu haben.

But Er hatte nichts zu sagen. Er hoffte sie zu Hause zu finden. Er pflegte sie jeden Tag zu besuchen. Er glaubte kommen zu können.

vii After an infinitive (simple with *zu* or extended) when this comes first in the sentence immediately followed by a demonstrative (*das, daran, darauf*, etc.), but not otherwise:

Früh aufzustehen, das ist höchst unangenehm. Zu arbeiten, daran hatten wir wirklich nicht gedacht.

But Früh aufzustehen ist höchst unangenehm.

(b) Inverted commas (*Anführungszeichen*) are used as in English but are written and printed differently:

„Er kommt bald", sagte er. „Bleib da!"

(c) The colon (*der Doppelpunkt*) is used in German to introduce direct speech:

Er sagte zu mir: „Ich muß jetzt unbedingt nach Hause gehen."

(d) The exclamation mark (*das Ausrufezeichen*) is used after imperatives, optative clauses, exclamations and after the salutation in a letter:

Bleib sitzen! Wenn er doch käme! Auf Wiedersehen!
Schade! Wie blaß du aussiehst!
Liebe Trude! – Ich danke Dir ... Sehr geehrter Herr! (*Dear Sir*).

(e) The full-stop (*der Punkt*), semi-colon (*der Strichpunkt/das Semikolon*), question-mark (*das Fragezeichen*), dash (*der Gedankenstrich*), brackets (*Klammern*) and points of suspension (*Auslassungspunkte*) are used as in English.

(f) Hyphenation:

i The syllable after the hyphen should if possible begin with a consonant:

lie-gen; nä-hern; Bru-der

ii *ch, sch, ß, ph, th* are never separated:

Lö-cher; Fi-scher; Fü-ße; pro-phezeien; ka-tholisch

iii Of several consonants with other combinations the last follows the hyphen:

sin-gen; Fül-le; Wech-sel; Abwechs-lung

NOTE 1: *ck* becomes *k-k*: lok-ken; Bäk-ker
NOTE 2: *st* is never separated except in compound words: La-ster; Fa-sten; *but* Diens-tag

iv Suffixes beginning with a vowel take with them the preceding consonant:

Lehre-rin; Freun-din; Hoff-nung; Bäcke-rei

v A single vowel should not be separated from the rest of the word:

aber; *not* a-ber

vi A word may be hyphenated between two vowels only when there is a clear break between them:

be-enden; Genugtu-ung; Befrei-ung; Mau-er
But Waa-ge; Boo-te; Bei-ne; Häu-ser; Beu-tel

vii In compound words the division comes at the end of each constituent element:

Last-auto; dar-aus; wor-auf; Geburts-tags-geschenk

viii Hyphenation of the constituent elements themselves follows the same rules as those given above (i)–(vi):

Ge-burts-tags-ge-schenk; Auf-fas-sungs-ver-mö-gen

(g) The character *ß*

In printing, the character *ß* is used for *ss*:

i medially, when preceded by a long vowel or by a diphthong:

Maße; Größe; Muße; Füße; regelmäßig; fleißig; äußerst; draußen
But Mässe; Bissen; Flüsse; essen; lässig; Hausschlüssel

ii at the end of a word or syllable with or without *t* following, whether the vowel preceding is long or short:

däß; Maß; gewiß; Gewißheit; Mißachtung; Mißfallen; Kompromiß; laß; mußt; mußte
But gewisse; Kompromisse; lasse

NOTE: If, after a short vowel, the omission of a final *e* is indicated by an apostrophe, *ss* is used, not *ß*, e.g. *lass'*.

iii when followed by a consonant as a result of elision of unstressed *e*:

laßt; ein Gottverlaßner
But lasset; ein Gottverlassener

In writing it is not necessary to use the character *ß*. If, however, it is used the rules given above should be observed.

86 Strong and Weak Declension

(a) Strong Declension

| | sing. | | | pl. |
	m.	*f.*	*n.*	*m.f.n.*
N.	– er	– e	– es	– e
A.	– en	– e	– es	– e
G.	– es	– er	– es	– er
D.	– em	– er	– em	– en

(b) Weak Declension

| | sing. | | | pl. |
	m.	*f.*	*n.*	*m.f.n.*
N.	– e	– e	– e	– en
A.	– en	– e	– e	– en
G.	– en	– en	– en	– en
D.	– en	– en	– en	– en

NOTE 1: Though the terms 'strong' and 'weak' are also applied by grammarians to the declension of nouns (see *101*), the above inflections do not apply to nouns.

NOTE 2: The attributive adjective declined strong has in modern German the weak form *-en* and not the strong form *-es* in the genitive singular masculine and neuter (see *93*).

NOTE 3: A few other words, e.g. *jeder*, *aller*, when declined strong, are now often found with the weak ending *-en* in the genitive singular masculine and neuter in front of nouns that clearly show the genitive case. Thus:

> Die Lösung jedes/jeden Problems.
> Trotz alles/allen Widerstands.

But Die Aufgabe jedes einzelnen.
> Die Entbehrung alles Gewohnten.

87 Declension of the Definite Article

| | sing. | | | pl. |
	m.	*f.*	*n.*	*m.f.n.*
N.	der	die	das	die
A.	den	die	das	die
G.	des	der	des	der
D.	dem	der	dem	den

88 Declension of the Indefinite Article

	m.	*f.*	*n.*
N.	ein	eine	ein
A.	einen	eine	ein
G.	eines	einer	eines
D.	einem	einer	einem

NOTE: As with English 'a' there is no plural of *ein*. The plural of *ein Mann* is simply *Männer*.

89 Declension of the Possessive Adjective

	sing.			pl.
	m.	*f.*	*n.*	*m.f.n.*
N.	**mein**	meine	**mein**	meine
A.	mein**en**	mein**e**	**mein**	meine
G.	mein**es**	mein**er**	mein**es**	mein**er**
D.	mein**em**	mein**er**	mein**em**	mein**en**

Likewise: *dein, sein, ihr, unser, euer, Ihr* and *kein.*

90 Declension of the Demonstrative Adjective and Pronoun

	sing.			pl.
	m.	*f.*	*n.*	*m.f.n.*
N.	dies**er**	dies**e**	dies**es**	dies**e**
A.	dies**en**	dies**e**	dies**es**	dies**e**
G.	dies**es**	dies**er**	dies**es**	dies**er**
D.	dies**em**	dies**er**	dies**em**	dies**en**

Likewise: *jener, welcher, solcher, mancher, jeder* (sing.), *allé* (pl.), *einige* (pl.), *etliche* (pl.), *mehrere* (pl.), *viele* (pl.), *wenige* (pl.). (See also *51.*)

91 Inflection of the Adjective after the Definite Article

	sing.			pl.
	m.	*f.*	*n.*	*m.f.n.*
N.	der – **e**	die – **e**	das – **e**	die – **en**
A.	den – **en**	die – **e**	das – **e**	die – **en**
G.	des – **en**	der – **en**	des – **en**	der – **en**
D.	dem – **en**	der – **en**	dem – **en**	den – **en**

Likewise after: *dieser, jener, welcher, solcher, derselbe, derjenige, jeder* (sing.), *alle* (pl.), *mancher* (sing.)

92 Inflection of the Adjective after the Possessive Adjective

	sing.			pl.
	m.	*f.*	*n.*	*m.f.n.*
N.	mein – **er**	meine – **e**	mein – **es**	meine – **en**
A.	meinen – **en**	meine – **e**	mein – **es**	meine – **en**
G.	meines – **en**	meiner – **en**	meines – **en**	meiner – **en**
D.	meinem – **en**	meiner – **en**	meinem – **en**	meinen – **en**

Likewise after: *dein, sein, ihr, unser, euer, Ihr, ein* (sing.) and *kein.*

93 Inflection of the Adjective when standing alone before a Noun

	sing. m.	*f.*	*n.*	*pl.* m.f.n.
N.	– er	– e	– es	– e
A.	– en	– e	– es	– e
G.	– en	– er	– en	– er
D.	– em	– er	– em	– en

Likewise after the plurals: *2, 3, 4,* etc. (but no genitive except with 2 and 3) *ein paar, einige, etliche, manche, mehrere, viele* and *wenige.*

94 Declension of *derselbe* and *derjenige*

	sing. m.	*f.*	*n.*	*pl.* m.f.n.
N.	derselbe	dieselbe	dasselbe	dieselben
A.	denselben	dieselbe	dasselbe	dieselben
G.	desselben	derselben	desselben	derselben
D.	demselben	derselben	demselben	denselben

Likewise: *derjenige.*

95 Declension of the Relative Pronoun

		sing. m.	*f.*	*n.*	*pl.* m.f.n.
(a)	N.	der	die	das	die
	A.	den	die	das	die
	G.	dessen	deren	dessen	deren
	D.	dem	der	dem	denen
(b)	N.	welcher	welche	welches	welche
	A.	welchen	welche	welches	welche
	G.	(dessen)	(deren)	(dessen)	(deren)
	D.	welchem	welcher	welchem	welchen

96 Declension of *wer, was*

	m.f.	n.
N.	wer	was
A.	wen	was (wodurch, worein, etc.)
G.	wessen	wessen
D.	wem	(womit, worauf, etc.)

97 Declension of the Demonstrative Pronoun

	sing.			*pl.*
	m.	*f.*	*n.*	*m.f.n.*
N.	der	die	das	die
A.	den	die	das	die
G.	**dessen**	**deren**	**dessen**	**deren/derer**
D.	dem	der	dem	**denen**

NOTE: The genitive plural of the demonstrative pronoun is **derer** when followed by a relative pronoun.

98 Declension of the Personal Pronouns

sing.							
	N.	ich	du	Sie	er	sie	es
	A.	mich	dich	Sie	ihn	sie	es
	G.	meiner	deiner	Ihrer	seiner	ihrer	seiner
	D.	mir	dir	Ihnen	ihm	ihr	ihm

pl.					
	N.	wir	ihr	Sie	sie
	A.	uns	euch	Sie	sie
	G.	unser	euer	Ihrer	ihrer
	D.	uns	euch	Ihnen	ihnen

99 Declension of the Reflexive Pronouns

sing.				
	A.	mich	dich	sich	sich
	G.	meiner	deiner	Ihrer selbst	seiner/ihrer selbst
	D.	mir	dir	sich	sich
pl.	A.	uns	euch	sich	sich
	G.	unser	euer	Ihrer selbst	ihrer selbst
	D.	uns	euch	sich	sich

100 Declension of the Possessive Pronouns

		sing.			*pl.*
		m.	*f.*	*n.*	*m.f.n.*
(a)	N.	mein**er**	mein**e**	mein(**e**)**s**	mein**e**
	A.	mein**en**	mein**e**	mein(**e**)**s**	mein**e**
	G.	mein**es**	mein**er**	mein**es**	mein**er**
	D.	mein**em**	mein**er**	mein**em**	mein**en**
(b)	N.	der mein**e**	die mein**e**	das mein**e**	die mein**en**
	A.	den mein**en**	die mein**e**	das mein**e**	die mein**en**
	G.	des mein**en**	der mein**en**	des mein**en**	der mein**en**
	D.	dem mein**en**	der mein**en**	dem mein**en**	den mein**en**
(c)	N.	der mein**ige**	die mein**ige**	das mein**ige**	die mein**igen**
	A.	den mein**igen**	die mein**ige**	das mein**ige**	die mein**igen**
	G.	des mein**igen**	der mein**igen**	des mein**igen**	der mein**igen**
	D.	dem mein**igen**	der mein**igen**	dem mein**igen**	den mein**igen**

Likewise: *deiner, seiner, ihrer, unserer, eurer, Ihrer.* Like (a): *einer, keiner.*

101 Declension of Nouns

	STRONG						WEAK	MIXED	
	Ia		**Ib**		**Ic**		**II**	**IIIa**	**IIIb**
	Pl. not modified	*Pl. modified*	*Pl. not modified*	*Pl. modified*	*Pl. not modified*	*Pl. modified*			
Masc.			(3)	(1o)		(2)			(1o)
Sing. N.	Tag	Sohn	Geist	Wald	Onkel	Apfel	Mensch	Staat	Name
A.	Tag	Sohn	Geist	Wald	Onkel	Apfel	Menschen	Staat	Namen
G.	Tag(e)s	Sohn(e)s	Geistes	Wald(e)s	Onkels	Apfels	Menschen	Staat(e)s	Namens
D.	Tag(e)	Sohn(e)	Geist(e)	Wald(e)	Onkel	Apfel	Menschen	Staat(e)	Namen
Pl. N.	Tage	Söhne	Geister	Wälder	Onkel	Äpfel	Menschen	Staaten	Namen
A.	Tage	Söhne	Geister	Wälder	Onkel	Äpfel	Menschen	Staaten	Namen
G.	Tage	Söhne	Geister	Wälder	Onkel	Äpfel	Menschen	Staaten	Namen
D.	Tagen	Söhnen	Geistern	Wäldern	Onkeln	Äpfeln	Menschen	Staaten	Namen
Fem.	(1o)	(3o)				(2)			
Sing. N.	Trübsal	Stadt	None	None	None	Mutter	None	Frau	None
A.	Trübsal	Stadt				Mutter		Frau	
G.	Trübsal	Stadt				Mutter		Frau	
D.	Trübsal	Stadt				Mutter		Frau	
Pl. N.	Trübsale	Städte				Mütter		Frauen	
A.	Trübsale	Städte				Mütter		Frauen	
G.	Trübsale	Städte				Mütter		Frauen	
D.	Trübsalen	Städten				Müttern		Frauen	
Neut.		(1)	(1)			(1)		(7)	(1)
Sing. N.	Tier	Floß	Kind	Haus	Fenster	Kloster	None	Bett	Herz
A.	Tier	Floß	Kind	Haus	Fenster	Kloster		Bett	Herz
G.	Tier(e)s	Floßes	Kind(e)s	Hauses	Fensters	Klosters		Bett(e)s	Herzens
D.	Tier(e)	Floß(e)	Kind(e)	Haus(e)	Fenster	Kloster		Bett(e)	Herzen
Pl. N.	Tiere	Flöße	Kinder	Häuser	Fenster	Klöster		Betten	Herzen
A.	Tiere	Flöße	Kinder	Häuser	Fenster	Klöster		Betten	Herzen
G.	Tiere	Flöße	Kinder	Häuser	Fenster	Klöster		Betten	Herzen
D.	Tieren	Flößen	Kindern	Häusern	Fenstern	Klöstern		Betten	Herzen

NOTE: The approximate number of nouns, excluding compound nouns, in the various groups is given where this is not large.

Infinitive	3rd Pers. Sing. Pres.	3rd Pers. Sing. Impf.	Past Part.	Meaning
backen	bäckt[1]	buk[1]	gebacken	bake
befehlen	befiehlt	befahl[2]	befohlen	order
beginnen	beginnt	begann	begonnen	begin
beißen	beißt	biß	gebissen	bite
bergen	birgt	barg	geborgen	shelter; contain
*bersten	birst	barst	geborsten	burst (intr.)
betrügen	betrügt	betrog	betrogen	deceive, cheat
bewegen	bewegt	bewog	bewogen	induce
(*)biegen	biegt	bog	gebogen	bend, turn
bieten	bietet	bot	geboten	offer, bid
binden	bindet	band	gebunden	tie
bitten	bittet	bat	gebeten	ask, request
blasen	bläst	blies	geblasen	blow, sound
*bleiben	bleibt	blieb	geblieben	remain, stay
braten	brät	briet	gebraten	roast
(*)brechen	bricht	brach	gebrochen	break
brennen	brennt	brannte[3]	gebrannt	burn
bringen	bringt	brachte[3]	gebracht	bring, take
denken	denkt	dachte[3]	gedacht	think
(*)dringen	dringt	drang	gedrungen	press; insist
dürfen[4]	darf	durfte	gedurft	be allowed to
empfehlen	empfiehlt	empfahl[2]	empfohlen	recommend
*erlöschen[5]	erlischt	erlosch	erloschen	be extinguished
*erschrecken[6]	erschrickt	erschrak	erschrocken	be frightened
erwägen	erwägt	erwog	erwogen	think over, weigh
essen	ißt	aß	gegessen	eat
(*)fahren	fährt	fuhr	gefahren	go (not on foot); drive
*fallen	fällt	fiel	gefallen	fall
fangen	fängt	fing	gefangen	catch
fechten	ficht[7]	focht	gefochten	fight, fence
finden	findet	fand	gefunden	find
flechten	flicht[8]	flocht	geflochten	wreathe
(*)fliegen	fliegt	flog	geflogen	fly
(*)fliehen	flieht	floh	geflohen	flee
*fließen	fließt	floß	geflossen	flow
fressen	frißt	fraß	gefressen	eat (of animals)
(*)frieren	friert	fror	gefroren	freeze, be cold

[1] Also: backt, backte
[2] See 70 (e)
[3] See 70 (f)
[4] See 67

[5] Weak = extinguish
[6] Weak = frighten
[7] 2nd person singular du fichtst
[8] 2nd person singular du flichtst

Infinitive	3rd Pers. Sing. Pres.	3rd Pers. Sing. Impf.	Past Part.	Meaning
gebären	gebiert	gebar	geboren	*give birth, bear*
geben	gibt	gab	gegeben	*give*
*gedeihen	gedeiht	gedieh	gediehen	*prosper, flourish*
*gehen	geht	ging	gegangen	*go, walk*
*gelingen[1]	gelingt	gelang	gelungen	*succeed*
gelten	gilt	galt	gegolten	*be valid, worth*
*genesen	genest	genas	genesen	*grow well, recover*
genießen	genießt	genoß	genossen	*enjoy*
*geschehen	geschieht	geschah	geschehen	*happen*
gewinnen	gewinnt	gewann	gewonnen	*win, gain*
gießen	gießt	goß	gegossen	*pour*
gleichen	gleicht	glich	geglichen	*resemble*
*gleiten	gleitet	glitt	geglitten	*glide, slide*
glimmen	glimmt	glomm	geglommen	*glow*
graben	gräbt	grub	gegraben	*dig*
greifen	greift	griff	gegriffen	*grasp, seize grab*
haben[2]	hat	hatte	gehabt	*have*
halten	hält	hielt	gehalten	*hold, stop (intr.)*
hängen[3]	hängt	hing	gehangen	*hang (intr.)*
hauen	haut	hieb[4]	gehauen	*hew; beat; chop*
heben	hebt	hob	gehoben	*raise, lift*
heißen	heißt	hieß	geheißen	*be called; bid*
helfen	hilft	half[5]	geholfen	*help*
kennen	kennt	kannte[6]	gekannt	*know (see 84)*
klingen	klingt	klang	geklungen	*sound*
*kommen	kommt	kam	gekommen	*come*
können[7]	kann	konnte	gekonnt	*can, be able to*
*kriechen	kriecht	kroch	gekrochen	*crawl, creep*
laden	lädt[8]	lud	geladen	*load; invite*
lassen	läßt	ließ	gelassen	*let, leave (behind)*
*laufen	läuft	lief	gelaufen	*run*
leiden	leidet	litt	gelitten	*suffer, bear*
leihen	leiht	lieh	geliehen	*lend*
lesen	liest	las	gelesen	*read*
liegen	liegt	lag	gelegen	*lie*
lügen	lügt	log	gelogen	*tell lies*
messen	mißt	maß	gemessen	*measure*
mögen[7]	mag	mochte	gemocht	*may; like*
müssen[7]	muß	mußte	gemußt	*must, have to*
nehmen	nimmt	nahm	genommen	*take*

[1] See *62 (c)*
[2] See *57 (a)*
[3] Or *hangen*. Weak = hang (tr.)
[4] Weak = beat; chop

[5] See *70 (e)*
[6] *70 (f)*
[7] See *67*
[8] Also: *ladet*

E

Infinitive	3rd Pers. Sing. Pres.	3rd Pers. Sing. Impf.	Past Part.	Meaning
nennen	nennt	nannte[1]	genannt	*name, call*
pfeifen	pfeift	pfiff	gepfiffen	*whistle; pipe*
preisen	preist	pries	gepriesen	*praise*
*quellen	quillt	quoll	gequollen	*spring, gush up*
raten	rät	riet	geraten	*advise; guess*
reiben	reibt	rieb	gerieben	*rub*
(*)reißen	reißt	riß	gerissen	*tear*
*reiten	reitet	ritt	geritten	*ride (on animal)*
*rennen	rennt	rannte[1]	gerannt	*run*
riechen	riecht	roch	gerochen	*smell*
ringen	ringt	rang	gerungen	*wrestle, struggle*
*rinnen	rinnt	rann	geronnen	*flow, trickle*
rufen	ruft	rief	gerufen	*call*
saufen	säuft	soff	gesoffen	*drink (of animals)*
saugen	saugt	sog	gesogen	*suck*
schaffen[2]	schafft	schuf	geschaffen	*create*
(*)scheiden	scheidet	schied	geschieden	*separate; part*
scheinen	scheint	schien	geschienen	*seem; shine*
schelten	schilt	schalt[3]	gescholten	*scold, blame*
scheren	schert	schor	geschoren	*shear, cut*
schieben	schiebt	schob	geschoben	*shove, push*
(*)schießen	schießt	schoß	geschossen	*shoot*
schinden	schindet	schund	geschunden	*flay, rub off skin*
schlafen	schläft	schlief	geschlafen	*sleep*
schlagen	schlägt	schlug	geschlagen	*beat, strike*
*schleichen	schleicht	schlich	geschlichen	*creep, slink*
schließen	schließt	schloß	geschlossen	*shut, conclude*
schlingen	schlingt	schlang	geschlungen	*coil; devour*
schmeißen	schmeißt	schmiß	geschmissen	*fling, chuck*
(*)schmelzen	schmilzt[4]	schmolz	geschmolzen	*melt*
schneiden	schneidet	schnitt	geschnitten	*cut*
schreiben	schreibt	schrieb	geschrieben	*write*
schreien	schreit	schrie	geschrie(e)n	*shout, shriek*
*schreiten	schreitet	schritt	geschritten	*stride, proceed*
schweigen	schweigt	schwieg	geschwiegen	*be(come) silent*
*schwellen[5]	schwillt	schwoll	geschwollen	*swell (intr.)*
(*)schwimmen	schwimmt	schwamm	geschwommen[6]	*swim*
schwingen	schwingt	schwang	geschwungen	*swing*
schwören	schwört	schwur	geschworen	*swear (on oath)*
sehen	sieht	sah	gesehen	*see*

[1] See 70 (f).
[2] Weak = do, achieve
[3] See 70 (e)
[4] Also *schmelzt* when transitive
[5] Weak = swell (tr.)
[6] 57 (c) (f)

Infinitive	3rd Pers. Sing. Pres.	3rd Pers. Sing. Impf.	Past Part.	Meaning
*sein[1]	ist	war	gewesen	*be*
senden	sendet	sandte[2,3]	gesandt[3]	*send*
singen	singt	sang	gesungen	*sing*
*sinken	sinkt	sank	gesunken	*sink (intr.)*
sinnen	sinnt	sann	gesonnen	*think, meditate*
sitzen	sitzt	saß	gesessen	*be sitting, sit*
sollen[4]	soll	sollte	gesollt	*be obliged to*
speien	speit	spie	gespien	*spit, spew out*
spinnen	spinnt	spann[5]	gesponnen	*spin, spin round*
sprechen	spricht	sprach	gesprochen	*speak*
*sprießen	sprießt	sproß	gesprossen	*sprout*
*springen	springt	sprang	gesprungen	*jump, spring*
stechen	sticht	stach	gestochen	*prick, sting; trump*
stehen	steht	stand	gestanden	*stand*
stehlen	stiehlt	stahl	gestohlen	*steal*
*steigen	steigt	stieg	gestiegen	*mount, rise*
*sterben	stirbt	starb[5]	gestorben	*die*
*stieben	stiebt	stob	gestoben	*scatter (intr.)*
(*)stoßen	stößt	stieß	gestoßen	*push; stumble on*
(*)streichen	streicht	strich	gestrichen	*stroke; wander*
streiten	streitet	stritt	gestritten	*argue, quarrel*
tragen	trägt	trug	getragen	*carry, bear; wear*
treffen	trifft	traf	getroffen	*meet; hit*
(*)treiben	treibt	trieb	getrieben	*drive, do; drift*
(*)treten	tritt	trat	getreten	*step, go; kick*
trinken	trinkt	trank	getrunken	*drink*
tun	tut	tat	getan	*do*
(*)verderben	verdirbt	verdarb[5]	verdorben	*spoil, ruin*
verdrießen	verdrießt	verdroß	verdrossen	*vex*
vergessen	vergißt	vergaß	vergessen	*forget*
verlieren	verliert	verlor	verloren	*lose*
vermeiden	vermeidet	vermied	vermieden	*avoid*
*verschwin- den	verschwin- det	ver- schwand	verschwun- den	*disappear*
verzeihen	verzeiht	verzieh	verziehen	*pardon*
*wachsen	wächst	wuchs	gewachsen	*grow (intr.)*
waschen	wäscht	wusch	gewaschen	*wash (tr.)*
weben[6]	webt	wob	gewoben	*weave*
*weichen[7]	weicht	wich	gewichen	*give way to*
weisen	weist	wies	gewiesen	*point, show*

[1] See 57 (*a*)
[2] 70 (*f*)
[3] Also: *sendete, gesendet*
[4] See 67
[5] See 70 (*e*)
[6] Usually weak except in non-literal sense
[7] Weak = soften

Infinitive	3rd Pers. Sing. Pres.	3rd Pers. Sing. Impf.	Past Part.	Meaning
wenden	wendet	wandte[1,2]	gewandt[2]	*turn (tr.)*
werben	wirbt	warb[3]	geworben	*woo, enlist*
*werden[4]	wird	wurde	geworden	*become*
werfen	wirft	warf[3]	geworfen	*throw*
wiegen[5]	wiegt	wog	gewogen	*weigh (intr.)*
winden	windet	wand	gewunden	*wind, twist*
wissen	weiß[6]	wußte	gewußt	*know (see 84)*
wollen[7]	will	wollte	gewollt	*want to*
zeihen	zeiht	zieh	geziehen	*accuse*
(*)ziehen	zieht	zog	gezogen	*draw, pull; grow (tr.); go, move*
zwingen	zwingt	zwang	gezwungen	*compel, force*

[1] 70 (f)
[2] Also: *wendete, gewendet*
[3] See 70 (e)
[4] See 57 (a)

[5] Weak = rock
[6] See 58 (a) (vi)
[7] 67

Part Two

Exercises in German Grammar and Syntax

(The *italic numbers* in brackets after the heading of each exercise refer to the paragraphs of *Part One* Grammar and Syntax)

1 Word Order *(1)*

TRANSLATE INTO GERMAN:

1. We came back early. 2. We shall come back tomorrow. 3. He had seen her at the window. 4. You must come back tomorrow. 5. That he has not come back is surprising. 6. To be always punctual is unusual. 7. This book you must read. 8. 'There they are,' he said. 9. 'He has *stolen* the money!' 10. '*Him?*' he said. 'I don't know *him*.' 11. 'Come you must!' 12. This morning we got up late. 13. The book I have just read is very interesting. 14. The book, the only one in the house, had disappeared. 15. This morning when we woke up the sun was shining. 16. 'Who can come today?' 17. 'Have the books arrived already?' 18. How difficult that is! 19. Yes, that is true. 20. In a word, you do not want to come.

2 Word Order *(2-5)*

TRANSLATE INTO GERMAN:

1. He got up early, dressed quickly and left the house before 8 o'clock. 2. Although he works hard he does not earn very much. 3. I know that he is very ill. 4. I had to wait a long time till he came home. 5. I have at last finished reading (*auslesen*) the book that I bought a month ago. 6. Before he woke up and could ask questions we hid the money. 7. I said that because I wanted to help him. 8. After he had written the letter and posted it he went to bed. 9. Whatever he says, I don't believe him. 10. Wherever you are you must obey me.

3 Word Order *(6, 75)*

TRANSLATE INTO GERMAN:

1. I owe the job to him. 2. I owe the job to my friend. 3. He brought it to me. 4. He read her the book. 5. I teach them German. 6. He inspired his

soldiers with new courage. 7. 'Pass your mother the salt, John.' 8. Everybody prefers peace to war. 9. He suggested that to us. 10. I promised him it. 11. I recognised your friend by his hat. 12. He prevented his brother from reading. 13. Then his mother lay down on the bed. 14. Then she lay down on the bed. 15. Then his mother washed him. 16. After his mother had lain down on the bed she fell asleep. 17. Don't go away. 18. He is not at home. 19. I haven't found it. 20. I haven't the book. 21. That isn't my book. 22. He couldn't come today. 23. He hasn't eaten lunch. 24. If he doesn't write I shall ring up. 25. Since he hadn't written I rang up. 26. Since it was so cold this morning I stayed at home. 27. Since he didn't go by car I stayed at home. 28. He didn't come today, he came yesterday. 29. I didn't see his brother but his sister. 30. We had for this reason to go home early. 31. We must go to bed early today. 32. We drove to town slowly. 33. We are invited there to tea today. 34. I have only worked a little today. 35. I rang her up yesterday. 36. When I got up this morning at six o'clock the sun was shining. 37. I don't dare to ring up. 38. I have worked harder today than yesterday. 39. He is, I think, rather stupid. 40. He is – his teacher has told me so more than once – rather stupid.

4 Conjunctions *(7-9)*

TRANSLATE INTO GERMAN:

1. He is old and ill. 2. He got into the car and drove off. 3. I like him but I do not know him well. 4. In the evening he goes to the cinema or (else) stays at home and reads a book. 5. He is not stupid but clever. 6. He did not go there by car but went on foot. 7. He is too young, for he is only six years old. 8. He is stupid but hardworking.

9. If you have time come tomorrow. 10. While I was talking with him Mary came into the room. 11. Instead of being grateful he treats her badly. 12. Only when we came close up did we see that the house was empty. 13. According to the way the decision goes (say: 'falls') we must execute the one plan or the other. 14. He went through the room without her noticing it. 15. Whether it happened intentionally or by mistake, it amounts to the same thing *(49(e))*. 16. In so far as he sticks *(79(b))* closely *(genau)* to the rules nothing can happen to him. 17. Be quick so that we are not late. 18. Even before the man could say anything they gave him some money. 19. You can walk in without ringing except of course when the door is locked. 20. I'll come immediately you ring up (add: 'as soon as'). 21. Although it was very cold he went out without a coat. 22. He ate with great enjoyment, especially as he had not had breakfast. 23. After you have unpacked come into the garden. 24. As the others grew more excited he regained his self-control. 25. He must exert himself all the more because his whole career depends on it. 26. Provided you don't get wet you won't catch cold. 27. He was in so far placed at a disadvantage as he was the youngest son. 28. I'll wait till you are ready. 29. He will not come before tomorrow

unless he takes an earlier train. 30. I cannot come now because I have too much work to do.

31. However much he wants it he cannot buy it. 32. Whenever we want to go out it always rains. 33. Whatever dress she puts on she always looks untidy. 34. However difficult it is he tries again and again (*34(d)*). 35. Whoever said that about him must have misunderstood him. 36. However warm it is it is never warm enough for her. 37. Whatever she says nobody believes her now. 38. Wherever we spend our holidays it always rains. 39. Wherever they go they are always popular. 40. Even if it rains we go out every day.

5 Conjunctions *(9)*

TRANSLATE INTO GERMAN:

1. As you see I am not free. 2. As they advanced the forest got thicker. 3. Just as you have recovered so I feel better now. 4. As he didn't come we went to the theatre without him. 5. As he said that he opened the door. 6. I know it isn't good but I do it nevertheless. 7. That is not true but a great lie. 8. The materials are anything but what we are looking for. 9. One could see nothing but trees. 10. He is not old, but she is much younger. 11. Since he has drunk too much he must not drive. 12. Since I have known that I forgive him a lot. 13. It was a long time now since they had seen one another. 14. Put the lamp on the table so that I can see better. 15. I exchanged my umbrella so that it now matches my coat. 16. She has so many visits to make so that she is hardly ever at home. 17. When you are well again you may get up. 18. When he comes he always brings me flowers. 19. When he finally came it was too late. 20. When he had said that he went out of the room. 21. When can I have a reply? 22. Hardly had they caught sight of him when they all began to run to him. 23. The hour came when they had to part. 24. While they were sitting in the train they did not say a word to one another. 25. He was talking outside while I was waiting for him with the meal.

6 Conjunctions *(10-11)*

TRANSLATE INTO GERMAN:

1. All the same I must decline the invitation. 2. I am as it is very busy. 3. I hardly know what I am to say. 4. Consequently I had to remain another hour. 5. Particularly is that the case when it rains. 6. Nevertheless he did pay the money. 7. Nor was the weather fine. 8. He writes books, biographies to be precise. 9. That is why he cannot come today. 10. And so we separated. 11. Either you pay the money now or you can send me a cheque. 12. I said nothing either yesterday or today. 13. There are not

enough pencils, let alone pens. 14. Neither he nor I said a word. 15. The later I get up the more tired I feel. 16. She isn't beautiful nor is she clever. 17. Just as there are many who like jazz, so there are many others who only like classical music. 18. Whether because he has no money or because he prefers to remain at home, he never goes out in the evening. 19. Both he and I failed (the examination). 20. On the one hand I have no money, on the other I have no time. 21. Now we would make long excursions, now we would stay all day at home. 22. It is one thing to talk, it is another to act. 23. Partly they came on foot, partly by car (*12(b)i*). 24. It is true that he is very clever, but he doesn't make any progress. 25. He enjoyed himself just as much as you were bored.

7 The Articles *(12)*

TRANSLATE INTO GERMAN:
1. Man proposes (= 'thinks'), God disposes. 2. Catholic Germany. 3. He lives in Goethe Street. 4. After breakfast we went to school immediately. 5. Send it to me by post. 6. I can come either at the beginning of May, in the middle of June or at the end of September. 7. After the end of the opera I couldn't get a taxi. 8. This road goes due (*gerade*) north. 9. For the above reason I can only come towards the end of the month. 10. He as a former Member of Parliament was heartily welcome. 11. He would like to become a doctor. 12. She was disguised as a gipsy. 13. He is always in a hurry. 14. We cannot come today since we have visitors. 15. He spoke in a low voice. 16. I drank some of the wine. 17. I never drink any milk. 18. I have some bread and cheese. 19. We were going 80 miles an hour. 20. How much do you earn a year? 21. I only said it for a joke. 22. For a change we ate at the restaurant. 23. It costs 5 marks a kilo. 24. I always change my clothes twice a day. 25. He stood there with his pipe in his mouth.

8 Nouns *(13)*

Add the appropriate definite article before each noun:

Käfig	Palast	Prämisse	Waise
Materie	Kamille	Königin	Opfer
Benzin	Reisig	Konsonant	Etikette
Absolutismus	Person	Lektüre	Genie
Politik	Regisseur	Christentum	Irrtum
Teppich	Literatur	Jüngling	Ende
Erkennen	Pensionär	Maschine	Dosis
Parlament	Gebüsch	Philosophie	Instrument
Intelligenz	Diskussion	Schnaps	Natur
Bankier	Mädchen	Affe	Geburt

Dickicht	Bewohner	Flamme	Fanatiker
Garage	Botschaft	Fünftel	Kontrast
Einzelheit	Pastor	Reichtum	Wache
Habicht	Datum	Initiative	Gebäude
Nichts	Universität	Gedanke	Honig
Fräulein	Anarchist	Tragödie	Lyrik
Toleranz	Tuberkulose	Erlaubnis	Renaissance
Schlägerei	Bukett	Komponist	Schokolade
Thema	Komma	Archäologe	Ordonnanz
Offizier	Bronchitis	Zement	Weib
Trübsal	Name	Auge	Hindernis
Teenager	Lamm	Stier	Schweigen
Kadett	Schmetterling	Phantasie	Finsternis
Fontäne	Knicks	Staffelei	Scheusal
Klima	Hoffnung	Fohlen	Basis

9 Nouns *(14-16)*

TRANSLATE INTO GERMAN:

1. I have a selection of Goethe's works in twenty volumes. 2. She had a red ribbon in her hair. 3. They had removed the book-shelf. 4. She had a bunch of keys in her hand. 5. The League of Nations had its seat in Geneva. 6. He is his grandfather's sole heir. 7. He squandered his inheritance in a short time. 8. In the hall of our house is a very old clock. 9. They went through the meadows and fields. 10. Do me the favour. 11. She has great pleasure in *(an + D)* beautiful clothes. 12. The contents of the bottle were given on the label. 13. The salary for this post was not very attractive. 14. He is a real heathen. 15. We walked over the moor. 16. He was not on his (say: 'the') guard and lost his hat. 17. The boy went into the kitchen to see the cat's kittens. 18. He has strong jaws. 19. This is a spruce-fir forest. 20. A customer came into the shop. 21. The news of the mishap spread quickly. 22. The manager of the factory is away ('absent'). 23. He put the ladder against the wall. 24. From the marrow of these bones you can make a very good soup. 25. In the March of Brandenburg there is a lot of sand. 26. The mark is a German coin. 27. The surveyor hasn't come yet. 28. Give me a knife. 29. The decisive moment had come. 30. The most important factor in the discussion had been overlooked. 31. Rice comes mostly from China. 32. She planted a shoot and a tree grew from it (say: 'out of it'). 33. The knight had lost his shield. 34. There is a new name-plate on the door. 35. On the lake there are a lot of boats today. 36. The sea was stormy. 37. My brother sat at the steering-wheel. 38. Taxes are very high in England. 39. Towards morning heavy (say: 'strong') dew fell. 40. He fastened the boat with a rope. 41. A deaf man was leading a blind man. 42. A pigeon has a nest in our tree. 43. Don't be a fool. 44. The gates of the city were shut. 45. His earnings are negligible. 46. He has been treated according to

E*

his deserts. 47. Above the weir is a swimming-pool. 48. He offered (use: '*sich setzen zu*') resistance. 49. The seven wise men of Greece. 50. This song is an old melody.

51. He is always looking for his spectacles. 52. The barracks have been modernised. 53. The children had no toys. 54. He came down the stairs. 55. Have you borrowed my scissors? 56. Take the ashes from the fireplace. 57. The town has beautiful surroundings. 58. His sorrows had made him old. 59. He got his wages paid (*ausgezahlt*) weekly. 60. Politics is the art of the possible.

10 Proper Nouns and Adjectives derived therefrom (17-18)

TRANSLATE INTO GERMAN:

1. Asia; Europe; South Africa; North America; West Africa. 2. France; Norway; Poland; Switzerland; the United States. 3. Prussia; Bavaria; Alsace-Lorraine; Styria; Carinthia. 4. Brunswick; Lisbon; Munich; Venice; Warsaw. 5. The Thames; the Moselle; the Rhine; the Danube; the Main. 6. Of the Bavarian; the Danes; the Asians; of the Frenchman; a German. 7. He speaks French, German, Polish, Russian and Chinese. 8. In this library there are Greek, Italian, Spanish, Dutch, Russian and German books as well as English and French ones (50(*b*), note). 9. The Age of Enlightenment; The Thirty Years' War; the Counter Reformation; the Elizabethan Age; the Victorian Age; the Hegelian philosophy. 10. Lessing's works; Leibniz's works; Frederick's car; Gertrude's new dress. 11. The Brauns are coming this evening. 12. In the reign of Elizabeth the Second of England. 13. In the reign of King Charles the First. 14. Professor Hafner's writings; the works of Wilhelm von Scholz; uncle Peter's house. 15. The last days of September; the first days of the month of April; on the evening of the following Wednesday.

11 The Cases (19-23)

TRANSLATE INTO GERMAN:

1. He became the next president. 2. I can only stay a moment. 3. It must not be more than an inch thick. 4. It only costs three shillings a bottle. 5. He came every evening. 6. Expect me next Sunday. 7. He ran up the stairs. 8. He stood there with his hat in his hand. 9. I have at last got rid of him. 10. One fine morning he knocked at my door. 11. He looked at her with steady gaze. 12. Mindful of the fact that ... 13. Ignorant of the language I could understand nothing. 14. He is worthy of the honour he was shown. 15. He was here the other day. 16. Give me a cigarette. 17. I am very grateful to you. 18. That is repugnant to all men. 19. Everything is

subject to decay. 20. He was standing nearest to me. 21. He was superior to all others in (an) wisdom. 22. That is a song very familiar to me. 23. These insects are harmful to man. 24. Vanity is alien to her. 25. He is an equal of the greatest poets of the past. 26. The skirt is too long for her. 27. My library is at your disposal. 28. You are free to believe it or not. 29. However that may be. 30. I feel in low spirits this morning.

31. Do you know his son, the famous doctor? 32. I gave it to his brother, the bookseller. 33. He is coming on Monday the 8th January. 34. She came with a dozen eggs. 35. She bought two pairs of black gloves. 36. He as the youngest brother had to obey everybody. 37. I as the youngest child was given (69(d)) the biggest piece of cake. 38. He looks a poet. 39. I recognised him as the thief. 40. He was looked upon as a successful man.

12 The Adjective *(24-30)*

TRANSLATE INTO GERMAN:

1. Successful; unsuccessful; amiable; praiseworthy; fireproof; duty-free. 2. Patient; childish; Dutch; geographical; iron; silk; woollen. 3. Childlike; daily; yearly; weekly; monthly; questionable; fragile; ridiculous; frightful. 4. The London theatres; the Paris police; the New York skyscrapers; (the) Brunswick cathedral. 5. Fertile; eatable; drinkable; recognisable; unmistakable; nutritious; morbid; economical. 6. Impossible; unhealthy; dissatisfied; improbable; inhuman; unhappy. 7. Light blue; light green; dark blue; light brown; pale yellow. 8. Snow-white; sea-green; colour-blind; rose-red; ash-grey, dove-grey; house-trained. 9. A three-cornered hat; a five-storied house; a two-hour journey; a three-year stay. 10. A very promising beginning; far-reaching consequences; a breath-taking sight; a hair-raising story. 11. It is pitch dark. 12. He is as deaf as a post. 13. The cheese is as hard as rock. 14. Is the meat done? 15. You are to blame. 16. We are now quits. 17. Many books worth reading; these ridiculous hats; a dark red dress. 18. Your new waterproof coat; her snow-white hair; which revealing remarks? 19. All duty-free goods; revolutionary movements; every musical evening. 20. At the end of a three-day journey; in a three-storied house; a woman of breath-taking beauty. 21. These big black chimneys; these black and white cows. 22. All our friends; this my signature; with all his strength; the pages of all these books. 23. He poor man; I poor woman; to me poor woman; to us Germans. 24. We Germans; we poor people; to him poor man. 25. My sister whose eldest child ...; my sister, with whose eldest child ...; the combined strength of two great European powers. 26. Old and young; the old and young; many old and young. 27. A traveller; with the traveller; some travellers; all travellers; which travellers? 28. The good, the true and the beautiful; in the interior of the country. 29. Nothing new; with something interesting; everything possible; something else. 30. All sorts of interesting things; little that is interesting; much that is dramatic. 31. The only thing; the first thing; the

most necessary thing. 32. The most striking phenomenon; the safest course; conflicting elements; what is thought and said. 33. A lilac hat; a pink dress; a cream coloured shirt. 34. Tall and slim, there she stood. 35. There were once many Berlin newspapers.

13 Comparison of Adjectives and Adverbs *(31, 36)*

TRANSLATE INTO GERMAN:

1. He is just as clever as you. 2. He is far from being as industrious as his sister. 3. They are the same age. 4. He is even younger than you. 5. He is anything but stupid. 6. It is all the more amusing because he did not know who she was. 7. He had better write immediately. 8. After a prolonged stay in Germany he speaks German very fluently. 9. Most of the time he does nothing. 10. He is most cautious. 11. It would be best of all to write immediately. 12. I think it best if you come immediately. 13. You had best go by car. 14. He was not in the least pleased. 15. I'll come as quickly as I can.

14 Adverbs *(32-35)*

TRANSLATE INTO GERMAN:

1. As is well known girls are more conscientious than boys. 2. He was deservedly punished. 3. Strange to relate he returned the money. 4. For once in a while (= 'exceptionally') he came to the cinema with us last night. 5. He happened to be standing (say: 'stood by chance') at the corner of the street. 6. Strictly speaking I ought to go there today. 7. He looked at her a moment. 8. Stay upstairs, don't come down. 9. She was walking along beside him. 10. It came to the same thing. 11. We drove past the station. 12. They came up to us. 13. I looked in her direction. 14. I must go upstairs. 15. At the risk of offending him I sent him back the cheque. 16. On my advice he declined the offer. 17. From that day onwards he never spoke to him. 18. Now and again he visits us. 19. We drove along the shore of the lake. 20. As far as I am concerned you can accept it.

15 Numerals, etc. *(37-42)*

TRANSLATE INTO GERMAN:

1. Bring another two cups of coffee. 2. That is the boy whose one wish is *(43(i)i)* to become a doctor. 3. She is a woman in her middle thirties. 4. They came in thousands. 5. That was in the 'forties of this century. 6. 'You stay with us, you other two can go home,' said their mother. 7. When I saw him for the first time he looked very ill. 8. He left his friend a fifth of his fortune. 9. I'll be back in a quarter of an hour. 10. His house is twice as big as

ours. 11. You don't need to go into details. 12. That was the only thing he said. 13. This room is ten yards by six and a half. 14. He arrived at 2 o'clock in the morning. 15. What was the date of the Battle of Hastings? 16. She is getting on in years. 17. He died in the prime of life. 18. When is Easter this year? 19. She is coming in a fortnight's time. 20. He visited us last Wednesday.

16 Personal, Reflexive, Possessive and Reciprocal Pronouns (43-45, 89, 98-100)

TRANSLATE INTO GERMAN:

1. Did you get the letter? – Yes, I got it this morning. It was very interesting. 2. He paints pictures such as his father used to paint. 3. I am sure of it. 4. I don't mind, you can do what you like. 5. People like us must hold their tongues. 6. I have no objection to it. 7. And into the bargain he was insolent. 8. I hate going out in the evenings. 9. Did you know that they were my pictures? 10. Did you know that there aren't any books on the table? 11. In the evening there was singing and dancing. 12. There was once upon a time a poor man who ... 13. What is there to eat? 14. There are people who still prefer to stay at home in the weekend(s). 15. Was it you who wrote the letter? 16. My hat was cheaper than yours. 17. There are more trees in your garden than in ours. 18. This watch is mine. 19. The books are hers. 20. Have you a car of your own? 21. He could see the sea beneath him. 22. He only thinks of himself. 23. He saw her beckoning to him. 24. What the thing in itself is nobody knows. 25. They don't like one another.

17 Interrogatives and Relative Pronouns (47-48, 90, 95-96)

TRANSLATE INTO GERMAN:

1. Which books do you prefer? 2. In which street do you live? 3. What is the capital of Switzerland? 4. What sort of a man is your cousin? 5. What sort of ones are these? 6. Whose watch is this? 7. What is your father? 8. What is he accused of? 9. The knife I cut my finger with was very sharp. 10. The house whose windows were all shut looked uninhabited. 11. His wife, for whose sake he had sacrificed everything, left him. 12. Those are books I know I shall never be able to read. 13. We who knew him well are not at all surprised. 14. Was it you who rang up? 15. Everything he showed us was most interesting. 16. That is the only thing I can remember. 17. Much that has been written about it is untrue. 18. What he spoke about I have now forgotten. 19. Nobody who has tried to help them can know how difficult it is. 20. Say what you will, I still cannot believe it.

18 Demonstratives and Indefinite Adjectives and Pronouns (49-51, 90, 94, 97)

TRANSLATE INTO GERMAN:

1. I write better with this pen than with that one. 2. That hat is very pretty. 3. It was such bad weather that we stayed at home. 4. I get such letters every day. 5. Those are his. 6. People who go there enthuse about it. 7. Some of those who came regretted it. 8. My garden is much bigger than my daughter's. 9. There are more fruit-trees in my garden than in my neighbour's. 10. His only pleasure is to play chess. 11. He always uses the same expressions. 12. He returned the same day. 13. You yourself wrote the letter. 14. There was a knock. 15. Only one thing is necessary. 16. One of the tables is rickety. 17. Give me white cups, I don't like blue ones. 18. Did anybody else ask a question? 19. That is somebody else. 20. I can come any other time, only not this afternoon. 21. You must each work for an hour. 22. I haven't any matches – Have you any? 23. All these are my children and grandchildren. 24. It must have been something of the sort. 25. No, it was something else. 26. I should like a little more, please. 27. We have some experience in such matters. 28. Quite a number of young people nowadays do not smoke. 29. In the whole of England you won't find anybody who will agree with you. 30. Some maintain this, others that.

19 Prepositions (52-54)

TRANSLATE INTO GERMAN:

1. It will last two to three hours. 2. At about six o'clock he left the house against my express order(s). 3. She will be back by next Saturday. 4. He must have met her round about the year 1960. 5. All were singing merrily except the little girl. 6. He said a few words to everybody except to me. 7. I wouldn't live in a town for anything in the world. 8. He was woken up by the noise. 9. I would go to the end of the world with you. 10. He was driving much too fast down the narrow street. 11. She lived there all alone till her death. 12. What we spend is nothing compared to what they spend.

13. In spite of the large amount of (51(d)) work he always remains cheerful. 14. Instead of to me she gave it to my younger brother. 15. During the winter all the hotels are closed, 16. As long as he lived he never opened a book. 17. Because of mother we had to stay at home. 18. With the aid of a dictionary we managed to translate the letter. 19. As a result of the gale many houses were destroyed. 20. On the occasion of the celebration the children had a holiday. 21. She came instead of her father. 22. In view of the circumstances we must accept (84) the situation. 23. He did it for her sake. 24. In accordance with the order I must arrest you.

25. I did it for a different reason. 26. On closer examination he found

that it was made of leather. 27. He interrupted me at every second word. 28. Within a year he had fully recovered. 29. Thanks to his help I was able to finish the work in time. 30. Contrary to all appearances he is very humble. 31. Like you I came by car. 32. He spoke in a deep voice. 33. You'll understand that in time. 34. She passed her hand over her hair. 35. He did it on purpose. 36. I prefer to write in pencil. 37. To all appearances he is very rich. 38. We'll go for a walk tomorrow or remain at home, depending on the weather. 39. I don't know him by sight, I only know him by name. 40. He was standing next to her. 41. All the crew were there together with officers and captain. 42. I have known him for many years. 43. That lies to the south of Brunswick. 44. Which is the nearest way to the station? 45. If need be we can come tomorrow. 46. That we shall never see in our lifetime. 47. You must go to the doctor's. 48. He always arrives home in time. 49. That is against the law. 50. He did it by mistake.

20 Prepositions *(55)*

TRANSLATE INTO GERMAN:

1. She lay down on the bed. 2. She was lying on the bed. 3. He sat down between them. 4. He was sitting between them. 5. She sat down at the table. 6. He was working at the table. 7. He threw it under the table. 8. The dog was lying under the table. 9. He came into the room. 10. He was working in the room.

11. It is my turn. 12. That afternoon we went to London. 13. There are no stars in the sky tonight. 14. The houses along the bank of this river are old and picturesque. 15. We like going into the country. 16. When we are in the country we go for long walks. 17. When we are at the seaside we bathe every day. 18. It is time she wrote (59(a)v). 19. In the long run that is impossible. 20. From time to time one must chance it. 21. He was caught in the act. 22. We eat out on Sundays. 23. It must be done in this way. 24. I met him at the station this morning. 25. Apart from my brother everybody was there. 26. He disappeared behind the house. 27. We go abroad every year. 28. I have cut my finger again. 29. I have to go to the office every day. 30. I saw that on TV. 31. On the average I go twice a week to the theatre. 32. He jumped out at the last moment. 33. Unlike most English authors he does not live abroad. 34. He stayed throughout the summer. 35. We go out (for a drive) during the week but stay at home at the weekend. 36. That happened in the reign of Charles I. 37. Only on this condition could he accept. 38. Between ourselves he should not say that sort of thing. 39. He arrived in the town two months ago. 40. There are people who cannot see the wood for the trees.

21 Nouns and Adjectives
with Prepositional Objects *(56, 79(v))*

TRANSLATE INTO GERMAN:

1. I have a request (to make) to you. 2. He has had a great influence on her. 3. It was a mixture of fear and envy. 4. He makes no allowance for weakness. 5. He gave a lecture on Goethe. 6. His dependence on his mother was obvious. 7. He has no sympathy for such people. 8. His concern for his children was touching. 9. Her attitude to her subordinates was cool and unfriendly. 10. He had (a) great fear of dogs. 11. That was the occasion for the celebration. 12. This demanded submission to his father's will. 13. Most young people have a longing for adventure. 14. His indignation at her words knew no bounds. 15. This would mean a relapse into barbarism. 16. His conviction as to the efficacy of the means is unshakable. 17. The remedy for such illnesses is simple. 18. The measure of success is quite a different one. 19. This is a translation from the English. 20. There is no reliance (to be placed) on him. 21. It is a matter of adaptation of means to ends. 22. He took a cruel revenge on his brother. 23. This puts *(stellen)* high demands on the citizen. 24. I put *(setzen)* all my confidence in you. 25. His dislike of work is well known. 26. He conceived (*fassen*) a great affection for her. 27. He raised all sorts of objections to it. 28. There was a violent dispute as to the meaning of the word. 29. His hatred of insincerity grew more and more. 30. That is a striking proof of the correctness of his views.

31. He is blind in one eye. 32. I am ready for anything. 33. He is susceptible to flattery. 34. She is very sensitive to cold. 35. He was in love with her. 36. He is above all suspicion. 37. She is never at a loss for words. 38. He is well *(wohl)* versed in history. 39. That is incompatible with his views. 40. I was incensed at his behaviour.

41. He is accustomed to going to bed late. 42. He is to blame for her coming home so late. 43. He was intent on making a good impression. 44. He was entitled to travel first class. 45. He was safe from being seen. 46. The memory of having offended her never left him. 47. The hope that he would get a holiday proved to be very foolish. 48. That was the reason for his declining the invitation. 49. The views as to how that should be done were conflicting. 50. The condition of (*für*) my going with you is that you pay for everything.

22 Haben, Sein, Werden *(57)*

TRANSLATE INTO GERMAN using the perfect where possible:

1. He has bought the house. 2. He has hurt himself. 3. He has gone down the mountain. 4. He has run (a) great risk. 5. He has been driving the car. 6. He has worked hard. 7. He has been dancing a lot. 8. He has come. 9. He has woken up. 10. Who has stayed? 11. What has happened? 12.

Where have you been? 13. He has gone by car. 14. He will do it. 15. The table is being laid.

23 The Tenses *(59)*

TRANSLATE INTO GERMAN:

1. He reads the paper every morning. 2. He has been reading since 8 o'clock. 3. He is reading the paper now. 4. I'll come again tomorrow. 5. It is the first time he has written. 6. It is time we went. 7. He got up at seven, washed, dressed, breakfasted and left the house at eight. 8. He used to visit us every week. 9. He would come home at eight o'clock, and then he would take a bath, eat something and go out and not come back before midnight. 10. He had been driving for more than two hours. 11. I came this morning. 12. I expect you have read the novel. 13. He won't obey me. 14. He is about to leave Paris. 15. He is on the point of moving house. 16. He would do it if he had time. 17. He said he would do it. 18. He wouldn't answer my question. 19. He would have said nothing. 20. He could have come earlier.

24 Compound Verbs *(60)*

TRANSLATE INTO GERMAN:

1. Don't exaggerate. 2. He repeats everything. 3. He has filled up the form. 4. She embraced her mother. 5. Where did it take place? 6. Don't contradict me. 7. He has just gone past. 8. Don't interrupt me. 9. He gets up at 7 o'clock. 10. He switched on the light. 11. He bequeathed her his whole fortune. 12. What did you discover? 13. He looked up at her. 14. He has just woken up. 15. He has not convinced me. 16. Don't misunderstand me. 17. He has let the house. 18. It is impossible to resist that. 19. He has promised it to me. 20. Who took part? 21. We have lost our way. 22. He went away. 23. He tore the paper up. 24. It is impossible to distinguish them. 25. He has at last acknowledged her. 26. Don't over-exert yourself. 27. He refuted my argument. 28. Shut the door. 29. He was run over. 30. The library comprises all sorts of books.

25 Reflexive and Impersonal Verbs *(61-62)*

TRANSLATE INTO GERMAN:

1. Just imagine (*3 forms*). 2. Don't catch cold (*3 forms*). 3. You must change (your clothes). 4. After he had undressed he lay down. 5. He sat down on the chair. 6. You haven't washed your face. 7. It is said that he ran away. 8. It depends on how one says it. 9. Shut the door, there is a draught.

10. He lacks courage. 11. I am two marks short. 12. You are free to come or stay at home. 13. How are you? – I am very well, thank you. 14. She felt apprehensive. 15. He succeeded in getting there in time. 16. At first it rained, but soon afterwards the weather cleared up. 17. It is a matter of life or death. 18. I am astonished that he doesn't come. 19. It occurred to me that he hadn't said anything. 20. My finger itches.

26 The Infinitive *(63)*

TRANSLATE INTO GERMAN:

1. He is unable to come tonight. 2. I should like to meet her. 3. I had to hold my tongue. 4. He did not want to go to the theatre. 5. They go dancing every Saturday night. 6. They saw me coming. 7. Help me make the bed. 8. He has a lot of books lying around. 9. It is quite useless to write to him. 10. He seems to have forgotten us. 11. I have no time to lose. 12. He came in without knocking at the door. 13. He rang up instead of writing. 14. In order to arrive in time I left the house at nine o'clock. 15. He is not yet old enough to be able to understand that.

27 Participles *(64)*

TRANSLATE INTO GERMAN, using participles:

1. Having arrived in the town he looked for a hotel. 2. Stimulated by the discussion he was able to finish his article. 3. They lived there for months vainly waiting for news. 4. Giving up the effort he sank back on his bed. 5. Leaning back in his chair he went on smoking his pipe. 6. Passing (*54(k)*) his hand over his forehead he said he felt unwell. 7. Suddenly sitting up in bed he shouted that he had seen a ghost. 8. Blushing she looked down and said nothing. 9. The village, completely destroyed by bombs in 1941, has now been rebuilt. 10. Although deeply moved he seemed quite calm. 11. Some stayed a bit longer reading newspapers, playing cards or bent over chess boards (say: 'the chess board'). 12. The book which appeared in 1959 has had a great success. 13. That is a situation that can now scarcely be changed. 14 They spoke of the guests that were to be invited. 15. She came running up to him.

28 The Imperative and Interrogative *(65-66)*

TRANSLATE INTO GERMAN, giving the three forms of the imperative:

1. Stay. 2. Look at me. 3. Don't run away. 4. Listen. 5. Pay attention. 6. Don't catch cold. 7. Calm yourself. 8. Do ('act') as you like. 9. Don't pity him. 10. Be glad that it is not worse. 11. Let us eat (*all possible*

forms). 12. Do be careful. 13. Go on, offer it to him. 14. Now don't be late. 15. Mind you don't forget. 16. Be sure to let him know that you are coming. 17. See to it that you don't fail (your exam). 18. Come along now. 19. Just stay quiet. 20. Just imagine. 21. Come on, don't be afraid. 22. Help yourself, do. 23. All right, go. 24. Go on, laugh away. 25. Just you wait, I'll have my revenge.

26. Haven't you read the book? 27. Why doesn't he come? 28. You have read the book, haven't you? 29. You will be seeing him, won't you? 30. You didn't come yesterday, did you? – Yes, I did.

29 Auxiliary Verbs of Mood *(67)*

TRANSLATE INTO GERMAN:

1. May he come tomorrow? – He may. 2. May I come in? 3. That may well be. 4. He may have gone away. 5. It may have been 10 o'clock when he got back. 6. He may have been forty when I met him for the first time. 7. Long may he flourish. 8. He might have written, for it looks like his handwriting. 9. He need only say so. 10. They cannot help it. 11. We don't know Italian. 12. He might still come. 13. He might have accepted the invitation if we had written in time. 14. He can speak French, Spanish and Russian. 15. He cannot possibly arrive before 6 o'clock. 16. I must now ring up. 17. Are you to ring up this afternoon? 18. We could come earlier. 19. We could have come earlier. 20. He ought really to be going now. 21. He ought to have come earlier. 22. Tell him to write the letter immediately. 23. What would you like me to give you as a present? 24. You must not say anything. 25. Ought we to have declined the invitation? 26. Did he have to sell it? 27. We could not help laughing. 28. What is the meaning of that? 29. What was I to say? 30. You don't have to come with us. 31. He must have known. 32. Would you like to eat a piece of cake? 33. He didn't like to admit it. 34. Let's go for a walk today. 35. He wouldn't wait any longer. 36. Shall we go to the cinema? 37. Shall we go home now? 38. He asserts that he came earlier. 39. I had intended to come earlier but I couldn't. 40. He is said to be very clever. 41. Children ought not to play with matches. 42. I ought to write the letter this evening. 43. What was to become of *(79(f))* him? 44. Didn't you want to go out today? 45. I should like to have prevented it. 46. He might just as well have written. 47. The rain shows no signs of stopping. 48. That shouldn't be difficult. 49. Can he want to do it? 50. You must not always want to interfere in *(79(j))* everything.

30 Lassen *(68)*

TRANSLATE INTO GERMAN:

1. Where did you leave it? 2. We left the children at home. 3. I made them learn the poem by heart. 4. My wife always keeps me waiting. 5. That

makes me suspect that he does not intend to come. 6. What made you say that? 7. He got her to do it for him. 8. They have had a new house built for them. 9. Get your hair cut. 10. I always get that sort of thing done for me. 11. I have had to have a tooth extracted. 12. He didn't let them go without first warning them. 13. Let us go there. 14. He let the water run into the bath. 15. He didn't let me know when he intended to come. 16. That could not be proved. 17. I sent her my regards. 18. We sent for the doctor. 19. He sent word to us that he would not be able to come on Tuesday. 20. He'll not put up with that.

31 The Passive Voice (69)

TRANSLATE INTO GERMAN:

1. The table is being laid. 2. When was the school founded? 3. Everything has been destroyed. 4. Will it ever be rebuilt? 5. He said it would be rebuilt. 6. It has been entirely rebuilt. 7. Can it be restored? 8. It must be restored. 9. It could not be restored. 10. The book had to be completely revised. 11. It ought not to have been restored. 12. It will have to be destroyed. 13. The cathedral has been restored by the very best craftsmen. 14. He was wounded by a bullet. 15. The window was broken by the gale. 16. I was given the biggest piece of cake. 17. He was advised to stay at home. 18. Although he was advised to stay at home he went out. 19. There was dancing and singing in the streets. 20. That had been thought of too. 21. They must be shown how it is done. 22. It remains to be seen how many can come. 23. It is to be regretted that they behaved so badly. 24. This book is to be taken seriously. 25. It cannot be denied that they behaved badly. 26. When we came into the room the tables were being laid. 27. When we came into the room the tables were already laid. 28. This song is sung everywhere today. 29. He was firmly resolved to say nothing. 30. She was inclined to stay at home. 31. They were forced to remain at home. 32. The house was surrounded by a hedge. 33. He was filled with (*von*), enthusiasm. 34. She was dressed in black. 35. It was found to be defective. 36. Where was he drowned? 37. Don't be frightened. 38. He is not allowed to drink wine. 39. He is said to be cleverer than he looks. 40. He was expected to hold his tongue. 41. They expect to be invited. 42. We are told that ministers know (add: 'it') better. 43. That is what is needed above all. 44. That was a journey never to be forgotten. 45. That is a book to be taken seriously.

32 Indirect Speech (70-71)

TRANSLATE INTO GERMAN both with and without *daß* wherever possible:

1. He says he doesn't know her. 2. She says she has never been to France. 3. He says he came at 6 o'clock. 4. He says he wants to sleep. 5. He says he

wanted to write immediately. 6. They say the queen is coming tomorrow. 7. He said he must leave tomorrow. 8. She said she would be writing later. 9. They said they called on us yesterday. 10. He said that if he wrote immediately he would have a reply on Wednesday. 11. He said they were books he had just bought. 12. He asked me if he could come tomorrow. 13. He asked her if she felt unwell. 14. She asked him for whom he had bought the present. 15. He asked her how long she had been learning German. 16. I asked him who he was, what he wanted, why he looked so pale and if I could help him. 17. He asked her who the man was who had just left the room. 18. Tell her to come at once. 19. He told him to sit down. 20. He told me that the boys were not working hard. 21. He said that they would come back tomorrow. 22. He said that they had declined the invitation. 23. I think he has come. 24. He thought she had come. 25. I know that it is true.

33 Conditional Sentences *(70, 72)*

TRANSLATE INTO GERMAN:

1. If you ring up I'll come at once. 2. If you rang up I'd come at once. 3. If you had rung up I should have come at once. 4. If he is at home I'll come. 5. If he were at home I'd come. 6. If he had been at home I should have come. 7. I shall have time for you if you come tomorrow. 8. I should have time for you if you came tomorrow. 9. He would have had time for you if you had come on Tuesday. 10. If you want I can come tomorrow. 11. If you wanted I could come tomorrow. 12. If you had wanted I could have come last Saturday. 13. If one can see ahead one can take steps. 14. If one could see ahead one could take steps. 15. If one could have seen ahead one could have taken steps. 16. If the telegram comes he is to let me know. 17. If the telegram came I should know what to do. 18. If the telegram had come I should have known what to do. 19. If he were to write his mother would be reassured. 20. Had he started earlier he might have been able to avoid the traffic jam. 21. Had he written we could have fetched him from the station. 22. Had he been able to drive he could have saved a lot of time. 23. If he did obey he did so only because of *(aus)* fear. 24. If he refused it was only because he was ill. 25. If he didn't write it was only because he had no time.

34 Other Uses of the Subjunctive *(70, 73)*

TRANSLATE INTO GERMAN:

1. May he come in time! 2. Long live the queen! 3. Let us stay at home. 4. Let us be quick. 5. Had I only thought of it before! 6. If only one didn't forget so easily! 7. Well, that's all. 8. I almost came too late. 9. She wanted me to go away immediately. 10. I wish it would stop raining. 11. He would

like her to wear her hair long. 12. I want him to tell the truth. 13. She went straight away into the kitchen so that the meal should be ready in time. 14. I know nobody who is as clever as that young man. 15. I knew nobody who looked as beautiful as that woman. 16. Not that I took it amiss. 17. He would not admit that it could be done like that too. 18. A boy who only went in for (*treiben*) sport would not be able to pass his examination. 19. The book was too heavy for the child to be able to carry. 20. Not a day passes without his mentioning it. 21. Not a day passed without his mentioning it. 22. Instead of his answering the letter his son had to sit down and write. 23. He nearly ran us over. 24. He looks as if he wants to sleep. 25. He pretended to know nothing about it.

35 Government of Verbs (74-78)

TRANSLATE INTO GERMAN:

1. That impressed him very (much). 2. Her pale face struck him. 3. Don't contradict your father. 4. What is the matter with you? 5. He doesn't believe me. 6. He preceded the others. 7. He has succumbed to his wounds. 8. They were approaching the castle. 9. I have just met him in the street. 10. That would never have occurred to me. 11. Wednesday will suit us very well. 12. He pleases the ladies because he flatters them. 13. Many royal personages were present at the ceremony. 14. She devoted herself to the study of history. 15. She smiled at her companion.

16. You must impress on him to come back immediately. 17. You can leave that to me. 18. Certain facts have been withheld from them. 19. You expect too much of him. 20. I owe him my life. 21. He has refused her (the) permission to leave before 5 o'clock. 22. He has imposed impossible conditions on them. 23. Can you recommend me an exciting novel? 24. We had to show them the door. 25. He managed to get them two theatre tickets. 26. She has quite fascinated him. 27. May I introduce my friend to you? 28. I have nothing to reproach myself for. 29. How can you prove that to him? 30. You can save yourself the trouble.

31. He used the opportunity to escape. 32. The younger son usurped the throne. 33. He has fulfilled his task most speedily. 34. She had to take charge of the child. 35. She took pity on the poor old man. 36. There is no need of this explanation. 37. He boasted of always having money in his pocket. 38. She couldn't hold back her tears. 39. Bear in mind the difficulties that might arise therefrom (79(*f*)). 40. We have assured ourselves of his help.

41. He was accused of the murder. 42. He was deprived of his office. 43. He was suspected of high treason. 44. He had to be broken of the habit of smoking. 45. He deemed her unworthy of an answer. 46. The letter robbed her of all hope.

47. He called the man a fool. 48. That will teach you obedience. 49. That has cost me too much time already. 50. He calls himself a poet.

36 Government of Verbs *(79)*

TRANSLATE INTO GERMAN:

(b)–(k)

1. Mother always thinks of my birthday. 2. Look after the baby. 3. They think him honest. 4. What objection have you got to him? 5. The driver apologised to the woman. 6. Initiate them into the secret. 7. We have been working for a long time at this book. 8. The aeroplane disappeared into the clouds. 9. Thieves had burgled the house. 10. His assertion is based on a false premise. 11. My wife suffers from headaches. 12. What he said is also true of other cases. 13. Remind me of it again before you go. 14. They drank to his success. 15. She thanked him for the lovely present. 16. He stuck obstinately to his point of view. 17. She died of the same illness as her mother. 18. Her brother renounced his share of the inheritance. 19. He finds it difficult to get used to early rising. 20. Do answer my question.

(l)–(u)

21. The whole house smelt of cigars. 22. The guests complained of the bad food. 23. What do you think of the new school? 24. The dark mountains stood out against the silver grey of the sea. 25. When my sister applied for the post she got it immediately. 26. He had to suffer a good deal from the consequences. 27. He set off for Paris yesterday. 28. He has been cheated out of his fortune. 29. I will willingly help you to (get) a seat. 30. That depends entirely on his mood. 31. Don't blame him for his absence, he was ill. 32. When the mother saw her child again she wept for joy. 33. God preserve us from false friends. 34. We congratulated her on her success. 35. All her life she had striven for this goal. 36. You grumble about every trifle. 37. Then she turned to her neighbour and took his arm. 38. The dog was wagging its tail. 39. Many people lost their lives. 40. He was elected president.

(v)

41. I insist on your showing it to me. 42. Don't compel me to use force. 43. The teacher indicated where the mistake lay. 44. He doesn't believe that she is really ill. 45. Mary thought a long time about what he had said. 46. He doubts whether the house can be finished (say: 'built') in time. 47. The doctor warned him against smoking too many cigarettes. 48. That kept him from wasting his money. 49. He called my attention to the fact that I had not replied to his letter. 50. It is a question of finding time. 51. You must beware of annoying him. 52. I rely on your writing immediately. 53. He saw to it that they got there in time. 54. He concluded from this that she did not want to come. 55. They tried to force her to sing a song. 56. He pressed for it to be done immediately. 57. We envied his being so rich. 58. He prevented us from leaving in time. 59. He spoke of the way in which he had escaped from prison. 60. He thanked me for sending him the books.

37 The Infinitive-Noun *(80)*

TRANSLATE INTO GERMAN, using infinitive-nouns:

1. Getting up early has exhausted me. 2. Shopping in a big city is time-absorbing. 3. This long wait is unbearable. 4. I have never been able to get used to bathing in cold water. 5. Before working in the garden it is better to put on old clothes. 6. He cut himself while shaving. 7. I have no time for reading. 8. He prevented me from making headway. 9. After reflecting a long time he decided not to send the letter. 10. In spite of listening intently he could hear nothing. 11. There is nothing to eat in the house. 12. That made (79(*u*)) them stop talking. 13. He was ready to go out. 14. I have no time to write letters. 15. He helped me to plant flowers.

38 Translation of English Present Participle and Gerund *(81)*

TRANSLATE INTO GERMAN without using the participle forms:

1. It is strange being alone in this house. 2. I intended coming tomorrow. 3. He won't succeed in finding me at home. 4. Most people prefer getting up late. 5. Children hate going to bed early. 6. He went out without waiting for us. 7. Instead of ringing up immediately he sent a postcard. 8. I came into the room without their noticing it. 9. Instead of his paying for me I had to pay for him. 10. He tried to deceive us by pretending to be asleep. 11. By insisting on the money you only annoy him. 12. Being sleepy he went to bed early. 13. Having paid the bill he left the shop and went home. 14. After finishing (*auslesen*) the book he went to bed. 15. Before going to bed he finished the book. 16. When driving a car one must pay attention. 17. They listened attentively, looking at him all the time. 18. He heard his mother coming up the stairs. 19. We saw them driving past in their new car. 20. He watched them playing football. 21. He listened to her playing the piano. 22. The man standing by her side seemed not to notice anybody. 23. He caught sight of his sister standing at the corner of the street. 24. She sat there listening to them. 25. While getting out he fell and was run over. 26. On catching sight of his wife he stopped the car. 27. When skiing one must be warmly dressed. 28. He likes dancing. 29. Some people prefer reading. 30. I like swimming best.

39 Exclamations *(82)*

TRANSLATE INTO GERMAN:

1. How time flies! 2. How beautiful she is! 3. What a beautiful picture that is! 4. What a long time ago that was! 5. How beautifully she sings! 6. Isn't that exquisite! 7. Aren't I glad! 8. What a beautiful picture! 9. What lovely weather! 10. What an extraordinary idea!

40 Some difficult German Words *(83)*

TRANSLATE INTO GERMAN:

1. I did not say anything. – Nor did I. 2. You are getting younger and younger. 3. Be sure to write again soon. 4. I had never seen that before. 5. I am truly sorry. 6. I expect you know him. 7. Just one more cup of coffee and then I'll go. 8. The letter must be there by now. 9. Could you perhaps lend me five marks? 10. I'll come if I possibly can. 11. He repeated the sentence again and again. 12. Somehow or other it must be done. 13. About twenty people were in the room. 14. He waited as long as he possibly could. 15. Don't you remember, we saw it yesterday. 16. He said yes straight away without even reflecting for a moment. 17. His son considered him more as a friend than as a father. 18. However idle he is he always gets good marks (sing.). 19. It is surely time he came. 20. He'll come all right. 21. Well, what do you think? 22. We had quite nice weather. 23. That is true enough, but despite that he ought not to have done it. 24. He is far from being old enough. 25. Just lie down. 26. You really ought to write. 27. Just one second more! 28. However that may be. 29. He did see it after all. 30. We'll meet again some time or other.

41 Synonyms *(84)*

TRANSLATE INTO GERMAN
(ACCEPT – BOX)

1. We accepted their invitation. 2. He calmly accepted all these insults. 3. I cannot accept such a situation. 4. He was accepted everywhere. 5. He has a pleasant appearance. 6. He was a man of pleasant appearance. 7. It has every appearance of rain (say: 'entirely the appearance as if it were about to rain'). 8. To all appearances he is a Frenchman. 9. Appearances are against him, but appearances are deceptive. 10. After the appearance of the book he was fêted everywhere. 11. She did not notice his appearance. 12. He seized her arm. 13. They took up arms. 14. He seized the arm of his chair. 15. He asked me if I could come. 16. He asked me to (go and) visit them. 17. She asked him the way to the hospital. 18. They asked us for petrol. 19. They have asked me to dinner. 20. He was asked to apologise. 21. He said that that was asking too much. 22. How many people were there in the concert hall? 23. There are many people who never go to the theatre. 24. Several books were on the table. 25. There are no stars in the sky tonight. 26. Their house is at the end of the village. 27. There was a pause and then she asked another question. 28. The facts of the matter are like this: her father went ... 29. He knows how to behave. 30. Why did he behave so badly to her? 31. You/England ought to have behaved differently. 32. She got a 'two' for conduct. 33. He has got no manners. 34. The car belongs to his mother. 35. I am one of his admirers. 36. He is a French national (say: 'belongs to the French state'). 37. They stood there

surrounded by trunks and suitcases. 38. I have lost my cigarette-case. 39. There is a letter-box at the corner of the road. 40. Where did I put the box of matches?

(CATCH – MAN)

41. We just managed to catch the train. 42. We just caught a glimpse of them as they drove past. 43. Mind you don't catch cold. 44. The police caught the thief. 45. I could only catch a few words now and again. 46. At what time did you get home? 47. He has got very old. 48. There are people that one gets on well with. 49. How did the letter get among these papers? 50. During the interval we drank coffee. 51. The second car followed at an interval of a hundred yards. 52. She had no jewelry on. 53. The ring was set with jewels. 54. Do you know Paris? 55. What do you know about it? 56. Do you know French? 57. He knows how to talk. 58. I have a very limited knowledge of this subject. 59. He has devoted his life to the advancement of knowledge ('learning'). 60. I've left it at home. 61. When I left home it was raining. 62. He left it to us (to do). 63. He left her nothing. 64. Don't leave us in the lurch. 65. She looks very young. 66. She looked straight at him. 67. She looked up at him. 68. We had a good look at the museum. 69. Where did you look for it? 70. That is another matter. 71. Those are matters of state (use compound noun). 72. As a matter of fact he is very young. 73. A man who maintains that sort of thing nowadays is very far behind the times. 74. People who prefer to stay at home at the weekend are wise. 75. Man is mortal. 76. People say that royal personages are just like ordinary people. 77. There was a great crowd of people in the square. 78. The English are a strange people. 79. There were women there as well as men. 80. All men are equal.

(NEED – SEE)

81. I need a lot more time. 82. We don't need to leave before 6 o'clock. 83. She is in need of consolation. 84. It needs all your strength. 85. What is needed above all is that you should come immediately. 86. He saw the need for this step. 87. There are still many people who are in need. 88. He ordered a glass of wine. 89. He ordered them to stand up. 90. He likes giving orders. 91. You must not do that even in play. 92. He gives (*gewähren*) free play to his imagination. 93. He put the book on the shelf. 94. Put the paper on the table. 95. He put the money in his pocket. 96. He put the chair up against the table. 97. Just a moment, I must put my glasses on. 98. I was so ill that they had to put me to bed. 99. It has got rather dark. 100. I'd rather come later. 101. It was all rather vague. 102. He is clever rather than stupid. 103. When will you realise that I cannot bear her. 104. She hardly realises the consequences of her behaviour. 105. He finally realised that she didn't like him. 106. Can't you realise what will happen? 107. I really shouldn't say so, but I like him very much. 108. Do you really like him? 109. You really must (come and) visit us. 110. I couldn't see anything. 111. I see it is impossible. 112. I don't see why we

shouldn't visit them. 113. See to it that everything is ready when we get home. 114. Oh, I see, you wanted another piece of cake. 115. Yes, I see, that would be much better.

(SO – WELL)

116. We were very tired and so we went to bed. 117. Will you take us? 118. When does the prime minister take office? 119. What do you take me for? 120. He took it as an insult. 121. I take the view that art is more than amusement. 122. He took more than three years to write the book. 123. His face took on a severer expression than usual. 124. She was quite taken in by his behaviour. 125. I don't like taking part in political discussions. 126. Won't you take off your hat? 127. He took a step back. 128. We shall have to take steps. 129. People who think too much are dangerous. 130. Who were you thinking of? 131. Do you think he will come? 132. It would be better to think it over first. 133. The very thought of it made me sad. 134. Thought and action are two different things (40(d)). 135. That very morning the very worst happened. 136. I knew quite well that he hadn't meant it. 137. He is not so well now as a year ago. 138. They as well as we were very impatient. 139. Well, can you make a suggestion? 140. Can you come too? – Well, it all depends.

Part Three

English Prose Passages
for Translation into German

1 The Looking-glass

People should not leave[1] looking-glasses hanging in their rooms any more than they should leave[1] open cheque books or letters confessing[2] some hideous crime. One could not help[3] looking, that[4] summer afternoon, in the long glass that hung outside in the hall. Chance had so arranged it. From the depths of the sofa in the drawing-room one could see reflected in the Italian glass not only the marble-topped table[5] opposite, but a stretch of the garden beyond. One could see a long grass path leading between banks of tall flowers until the gold rim cut it off.[6]

VIRGINIA WOOLF, *A Haunted House*

1. (63(a)iv). 2. Care: contrive that this verb refers only to 'letters' and see 6(h)ii. 3. (67(e)). 4. (55(d)). 5. Say: 'the with a marble-top provided table' and see 64(c). 6. (60(h)).

2 The Bridge

'What a[1] beautiful bridge,' Aymo said. It was a long plain iron bridge across what[2] was usually a dry river bed.

'We better hurry and get across before they blow it up,' I said.

'There's nobody to blow it up,' Piani said. 'They're all gone.'

'It's probably mined,'[3] Bonello said. 'You cross[4] first, Tenente.'

'Listen[5] to the anarchist,' Aymo said. 'Make[6] him go first.'

'I'll go,' I said. 'It won't be mined[7] to blow up with[8] one man.'

'You see,' Piani said. 'That is[9] brains. Why haven't you brains, anarchist?'

'If I had brains I wouldn't be here,' Bonello said.

ERNEST HEMINGWAY, *A Farewell to Arms*

1. (82). 2. Say: 'across a river bed that was usually dry'. 3. Say: 'they have ... laid mines'. 4. (65(d)). 5. Say: 'hear'. 6. (67(f)). 7. Say: 'so mined that it blows up immediately....' 8. *bei*. 9. Say: 'that I call brains'.

3 Difficulties of Understanding [1]

I drank slowly the green bitter tea, shifting[2] the handleless cup from palm
to palm as[3] the heat scorched my[4] fingers, and I wondered how long I
ought to stay. I tried the family[5] once in French, asking[6,7] when[8] they
expected[9] M. Chou to return,[9] but no one replied: they had probably
not understood. When[8] my cup was empty they refilled it and continued[10]
their own occupations: a woman ironing,[11] a girl sewing,[11] the two boys
at their lessons,[12] the old lady looking[7,11] at her feet, the tiny crippled feet
of old China[13] – and the dog watching[11] the cat, which stayed[14] on the
cardboard boxes.[7]

GRAHAM GREENE, *The Quiet American*

1. Say: 'difficult understanding'. 2. (*64(b)i*). 3. Say: 'when' and see *9(e)*.
4. (*12(b)vi*). 5 Say: 'I tried it once in (*55(e)*) French with the family'.
6. (*81(g)*). 7. (*84*). 8. (*9(e)*). 9. Say: 'expect back'. 10. Add: 'to pursue'.
11. Use finite form of these verbs. 12. Say: 'did their schoolwork'. 13.
(*18(e)*). 14. Add: 'sitting' or 'lying'.

4 The Three-legged Toad

The philosopher Pi-Fu one day[1] committed a fault, and God, looking[2]
down[3] from Heaven, laughed and said to him: 'In your well there is a
three-legged toad. I command you to fish for[4] him every day until you
succeed[5] in bringing him up.'[3] The philosopher spent many weary days
by[6] the well, until at last he sat down to[7] think.[8] 'My fault,' he said to
himself, 'came from the love of[9] money; the love of[9] money makes[10] a
man walk crookedly; the three-legged toad must of necessity walk
crookedly; perhaps he is afflicted as I was.'[11] So he let down[3] into the well
a coin, and sure enough up[3] came the three-legged toad clinging[12] tight
to the coin. Then a peal of laughter came down[3] from Heaven and the
philosopher was once more a free man.

L. H. MYERS, *The Near and the Far*

1. (*21(b)*). 2. (*81(f)*). 3. (*35(d)*). 4. (*79(m)*). 5. (*62(c)*). 6. (*55(d)*). 7. (*63(d)i*).
8. (*84*). 9. (*56(v)*). 10. (*68(b)*). 11. (*43(i)i*). 12. (*79(b)*) and (*64(b)i*).

5 In the Oberammergau [1] Country [1]

I am here in Bavarian[1] Tyrol,[1] near the mountains. They stand up streaked
with snow,[2] so blue, across[3] the valley. The Isar[1] is a quick stream, all
muddy with glacier water now. If ever you come to Germany,[1] come down[4]
the Isarthal.[1] The flowers are in masses, masses, enough to satisfy any
heart[5] alive, and so beautiful.[6] And the clear, clean atmosphere, and the

peasants bare-footed,[7] and the white cows with their cow-bells, it is all so delightful. Yesterday we were at[8] a peasant play – you know this is the Ober-Ammergau[1] country.[1] It was an old Miracle play, with the Devil and Death, and Christ,[1] and Maria – quaint and rather[9] touching. You would like it very much. Some time, come to Bavaria.[1] It is the Minne-singer country. I have been in the Rhineland,[1] and the Mosel[1] land,[10] but I like Bavaria[1] best....

D. H. LAWRENCE, Letters

1. (*17*). 2. Say: 'snow-streaked'. 3. Say: 'over there (*35(a)*) on (*55(f)*)) the other side of'. 4. (*35(d)*). 5. Say: 'soul' and omit 'alive'. 6. Say: 'beautiful ones' (*50(b)*), note). 7. Use attributive adjective. 8. Say: 'in'. 9. (*84*). 10. Say: 'by (*55(d)*)) the Mosel'.

6 Stranded in the East

His history was curious. He had been born[1] in Bavaria[2] and when a[3] youth of twenty-two had taken[4] an active part[4] in the revolutionary movement of 1848. He managed[5] to make his escape and at first found a refuge with a poor watchmaker in Trieste.[2] From there he made his way to Tripoli[2] with a stock of[6] cheap watches to hawk about.[7] It was there[8] he came upon a Dutch[2] traveller – a rather famous man[9] I believe,[10] but I don't remember[11] his name. Engaging[12] him as a sort of assistant[13] the Dutchman[2] took[14] him to the East. They travelled together and[15] separately, collecting[16] insects and birds for four years and more. Then the Dutchman went home[17] and Stein, having[18] no home to go to,[19] remained with an old trader he had come across in his journeyings in the interior[20] of Celebes.[2]

JOSEPH CONRAD, Lord Jim (adapted)

1 (*42(b)ii*). 2. (*17*). 3. Say: 'as a' (*23(b)i*). 4. (*79(c)*). 5. (*62(c)*). 6. Say: 'supply of' (*56(d)*). 7. Say: 'as a hawker'. 8. Say: 'There it was where'. 9. (*23(a)i*). 10. (*6(i)*). 11. (*79(b)*). 12. Say: 'The Dutchman engaged him...and took'. 13. (*23(b)i*). 14. (*84*). 15. Say: 'or also'. 16. (*81(g)*). 17. Add: 'back'. 18. (*81(f)*). 19. Say: 'where he could go to' (*35(b)*). 20. (*29(a)*).

7 A Place to Cross

Later we were[1] on a road that led to a river. There was[1] a long line of abandoned trucks and carts on the road leading[2] up to[3] the bridge. No one was in sight.[4] The river was[1] high and the bridge had been blown up in the centre; the stone[5] arch was fallen into the river and the brown water was going over it.[6] We went on up[7] the bank looking[8] for a place to cross. Up above[9] I knew there was a railway bridge and I thought we might be able[10] to get[8] across there. The path was wet and muddy. We did not see any troops; only abandoned trucks and stores. Along the riverbank there was nothing and no one but[11] the wet brush and muddy ground. We went up to[12] the bank and finally we saw the railway bridge.

ERNEST HEMINGWAY, A Farewell to Arms

1. (*84*) 'be'. 2. (*81(f)*). 3. (*35(e)ii*). 4. Say: 'was to be seen' (*69(f)*). 5. (*24(a)ii*). 6. (*35(e)iii*). 7. (*35(d)*). 8. (*84*). 9. Say: 'further upstream'. 10. (*67(c)*). 11. (*9(b)*). 12. (*52(b)*).

8 Karl Valentin

The late Munich[1] comedian, Karl Valentin – one[2] of the greatest of[3] the rare race of metaphysical clowns – once enacted the following[4] scene: the curtain goes up and reveals darkness; and in this darkness is a solitary[5] circle of light[6] thrown by a street lamp. Valentin, with his long-drawn and deeply worried face, walks round and round[7] this circle of light,[6] desperately looking[8] for something. 'What have you lost?' a policeman asks who has entered the scene.[9] 'The key to my house,'[6] upon which the policeman joins him in his search.[10] They find nothing; and after a while he enquires: 'Are you sure you lost it here?' 'No,' says Valentin, and pointing[11] to a dark corner of the stage: 'Over there.' 'Then why on earth[12] are you looking[8] for it here?' 'There is[13] no light over there,' says Valentin.

ERICH HELLER, The Disinherited Mind

1. (*24(a)iv*). 2. (*50(b)*). 3. Say: 'out of'. 4. (*12(b)ii*). 5. (*40(e)*). 6. Compound noun. 7. Say: 'again and again (*83(e)*) round'. 8. (*84*). 9. Say: 'a policeman who had just supervened' and see *64(c)*. 10. Say: 'helps him to look' (*80(b)*) or (*63(a)iii*). 11. Say: 'and points' and see *79(d)*. 12. (*83(b)*). 13. Start with: 'Over there' and see *43(i)iii* and *83(g)*.

9 Gloomy Forebodings

Esther was not listening. She was thinking[1] of what[2] would happen[3] to her. Would they send her away at the end of the week, or that very[1] afternoon? Would they give her a week's wages,[4] or would they turn her out to find[5] her way back to London as best she might?[6] What should she do if they turned her out-of-doors that very[1] afternoon? Walk back to London? She didn't know how far[7] she had come – a long distance,[8] no doubt, for she had seen woods, hills, rivers, and towns flying[9] past. She'd never be able to find her way back through them[10] miles of country;[11] besides, she couldn't carry her box[1] on her back. What was she to[12] do? Not a friend, not a penny in the world.[13] Now[14] why did[15] such misfortune fall on[16] a poor girl who had never harmed anyone in the world!

GEORGE MOORE, *Esther Waters*

1. (*84*). 2. (*79(a)ii*). 3. (*79(l)*). 4. Say: 'wages (*16*) for a week'. 5. Say: 'so that (*9(d)*) she would have to (*67(e)*) find'. 6. Say: 'as well (*84*) as she could'. 7. Say: 'from how far (*weither*)'. 8. Say: 'very far'. 9. (*63(a)ii*). 10. Say: 'those'. 11. Genitive. 12. (*67(f)*). 13. Expand: 'She had not a single friend in the world and not a single penny in her pocket.' 14. *Ach!* 15. Say: 'had to'. 16. (*79(n)*).

10 In the Drawing-room

It was a large room and most opulently[1] furnished. Men were standing in groups or leaning over the backs of chairs and sofas where[2] ladies were sitting with small cups[3] of coffee in their hands.[3] I noticed[4] in particular an old man with grizzled hair, who was sitting on the arm of a large armchair by the fireplace. He was hale and vigorous, and, from[5] the ease of his position and from the deference with which he seemed to be regarded[6] by the rest, I took[7] him to be the master of the house. He[8] it was who had been strumming on the guitar, but now he had put the instrument down across his knees, and close to it,[9] gently fingering[10] one of the strings, stood a little boy of five or six years old, dressed again most oddly to my notions,[11] whose face immediately interested me, since it reminded[12] me of something which I had already seen.

REX WARNER, *Why Was I Killed?*

1. (*36(b)*). 2. Say: 'on which'. 3. Singular or plural? 4. (*74*). 5. Say: 'as a result of' (*53*). 6. Say: 'treated'. 7. (*79(h)*). 8. (*48(f)ii*). 9. (*43(h)*). 10. (*64(b)i*). 11. Singular, and see *54(l)*. 12. (*79(b)*) and (*48(f)iii*).

11 Pure Reason

Reason[1] is always right. To[2] every question there is[3] only one true[4] answer[2] which with sufficient assiduity can be infallibly discovered, and[5] this applies[6] no less to[6] questions of ethics[7] or politics,[7] of personal and social life, than to[6] the problems of physics[7] or mathematics.[7] Once found,[8] the putting of a solution into practice is a matter[9] of mere technical skill; but the traditional enemies of progress must first be removed, and men[9] taught[10] the importance of acting[11] in all questions on[12] the advice of disinterested scientific experts, whose knowledge[9] is founded[13] on reason and experience. Once this has been achieved, the path is[14] clear[15] to the millennium.

ISAIAH BERLIN, *Karl Marx*

1. (*12(b)i*). 2. (*56(e)*). 3. (*43(i)ii*). 4. Say: 'right'. 5. Omit, and start a new sentence. 6. (*79(d)*). 7. (*16(a)*). 8. Say: 'once (*8(a)*) one has found the solution'. 9. (*84*). 10. (*75*) and (*69(e)*). 11. Say: 'how important it is to act'. 12. Say: 'according to'. 13. (*79(d)*). 14. (*84*): 'be'. 15. Say: 'quite open'.

12 The Return Journey

She got in and put[1] her case[1] in the rack, and the brace of pheasants[2] on top of it.[3] Then she sat down in the corner. The train was rattling through the midlands,[4] and the fog, which came[5] in when she opened the door, seemed to enlarge the carriage and set the four travellers[6] apart. Obviously M.M. – those were the initials on the suit case – had been staying the week-end with[7] a shooting party. Obviously, for she was telling over the story[8] now, lying back[9] in her[10] corner. She did not shut her eyes. But clearly she did not see the man opposite, nor[11] the coloured photograph of York Minster. She must[12] have heard, too, what they had been saying. For as she gazed, her lips moved; now and then she smiled.

VIRGINIA WOOLF, *A Haunted House*

1. (*84*). 2. (*23(a)i*). 3. (*43(h)*). 4. (*17*). 5. Say: 'had come in'. 6. (*29(a)(b)*). 7. *auf.* 8. Say: 'telling to herself in thoughts the whole story'. 9. Say: 'leaning back' and use a past participle. 10. Case? 11. (*10*). 12 (*67(e)*).

13 The Good [1] Samaritan [2]

A man was on his[3] way from Jerusalem down to Jericho when he fell in with[4] robbers, who stripped him, beat him and went off leaving[5] him half dead. It so happened that[6] a priest was going down by[7] the same road; but when he saw him, he went past on the other side. So too a Levite[2] came to the place, and when he saw him went past on the other side. But a Samaritan[2] who was making the journey came upon him,[8] and when he saw him was moved to[9] pity. He went up and bandaged his wounds, bathing them with oil and wine. Then he lifted him on to his own beast, brought him to an inn, and looked after him there. Next day[10] he produced two silver pieces and gave them to the innkeeper, and said, 'Look[5] after him: and if you[11] spend any more, I will repay you on my way back.'

St Luke 10: 30–36 (New English Bible version)

1. Say: 'merciful'. 2. (*17*). 3. Say: 'the'. 4. (*79(p)*). 5. (*84*). 6. Say: 'By chance a …'. 7. Omit. 8. Say: 'found him there'. 9. Say: 'by'. 10. (*55(d)*). 11. (*43(b)*, note 2).

14 Murder?

He devoted[1] himself to the viands with a[2] ravenous gusto, while the old man, leaning backward, watched him with steady, curious eyes.[3]

'You[4] have blood on[5] your shoulder, my[2] man,' he said.

Montigny must[6] have laid[7] his wet right hand upon him as[8] he left the house. He cursed Montigny in his heart.

'It was none of my shedding,'[9] he stammered.

'I had not supposed so,'[10] returned his host quietly. 'A brawl?'

'Well,[10] something of that sort,'[11] Villon admitted with a quaver.[12]

'Perhaps a fellow murdered?'

'Oh, no, not murdered,' said the poet, more and more confused.[13] 'It was all fair play – murdered by accident.[14] I had no hand in it, God strike me dead!'[15] he added fervently.

'One rogue the fewer, I dare say,'[16] observed the master of the house.

'You may dare to say that,'[17] agreed Villon, infinitely relieved.

R. L. STEVENSON, New Arabian Nights

1. Say: 'fell upon' (79(n)). 2. Omit. 3. Say: 'with unaverted gaze (21(c)) inquisitively'. 4. (43(b), note 2). 5. (55(d)). 6. (67(e)). 7. Say: 'touched ... with'. 8. (9(a)). 9. Say: 'It was not I (43(i)v) who ...'. 10. (84). 11. (51(b)). 12. Say: 'with a quavering voice' (12(b)iii). 13. Add: 'becoming' and see 31(d)ii. 14. (54(a)). 15. Say: 'God strike me dead (73(a)i) if I had anything to do with it'. 16. Say: 'if I may (67(b)) say so'. 17. Say: 'you may well say that'.

15 View from the Veranda

In front of the house where[1] we lived the mountain went down[2] steeply to the little plain along[3] the lake and we sat on the porch[4] of the house in the sun and saw the winding[5] of the road down[6] the mountain-side and the terraced vineyards[7] on the side of the lower mountain, the vines[8] all dead now for the winter and the fields[9] divided[10] by[11] stone walls, and below the vineyards the houses of the town on the narrow plain along[3] the lake shore. There was[12] an island with two trees on[13] the lake and the trees looked[14] like the double sails[15] of a fishing boat. The mountains were sharp and steep on the other side of the lake and down at the end of the lake was[12] the plain of the Rhone valley flat between the two ranges of mountains; and up the valley where the mountains cut it off was the Dent du Midi.[16] It was a high snowy mountain and it dominated the valley but it was so far away that it did not make[17] a shadow.

ERNEST HEMINGWAY, A Farewell to Arms

1. Say: 'in which'. 2. (60(h)). 3. (55(d)). 4. American English for 'veranda'. 5. Plural. 6. (35(d)). 7. Compound noun: 'vineyard-terraces'. 8. Add:

'which were'. 9. Say: 'vineyards', since *Felder* suggests 'arable fields'.
10. *(64(c))*. 11. *(69(c))*. 12. *(84)*: 'be'. 13. Say: 'in'. 14. *(84)*. 15. *(15 II(c)iii)*.
16. Masculine. 17. Say: 'cast'.

16 The Elm

The charm of the English scene owes[1] more to the elm than any other tree,
not least[2] in[3] winter or in[3] early spring when the tracery of its aspiring
boughs is topped with a purple mist of flowers. Nevertheless, the tree is as[4]
dangerous as[4] precious, and often becomes[5] a threat before its days of
decay[6] set in. A few years ago, on a singularly hot September day, lunch-
eon[7] for a shooting party was spread[7] out of doors.[8] The noble lord, on
returning[9] with his guests, was horrified to see that the table had been
placed under an elm. Being[10] an observant[11] countryman he endorsed
the maxims of both Kipling and Jeffries, stressing[12] the hostility of
'ellum' to[13] man. He ordered[14] an immediate change of site, which[15] was
regarded as a superfluous excess of[16] care. In the midst of[17] the meal a
crash was heard and a heavy elm bough fell[18] where the table had been.[19]

W. BEACH THOMAS, (*in*) *The Observer*

1. *(75)*. 2. *(36(c)i)*. 3. *(12(b)i)*. 4. *(31(d)i)*. 5. *(79(u))*. 6. Say: 'the days of its
decay'. 7. Say: 'the table was laid for lunch' *(12(b)i)*. 8. *(55(l))*. 9. *(54(b))*.
10. *(81(c))*. 11. Say: 'attentively observing'. 12. *(81(f))*. 13. *(56(k))*. 14. *(84)*.
15. *(48(f)vii)*. 16. *(56(d))*. 17. *(53(b))*. 18. Add: 'just there'. 19. *(84)* 'be'.

17 The Apparition

I looked[1] up and saw descending[2] the wide staircase in front of me a tall
and beautiful woman, whose appearance[3] at once surprised me, for her
clothes were like none[4] which I had ever seen, but reminded me of the
pictures in old books which I used to[5] read in my childhood -- pictures of
the men and women who lived sixty or seventy years ago.

The lady reached the bottom of the stairs and, as[6] she walked slowly
towards[7] me, I took a step[8] to meet[9] her, being uncertain as to[10] how I
should explain my appearance[1] here, and yet strangely unembarrassed by[11]
the evident necessity for doing so.[12] She looked directly[13] into my eyes,
smiling very sweetly, but without showing[14] the least awareness[14] of
my presence, so that[15] I realized[1] once more that I was invisible to her, and
I stepped aside to let her pass towards the door on my left.[15]

REX WARNER, *Why Was I Killed?*

1. *(84)*. 2. *(81(f)* or *(e))*. 3. Omit 'whose' and begin a new sentence: 'Her
appearance' *(84)*. 4. Say: 'were such as I had never yet seen' and see *43(d)*.

5. ($59(b)i$). 6. ($9(a)$). 7. ($79(d)$). 8. Say: 'went a step' and see $20(b)$. 9. ($60(h)$). 10. Omit 'as to'. 11. ($56(u)$). 12. Use infinitive construction. 13. Omit. 14. Say: 'showing in the least ($36(c)i$) that she was in any way ($83(f)$) aware ($21(d)$) of'. 15. ($9(d)$). 16. ($55(d)$).

18 Work

Work is of two kinds[1]: first,[2] altering[3] the position of matter[4] at or near the earth's[5] surface[5] relatively[6] to other such matter; second,[2] telling other people to do so.[4] The first kind is unpleasant and ill paid;[7] the second is pleasant and highly paid.[7] The second kind is capable[8] of indefinite extension: there are not only those[9] who give orders, but[10] those[9] who give advice[11] as to what[11] orders should be given. Usually two opposite kinds of advice[12] are given[7] simultaneously by two organised bodies of men; this is called politics. The skill required[13] for this kind of work is[14] not knowledge[4] of the subjects as to[15] which advice is given,[7] but[10] knowledge[4] of the art of persuasive speaking and writing,[16] i.e. of advertising.

BERTRAND RUSSELL, *In Praise of Idleness*

1. Say: 'There are ($43(i)iii$, note) two kinds of ($40(d)$) work'. 2. ($40(h)$). 3. Use infinitive + *zu* construction. 4. (84). 5. Compound noun. 6. Say: 'in relatio to' and see $56(v)$. 7. Statal or actional passive? See $69(g)$. 8. ($21(d)$, note). 9. ($49(d)$). 10. ($9(b)$). 11. ($79(v)i$). 12. Omit: 'kinds of' and use plural form. 13. Add: 'which is'. 14. Say: 'is not based on' ($79(e)$). 15. ($56(p)$). 16. Say: 'of the art of persuasion (compound noun) in word and writing'.

19 The Professor's Beard

'Listen,[1] Inglés,' Agustin said. 'How did you happen to[2] come to Spain? Pay no attention[3] to Pablo. He is drunk.'

'I came first[4] twelve years ago to study the country and the language,'[5] Robert Jordan said. 'I teach Spanish in[6] a university.'

'You look[7] very like a professor,' Primitivo said.

'He has no beard,' Pablo said. 'Look at him. He has no beard.'

'Are you truly a professor?'

'An instructor.'[8]

'But you teach?'

'Yes.'

'But why Spanish?' Andrés asked. 'Would it not be easier to teach English since you are English?'[9]

'He speaks Spanish as we do,'[10] Anselmo said. 'Why should he not teach Spanish?'

'Yes. But it is, in a way,[11] presumptuous[12] for a foreigner to teach Spanish,' Fernando said. 'I mean nothing against you,[13] Don Roberto.'

'He's a false professor,' Pablo said, very pleased with himself. 'He hasn't got a beard.'

ERNEST HEMINGWAY, *For Whom the Bell Tolls*

1. Say: 'just (65(g)) hear'. 2. For 'happen to' use *eigentlich*. 3. (79(d)). 4. Say: 'the first time'. 5. Say: 'to get to know the country and study the language'. 6. (55(d)). 7. (84). 8. American English for 'university teacher'. 9. Use the noun here. 10. Say: 'exactly as we'. 11. (83(f)). 12. Say: 'a presumption'. 13. Say: 'no harm meant'.

20 Rest in the Desert

Night came upon us whilst labouring across gullies and sandy mounds, and we were obliged[1] to come to a standstill[2] quite suddenly, upon the very[3] edge of a precipitous descent. Every step towards[4] the Dead Sea had brought us into a country more and more dreary; and this sand hill which we were forced to choose for[5] our resting-place was dismal enough. A few slender blades of grass which here and there singly[6] pierced the sand, mocked bitterly[7] the hunger of our jaded beasts, and with our small remaining fragment of goat's milk rock[8] by way of[9] supper, we were not much better off than our horses; we wanted,[10] too, the great requisite[11] of a cheery bivouac – fire! Moreover, the spot on[12] which we had been so suddenly brought to a standstill[13] was relatively high, and unsheltered, and the night wind blew swiftly and cold.

A. W. KINGLAKE, *Eothen*

1. (69(g)). 2. Say: 'stop'. 3. (84). 4. (54(e)). 5. Say: 'as' and see 23(b). 6. (40(f)). 7. Say: 'were bitter mockery for'. 8. Say: 'of very hard (24(d)) goat's cheese' (compound noun). 9. Say: 'as'. 10. Care! (62(e)). 11. Say: 'the very (84) most necessary thing for' and see 29(f) and 56(v). 12. (55(d)). 13. Say: 'had to stop'.

21 Queen Victoria in Germany

Another year,[1] Germany was visited, and Albert displayed the beauties of his home. When Victoria crossed the frontier, she was much excited – and she was astonished as well. 'To hear the people speak German,' she noted[2] in[3] her diary, 'and to see the German soldiers, etc., seemed to me so singular.' Having recovered[4] from this slight shock, she found the country charming. She was fêted everywhere, crowds[5] of the surrounding royalties[6] swooped down[7] to welcome her, and the prettiest groups of children, dressed[8] in their best clothes, presented her with bunches of flowers. The principality of Coburg,[9] with its romantic scenery and its well-behaved inhabitants, particularly delighted her; and when she woke up one morning[10] to[11] find herself in 'dear Rosenau, my Albert's birth-place,'[12] it was 'like a beautiful dream.' On[13] her return home, she expatiated, in a letter to[14] King Leopold, upon the pleasures of the trip, dwelling[4] especially upon the intensity of her affection for[15] Albert's native land.

LYTTON STRACHEY, Queen Victoria

1. (42(c)iii). 2. Say: 'wrote'. 3. Case? See 55(a). 4. (81(c)). 5. Say: 'a whole crowd'. 6. Say: 'royal personages (84: 'man') of the surroundings (16). 7. Add: 'on her' and see 55(a). 8. Omit and replace by 'all'. 9. (17). 10. (21(b)). 11. Say 'and found herself'. 12. (23(a)). 13. Say: 'after'. 14. (56(c)). 15. (56(v)).

22 Faust

Such[1] is the spirit, and such are the conditions, in which Faust[1] undertakes his adventures. He thirsts[2] for all experience, including[3] all experience of evil;[4] he fears no hell; and he hopes[5] for no happiness. He trusts[5] in magic; that is, he believes, or is willing to make believe,[6] that apart from any settled conditions laid down by[7] nature or God, personal will can evoke the experience it covets[8] by its sheer force[9] and assurance. His bond with Mephistopheles is an expression of this romantic faith. It[10] is no bargain to buy[10] pleasures on earth[11] at the cost of[12] torments hereafter; for neither Goethe, nor Faust, nor Mephistopheles believes[13] that such pleasures are[14] worth having,[15] or such torments possible.

GEORGE SANTAYANA, Three Philosophical Poets

1. Say: 'in such spirit and in such circumstances (55(o)) Faust ...'. 2. (62(e)). 3. (53). 4. (29(a)). 5. (79(d)). 6. (73(b)iii). 7. (64(c)). 8. Say: 'the coveted experience'. 9. Say: 'through its very (84) force ... alone'. 10. Make the infinitive phrase the subject and omit 'it'. 11. Say: 'earthly joys'. 12. = 'with'. 13. Singular or plural   See 11. 14. Mood   See 71(d). 15. Say: 'worth the trouble' (21(e)).

23 The Way Out

'What would you like[1] me to read to you, Uncle Hector?' asked Jasmine when the house was silent.[2]

'Well,[3] really, I don't know,' he said. 'I don't think there's anything nowadays worth reading.[4] I don't care[5] about these modern writers. I don't understand them. But if they came to me as patients I should know how[6] to prescribe for them.'

'Shall[1] I read you some[7] Dickens?' Jasmine suggested.

'It's hardly worth while[8] beginning[9] a long novel at this time of evening.'[10]

'I might[11] read you *The Christmas Carol*.'

'Oh, I know[3] that by heart,' said Sir Hector.

'Well,[3] what shall[1] I read you? Shall[1] I read you something from[12] Thackeray's *Book of Snobs*?'

'No, I know that by heart, too,' said Sir Hector.

'If you don't like[5] modern writers, and you know all the other writers by heart ...'

'Well,[3] if you want to read something,' said Sir Hector at last, as if he were gratifying a spoilt child, 'you had better read[13] me Mr. Balfour's speech[14] in the House last night.'

COMPTON MACKENZIE, Rich Relatives

1. (*67(f)*). 2. Say: 'when everything was quiet in the house'. 3. (*84*). 4. (*24(a)i*). 5. (*67(d)*). 6. Say: 'what I ought to (*67(e)*) prescribe to them'. 7. Say: 'something from'. 8. (*62(b)*). 9. Construction? 10. Say: 'so late in the evening'. 11. (*67(c)*). 12. Say: 'out of'. 13. Say: 'you might (*67(c)*) rather (*84*) read'. 14. Say: 'speech which Mr. B. made'.

24 Revolutions in Germany

There has never been[1] a successful revolutionary movement in Germany based[2] on the desire for[3] political and social liberty. The revolution of 1848 cost few lives and failed for[4] lack of[5] unity of[6] aim and strength of purpose. That[7] of November[8] 1918 was ... largely the result of defeat and war weariness and, when it occurred, the republican parties were more concerned[9] to secure internal order than to break the power of the ruling classes of Imperial Germany.[10] The sense of[11] reverence for[12] the army, as the one[13] great instrument of national unity, transcending[14] all their social, religious and political differences, of which the Germans were acutely[15] aware, survived the revolution and carried with it the acceptance of a hierarchical society in which leadership was the function of an 'officer' class, whether[16] in the army or[16] the civil service, in agriculture or in industry.

E. J. PASSANT, A Short History of Germany, 1815–1945

1. (*43(i)iii*, note). 2. (*79(e)*) and use a relative clause. 3. (*56(o)*). 4. (*54(a)*). 5. (*56(d)*). 6. Say: 'a united'. 7. (*49(c)*). 8. (*12(b)i*). 9. (*79(d)*). 10. (*12(b)i*) and (*18(e)*). 11. Omit 'sense of'. 12. (*56(t)*). 13. (*23(b)*). 14. Say: 'superior to' (*56(p)*). 15. Say: 'extraordinarily'. 16. (*11*).

25 After the Quarrel

For a moment[1] she looked[2] at him with the utmost[3] compassion. Then her eyes filled with tears. She covered her face with her hands and went quickly out of the room. The man took a pace forward as[4] though to follow[4] her.

But it seemed that he realized[5] that further argument would be unfruitful and even comfort, at[6] the moment, misplaced. He stepped[7] back again to the fireplace and sat down. For some seconds[1] he stared into the fire, and then took up as it were idly with[8] one hand a copy of an illustrated magazine from a table at his side. As he turned over the leaves I noticed what seemed[9] to me quaint photographs of bearded generals, of horses galloping madly[10] as in long trains they drew small and old-fashioned guns, of antiquated warships and of royal personages. The man looked[2] intently at these photographs, and when, in[11] his perusal of the magazine, he came upon[12] a recruiting advertisement, he surveyed it thoughtfully for some time.[1]

REX WARNER, Why Was I Killed?

1. $(34(c))$. 2. (84). 3. Say: 'with the deepest'. 4. $(73(b)iii$, note). 5. Say: 'he seemed to realise' (84). 6. Say: 'at this moment' $(55(l))$. 7. Say: 'went'. 8. Add: 'only'. 9. Say: 'saw to me quaintly appearing photographs' and see $64(c)$. 10. $(55(l))$. 11. $(54(b))$. 12. $(79(d))$.

26 The Lighthouse

So fine was the morning except for a streak of wind here and there that the sea and sky looked[1] all one fabric, as if[2] sails were stuck high up in[3] the sky, or[4] the clouds had dropped down into the sea. A steamer far out[5] at[6] sea had drawn in[7] the air a great scroll of smoke which stayed there curving[8] and circling[8] decoratively, as if[2] the air were a fine gauze which held things and kept them softly in its mesh,[9] only gently swaying them this way and that.[10] And as[11] happens sometimes when the weather is very fine, the cliffs looked as if[2] they were conscious of the ships, and the ships looked as if[2] they were conscious of the cliffs, as if[2] they signalled to each other some secret message of their own.[12] For[13] sometimes quite close to[3] the shore, the Lighthouse looked this morning in the haze[14] an enormous distance away.[15]

VIRGINIA WOOLF, To the Lighthouse

1. Say: 'looked as if $(73(b)iii$, note) made of $(54(a))$ one fabric'. 2. $(73(b)iii)$. 3. $(55(d))$. 4. Repeat: 'as if'. 5. $(35(a))$. 6. $(55(f))$. 7. $(55(b))$. 8. $(81(g))$. 9. Plural. 10. $(35(e)i)$. 11. $(9(a))$. 12. $(44(c))$. 13. Say: 'although the lighthouse seemed sometimes to be'. 14. Add: 'as if it were'. 15. Say: 'enormously far away'.

27 Germany before the Thirty Years' War

Germany was a network of roads knotted[1] together at the intersections by the great clearing-houses at Frankfort on the Main,[2] Frankfort on the Oder,[2] Leipzig, Nuremberg,[2] Augsburg. West Indian[2] sugar reached Europe[2] from[3] the refineries of Hamburg, Russian[2] furs from Leipzig, salt fish from Lübeck, oriental silks and spices from Venice[2] through Augsburg, copper, salt, iron, sandstone, corn were carried down the Elbe[2] and Oder,[2] Spanish[2] and English[2] wool woven[4] in Germany competed with Spanish and English cloth in[5] the European[2] market, and the wood that built[6] the Armada was shipped from Danzig. The continual passage of merchants, the going and coming[7] of strangers had more powerfully affected German development than any other single[8] cause. Commerce was[9] her[10] existence, and her[10] cities were more thickly spread[11] than those[12] of any[13] country in Europe. German[14] civilisation centred in the small town, but the activities[15] of her[10] traders, the concourse of foreigners to the fairs at Leipzig and Frankfort, drew the interests[15] of the Germans outwards and[16] away from their own country.

C. V. WEDGWOOD, The Thirty Years War

1. Use a relative clause. 2. (*17*). 3. Say: 'via' (*55(m)*). 4. (*64(c)*). 5. (*55(f)*). 6. Say: 'of which the Armada was built'. 7. Say: 'the coming and going'. 8. (*40(e)*). 9. Say: 'Her existence was based on (*79(e)*) commerce'. 10. Care! 11. Say: 'lay more thickly together (*beieinander*)'. 12. (*49(c)*). 13. Say: 'any other' and see *83(f)* or *50(d)*. 14. Say: 'of Germany'. 15. Singular. 16. Omit.

28 Everywhere at Home

'Pleasant place, Rome,'[1] he murmured: 'you'll like[2] it.' It was[3] some minutes later that[3] he added: 'But I wouldn't go just now, if I were you:[4] too jolly hot.'

'*You* haven't been to Rome,[1] have you?' I inquired.

'Rather,'[5] he replied briefly: 'I live there....'

'But you don't really live there, do you?'

'Well,'[5] he said, 'I live there as much as[6] I live anywhere. About half the year sometimes. I've got a sort of a[7] shanty there. You must come and see[5] it some day.'

'But do you live anywhere else[8] as well?' I went on.

'O yes, all over the place,'[9] was his vague reply. 'And I've got a diggings somewhere off[10] Piccadilly.'

'Where's that?' I inquired.

'Where's what?' said he. 'O, Piccadilly! It's in London.'

'Have you a large garden?' I asked; 'and how many pigs have you got?'

'I've got no garden at all,' he replied sadly, 'and they don't allow[11] me to keep pigs, though I'd like too, awfully. It's very hard.'

KENNETH GRAHAME, The Golden Age

N.B. (*83*) should be consulted for the use of such words as *denn, doch, etwa, ja, mal, nun, schon.*

1. (*17*). 2. (*74*). 3. (*43(i)vi*). 4. (*55(d)*). 5. (*84*). 6. Say: 'as good as'. 7. Omit. 8. (*35(a)*). 9. Say: 'here, there and everywhere' (*35(a)*). 10. Say: 'in the region of'. 11. Say: 'I'm not allowed to' (*67(b)*).

29 Life [1]

Life,[1] at[2] all times full of pain, is more painful in[2] our time than in the two centuries that preceded[3] it. The attempt to escape[3] from pain drives men[4] to triviality, to self-deception, to the invention of vast collective myths. But these momentary alleviations do but[5] increase the sources of suffering in the long run.[6] Both private and public misfortune can[7] only be[7] mastered by a process[8] in which[8] will and intelligence interact: the part of will is[9] to refuse to shirk the evil or accept[4] an unreal solution, while the part of intelligence is to understand it, to find a cure if it is curable, and, if not, to make it bearable by seeing[8] it in its relations,[10] accepting[4] it as unavoidable, and remembering[11] what lies outside it in other regions, other ages, and the abysses of interstellar space.

BERTRAND RUSSELL, *In Praise of Idleness*

1. *(12(b)i)*. 2. *(54(r))*. 3. *(74)*. 4. *(84)*. 5. *(63(c)ii)*. 6. *(55(e))*. 7. *(68(f))*. 8. *(81(b))*. 9. *(43(i)i)*. 10. Add: 'to the whole' *(29(a))*. 11. *(48(f)vi)*.

30 The Prime Minister

Meantime Monostatos was reporting[1] to the Queen what had occurred. He began by[2] complaining of[3] Papageno, as he had often done[4] before. But on[5] that point the Queen was obdurate. She said that she liked[6] Papageno and that was[6] the long and short of it,[7] and if he misbehaved[6] himself, it couldn't[6] be helped.[8] So Monostatos shrugged his shoulders and went on to more important matters. Being an able and ambitious man, he was impatient[9] of all this business of love,[10] in which he was expected to mix himself up.[11] Power was his aim, and, as he well knew, the surest way to power was war. He proposed therefore to the Queen that he should take[12] up arms against Sarastro, pretending[13] that, in[14] this way, he could compel[15] him to give up Pamina. Since he was an intelligent man he knew that this was nonsense; for he knew that Sarastro would not fight, in that way, nor[16] could Pamina so be won. But he knew also that the Queen, being romantic, loved war; that she would believe that the right[17] cause must[6] triumph; and that she would be sure her own cause must[6] be right.[17]

G. LOWES DICKINSON, *The Magic Flute*

1. *(75)*. 2. *(79(l))* and *(79(a)ii)*. 3. *(79(n))*. 4. *(43(i)i)*. 5. *(55(l))*. 6. *(71(a)i)*. 7. Say: 'that was finally everything'. 8. Say: 'one must accept *(84)* the situation'. 9. Say: 'he had no patience with'. 10. Say: 'this whole chapter concerning love'. 11. Say: 'to mix himself up in which one expected of him'. 12. *(84)*. 13. *(73(b)iii)* and *(81(b))*. 14. *(55(e))*. 15. *(79(u))* and *(79(a)ii)*. 16. *(10)*. 17. Say: 'just'.

31 The Englishman

Instinctively the Englishman is no missionary, no conqueror. He prefers[1] the country to the town, and home to foreign parts. He is rather glad and relieved if only natives will remain natives and strangers strangers, and[2] at[3] a comfortable distance from himself.[4] Yet outwardly[5] he is most[6] hospitable and accepts[7] almost anybody[8] for the time being; he travels and conquers without a settled design, because he has the instinct of[9] exploration. His adventures are all external; they change him so little that he is not afraid[10] of them. He carries his English weather in his heart wherever[11] he goes, and it becomes[12] a cool spot in the desert, and a steady and sane oracle amongst[13] all the deliriums of mankind. Never since the heroic days[14] of Greece[15] has the world had such a sweet, just, boyish master. It will be a black day for the human race when scientific blackguards, conspirators, churls, and fanatics manage[16] to supplant him.

GEORGE SANTAYANA, *Soliloquies in England*

1. (6(*b*)). 2. Say: 'to be precise' (*10*). 3. (55(*l*)). 4. (49(*f*)). 5. (35(*e*)*ii*). 6. (36(*c*)*ii*). 7. (*84*). 8. (50(*d*)). 9. Say: 'for'. 10. (79(*s*)). 11. Care! See 5, *8(a)* and 35(*b*). 12. (79(*u*)). 13. Say: 'in the midst of' (*53*). 14. Say: 'time'. 15. (*17*). 16. (62(*c*)).

32 The Clerk

I knew a man, said the voice, and he was a clerk. He had[1] thirty shillings[2] a[3] week and for[4] five years he had never missed a day going[5] to his work. He was a careful man, but a person[6] with[7] a wife and four children cannot save much out of[8] thirty shillings[2] a[3] week. The rent of a house is high, a wife and children must be fed, and they have to get[9] boots and clothes, so that at the end of each week that man's thirty shillings used to be[10] all gone. But they managed to get along somehow – the man and his wife and the four children were fed and clothed and educated, and the man often wondered how so much could be done with so little money; but the reason[11] was that his wife was a careful woman ... and then the man got[9] sick. A poor person[6] cannot afford to get sick, and a married man cannot leave[9] his work. If he is sick he has to be sick; but he must go to his work all the same,[12] for if he stayed away, who would pay the wages[13] and feed his family? and when[14] he went back to work he might[15] find that there was[16] nothing for him to do.

JAMES STEPHENS, *The Crock of Gold*

1. Say: 'earned'. 2. (*41*). 3. (*12(b)v*). 4. (*34(c)*). 5. Say: 'to go'. 6. (*84*): 'man'. 7. Say: 'who has'. 8. Say: 'from'. 9. (*84*). 10. Say: 'was always'. 11. Add: 'for it'. 12. (*10*). 13. (*16(a)*). 14. Use *wenn*. Mood? 15. (*67(c)*). 16. (*43(i)ii*).

33 Humpty Dumpty

There was[1] a long pause.

'Is that all?' Alice timidly asked.

'That's all,' said Humpty Dumpty. 'Good-bye'.

This was rather[2] sudden, Alice-thought: but after such a *very* strong hint that she ought to be going, she felt that it would hardly be civil to stay. So she got up and held out her hand. 'Good-bye, till we meet[3] again!' she said as cheerfully as she could.

'I shouldn't know[4] you if we *did*[5] meet,' Humpty Dumpty replied in a discontented tone, giving her one of his fingers to shake:[6] 'you're so exactly like other people.'

'The face is what one goes by, generally,'[7] Alice remarked in a thoughtful tone.

'That's just what[8] I complain of,'[8] said Humpty Dumpty, 'Your face is the same as everybody has[9] – the two eyes, so – ' (marking the places in the air with his[10] thumb) 'nose in the middle, mouth under. It's always the same. Now if you had the two eyes on the same side of the nose, for instance – or the mouth at the top[11] – that would be *some* help.'[12]

'It wouldn't look nice,' Alice objected. But Humpty Dumpty only shut his[10] eyes and said, 'Wait till you've tried.'[13]

LEWIS CARROLL, *Through the Looking-glass*

1. *(84)*: 'be'. 2. Say: 'but'. 3 *(61(b))*. 4. Say: 'recognise'. 5. *(59(b)i)*. 6. Use the phrase *zum Abschied reichen*. 7. Say: 'One generally recognises people by *(79(c))* their face'. 8. *(48(f)v)* and *(79(n))*. 9. Say: 'You have a face like everybody else' *(50(d))*. 10. *(12(b)vi)*. 11. *(35(a))*. 12. Say: 'that would at least help *something*'. 13. *(43(i)i)*.

34 The Beginning of a New Epoch

With few exceptions Germany's intellectual spokesmen welcomed the downfall of absolutism as a[1] blessing for France and an[1] omen of[2] German liberty; but the rapid change in[3] the character of the movement was followed[4] by a revulsion on the part of[5] the spectators, and men like Klopstock who had led the applause,[6] now hurled their thunderbolts against the savages on[7] the Seine.[8] After the outbreak of war, the September[9] massacres, and the execution of the King, few voices were raised[10] on behalf of[11] French principles. Yet the impressions produced by the events of 1789 were never effaced, for the subjects had learned to hope and rulers to fear. Moreover the failure of Brunswick's[8] invasion showed that the Revolution could not be suppressed by foreign arms. On the evening of[12] Valmy, Goethe, who had accompanied Karl August of Weimar to[13] the front, was asked[14] what he thought[15] of the situation. 'Here and today commences a new epoch of world-history,' he replied, 'and you can boast that you were present at its birth.'

G. P. GOOCH, *Germany*

1. (*23(b)ii*). 2. (*56(i)*). 3. Say: 'of'. 4. Use the construction: *zur Folge haben*. 5. Say: 'among' (*55(o)*). 6. Say: 'who had been the first to applaud' (*38(g)*). 7. (*55(d)*). 8. (*17*). 9. Say: 'of September' (*18(h)*). 10 (*69(h)i*). 11. (*53(a)*). 12. Say: 'after' 13. (*55(c)*). 14. (*69(h)iv*). 15. (*79(r)*).

35 Rain in the Holidays

Their room, though[1] it was a back room facing[1] into the pinewoods, had a balcony; they would[2] run away from[3] the salon and spend the long wet afternoons there. They would[2] lie down covered[4] with coats, leaving the window open, smelling the wet woodwork, hearing the gutters run. Turn abouts, they would[2] read aloud to each other[5] the Tauchnitz novels[6] they had bought in Lucerne.[7] Things for tea,[8] the little stove, and a bottle of[9] violet methylated spirits stood on the wobbly commode between their beds, and at four o'clock Portia would[2] make tea. They ate, in alternate mouthfuls,[10] block chocolate and brioches. Postcards they liked, and Irene's[11] and Portia's[11] sketches were pinned[12] to the pine walls; stockings they had just washed would[2] be exposed[13] to dry[14] on the radiator, although the heating was off.[15] Sometimes they heard a cow bell in the thick[16] distance, or people talking German in the room next door. Between five and six the rain quite[17] often stopped, wet light crept[18] down the trunks of the pines. Then they rolled[19] off their beds, put their shoes on, and walked down the village street to the view-point[20] over[21] the lake.

ELIZABETH BOWEN, *The Death of the Heart*

1. Say: 'Though their room at the back (*35(e)ii*) faced the'. 2. Care! (*59(b)i*, note). 3. Say: 'steal away out of'. 4. Say: 'and cover themselves with their'. 5. (*46(a)*). 6. Use compound noun. 7. (*17*). 8. Say: 'everything for (*zum*) tea'. 9. Say: 'with'. 10. Say: 'in mouthfuls (*33(a)*) alternately'. 11. (*18(a)*). 12. (*79(b)*). 13. Say: 'spread out'. 14. (*80(b)*). 15. Say: 'turned off'. 16. Say: 'fog-thick'. 17. Say: 'fairly'. 18. Say: 'seeped down'. 19. Say: 'rolled down from'. 20 Say: 'to the point where one had a view'. 21. (*56(p)*).

36 Outside the School

I was standing outside[1] a large building of red brick[2] which was evidently a school. In front of me, through two or three congested exits, boys and girls were streaming out on to the black asphalt playground, jostling,[3] screaming,[3] pushing[3] each other, laughing,[3] forming[3] into small groups or darting[3] hither and thither[4] over[5] the hard black ground. Behind my back[6] a red winter sun was setting and was now near[7] the horizon, so that, as[8] I stood at the top of a short flight of steps overlooking the playground, my shadow seemed monstrously enlarged, cutting[9] right across the asphalt and the eager bodies and faces of the children. The door nearest[7] to me seemed to be confined[10] to the use of[11] boys, and nearly all of those[12] who came out of it[13] passed through or along[14] my shadow. Some of these would[15] look up suddenly in my direction[16] almost as if they had been momentarily startled, but no one showed me any sign of recognition.

REX WARNER, Why Was I Killed?

1. (55(p)). 2. Plural. 3. Use *wobei* and see 81(c). 4. (35(e)i). 5. (55(a)). 6. Say: 'behind me'. 7. (22(d)). 8. (9(a)). 9. Say: 'and fell hard and sharp'. 10. (79(d)). 11. Say: 'for'. 12. (49(d)). 13. Say: 'this door'. 14. Say: 'through my shadow or along it' and see 35(e)ii. 15. Care! See 59(b)i, note. 16. Say: 'towards me' (35(e)ii).

37 Visit at Night

The sound of his blows echoed through the house with thin, phantasmal reverberations,[1] as though it were quite empty; but these[2] had scarcely[3] died away before[3] a measured tread drew near, a couple of bolts were withdrawn, and one wing was opened broadly, as though no guile or fear of guile were known[4] to those[5] within.[6] A tall figure of a man,[7] muscular and spare, but a little bent, confronted Villon. The head was massive in bulk,[8] but finely sculptured; the nose[9] blunt at the bottom,[6] but refining upwards[10] to[11] where it joined a pair of strong and honest eyebrows; the[11] mouth and eyes[12] surrounded with delicate markings, and the whole face based[13] upon a thick white beard, boldly and squarely trimmed. Seen as it was[14] by the light of a flickering hand-lamp,[15] it looked[16] perhaps nobler than it had a right to do;[17] but it was a fine face, honourable rather[16] than intelligent, strong, simple and righteous.

R. L. STEVENSON, New Arabian Nights

1. Say: 'echo'. 2. Say: 'this'. 3. (9(e)). 4. (22(d)). 5. (49(c)). 6. (35(a)). 7. Say: 'a man of tall figure'. 8. Omit 'in bulk'. 9. Add: 'was'. 10. (35(b)). 11. Omit. 12. Add: 'were'. 13. Say: 'rested'. 14. Omit 'as it was'. 15. Say: 'by (54(b)) the flickering light of a hand-lamp'. 16. (84). 17. Say: 'that it should have (67(f)) looked by right' (53(b)).

38 Advice to [1] Foreigners

If you[2] are learning English because you intend to travel in England and wish to be understood there, do not try to speak English perfectly, because, if you do,[3] no one will understand you.

No foreigner can ever stress the syllables and make[4] the voice rise and fall in question and answer, assertion and denial, refusal and consent, exactly[5] as a native does.[5]

Therefore the first thing[6] you have to do is to speak with a strong foreign accent, and speak broken English: that is, English without grammar. Then every English person to whom you speak will at once know that you are a[7] foreigner, and try to understand you and be ready to help you. He will not expect you to be[8] polite and to use elaborate grammatical phrases. He will be interested in[9] you because you are a stranger, and pleased by[10] his own cleverness in[11] making out your meaning and being able[11] to tell you what you want to know.

If you say 'Will you have the goodness, Sir, to direct[12] me to the railway terminus at Charing Cross?' pronouncing[13] all the vowels and consonants beautifully, he will not understand you, and will suspect you of being[14] a beggar. But if you shout, 'Please! Charing Cross! Which way?' you will have no difficulty. Half a dozen[15] people will immediately overwhelm you with directions.

GEORGE BERNARD SHAW, *Spoken and Broken English*

1. (*56(i)*). 2. (*43(b)*, note 3). 3. Add: 'that'. 4. (*68(b)*). 5. Place this clause immediately after 'ever' and omit 'does'. 6. (*48(f)iv*). 7. (*12(b)iii*). 8. Say: 'that you are polite and use'. 9. (*56(d)*). 10. (*79(n)*). 11. Say: 'with which he makes out ... and can'. 12. Say: 'tell me how one gets (*79(u)*) to'. 13. (*81(g)*) and add: 'in doing so' (*43(h)*, note 2). 14. Say: 'that you are'. 15. (*39(a)*).

39 Thought [1]

But though our thought[1] seems to possess this unbounded liberty, we shall find, upon[2] a nearer examination, that it is really confined within[3] very narrow limits, and that all this creative power[4] of the mind[4] amounts[5] to no more[6] than[7] the faculty of compounding,[8] transposing,[8] augmenting,[8] or diminishing[8] the materials afforded[9] us by[10] the senses and experience. When we think[1] of a golden mountain, we only join two consistent ideas, *gold* and *mountain*, with which we were formerly acquainted. A virtuous horse we can conceive; because, from our own feeling,[11] we can conceive virtue; and this we may[12] unite to the figure and shape of a horse, which is an animal familiar to us. In short,[13] all the materials of thinking are derived either[14] from our outward or[15] inward sentiment: the mixture and composition of these belongs[1] alone to the mind and will.

DAVID HUME, *Enquiries*

1. (*84*). 2. (*54(b)*). 3. Use *in* + A. 4. Compound noun. 5. (*79(d)*). 6. Say: 'nothing further'. 7. Repeat the preposition. 8. (*81(a)*). 9. (*64(c)*). 10. Say: 'through'. 11. (*35(e)ii*). 12. Say: 'are able to'. 13. (*1(g)*). 14. (*11*). 15. Add: 'from our'.

40 The Habsburgs [1]

The Habsburgs,[1] in their time, discharged many missions. In the sixteenth century they defended Europe[1] from[2] the Turk;[3] in the seventeenth century they promoted[4] the victory of the Counter-Reformation;[1] in the eighteenth century they propagated the ideas of the Enlightenment;[1] in the nineteenth century they acted[5] as a barrier against a Great German[6] national state.[6] All these[7] were casual associations. Their enduring aim was to exist in greatness; ideas, like peoples, were exploited for the greatness of their house. Hence the readiness to experiment, which[8] made[9] Francis Joseph,[1] for example, at the end of his reign the exponent of universal suffrage. They changed[10] ideas, territories, methods, alliances, statesmen, whenever[11] it suited dynastic interests to do so.[12] Only 'the August House' was permanent. The Habsburg[1] lands were a collection of entailed estates, not a state; and the Habsburgs[1] were landlords, not rulers – some were benevolent landlords, some incompetent, some rapacious and grasping, but all intent[13] on extracting the best return from their tenants so as to[14] cut a great figure[15] in Europe.[1] They could compound[16] with anything, except with the demand to be free[17] of landlords; this demand was their ruin.

A. J. P. TAYLOR, The Habsburg Monarchy

1. (*17*). 2. Say: 'against'. 3. Plural, and see *17*. 4. Say: 'helped the C.R. to victory' and see *79(u)*. 5. Say: 'served'. 6. Compound adjective and noun. 7. (*51(a)*). 8. (*48(f)vii*). 9. Say: 'made (*68(b)*) ... become (*79(u)*) the exponent'. 10. Say: 'They changed and exchanged'. 11. (*9(e)*). 12. Say: 'this suited (*74*) their interests'. 13. (*56(e)*) and (*79(a)ii*). 14. (*63(d)i*). 15. Say: 'play a great part'. 16. (*79(l)*). 17. Say: 'independent of' (*56(s)*).

41 Inert Ideas

In the history of education, the most striking phenomenon is that schools of learning, which at one epoch are alive with a ferment of genius, in a succeeding generation exhibit merely pedantry and routine. The reason is, that they are overladen with inert ideas. Education with inert ideas is not only useless: it is, above all things, harmful – *Corruptio optimi, pessima*. Except at rare intervals of intellectual ferment, education in the past has been radically infected with inert ideas. That is the reason why uneducated clever women, who have seen much of the world, are in middle life so much the most cultured part of the community. They have been saved from this horrible burden of inert ideas. Every intellectual revolution which has ever stirred humanity to greatness has been a passionate protest against inert ideas. Then, alas, with pathetic ignorance of human psychology, it has pro-

ceeded by some educational scheme to bind humanity afresh with inert
ideas of its own fashioning.

A. N. WHITEHEAD, The Aims of Education

42 A Natural Amphitheatre

The sun had sunk[1] behind the western wall, leaving the pit in shadow; but
its[2] dying glare flooded with startling red the wings each side[3] of the entry,
and the fiery bulk of the further wall across the great valley. The pit-floor
was of[4] damp sand, darkly wooded with shrubs; while about the feet of all
the cliffs lay boulders[5] greater than houses, sometimes, indeed, like[6]
fortresses which had crashed down from the heights above.[7] In front of us a
path, pale with[8] use, zigzagged up the cliff-plinth to[9] the point from which[10]
the main face rose, and there[11] it turned precariously southward along a
shallow ledge outlined[12] by occasional leafy trees.[12] From between[13] these
trees, in hidden crannies of the rock, issued strange cries; the echoes,[14]
turned into music,[15] of the voices of the Arabs[16] watering camels at the
springs which there flowed[15] out three hundred feet[17] above ground.[18]

T. E. LAWRENCE, Seven Pillars of Wisdom

1. Say: 'set'. 2. Say: 'the dying glare of the sun'. 3. Say: 'on each side'.
4. Omit, or say 'consisted (79(f)) of'. 5. Add: 'which were'. 6. Say: 'looked
like'. 7. Add: 'it' and see 43(h). 8. Say: 'from'. 9. Say: 'as far as (52(b)) to
the spot'. 10. Say: 'spot where'. 11. Say: 'from there'. 12. Say: 'whose
outline occasional leafy trees indicated'. 13. *Zwischen* + D *hindurch*. 14.
Singular. 15. (64(c)). 16. (17). 17. (41). 18. Say: 'over the valley-bottom'.

43 Peacemaking

People who study the past under the conviction that they themselves would
automatically behave better in the present are adopting a dangerous habit
of mind. They are importing the ethical standards of tranquillity into the
emotional atmosphere of danger. It would be better were the student of
international affairs to concentrate less upon comparative ethics and more
upon the problem of human behaviour at periods when humanity is
strained. Highmindedness, once it becomes involved in the machines of
human necessity, is not strong enough. Other reinforcements, when it
comes to peacemaking, are also required. The elder statesmen will need
foresight, planning, rigid programmes, time, obduracy, independence,
method, and a faculty for insisting upon the most inconvenient precisions.
He will also require a trained and numerous staff of expert assistants.

HAROLD NICOLSON, Peacemaking, 1919

44 The Arrival

'We shall not be able[1] to unpack,' said Ethel, in a tone without feeling.

'Did you not bring your luggage?' said Anna. 'Is that all you brought in the cab? You might[1] as well have[1] walked.'

'Cook could[1] not have[1] walked, Miss Anna. A quarter of a mile is her limit.'

'But the man could[1] have[1] put your luggage[2] on the cab. That would not[3] have imposed much strain upon her.'[3]

'The fly could not take our large trunks, Miss Anna. So we thought we might[1] as well bring what we needed[4] for the night,' said Ethel, her tone not disguising[5] the ominous[6] touch[6] in her words.

'Well,[7] I would not waste[8] a cab like that.'

'Oh, Cook has often hailed a fly to save her a hundred yards, Miss Anna,' said Ethel, sufficiently exhilarated by this difference for her face to clear.[9]

'Well,[10] it is your own fault that[11] you can't get properly established.'

IVY COMPTON-BURNETT, *Elders and Betters*

1. (*67(c)*). 2. Add: 'on top' (*35(a)*). 3. Say: 'would have been no great strain for her'. 4. Say: 'we just need'. 5. (*81(c)*). 6. (*29(f)*). 7. Say: 'but'. 8. Say: 'be so wasteful with'. 9. Say: 'that her face cleared'. 10. (*84*). 11. Say: 'if'.

45 The Kingfisher

The girl at my side stopped suddenly, and, turning away from me, gripped her companion's arm. 'Oh, look!' she said. 'Look!' And in her voice both excitement and a kind of reverence were curiously blended.

I followed the direction of her outstretched hand and saw skimming the shining surface of the water, past the sedges and the cavernous opening of a boat-house and the earthy river banks now reddened by the sun's departing glow, like a jewelled dart flying, the flashing shape of a kingfisher following the river in a breathless instant till he rounded the bend. We stood still for a moment after the bird had disappeared, and then the girl looked up into her companion's face and he looked at her, still silent. It appeared to me that they were in love, amazed with the excitement of it, and that they regarded this phenomenon of nature, this flying bird, as some kind of a mystery or sacrament whose appearance filled them with wonder and delight, binding them even more closely together than heretofore.

REX WARNER, *Why Was I Killed?*

46 Goethe's Lyric Poetry

If in spite of all Goethe says to the contrary[1] his poetry continues[2] to impress[3] us as being frequently remote from the scientist, rarely touching on anything that pertains obviously to science and devoting[4] itself for the most part to matters[5] that seem alien[6] to it, it is not without good reason. He had begun[7] as a poet by[7] exploring the richness of sentiment[8] that he discovered in himself, and it was[9] in his ability to express its variations so perfectly, with a purity, an immediacy, rivalling[10] the great musical[11] composers, that[9] he may be said[12] to have first shown himself supreme.[13] Whatever[14] promise[15] he may have shown here and there of[15] gifts of another sort, dramatic[16] or narrative,[16] they are completely overshadowed by his lyrical gift and his command[5] of the emotions.

BARKER FAIRLEY, *A Study of Goethe*

1. (*43(h)*, note 2). 2. Use *weiterhin* instead of verb. 3. Say: arouse the impression in us as if'. 4. Say: 'dealing with' (*79(l)*). 5. (*84*). 6. (*22(d)*). 7. (*79(l)*) and (*79(a)ii*). 8. Say: 'the richness of his feelings'. 9. (*43(i)vi*). 10. Use a relative clause and see *22(d)*. 11. Omit. 12. (*83(o)*). 13. Say: 'far superior (*22(d)*) to all others'. 14. (*5*). 15. Plural and see *56(d)*. 16. Say: 'as a dramatist or narrator'.

47 The Secret

'Be so good as to let me know what is going on in the house,' he said to her, in a tone which, under the circumstances, he himself deemed genial.

'Going on, Austin?' Mrs. Penniman exclaimed. 'Why, I am sure I don't know! I believe that last night the old grey cat had kittens!'

'At her age?' said the Doctor. 'The idea is startling – almost shocking. Be so good as to see that they are all drowned. But what else has happened?'

'Ah, the dear little kittens!' cried Mrs. Penniman. 'I wouldn't have them drowned for the world!'

Her brother puffed his cigar a few moments in silence. 'Your sympathy with kittens, Lavinia,' he presently resumed, 'arises from a feline element in your own character.'

'Cats are very graceful, and very clean,' said Mrs. Penniman, smiling.

'And very stealthy. You are the embodiment both of grace and of neatness; but you are wanting in frankness.'

'You certainly are not, dear brother.'

'I don't pretend to be graceful, though I try to be neat. Why haven't you let me know that Mr. Morris Townsend is coming to the house four times a week?'

HENRY JAMES, *Washington Square*

48 The Peace of Westphalia[1]

As for the results, however, the peace of Westphalia[1] was in[2] itself a compromise: the Thirty Years' War[1] contains much[3] that is dramatic,[3] but it has no pretensions[4] to the character of a drama itself.[5] Its results were what neither[6] party was struggling for; they are decisive for neither[7] side; but they are marked and lasting. The peace drew a decided and permanent line between Protestant[8] and Catholic[8] Germany. What was left[9] Protestant continues[10] so, and what was left[11] Catholic continues[12] Catholic; it[13] stopped the process of robbery[14] on the Protestant side; what was secularized then remained secular, and what was kept ecclesiastical[15] then remained ecclesiastical[16] to[17] the end of the Empire. It[13] settled the boundaries of Germany from that day to[17] the same period;[18] for Lorraine,[1] the only subsequent addition to France,[19] had long been[20] French to all intents and purposes, and the seizure of Strassburg remains the only considerable infringement of the rule. But, further, it[13] settled[21] the constitution of the Empire to be[21] but *primus inter pares*: the chief state of[22] a confederation in which the[23] pre-eminence was but nominal and the reality[24] of the power due[24] to the possessions of the reigning house outside Germany.

W. STUBBS, *Lectures on European History*

1. *(17)*. 2. *(45(d))*. 3. *(29(f))*. 4. *(56(e))*. 5. Say: 'of a real drama'. 6. Say: 'not what *(48(f)v)* each party'. 7. *(37(p)ii)*. 8. *(12(b)i)*. 9. Say: 'had then remained'. 10. Say: 'is so *(84)* even today'. 11. Omit. 12. Say: 'remains'. 13. Say: 'the peace'. 14. Omit 'process of' and say: 'robberies'. 15. Say: 'had remained preserved to the church'. 16. Say: 'remained to it'. 17. *(52(b))*. 18. Say 'point of time'. 19. Say: 'the only thing that *(48(f)iv)* was subsequently added to France'. 20. Say: 'belonged (see *79(u)* and *59(b)iii*) to France'. 21. Say: 'that the Empire should be constitutionally only ...'. 22. Say: 'in'. 23. Say: 'its'. 24. Say: 'and in which it owed *(75)* its real power ...'.

49 A Lonely Seashore

We have lived a few days on the seashore, with the waves banging up at us. Also over the river, beyond the ferry, there is the flat silvery world, as in the beginning, untouched: with pale sand, and very much white foam, row after row, coming from under the sky, in the silver evening: and no people, no people at all, no houses, no buildings, only a haystack on the edge of the shingle, and an old black mill. For the rest, the flat unfinished world running with foam and noise and silvery light, and a few gulls swinging like a half-born thought. It is a great thing to realise that the original world is still there – perfectly clean and pure, many white advancing foams, and only the gulls swinging between the sky and the shore; and in the wind the yellow sea poppies fluttering very hard, like yellow gleams in the wind, and the windy flourish of the seed-horns.[1]

D. H. LAWRENCE, *Letters*

1. Say: 'the dance of the wind-shaken seed-horns'.

50 The Oriental Capital

There it was, spread largely on both banks, the Oriental capital which had as
yet suffered no white conqueror; an expanse of[1] brown houses of bamboo,
of mats, of leaves, of a vegetable-matter style[2] of architecture, sprung out
of the brown soil on the banks of the muddy river. It was amazing to think[3]
that in those miles of[4] human habitations there was not probably half a
dozen pounds of nails. Some of those houses of sticks and grass, like[5]
the nests of an aquatic race, clung[6] to the low shores. Others seemed to
grow out[7] of the water; others again floated in long anchored rows in the
very[3] middle of the stream. Here and there in the distance, above the
crowded mob of low, brown roof ridges, towered great piles of masonry,
King's Palace, temples, gorgeous and dilapidated, crumbling under the
vertical sunlight, tremendous, overpowering, almost palpable, which
seemed to enter one's breast with the breath of one's nostrils[8] and soak
into one's limbs through every pore of one's skin.

JOSEPH CONRAD, *The Shadow Line*

1. Say: 'in wide expanse lay there'. 2. Say: 'in a style of architecture
dependent on (see *56(e)* and *64(c)*) vegetable-matter'. 3. (*84*). 4. Say: 'for
miles in those'. 5. (*22(d)*). 6. (*79(b)*). 7. *aus . . . heraus*. 8. Say: 'with every
breath through the nose.'

51 A Visit to Klopstock

Believe me, I walked with an impression of awe on my spirits, as W— and
myself accompanied Mr. Klopstock to the house of his brother, the poet,
which stands about a quarter of a mile from the city gate. It is one of a
row of little common-place summer-houses (for so they looked) with four
or five rows of young meagre elm trees before the windows, beyond which
is a green, and then a dead flat intersected with several roads. Whatever
beauty (thought I) may be before the poet's eyes at present, it must certainly be purely of his own creation. We waited a few minutes in a neat
little parlour, ornamented with the figures of two of the Muses and with
prints, the subjects of which were from Klopstock's odes. The poet entered.
I was much disappointed in his countenance, and recognised in it no likeness to the bust. There was no comprehension in the forehead, no weight
over the eye-brows, no expression of peculiarity, moral or intellectual, in
the eyes, no massiveness in the general countenance. He is, if anything,
rather below the middle size. He wore very large half-boots, which his legs
filled, so fearfully were they swoln. However, though neither W— nor
myself could discover any indication of sublimity or enthusiasm in his
physiognomy, we were both equally impressed with his liveliness, and his
kind and ready courtesy.

S. T. COLERIDGE, *Biographia Literaria*

52 Hypocrisy

In London a considerable body of persons[1] go to the theatre as many others go to church, to display their best clothes and compare them with other people's[1,2] to be in the fashion, and have something to talk about at[3] dinner parties; to adore a pet performer; to pass the evening anywhere rather than[4] at home: in short, for any or every reason[5] except[6] interest[7] in dramatic art as such.[8] In fashionable centres[9] the number of irreligious people[1] who go to church,[10] of unmusical people[1] who go to concerts[11] and operas[11] and of undramatic people[12] who go to the theatre,[11] is so prodigious that sermons have been cut down[13] to ten minutes and plays to two hours; and, even at that,[14] congregations sit longing[15] for the benediction and audiences for the final curtain, so that[16] they may get[1] away to the lunch or supper they really crave for, after arriving[17] as late as (or later than) the hour of beginning can possibly be made for them.[18]

GEORGE BERNARD SHAW, *Saint Joan* (*Preface*)

1. (*84*). 2. (*49(c)*). 3. Say: 'a topic of conversation for'. 4. Say: 'anywhere else (*83(f)*), only not'. 5. (*83(f)*). 6. Say: 'only not from' (*54(a)*). 7. (*56(d)*). 8. (*23(b)i*). 9. Say: 'circles'. 10. (*12(b)i*). 11. (*55(k)*). 12. Say: 'of people uninterested in (*56(d)*) the drama'. 13. (*79(d)*). 14. Say: 'even then'. 15. Say: 'congregations long (*79(m)*) on their seats for'. 16. (*9(d)*). 17. Say: 'and this, after coming (*81(c)*) anyhow so late as the time ... or even (*31(d)ii*) later'. 18. Say: 'could for them (*43(g)*) possibly be fixed'.

53 The Outsider

'I've been thinking,' he said, 'about a clock. We could make a sundial. We could put a stick in the sand, and then — '

The effort to express the mathematical processes involved was too great. He made a few passes instead.

'And an airplane, and a TV set,' said Ralph sourly, 'and a steam engine.' Piggy shook his head.

'You have to have a lot of metal things for that,' he said, 'and we haven't got no metal. But we got a stick.'

Ralph turned and smiled involuntarily. Piggy was a bore; his fat, his ass-mar,[1] and his matter-of fact ideas were dull; but there was always a little pleasure to be got out of pulling his leg, even if one did it by accident.

Piggy saw the smile and misinterpreted it as friendliness. There had grown up tacitly among the biguns the opinion that Piggy was an outsider, not only by accent, which did not matter, but by fat, and ass-mar, and specs, and a certain disinclination for manual labour. Now, finding that something he had said made Ralph smile, he rejoiced and pressed his advantage.

'We got a lot of sticks. We could have a sundial each. Then we should know what the time was.'

'A fat lot of good that would be.'[2]

'You said you wanted things done. So as we could be rescued.'

'Oh, shut up.'

WILLIAM GOLDING, Lord of the Flies

1. = 'asthma'. 2. Say: *Das würde uns einen Dreck nützen.*

54 The Prussians [1]

As you travel through the unprepossessing country which formed the original domain of Frederick the Great[1] – Brandenburg,[1] Pomerania[1] and East Prussia[1] – with its starveling pine plantations and sandy fields, you might fancy you were traversing some outlying portion of the Eurasian[1] Steppes. In whichever[2] direction you travel out of it,[3] to the pastures and beechwoods of Denmark,[1] the black earth of Lithuania[1] or the vineyards of the Rhineland,[1] you pass[4] into easier and pleasanter country. Yet the descendants of the medieval colonists who occupied these 'bad lands' have played an exceptional part in the history of our Western Society. It is[5] not only that in the nineteenth century they mastered Germany and in the twentieth led the Germans in a strenuous attempt to provide our society with its universal state. The Prussian[6] also taught his[6] neighbours how to make sand produce cereals[7] by enriching[8] it with artificial manures;[9] how to raise[10] a whole population to a standard[10] of unprecedented social efficiency by a system of compulsory education and of unprecedented security by a system of compulsory[11] health and unemployment insurance. We may[12] not like him[13] but we cannot deny that we have learnt from him[13] lessons of importance[14] and value.[14]

A. J. TOYNBEE, A Study of History

1. (*17*). 2. (*5*). 3. Omit 'of it'. 4. Say: 'come'. 5. Omit 'it is'. 6. Say: 'Prussians ... their'. 7. Say: 'how on sand cereals (singular) can be grown'. 8. (*81(b)*). 9. Singular. 10. Say: 'how one can bring ... on to a level'. 11. Say: 'universal'. 12. (*67(d)*). 13. Say: 'them'. 14. Omit 'lessons of' and use noun-adjectives (*29(f)*).

55 Thoughts of Revenge

When they put me to bed they found I had a broken nose, a broken arm, a broken collar bone, four broken ribs, three broken fingers, three or four square yards of serious contusions and a double rupture. The Sister thought I ought to die, the house surgeon thought I was dying, and the nurse was sure I ought to be going off before tea-time, as she hadn't a relief. And I was so angry that I might have done myself a serious injury, if I hadn't said to myself, Hold on, Gulley. Don't lose your presence of imagination. Wash out that blackguard till you're well again and get a new pair of boots. With nails in them. Forgive and forget. Till you have him set. Remember that he had a certain amount of excuse for his actions. Give him his due, but not till you are ready with a crowbar. Don't get spiteful. Keep cool. It's the only way to handle a snake like that. Approach the matter in a judicious spirit, meet him with a friendly smile, and a couple of knuckledusters.

JOYCE CARY, The Horse's Mouth

56 Prejudice

Prejudice, in its[1] ordinary and literal sense, is *prejudging*[2] any question without having sufficiently examined it, and adhering[2] to our opinion upon it, through ignorance, malice, or perversity, in spite of every evidence to the contrary.[3] The little that[4] we know has a strong alloy of misgiving and uncertainty in it; the mass of things of which we have no means of judging,[5] but of which we form a blind and confident opinion,[6] as if we were thoroughly acquainted[7] with them, is monstrous. Prejudice is the[8] child of ignorance; for as[9] our actual knowledge falls short of our desire to know,[10] or curiosity and interest in the world about us,[11] so[9] must we be tempted to decide[12] upon a greater number of things at a venture; and having[13] no check from reason or[14] inquiry, we shall grow more obstinate and bigoted in our conclusions, according as[15] we have been rash and presumptuous.

WILLIAM HAZLITT, On Prejudice

1. Say: 'the'. 2. Use the infinitive and see 63(c)i. 3. Say: 'in spite of all contrary proofs adhering (79(e)) to this opinion'. 4. (48(f)iii). 5. Say: 'as to which we can form no judgment' (56(p)). 6. (56(p)). 7. Say: 'familiar' (56(n)). 8. Say: 'a'. 9. (11). 10. Compound noun. 11. Say: 'our curiosity (56(p)) in our surrounding world (15 II(c)v) and our interest (56(d)) in it'. 12. (79(n)). 13. (81(c)). 14. Say: 'check either through ... or through'. See 11, last example but one. 15. Say: 'to the same extent as' (8(a)).

57 In the Moonlight

The night came.

He descended noiselessly into the cool and dark chasm, resting awhile on a ledge about half-way down, to drink in the spirit of the place. All was silent. Dim masses towered overhead; through rifts in the rocky fabric he caught glimmerings, strange and yet familiar, of the landscape down below.

It swam in the milky radiance of a full moon whose light streamed down from some undiscoverable source behind the mountain, suffusing the distant vineyards and trees with a ghostly tinge of green. Like looking into another world, he thought; a poet's world. Calmly it lay there, full of splendour. How well one could understand, in such a place, the glamour, the romance, of night! Romance ... What was left of life without romance? He remembered his talk with Marten; he thought of the scientist's crude notions of romance. He pitied the materialism which denied him joys like these. This moonlit landscape – how full of suggestions! That grotto down below – what tales it could unfold!

NORMAN DOUGLAS, *South Wind*

58 The New Captain

The ridiculous victim of jealousy had for some reason or other to stop his engines just then. The steamer drifted slowly up with the tide. Oblivious[1] of my new surroundings I walked the deck,[2] in anxious, deadened abstraction, a commingling of[3] romantic reverie with a very practical survey[4] of my qualifications. For the time was approaching for me[5] to behold my command[6] and to prove my worth in the ultimate test of my profession.

Suddenly I heard myself called by that imbecile. He was beckoning me to come up on his bridge.

I didn't care very much for that, but as it seemed that he had something particular to say I went up the ladder.

He laid his hand on my shoulder and gave me a slight turn,[7] pointing[8] with his other arm at the same time.[9]

'There! That's your ship, Captain,' he said.

I felt a thump in my breast – only one, as if my heart had then ceased to beat. There were ten or more ships moored along[10] the bank, and the one he meant was partly hidden from my sight[11] by her next astern.[12] He said: 'We'll[13] drift abreast her[14] in a moment.'

What was[15] his tone? Mocking? Threatening? Or only indifferent? I could not tell. I suspected some malice[16] in this unexpected manifestation of interest.

JOSEPH CONRAD, *The Shadow Line*

1. Say: 'Without being aware (*21(d)*) of'. 2. Say: 'walked on the deck up and down'. 3. Say: 'a mixture of' (*56(g)*). 4. (*56(p)*). 5. Say: 'the moment had almost come when (*9(e)*) I was to' (*67(f)*). 6. Say: 'the ship to be committed to my command' (*64(d)*). 7. Say: 'turned me a little'. 8. (*81(g)*). 9. (*43(h)*, note 2). 10 (*55(d)*). 11. Say: 'my eyes'. 12. Say: 'by the next one lying astern' (*64(c)*) and (*50(b)*, note). 13. (*59(a)iii*). 14. Omit. 15. Say: 'How did his tone sound?' 16. Say: 'something malicious'.

59 Jealousy

They had to catch the train early next morning. At the little station, they stood with their suitcases in a crowd of people who regretted the holiday was over. But Mary was regretting nothing. As soon as the train came in, she got in, and left Tommy shaking hands with crowds of English people whom apparently he had met the night before. At the last minute, the young Clarkes came running up in bathing costumes to say goodbye. She nodded stiffly out of the train window and went on arranging the baggage. Then the train started and her husband came in.

The compartment was full and there was an excuse not to talk. The silence persisted, however. Soon Tommy was watching her anxiously, and making remarks about the weather, which worsened steadily as they went north.

In Paris there were five hours to fill in.

They were walking beside the river, by the open-air market, when she stopped before a stall selling earthenware.

'That big bowl,' she exclaimed, her voice newly alive, 'that big red one, there – it would be just right for the Christmas tree.'

'So it would, go ahead and buy it, old girl,' he agreed at once, with infinite relief.

DORIS LESSING, *The Habit of Loving*

60 A Boarding-house

Mrs. Alden's younger brother Harry was at that time pursuing his theological studies at Göttingen. Among those red-tiled roofs and modest gardens, he lodged in the house of the widowed Frau Pastor Schlote, whose elder daughter gave German lessons to the foreign boarders. There was also a much younger daughter, Irma, who had recently returned from England, where for some years she had been a teaching pupil at St. Felix's School for young ladies[1] at Southwold in Suffolk. Irma, too, sometimes gave German lessons; but her chief employment was to help in the household. Sometimes she even waited at table; and then, flushed with the heat of the kitchen and the pride of making herself[2] useful, she would sit down at her place at the foot of the board,[3] and enthusiastically and accurately[4] impart all the miscellaneous information which travel and foreign residence had given her.[5] She was just as happy in knowing[6] how to make perfect Eierkuchen or to carve a goose, as in knowing[6] the beauties of English literature and even the splendours[7] of English society.

GEORGE SANTAYANA, *The Last Puritan*

1. Say: 'girls from genteel families'. 2. Say: 'being useful'. 3. Say: 'at the lower end of the table'. 4. Say: 'with great accuracy'. 5. Say: 'which she had acquired on her travels and through (*bei*) her residence abroad'. 6. Say: 'in her knowledge how one ... or carves ... as in her knowledge of'. 7. Say: 'brilliant life'.

61 Bismarck

Bismarck was 47 when he became prime minister. No man has taken supreme office with a more slender background of experience. He had never been a minister and had spent only a few months of rebellious youth in the bureaucracy nearly twenty years before. During his short time in parliament he had merely voiced extreme reactionary views; he had not tried to win votes or to work with others. At Frankfurt he had fought Austria, not practised diplomacy in the usual sense. He had no friends or social circle, except for a few sycophants who wrote at his dictation.[1] Where an English prime minister spent the recess going from one great country house to another, Bismarck withdrew to his own estate and saw no one. In later years he was absent from Berlin for months, once for ten months, at a time. He is often called a Junker and certainly he liked to present himself as a landowner. But he had a poor opinion of his fellow Junkers and jettisoned their interests without hesitation whenever it suited his policy. His aim was to succeed in whatever he turned his hand to or, as he called it, 'to accomplish God's purpose'; and he certainly did not think that every Junker prejudice was a divine ordinance. The only check on him[2] was the king's will, but he meant[3] to see to it that the king should will what he wanted.

A. J. P. TAYLOR, *Bismarck*

1. Say: 'did what he dictated'. 2. Say: 'the only thing that checked him'
3. Say: 'was firmly resolved'.

62 Dialogue

'So then you rang off?'
'No, he did. It was his tea time, no doubt.'
'Did he say he'd ring up again?'
'No, he left[1] what he had to say.'
'Did you say I was on my way back?'
'No, why should I?[2] He didn't ask.'[3]
'When did he *think*[2] I'd be back?
'Oh, I couldn't tell you, I'm sure.'[4]
'What made[5] him be going away on a *Friday* morning?'
'I couldn't[6] tell you that, either.[7] Office business,[8] no doubt.'
'It seems[9] to me very odd.'
'A good deal in that office seems to me very odd. However, it's not for me to say.'[10]
'But,[11] Matchett – just[12] one thing more: did he realize I'd be back that very night?'[13]
'What he realized or didn't realize I couldn't[6] tell you. All I know is he kept chattering on.'[14]

'He does[15] chatter, I know. But you don't think — '

'Listen:[16] I don't think:[17] I haven't the time[18] to, really. What I don't think I don't think – you ought to know that.[19] I don't make mysteries, either.[7] I suppose,[20] if I hadn't thought to say, *you'd* never have thought to tell me he'd been there at Mrs Heccomb's? Now, you get off my table, there's a good girl,[21] while I plug in the iron: I've got some pressing to do.'

ELIZABETH BOWEN, *The Death of the Heart*

1. Say: 'he didn't say what he had wanted to say'. 2. (*83(b)*). 3. (*83(g)*). 4. Say: 'definitely not'. 5. (*79(u)*) and (*79(a)ii*). 6. Say: 'I cannot'. 7. (*10*). 8. Say: 'Business (*pl.*) in the office'. 9. (*74*). 10. Say: 'It does not concern me'. 11. Say: 'Listen'. 12. Say: 'only'. 13. (*42(c)iii*). 14. Say: 'chattered endlessly on'. 15. Say: 'He can'. 16. Say: 'Now just (*83(h)*) listen'. 17. Say: 'I think nothing at all'. 18. Say: 'time for that' (*56(v)*). 19. (*67(e)*). 20. Say: '*you'd* presumably'. 21. Say: 'be (*83(h)*) so good (*or* sensible) and get (*84*) off from my table'. 22. Say: 'I must still iron something'.

63 A Strange Couple

As the streets that lead from the Strand to the Embankment are very narrow, it is better not to walk down them arm-in-arm. If you persist, lawyers' clerks will have to make flying leaps into the mud; young lady typists will have to fidget behind you. In the streets of London where beauty goes unregarded, eccentricity must pay the penalty, and it is better not to be very tall, to wear a long blue cloak, or to beat the air with your left hand.

One afternoon in the beginning of October when the traffic was becoming brisk a tall man strode along the edge of the pavement with a lady on his arm. Angry glances struck upon their backs. The small, agitated figures – for in comparison with this couple most people looked small – decorated with fountain pens, and burdened with despatch-cases, had appointments to keep, and drew a weekly salary, so that there was some reason for the unfriendly stare which was bestowed[1] upon Mr Ambrose's height and upon Mrs Ambrose's cloak. But some[2] enchantment had put both man and woman beyond the reach of malice and unpopularity.

VIRGINIA WOOLF, *The Voyage Out*

1. Say: 'for the unfriendliness with which ... were stared at'. 2. Say: 'a kind of'.

64 The Absent Host

The house stood[1] with its back, as it were, to the river, and the only landing-stage; the main entrance was on the other side, and looked down the long island garden. The visitors approached it, therefore, by a small path running round nearly three sides of the house, close under the low eaves. Through three different windows on three different sides they looked in on the same long, well-lit room, panelled[2] in light wood, with[2] a large number of looking-glasses, and laid out[2] as for an elegant lunch. The front door, when they came round to it[3] at last, was flanked by two[4] turquoise-blue flower-pots. It was opened by a butler of the drearier type – long, lean, grey and listless – who[5] murmured that Prince Saradine was from home at present, but was expected hourly; the house being kept ready for him and his guests. The exhibition of the card with the scrawl of[6] green ink awoke a flicker of life in the parchment face of this depressed retainer, and it was[7] with a certain shaky courtesy that[7] he suggested that the strangers should remain. 'His Highness may be here any minute,' he said, 'and would be distressed to have just missed any gentleman he had invited. We have orders always to keep a little cold lunch[8] for him and his friends, and I am sure he would wish it to be offered.'

G. K. CHESTERTON, The Innocence of Father Brown

1. Say: 'turned as it were its back on the river'. 2. Say: 'which was panelled ..., contained ... and was laid out'. 3. Say: 'had arrived at (*bei*) it'. 4. Say: 'was flanked on (*54(r)*) both sides by turquoise-blue'. 5. Say: 'he murmured'. 6. Say: 'in'. 7. (*43(i)vi*). 8. Say: 'a cold snack'.

65 Luther

When Luther was discussing the value of indulgences here and in the other world he meant no more and saw no farther. But now he saw the chasm, and possessed a principle on which to found his theology, his ethics, his politics, his theory of Church and State, and he proceeded to expound his ideas thoroughly in three celebrated works, known as his *Reformation Tracts* which appeared in 1520. Luther's fundamental doctrine had come to him in early life, not from books, but from[1] a friend. When all the efforts and resources of monastic criticism had led him only to despair, one of the brethren told him that his own works could not bring relief from the sense of unforgiven sin, but only faith in the merits of Christ. He found such comfort in this idea, which became the doctrine of imputation, and he grasped it with such energy that it has transformed the world. Predestination[2] seemed to follow logically, and the rejection of free-will; and, as the office of the ordained priest became superfluous, the universal priesthood, with[3] the denial of Prelacy.[4] All this was fully worked out in the writings of 1520.

LORD ACTON, Lectures on Modern History

1. Say: 'incited thereto (*43(h)*) by a friend'. 2. Add: 'The doctrine of'. 3. Say: 'and'. 4. Add: 'also followed logically'.

66 Three Women

Anna Donne was a short, high-shouldered woman of thirty, with a large head that seemed to dwarf[1] her height; round,[2] open hazel eyes set[3] under a receding forehead and[3] close to an irregular nose; and an[2] unusual reddish tinge in her[3] hair and brows, that[4] contributed[5] to an odd appearance.[6] Her father's first[3] cousin, Clara Bell, known as[7] Claribel to the family, and to as many people outside it as she could contrive,[8] was a tall, thin, upright woman of fifty-six, with an air[9] of being distinguished and good-looking, that made[10] her small, rough features a surprise;[10] carefully dressed grey hair,[11] that she frequently touched with a view to her reassurance;[12] and a rather discordant voice, that was generally used, and often raised,[13] to draw attention to herself. Maria Jennings, whose daily name was Jenney, and who was[14] housekeeper in the motherless home, was a woman of similar age but small and strong; prominent features[11] that seemed to rise from her face with[15] eagerness or[16] interest; large, gentle, happy eyes, an even, almost absent manner,[17] and an air[18] of asking little from life, and being content and almost excited when she got[19] it.

IVY COMPTON-BURNETT, *Elders and Betters*

1. Say: 'to make her small'. 2. Add: 'with'. 3. Omit. 4. (*48(f)vii*). 5. (*79(u)*). 6. (*84*). 7. (*55(o)*). 8. Say: 'as she could induce (*79(u)*) thereto'. 9. Say: 'with the appearance (*84*) of distinction and beauty'. 10. Say: 'whereby her ... features produced a surprising expression'. 11. Start a new sentence: 'She had ...'. 12. Use an infinitive construction. 13. Add: *deswegen*. 14. Omit 'and who was' and say: 'the'. 15. *im*. 16. Add: *bei*. 17. (*84*): 'behaviour'. 18. Say: 'an appearance (*84*) as if she were asking ... and as if she were'. 19. Stress this and see *83(c)*.

67 Nietzsche

He condemns Christian love because he thinks it is an outcome of fear: I am afraid my neighbour may injure me, and so I assure him that I love him. If I were stronger and bolder, I should openly display the contempt for him which of course I feel. It does not occur to Nietzsche as possible that a man should genuinely feel universal love, obviously because he himself feels almost universal hatred and fear, which he would fain disguise as lordly indifference. His 'noble' man – who is himself in day-dreams – is a being wholly devoid of sympathy, ruthless, cunning, cruel, concerned only with his own power. King Lear, on the verge of madness, says:

> I will do such things –
> What they are yet I know not – but they shall be
> The terror of the earth.

This is Nietzsche's philosophy in a nutshell.

It never occurred to Nietzsche that the lust for power, with which he endows his superman, is itself an outcome of fear. Those who do not fear their neighbours see no necessity to tyrannize over them. Men who have conquered fear have not the frantic quality of Nietzsche's 'artist-tyrant' Neros, who try to enjoy music and massacre while their hearts are filled with dread of the inevitable palace revolution. I will not deny that, partly as a result of his teaching, the real world has become very like his nightmare, but that does not make it any the less horrible.

BERTRAND RUSSELL, *History of Western Philosophy*

68 The Distant View

It was a region that seemed to promise him a disembodied nimbleness, an unearthly freedom. Its very boundaries were unsubstantial – lines of hills pencilled so lightly along the horizon that noonday melted them into[1] the white-hot sky. Only at sunset did those hills become real. Then it was that they emerged serenely, yet with melancholy, out of nothingness into[2] beauty. Cliffs, battlements, ranges, then took on a substance just solid enough to catch the tints of gold and rose that streamed through the air. The watery glitter of mirage was withdrawn from about their feet.[3] They gave, in their remoteness, a measure of the desolate space in between. But this lasted for a few minutes only. Swiftly rising, the dusk submerged them, and what had been hidden daylong under[4] the glare from above was now drowned in a darkness from underneath. Night rolled across the plain, sharp stars pricked the blue; in a moment nothing was left but the twin darkness of earth and sky.

L. H. MYERS, *The Near and the Far*

1. Say: 'with'. 2. Add: 'and turned (79(*j*)) into'. 3. Say: 'glitter of mirage at their feet was withdrawn'. 4. Say: 'in'.

69 The Night-class

That Mr. B. had been shut in became, however, almost instantly known, and the night-class, usually so unruly, was awed[1] by the event into exemplary decorum.[1] There, with no master near us, in a silence rarely broken by a giggle or a cat-call, we sat diligently working, or pretending to work. Through my brain, as I hung over my book, a thousand new thoughts began to surge. I was the liberator, the tyrannicide; I had freed all my fellows from the odious oppressor. Surely, when they learned[2] that it was I, they would cluster round me; surely, now I should be somebody[3] in the school-life, no longer a mere trotting shadow or invisible presence. The interval seemed long; at length Mr. B. was released by a servant, and he came up into the school-room to find us in that ominous condition of suspense.

At first he said nothing. He sank upon a chair in a half-fainting attitude, while he pressed his hand to his side;[4] his distress and silence redoubled the boys' surprise and filled me with something like remorse. For the first time, I reflected that he was human,[5] that perhaps he suffered. He rose presently and took a slate, upon which he wrote two questions: 'Did you do it?' 'Do you know who did?' and these he propounded to each boy in rotation. The prompt, redoubled 'No' in every case seemed to pile up his despair.

EDMUND GOSSE, *Father and Son*

1. Say: 'so awed ... that it behaved with exemplary decorum'. 2. Say: 'as soon as they would learn'. 3. Say: 'something' and stress it; see *83(o)*. 4. Say: 'held his side with his hand' and see *45(e)*. 5. Say: 'a human being'.

70 Goethe as a Scientist

The extent of Goethe's unusualness[1] in scientific matters is not fully shown till he comes to deal with the scientist himself. Here he takes an unexpected, but quite consistent stand. If the aim of science, as he conceived it, was[2] to apprehend the infinite variety and detail[3] of the natural universe in its quality of[4] oneness or wholeness, then the person who seeks to apprehend it, being himself part of the natural universe, must partake of this wholeness or he is unfitted[5] for the task. All the isolated findings in the world will not avail if the living and undivided personality is lacking to receive them. It was in accordance with this criterion, which is appropriate to Goethe, though difficult of application[6] to others unless they have it in them to follow and be like him, that he distrusted any merely intellectual or manipulatory endowment in the scientist and demanded that he bring all his faculties, his combined faculties, to bear on the problems he undertakes.

BARKER FAIRLEY, *A Study of Goethe*

1. Say: 'To what degree Goethe was unusual in'. 2. Say: 'consists (see *79(k)* and *79(a)ii* in apprehending'. 3. Say: 'the infinite details'. 4. Omit 'its quality of'. 5. Say: 'not a match for' (*22(d)*). 6. Say: 'with difficulty applicable to' (*56(e)*).

71 The Refusal

'What has he done – what do you know?'

'He has never done anything – he is a selfish idler.'

'Oh, father, don't abuse him!' she exclaimed pleadingly.

'I don't mean to abuse him; it would be a great mistake. You may do as you choose,' he added, turning away.

'I may see him again?'

'Just as you choose.'

'Will you forgive me?'

'By no means.'

'It will only be for once.'

'I don't know what you mean by once. You must either give him up or continue the acquaintance.'

'I wish to explain – to tell him to wait.'

'To wait for what?'

'Till you know him better – till you consent.'

'Don't tell him any such nonsense as that. I know him well enough, and I shall never consent.'

'But we can wait a long time,' said poor Catherine, in a tone which was meant to express the humblest conciliation, but which had upon her father's nerves the effect of an iteration not characterized by tact.[1]

The Doctor answered, however, quietly enough: 'Of course you can wait till I die, if you like.'

Catherine gave a cry of natural horror.

'Your engagement will have one delightful effect upon you; it will make you extremely impatient[2] for that event.'

HENRY JAMES, *Washington Square*

1. Say: 'of a by no means tactful iteration'. 2. Say: 'make you wait ... impatiently' and see *68(b)*.

72 English Schoolmaster in India [1]

His career, though scholastic, was varied, and had included[2] going to the bad and repenting thereafter. By now he was a hard-bitten, good-tempered, intelligent fellow on the verge of middle age, with a belief in[3] education. He did not mind whom he taught: public schoolboys, mental defectives and policemen had all come his way, and he had no objection to adding Indians.[1] Through the[4] influence of friends, he was nominated[5] Principal of the little college of Chandrapore,[1] liked it, and assumed he was a success.[6] He did[7] succeed with[8] his pupils, but the gulf between himself and his countrymen, which he had noticed in the train, widened distressingly. He could not at first see what was wrong.[9] He was not unpatriotic, he always got on with Englishmen[1] in England, all his best friends were English,[1] so[10] why was it not the same out here? Outwardly of the large shaggy type,[11] with sprawling limbs and blue eyes, he appeared to inspire confidence until he spoke. Then something in his manner[12] puzzled people and failed to allay the distrust which his profession naturally inspired. There needs[13] must be this evil of brains in India, but woe to him[14] through whom[15] they are increased! The feeling grew that Mr. Fielding was a disruptive force, and rightly, for ideas are fatal to caste, and he used ideas by[16] that most potent method – interchange.

E. M. FORSTER, A Passage to India

1. (*17*). 2. Say: 'and to it had belonged' (*79(u)*). 3. Say: 'and set great value on'. 4. Omit. 5. (*79(u)*). 6. Say: 'was successful'. 7. (*59(b)i*). 8. Say: 'with regard to'. 9. Say: 'had gone wrong'. 10. (*83(b)*). 11. Say: 'according to (*54(l)*) the outward appearance (*84*) large and shaggy'. 12. (*84*): 'behaviour'. 13. Omit. 14. (*49(c)*). 15. Say: 'through whose help'. 16. Say: 'in'.

73 Perception

We perceive things in space. For example, among such things are dogs, chairs, curtains, drops of water, gusts of air, flames, rainbows, chimes of bells, odours, aches and pains. There is a scientific explanation of the origin of these perceptions. This explanation is given in terms of[1] molecules, atoms, electrons, and their mutual relations, in particular of[2] their space-relations, and waves of disturbance of these space-relations which are propagated through space. The primary elements of the scientific explanation – molecules, etc. – are not the things directly perceived. For example, we do not perceive a wave of light; the sensation of sight is the resultant effect of the impact of millions of such waves through a stretch of time. Thus the object directly perceived corresponds to a series of events in the physical world, events which are prolonged through[3] a stretch of time. Nor is it true that a perceived object always corresponds to the same group of molecules. After a few years we recognise the same cat, but we are thereby related to different molecules.

A. N. WHITEHEAD, The Aims of Education

1. Say: 'terms like'. 2. Omit. 3. Say: 'which last for'.

74 The Farmhouse

We came to an old farm that stood on the level brow of the hill. The woods swept away from it, leaving a great clearing of what[1] was once cultivated land. The handsome chimneys of the house, silhouetted against a light sky, drew my admiration. I noticed that there was no light or glow in any window, though the house had only the width of one room,[2] and though the night was only at eight o'clock. We looked at the long, impressive front. Several of the windows had been bricked in, giving a pitiful impression of blindness; the places where the plaster had fallen off the walls showed blacker in the shadow. We pushed open the gate, and as we walked down the path, weeds and dead plants brushed our ankles. We looked in at a window. The room was lighted also by a window from[3] the other side, through which the moonlight streamed on to the flagged floor, dirty, littered with paper, and wisps of straw. The hearth lay in the light, with all its distress of grey ashes, and piled cinders of burnt paper, and a child's headless doll, charred and pitiful. On the borderline of shadow lay a round fur cap – a gamekeeper's cap. I blamed the moonlight for entering the desolate room; the darkness alone was[4] decent and reticent. I hated the little roses on the illuminated piece of wallpaper, I hated that fireside.

D. H. LAWRENCE, *The White Serpent*

1. Replace 'of what' by 'there where'. 2. Say: 'one room wide' (*20(c)*). 3. Say: 'on'. 4. Use the subjunctive = 'would be'.

75 Two Generations

'Look[1] here, cock,' he said, 'I don't know what your name is, but ...'

'Fothey, my dear sir,' replied the prosperous looking man immediately. 'FOTHEY, Fothey.' He bowed slightly and, on straightening his back, began nervously to pat the top of his head with his left hand.

He bowed again when the girl, looking at him fiercely, said '*His* name's Mr. Clark, Bob Clark.' She turned her head and smiled proudly at her escort, who appeared somewhat taken aback by these introductions,[2] and to have for the moment lost the thread of his discourse. After a short pause he began again. 'Well, Mr. Fothey,' he said, 'or Lord Fothey ...'

'Sir Alfred Fothey, as a matter of fact,' replied the other. Again he showed his embarrassment by patting furiously the top of his head. He looked imploringly at the young man, who again was at a loss for words. After a pause he added sadly: 'Yes, Sir Alfred Fothey. You may have heard of my young cousin, perhaps. He was a cricketer.'

Bob Clark now spoke again. 'Well,' he said. 'Sir Alfred Fothey. Got it right this time.' He grinned at the girl. 'What I was going to say when I was interrupted ...'

'I beg your pardon, I'm sure, my dear fellow,' interjected Sir Alfred.

'Don't mention it, cock. What I was going to say was that you really must come off it. All this patriotism[3] stuff, I mean, and "do[4] or die" and all the rest of it. It's all bunk. You're behind the times, old boy. That's about[5] it.'

REX WARNER, *Why Was I Killed?*

1. (*83(h)*). 2. Singular. 3. Say: 'patriotic'. 4. Say: 'fight'. 5. Omit.

76 Winckelmann

Soon after we find Winckelmann in the library at Nöthenitz. Thence he made many visits[1] to the collection of antiquities at Dresden. He became acquainted with many artists, above all with Oeser, Goethe's future friend and master, who, uniting a high culture with the[2] practical knowledge of art, was fitted to minister to Winckelmann's culture. And now a new way of[3] communion with the Greek life was opened[4] for him. Hitherto he had handled the words only of Greek poetry, stirred indeed and roused by them, yet divining beyond the words an unexpressed pulsation of sensuous life. Suddenly he is in contact with that life, still fervent in the relics of plastic art. Filled[5] as our culture is with the classical spirit, we can hardly imagine how deeply the human mind was moved, when, at[6] the Renaissance, in the midst of a frozen world, the buried fire of ancient art rose up from under[7] the soil.

WALTER PATER, *The Renaissance*

1. Say: 'he visited frequently'. 2. Omit. 3. Say: 'to'. 4. (*69(h)i*). 5. Say: 'As our culture is now so filled'. 6. Say: 'in'. 7. (*35(e)ii*).

77 Early in the Morning

John Sands shook the pyjama jacket off his back and stood for a moment in front of the window. Hail[1] was prattling in the gutter outside, and the wind thudded against the stained-glass panes of the window, sending spines of draught through every cranny and a rush of damp air through the high, open pane, making the flesh shiver on his thighs[2] and along the sides of his chest. The air smelt of soot. He pressed his head against the chilly glass. Drifts of hail[3] were sweeping in whirls between the houses, bouncing up from the asphalt pavement, veiling the slate roofs in a dense covering of ricocheting white stones. In Mission Road a single forlorn figure huddled under a cape was splashing through the puddles to work, hurrying to catch the half-past-seven ferry to the city. John stepped back to bang the open pane shut and stood staring at the storm, letting the stained glass order its madness into a pattern of colours – pale ruby red, turquoise and rusty gold. 'Magnificent,' he said out loud, 'magnificent,' as he wrapped his dressing-gown round his shoulders and padded away to his bath.

ALASDAIR CLAYRE, *The Window*

1. Say: 'hailstones'. 2. Omit 'the flesh' and say: 'so that he shivered on thighs'. 3. Say: 'hail-showers driven by the wind' and see *64(c)*.

78 The Educated Man [1]

No one is educated who does not know the meaning,[2] and realize[1] the importance, of two words: standards and leisure. A man knows the

meaning of[3] standards when he realizes[1] that in all pursuits and activities
there is a first-rate, that it differs from the second-rate and the third-rate
and that the road to a good life is[4] to know and choose it. This knowledge,[1]
important at all times, is especially so in an age which puts within our reach
in every field an indiscriminate profusion of the fine and shoddy, the choice
and the worthless. Never was it more difficult to 'refuse the evil and choose
the good.' ... Now[5] a chief weakness of our present civilization lies largely
in the misuse of leisure, in the failure to distinguish it from 'play'. There
are countless ways of using it well. Some may use[6] it in philosophy or
science, in music, art and literature; others in experimenting with radio,
in photography, botanizing, gardening, beekeeping, breeding animals,
etc. But the right use of leisure has two characteristics; it is not pursued
in order to make money, even if money may incidentally be made from it,
and it gives scope, as 'play' does not, for the intelligence, imagination, and
creative power, whose exercise enriches human life.

R. W. LIVINGSTONE

1. (84). 2. Say: 'meaning of the two words ... and realize their (43(e)) importance'. 3. Say: 'of the word "standard"'. 4. Add: 'that one' (49(c)).
5. Omit. 6. Say: 'spend'.

79 Frederick the Great's Political Maxims

In the sphere of foreign relations Frederick's maxims are unfortunately
much less out of date. He would have approved Palmerson's aphorism
that England had no eternal enemies and no eternal friends – only eternal
interests. A country must always be ready for war, offensive or defensive,
and preparedness depends on the condition of the army and the finances.
Diplomacy[1] without armaments, he declared, is like music without in-
struments. The most difficult of the ruler's tasks is to conduct his country's
relations with other states, for it is surrounded by jealous and greedy
neighbours. The condition of survival is eternal vigilance. Full and up-to-
date knowledge is required of the resources of every political unit in
Europe, of the characteristics of their people,[2] the temperament of their
rulers,[2] the political tradition and the dominant aims. Few, if any, states
are satisfied with their lot, for they wish either to enlarge their territory or
to recover what they have lost. Since man is a fighting animal, peace is
envisaged, not as the normal experience of a community, but as a precarious
interval spent[3] in recovering from the last round and preparing for the
next.

G. P. GOOCH, Frederick the Great

1. Say: 'A diplomacy'. 2. Say: 'of the peoples ... of the rulers'. 3. Omit,
and say: 'in which one recovers ... and prepares'.

80 The Universe

Do you not think that we should look[1] with a disapprobation amounting to scorn, upon the[2] father who allowed his son, or[3] the[2] state which allowed[4] its members, to grow up without knowing[5] a pawn from a knight?

Yet it is a very plain and elementary truth that the life, the fortune,[6] and the happiness of every one of us, and, more or less, of those[7] who are connected with us, do depend upon our knowing something of the rules of a game infinitely more difficult and complicated than chess. It is a game which has been played[8] for untold ages, every man and woman of us being[9] one of the two players in a game of his or her own. The chess-board is the world, the pieces are the phenomena of the universe, the rules of the game are what we call the laws of Nature.

The player on the other side is hidden from us. We know that his play is always fair, just, and patient. But also we know, to our cost,[10] that he never overlooks a mistake, or makes the smallest allowance for ignorance. To the man who[11] plays well, the highest stakes are paid,[12] with that sort of[13] overflowing generosity with which the strong shows delight in strength.[14] And one who plays ill is checkmated – without haste, but without remorse.

T. H. HUXLEY, *Lay Sermons*

1. Say: 'look down' (*84*) and place immediately after 'father'. 2. Say: 'a'. 3. Repeat 'on'. 4. (*68(e)*)) and (*73(b)ii*). 5. Say: 'so to grow ... that they could not even distinguish'. 6. Meaning? 7. Care! See *49(c)*. 8. (*59(a)ii*). 9. Say: 'in which every man, every woman among us is one ...'. 10. (*54(r)*). 11. (*49(d)*). 12. Say: 'paid out'. 13. Omit 'sort of'. 14. Say: 'gives (*verleiht*) expression to his joy (*56(p)*)) at the display of strength'.

81 Theatres of the Future

For all the use[1] it is to the theatre of today, the drama[2] of the last fifty years might never have been written.[1] And the waste goes on. As good plays are being written, it may be; but good and bad alike, when they have served their turn, are thrown aside and forgotten. We win victories, but we never consolidate our gains. What demoralises the theatre today is the fact that work for it, however fine, however devoted, is but a ploughing of the sands.

The remedy is simple. The majority of the theatres in a great city only need be concerned with the drama of the moment. This can be excellent in its kind; and indeed, the very greatest plays were once the drama[2] of the moment, since the dramatist who pretends to write for posterity generally misses that mark also. All that is needed is for two or three theatres – or as many more as may find a public – to be organised in the permanent interests of the drama. It does not matter what we call the theatres; National, Municipal or Repertory.[3] Nor is there any one way to organise them (though there are several ways not to). We only need to keep their purpose in mind, and to realise that the more permanent interests of the drama cannot be identical – even though the two things may occasionally coincide – with its exploiting for the maximum financial profit of the moment.

HARLEY GRANVILLE-BARKER

1. Say: 'If one considers how little use the plays ... they need just as well not have been written' (*69(b)*). 2. Plural. 3. Add: 'theatres' and use compound nouns.

82 Unexpected Ending

While I was performing these manoeuvres I saw Sammy's face soften into a look of affected incomprehension.

'What[1] do you think you're doing?' he asked.

I wasn't quite ready for this, and felt let down. 'Don't[1] you want to fight?' I replied, with irritation.

Sammy stared at me, and then broke into a roar of laughter. 'My, my!' he said. 'Whatever gave you that idea?[2] You're Donaghue, aren't you? Here, have a lotion.' And quick as a flash he put[3] a glass of whiskey into my free hand. You can imagine what a fool I felt,[4] with the whiskey in one hand and my belt in the other.

When I had re-organized myself, I said, hoping that I didn't sound sheepish, 'I suppose you're Starfield?'[5] I felt thoroughly at a loss. I suspected that it ought to be up to me[6] whether we fought or not. I certainly didn't want to fight, but I had let[7] Sammy get the initiative now, and no mistake,[8] and I hated that too.

'That's me,' said Sammy, 'and you're young Donaghue. Well,[9] what a fire-eater!' and he went off into another explosion of laughter. I took a gulp of the whiskey and put on my belt, endeavouring to wear the expression of one who, contrary to appearances,[10] is master of the situation. The films[11] provide one with useful conventions of this kind. I looked[3] Sammy up and down with deliberation. He was rather[3] a handsome creature in the style already indicated.[12]

IRIS MURDOCH, *Under the Net*

1. (*83(b)*). 2. Say: 'How on earth (*83(b)*) did you hit (*79(d)*) upon it?' 3. (*84*). 4. (*74*). 5. (*83(o)*). 6. (*79(c)*). 7. Say: 'had left (*84*) it to Sammy to seize the initiative'. 8. Say: 'about that there could certainly (*83(o)*) be no doubt' (*56(p)*). 9. Say: 'My goodness!' 10. (*54(e)*). 11. Singular. 12. Say: 'of the kind such as I (*43(d)*) have already indicated'.

83 Death of a Ship

Between the darkness of earth and heaven she[1] was burning fiercely upon a disc of purple sea shot by the blood-red play of gleams; upon a disc of water, glittering and sinister. A high, clear flame, an immense and lonely flame, ascended from the ocean, and from its summit the black smoke poured continuously at the sky. She burned furiously; mournful and imposing like a funeral pile kindled in the night, surrounded by the sea, watched over by the stars. A magnificent death had come[2] like a grace, like a gift, like a reward to that old ship at the end of her laborious days. The surrender of her weary ghost to the keeping of stars and sea was stirring like the sight of a glorious triumph. The masts fell just before daybreak, and for a moment there was a burst and turmoil of sparks that seemed to fill with flying fire the night patient and watchful, the vast night lying silent upon the sea. At daylight she was only a charred shell, floating still under a cloud of smoke and bearing a glowing mass of coal within.

JOSEPH CONRAD, *Youth*

1. Say: 'the ship'; care! 2. Say: 'had been allotted' (*22(c)*).

84 A Portrait

Benjamin Donne was a short, thickly-built man of sixty, with black hair that was not so much varied as confused[1] by streaks of white; round,[2] hazel eyes like his daughter's, but of a darker shade,[3] and set[4] in a network of wrinkles from which hers might[5] always be free; a nose[2] that overshadowed and[6] almost distorted his face; sudden,[2] uncontrolled movements, and[2] an expression rendered enigmatic[7] both by nature and himself. He bent over Anna with his hand on her shoulder, and listened to Jenney with the interest accorded[8] to a guest, the ironic atmosphere pervading[9] all that he did. He was a man at war with himself, and tended[10] to find himself in this relation[11] to other people. His friends took different views[12] of him, some seeing[13] him as harsh and forbidding, and others as a man of natural, if suppressed affections, and both being[13] right. He had been[14] a widower for twelve years, and had not thought[15] of marrying again, having found the conflicting elements[16] of[17] married life too much. He had greatly desired children, but was sufficiently provided with these.

IVY COMPTON-BURNETT, *Elders and Betters*

1. Say: 'was rather (*84*) confused than varied'. 2. Add: 'with'. 3. Say: 'only rather (*84*) darker'. 4. Say: 'lying'. 5. Say: 'would perhaps be'. 6. (*83(g)*). 7. Say: 'which had by nature (*35(e)ii*) as well as intended by himself an enigmatic effect'. 8. Say: 'due to' (*64(c)*). 9. Say: 'irony was to be felt in all ...' (*81(c)*). 10. (*79(u)*). 11. (*56(k)*). 12. Say: 'were of different opinion (*56(p)*) about him'. 13. Say: 'thought (*79(h)*) him to be ... and both were'. 14. (*59(b)iii*). 15. (*79(b)*) and (*79(a)ii*). 16. (*29(f)*). 17. Say: 'in'.

85 Democracy

Democracy demands a great deal of the citizen. It demands self-discipline, submission to laws democratically established, willingness to participate in political discussion,[1] willingness to serve others and thus to encourage in oneself those friendly feelings for other persons which find their highest expression in love. The sacrifices required of the individual by a community at war are hard to endure, but they are not always hard to make; the sacrifices required in a democracy at peace seem easy to make because we have not seriously considered what they involve and how humdrum and irksome may be the enduring of them. To co-operate voluntarily with free men in a free community seems attractive because 'to act voluntarily' and 'to be free' are pleasant sounding phrases. Then comes the clash of interests. *I* want what will frustrate *you*;[2] to surrender my claim, however feeble the claim may be, is difficult; to know whether it ought to be surrendered may need intelligence and imagination. My natural egoism will not be gratified, as in war, by its enlargement in[3] the notion of *my* country against an enemy, for both you and I are, *ex hypothesi*, citizens of a State at peace. Nor is it a matter of a single decision – one hurdle to be jumped[4] and the race is won. The need[5] for decisions[5] recurs and the struggle is renewed. Only a sense of good-fellowship and faith in our ideal of free men freely associated can carry us through these difficult moments.

L. S. STEBBING, *Ideals and Illusions*

1. Plural. 2. Say: '*your plans*'. 3. Say: 'through'. 4. Say: 'one more jump over a last hurdle'. 5. Say: 'the need (*84*) to make decisions'.

86 Bullying

'There's very little bullying here,' said Agnes.
'There was very little bullying at my school. There was simply the atmosphere of unkindness, which no discipline can dispel. It's not what people do to you, but what[1] they mean, that hurts.'
'I don't understand.'
'Physical pain doesn't hurt – at least not what I call[2] hurt – if a man hits you by accident or in play. But just a little tap, when you know it comes from hatred is too terrible. Boys do hate each other: I remember it, and see it again. They can make strong isolated friendships, but of general good-fellowship they haven't a notion.'
'All I know is there's very little bullying here.'
'You see, the notion of good-fellowship develops late: you can just see its beginning here among the prefects: up at Cambridge it flourishes amazingly. That's why I pity people who don't go up[3] to Cambridge: not because a University is smart,[4] but because those are the magic years, and –

with luck – you see up[3] there what you couldn't see before and mayn't ever see again.'

'Aren't these the magic years?' the lady demanded.

He laughed and hit at her.[5] 'I'm getting somewhat involved. But hear me, O Agnes, for I am practical. I approve of our public schools. Long may they flourish. But I do not approve of the boarding-house system. It isn't an inevitable adjunct.'

'Good gracious me!' she shrieked. 'Have you gone mad?'

E. M. FORSTER, *The Longest Journey*

1. Say: 'how they mean it, that is what hurts'. 2. Say: 'would call'. 3. Omit. 4. Say: 'because it is smart to go to the university' (*55(e)*). 5. Say: 'he pretended (*73(b)iii*) to be about to (*67(g)*) give her a slap'.

87 Advertisements

Nobody who[1] has not tried to write an advertisement has any idea of the delights and difficulties presented by this form of literature – or shall I say of 'applied literature', for the sake of those[2] who still believe in the romantic superiority of the pure, the disinterested, over the immediately useful? The problem that confronts the writer of advertisements is an[3] immensely complicated one,[3] and by reason of its very arduousness[4] immensely interesting. It is far easier to write ten passably effective Sonnets, good enough to take in the not too inquiring critic, than one effective advertisement that will take in a few thousand of the uncritical buying public. The problem presented by the Sonnet is child's play compared with the problem of the advertisement. In writing[5] a Sonnet one need think only of oneself. If one's readers find one boring or obscure, so much the worse for them. But in writing an advertisement one must think of other people. Advertisement writers may not be lyrical, or obscure, or in any way esoteric. They must be universally intelligible. A good advertisement has this in common with drama and oratory, that it must be immediately comprehensible and directly moving. But at the same time it must possess all the succinctness of epigram.

ALDOUS HUXLEY, *On the Margin*

1. (*48(f)viii*). 2. Say: 'to meet half-way those'. 3. Omit. 4. Say: 'precisely because of the trouble it costs'. 5. (*81(c)*).

88 Opposite Views

Dear Isobel,

I have been so sad that our meeting should have ended on such an unhappy note.[1] It was dear and good of you to come down and wish me so well[2] and it was very foolish of me to let an unimportant argument prevent me from[3] expressing my gratitude.

If I cannot believe as you do, you must not think that I have ever ceased to be on the side of the oppressed, the weak and the misfits. I have lived long enough to know that many of them are so from their own doing, that many of the strong and fortunate are finer people, but still I must stand with the unfortunate. We shall not see anything of what we wish come in our lifetime, and, of what happens after we are gone, we are free[4] to make what pleasant dreams we will.[5] If I am right about[6] those you believe in, you will be the first to denounce them, I know. If I am wrong, you will forgive me and understand why.

I have thought so much about you and how wonderfully you have coped. Neither you nor I were born to be[7] teachers. By the lucky fluke[8] of being able to write, I got out.[9] Surely[10] it is time you did[11] the same. Your life is a very full one,[12] full enough to do without the grind of work that has gone stale on you.[13] If you should think of retiring, perhaps we could start your new life by a trip abroad together. Let us meet soon. My good[14] wishes[15] to Miss Randall, if she will accept them.

All my love,[16]

Bernard.

ANGUS WILSON, *Hemlock and After*

1. Say: 'meeting ended so unhappily'. 2. Say: 'so much good' (*29(d)*). 3. Say: 'let myself be prevented from' (*79(r)*). 4. (*22(e)*). 5. Say: 'to give ourselves up to such pleasant dreams as ever (*immer*) we wish'. 6. = 'with regard to' (*53*). 7. Omit. 8. Say: 'Since I had the luck'. 9. Say: 'I could give up'. 10. (*83(o)*). 11. (*59(a)v*). 12. (*50(b)*, note). 13. Say: 'that has lost all charm for you'. 14. Say: 'best'. 15. (*56(i)*). 16. Say: 'In love, your Bernard'.

89 *Elpenor*

Out of this reading of Greek tragedy there arose in Goethe's mind the idea for a new play – *Elpenor*. The names and setting are Greek, but unlike *Prometheus* and *Iphigenie* the plot is not taken from Greek mythology; it is an invention of Goethe's which he chose to cast[1] in Greek costume. This fact might be taken as being proof[2] of a growing tendency in him to regard Greek art in all its forms as an absolute model. When in the days of *Sturm und Drang* he had used a Greek setting he had done so because some Greek story best expressed what he wanted to say; for *Iphigenie* too the Tantalid[3] myth was ready to his hand. For his new idea there was no suitable Greek myth; but Goethe was determined to have[4] the setting Greek, so he invented a story and gave the characters Greek names. It is true that he was determined to cast the new play in Greek costume despite the fact that there was no Greek myth available to symbolise the idea, but the reason was not that he was coming to regard a Greek setting as indispensable. The reason for his choice of Greek costume lay, as we shall see, in the idea which he was trying to express.

HUMPHREY TREVELYAN, Goethe and the Greeks

1. Say: 'clothe' and see (79(j)). 2. (56(i)). 3. Tantaliden-. 4. Say: 'fashion'.

90 The Adversaries

I bounded[1] into the sitting-room, and was well inside[2] the door when I saw a man standing on the other side of the room with a bottle in his hand. It needed but one glance to tell me that this was Sacred Sammy. He was dressed[3] in tweeds and had the look[4] of an outdoor[5] man who had lived[6] too much by[7] electric light. He had a heavy reddish face and a powerful spread of[8] nose. His hair was only slightly grey. He held his head well[9] and the bottle by the neck. He looked at me now with a calm bland dangerous look. It was evident to me that he knew who I was. I hesitated. Sammy has his name in lights, but he used to be a real race-course bookie, and there was no doubt that he was a tough customer. I estimated the distance between us and took a step back. Then I took off my belt. It was a rather heavy leather belt with a strong brass buckle. This was only a feint. I have seen Guardsmen do this before a fight and it's an impressive gesture. I had no intention of using it[10] as a weapon, but prevention is better than a fracas and Sammy, who perhaps didn't know that I was a Judo expert, might have it in mind to start something. If[11] he came at me I had already planned to give[12] him an old-fashioned flying mare.

IRIS MURDOCH, Under the Net

1. Say: 'With one bound I was in.' 2. Say: 'was fairly far away from'. 3. (69(h)ii). 4. (84). 5. Say: 'who was used to living out of doors'. 6. Say: 'spent too much time'. 7. (54(b)). 8. Say: 'powerfully spreading'. 9. Say: 'upright'. 10. Make clear! 11. Say: 'In case'. 12. Say: 'to receive him with a good old flying-mare' (der Pferdekopfsturz).

91 Honorary Citizen

Whenever and wherever[1] tyranny threatened, he has always championed liberty. Facing firmly toward the future, he has never forgotten the past. Serving six monarchs of his native Great Britain, he has served all men's freedom and dignity.

   In the dark days and darker nights when Britain stood alone – and most men save Englishmen despaired of England's life – he mobilized the English language and sent it into battle. The incandescent quality of his words illuminated the courage of his countrymen.

Given unlimited power by his citizens, he was ever vigilant to protect their rights. Indifferent himself to danger, he wept over the sorrows of others. A child[2] of the House of Commons, he became in time its father. Accustomed to the hardships of battle, he has no distaste for pleasure.

Now his stately ship of life, having weathered the severest storms of a troubled century, is anchored in tranquil waters, proof that courage and faith and the zest for freedom are truly indestructible. The record of his triumphant passage will inspire free hearts of all time.

By adding his name to our rolls, we mean to honour him – but his acceptance honours us far more. For no statement or proclamation can enrich his name now – the name Sir Winston Churchill is already legend.

JOHN F. KENNEDY

1. Say: 'from wherever'. 2. Say: 'son'.

92 A Comparison

There is no need to argue the point that Scotland[1] is a 'harder' land than England,[1] nor to elaborate the notorious difference of[2] temperament between the traditional Scotsman[1] – solemn, parsimonious, precise, persistent, cautious, conscientious and well educated – and the traditional Englishman[1] – frivolous, extravagant, vague, spasmodic, careless, free and easy and ill grounded in book-learning. The English[1] may regard this traditional comparison as rather a joke; they regard most things as rather a joke; but the Scots[1] do not. Johnson used to chaff Boswell with his apparently oft repeated *mot* that the finest prospect a Scotsman ever sees is the road to England; and before Johnson was born a wit of Queen Anne's day said that,[3] if Cain[1] had been a Scotsman, his punishment would have been reversed[4] and, instead of being condemned to be a wanderer on the face of the Earth, he would have been sentenced to stay at home. The popular impression that[5] the Scots have played a part disproportionate to their numbers in the making of the British Empire,[5,1] and in the occupancy of the high places of church and state[5] is undoubtedly well founded. The classical parliamentary conflict of[2] Victorian[1] England was between a pure-bred Scot and a pure-bred Jew,[1] and, of Gladstone's successors in the premiership of the United Kingdom[1] down to this day, nearly half have been Scots.

A. J. TOYNBEE, *A Study of History*

1. (*17*). 2. Say: 'in'. 3. Omit 'that'. 4. Say: 'he would have received an opposite punishment'. 5. Say: 'that the share of the Scots in the making of the ... stands in no relation to their number'.

93 A Strange Custom

They do not put up monuments, nor write epitaphs, for their dead, though in former ages their practice was much as ours, but they have a custom which comes to much the same thing, for the instinct of preserving the name alive after the death of the body seems to be common to all mankind. They have statues of themselves made while they are still alive (those, that is, who can afford it), and write inscriptions under them, which are often quite as untruthful as are our own epitaphs – only in another way. For they do not hesitate to describe themselves as victims to ill temper, jealousy, covetousness, and the like, but almost always lay claim to personal beauty, whether they have it or not, and, often, to the possession of a large sum in the funded debt of the country. If a person is ugly he does not sit as a model for his own statue, although it bears his name. He gets the handsomest of his friends to sit for him, and one of the ways of paying a compliment to another is to ask him to sit for such a statue. Women generally sit for their own statues, from a natural disinclination to admit the superior beauty of a friend, but they expect to be idealized. I understood that the multitude of these statues was beginning to be felt as an encumbrance in almost every family, and that the custom would probably before long fall into desuetude.

SAMUEL BUTLER, Erewhon

94 Vernon Passenger

People in the neighbourhood were accustomed to say that Vernon Passenger's manner was due[1] to the disappointing life that he had lived. Hardly anything[2] in his career had turned out[3] as he had intended. As a young man he had become tired of London society and had gone out to[4] the Boer war[5] as a volunteer, but a few days after his arrival in South Africa[5] he had[6] nearly died of measles. When he came back to England and before he had fully recovered his health he began to edit the works of a seventeenth-century minor poet. But his convalescence had allowed him little time for research and the edition was found on publication to contain[7] so many errors that he withdrew the whole of it[8] at his own expense. This incident had given him a distaste for the life of the mind from which he had never wholly recovered and, as his father died about this time and he came into the property, he married at once and went to live in the country.[9] There he occupied himself with the scientific growing of apples, crop after crop of which were destroyed every year by germs. Then the war came. Mr Passenger had pro-German sympathies. Again he backed the wrong horse. It was no wonder that he was often morose. In winter he hunted, although the hunting in this part of the country was poor. He was Master of the local pack. In summer he prowled about quarrelling with his neighbours. He was an easy-going landlord, very popular with the cottagers, because he had once spoken over the wireless on an agricultural subject.

ANTHONY POWELL, From a View to a Death

1. Say: 'was to be attributed to' (79(*d*)) and (69(*f*)). 2. Say: 'almost nothing'. 3. Say: 'had come so'. 4. Say: 'into'. 5. (*17*). 6. (*73*(*a*)*ii*). 7. Say: 'and it was found . . . that the edition contained' and see *69*(*h*)*i*. 8. Say: 'the whole thing'. 9. Say: 'and moved into (*55*(*e*)) the country'.

95 The City of Mandalay

Fanny hardly heard what her father was saying, she was gazing with the whole of what soul she possessed[1] in her eyes, and indeed nothing stranger and lovelier than the Gem City of Mandalay could be found upon the earth. The high rose-red walls, crowned at intervals by soaring spires with upcurving pagoda-like roofs, stretched all along above the moat, which shone in limpid patches between outflung masses of pink lotus. And moored all along the gleaming leafy mile of water were golden barges with high prows, decked with golden dragons that sparkled and glittered in the sunlight till they were mere twinkling points of light in the far distance, points that gleamed like flame against the soft blue of the Shan mountains. Beside the moat was a strip of vivid green, dappled with shade from the dark clump of mango trees that hung their heavy pointed leaves in the still air. Further down the moat a bridge, washed a dazzling snow-white, spanned the lily-strewn water. As Fanny gazed the deep notes of a gong sounded from beyond the rose-red walls.

F. TENNYSON JESSE, The Lacquer Lady

1. Say: 'gazing, all that she possessed in the way of (*an*) soul in her eyes'.

96 Intellectualism

The dominant intellectual influence in the University of Berlin, as indeed in every other German university at this time, was the Hegelian[1] philosophy. The soil for this had been prepared by gradual revolt from the beliefs and idiom of the classical period, which had begun in the seventeenth, and was consolidated and reduced to a system in the eighteenth century. The greatest and most original figure in this movement among the Germans was Gottfried Wilhelm Leibnitz,[1] whose ideas were developed by his followers and interpreters into a coherent and dogmatic metaphysical system, which, so their popularisers claimed, was logically demonstrable by deductive steps[2] from simple premises, in their turn self-evident to those who could use that infallible intellectual intuition with which all thinking beings were endowed at birth. This rigid intellectualism was attacked in England, where no form of[3] pure rationalism had ever found a congenial[4] soil, by the most influential philosophical writers of the age. Locke, Hume, and, towards the end of the century, Bentham and the philosophical radicals agreed in denying[5] the existence of any such faculty as an intellectual intuition into the real nature of things. No faculty other than the familiar physical senses[6] could provide that initial empirical information on which all other knowledge of the world is ultimately founded. Since all information was conveyed by the senses, reason could not be an independent source of knowledge, and was responsible only for arranging, classifying and fitting together such information, and drawing deductions from it, operating upon material obtained without its aid.

ISAIAH BERLIN, *Karl Marx*

1. (*17*). 2. Say: 'by step-by-step (*33(a)*) deduced conclusions'. 3. Add: 'a'. 4. Say: 'receptive'. 5. Say: 'the denial that there is' (*73(b)ii*). 6. Say: 'sense-organs'.

97 Wealth

A few months later he reached the age of twenty-one, and came into his money. Wealth didn't ruin him. The only charm of money for him was liberty; he hated worse than poverty all the constraints to which your conventional rich man was subjected: pompous business, pompous society, pompous speeches, and a gold watch-chain heavily festooning a big paunch.[1] Peter's impulse was to ramble, to observe, to follow up, not too hopefully, little casual adventures and acquaintances. But how to justify such a life of idleness? His liberty dragged the lengthening chain of a bad conscience. In vain he alleged to himself that his health was frail and rather cultivated frailness. In vain he made some attempt to serve the sacred cause of science as an explorer or a collector. He could explore only what others had discovered, and collect what they had thrown away. His modesty disinclined him to that voluminous nullity[2] which fills so many books of travel: yet the sidelights of any undertaking interested him more than its alleged purpose. He vegetated, physically lazy and mentally restless; grew stale while still half-baked; heard something of everything and learned nothing well. It was universally agreed among his Boston friends, whenever they still mentioned him, that he had turned out badly. Only one circumstance preserved him from complete condemnation: his life in remote parts and even his most ambitious journeys absorbed only a fraction of his income. He was growing richer and richer.

GEORGE SANTAYANA, *The Last Puritan*

1. Say: 'hanging over a big paunch like a heavy garland'. 2. Plural.

98 Tolerance

The degree of tolerance attainable at any moment depends on the strain[1] under which society is maintaining its cohesion. In war, for instance, we suppress the gospels and put Quakers[2] in prison, muzzle the newspapers, and make it a serious offence to shew a light at night. Under the strain[1] of invasion[3] the French Government in 1792 struck off[4] 4000 heads, mostly on grounds that would not in time of settled peace have provoked any Government to chloroform a dog; and in 1920 the British Government slaughtered and burnt in Ireland[2] to persecute the advocates of a constitutional change which it had presently to effect itself. Later on the Fascists[2] in Italy[2] did everything that the Black and Tans[2] did[5] in Ireland, with some grotesquely ferocious variations, under the strain[1] of an unskilled attempt at industrial revolution by Socialists who understood Socialism even less than Capitalists understand Capitalism. In the United States[2] an incredibly savage persecution of Russians[2] took place during the scare spread by the Russian[2] Bolshevik[2] revolution after 1917. These instances could[6] easily be multiplied; but they are enough to shew that between a maximum of indulgent toleration and a ruthlessly intolerant Terrorism there is a scale through which toleration is continuously rising and falling, and that there was not the smallest ground for the self-complacent conviction of the nineteenth century[7] that it was[8] more tolerant than the fifteenth, or that such an event as the execution of Joan[2] could[8] not possibly[9] occur in what we call our own enlightened[10] times.

GEORGE BERNARD SHAW, *Saint Joan*

1. Say: 'pressure'. 2. (*17*). 3. Add: 'hostile'. 4. (*68(d)*). 5. Say: 'had done'. 6. (*68(f)*). 7. Say: 'that the nineteenth century had not the least ground'. 8. (*73(b)ii*). 9. (*67(c)*). 10. Say: 'in our so-called more enlightened'.

99 The Telegram

'Your son passed painlessly away on June 20th.' ...
He dropped the telegram, spun round, stood motionless. The moon shone in on him; a moth flew in his face. The first day of all that he had not thought almost ceaselessly of Jolly. He went blindly towards the window, struck against the old arm-chair – his father's – and sank down on to the arm of it. He sat there huddled forward, staring into the night. Gone out like a candle flame; far from home, from love, all by himself, in the dark! His boy! From a little chap always so good to him, so friendly! Twenty years old, and cut down like grass – to have no life at all! 'I didn't really know him,' he thought, 'and he didn't know me; but we loved each other. It's only love that matters.'
The moon had passed behind the oak-tree now,[1] endowing it with uncanny fire, so that it seemed watching him – the oak-tree his boy had been

so fond of climbing, out of which he had once fallen and hurt himself, and hadn't cried!

The door creaked. He saw Irene come in, pick up the telegram and read it. He heard the faint rustle of her dress. She sank on her knees close to him, and he forced himself to smile at her. She stretched up her arms[2] and drew his head down on her shoulder. The perfume and warmth of her encircled him; her presence gained[3] slowly his whole being.

JOHN GALSWORTHY, *The Forsyte Saga*

1. Say: 'The moon now stood behind the oak'. 2. Say: 'stretched out her arms towards him'. 3. Say: 'took possession of'.

100 Europe in the Eighteenth Century

The years which followed the Seven Years' War[1] were a time of peace for a great part of the Continent, in the course of[2] which a memorable change took place in European[1] polity. It was the age of what[3] may be called the Repentance of Monarchy. That which had been selfish, oppressive, and cruel became impersonal, philanthropic, and beneficent. The strong current of eighteenth-century opinion left the State omnipotent, but obliged it to take account of public, as distinct from dynastic, interests. It was employed more or less intelligently, for the good of the people. Humanity contended for the mastery with ambition. It was still a despotism, but an enlightened despotism. The competent expert was supreme, but he was influenced by great writers – Locke, Montesquieu, Turgot, Beccaria, Adam Smith. There was a serious tendency to increase popular education, to relieve poverty, to multiply hospitals, to promote wealth by the operations of the engineer, to emancipate the serf, to abolish torture, to encourage academies, observatories, and the like. Prisons had never been so bad – attempts were made to reform them. The slave trade had never been so prosperous; people began to doubt whether it was moral. Laws were codified, and though the codes were surprisingly bad, the laws were improved by them. The movement was almost universal,[4] from Spain[1] to Denmark[1] and Russia[1].... Society was enjoyable, apart from politics,[5] and was studied like a fine art[6] in the homes of luxury – Paris, Brussels,[1] Rome,[1] and Venice.[1] Things went very well in those days with any man who was not a Whig, and had no views as to what makes governments legitimate and averts revolution.

LORD ACTON, *Lectures on Modern History*

1. (*17*). 2. Omit 'the course of'. 3. Say: 'of a happening (*Geschehen*) that'. 4. Say: 'an almost universal one'. 5. Say: 'Life in good society was, except in the realm of politics, a pleasure and was'. 6. Say: 'one of the fine arts'.

Part Four

Subjects for Free Composition

I Narratives

1. Sie sind an Bord Schiff und bemerken plötzlich große Unruhe und viel Hin- und Herlaufen und hören kurze Kommandobefehle. Erzählen Sie, was passiert ist und was Sie tun!

2. Motorradfahrer fahren sehr schnell durch ein Dorf, das sie nicht kennen, und wissen nicht, daß dieser Weg im Fluß endet. Erzählen Sie weiter!

3. Beim Spielen hat ein Junge den Ball über eine Mauer geworfen. Die Jungen steigen über die Mauer und haben das Warnungsschild nicht bemerkt, daß das Betreten des Grundstücks lebensgefährlich ist. Erzählen Sie weiter!

4. Sie fahren auf einer Straße, auf der anscheinend nur schneller Verkehr ist, und es dämmert Ihnen plötzlich, daß Sie mitten in ein Wettrennen geraten sind. Erzählen Sie weiter!

5. Sie fahren nachts mit dem Auto nach Hause. Sie halten, um Kaffee zu trinken, damit Sie nicht am Steuer einschlafen. Da kommt aus dem Dunkel eine Frau und bittet mit verdächtig tiefer Stimme darum, sie mitzunehmen. Erzählen Sie weiter!

6. Sie sind im Ausland und bemerken plötzlich, daß Sie Ihren Paß nicht bei sich haben. Erzählen Sie weiter!

7. Sie telefonieren nachts mit einem Freund. Mitten im Gespräch sagt Ihr Freund erschrocken: „O mein Gott!", und Sie hören nichts mehr. Erzählen Sie weiter!

8. Sie überhören ein Gespräch, in dem ein Einbruch in ein Juweliergeschäft geplant wird. Erzählen Sie weiter!

9. Der Direktor einer Internatsschule wacht nachts auf. Er hört ein sonderbar rauschendes Geräusch, und sein Schlafzimmer ist hell erleuchtet. Plötzlich ist er ganz wach, springt aus dem Bett und geht zum Fenster. Erzählen Sie weiter!

10. Ihre Mutter hat seit ein paar Tagen einen kleinen Sack im Garten bemerkt. Sie denkt, er gehört dem Gärtner, aber dieser weiß nichts davon. Erzählen Sie weiter!

11. Sie hören nachts ein Geräusch. Sie stehen auf und gehen ans Fenster. Sie sehen Ihnen unbekannte Menschengestalten im Garten. Erzählen Sie weiter!

12. Auf einer sehr engen einsamen Landstraße fahren Sie an einem stehengebliebenen Auto vorbei, in dem scheinbar ein Mann schläft. Sie

bemerken noch, daß die Scheibe der Vordertür zersplittert ist. Erzählen Sie weiter!

13. Sie fahren mit dem Zuge. Sie sind müde und schlafen ein. Sie wachen auf, weil der Zug hält. Sie sehen das Namenschild des Bahnhofs. Sie sind weit über Ihr Ziel hinausgefahren. Erzählen Sie weiter!

14. Sie helfen in einem Lager bei römischen Ausgrabungen. Plötzlich stoßen Sie auf einen großen Gegenstand. Sie glauben, daß Sie diesmal wirklich Glück haben. Erzählen Sie weiter!

15. Ihre Familie plant wie gewöhnlich die gemeinsamen Sommerferien. Sie weigern sich mitzugehen. Erzählen Sie, was geschieht!

16. Im letzten Augenblick läutet das Telefon, und ein Ball, zu dem Sie gerade gehen wollten, wird hastig und ohne Erklärungen abgesagt. Erzählen Sie, was passiert ist!

17. Sie wetten, daß Sie einen ganzen Tag nur die Wahrheit sprechen werden. Erzählen Sie, wie der Tag verläuft!

18. Es kommt unerwarteter und unerwünschter Besuch. Erzählen Sie, was Sie tun, um ihn loszuwerden!

19. Sie treffen zufällig einen Herrn in der Bahn. Es stellt sich heraus, daß er ein langvergessener Onkel ist, der früh in seinem Leben auswandern mußte. Erzählen Sie, was er Ihnen von seinem Leben berichtet!

20. Erzählen Sie von einer Situation in Ihrem Leben, wo Sie heute noch rot werden, wenn Sie daran denken!

21. Sie sind auf der Reise nach Deutschland und entdecken, daß Sie den Brief Ihrer deutschen Freunde zu Hause gelassen haben, in dem die komplizierten Anweisungen stehen, wie Sie zu dem entlegenen Sommersitz der Familie gelangen können. Erzählen Sie, was Sie machen!

22. Sie haben eine Einladung zum Tee in einem Vorort. Aus Versehen steigen Sie in einen Fernzug ein. Erzählen Sie weiter!

23. Erzählen Sie kurz ein Begebnis und wie es durch Klatsch völlig entstellt wird!

24. Zwei junge Leute haben sich in den Bergen verirrt. Es wird schon dunkel, und Schnee liegt auf der Erde. Erzählen Sie, was sie machen!

25. Denken Sie sich einen ganz verrückten Traum aus!

II Descriptions

26. Geben Sie die Charakterbeschreibung eines despotischen Vaters oder einer despotischen Mutter!

27. Geben Sie das Bild einer vollkommenen alten Jungfer!

28. Beschreiben Sie einen eingefleischten Junggesellen!

29. Geben Sie das Charakterbild eines Sonderlings!

30. Geben Sie die Beschreibung einer älteren Dame, die jemand, der sie nicht kennt, vom Bahnhof abholen soll, weil Sie selbst nicht gehen können.

31. Schreiben Sie das Porträt von einem Ihrer Lehrer (oder von einer Ihrer Lehrerinnen)!

32. Ihre Großmutter erzählt Ihnen von dem idealen Dienstmädchen der alten Zeit. Wie unterschied sich das damalige Dienstmädchen vom heutigen?

33. Ein Mann in einem Abteil erzählt Ihnen, daß er eben ein vollkommenes Verbrechen begangen hat. „Ich sehe so aus wie tausend andere. Ich habe keine Angst, daß Sie mich so beschreiben können, daß man mich findet", sagt er, und steigt auf einem großen Bahnhof aus. Beschreiben Sie der Polizei den Mann!

34. Was ist nach Ihrem Begriff ein idealer Freund (eine ideale Freundin)?

35. Beschreiben Sie ausführlich, wie Sie oder wie Freunde von Ihnen wohnen!

36. Wie sieht Ihre Schule aus?

37. Beschreiben Sie einen Dom, den Sie gut kennen!

38. Geben Sie eine ausführliche Beschreibung von einem Bild, das Ihnen imponiert hat!

39. Beschreiben Sie, wie eine Mahlzeit in einem deutschen Haushalt verläuft!

40. Wenn Sie viel Geld hätten und einen Garten von Grund auf anlegen könnten, wie würde er aussehen?

41. Erklären Sie einem deutschen Freund das Kricketspiel!

42. Wenn Sie der Redakteur einer Zeitung wären, wie würde Ihre Zeitung aussehen?

43. Erzählen Sie, wie Ihre erste Autofahrstunde verlief!

44. Sie sehen, daß in einem Preisausschreiben eine beliebige Auslandsreise gewonnen werden kann. Beschreiben Sie Ihre Gedanken und Pläne!

45. Sie müssen eine Mahlzeit kochen. Erzählen Sie, wie Sie das machen!

46. Inhaltsangabe eines „klassischen" Theaterstücks.

47. Inhaltsangabe eines zeitgenössischen Theaterstücks.

48. Inhaltsangabe einer deutschen Novelle, die Ihnen gefallen hat.

49. Inhaltsangabe eines deutschen, englischen oder amerikanischen Films, der großen Eindruck auf Sie gemacht hat.

50. Beschreiben Sie einen Tag aus dem Leben eines Geschäftsmanns!

III Letters (see pp. 215–217)

51. Ihr Freund schreibt Ihnen einen Brief über das neue Haus, das er bauen lassen will.

52. Schreiben Sie einen Brief, in dem Ihre deutschen Gastgeber sich über Ihr Betragen beklagen!

53. Sie berichten Ihrer Mutter in einem Brief von Ihrer Reise nach Deutschland einschließlich Ihrer Erlebnisse mit deutschen Zollbeamten.

54. Schreiben Sie einen Brief an einen Freund (eine Freundin), in dem Sie über deutsche Sitten und Gebräuche berichten, die Ihnen bei Ihrem Aufenthalt in Deutschland aufgefallen sind.

55. Sie schreiben einen Brief an Ihre deutschen Gastgeber, in dem Sie sich wegen einer von Ihnen verursachten peinlichen Situation entschuldigen.

56. Schreiben Sie eine Einladung an einen deutschen Freund (eine deutsche Freundin) und erzählen Sie ihm (ihr), was Sie alles in den Ferien machen wollen!

57. Ein deutscher Freund (eine deutsche Freundin) lädt Sie für die Sommerferien ein und gibt Ihnen genaue Auskunft darüber, wie Sie dorthin kommen und was Sie dort erwartet. Schreiben Sie diesen Brief!

58. Schreiben Sie einen Brief für Ihre Mutter an ein deutsches Mädchen, von dem Ihre Mutter gehört hat, daß sie nach England kommen möchte. Versuchen Sie, sie dazu zu überreden, *au pair* zu Ihnen zu kommen!

59. Sie haben gehört, daß eine wohlhabende deutsche Familie einen englischen Studenten als Hauslehrer für ihren Sohn für die Sommerferien sucht. Schreiben Sie einen Bewerbungsbrief und auch die Antwort, die Sie darauf bekommen!

60. Sie sind bei deutschen Freunden eingeladen, die immer ein offenes Haus haben. Kurz vor Ihrer Abreise bekommen Sie plötzlich Besuch von einem ausländischen Vetter. Eigentlich müßten Sie jetzt zu Hause bleiben. Schreiben Sie einen Brief an Ihre deutschen Freunde! Erklären Sie die Situation und spielen Sie darauf an, daß Sie den Vetter gerne mitbringen möchten!

61. Sie lesen eine Anzeige in einer englischen Zeitung, in der die Vorteile und Bequemlichkeiten der deutschen Schlafwagengesellschaft angepriesen werden. Sie sind gerade von einer Reise in Deutschland zurückgekommen und hatten das Unglück, in einem ganz veralteten und äußerst unbequemen Schlafwagen fahren zu müssen. Schreiben Sie einen sarkastischen Brief an die Gesellschaft und auch die Antwort, die Sie darauf bekommen!

62. Sie haben im Ausland auf Empfehlung des Geschäftsinhabers eine Kamera gekauft. Sie haben auf der Rückfahrt viel Zoll dafür bezahlt und finden zu Hause heraus, daß die Kamera fehlerhaft ist. Beschweren Sie sich bei dem Inhaber des deutschen Geschäfts und schreiben Sie auch seine Antwort auf Ihre Beschwerde!

IV Discussions and Dialogues

63. Eine Diskussion zwischen Vater und Sohn (Tochter) über dessen (deren) zukünftigen Beruf.

64. Eine Diskussion zwischen den Eltern und ihrem siebzehnjährigen Sohn (ihrer siebzehnjährigen Tochter) über die ideale Art und Weise, die Sommerferien zu verbringen.

65. Eine Diskussion zwischen einem älteren Ehepaar und jungen Leuten über die Musik von heute und gestern.

66. Eine Diskussion zwischen Primanern über realistische und abstrakte Malerei.

67. Sie haben beim Spaziergang einen Schal verloren. Sie gehen zum Fundbüro. Erzählen Sie den Vorgang in Dialogform!

68. Dialog mit einem Polizisten über einen Unfall auf der Straße.
69. Dialog mit dem Tischnachbarn beim Abendessen.
70. Ein Telefongespräch mit einem Freund (einer Freundin).

V Germany and the Germans

71. Beschreiben Sie Ihren Aufenthalt in einer deutschen oder österreichischen Stadt!
72. Ein Abend in einem deutschen Restaurant.
73. Fastnacht am Rhein oder in Bayern.
74. Der Rhein.
75. Wintersport in den Alpen.
76. Unterschiede zwischen Nord- und Süddeutschland oder zwischen Deutschland und Österreich, die Ihnen aufgefallen sind.
77. Österreich als Reiseziel.
78. Das Oberammergauer Passionsspiel.
79. Ein Opernbesuch in Deutschland oder in Österreich.
80. Ein Festspiel in Deutschland oder in Österreich, dem Sie beigewohnt haben.

VI General Subjects

81. Ein Typ, der den heutigen Mädchen (Jungen) gefällt.
82. Man hat irgendwo Autofahrer, die zu schnell fahren, je nach der Schwere ihrer Übertretung, als Strafe eine Stunde oder mehr in einem Pferch (*pen*) warten lassen. Schlagen Sie andere originelle und praktisch geeignete Maßnahmen vor, die in solchen Fällen getroffen werden könnten!
83. Kann der Amateur heute noch eine Rolle im Sport spielen?
84. Sollte ein Student (eine Studentin) in den Ferien Geld verdienen?
85. Welche Form der Geselligkeit sagt Ihnen am meisten zu?
86. Soll man sich mit seiner Kleidung nach der Mode richten?
87. Kann man immer zugleich ehrlich und höflich sein?
88. Kann zu große Intimität eine Freundschaft zerstören?
89. Verdirbt Reichtum den Menschen?
90. Ist es nach Ihrer Meinung entwürdigend für eine Frau, die studiert hat, nur den Haushalt zu führen?
91. Lohnt sich für eine Schülerschaft der Aufwand an Zeit und Kraft, der mit einer Theateraufführung verbunden ist?
92. „Kann uns zum Vaterland die Fremde werden?" (GOETHE)
93. Kann man den Naturforscher verantwortlich machen für die Folgen seiner Entdeckung?
94. „Mehrheit ist der Unsinn. Verstand ist stets bei wen'gen nur gewesen." (SCHILLER)
95. Warum wird Neues so oft zuerst abgelehnt?

96. „Wir lernen die Menschen nicht kennen, wenn sie zu uns kommen. Wir müssen zu ihnen gehen, um zu erfahren, wie sie sind." (GOETHE)

97. Kann Mord aus politischen Gründen gerechtfertigt sein?

98. Sollte man nur aus finanziellen Gründen alte architektonisch wertvolle Häuser abreißen, um Neues zu schaffen?

99. Können Sie heutzutage mit der Forderung „Zurück zur Natur" einen Sinn verbinden?

100. „Durch das, was wir Betragen oder gute Sitten nennen, soll das erreicht werden, was außerdem nur durch Gewalt oder nicht einmal durch Gewalt zu erreichen ist." (GOETHE)

101. Gibt es zuverlässige Zeichen der Schundliteratur?

102. Mit welchem Recht verlangen asoziale Leute, daß man sich mit ihnen abfindet?

103. Die Rolle der heutigen Frau im sozialen Leben.

104. Kann ein Selbstmord sittlich gerechtfertigt werden?

105. Hat der aristokratische Begriff „noblesse oblige" heute noch irgendwelche Bedeutung?

106. Kann nach Ihrer Erfahrung der Spielfilm mehr als bloß unterhaltenden Wert haben?

107. „Wenn man von den Leuten Pflichten fordert und ihnen keine Rechte zugestehen will, muß man sie gut bezahlen." (GOETHE)

108. „Das einzig Unmoralische ist anderen unnötig seelischen oder körperlichen Schmerz zuzufügen."

109. Was verstehen Sie unter Etikette? Finden Sie sie heutzutage sinnlos?

110. „Jeder hat etwas in seiner Natur, das, wenn er es öffentlich aussprächе, Mißfallen erregen müßte." (GOETHE)

111. Definieren Sie Vulgarität!

112. „Unsere Zeit fühlt sich stolz auf ihre Kräfte, und doch hat sie Angst vor ihnen." (ORTEGA Y GASSET)

113. „Wenn die Freiheit zur Plage wird, muß das Gesetz sprechen." (BERTRAND RUSSELL)

114. „Alle Fortschritte des Wissens und Könnens wirken sich zuletzt verhängnisvoll aus, wenn wir nicht durch entsprechenden Fortschritt unserer Geistigkeit Gewalt über sie behalten." (ALBERT SCHWEITZER)

115. „Die Hand, die die Wiege bewegt, bewegt die Welt." (SPANISCHES SPRICHWORT)

116. Mit welcher Berechtigung kann man die Erziehung überhaupt als eine Art von Gehirnwäsche betrachten?

117. Muß die Popularisierung einer jeden Sportart unvermeidlich zu deren Degradierung führen?

118. „Mit Vergeltung ist es nicht getan." Wie ist denn die Kriminalität zu mindern?

119. „Soll alles gedruckt, gespielt und geschaffen werden, was irgendwelchen Intellektuellen und Künstlern wichtig dünkt?" (Kurt Sontheimer)

120. Was für Maßnahmen sollten getroffen werden, um die aus der Bevölkerungsexplosion entstandenen Probleme bewältigen zu können?

121. Führt die Rationalisierung in der Wirtschaft unvermeidlich zur Arbeitslosigkeit?

122. Muß denn Werbung Sünde sein?

123. Wie ist den Entwicklungsländern am besten zu helfen?

124. Vermag Ihrer Erfahrung nach die Einrichtung der höheren Schule dem Wesen des heutigen jungen Menschen gerecht zu werden?

125. Sollte unsere Demokratie grenzenlos tolerant sein in der Frage der politischen Weltanschauung und Parteienbildung?

126. „Gerechtigkeit ist ein Ideal, dem sich der Lehrer nähern sollte; daß er absolut gerecht urteilt, ist ausgeschlossen." (Werner Klose)

127. Warum scheut man sich in England davor, Geschäftsmann oder Techniker zu werden?

128. „Mit Überschall ins Defizit" – ist das das Ende vom Concorde-Lied?

129. Sind Verpestung und Verschmutzung unvermeidliche Begleiterscheinungen der modernen Technik?

130. Was verstehen Sie unter „Mitbestimmung"?

Note on Letter-writing

The Envelope

(a) Name: Herrn Friedrich Keller; Frau Trude Keller; Fräulein Karin Keller; Herrn Professor Müller; Herrn Dr. Ing. Herbert Kind

(b) Address: The recommended way of addressing the envelope in West Germany is as follows:

Frau
Elisabeth Steiniger
Widenmayerstraße 35

8000 München 22

The *Postleitzahl* (postcode) precedes the name of the town, which is followed by the number of the *Zustellpostamt* (district post-office) when the town has more than one of these. A space should be left between the line giving the town and the line giving the name and number of the street.

(c) Sender: The name and address of the *Absender* (sender) should be written or typed either in the top left-hand corner of the envelope or on the back of it:

Bruno Hage
Gerichtstraße 13
4730 Ahlen

The *Postleitzahl* now always consists of four figures, not one, two or three as well, as hitherto. Where necessary one, two or three noughts are added in order to make the *Postleitzahl* a four-figure number.

The Letter

(a) Since one's address is written on the envelope one normally writes only the name of the town and the date at the top of the letter or just the date; e.g. (Göttingen), (den) 10. August, 1977

(b) Modes of Address:

i   when writing to a business firm:

Sehr geehrte Herren! Sehr geehrte Damen und Herren!

ii   when writing to an individual one doesn't know:

Sehr geehrter Herr Hilpert! Sehr geehrte Frau Hilpert!
Sehr geehrtes Fräulein Hilpert!
Sehr geehrter Herr Professor!
Sehr geehrte gnädige Frau!
Werter Kollege! Werte Kollegin!

iii   when writing to an acquaintance:

Lieber Herr Hilpert! Liebe Frau Hilpert! Lieber Kollege Hilpert!
Liebes Fräulein Hilpert! Liebe, verehrte Frau Hilpert!
Sehr verehrte gnädige Frau! Sehr verehrtes gnädiges Fräulein!

iv   When writing to a friend or relation:

Lieber Hans! Liebe Erika! Meine liebe Mutter! Liebe Mutter!

(c) Endings·

i   when writing to a business firm or a stranger:

Mit freundlichen Grüßen
    E. Sachs
Hochachtungsvoll
    E. Sachs

ii   when a man writes to a woman acquaintance:

Ihr (sehr) ergebener
    Friedrich Keller
In Verehrung
    Ihr Friedrich Keller
Ihr Ihnen sehr ergebener
    Friedrich Keller

iii   when a woman writes to an acquaintance:

(Ihre) Trude Keller
Von ganzem Herzen Ihre Trude Keller

iv when writing to a friend:

(Dein) Friedrich
(Deine) Ille

v when writing to a close relative:

Dein Dich liebender Sohn

(d) When writing to acquaintances such endings are commonly preceded by expressions like:

Eine schöne Empfehlung an Ihren Herrn Gemahl/an die verehrte Frau Gemahlin/an Ihr Fräulein Tochter.
Bitte empfehlen Sie mich Ihren werten Eltern unbekannterweise!
Mein Mann und ich grüßen Sie und Ihren Mann sehr herzlich.
Mit vielen herzlichen Grüßen bin ich Ihr/Ihre ...
Mit verbindlichen Grüßen Ihr sehr ergebener ...
Mit herzlichen Grüßen und besten Empfehlungen bin ich Ihr ...

(e) When writing to friends and relatives such formulas (according to the degree of intimacy) as the following are met with:

Dir und Bodo alles Gute und tausend herzliche Grüße.
Seid beide in Liebe umarmt!
In treuer/alter Freundschaft.
Kuß von Deiner Trude.
Von ganzem Herzen Ihre Trude Keller
Herzlichst Trude Keller
Dein Sohn Max
Es grüßt Dich herzlich Dein Paul.
Es grüßen freundschaftlich verbunden Eure Trude und Euer Bodo.

Part Five

German Prose Passages for Translation into English

Section A

1 Die deutsche Sprache

Französisch ist ein edler Park, Italienisch ein großer, heller, bunter Wald. Aber Deutsch ist beinahe noch wie ein Urwald, so dicht und geheimnisvoll, so ohne großen Durchgang und doch tausendpfadig. Im Park kann man sich nicht verirren, in der italienischen Waldhelle nicht so leicht und gefährlich; aber im Deutsch kann einer in vier, fünf Minuten im Dickicht verschwinden. Darum, weil der Weg so schwierig scheint, suchen die meisten möglichst gradlinig hindurchzumarschieren, was eigentlich gegen die Natur dieser Sprache ist. Sie will gewiß eine Hauptrichtung, aber ladet durch hundert Pfade und Pfädchen nach links und rechts bald aus ihr heraus, bald wieder in sie hinein.

HEINRICH FEDERER (1866–1928), *Aus jungen Tagen*

2 Der Klebstoff

Ein Mann namens Rotnagel erfand einen neuen Klebstoff, der sehr vertrauenswürdig aussah und nach Oleander duftete; viele Frauen bedienten sich seiner, um angenehm zu riechen. Gegen diese Unsitte kämpfte Rotnagel heftig an – er wünschte, daß seine Erfindung sinngemäß verwendet werde. Gerade das aber bot Schwierigkeiten, denn der neue Klebstoff klebte nichts, jedenfalls nichts Bekanntes. Ob Papier oder Metall, Holz oder Porzellan – keines von ihnen haftete am gleichen oder an einem fremden Material. Bestrich man einen Gegenstand mit dem Klebstoff, so glitzerte dieser vielversprechend, aber er klebte nicht, und darauf kam es ja eigentlich an. Trotzdem wurde er viel benutzt, weniger aus praktischen Gründen, sondern wegen des herrlichen Oleanderduftes.

KURT KUSENBERG (geboren 1904), *Nihilit*

3 Das Wasser

Das Wasser, ein wertloser Stoff von verschiedener Güte, ohne Gestalt und Farbe, ist von größter Wichtigkeit. Es ermöglicht erst das Leben; wo es fehlt, herrscht der Tod. Aus ihm stammt alles Lebendige, und Pflanzen und Tiere sind einst aus dem Meer herausgestiegen. Es war zuerst auf der Welt, ja, ursprünglich machte es die Welt aus. „Der Geist Gottes schwebte über den Wassern", heißt es über die Entstehung der Erde. Es ist mit dem Licht das einzige, das vom Himmel fällt und das einzig Körperliche überhaupt, ein ewiges Manna. Mit Wasser tauft man die Menschen, damit sie wiedergeboren werden im Geiste.

RICHARD GÄNG (geboren 1899), Verbotener Fischfang

4 Der ewige Kampf

Der Kampf des Alten, Bestehenden, Beharrenden mit Entwicklung, Aus- und Umbildung ist immer derselbe. Aus aller Ordnung entsteht zuletzt Pedanterie; um diese loszuwerden, zerstört man jene, und es geht eine Zeit hin, bis man gewahr wird, daß man wieder Ordnung machen müsse. Klassizismus und Romantizismus, Innungszwang und Gewerbsfreiheit,[1] Festhalten und Zersplittern des Grundbodens: es ist immer derselbe Konflikt, der zuletzt wieder einen neuen erzeugt. Der größte Verstand des Regierenden wäre daher, diesen Kampf so zu mäßigen, daß er ohne Untergang der einen Seite sich ins gleiche stellte; dies ist aber den Menschen nicht gegeben, und Gott scheint es auch nicht zu wollen.

JOHANN WOLFGANG VON GOETHE (1749–1832),
Maximen und Reflexionen

5 Unerwarteter Empfang

Wenige Tage nach der Schlacht bei Fehrbellin, als die schwedische Armee auf ihrem hastigen Rückzug vielfach versprengte, einzelne Reiter zurücklassen mußte, die entweder von den erbitterten Bauern erschlagen oder von den brandenburgischen Regimentern in die Sümpfe gejagt wurden, pochte an das Tor des Gutshofes von Golzow ein blutjunger, zu Tode erschöpfter schwedischer Kornett. Als man ihm öffnete, prallte er entsetzt zurück, denn er hatte erwartet, hier noch ein Detachement seiner eigenen Waffengefährten anzutreffen, das auch bis vor wenigen Tagen dort gelegen hatte. Statt dessen stand er einem finster blickenden Mann in der bäuerlichen Tracht des Landes gegenüber, in dem er ohne Zweifel einen feindseligen Brandenburger zu erkennen hatte. Der Mann schlug denn auch sofort das Hoftor hinter dem Schweden zu und schob den schweren Balken vor.

GERTRUD VON LE FORT (1876–1971), Die Verfemte

6 Mittag im Walde

Vor mir lag der Bärenwald. In seinem dichten, schwarzen Tannenpelz, den er über das langgestreckte Plateau breitete, barg er nur noch in ordentlichen Gehegen Hirsche und Rehe. Der Pfad trug in seiner trockenen

---

[1] Veraltet. Jetzt *Gewerbefreiheit*

fleischfarbenen Erde die Rillen von Holzfuhren wie verharschte Wunden, und es ging sich nicht so gut. Gegen Mittag saß ich auf einem Hang zwischen blühenden Walderdbeeren, sah den schmausenden Insekten in den weißen Sternen zu und öffnete den Rucksack. Der Fingerhut hielt, ganz von Sonne vollgelaufen, seine glühenden Becher unverwandt und still gegen Süden, so daß er an der Nordseite des Stengels fast wie geschoren erschien. Man sah von hier weit über den Bärenwald hinaus, – der Hang war baumlos und höher gelegen. Der Kuckuck läutete in seinen fallenden Terzen das große Schweigen des Mittags ein; die Sonne fiel durch den fast südlich blauen Himmel herab; nahebei pochte ein Specht in seiner schattigen Werkstatt.

STEFAN ANDRES (1906–1970), *Das Wirtshaus zur weiten Welt*

7 Der General

Zum ersten Male schien der General seinem Adjutanten ein müder, kranker Mann zu sein, als sie miteinander die Treppe in den Hof hinabgingen. Patkul nahm jede der Stufen langsam und schwerfällig. Seine Rechte suchte tastend mehr Halt am Geländer, als daß sie gewohnheitsmäßig danach gegriffen hätte. Bexelius und Schmid, die fröstelnd und mißgelaunt schon seit langer Zeit unten vor dem Ausgang in den Hof gewartet hatten, schien er kaum zu bemerken. Im Hofe selbst betrachtete er einen Augenblick geistesabwesend die neben ihren Pferden abgesessenen Reiter, deren Reihen bei dem langen Warten schon in Auflösung geraten waren, sagte aber kein Wort, wie er's sonst wohl getan hätte, und ließ sich von Horn zu seiner Sänfte geleiten, die vor den Sänften der beiden Kommissarien abgesetzt stand. Inzwischen hallten auch die Befehle zum Aufsitzen, und bevor Patkul steifbeinig in dem engen Gehäuse Platz genommen hatte, waren die Sättel besetzt.

EDZARD SCHAPER (geboren 1908), *Der Gouverneur*

8 Die Schnecke

Eben meinte er noch, es sehe fahlgelb aus, und nun erkennt er, daß es in Wahrheit ein Wunder von goldenem Licht und gläserner, perlmutterfarbener Trübung ist. Und diese Spirale, wie unsagbar leicht und genau sie sich aus dem Mittelpunkt nach außen dreht gleich einer unwirklichen mathematischen Kurve! Quer zu ihr laufen kleine, gebogene Rillen, eine unmittelbar neben der anderen. Insgesamt bilden sie ein von innen nach außen breiter werdendes Wellenband. Dort, wo die Spirale beginnt, in der Mitte, sind graublaue und silberne Flecken in das Band eingesprengt, die, wenn der Einfall des Lichtes sich nur um eine Kleinigkeit ändert, ihren Schimmer wechseln wie Opale. Weiter am Rande besteht das Gehäuse gleichsam aus Antikglas, das den von drinnen heraufdämmernden

Goldglanz in ein unregelmäßiges, feuchtes Funkeln auflöst. Jeweils am
Grunde einer Querrille ist das Funkeln und Leuchten besonders stark.

MANFRED HAUSMANN (geboren 1898), Einer muß wachen

9 Schraubenbruch auf hoher See

In dem innerlich nicht mehr pulsierenden Schiff war jetzt eine tiefe Stille
verbreitet: eine Stille, darin das bange Leben der Bewohner nun doppelt
bemerkbar ward. Türen schlugen, und wenn sie sich öffneten, drangen
kurze, abgerissene Laute aus den Kabinen, die von der Verwirrung und
Angst der Bewohner zeugten. Ganz besonders war Friedrichen in diesem
durch elektrisches Licht erleuchteten, wie ein neuer Stiefel knarrenden,
schwankenden Korridor der unablässige Laut der elektrischen Klingeln
schauerlich. In hundert Kabinen zugleich schienen von angstvollen Menschen, die ihre Kajütplätze teuer bezahlt und Anspruch auf gute Bedienung
hatten, die Klingelknöpfe gedrückt zu werden. Keiner von ihnen war
geneigt, die force majeure des Atlantischen Ozeans, des Zyklons, eines
Schraubenbruchs, oder irgendeines möglichen Unglücksfalles anzuerkennen. Sie glaubten, wenn sie klingelten, so gäben sie der unwiderstehlichen Forderung Ausdruck, von einem durchaus verantwortlichen Retter
unbedingt aufs Trockene gebracht zu sein.

GERHART HAUPTMANN (1862–1946), Atlantis

10 Unschlüssigkeit

Er betrachtete die Häuser. Es fand sich kein Hotel darunter, ja, nicht einmal
Geschäftsläden gab es hier. Auch dies war in Ordnung. Wenn er nicht
irrte, hatte er einen Gasthof gleich bei der Bahn bemerkt, aber der gehörte
schon nicht mehr zum Platz; Fenster und Eingang waren der Bahn
zugekehrt gewesen. Wollte man hier auf dem Platze wohnen, wollte man
Fenster haben, die hinausschauen auf die grüne feuchtglänzende Fläche
des Rasens, wollte man an diesen Ufern weilen, so hieß es auf jene Bequemlichkeit verzichten, mit der einem bei der Ankunft im Hotel die Sorge um
das eigene Schicksal abgenommen wird. Vor allem mußte man wohl die
beiden Häuserzeilen abgehen und suchen, ob nicht irgendwo ein Vermietungszettel heraushänge; das war sicherlich nicht bequem, doch A. hatte
nun einmal, da er von der Reihe der Hoteldiener abgeschreckt worden
war, auf Bequemlichkeiten verzichtet, und er mußte nun wohl oder übel
die Konsequenzen daraus ziehen.

HERMANN BROCH (1886–1951), Verlorener Sohn

11 Die Arbeiter

Im Dunste eines schwachen künstlichen Lichtes flutete ein unablässiger
Verkehr von Arbeitsmännern vorüber, die Loren, Karren, Behälterwagen

mit aufgestapelten Mauersteinen vorwärts schoben, während auf dem anderen Strang ein Menschenzug in entgegengesetzter Richtung auf gleichen Räderkasten Massen von Schutt heranschaffte. Die nackten Oberkörper glänzten von Schweiß, die schweren Holzschuhe stampften dumpf im Takt wie Hufe. Die meisten Arbeitsmänner hielten die Gesichter vor Anstrengung gesenkt, sie schoben zu mehreren die Lastgefährte vorwärts, deren Räder im Laufe der Zeiten tiefe Rinnen in den steinernen Damm gefurcht hatten. Kolonne nach Kolonne trieb in den beiden Richtungen vorüber, ohne Anfang, ohne Ende. Zwischen den einzelnen Staffeln ging oft ein Vormann mit einer Grubenlaterne, wie sie Bergleute tragen, der dafür sorgte, daß der Abstand von wenigen Metern zwischen den Fahrzeugen genau innegehalten wurde. Einige der Bewacher hatten kurzgestielte Drahtkörbe wie Gewehre geschultert, die dazu dienten, etwa herunterfallende Kunststeine aufzusammeln.

HERMANN KASACK (1896–1966), *Die Stadt hinter dem Strom*

12 Der Maler

Anatol stand vor uns, zwischen Bett und Schrank, neben dem Stuhl, den er als Staffelei benutzte. Auf dem Stuhl lagen Tuben und Pinsel und Zeitungspapier, dick mit Farben verschmiert. Anatol war von untersetzter, breitschultriger Gestalt. Sein Hals war kurz und kräftig, sein Gesicht rund und großflächig, mit schweren, etwas trüben Zügen. Seine Stirn war bis zur Mitte des Schädels kahl, und auf ihrer Höhe zeichnete sich im scharfen Licht der Glühbirne, die von der Decke herabhing, eine kreisrunde Vertiefung ab. Seine Ohren waren klein und unentwickelt. Das dünne rote Haar kräuselte sich im Nacken und an den Schläfen. In den nikotingefärbten Fingern seiner hellen fleischigen Hand hielt er die Zigarette, die er kettenweise rauchte, eine an der andern entzündend, obgleich er hin und wieder geschüttelt wurde von Hustenanfällen, bei denen sein Gesicht sich dunkelrot färbte und die Tränen ihm in die Augen schossen. Auf dem Schrank, auf der Kommode und an den Wänden standen die Bilder dicht geschichtet.

PETER WEISS (geboren 1916), *Fluchtpunkt*

13 Die Gabe des Dichters

Diese Gabe, Leid und Lust so aussagen zu können, daß die Gefühle ihren wahrsten und schönsten Ausdruck finden, ist eine doppelte. Es ist einmal eine über menschliches Durchschnittsmaß hinausgesteigerte Kraft, auf alle Erlebnisse mit lebhaftester Gefühlsanteilnahme zu antworten, sei es nun mit der leidenschaftlichen Gegenregung des starken und tätigen oder mit der duldenden Hinnahme des dünnhäutigen und empfindlichen Menschen; und in diesem zweiten Fall kann die Reizbarkeit dem Dichter zum Fluche werden. Und ferner ist es das Vermögen, da, wo die übrigen Menschen mit sprachlichen Notbehelfen ungeschickt nach dem Ausdruck ihres Gefühls tasten – oder verstummen – mit sinnschweren und klangvollen Worten die ganze Tiefe des Gefühls auszuschöpfen. Und wenn wir die Dichterworte hören, lesen oder nachsprechen, dann ist uns, als wäre uns die Zunge gelöst, dann können wir aussprechen, was vordem unaussprechlich war; und was vorher dunkel und halbbewußt in uns war, ist nun hell und klar, weil die Worte des Dichters es aus Dämmer und Dunkel erlöst haben.

WILHELM SCHNEIDER (geboren 1885), *Liebe zum deutschen Gedicht*

14 Der Adler

Und vielleicht war es deshalb gut, daß ich diesen Adler niemals geschossen habe. Nach keiner Beute hat mich in meinem Leben leidenschaftlicher verlangt als nach ihm. Jedesmal hörte mein Herzschlag auf, wenn in unendlicher Höhe der Adler plötzlich seine Flügel anzog und in fast senkrechtem Sturze auf den Fisch herabstieß, den er gesehen hatte. Wie ein weißfunkelnder Blitz schoß er hernieder, eine Schaumwolke brauste auf, und langsam, schwer und majestätisch hoben sich seine Schwingen aus ihr auf, während in seinen Fängen der riesige Fisch sich noch wand, den er geschlagen hatte. Jedesmal zielte meine Büchse nach der Stelle, an der er wieder auftauchen mußte, und jedesmal ließ ich sie wieder sinken, weil ich fürchtete, ihn zu fehlen, vielleicht weil ich fürchtete, ihn zu treffen. Auch seinen Horst habe ich nie entdeckt, und so ist er in meiner Erinnerung das Stolzeste und Unerreichbarste geblieben, das meine Heimat besaß und das sie auf eine gütige Weise mir vorenthielt, damit die Hand nicht entweihte, was nur der Seele gehören sollte.

ERNST WIECHERT (1887–1950), *Wälder und Menschen*

15 Barbaren im Zeitalter der Aufklärung

Das Zeitalter ist aufgeklärt, das heißt, die Kenntnisse sind gefunden und öffentlich preisgegeben, welche hinreichen würden, wenigstens unsre praktischen Grundsätze zu berichtigen; der Geist der freien Untersuchung hat die Wahnbegriffe zerstreut, welche lange Zeit den Zugang zu der Wahrheit verwehrten, und den Grund unterwühlt, auf welchem Fanatismus und Betrug ihren Thron erbauten; die Vernunft hat sich von den Täuschungen der Sinne und von einer betrüglichen Sophistik gereinigt, und die Philosophie selbst, welche uns zuerst von ihr abtrünnig machte, ruft uns laut und dringend in den Schoß der Natur zurück – woran liegt es, daß wir noch immer Barbaren sind?

Es muß also, weil es nicht in den Dingen liegt, in den Gemütern der Menschen etwas vorhanden sein, was der Aufnahme der Wahrheit, auch wenn sie noch so hell leuchtete, und der Annahme derselben, auch wenn sie noch so lebendig überzeugte, im Wege steht. Ein alter Weiser hat es empfunden, und es liegt in dem vielbedeutenden Ausdrucke versteckt: *sapere aude.*

Erkühne dich, weise zu sein. Energie des Muts gehört dazu, die Hindernisse zu bekämpfen, welche sowohl die Trägheit der Natur als die Feigheit des Herzens der Belehrung entgegensetzen.

FRIEDRICH VON SCHILLER (1759–1805),
Über die ästhetische Erziehung des Menschen

16 Der Eisenbahnkönig

Er war zierlich gebaut und von eigenartiger Physiognomie. Aus seinem glatt rasierten Gesicht mit den hitzigen Wangen sprang die Nase ungewöhnlich waagerecht hervor, und darüber lagen nahe beieinander seine kleinen Rundaugen, die von metallisch unbestimmtem Blauschwarz waren, wie bei kleinen Kindern und Tieren, und zerstreut und ärgerlich blickten. Der obere Teil seines Schädels war kahl, aber am Hinterkopf und an den Schläfen besaß Herr Spoelmann reichliches graues Haar, das auf eine bei uns nicht übliche Art gehalten war. Er trug es weder kurz noch lang, sondern hochaufliegend, voll, nur im Nacken geschnitten und um die Ohren rasiert. Sein Mund war klein und fein geschnitten. Gekleidet in einen schwarzen Schoßrock mit samtener Weste, auf der eine lange, dünne, altmodische Uhrkette lag, und weiche Lederschuhe an seinen kurzen Füßchen, näherte er sich mit mißmutigem und beschäftigtem Gesichtsausdruck rasch dem Teetisch; aber seine Miene erhellte sich, sie gewann Weichheit und Freude, sobald er seiner Tochter ansichtig wurde.

THOMAS MANN (1875–1955), *Königliche Hoheit*

17 Weltentrückt

Vor dem Balkon fällt ein alter südlicher Baumgarten steil den Berg hinunter: Palmen mit dicken Fächerkronen, Kamelien, Rhododendren, Mimosen, Judasbaum, dazwischen einige Tannen und Eiben, von Glyzinien überklettert, und schwebende Rosenterrassen. Dieser steile, verschlafene Garten hängt zwischen mir und der Welt, er und ein paar stille Bachschluchten, mit Kastanienwald bestanden, auf ihre Wipfel blicke ich hinab, ihr Laub rauscht mir Tag und Nacht, aus ihnen tönt am Abend der traurige Eulenschrei herüber, sie schützen mich vor der Welt, vor den Häusern und Menschen, vor Lärm und Staub, Gestank und Geschmetter. Ganz und gar zwar konnte ich der Welt nicht entfliehen, ich bin auch hier oben noch allzu eng und gut mit ihr verbunden, durch eine Fahrstraße, auf welcher täglich mehrmals ein Postauto entbehrliche Briefe und Besuche heraufbringt. Zum Glück bringt dieselbe Post zuweilen auch

schöne Bücher, und zur Zeit sitze ich die **Abende mit Vergnügen** über
einigen historischen Werken, die mir Freude machen.

HERMANN HESSE (1877–1962), Die Goldfisch-Wolke

18 Der erste Reisetag

Am andern Tag, in aller Frühe, von der Mutter vorher noch mit vielen
Ermahnungen bedacht, ging ich mit meinem Vater zur Bahn. Die Schlitt-
schuhe hatte ich nicht in den Koffer packen lassen, ich trug sie an einem
hellbraunen, noch etwas steifen Lederriemen über der Schulter, und im
Zug hing ich sie über meinem Kopf an einem der Messinghaken des
Gepäcknetzes auf. So oft sie dann aneinanderstießen, die glänzenden,
erinnerte mich ihr leises Klirren an ihr glückverheißendes Vorhandensein.

Wir waren bei völliger Dunkelheit abgefahren, im Abteil brannte noch
Licht, und ich schlief immer wieder einmal ein wenig ein, wachte aber
auf, sooft der Zug am Bahnhof einer kleinen Ortschaft hielt, und sah dann
draußen die trüb erleuchteten Fensterscheiben der Häuser und schwarze
Gestalten im tiefen Schnee, die sich durch Aufstampfen warm zu machen
versuchten oder ihre frierenden Hände behauchten. Dann kam die Dämmerung, das Zwielicht wich einer blendenden Schneehelle, der Tag war da,
der erste Tag unserer Reise, und der Schlaf war mir nun gänzlich vergangen.

GEORG BRITTING (1892–1964), Der Eisläufer

19 Der Verfassungsstaat

Das politische Freiheitsideal, zu dem Aufklärung und Sturm-und-Drang
gleichermaßen emporsehen, ist die demokratische Idee des Rechts- und
Verfassungsstaates. Differiert man zwar in mannigfacher Weise, was als die
beste Verfassung anzusehen sei, die konstitutionelle Monarchie oder die
Republik, so ist man um so einiger in dem Grundgedanken, daß jedes
staatliche Leben auf einer freiwilligen Unterordnung aller Teile, vom
Fürsten bis zum letzten Tagelöhner, unter eine selbstgeschaffene Verfassung beruhen müsse, durch welche jede Willkür ausgeschaltet wird.
Nur dann ist der Staat die Verwirklichung der Freiheit und der Vernunft,
wenn er als ein Gesellschaftsvertrag zwischen Volk und Fürst und zwischen
den Volksgenossen untereinander betrachtet wird. Wie Montesquieu, der
erste kontinentale Verfechter des modernen Verfassungsstaates, gesagt
hat, besteht das Wesen der politischen Freiheit in dem Rechte, alles tun zu
können, was die Gesetze erlauben: ein Recht, das also auch den Fürsten
unter die Idee eines Gesetzes, der von ihm beschworenen Verfassung,
beugt und ihn aus einem absoluten Herrn in den ,,ersten Diener seines
Staates" verwandelt.

H. A. KORFF (1882–1963), Geist der Goethezeit

20 Die webende Natur

Freilich, man wußte so halb und halb, worin man lebte, ganz beiläufig, aus dem Augenwinkel gesehen: in Umgebungen, die, an Schweigsamkeit nicht zu überbieten, sich dennoch unaufhörlich mit Übergewalt aussprachen. In den Schluchten und Rissen nah an den Wänden des Bergs, in diesen Wunden des Walds, die jeder Frühling wieder mit dumpf trommelnden Wassermassen neu aufriß, lag jetzt, da sie sommerlich grün zum Teil wieder heilten, der verlassene und trockene feine Sand in den großen Becken zwischen glattgewaschenen Blöcken. Längst hatten Gebüsch und Geäst von beiden Seiten das leere Bachbett neuerlich überwölbt. Auch hier stand die Zeit nicht, wenn auch viele Stunden von vielen Stunden durch nichts getrennt wurden als etwa einmal durch den piependen Schrei des hochfliegenden Bussards. Die Zeit erschien hier nur auf jene Regelmäßigkeit gebracht, wie sie der Atem eines Tiefschlafenden hat. Morgens zeigte ein erster Sonnenfinger an einem bestimmten Stamm vorbei in den verborgenen Graben auf einen gewissen Stein; abends grüngolden von anderer Seite ein Gleiches.

HEIMITO VON DODERER (1896–1966), *Die Strudlhofstiege*

21 Ärger mit Tieren

Warum ich zuerst von den Schattenseiten des Zusammenlebens mit Tieren erzähle? Weil das Maß der Bereitschaft, diese Schattenseiten zu ertragen, Opfer zu bringen, auch ein Maß der Tierliebe ist. Unsterbliche Dankbarkeit meinen geduldigen Eltern, die nur den Kopf schüttelten oder nachgiebig seufzten, wenn ich als Schüler oder junger Student schon wieder einen neuen und voraussichtlich schadenstiftenden künftigen Hausgenossen heimbrachte. Und was hat meine Frau im Laufe der Jahre erund geduldet! Denn wer dürfte wohl seiner Gattin zumuten, daß eine zahme Ratte in der Wohnung frei herumläuft, aus den Bettüchern nette kleine Scheibchen nagt, um damit ihr Nest zu tapezieren? Oder, daß ein Kakadu von der Wäsche, die zum Trocknen im Garten hängt, sämtliche Knöpfe abbeißt? Oder, daß eine zahme Wildgans im Schlafzimmer nächtigt, welches sie morgens durch das Fenster fliegend verläßt? (Wildgänse sind nicht zimmerrein!) Oder: was würde eine andere Frau sagen, wenn sich herausstellt, daß die hübschen blauen Tupfen, mit denen Singvögel nach dem Genuß von Hollunderbeeren sämtliche Möbel und Vorhänge verziert haben, absolut nicht „herausgehen"? Was würde sie sagen, wenn ... und so weiter über zwanzig Seiten!

KONRAD LORENZ (geboren 1903),
Er redete mit dem Vieh, den Vögeln und den Fischen

22 Ein Gewitter

Atemlos stürzte ich in die Hütte und warf mich auf einige Heu- und Laub-
bündel an die Erde. Ein altes Weib, das auf dem Herde saß, machte
Gebärden des Erstaunens und zeigte hinaus und nach oben; denn sprechen
konnte man nicht wegen des Tobens der Elemente, die ich in solcher
Entfesselung noch nie gesehen hatte. Der Regen trommelte und rasselte
auf das Schindeldach; bald strömte er an vielen Stellen hindurch, und ich
mußte mein Lager deshalb mehrmals ändern. Die Alte setzte an die
gefährdeten Stellen Schüsseln und Mulden, um die Überschwemmung
im Innern abzuhalten, und kehrte dann auf ihren Herdsitz zurück, wo sie
wieder ihren Rosenkranz nahm und betete. Doch ärger und ärger wurde
das Toben. Da nahm sie eine Schachtel vom Gesims, holte ein paar kurze
schwarze Wachslichtchen heraus, zündete diese an, nahm trockene
Kräuter und warf sie, Sprüche murmelnd, in das Herdfeuer, von wo aus
alsbald ein dicker Dampf den ganzen Raum erfüllte. Von mir hatte sie
noch keine Notiz genommen. Es war eine wunderliche Szene!

LUDWIG RICHTER (1803–1884), *Von München auf den Wendelstein*

23 Wort und Begriff

Das Problem des Verhältnisses zwischen Wort und Begriff durchzieht
Goethes ganzes Denken und künstlerisches Ringen. Daß Wort und Begriff
nicht identisch sein können, wurde eigentlich schon dem Knaben klar,
der in vielerlei Sprachen sich ausbildete, ,,mit einer angeborenen Gabe,
leicht den Schall und Klang jeder Sprache, ihre Bewegung, ihren Akzent,
den Ton und sonstige äußere Eigentümlichkeit zu fassen". Daß Gegenstände
und Begriffe in jeder Sprache anderen Wortausdruck finden, beweist ja eben,
daß höchstens ein sinnlicher Annäherungsversuch, aber keine vollgültige
Wiedergabe des Begriffsinhaltes in sprachlicher Lautgebung möglich ist.
Man müßte also die Ausdrucksmöglichkeit mehrerer Sprachen zur Hand
haben, um den Dingen nahe zu kommen. Im Alter hat Goethe tatsächlich
solche Polyglottie empfohlen, weil jede Sprache ihren eigenen Ideenkreis
habe. ,,Wer fremde Sprachen nicht kennt, weiß nichts von seiner eigenen",
heißt es in einem Spruch. Auch in der pädogogischen Utopie der ,, Wander-
jahre" wird Sprachübung und Sprachbildung gleichmäßig in verschiedenen
Sprachen getrieben. ,,Damit jedoch keine babylonische Verwirrung, keine
Verderbnis entstehe, so wird das Jahr über monatweise nur eine Sprache im
allgemeinen gesprochen."

JULIUS PETERSEN (1878–1941), *Aus der Goethezeit*

24 Ein seltsames Land

Es ist ein seltsames Land. Wenn man auf dem kleinen Sandberg von
Worpswede steht, kann man es ringsum ausgebreitet sehen, ähnlich jenen

Bauerntüchern, die auf dunklem Grund Ecken tiefleuchtender Blumen zeigen. Flach liegt es da, fast ohne Falten. Der Sandberg war eine Düne des Meeres, das einmal vor Jahrtausenden hier stieg und fiel. Einst, als das Meer zurücktrat, da begann sich das Land zu formen. Pflanzen, die wir nicht kennen, erhoben sich, und es war ein rasches und hastiges Wachsen in dem fetten, faltigen Schlamm. Aber das Meer kam immer wieder mit seinen äußersten Wassern in die verlassenen Gebiete, und endlich blieben schwarze schwankende Sümpfe zurück; das Moor bildete sich; es begann sich an einzelnen Stellen zu schließen, leise, wie eine Wunde sich schließt. Um diese Zeit, man nimmt das dreizehnte Jahrhundert an, wurden in der Weserniederung Klöster gegründet; aber erst im achtzehnten Jahrhundert folgen neue Ansiedlungsversuche nach einem bestimmten Plan; heute sind die Ländereien an der Weser ziemlich bevölkert.

RAINER MARIA RILKE (1875–1926), *Worpswede*

25 Bismarck und die Militärs

Am 30. Juni 1866 abends traf Seine Majestät mit dem Hauptquartier in Reichenberg ein. Die Stadt von 28 000 Einwohnern beherbergte 1 800 österreichische Gefangene und war nur von 500 preußischen Trainsoldaten mit alten Karabinern besetzt; nur einige Meilen davon lag die sächsische Reiterei. Diese konnte in einer Nacht Reichenberg erreichen und das ganze Hauptquartier mit Sr. Majestät aufheben. Daß wir in Reichenberg Quartier hatten, war telegraphisch publiziert worden. Ich erlaubte mir den König hierauf aufmerksam zu machen, und infolge dieser Anregung wurde befohlen, daß die Trainsoldaten sich einzeln und unauffällig nach dem Schlosse begeben sollten, wo der König Quartier genommen hatte. Die Militärs waren über diese meine Einmischung empfindlich, und um ihnen zu beweisen, daß ich um meine Sicherheit nicht besorgt sei, verließ ich das Schloß, wohin Seine Majestät mich befohlen hatte, und behielt mein Quartier in der Stadt. Es war damit schon der Keim zu einer der Ressort-Eifersucht entspringenden Verstimmung der Militärs gegen mich wegen meiner persönlichen Stellung zu Seiner Majestät gelegt, die sich im Laufe des Feldzugs und des französischen Krieges weiter entwickelte.

OTTO VON BISMARCK (1815–1898), *Gedanken und Erinnerungen*

26 Die Eigenschaften der deutschen Sprache

In der Tat: die deutsche Sprache bietet dem einzelnen eine grenzenlose Fülle von Ausdrucksmöglichkeiten; sie führt ihn in das blühende Leben hinein und läßt den Armen dort glücklich und – schuldig werden. Ihre Begriffe haben nicht den scharfen Umriß der französischen, weil die bildliche Bedeutung ihrer Wurzel mitschwingt; sie sind weniger konventionell, weil sie nicht aus der Schule einer unermüdlichen Geselligkeit kommen; sie sind keine bloßen abstrakten Rechenpfennige, sondern jedermann kann selbst die Münzen prägen, die er ausgibt. Französisch schreibt gut, wer so schreibt wie die andern; nur die unauffällige Schönheit ist gestattet. Deutsch kann man nur gestaltend, nur individuell schreiben. Darum widerstrebt das Deutsche der Vollkommenheit; in einer so wunderlichen Sprache wie der deutschen, sagt Goethe, bleibt immer etwas zu wünschen übrig. Sie ist nie abgeschlossen, sondern stets im Aufbruch. Sie ist nicht so prächtig wie die italienische, nicht so klar wie die französische und nicht so handlich wie die englische. Aber das Raunende und Dämmernde, der Traum und die Ahnung,

> die große Kunst des Hintergrundes
> und das Geheimnis zweifelhafter Lichter,

sie gewinnen im Deutschen Gestalt.

LUDWIG REINERS (1896–1957), Stilkunst

27 Am Waldsee

Ein dichter Anflug junger Fichten nimmt uns nach einer Stunde Wanderung auf, und von dem schwarzen Samte seines Grundes herausgetreten, steht man an der noch schwärzern Seesfläche.

Ein Gefühl der tiefsten Einsamkeit überkam mich jedesmal unbesieglich, sooft und gern ich zu dem märchenhaften See hinaufstieg. Ein gespanntes Tuch ohne eine einzige Falte, liegt er weich zwischen dem harten Geklippe, gesäumt von einem dichten Fichtenbande, dunkel und ernst, daraus manch einzelner Urstamm den ästelosen Schaft emporstreckt, wie eine einzelne altertümliche Säule. Gegenüber diesem Waldbande steigt ein Felsentheater lotrecht auf, wie eine graue Mauer, nach jeder Richtung denselben Ernst der Farbe breitend, nur geschnitten durch zarte Streifen grünen Mooses und sparsam bewachsen von Schwarzföhren, die aber von solcher Höhe so klein herabsehen wie Rosmarinkräutlein. Auch brechen sie häufig aus Mangel des Grundes los und stürzen in den See hinab; daher man, über ihn hinschauend, der jenseitigen Wand entlang in gräßlicher Verwirrung die alten, ausgebleichten Stämme liegen sieht, in traurigem, weißleuchtendem Verhack die dunklen Wasser säumend. Rechts treibt die Seewand einen mächtigen Granitgiebel empor, Blockenstein geheißen; links schweift sie sich in ein sanftes Dach herum, von hohem Tannenwald bestanden und mit einem grünen Tuche des feinsten Mooses überhüllet.

ADALBERT STIFTER (1805–1868), Der Hochwald

28 Wagner und Nietzsche

Nietzsche warf dem einstigen Freunde heftig vor, daß er mit seiner Musik verzaubere, umnebele, narkotisiere, um so zum Ende zu verführen.

Daß Nietzsche nicht zum Ende verführen wollte, sondern zu einem neuen, wenn auch tragischen Leben, das ist klar. Aber war er nicht auch ein Rattenfänger, ein Zauberer und ein Verführer? Welch merkwürdige Ähnlichkeit besteht doch zwischen dem „dithyrambischen Tragiker" Wagner und dem dithyrambischen Philosophen Nietzsche, zwischen dem dichtenden Denker und dem musizierenden Dichter! Wenn überhaupt einer, so hat Nietzsche gar nicht versucht, mit dem einfachen, klaren, logischen Wort die philosophische Vernunft zu überzeugen. Seine Sprache überredet, verzaubert, umnebelt, berauscht, narkotisiert. Es gibt kein einziges Wort in Nietzsches Charakteristik der Wagnerschen Musik, das nicht auf seinen eigenen Stil anzuwenden wäre. Philosophie wird Lyrik und Musik in seinem Munde. Er selbst sagte einmal von sich: „Sie hätte singen, nicht reden sollen, diese neue Seele." *Hätte* singen sollen? Sie *hat* gesungen, und wahrlich einen Gesang von verführerischer Schönheit, und auch wenn Nietzsche „mit dem Hammer" philosophierte und Blitze schleuderte, so steht er den Blitz- und Donnergöttern und den hammerschwingenden Helden Wagners gar nicht so fern. Ob es nun um Verführung zum Ende oder zu einem moralbefreiten Leben ging, die Instrumente der Verführung waren nicht so sehr verschieden. Sirenengesang war beides.

FRITZ STRICH (1882–1963), *Der Dichter und die Zeit*

29 Was wir anderen Menschen verdanken

Noch ein anderes bewegt mich, wenn ich an meine Jugend zurückdenke: die Tatsache, daß so viele Menschen mir etwas gaben oder etwas waren, ohne daß sie es wußten. Solche, mit denen ich nie ein Wort gewechselt habe, ja auch solche, von denen ich nur erzählen hörte, haben einen bestimmten Einfluß auf mich ausgeübt. Sie sind in mein Leben eingetreten und Kräfte in mir geworden. Gar manches, was ich sonst nicht so klar empfunden und so entschieden getan hätte, empfinde und tue ich so, weil ich wie unter dem Zwang jener Menschen stehe. Darum kommt es mir immer vor, als ob wir alle geistig von dem lebten, was uns Menschen in bedeutungsvollen Stunden unseres Lebens gegeben haben. Diese bedeutungsvollen Stunden kündigen sich nicht an, sondern kommen unerwartet. Auch nehmen sie sich nicht großartig aus, sondern unscheinbar. Ja, manchmal bekommen sie ihre Bedeutung für uns erst in der Erinnerung, wie uns die Schönheit einer Musik oder einer Landschaft manchmal erst in der Erinnerung aufgeht. Vieles, was an Sanftmut, Gütigkeit, Kraft zum Verzeihen, Wahrhaftigkeit, Treue, Ergebung in Leid unser geworden ist, verdanken wir Menschen, an denen wir solches erlebt haben, einmal in einem großen, einmal in einem kleinen Begebnis. Ein Leben gewordener Gedanke sprang wie ein Funke in uns hinein und zündete.

ALBERT SCHWEITZER (1875–1965), *Aus meiner Kindheit und Jugendzeit*

30 Die höchste Ursache

Die gegenwärtige Welt eröffnet uns einen so unermeßlichen Schauplatz von Mannigfaltigkeit, Ordnung, Zweckmäßigkeit und Schönheit, man mag diese nun in der Unendlichkeit des Raumes, oder in der unbegrenzten Teilung desselben verfolgen, daß selbst nach den Kenntnissen, welche unser schwacher Verstand davon hat erwerben können, alle Sprache, über so viele und unabsehlich große Wunder, ihren Nachdruck, alle Zahlen ihre Kraft zu messen, und selbst unsere Gedanken alle Begrenzung vermissen, so, daß sich unser Urteil vom Ganzen in ein sprachloses, aber desto beredteres Erstaunen auflösen muß. Allerwärts sehen wir eine Kette von Wirkungen und Ursachen, von Zwecken und den Mitteln, Regelmäßigkeit im Entstehen oder Vergehen, und indem nichts von selbst in den Zustand getreten ist, darin es sich befindet, so weiset er immer weiter hin nach einem anderen Dinge als seiner Ursache, welche gerade eben dieselbe weitere Nachfrage notwendig macht, so, daß auf solche Weise das ganze All im Abgrunde des Nichts versinken müßte, nähme man nicht etwas an, das außerhalb diesem unendlichen Zufälligen, für sich selbst ursprünglich und unabhängig bestehend, dasselbe hielte und als die Ursache seines Ursprungs ihm zugleich seine Fortdauer sicherte.

IMMANUEL KANT (1724–1804), *Kritik der reinen Vernunft*

31 Freud

Der Mann, der nun aus seiner Heimat, der er Ruhm über die Erde und durch die Zeiten geschenkt, nach London flüchtete, war den Jahren nach längst ein alter und außerdem ein schwerkranker Mann. Aber es war kein müder Mann und kein gebeugter. Ich hatte mich im geheimen ein wenig gefürchtet, ihn verbittert oder verstört wiederzufinden nach all den quälenden Stunden, durch die er in Wien gegangen sein mußte, und fand ihn freier und sogar glücklicher als je. Er führte mich hinaus in den Garten des Londoner Vorstadthauses. „Habe ich je schöner gewohnt?" fragte er mit einem hellen Lächeln um den einstmals so strengen Mund. Er zeigte mir seine geliebten ägyptischen Statuetten, die ihm Maria Bonaparte gerettet. „Bin ich nicht wieder zu Hause?" Und auf dem Schreibtisch lagen aufgeschlagen die großen Folioseiten seines Manuskripts, und er schrieb, dreiundachtzigjährig, mit derselben runden klaren Schrift jeden Tag, gleich hell im Geiste wie in seinen besten Tagen und gleich unermüdlich; sein starker Wille hatte alles überwunden, die Krankheit, das Alter, das Exil, und zum erstenmal strömte jetzt die in den langen Jahren des Kampfes zurückgestaute Güte seines Wesens frei von ihm aus. Nur milder hatte ihn das Alter gemacht, nur nachsichtiger die überstandene Prüfung.

STEFAN ZWEIG (1881–1942), *Die Welt von gestern*

32 Körperliche Schönheit und der Dichter

Ohne hier zu untersuchen, wie weit es dem Dichter gelingen kann, körperliche Schönheit zu schildern, so ist so viel unstreitig, daß, da das ganze unermeßliche Reich der Vollkommenheit seiner Nachahmung offen steht, diese sichtbare Hülle, unter welcher Vollkommenheit zu Schönheit wird, nur eines von den geringsten Mitteln sein kann, durch die er uns für seine Personen zu interessieren weiß. Oft vernachlässigt er dieses Mittel gänzlich, versichert, daß, wenn sein Held einmal unsere Gewogenheit gewonnen, uns dessen edlere Eigenschaften entweder so beschäftigen, daß wir an die körperliche Gestalt gar nicht denken, oder, wenn wir daran denken, uns so bestechen, daß wir ihm von selbst, wo nicht eine schöne, doch eine gleichgültige erteilen. Am wenigsten wird er bei jedem einzelnen Zuge, der nicht ausdrücklich für das Gesicht bestimmt ist, seine Rücksicht dennoch auf diesen Sinn nehmen dürfen. Wenn Virgils Laokoon schreit, wem fällt es dabei ein, daß ein großes Maul zum Schreien nötig ist, und daß dieses große Maul häßlich läßt? Genug, daß *clamores horrendos ad sidera tollit*[1] ein erhabener Zug für das Gehör ist, mag er doch für das Gesicht sein, was er will. Wer hier ein schönes Bild verlangt, auf den hat der Dichter seinen ganzen Eindruck verfehlt.

GOTTFRIED EPHRAIM LESSING (1729–1843), *Laokoon*

33 Ein beruhigender Mensch

Man ist manchmal bei sich selber uneins über die Vorzüge verschiedener Menschen. Jeder hat seine Vortrefflichkeit und dabei seinen eigenen Mangel. Dieser gefällt uns durch die Einfachheit und Akkuratesse und Unbefangenheit, womit er in einer bestimmten Richtung fortgeht, der er sich hingab; die Momente seines Lebens folgen sich ununterbrochen und leicht, alles hat bei ihm seine Stelle und seine Zeit; nichts schwankt, nichts stört sich, und weil er beim Gewöhnlichen bleibt, so ist er auch selten großer Mühe und großem Zweifel ausgesetzt. Und wie er für sich selbst ist, so hält er es auch mit andern, so wirkt er auf sie. Bestimmt, klar, nicht sehr bekümmert, immer gerade und moderat, und der Stelle und dem Augenblick angemessen und ganz in der Gegenwart, ist er uns, wenn wir nicht zu gespannt und hochgestimmt sind, auch niemals ungelegen; er läßt uns, wie wir sind, wir vertragen uns leicht mit ihm, er bringt uns nicht gerade um Vieles weiter, interessiert uns eigentlich auch nicht tief; aber dies wünschen wir ja auch nicht immer und besonders unter gewaltsamen Erschütterungen haben wir vorerst kein echteres Bedürfnis, als einen solchen Umgang, einen solchen Gegenstand, bei dem wir uns am leichtesten in einem Gleichgewichte, in Ruhe und Klarheit wiederfinden.

FRIEDRICH HÖLDERLIN (1770-1843),
Über die verschiedenen Arten zu dichten

[1] 'He lifts to heaven hideous cries' (Aeneid, Bk. II, l. 222)

34 Ein byzantinisches Kloster

Wir sind an diesem Tag mit Freunden in das Hymettosgebirge gefahren, um ein byzantinisches Kloster zu sehen. Diese alten griechischen Klosterkirchen sind sehr klein und dunkel, sehr gedrungen und fest, wie in den Boden gerammt. In der Kirche von Kaisariani nun haben wir jeder ein paar lange dünne Kerzen gekauft, sie angezündet und, ein wenig nach außen geneigt, um einen Leuchter gesteckt. Danach haben wir die früheren Mönchszellen angeschaut, sind unter den herrlichen alten Platanen umhergegangen und haben die Hände auf den von einer fruchtbarkeitbewirkenden Quelle überronnenen marmornen Widderkopf gelegt. Viel später, als es schon dunkel war und wir fort und auseinandergehen wollten, kamen wir noch einmal bei der Kirche vorbei. Da sahen wir nun durch ein vorher gar nicht bemerktes kleines Fenster gerade auf unsere Lichter, die, noch kaum kürzer geworden, still in der inzwischen geschlossenen Kirche brannten. Dieser Anblick hatte etwas seltsam Erregendes, so als sei schon eine lange Zeit verstrichen und als seien wir selbst nur Geister, die vorbeiziehen an der Stätte ihres menschlichen Tuns. Aber zugleich hatte doch jeder von uns ein beglückendes Gefühl: daß nämlich jedes echte Zusammensein über seine eigentliche Dauer aufrechterhalten bleibt und daß auch die von uns angezündeten Lichter noch fortleuchten, wenigstens für ein paar nächtlich Vorübergehende und für eine kleine Zeit.

MARIE LUISE KASCHNITZ (geboren 1901), *Darmstädter Rede*

35 Eine junge Dame

Adele Schopenhauer, von Mager eingelassen, versank in tiefem Knicks, aus dem Charlotte, die ihr die Hand bot, sie freundlich emporhob. Die junge Dame, Anfang Zwanzig nach Charlottens Schätzung, war recht unschönen aber intelligenten Ansehens, – ja, schon die Art, wie sie vom ersten Augenblick an und dann immerfort das doch unverkennbare Schielen ihrer gelb-grünen Augen teils durch häufigen Lidschlag, teils durch hurtiges Umher- und namentlich Emporblicken zu verbergen suchte, erweckte den Eindruck einer nervösen Intelligenz, und ein zwar breiter und schmaler, aber klug lächelnder und sichtlich in gebildeter Rede geübter Mund konnte die hängende Länge der Nase, den ebenfalls zu langen Hals, die betrüblich abstehenden Ohren übersehen lassen, neben denen gelockte accroche-coeurs unter dem mit Röschen umkränzten, etwas genialisch geformten Strohhut hervorkamen und in die Wangen fielen. Die Gestalt des Mädchens war dürftig. Ein weißer, aber flacher Busen verlor sich in dem kurzärmeligen Batistmieder, das in offener Krause um die mageren Schultern und den Nacken stand. Durchbrochene Halbhandschuhe, am Ende der dürren Arme, ließen ebenfalls dürre, rötliche Finger mit weißen Nägeln frei. Sie umfaßte damit, außer dem Griff ihres

Sonnenschirms, auch die in Seidenpapier gehüllten Stengel einiger Blumen nebst einem rollenförmigen Päckchen.

THOMAS MANN (1875–1955), *Lotte in Weimar*

36 Begegnung am Berghang

Die Stille war derart, daß ich Schritte, die gegen mich kamen, schon auf großen Abstand hörte, und sogleich blieb ich stehen, da mich wunderte, wer jetzt in der Herbstzeitlosenzeit und nach dem Abtrieb des Viehs diesen Weg noch benützen mochte; zugleich beunruhigte mich das Geräusch. Der Mensch, der sich von oben her zeigte, kam wie alle Erscheinungen vom Nebel vergrößert. Erst in der Nähe wurde er kleiner und sah endlich wie ein Bergamaskerhirt[1] aus; auf dem Kopf trug er einen Hut ohne Band und am Leib eine graue Montur, deren Nähte ausgebleicht waren, ein Abfallstück des vergangenen Krieges; ein Hund begleitete ihn. Wir grüßten uns, und er fragte, welche Zeit es sei. Erst da merkte ich, daß ich ohne Uhr unterwegs war; ich mußte sie vergessen haben in dem mühseligen und verwirrten Zustand, in dem ich mich zu diesem Aufbruch entschlossen hatte. Mann und Hund blickten mich an; es kam mir vor, als müßte ich mich entschuldigen. Dann stieg ich weiter. Wieviel Uhr mag es sein? sagte ich zu mir selbst. Ich spürte es nicht. Unter mir entfernten sich keine Schritte. Als ich zurückblickte, hatte der Hirt sich nicht gerührt; er stand noch, wo wir uns begegnet waren, wie in Gedanken, doch ohne mir nachzublicken; nur der Hund hatte den Kopf gewandt.

GERD GAISER (1908–1976), *Am Paß Nascondo*

37 Gemütswechsel

Dort hatten sich mittlerweile die Gäste zum Tee versammelt. Man konnte Livia nicht die geringste Unruhe anmerken. Sie tat nicht einmal des Unfalls Erwähnung. Freundlich schenkte sie die Tassen voll, bot Butter und Toast an und führte die Unterhaltung, als habe sie keinen einzigen Nebengedanken. Jene übertriebene Sorge von vorhin schien gänzlich von ihr gewichen zu sein. Die Unterhaltung freilich war welk und schleppend. Der Enthusiasmus unserer Festnacht lag mit den Aschenresten und Zigarettenstummeln auf dem Mist des Gewesenen. Der große Lacher hatte sich in einen kleinen Stummen verwandelt, der den wurstigen Gesprächen mit emsigem, aber verständnislosem Augenblinzeln folgte. Die Schönheit von gestern war nun eine verdrossene Abgeblühtheit von vorgestern. Da half kein Spiegel und Lippenstift mehr, wenn er auch doppelt so häufig gezückt wurde wie während der strahlenden Festnacht. Das langbefreundete Ehepaar saß grau und trübsinnig herum und war

[1] Hirt aus Bergamo

vollauf damit beschäftigt, ein gegenseitig ansteckendes Gähnduett erschrocken zu unterdrücken. Der witzige Kopf mit dem Tick hatte seinen Witz verloren, seinen Tick behalten. Nur manchmal platzte eine matte Pointe, zu deren Lieferung er sich verpflichtet fühlte, wie eine fade Wasserblase in der Windstille des Gesprächs. Die Luft im Zimmer war stickig und grau wie wir selbst. Auf allen Möbeln schien dicker Staub der Müdigkeit zu liegen. Seit Stunden grollten ferne Gewitter am Himmel ratlos umher. Sie hatten nicht Kraft und Jugend genug, um auszubrechen.

FRANZ WERFEL (1890–1950), *Der veruntreute Himmel*

38 Wie Beethoven Musik komponierte

Ich trage meine Gedanken lange, oft sehr lange mit mir herum, ehe ich sie niederschreibe. Dabei bleibt mir mein Gedächtnis so treu, daß ich sicher bin, ein Thema, das ich einmal erfaßt habe, selbst nach Jahren nicht zu vergessen. Ich verändere manches, verwerfe und versuche aufs neue, so lange, bis ich damit zufrieden bin. Dann aber beginnt in meinem Kopfe die Verarbeitung in die Breite, in die Enge, Höhe und Tiefe, und da ich mir bewußt bin, was ich will, so verläßt mich die zugrundeliegende Idee niemals, sie steigt, sie wächst empor, ich sehe und höre das Bild in seiner ganzen Ausdehnung wie aus einem Gusse vor meinem Geiste stehen, und es bleibt nur die Arbeit des Niederschreibens, die rasch vonstatten geht, je nachdem ich die Zeit erübrige, weil ich zuweilen mehreres zugleich in Arbeit nehme, aber sicher bin, keins mit dem anderen zu verwirren.

Woher ich meine Ideen nehme? Das vermag ich mit Zuverlässigkeit nicht zu sagen; sie kommen ungerufen, mittelbar, unmittelbar, ich könnte sie mit Händen greifen in der freien Natur, im Walde, auf Spaziergängen, in der Stille der Nacht, am frühen Morgen, angeregt durch Stimmungen, die sich bei dem Dichter in Worte, bei mir in Töne umsetzen, klingen, brausen, stürmen, bis sie endlich in Noten vor mir stehen.

LUDWIG VAN BEETHOVEN (1770–1827), *Aufzeichnungen*

39 Der österreichische Offizier

Nachts, beim Lesen der Ilias, befiel mich Erinnerung an den jungen österreichischen Offizier, der uns auf dem Berge Carunta so freundlich bewirtete. Ob wir uns heute noch so gut verstünden? Sein schmales Gesicht ist mir nicht mehr so deutlich wie die lange knochige, durch Narben verzogene Hand, die beim Sprechen sehr schüchterne Bewegungen ausführte. Ein Buch mit italienischen Gedichten lag vor ihm aufgeschlagen. Von Zeit zu Zeit sah er durch ein Scherenfernrohr in das feindliche Gebiet hinüber, wo er schließlich eine Truppenansammlung entdeckte. Pflichtgemäß rief er durch den Fernsprecher zu dem Geschütz hinunter,

bezeichnete nach der Karte einen Punkt und gab an, mit wie vielen Grana-
ten dieser belegt werden sollte. Dann goß er wieder Tee in die Feldbecher
und erzählte sehr anmutig von seiner Frau und seinen Kindern, indessen
die Luft von den Abschüssen bebte. Er war ein ausgezeichneter Soldat
und hatte wieder einmal das Nötige getan, obendrein auf die sauberste,
sachlichste Weise; kein Tröpfchen Blut haftete an seinem grauen Rock.Ihm
wäre auch nicht eingefallen, ein unfreundliches Wort über den Gegner zu
äußern, er dachte wohl gar nicht an die zerfetzten Leiber, die drüben
verendeten. Was konnten sie ihm bedeuten? Schwerlich mehr als ein
Schwarm schädlicher Insekten, der nun, Gott sei Dank, beseitigt war.

HANS CAROSSA (1878–1956), *Geheimnisse des reifen Lebens*

40 Franz Kafka

Franz Kafka ist der einzige Dichter unseres Jahrhunderts, der die immanenten Gesetze unserer sozialen und persönlichen Wirklichkeit kritisch
erkannt und anschaulich ins Bild gebracht hat. Daher ist er der realistisch-
ste Dichter unserer Zeit. Daher ist er aber auch zugleich der rätselhaf-
teste und erschreckendste Dichter für alle diejenigen, die mehr oder weniger
bewußtlos oder unkritisch in diese Gesetze der Wirklichkeit verstrickt
sind oder sich gar mit ihnen identifizieren, sich als ihre Vollzugsorgane
bezeichnen, als die wahren Lenker der Geschichte aufgrund ihrer Einsicht
in die Gesetzmäßigkeit ihrer Abläufe. Diesen Lenkern der Geschicke, die
sich in Übereinstimmung wähnen mit dem notwendigen Gang der historischen Entwicklung, mußte und muß bis heute Franz Kafkas kritische
Entlarvung ihres Realitätsbewußtseins das große und gefährliche Ärgernis
ihres Denkens und Handelns darstellen. Denn sie mußten, genau wie die
von ihnen Verachteten, die mehr oder weniger ahnungslos oder mit einem
angeblich „falschen Bewußtsein" den immanenten Gesetzen der Wirklichkeit verfallen und ihnen ausgeliefert bleiben, bei der Lektüre Franz
Kafkas den unabweisbaren Chock erfahren, daß Franz Kafka die Wahrheit
der Wirklichkeit enthüllt, die Wahrheit, die jedoch so unerträglich ist, daß
ihr Bewußtsein sich gegen sie sperren und sie abdrängen muß ins Verließ
des Verbotenen, Anrüchigen, Grauenhaften, Irrationalen oder gar pervers
Dekadenten.

WILHELM EMRICH (geboren 1909), *Franz Kafka*

Section B

1 Was Sekretärinnen alles wissen müssen

Wieviel mehr eine Sekretärin können muß als Maschinenschreiben und Stenographieren, zeigt das jetzt erschienene Heyne-Taschenbuch über „Das grundlegende Sekretärinnenwissen". Es ist ein nützliches Handbuch für Sekretärinnen, da es Auskunft gibt über Postgebühren und Handelsabkürzungen, über die Währungen der verschiedenen Länder, Impfvorschriften, die Anschriften wichtiger Behörden, die Geheimsprache der Zeugnisse und anderes. Darüber hinaus informiert es über die verschiedenen Arbeitsbereiche der Sekretärin und gibt psychologische Tips für den Umgang mit dem Chef, mit Besuchern und Kollegen. Jungen Mädchen, die sich für diesen Beruf interessieren, gibt es eine Vorstellung von seiner Vielseitigkeit.

Stuttgarter Zeitung

2 Streß

Als besonders üble Kombination der Streßfaktoren Hetze, Angst, Isolation und Lärm gilt den Forschern das Autofahren. Aufzeichnungen der Herzstromkurven gesunder Fahrzeuglenker bestätigen den schlimmen Verdacht: Stets ist der Puls beschleunigt, der Blutdruck erhöht, die Sauerstoffversorgung des hohlen Muskels gemindert. Berufskraftfahrer werden deshalb bevorzugt Opfer eines Herzinfarkts . . .

Was aber das Streßphänomen so unheimlich, so ungreifbar macht, ist die Tatsache, daß jeder Mensch in individueller Weise auf die verschiedenen Streßfaktoren reagiert: Beat ist dem Beatle Wohlklang und kein Streß . . .

Aber nicht nur die Empfindsamkeit des einzelnen gegenüber Streßfaktoren ist unterschiedlich – mindestens ebenso große Differenzen zeigen sich auch in der Art, wie der Organismus reagiert.

Der Spiegel

3 Kunstdiebstähle

Kunstdiebstähle werden heute oft mit einer geradezu verblüffenden Sachkenntnis durchgeführt. Bei Einbrüchen bleiben immer wieder Bilder, die mit großem Geschick an den populären Geschmack appellieren, unangetastet, während verhältnismäßig unscheinbare Werke von wirklichem Wert gestohlen werden. In einem bestimmten Fall ließen sich die Connoisseure der Diebsgilde auch durch die etwas zweifelhaften Bezeichnungen „P. P. Rubens" und „Claude Lorraine" auf dem Goldrahmen zweier Bilder nicht imponieren. Sie legten kritischere Maßstäbe an als die Eigentümer und ignorierten die Gemälde.

Ist es wirklich denkbar, daß die Einbrecher Kunstexperten sind? Viel wahrscheinlicher ist es, daß die Spezialkenntnis von ihren Hintermännern und Auftraggebern beigesteuert wird. Jedenfalls werden die Raubzüge der Kunstgangster sorgfältig organisiert und mit geradezu wissenschaftlicher Gründlichkeit vorbereitet.

Die Zeit

4 Erstaunliche Erholungsmöglichkeiten des Gehirns

Der Hirnschaden, den Kinder erleiden, wenn sie bis zu ihrem zweiten Lebensjahr unzureichend ernährt werden, kann in beträchtlichem Ausmaß behoben werden, wenn die Kinder nachher in eine Umgebung kommen, die ihnen geistige Anregungen bietet. Das Gehirn ist eben eine Struktur, die zu erstaunlichen Ausgleichsmaßnahmen fähig ist. Zu dieser Aussage kommen englische und amerikanische Ärzte und Psychologen, die die Entwicklung koreanischer Kinder studiert haben, die von amerikanischen und europäischen Familien adoptiert wurden. Wenn ein Elternpaar ein fernöstliches elternloses Kind adoptiert, so folgern die Gelehrten, ist damit *eo ipso* eine gewisse Gewähr dafür gegeben, daß das Kind in eine anregende Umgebung kommt. Nach einigen Jahren haben die Kinder, wie die Untersuchungen ergaben, den Standard ihrer Altersgenossen erreicht, hinter dem sie anfangs beträchtlich zurückstanden.

Die Zeit

5 Schwere Tresorknacker-Laufbahn

Wie schwer und reich an Enttäuschungen eine Tresorknacker-Laufbahn sein kann, schilderte die Züricher Polizei. Ein Einbrechertrio, jetzt hinter Schweizer „schwedischen Gardinen", stahl in Zürich zunächst einen Personenwagen, um nächtens ins knapp 30 Kilometer entfernte Wädenswil zu brausen. Dort hatten es die Männer auf einen Tresor in einer Fabrik abgesehen, für dessen Abtransport allerdings erst ein Lieferwagen „den Besitzer wechseln" mußte. In einem Waldstück angekommen, erwies sich das mitgebrachte Werkzeug für die „Schränker-Arbeiten" als unbrauchbar. Im nahen Horgen suchten sie deshalb eine Werkstatt heim. Doch auch mit den neuen Instrumenten kamen sie nicht ans Ziel. Ein weiterer Einbruch verhalf ihnen zu einem Schneidbrenner, dem der Tresor schließlich nicht widerstand. Ebensowenig widerstand der gestohlene Lieferwagen einem Feuer: Das Trio steckte ihn aus Wut darüber, daß der Geldschrank leer war, in Brand.

Stuttgarter Zeitung

6 Wer zu dicht auffährt, fährt auf!

„. . . kam nicht mehr rechtzeitig zum Stehen und fuhr auf seinen Vordermann auf." Es ist fast schon langweilig, diesen Satz wieder und wieder in Unfallberichten lesen zu müssen. Speziell auf Autobahnen und Schnellverkehrsstraßen zählen Auffahrunfälle nach Bremsmanövern des Vordermanns zu den häufigsten Unfällen überhaupt.

Und warum donnern so viele ihrem Vorausfahrenden ins Heck? In den allermeisten Fällen weil sie sich zu dicht hinter den Vordermann geklemmt, weil sie einen zu geringen Abstand gehalten hatten.

Die Sache ist ganz einfach: Schreckspanne, Reaktionszeit und Bremsenansprechzeit machen zusammen beim Durchschnittsfahrer 1,0 bis 1,5 Sekunden aus. Fährt man mit 120 km/h hinter einem anderen her und bremst dieser andere, so rollt man noch 33 bis 50 Meter weiter, ehe die eigenen Bremsen zupacken. Um diese Meterzahl ist somit bei Bremsmanövern der Hinterherfahrer unabänderlich im Minus. Einziges Gegenrezept: Genug Abstand halten.

Rhein-Neckar-Zeitung

7 Die Kommunisten in der DDR[1]

Bei uns in der BRD[2] herrscht im allgemeinen die Vorstellung, Kommunisten seien bar jeder Moral. Man glaubt, für sie existiere überhaupt keine ethische Weltvorstellung, es gehe ihnen vielmehr nur um materielle Herrschaft und Machtausübung und also darum, ihre Bevölkerung physisch zu beherrschen und geistig zu bevormunden. Wenn dies so wäre, wenn der Fortschrittsglaube wirklich nur Tarnung der Herrschaftsgelüste wäre, dann wäre es verhältnismäßig leicht, sie zu entlarven und mit ihnen fertig zu werden. Die Schwierigkeit aber liegt gerade darin, daß die Kommunisten von der moralischen Berechtigung ihrer Handlungsweise fest überzeugt sind, daß sie ferner ihre Gläubigen zu größter Hingabe und Opferbereitschaft zu inspirieren vermögen und daß schließlich in mancher Hinsicht der Idealismus drüben viel größer ist als auf unserer Seite. Die drüben glauben wirklich, man könnte die Welt verändern und die Menschheit von der Versuchung des Bösen befreien.

MARION GRÄFIN DÖNHOFF, *Reise in ein fernes Land*

[1]DDR: Deutsche Demokratische Republik (German Democratic Republic/E. Germany)
[2]BRD: Bundesrepublik Deutschland (Federal Republic of Germany/W. Germany)

8 Die Bevölkerungsexplosion

In knapp 16 Jahren hat die Menschheit um abermals eine Milliarde zugenommen, und die Entwicklung geht mit wachsender Geschwindigkeit weiter – wenn nichts geschieht.

Etwas aber muß geschehen. Rohstoffe und Nahrung gibt es nicht unbegrenzt, und ihre Produktion läßt sich auch nicht im gleichen Maße steigen, wie die Bevölkerung zunimmt. Die tiefe Spaltung der Länder dieser Erde in immer Reichere und immer ärmere Habenichtse würde durch ein weiter ungehemmtes Bevölkerungswachstum so verstärkt werden, daß schließlich ein Weltbrand als Kampf um die bloße Existenz abzusehen wäre. Gegen solche heillose Entwicklung gilt es einen Damm zu errichten. Und wie ein Damm gepflegt und behütet werden muß, soll er den Stürmen trotzen, so bleibt den Staaten dieser Welt trotz aller unterschiedlicher Interessen künftig gar nichts anderes übrig, als gemeinsam das mühsame Werk gegen Hunger, Armut und Radikalismus zu vollenden und dann immer wieder auf Schwachstellen zu klopfen.

Hessische Allgemeine

9 Versuchung im Kaufhaus

Die Zahl stehlender Kinder nahm in den letzten Jahren besorgniserregend zu, jedenfalls wurden mehr Kinder erwischt als früher. Ihre Lieblingsobjekte sind Schallplatten und Kosmetika, Dinge, die „man" haben muß, wenn man „in" sein will, und für die das Taschengeld nicht reicht. Nicht selten sind Kinder aber auch „Erfüllungsgehilfen" ihrer Eltern. Denn Kinder anschaffen zu lassen, ist weniger riskant. In der Regel werden sie nämlich nicht der Polizei und auch nicht der Schule gemeldet – der Kaufhof-Konzern gehört zu den Ausnahmen. Die meisten Firmen benachrichtigen nur die Eltern, die ihre Kinder dann abholen müssen. Und was die in den häuslichen vier Wänden mit ihnen machen, geht niemand was an.

Gezielte Kampagnen wie die der Hamburger Schulbehörde sollen Kindern zum Unrechtsbewußtsein verhelfen. Aber der Sog der Sachen ist eben stark, und das „Zeige mir, was du hast, und ich will dir sagen, wer du bist" – diese Wertskala leben ihnen ja die Erwachsenen vor.

RUTH HERRMANN, *Tatort: Das Kaufhaus* (Die Zeit)

10 Kein Alibi

Früher, in der guten alten, computerlosen Zeit, wurden Reklamationsbriefe etwa so beantwortet: „. . . und bitten wir Sie höflich um Nachsicht. Wir sind der Sache nachgegangen und können uns die Verzögerung in der

Bearbeitung Ihres werten Auftrags nur so erklären, daß unserem Buchhalter ein Irrtum unterlaufen ist, was wir bedauern. Indem wir nochmals um Entschuldigung bitten . . ." Und so weiter. Das waren noch Zeiten!

Heute, im Zeitalter des technischen Fortschritts, der Rationalisierung und der Automatisierung bekommt man immer häufiger – mitunter sogar auf vervielfältigte Weise – zu lesen: „Wir bitten Sie um Verständnis dafür, daß wir unser gesamtes Rechnungswesen auf moderne Computer umgestellt haben. Der Fortschritt der Technik bringt es leider mit sich . . ." Und so weiter. Zeiten sind das!

Computer hin, Computer her. Sie mögen zu manchem nützlich und zuweilen sogar unentbehrlich sein; aber als Alibi sollte man sie nicht mißbrauchen, jedenfalls nicht, solange sie noch von Menschen programmiert, und zwar oft genug *falsch* programmiert werden.

Die Zeit

11 Die Verantwortung des Naturwissenschaftlers

Wenn wir dem Naturwissenschaftler sagen, wie wichtig er ist, so müssen wir ihm eben darum auch sagen, welche Verantwortung er trägt. Die Verantwortung für die Sauberkeit seines wissenschaftlichen Denkens kennt er. Die Verantwortung für die Folgen seiner Handlungen im menschlichen Leben muß er kennen. Jeder Naturwissenschaftler weiß, daß ein physikalisches Experiment, das nicht mit aller Sorgfalt durchgeführt ist, wertlos ist; sonst messen wir, wie wir im Jargon sagen, nicht die wirklichen Effekte, sondern die Dreckeffekte. So lange unserem Stand, dem Stand der Naturwissenschaftler und Techniker, die Rücksicht darauf, was für Wirkungen unsere Apparaturen im menschlichen Leben anrichten, nicht ebenso selbstverständlich geworden ist wie die Sorgfalt im Experimentieren, so lange sind wir zum Leben im technischen Zeitalter nicht reif. Ich denke hier nicht nur an die großen politischen Entscheidungen. Wer mit dem Auto schneller fährt, als er bei den bekannten Eigenschaften dieses Apparats verantworten kann, verhält sich untechnisch. Die Zerstörung des Lebens durch Hast und Lärm wirkt subtiler als die Bomben, verdient aber nicht weniger Aufmerksamkeit.

CARL FRIEDRICH VON WEIZSÄCKER (geboren 1912),
Atomenergie und Atomzeitalter

12 Athletik, Artistik und Arithmetik bei den Europapokalspielen

Das Tempo der Polen in Hamburg, ihre glänzende Technik – jeder Spieler hatte den Ball in jeder Situation unter Kontrolle – und die disziplinierte Taktik – jeder Spieler widmete sich bei der Defensive einem ihm vom Trainer zugewiesenen HSV[1]-Spieler und löste sich sofort von ihm, wenn die eigene Offensive begann, waren im Stadion offensichtlich.

Das Spiel in Düsseldorf war eine Demonstration für den Fußball anno 1976: eine Mischung aus Athletik, Artistik und Arithmetik. Athleten und Artisten waren die Spieler beider Mannschaften. Die Gladbacher – das war auffällig, wenn sie in Ballbesitz waren – hatten in Ballnähe mindestens drei Spieler, die rannten. Dieses Tempo beeindruckte die Spanier zunächst sehr, weil ihre Spielweise ökonomischer angelegt ist. Sie haben ebenfalls viele Spieler in Ballnähe, aber die im Schrittempo. Den Torerfolg suchen dann Individualisten. Sowohl das Kopfballtor als auch das Ausgleichstor durch Pirri waren Ergebnisse von außergewöhnlichen Einzelleistungen. Gladbachs nachlassendes Tempo begünstigte dann Madrids Taktik.

Die Arithmetik hatte begonnen: Die Spieler spielten auf Zeit, simulierten Verletzungen, nahmen Drohgebärden ein – man rechnete mit Reaktionen.

JÜRGEN WERNER, Geld, Gefühl und Arithmetik (Die Zeit)

[1] HSV: Hamburger Sportverein

13 Bürger

Von fern schwingt noch etwas Positives im Wort Bürger mit: der Bürger als *citoyen*, als Staatsbürger, der bewußt Anteil nimmt an der Wohlfahrt der Allgemeinheit, der sich in Revolutionen gegen die Aristokratie durchgesetzt und „bürgerliche Ehrenrechte" erobert hat. Aber diese Bedeutungskomponente ist fast verschüttet.

Die Hauptkomponente ist die verwaschenste. In ihr ist die Verachtung des Außenseiters für alles enthalten, was er für banale Normalität hält. Seit anderthalb Jahrhunderten heben sich Künstler so vom Philister, vom Spießer, vom Bourgeois, vom Bürger ab. Wie beim Wort Kitsch, setzt jeder nach Belieben ein, was er selber für die miesesten Merkmale dieser Normalität hält. Eine Definition für das flexible Schimpfwort ist diesem Affekt unmöglich abzugewinnen. Bürger: das Operettenpublikum, die Kuchenesser bei Kranzler[1], die Leute, die nach Mallorca reisen, die Lesezirkeln angehören, die behäbig selbstgerecht sind . . . Menschen wie du, aber nicht ich . . .

Hinzu kommt als dritte die marxistische Komponente: der Bürger als Angehöriger der Schicht, die den Kapitalismus groß gemacht hat und beseitigt werden muß, wo der Kapitalismus verschwinden soll.

DIETER E. ZIMMER, Bürger! (Die Zeit)

[1] Kranzler: berühmte Konditorei

14 Neuakademiker in Wirtschaft und Verwaltung

Die Angst der Industrie vor zuviel Theorie der Hochschulen ist immer noch sehr groß und – wie böse Erfahrungen zeigen – sicherlich auch zum Teil berechtigt. Das führt bei einem Teil der Personalleiter dazu, daß sie *promovierte Bewerber* mit dem Hinweis ablehnen, diese seien noch mehr als alle anderen Hochschulabsolventen durch Theorie „verdorben" . . .

Ein Teil der Absolventenstellen ist deshalb dem Promovierten von vornherein verschlossen. Allerdings sind es meist Positionen, die für den jungen Doktor auch kaum noch attraktiv sind. Er wird aber – und das betrifft vor allem technische, naturwissenschaftliche und wirtschaftswissenschaftliche Richtungen – bei einer Anzahl von Positionen stark bevorzugt . . .

Für die meisten Promovierten bedeutet das einen Einkommensvorteil von 500 bis 1000 Mark pro Monat gegenüber Diplomierten, die allerdings drei bis vier Jahre jünger sind. Bei gleichrangigen Positionen gibt es kaum Einkommensunterschiede; allenfalls werden 100 bis 200 Mark Anerkennungszuschlag gezahlt. Untersucht man allerdings langfristig die Karriere von Promovierten, so ist festzustellen, daß sie meist schneller in höhere Funktionen gelangen und auch häufiger Top-Positionen erreichen als nicht promovierte Akademiker.

FRANZ GRÄTZ, *Praktische Erfahrungen bringen Geld* (Die Zeit)

15 Der manchmal giftige Schmetterling

Manche Kräuter wenden einige Energie auf, um Glykoside zu synthetisieren, die keine andere erkennbare Bedeutung haben, als die Pflanze immun zu machen gegen den Fraß von Rindern und Rehen; es sind Herzgifte für Wirbeltiere. Dann kommen Raupen und leihen sich diese kugelsichere Weste. Sie fressen von den Blättern und speichern das Gift, so daß auch der Falter noch für Vögel giftig und ungenießbar ist. Seine Färbung wird für die Vögel zur „Warnfarbe". Dieses Kostüm wiederum „leihen" sich andere ungiftige Schmetterlinge. Sie ahmen die Warnfärbung nach und genießen nun einen Schutz, den sie gar nicht selber verdient haben. Soweit das Täuschungssystem der klassischen Mimikry mit dem giftigen „Vorbild" und dem ungiftigen „Nachahmer".

Es funktioniert auch dann noch, so fand der amerikanische Biologe Professor Lincoln Pierson Brower in einer tiefschürfenden Analyse heraus, wenn gar nicht sämtliche Schmetterlinge des giftigen Vorbildes giftig und unschmackhaft sind. Es genügt durchaus, daß die Hälfte oder gar nur ein Viertel der Population an einem Giftkraut groß geworden ist und das Gift wirklich enthält.

GUSTAV ADOLF HENNING, *Der manchmal giftige Schmetterling* (Die Zeit)

16 Der Markt einst und jetzt

„Sehen Sie, wie war es früher? Mindestens vier Fragen stellte sich der Käufer, bevor er sich zum Kauf entschloß. Erste Frage: Brauche ich das Produkt? Zweite Frage: Ist es preiswürdig? Dritte Frage: Kann ich es mir leisten? Vierte Frage: Wie ermögliche ich mir den Kauf, ohne in Verschuldung zu geraten? Eventuell muß ich auf anderes verzichten. Auf was? – Von diesen Grundfragen wurde der Markt bestimmt. Die Wirtschaft aber produzierte, was dieser Markt verlangte. Mit anderen Worten: der Markt war von den Bedürfnissen des Verbrauchers bestimmt. Heute: die Wirtschaft hat sich auf Stückzahlen eingerichtet, die den echten Bedarf übersteigen. Also heißt es: Anreize schaffen, um neuen Bedarf zu wecken. Erzeugung von Bedürfnissen, und sei's um den Preis künstlicher Verschuldung. Und da, sehen Sie, hört meine Liebe auf. Jedenfalls meine Liebe zum Beruf. An dieser Grenzlinie rufe ich halt!"

„Sie meinen: wer bewußt über diese Grenzlinie wechselt, macht sich schuldig. Schuldig gegenüber der Gesellschaft?"

„Das meine ich: er verletzt ein fundamentales Moralgesetz dieser Gesellschaft, deren Teil er ist."

HORST MÖNNICH (geboren 1918)
Wir tüchtigen Deutschen (Bestandsaufnahme)

17 Mitbestimmung

Aus einem Vergleich der englischen und deutschen Stellungnahmen ergab sich, daß auf dem Gebiet der Hochschulen die Situation in England weit weniger revolutionär ist. Die gleiche Feststellung trifft im Grunde für die Wirtschaft zu.

Die Engländer sagten: Was wir brauchen, ist eine optimale Rationalisierung unserer Industrie und ein erstklassiges Management – beides können wir mit industrieller Demokratisierung, also mit Mitbestimmung, nicht erreichen. Eine saubere Konfliktsituation – hie Eigentümer, dort Arbeiter – ist viel besser.

Ein Mitglied der SPD[1] entgegnete ihnen, es sei falsch, das Problem auf die Ebene *Eigentümer und Nicht-Eigentümer* zu schieben: es sei nämlich ganz gleich, ob der Staat, die Aktionäre oder eine Privatperson der Eigentümer sei, worauf es ankommt, sei das Management und nicht die Frage, wem das Vermögen gehöre. Ausgangspunkt sei auch nicht die Konfliktsituation zwischen Kapital und Arbeit, die ja beide im Betrieb gleichermaßen unentbehrlich sind. Den Arbeitern, so sagte er, gehe es nicht um Opposition gegen das Kapital oder darum, selber das Management zu stellen, sondern darum, daß beide zusammen den Aufsichtsrat wählen, der seinerseits das Management bestimmt.

MARION GRÄFIN DÖNHOFF,
Participation – wie Deutsche und Engländer sie sehen (Die Zeit)

[1]SPD: Sozialdemokratische Partei Deutschlands

18 Liebe oder Vaterlandsliebe?

REA: Soll man denn nicht das Vaterland mehr lieben als alles in der Welt?

ROMULUS: Nein, man soll es weniger lieben als einen Menschen.

REA: Vater!

ROMULUS: Meine Tochter?

REA: Ich kann doch das Vaterland unmöglich im Stich lassen.

ROMULUS: Du mußt es im Stich lassen.

REA: Ich kann nicht ohne Vaterland leben!

ROMULUS: Kannst du ohne den Geliebten leben? Es ist viel größer und viel schwerer, einem Menschen die Treue zu halten als einem Staat.

REA: Es geht um das Vaterland, nicht um einen Staat.

ROMULUS: Vaterland nennt sich der Staat immer dann, wenn er sich anschickt, auf Menschenmord auszugehen.

REA: Unsere unbedingte Liebe zum Vaterland hat Rom groß gemacht.

ROMULUS: Aber unsere Liebe hat Rom nicht gut gemacht. Wir haben mit unseren Tugenden eine Bestie gemästet. Wir haben uns an der Größe unseres Vaterlandes wie mit Wein berauscht, aber nun ist Wermut geworden, was wir liebten.

REA: Du bist undankbar gegen das Vaterland.

ROMULUS: Nein, ich bin nur nicht wie einer jener Heldenväter in den Trauerspielen, die dem Staat noch einen guten Appetit wünschen, wenn er ihre Kinder fressen will. Geh, heirate Ämilian!

Schweigen

REA: Ämilian hat mich verstoßen, Vater.

FRIEDRICH DÜRRENMATT (geboren 1921), *Romulus der Große*

19 Keine Zeit zum Spielen

Die durch unser einseitig orientiertes Bildungssystem verursachte Perversion des Leistungsbegriffs hat dazu geführt, daß der persönliche Freiraum der Heranwachsenden beschnitten wird und die emotionalen, sozialen und kreativen Bedürfnisse der Schüler ins Hintertreffen geraten. Besonders verhängnisvoll wirkt sich dabei aus, daß der Leistungsdruck der Schule vor dem Familienleben nicht haltmacht, sondern durch die Hausaufgabenmisere ins Elternhaus hineingetragen wird. So finden die Schüler nach einem anstrengenden Unterrichtsvormittag in ihrer sogenannten Freizeit zu Hause vielfach keinen Ort der Entspannung, sondern eine Zweigniederlassung des Schulbetriebs vor.

Doch anstatt sich gegen diesen Übergriff der Schule zu wehren, drängen manche Eltern sogar darauf, daß ihre Kinder mit noch mehr Lernstoff vollgepfropft werden. ,,Ich bin froh, wenn meine Kinder eine Menge Hausaufgaben machen müssen. Dann tun sie wenigstens etwas Vernünftiges. Sonst wissen sie ja doch nichts mit sich anzufangen." Diese

Meinung wird von Müttern immer wieder geäußert. Und sie nehmen mit Genugtuung zur Kenntnis, wenn ihre Kinder nachmittagelang über Schulbüchern sitzen. Daß hier in vielen Fällen nicht für das Leben gelernt, sondern lediglich für die Schule gepaukt wird, ist den meisten Eltern gar nicht bewußt.

RUTH MARTIN, *Keine Zeit zum Spielen* (Die Zeit)

20 Gehirnwäsche

Die Verfahren der Gehirnwäsche dauern verschieden lange, je nach der individuellen Widerstandskraft. Sie werden auch miteinander vermischt angewendet. Zuerst wird mit einer einmaligen überraschenden Aktion die reine Existenz des Menschen gefährdet. Man gibt ihm zu verstehen, er werde nicht mehr lange leben . . . Schon in dieser Phase kann man dem Opfer zu verstehen geben, daß es unter gewissen Umständen doch eine Möglichkeit zu überleben gibt.

Ziel der zweiten Stufe der Gehirnwäsche ist es, ein Gefühl nicht näher definierbarer Schuld zu züchten: „Irgendeinen Fehler muß ich doch gemacht haben.“ Im nächsten Stadium liefert man dem Opfer entsprechende Informationen. Es kann sich beispielsweise um bewußt verdrehte Äußerungen des Angeklagten handeln oder um gefälschte Dokumente. In den meisten Fällen präsentiert man überzeugende Nachrichten darüber, daß seine Freunde und Familienangehörigen ihn denunziert haben.

Im nächsten Stadium versucht man, ihm direkt oder indirekt den Gedanken zu suggerieren: „Nur der, der sich ändert und einwandfrei mitarbeitet, kann überleben.“

Es geht um einen langsamen Aufbau von Paranoia und selbstanklägerischen Vorstellungen. Oft wird an den gesunden Menschenverstand appelliert und „Anpassung an die Realität“ als einziger Ausweg empfohlen.

IVO PLANAVA, *Gehirnwäsche* (Die Zeit)

21 Atomenergie und Atomzeitalter

„Wie schön wäre es, wenn es nur diese friedliche Verwendung der Atomenergie gäbe! Aber es gab ja auch die Bomben von Hiroshima und Nagasaki. Es gibt die Wasserstoffbombe, und es gibt die Atomraketen, strategische und taktische Atomwaffen . . .

Die Wissenschaftler können nicht verhindern, was mit den Ergebnissen ihrer Forschung geschieht. Aber sie können doch immer wieder versuchen, friedliche Gespräche vor kriegerische Maßnahmen zu stellen. Heute haben wir die Wasserstoffbombe als das drohende Gespenst der explosiven Vereinigung von Wasserstoff und Helium. Aber unsere Sonne zeigt uns ja etwas ganz anderes. Daß unsere Erde noch bewohnbar ist, daß sie nicht längst zu einem toten Steinhaufen erkaltet ist, verdanken wir der in der

Sonne seit einigen Millionen Jahren vor sich gehenden.geregelten¨ Verschmelzung des Wasserstoffs in Helium, also dem Vorgang, um den sich unsere Wissenschaftler jetzt bemühen. Und unsere Kinder und Enkel – oder ihre Kinder und Enkel – werden den Prozeß gemeistert haben. Dann bringen sie das, was die Sonne uns seit Milliarden geliefert hat, dann bringen sie die Sonne auf die Erde – wenn man ihnen ein Weiterleben auf der Erde gestattet."

OTTO HAHN (1879–1968), *Aus einem 1958 an die Gesellschaft Deutscher Naturforscher und Ärzte gehaltenen Vortrag* (Die Zeit)

22 Nachteile der Technik

Wären wir nun in den nichtkommunistischen Ländern wirklich frei, so könnten wir versuchen, auf die neuen Fragen, die der stürmische wissenschaftlich-technische Wandlungsprozeß der Gesellschaft aufgibt, die jeweils richtigen Antworten zu finden. In Wahrheit aber sind wir an veraltete wissenschaftliche und soziale Strukturen gebunden, die eine Bewältigung der Zukunftsaufgaben hemmen und in vielen Fällen fast unmöglich machen.

Ein besonders eklatantes Beispiel für dieses Versagen ist der mangelnde Schutz für das, was wir Europäer von den vorhergehenden Generationen erbten und den kommenden Generationen weitergeben sollten: Luft, Wasser, Boden, Kulturdenkmäler. Gerade diejenigen, die sich so gerne als Verteidiger von Tradition und Ordnung hinstellen, verhindern aus Geiz oder Habgier den wirkungsvollen Kampf gegen den Chaos verursachenden Einbruch antihumanistischer technischer Gewalten. Sie gestatten, ja fördern industrielle Luftverpestung, die ständig zunehmende Verschmutzung aller Gewässer, die große Landzerstörung, die vor keinem Wald mehr haltmachen will, die Verschändelung historischer Stadtlandschaften. Denn diesen Anhängern der freien Marktordnung und den Strategen, die ihre Unordnung zu verteidigen haben, wird der Himmel zum bloßen „Luftraum", der Strom zum „Abwasser", die Wiese zum „Gelände", das ehrwürdige Bauwerk zum Objekt einer Grundstückspekulation.

ROBERT JUNGK, *Unbewältigte Zukunft (Bestandsaufnahme)*

23 Die Intellektuellen und die Unternehmer

Aus einer Geburtstagsrede auf einen Freund, der seinen Weg als Kaufmann gemacht hat

... Durch meinen Beruf habe ich es ständig mit Künstlern, Schriftstellern, Schauspielern, Musikern und Wissenschaftlern zu tun – und wenn mich bei den zahllosen Gesprächen mit ihnen etwas, und zwar gar nicht so selten, geärgert hat, dann war es ihr Hochmut gegenüber den Menschen, die Geld verdienen . . . Ich habe es hundert Male erlebt, daß von Intellektuellen selbst über bedeutendste Persönlichkeiten der Wirtschaft Äußerungen gemacht wurden, die maßlos ungerecht waren und zudem eine völlige Ahnungslosigkeit in bezug darauf verrieten, was ein Kaufmann, ein Mann der Wirtschaft, ein Unternehmer heute ist und sein muß . . .

Für mich hat Dein Beruf, der Beruf . . . des Kaufmanns etwas Faszinierendes: es ist verbunden mit Kenntnis des Materials, mit Kenntnis des Menschen, mit Kenntnis des Marktes. Wer sind denn die weltpolitisch am besten informierten Freunde? Außer den Journalisten immer doch wieder die Kaufleute. Und Dein Beruf ist – wie immer so auch heute – verbunden mit dem Wagnis. Glaube mir, auch der Künstler, der Schauspieler, der Regisseur, der Intendant und sogar der Journalist wissen um das Wagnis. Aber gerade das sollte verbinden . . .

EDWIN KUNTZ, *Die Intellektuellen und die Unternehmer*
(Rhein-Neckar-Zeitung)

24 „Schüler reden nach dem Mund"

Die deutschen Schüler sind heute ganz erschreckend anpassungsfähig und verhalten sich, je näher sie dem Abitur kommen, immer mehr wie Duckmäuser. Zu diesem Ergebnis kamen die Hamburger Psychologen Manfred Amelang und Wolfgang Zaworka in einer großangelegten Untersuchung, in deren Verlauf 241 Oberschülern 223 Fragen vorgelegt wurden. „Mit zunehmender Nähe zum Abitur verschlechtert sich", so die Wissenschaftler, „die Solidarität zwischen den Schülern und die Güte des Klassenklimas rapide."

Die Untersuchung . . . bezog sich unter anderem auf das Verhalten der Schüler gegenüber ihren Lehrern und der Schüler untereinander. Eine erstaunlich hohe Prozentzahl (75 Prozent) beantwortete die Frage, ob zu einer guten Note auch „eine gehörige Portion nach dem Mund reden" gehöre, mit „ja". Daß, wer sich beliebt zu machen verstehe, auch bei geringerer Leistung eine gute Zensur erhalte, bestätigten sogar 80 Prozent. Und daß Lehrer einen guten Blick dafür hätten, ob ein Mitschüler ein „Schleimer" sei oder nicht, bestritten 77 Prozent der Gymnasiasten. 65 Prozent bestätigten die Behauptung, daß der Zusammenhalt der Schüler untereinander immer geringer werde, wenn die Anforderungen an ihre Leistungen steigen. „Immer ausgeprägter wird die Überzeugung", klagen die Autoren, „daß man sich selbst einen schlechten Dienst erweise, wenn man den Klassenkameraden abschreiben läßt."

Stuttgarter Zeitung

25 Die Notwendigkeit des technischen Fortschritts im modernen Leben

Das Tempo des technischen Fortschritts gestern und heute wird nicht etwa bestimmt durch Technokraten oder gar durch Professoren der technischen Hochschulen, sondern es wird erzwungen durch die anscheinend unaufhaltsame Bevölkerungsvermehrung der Welt. In dieser Hinsicht haben wir das Erbe eines ganzen Jahrhunderts zu tragen und müssen trachten, auf halbwegs menschenwürdige Weise damit fertig zu werden. Es wird niemand die Leistung von Semmelweis[1] und die Bekämpfung des Kindbettfiebers in ihrer Bedeutung verkleinern wollen; aber was eine außerordentliche, positive Leistung im Rahmen der Hygiene gewesen ist, hat die Möglichkeit der Bevölkerungsexplosion zunächst in den alten Industriestaaten und heute in den sogenannten Entwicklungsländern geschaffen.

Wenn man nicht der Meinung ist, daß diese Millionen und Milliarden, die infolgedessen die Erde bevölkern, nur dazu da sind, um als Ameisen oder Drohnen zu vegetieren, sondern wenn man es für·eine menschliche, gesellschaftliche und politische Aufgabe hält, diesen argen Zuwachs nicht mit Elendsnahrung und in Elendsquartieren verkommen zu lassen, dann bleibt gar nichts übrig, als auf sämtlichen Gebieten die Produktion so zu steigern, daß alles, was da kreucht und fleucht,[2] mit ungefähr den gleichen Produkten versorgt und in ungefähr die gleichen Wohnungen eingewiesen und mit ungefähr den gleichen Verkehrsmitteln befördert werden kann.

EDGAR SALIN, *Falsche Angst vor Größe* (Die Zeit)

[1] I.P. Semmelweis (1818–1865): ungarischer Gynäkologe, Entdecker der Ansteckungsweise und Ursache des Kindbettfiebers
[2] kreucht und fleucht: kriecht und fliegt

26 Mondscheingespräche

Lebt man etwas abseits der Großstadt, führt man keine Ortsgespräche. Fern sind alle Gesprächsteilnehmer. Diese Tatsache gestaltet seit Einführung des Mondscheintarifs unsere Abende wesentlich gemütlicher. Während früher Freunde und Verwandte höchstens bis nach den Abendnachrichten ihre Ungeduld zähmten, uns Glückwünsche und Neuigkeiten zu übermitteln, bleibt das Geklingel nun aus. Ungestört zieht der Saphir auf der Lieblingsplatte seine Bahnen, man wagt es, zu einem Buch zu greifen, dessen Lektüre Unterbrechungen ebenso schlecht verträgt wie die seltenen guten Filme im Fernsehen. Wie schön ist es, Briefe in einem Guß zu schreiben, ohne Gedankensprünge in verschiedene Himmelsrichtungen. Viele Jahre hatte das Telefon am Abend die Störfaktoren des Tages nahtlos abgelöst. Nun gehört der Abend uns wieder – bis 22 Uhr.

Mit dem Glockenschlag allerdings ist die Ruhe dahin. Die Großeltern sind die ersten, die noch schnell gute Nacht sagen wollen. Je weiter der Zeiger rückt, desto jünger werden die Anrufer. Vier von fünf Studenten – so hat es eine der zahllosen Umfragen ermittelt – telefonieren grundsätzlich nach 22 Uhr. Auch ich mache es mir nun auf dem Telefonsessel gemütlich, sortiere meine Lieben nach Frühaufstehern und Nachteulen und bewege nach dieser Skala die Wählscheibe. Der Mondscheintarif hat Ruhebedürfnis und Gesprächsbereitschaft in eine gute Balance gebracht.

Stuttgarter Zeitung

27 Das Problem der Arbeitslosigkeit in den hochentwickelten Ländern

Die Industrie ist an einer Lösung des Arbeitslosenproblems und der Ausbildung von Jugendlichen nur noch sehr begrenzt interessiert. Sie kann allein durch einen höheren Energie- und Kapitaleinsatz ihre Produktion steigern und somit höhere Umsätze und Gewinne erwirtschaften.

Sollen künftig ausreichend Arbeitsplätze für die Bevölkerung – die ja weiterarbeiten will – erhalten bleiben, so muß der Prozeß der Rationalisierung und der Einkommenssteigerung sehr rasch und sehr deutlich verlangsamt werden. Denn sonst wird in Bälde einer kleinen Gruppe von hochqualifizierten Spitzenverdienern ein Heer von Arbeitslosen gegenüberstehen. Die sozialen und politischen Auswirkungen lassen sich in ihrer Größe nur erahnen.

VOLKER ROETHER (Die Zeit)

. . . der beunruhigend großen Zahl von Arbeitslosen steht eine große Zahl von Menschen gegenüber, die bereit sind, ihren Arbeitsplatz zur Verfügung zu stellen. Der – von den Experten so nicht erwartete – starke Gebrauch von der flexiblen Altersgrenze beweist, daß mit einer nochmaligen Vorverlegung dieser Grenze eine rasche und nachhaltige Senkung der Arbeitslosigkeit möglich ist.

Daß die Realisierung dieses Gedankens nicht einfach ist, darf kein Argument dagegen, muß vielmehr ein Ansporn sein, Phantasie, Sachverstand und Fleiß walten zu lassen. Es gibt viele Möglichkeiten für das Verfahren und auch für die Finanzierung.

Vielleicht erkennt ein Politiker, welche Chancen für die nächste Bundestagswahl für seine Partei hier liegen.

ARNO HAUCK (Die Zeit)

28 „Der gewöhnliche Faschismus"

Neu ist er nicht, dieser Film von Michail Romm über den gewöhnlichen, den alltäglichen, den ordinären Faschismus, eine preisgekrönte Dokumentation, die sich in der deutschen Fassung am Schluß allgemein-menschlich und nicht politisch-aggressiv gab . . .

Neu waren die Bilder für uns, man kannte sie kaum, diese Archivphotos des geifernden Gliedermannes, der Hitler-Puppe mit den schnellenden Armen, den Marionettenschrittchen und den wie von Drähten gelenkten, sich in Rückchen und Zückchen äußernden Gesten. Nie wurde das Predigerhafte, die Mimik des völkischen Bußmönchs und chauvinistischen Kanzelredners, so deutlich wie im Film Michail Romms, doppelt deutlich durch einen witzig kommentierenden Text, der das Un-Angemessene, das Popanzhafte und Steif-Maschinelle national-sozialistischer Artikulationen heraushob, dieses Augenrollen von Automaten, die nicht erkennen, wie komisch sie wirken in ihrer Blutrunst und Feierlichkeit . . .

Einwände freilich bieten sich an . . .; die Guten und die Schlechten wurden gezeigt, die Henker hier, die Opfer dort, aber die 90 Prozent Gutschlechten traten nicht vor die Linsen. Auch der Zweiweltenmensch, am Tage das Mördergeschäft, am Abend Quartettmusik und deutsche Innerlichkeit, den Juden getötet und danach Dürer und Bach, den Führer bejubelt und daneben ein *ganz normales* Leben geführt, ein Leben, das sich nach 45 bruchlos fortsetzen ließ – auch der Zweiweltenmensch verbarg sein Gesicht.

Die Zeit

29 Die Bewältigung der Vergangenheit

„Natürlich war der Nazismus kein Amoklauf einzelner krimineller Psychopathen! Auch keine Infektionskrankheit, die Deutschland zufällig bekam. Er war das Syndrom chronischer Leiden."

„Welcher Leiden?" fragte Crispenhoven.

„Die Frage kann kein Jude für sich allein beantworten. Ebensowenig wie ein Deutscher. Die Antwort darauf kann, wenn überhaupt, nur im Gespräch zwischen Juden und Deutschen gefunden werden. Ich glaube, es war dieses Gespräch, wofür ich zurückgekehrt bin!"

„Haben Sie es gefunden?"

„Selten. Zu selten. Es ist für einen Juden oder einen Halbjuden kaum möglich, mit Deutschen in ein Gespräch über das Dritte Reich zu kommen."

„Das kann ich mir nicht vorstellen, Groenewold", sagte Violat, und schenkte nach.

„Natürlich können Sie mit den Leuten darüber reden, Violat, etwa wie man über einen Hochwasserschaden oder über ein Flugzeugunglück redet. Aber das ist kein Gespräch! Keins, das die Wahrheit ans Licht bringt."

„Und woran liegt das, nach Ihrer Erfahrung?" fragte Crispenhoven.

„Der Jude erinnert sich zu viel und der Deutsche zu wenig. Er hat sich in die Gleichgültigkeit begeben, wie in einen Heilschlaf."

„Gleichgültigkeit?"

„Nennen Sie mir ein anderes Wort, Crispenhoven, das genau diese entsetzliche Indifferenz vieler Deutscher gegenüber ihrer Vergangenheit bezeichnet! Gedächtnisschwund? Bewußtseinsspaltung? Verdrängung? Es läuft auf dasselbe hinaus."

„Ist das nicht, entschuldigen Sie, Groenewold, ein bißchen überempfindlich?"

„Ja, aber natürlich, Violat. Ich bin's . . ."

THOMAS VALENTIN (geboren 1922), *Die Unberatenen*

30 Wirtschaft und Qualität

In Wirklichkeit wird das, was wir kaufen, von dem Umstand bestimmt, daß eine Fabrik ihren Umsatz erhöhen will. Und sie gibt ihren Produkten das Aussehen und die technische Qualität, die ihr einen steigenden Umsatz sichern. Nun ist der Umsatz wohl in der Tat noch immer der beste Maßstab wirtschaftlicher Aktivität. Darüber zu moralisieren wäre müßig. Darf man überhaupt – ökonomisch gesehen – einen Qualitätsanspruch an die Wirtschaft stellen? Sollte man nicht so ehrlich sein zuzugeben, daß die Wirtschaft keine qualitativen Ansprüche zum Inhalt hat, sondern daß sie ganz einfach verkaufen will und soll?

Diese Tendenz der Wirtschaft ist korrekt, solange es neben ihr Maßstäbe und Kräfte gibt, die auch andere Kriterien ins Feld führen. Aber diese Maßstäbe anderer Art scheint es heute nicht zu geben. Qualität ist eine gesellschaftliche oder kulturelle Kategorie, nicht eine ökonomische. Diese Kategorie ist aber ohne institutionelle Wirksamkeit kraftlos und hängt in der Luft. Sie hat weder Autorität noch Organe.

Ist es sinnvoll, daß ein Auto mit allem Aufwand der Technik dazu gebracht wird, ein paar Kilometer schneller zu fahren? Ist es sinnvoll, daß fast nur für Alkoholika, Waschmittel, Zigaretten und Strümpfe die Reklamewände vollgeklebt werden? Ist es sinnvoll, daß mehr und mehr die Verpackung den Inhalt an Wert übersteigt? Diese und ähnliche Fragen werden in unserer Welt nicht, nicht mehr oder noch nicht gestellt.

INGE SCHOLL (geboren 1917),
Eine neue Gründerzeit und ihre Gebrauchskunst (Bestandsaufnahme)

31 Harold Lloyd und Buster Keaton

Fast zwanzig Jahre lang gehörte Harold Lloyd zu den gefeierten Film-
machern der Welt, verkörperte er in der Nachfolge Douglas Fairbanks
den ewig optimistischen, strebsamen, modernen jungen Mann, der nach
zwei erzamerikanischen Maximen lebte, die besagen, daß ein Weg sei, wo
ein Wille ist, und ein Freund dort, wo man sich um einen bemüht.
Einem Publikum, dessen Interesse in einer Zeit ungetrübten nationalen
Selbstbewußtseins und Fortschrittsglaubens vorwiegend auf das eigene
Vorwärtskommen gerichtet war, zeigte Harold Lloyd, daß man Erfolg hat,
wenn man nur will.

In ihrem Handlungsablauf ähneln seine Filme denen Buster Keatons:
Ein Mann muß eine Reihe von Prüfungen, auf die ihn sein bisheriges
Leben absolut nicht vorbereitet hat, überstehen. Seine Motivationen sind
jedoch – abgesehen davon, daß es für beide auch um eine Frau geht – sehr
verschieden. Während Keatons Abenteuer nur selten auf dessen eigenen
Willen zurückführen lassen, ist der Motor der Filme Lloyds . . . der
explizite Wunsch, sich im Leben durchzusetzen und dabei möglichst
viele Freunde zu gewinnen. Keatons Abenteuer dienen immer nur der
Bewältigung konkreter, meist von außen an ihn herangetragener Gefahren;
an ihrem Ende hat man den Eindruck, daß sie absolut noch nicht zu Ende
sind, wogegen fast alle Abenteuer Harold Lloyds zu einem Abschluß
kommen, an dem der Held am Ziel all seiner Wünsche ist und getrost der
Zukunft entgegenblicken kann.

WOLFRAM TICHY, *Der strebsame Optimist* (Die Zeit)

32 Folgenschwere Entdeckung

GROVE: Wenn du schon mein Sohn bist, dann solltest du versuchen, so zu
    sein, wie ich mir einen tüchtigen Kerl vorstelle.
AXEL: So wie du? Das wolltest du wohl sagen.
GROVE: Jawohl, meinetwegen. Sieh mich an, sprich mit mir, dann weißt du,
    wie man die Dinge anzupacken hat.
AXEL: Ich würde dich zum Beispiel gern was fragen.
GROVE: Schieß los, mein Junge.
AXEL: Da sitzen sieben Leute eingepfercht im Laderaum.
GROVE: Wer hat dir das erzählt?
AXEL: Niemand hat mir das erzählt. Ich bin selber unten gewesen.
GROVE: So? Herumgeschnüffelt also?
AXEL: Nein. Ich ging herum, und zufällig –
GROVE: Jetzt hör mal zu: Die Leute unten, – die gehen dich gar nichts an.
AXEL: Ich wollte dich nur fragen, ob du es weißt.
GROVE: Ja, glaubst du denn, jemand würde es wagen, hinter meinem
    Rücken irgendwas zu tun? Wann bist du unten gewesen?

AXEL: Zum ersten Mal war es –
GROVE: Was heißt das? Bist du mehrere Male dort gewesen? Was hattest du dort zu suchen?
AXEL: Einige Male.
GROVE: Ja, was denn? Wozu denn? Bei diesem Gesindel! Was wolltest du da?
AXEL: Sie schlafen auf dem nackten Boden. Bist du unten gewesen? Kennst du diese Menschen?
GROVE: Nein. Ich kenne sie nicht. Ich will sie nicht kennen. Und ich verbiete dir, daß du noch einmal hingehst.
AXEL: Warum denn?
GROVE: Abschaum. Gesindel, dem der Boden zu heiß geworden ist.
AXEL: Sie taten mir leid. Sie wußten nicht einmal, auf was für einem Schiff sie sind.
GROVE: Und das hast du ihnen gesagt?
AXEL: Ja. Warum nicht?
GROVE: Was hast du ihnen gesagt? Genau?
AXEL: Nichts Böses. Nur daß das Schiff Esperanza heißt und nach Wilmington unterwegs ist –
GROVE: Du Idiot! Und du kapierst womöglich gar nicht, was du damit angerichtet hast!

FRED VON HOERSCHELMANN (geboren 1901), *Das Schiff Esperanza*

33 Stoßseufzer vor dem Abitur

Ich bin achtzehn. Schüler an einem bundesdeutschen Gymnasium – humanistischer Zweig. Ich mache mein Abi, besser: ich stehe kurz davor. Knapp mehr als zwei Monate sind es noch, bis die „schriftliche Reifeprüfung" eingeläutet wird, zehn Wochen, die länger werden als die vergangene, immerhin dreizehnjährige Schulzeit. Ich hab's satt, mir steht's bis oben.

Dabei könnte ich mir – mittlerweile erwachsen und verständig geworden – eine Schule vorstellen, die Spaß macht. Mehr zu wissen, mehr zu verstehen, mehr zu können, das ist doch eigentlich etwas sehr Positives, etwas Gewinnbringendes für mich. Nach den Purbertätsquerelen wäre es jetzt möglich, in der Klassengemeinschaft Partnerschaftlichkeit und Vertrauen zu erfahren. Vielleicht noch mehr: Den Klassenkameraden als Persönlichkeit zu sehen, mit dem zu sprechen wertvoll ist. Was könnte es schön sein, den Lehrer da vorne am Pult zu erleben als Mehr-Wisser, als verständigen Informanten, als geduldigen Erklärer und Vermittler schwieriger Sachverhalte.

Aber wie sieht's aus? Der Numerus clausus ist kein anonymes Gespenst, sondern sehr harte und unmittelbare Realität in den Klassenzimmern. Es ist direkt verwunderlich – einsames Zeichen aufopfernder Menschlichkeit

– daß es noch Mitschüler gibt, die einem Unwissenden manchmal etwas erklären, obwohl sie damit ihre eigenen Chancen verschlechtern. Aber „hintenrum" wird ganz schön viel gemunkelt und geschaukelt. Und Tests – unangekündigte Überprüfung der Hausaufgaben – werden jetzt auch auf den Tisch des Hauses geknallt. Na ja, die Lehrer werden halt auch gebeutelt von den komischen Bestimmungen aus dem Ministerium. Von wegen objektiver Leistungsmessung!

Was bin ich froh, wenn's geschafft ist. Wenn das Notengerangel aufhört. Ich nicht mehr von einem Tag auf den anderen auswendig pauken muß, um mir – den NC[1] im Nacken – halt den Durchschnitt zu retten. Dabei ist es grundsätzlich egal, was ich in mich hineinschlinge – und am Tag nach dem Test ist es auch wieder vergessen. Was bin ich froh, wenn sich „nach der Schule" dann eine ganz neue Welt auftut. Eine Welt, in der Menschen auch anders als durch Leistungszwänge zu motivieren sind. In der Leben noch ein bißchen Spaß macht.

Grinst da jemand?

PETER FREY (18 Jahre), *Die Zeit*

[1]NC: Numerus clausus

Part Six

German Prose Passages
for Comment and Appreciation

Principles of Literary Analysis

The best way to set about the literary analysis of a passage of prose (or of verse) will depend on the nature of the passage; but generally speaking it is advisable to proceed methodically. Normally one would begin by stating briefly the theme or the specific character of the passage, or summarising the argument if it is an argument, go on then to an analysis of the manner in which it is presented, and finally give again in very summary form the conclusions one has reached.

The main part of the literary analysis will be concerned with such problems as (*a*) the author's presumed intention and the degree of his success in carrying it out; (*b*) the syntactical structure of the passage and its suitability for the presumed intention; (*c*) the imagery (metaphor, similes, personification, etc.), if any, and its appropriateness and originality; (*d*) the character of the various parts of speech – nouns, adjectives, etc., and their effectiveness; (*e*) the atmosphere, and how it is evoked; (*f*) the mood or tone, serious, humorous, ironic, witty, etc., and the way this is achieved.

There are certain dangers to guard against. One must avoid writing a paraphrase, i.e. saying again and at greater length in one's own words what the author almost certainly has said much better in his. One must realise too that there is no point in the mere *enumeration* of stylistic devices, that what matters is to discover exactly what effect has been produced by this or that device, to show how and for what purpose and with what measure of success such artistic devices have been employed. One must also refrain from making sweeping statements, from indulging in fulsome praise or total condemnation on little or no evidence. Generalisations can indeed often be made, but they must be demonstrably true, clear and specific reference being made to the evidence afforded by the text.

Examples of Literary Analysis of Prose

There is further the danger that literary analysis may be vitiated by preconceived ideas and stock reponses, a danger that can sometimes be averted simply by not knowing who wrote the passage. It is partly for this reason that the names of the authors of the passages that we have chosen for commentary have been omitted. The absence of such extraneous information

244

has, in our experience, often the effect of compelling the student to study the text more closely and thus to avoid trying to rely on 'critical' short-cuts.

We have ventured to offer our own literary analysis of two passages of prose, one a passage of descriptive prose, the other a passage of an argumentative nature. It was of course unavoidable that we should know who the authors of these passages were, but we have tried not to let this knowledge affect our judgment. The commentaries are offered not as 'models', for we are in the first place only too conscious of their shortcomings and in the second place have deliberately set ourselves limits of space corresponding roughly to those that examinations impose on candidates. We hope that they may serve to illustrate and perhaps make clearer some of the principles outlined above and also to stimulate further, and more penetrating, literary analysis.

(a) Das Totenmaar

Hoch oben in den Eifelbergen liegt ein See, dunkel, tief, kreisrund, unheimlich wie ein Kraterschlund.

Einst tobten unterirdische Gewalten da unten, Feuer und Lavamassen wurden emporgeschleudert; jetzt füllt eine glatte Flut das Becken, wie Tränen eine Schale. Es geht hinunter in bodenlose Tiefe.   5

Keine Bäume, keine Blumen. Nackte vulkanische Höhen, gleich riesigen Maulwurfshügeln, stehen im Kranz, zu nichts gut als zu armseliger Viehweide. Mageres Strandgras weht, blasses Heidekraut duckt sich unter Brombeergestrüpp. Kein Vogel singt, kein Schmetterling gaukelt. Einsam ist's, zum Sterben öde.   10

Das ist das Weinfelder Maar, das Totenmaar, wie's die Leute heißen. Es hat keinen Abfluß, keinen Zufluß anders als die Tränen, die der Himmel drein weint. Es liegt und träumt und ist todestraurig wie alles ringsumher.

Wenn Herbstwinde über die Eifel gehen und kalte Nebel in den Tälern hocken, ist's hier oben noch kälter. Hui, pfeift das! Wind, wilder Gesell,   15
stöhn nicht so laut! Zerre nicht die letzten braunen Blätter von den dornigen Ranken, stürze nicht die morschen Holzkreuze um, die dort um das Kirchlein stehen, das grau und düster am Seeufer trauert. Es ist das einzige Werk der Menschenhand hier oben, viel hundert Jahre alt, nicht schön, nicht häßlich, doch voll schwermütiger Poesie.   20

Einst lag hier das Dorf Weinfelden, seine Hütten scharten sich um das Gotteshaus wie Küchlein unter die Flügel der Glucke. Es ist lange her, das Dorf ist verschwunden – zerstört, versunken? Wer weiß! Am sichersten verhungert. Einzig das Kirchlein ist übriggeblieben und reckt seinen schwärzlichen Turm gen Himmel. Gottesdienst wird nicht viel darin   25
gehalten; die Lebenden kommen nur herauf, ihre Toten zu begraben.

                                                    CLARA VIEBIG

Commentary

In these opening paragraphs of a story the mood is set for what is to follow.
The mood is one of desolation and death. Time seems more or less to have
stopped. There is further a suggestion of the uncanny, or the inexplicable,
a hint that something cataclysmic has happened, may happen again.

The story is entitled *Das Totenmaar* and the lake appropriately stands in
the centre of the scene. In the first sentence we are given its position, high
up in the mountains, and three of the four predicative adjectives used –
'*dunkel*', '*tief*', '*kreisrund*' – describe its physical appearance, whilst the
fourth, together with the simile – '*unheimlich wie ein Kraterschlund*' – gives
us a subjective reaction of the author to its appearance, namely the feeling
of its eerie quality.

The next two paragraphs offer a contrast, suggested by the word '*Krater*'
used in the simile, the contrast between this place once seething with
violence and movement, now become still, barren and desolate. In the
third paragraph the detailed description of what is to be found there is
framed, as it were, by what is missing, starting with plant life ('*keine
Bäume*', '*keine Blumen*' – plural) and concluding with living creatures ('*kein
Vogel*', '*kein Schmetterling*' – singular). The writer is throughout specific;
what is to be seen there is indicated precisely ('*nackte vulkanische Höhen,
gleich riesigen Maulwurfshügeln, stehen im Kranz*'; '*mageres Strandgras*';
'*blasses Heidekraut*'; '*Brombeergestrüpp*'). Even what is missing is particu-
larised ('*kein Vogel singt*'; '*kein Schmetterling gaukelt*'). Colourless verbs are
avoided; instead we have '*tobten*', '*wurden emporgeschleudert*', '*geht hinunter*', '*weht*', '*duckt sich*', '*singt*', '*gaukelt*'.

Within this landscape the lake is situated, associated twice with tears,
first in the simile in which it is oddly and unconvincingly compared to
tears filling a bowl, then in the metaphor in the fourth paragraph, tears
that the sky 'weeps' into it; and the lake is cut off from all connection with
the rest of the world – '*kein Abfluß, kein Zufluß*'. It shares in the enveloping
desolation and is described as 'dreaming' and as 'mortally sad'.

In the third paragraph there is just the hint of movement, that of the
wind stirring in the long grass, otherwise stillness and desolation. But in the
autumn a new destructive force arises (paragraph five) in the form of the
autumnal gales that here rage even more fiercely than elsewhere in this
mountainous area. With the words '*Hui, pfeift das!*' the author has as it
were suddenly and unexpectedly found herself in the path of a howling
wind. But for all its destructiveness (against which the author pleads)
here is at least something alive. The wind is boldly personified as '*wilder
Gesell*', is bidden not to 'groan', not to 'tug at' the last brown leaves, not
to 'knock over' the dilapidated crosses. And in this oblique way we learn
that here a community must once have lived, whose only surviving monuments are graveyard crosses and a little church.

The final paragraph develops the theme of the life that was once lived
here, that has now disappeared no one quite knows how. Life has been blotted

out, and the living only come up from below to bury their dead and very occasionally to take part in divine service, perhaps to graze their cattle for a day or two. Again the characteristic of the writing in this paragraph is particularisation: the cottages *'scharten sich wie Küchlein unter die Flügel der Glucke'*, the hen being not just a hen but a sitting hen; the village has disappeared – how? 'destroyed'? 'engulfed'? 'starved to death'?; the little church *'reckt seinen Turm gen Himmel'*.

Two paragraphs, the second and the last, begin with the word *'einst'* ('once, years ago'). Is the word a reference to the same point of time in the past? Was it the volcanic eruption which once took place that destroyed the village, or was its destruction a further calamity, war, perhaps, or a failure to make even an exiguous living from a barren ungrateful soil? Presumably the answer to such questions as these that occur to the reader will be given later. At any rate, curiosity has been aroused, as one must suppose was the author's intention.

Much of the general effect of gloom and desolation is produced in the reader by the epithets used. There is throughout the passage a general absence of colour – the objects are *'dunkel'*, *'blaß'*, *'düster'*, *'grau'*, *'schwärzlich'*. Even the last leaves of the brambles suggest by the choice of the word *'braun'* nothing very vivid. The epithets *'dornig'*, *'morsch'*, *'alt'*, *'armselig'*, *'mager'* conjure up an atmosphere of life without sap, at best a sort of life-in-death; and *'unheimlich'*, *'bodenlos'*, *'einsam'*, *'schwermütig'*, *'todestraurig'*, *'zum Sterben öde'* insist, perhaps too directly, on the loneliness, melancholy and mystery of the scene. But at the same time the whole passage is imbued with a strange life of its own by the personification that plays so great a part throughout – the wind is a 'wild fellow' that 'whistles', 'groans', and 'tugs at' the leaves; the mists 'crouch', the rain 'weeps', the heather 'ducks down', the lake 'dreams', the church 'mourns' and 'stretches up', as it were pleadingly, its tower like an arm to the sky. A curious indeterminate state, neither quite alive, nor quite dead.

Syntactically, these paragraphs are composed almost entirely of main clauses, sometimes very short (e.g. *'kein Vogel singt'*), sometimes without a verb (e.g. *'keine Bäume'*, *'keine Blumen'*). One might expect in a descriptive passage as well as numerous adjectives a fair number of relative clauses; there are, however, only two, though there are instances of appositional adjective constructions, sometimes quite elaborate (*'ein See, dunkel, tief'*, etc.; *'Höhen ... zu nichts gut als ...'*; *'Werk ..., alt, nicht schön, nicht häßlich, doch voll'*) which are more effective, because more terse, equivalents of relative clauses. The passage does not consist only of statements, brief and simple as these are. Imperatives and questions give added vigour to the picture.

The scene is mainly an impressionistic one, constructed stroke by stroke (epithet, image, phrase, clause) appealing primarily to the eye, but also occasionally to the ear. Underlying the pictorial aspect, deriving in part from it but also in part added to it is the suggestion of a further historical dimension, conveyed by the past tenses in the second and last paragraphs.

The colloquialism 's' for 'es' (three times) and the 'poetical' 'gen' for
'gegen', the apt but rather hackneyed simile ('scharten sich wie Küchlein unter
die Flügel der Glucke'), the stock, hackneyed phrase 'voll schwermütiger
Poesie' and the somewhat unsatisfactory simile ('füllt ... wie Tränen eine
Schale') are minor blemishes perhaps in a passage that otherwise can be
considered to achieve its intention, despite the danger of 'poetical' prose
which can easily become slightly ridiculous.

(b) Die Eigenschaften der echten Form

„... Wenn ich beim Dichten in meinen Busen fassen, meinen Gedanken
ergreifen und mit Händen, ohne weitere Zutat, in den Deinigen legen
könnte: so wäre, die Wahrheit zu gestehn, die ganze innere Forderung
meiner Seele erfüllt. Und auch Dir, Freund, dünkt mich, bliebe nichts zu
5 wünschen übrig: dem Durstigen kommt es, als solchem, auf die Schale
nicht an, sondern auf die Früchte, die man ihm darin bringt. Nur weil der
Gedanke, um zu erscheinen, wie jene flüchtigen, undarstellbaren, chemi-
schen Stoffe, mit etwas Gröberem, Körperlichen, verbunden sein muß:
nur darum bediene ich mich, wenn ich Dir mitteilen will, und nur darum
10 bedarfst Du, um mich zu verstehen, der Rede. Sprache, Rhythmus,
Wohlklang usw., so reizend diese Dinge auch, insofern sie den Geist
einhüllen, sein mögen, so sind sie doch an und für sich, aus diesem höheren
Gesichtspunkt betrachtet, nichts als ein wahrer, obschon natürlicher und
notwendiger Übelstand; und die Kunst kann, in bezug auf sie, auf nichts
15 gehen, als sie möglichst *verschwinden* zu machen. Ich bemühe mich aus
meinen besten Kräften, dem Ausdruck Klarheit, dem Versbau Bedeutung,
dem Klang der Worte Anmut und Leben zu geben: aber bloß, damit diese
Dinge gar nicht, vielmehr einzig und allein der Gedanke, den sie einschließen, erscheine. Denn das ist die Eigenschaft aller echten Form, daß
20 der Geist augenblicklich und unmittelbar daraus hervortritt, während die
mangelhafte ihn, wie ein schlechter Spiegel, gebunden hält und uns an
nichts erinnert, als an sich selbst..."

HEINRICH VON KLEIST

Commentary

The argument of this passage is briefly as follows:

Ideally, communication of poetic experience should be direct, without
the need for any medium. Such communication is, however, impossible.
Language is a necessary evil. The function of art is to reduce this evil to a
minimum by seeing to it that language does not get in the way of such
communication. Various devices are available to the poet but these must
never be used for their own sake. Only that 'form' is genuine that makes
'matter' immediately apparent without any distorting or blurring effects.

One notices that the argument is addressed to one person, to a friend,
and it is not difficult to infer from the use of capital letters ('Du', 'Dir', 'den

Deinigen') that this passage is an extract from a letter. This may be in part the reason why the whole passage has powerful emotional overtones; but that it is so highly charged emotionally suggests that the subject is felt to be of great importance to the writer.

Though the argument proceeds through the six sentences by perfectly logical steps the fact that it starts from an ardent desire (*'die ganze innere Forderung meiner Seele'*) that is impossible of fulfilment (its impossibility being conveyed, but not stated in so many words, by the conditional: *'wenn ich ... könnte'*) transforms it into something much more than a mere logical argument.

In the first sentence the nature of ideal or absolute communication of poetic experience is conveyed by means of striking and highly individual imagery. Significantly the *locus* from which and to which the *'Gedanke'* is to be transferred is the *'Busen'*, the heart, not the head. No *'Zutat'* or garnishing is permissible or desirable; and the hands of the poet offer, as it were, lovingly, that which is most intimately his to a kindred soul, for safe keeping in his *'Busen'*.

The second sentence adds a further consequence that would follow from the 'impossible' protasis (*'wenn ich ... könnte'*). Not only would this perfect communication satisfy the poet, for it is his most ardent desire to communicate thus, but it would also completely satisfy the friend, the reader; and the metaphor that immediately follows suggests that the reader both 'thirsts' for this sort of experience and is satisfied only by the experience itself, not by the vehicle by which it is conveyed, though he may, the text seems to imply, perhaps not know this. The imagery is very pertinent to the argument: matter (*'die Früchte'*), not form (*'die Schale'*, the bowl in which it is offered, with its suggestion of useless beauty), is the only thing that has significance in the author's view. (It is worth noting that this sentence balances the first in presenting the receiving end of the communication – and moves, as it were, this time outwards from the statement of satisfaction to the imagery, which derives very naturally from that of hands presenting the truth at the beginning of the first sentence.)

The third sentence leaves the realm of the ideal and comes down to earth. A reason, given in the form of a striking but an apt simile (its scientific character stressing, as it were, the reality the poet is up against), is offered why perfect communication is impossible. The *'Gedanke'* like certain chemical substances is *'flüchtig'* ('volatile'), discernible only when compounded with other grosser and cruder substances, to which category *'Rede'* ('discourse') belongs. The sole justification (*'nur darum'*) for the vehicle of speech is that only thereby can the poet communicate his experience, and the reader understand and share it. Here again the poet-reader link is once more presented in a balanced way (lines 9–10).

The fourth sentence concedes the beauty of certain features of language – vocabulary, rhythm, euphony – but denies them any value in their own right; they are a 'natural and necessary evil'. The function of *'Kunst'*, by which here is meant the poet's technical skill, is to reduce this necessary evil to a minimum by seeing to it that such features or devices do not get in the way of communication, that they are not felt to be present at all. Here a new metaphor is introduced somewhat casually. Matter is now *'Geist'* ('spirit' or 'soul'), form is now that which envelops it ('body'), and this body has somehow to be made to disappear as much as possible, leaving us face to face with the spirit.

The fifth sentence, which is a statement of the poet's personal practice, after one generalisation and before another, shows how these devices can in fact serve the poet's purposes. The qualities aimed at are clarity, significance, grace and life. If one considers these qualities it is evident that they are such that will enable the experience to come across as immediately as possible, so that it shall be palpitatingly alive and pregnant with meaning. *'Anmut'*, associated with *'Leben'*, seems to smuggle in the notion of beauty for its own sake, but it is here probably conceived by the author as a quality of language without which experience could not be conveyed without loss of vitality.

The final sentence sums up the argument. True form is that which enables matter (*'Geist'*) or experience to emerge, directly and instantaneously, whereas defective form obstructs matter, diverts our attention from the end to the means. A new simile suggests now that true form is like a perfect mirror in which the image we see is so crystal clear and undistorted that we forget we are looking in a mirror at all.

The argument as a whole is clearly articulated as it proceeds from sentence to sentence; but the sentences themselves tend to be complex, with a strong forward movement, checked by parenthetical qualifications, by violently dislocated word order separating subjects of sentences from their verbs and verbs from their objects. Not that this is done arbitrarily. The end to which the argument is moving is never lost sight of and, when reached after many obstacles encountered and overcome, is all the more securely won. In the third sentence, for instance, the word *'Rede'*, which is the genitive object of two separate verbs (*'sich bedienen'* and *'bedürfen'*) whose subjects are *'ich'* and *'Du'*, i.e. poet and reader, is only finally and somewhat reluctantly reached after it has been made clear that it alone, alas, makes communication possible between poet and reader; and in the fifth sentence the verb *'erscheine'* finds itself, somewhat ungrammatically, in danger of having the wrong subject, and thus powerfully suggests by the word order a too easily possible confusion of ends and means.

Thus what might have been merely a cool logical argument has been given flesh and blood, has been transmuted by the variety, vigour and aptness of the imagery and by the virile forward thrust of the speech-rhythms into something powerfully persuasive. One is left with the feeling that something very important is at stake, that the function of art is for he writer of these lines not an aesthetic one at all; it is nothing les, than the communication of Truth.

I Descriptive

1 Der Nordwestwind

Tagelang sang der Nordwestwind seine grämlichen Lieder; wenn die Sonne mit rotem Gesichte über die Heidberge kam, stürmte er ihr entgegen und langweilte sie so lange mit seinem öden Gesinge, bis sie ärgerlich hinter den grauen Wolken verschwand. Dann hatte der Wind wieder Oberhand und goß Wasser über das Moor. Da kam der Mond der Sonne zur Hilfe, 5 er brachte den Südwestwind mit; der jagte die Wolken vom Himmel und trocknete das Wasser im Moore auf, und eines Morgens war das ganze Moor silberweiß von Rauhreif, so silbern, so weiß, daß die weißen Birkenstämme und die beiden silbernen Weidenbüsche völlig verschwanden.

Aber schon mittags war der trübsinnige Wind aus Nordwesten wieder 10 da; er wischte mit langen, nassen Nebellappen den Silberreif von Baum und Busch, Heide und Halm, schnaufte im Risch,[1] stöhnte in den Ellern[2] wehleidig und weinerlich und verleidete den wenigen Vögeln, die in das Moor zurückgekehrt waren, die Heimat wieder.

2 Der Frühling

Zuerst waren es die Nächte, die klar wurden; doch ihre Klarheit war sanfter als die winterliche. Alle Härte war aus dem Nachtfirmament gewichen, war gleichsam verdunstet oder hinweggeschmolzen, die Milde hatte endgültig die Oberhand gewonnen, und in einer Durchsichtigkeit, die der des menschlichen Auges glich, war die Sternenfülle lockerer geworden, 5 ihr Glanz satter und goldener, so daß vom Goldglanz getroffen, vergoldet ihr silbernes Strahlen, die Mondessichel zwischen den Gestirnen schwebte: der Frühling ruhte im Himmelsgewölbe und eines Tags kam er zur Erde herab. Da zogen weiße Wolken, Schub um Schub, gegen Westen und gegen den Kuppron zu; sie verloren sich hinter dem Gebirge, wie um den kühlen 10 blauen Himmelsraum für neue und wiederum neue Wolkenschübe freizumachen, und ihr Wehen, frühlingsgetragen, frühlingtragend, war das des wiedererstehenden Lebens. Es war nicht der explosive Frühling jener ersten Märztage, sondern ein haltbarer und richtiger, sanft und sachte unter einem heiterkühlen Wehen, und ebenso sanft, ebenso kühl rieselte 15 die Himmelsbläue in die kreatürliche Welt, rieselte über die Körper der Menschen, und war sachte wie ein leiser Regen, dem man gerne die Kleider öffnen will. – So wurde es Ostern.

3 Modernisierung einer Großstadt

Ich gehe durch eine Stadt, in der ich seit zwanzig Jahren ansässig bin und an deren Entwicklung ich teilgenommen habe. Ich gehe durch den ge-

---

[1] Der Risch, *reeds, sedge*.   [2] =Die Erle, *alder*.

steigerten Verkehr, die aufgerissenen Straßen entlang, vorbei an den
gläsernen Hochhäusern, im Lärm der Rammklötze und Preßluftbohrer,
5 im Rasseln der Zementmischer. Vom Bahnhof aus blicke ich über die
Neubauten, die Gerüste, die Überbrückungen und erweiterten Straßen-
züge. Das Hotel Continental, mit seinen Jugendstilranken,[1] seinem fließen-
den Stuckwerk, seinen schweren Draperien hinter den gewölbten Fenstern,
ist abgerissen. Ringsum liegen die Einstiegschächte zur neugelegten
10 Untergrundbahn und die Plattformen der Haltestellen, vom Wald der
Verkehrszeichen umgeben. Hinüber zur Altstadt und zum südlichen
Stadtteil strecken sich neue Brücken, breite Einfahrtsstraßen. Der schmale
Holzsteg an der Eisenbahnbrücke, dessen Pfosten beim Vorbeifahren
eines Zuges knarrten, ist einer modernen Konstruktion gewichen, man
15 kann auf säuberlich ausgerichteten Steinbänken sitzen und die Aussicht
über den Strom genießen, an dessen Südufer abends lange Reihen von
Lichtfäden hängen. Wo früher die dunklen Uferpfade unterhalb des
Ritterhauses lagen, rollen jetzt auf breiten, asphaltierten Wegen die Auto-
mobile in unaufhörlicher Folge hin und her, und über der Schleuse erhebt
20 sich ein Verkehrskarussell in zahlreichen Schichten. Nur das eiserne Gerüst
des Fahrstuhls, der zur Anhöhe des Südufers führt, steht noch wie ein
altertümliches Denkmal vor den leuchtenden Blöcken der neuerrichteten
Geschäftshäuser.

4 Der Mond geht auf

Als ich mich nun umwendete, rollte die obere Kuppe der Mondkugel mit
solcher Schnelligkeit, als werde sie durch eine Flutwelle von unten emporge-
spült, hinter den schräg seitlich aufsteigenden, sehr fernen Zacken des
Latemargrates entlang. Gleich darauf verschwand sie wieder zur Hälfte
5 hinter einem ihre Bahn deckenden, massiveren Felsenturm, auf dessen
anderer Seite, schon voller, gerundeter, scheibenhafter, sie dann heraus-
tauchte. Eine Zeitlang wanderte nun die unten noch abgeschnittene
Kreisfläche hinter dem immer steiler aufragenden Bergrücken, im Dunst
der Atmosphäre lampenhaft rötlich leuchtend, – bis endlich die volle
10 Frucht sich aus der steinernen Schale löste und das klare Gestirn, wie von
einem überirdisch leichten Gas gehoben, in den dunklen Raum hinauf-
schwebte. Rasch überflutet, füllte sich die ungeheure Weite des Tals mit
einem silbrig irisierenden Lichtnebel, und um uns her begannen alle
Gegenstände, Gläser und Flaschen, Stühle, Gesims, und Steinbrüstung,
15 auch unsre eigenen Körper, in ihren Umrissen scharf und kalt befunkelt,
lange Mondschatten zu werfen. Die Felsen des Latemar, fern hinterm
Waldgebirge, strahlten in einem geisterhaften fahlen Schein, und während
der Mond, schon schwanengleich in schwarzer Bläue schwimmend, immer
klarer wurde und immer größere Kraft gewann, verglasten die oberen

[1] Jugendstil, 'art nouveau'

Ränder der Berge mehr und mehr. Aber das schiefergedeckte Dach des 20
Haupthauses, das vom Altan der Rocca seitlich lag, gerann jetzt zu einer
einzigen metallisch glänzenden Schimmerfläche.

5 Die Maschine

Gestern, bei einem nächtlichen Spaziergang durch entlegene Straßen des
östlichen Viertels, in dem ich wohne, sah ich ein einsames ·und finsteres
Bild. Ein vergittertes Kellerfenster öffnete dem Blick einen Maschinenraum,
in dem ohne jede menschliche Wartung ein ungeheures Schwungrad um
die Achse pfiff. Während ein warmer, öliger Dunst von innen heraus durch 5
das Fenster trieb, wurde das Ohr durch den prachtvollen Gang einer
sicheren, gesteuerten Energie fasziniert, der sich ganz leise wie auf den
Sohlen des Panthers der Sinne bemächtigte, begleitet von einem feinen
Knistern, wie es aus dem schwarzen Fell der Katzen springt, und vom
pfeifenden Summen des Stahles in der Luft – dies alles ein wenig ein- 10
schläfernd und sehr aufreizend zugleich. Und hier empfand ich wieder,
was man hinter dem Triebwerk des Flugzeugs empfindet, wenn die Faust
den Gashebel nach vorn stößt und das schreckliche Gebrüll der Kraft, die
der Erde entfliehen will, sich erhebt; oder wenn man nächtlich sich durch
zyklopische Landschaften stürzt, während die glühenden Flammenhauben 15
der Hochöfen das Dunkel zerreißen und inmitten der rasenden Bewegung
dem Gemüte kein Atom mehr möglich erscheint, das nicht in Arbeit ist.
Hoch über den Wolken und tief im Innern der funkelnden Schiffe,
wenn die Kraft die silbernen Flügel und die eisernen Rippen durchströmt,
ergreift uns ein stolzes und schmerzliches Gefühl – das Gefühl, im Ernst- 20
fall zu stehen.

6 Das Boudoir der Fürstin

Das Zimmer … war klein im Verhältnis zu seiner Höhe, mit einem grau-
blauen Teppich versehen, und ausgestattet mit anmutig geformten und
silbergrau lackierten Möbeln, deren Sitze blasse Seidenbezüge zeigten. Ein
Lustre aus milchigem Porzellan hing von dem weiß umschnörkelten Mittelpunkt der Decke herab, und die Wände waren mit Ölbildern von verschiede- 5
ner Größe geschmückt, Erwerbungen des Fürsten Philipp, lichterfüllten
Studien im neuen Geschmack, die weiße Ziegen in der Sonne, Federvieh
in der Sonne, besonnte Wiesen und bäuerliche Menschen mit blinzelnden,
von der Sonne gesprenkelten Gesichtern zur Anschauung brachten. Der
dünnbeinige Damen-Sekretär beim weißverhangenen Fenster war bedeckt 10
mit hundert peinlich geordneten Sächelchen, Nippes, Schreibutensilien und
mehreren zierlichen Notizblocks … vorm Tintenfaß lag offen ein Wirt-
schaftsbuch, und neben dem Schreibtisch war an der Wand ein kleiner, mit
seidenen Schleifen verzierter Abreißkalender befestigt … Gegenüber der

15 weißen Flügeltür zum Empfangssalon war zwischen der Sofabank und
einem Halbkreis von Stühlen der ovale Tisch mit zartem Damast und
einem blauseidenen Läufer gedeckt; das blumige Teegeschirr, ein Aufsatz
mit Konfekt, längliche Schalen mit Zuckergebäck und winzigen Butter-
brötchen waren in ebenmäßiger Anordnung darauf verteilt, und seit-
20 wärts dampfte auf einem Glastischchen über einer Spiritusflamme der
silberne Teekessel. Aber überall, in den Vasen auf dem Schreibtisch, dem
Teetisch, dem Spiegeltisch, dem Glasschrank voll Porzellanfiguretten,
dem Tischchen neben der weißen Chaiselongue waren Blumen, und ein
Blumentisch voller Topfgewächse stand zum Überfluß auch hier vor dem
25 Fenster.

7 Einfühlung in die Natur

Eine wunderbare Heiterkeit hat meine ganze Seele eingenommen, gleich
den süßen Frühlingsmorgen, die ich mit ganzem Herzen genieße. Ich bin
allein und freue mich meines Lebens in dieser Gegend, die für solche
Seelen geschaffen ist wie die meine. Ich bin so glücklich, mein Bester, so
5 ganz in dem Gefühle von ruhigem Dasein versunken, daß meine Kunst
darunter leidet. Ich könnte jetzt nicht zeichnen, nicht einen Strich, und
bin nie ein größerer Maler gewesen als in diesen Augenblicken. Wenn das
liebe Tal um mich dampft und die hohe Sonne an der Oberfläche der
undurchdringlichen Finsternis meines Waldes ruht und nur einzelne
10 Strahlen sich in das innere Heiligtum stehlen, ich dann im hohen Grase am
fallenden Bache liege und näher an der Erde tausend mannigfaltige
Gräschen mir merkwürdig werden; wenn ich das Wimmeln der kleinen
Welt zwischen Halmen, die unzähligen unergründlichen Gestalten der
Würmchen, der Mückchen näher an meinem Herzen fühle und fühle die
15 Gegenwart des Allmächtigen, der uns nach seinem Bilde schuf, das Wehen
des Allliebenden, der uns in ewiger Wonne schwebend trägt und erhält;
mein Freund, wenn's dann um meine Augen dämmert und die Welt um
mich her und der Himmel ganz in meiner Seele ruhn wie die Gestalt einer
Geliebten, dann sehne ich mich oft und denke: Ach, könntest du das
20 wieder ausdrücken, könntest du dem Papiere das einhauchen, was so voll,
so warm in dir lebt, daß es würde der Spiegel deiner Seele, wie deine Seele
ist der Spiegel des unendlichen Gottes! – Mein Freund! – Aber ich gehe
darüber zugrunde, ich erliege unter der Gewalt der Herrlichkeit dieser
Erscheinungen.

8 Ein Hund begrüßt seinen Herrn

Unwillkürlich stelle ich mich seitlich gegen den Heranstürmenden, in
Abwehrposition, denn seine Scheinabsicht, mir zwischen die Füße zu
stoßen und mich zu Falle zu bringen, hat unfehlbare Täuschungskraft.

Im letzten Augenblick aber und dicht vor dem Anprall weiß er zu bremsen
und einzuschwenken, was sowohl für seine körperliche als seine geistige 5
Selbstbeherrschung zeugt; und nun beginnt er, ohne Laut zu geben – denn
er macht einen sparsamen Gebrauch von seiner sonoren und ausdrucks-
fähigen Stimme –, einen wirren Begrüßungstanz um mich herum zu
vollführen, bestehend aus Trampeln, maßlosem Wedeln, das sich nicht
auf das hierzu bestimmte Ausdruckswerkzeug des Schwanzes beschränkt, 10
sondern den ganzen Hinterleib bis zu den Rippen in Mitleidenschaft
zieht, ferner einem ringelnden Sichzusammenziehen seines Körpers
sowie schnellenden, schleudernden Luftsprüngen nebst Drehungen um
die eigene Achse, – Aufführungen, die er aber merkwürdigerweise meinen
Blicken zu entziehen trachtet, indem er ihren Schauplatz, wie ich mich 15
auch wende, immer auf die entgegengesetzte Seite verlegt. In dem Augenblick jedoch, wo ich mich niederbeuge und die Hand ausstrecke, ist er
plötzlich mit einem Sprunge neben mir und steht, die Schulter gegen mein
Schienbein gepreßt, wie eine Bildsäule: schräg an mich gelehnt steht er,
die starken Pfoten gegen den Boden gestemmt, das Gesicht gegen das 20
meine erhoben, so daß er mir verkehrt und von unten herauf in die Augen
blickt und seine Reglosigkeit, während ich ihm unter halblauten und guten
Worten das Schulterblatt klopfe, atmet dieselbe Konzentration und Leidenschaft wie der vorhergegangene Taumel.

9 Wesentliche Unveränderlichkeit

Und die Welt, verändert sie sich? Nein. Das Winterbild kann sich über die
Sommerwelt werfen; aus dem Winter kann Frühling werden; aber das
Gesicht der Erde ist dasselbe geblieben. Es legt Masken an und ab, es
runzelt und lichtet die große schöne Stirne, es lächelt oder es zürnt, aber
bleibt immer dasselbe. Es liebt die Schminke, es färbt sich bald bunter, 5
bald matt, bald ist es glühend und bald blaß; es ist nie ganz dasselbe, es
verändert sich immer ein wenig und bleibt doch immer lebendig und ruhelos
gleich. Es blitzt mit den Augen Blitze und donnert mit seiner gewaltigen
Stimme den Donner, es weint den Regen in Strömen herab und läßt den
saubern, glitzernden Schnee zu seinem Mund herauslächeln, aber an den 10
Zügen und Linien des Gesichtes verändert sich spurwenig. Manchmal nur
fährt ihm ein schauderndes Erdbeben, ein Hagelsturz, eine Flutenüber-
schwemmung oder ein Vulkanfeuer über die ruhige Oberfläche dahin, oder
es erbebt und erschaudert innerlich von Welt- und Erdempfindungen und
-zuckungen; aber es bleibt dasselbe. Die Gegenden bleiben dieselben, 15
Städteansichten allerdings weiten und runden sich aus; aber wegfliegen
und sich einen andern Ort aussuchen, von einer Stunde auf die andere, das
können Städte auch nicht. Die Ströme und Flüsse fließen dieselbe Bahn wie
seit Jahrtausenden; sie können versanden, aber sie stürzen nicht plötzlich
über ihre Strombetten an die offene leichte Luft hinaus. Das Wasser muß 20
sich durch Kanäle und Höhlen hindurcharbeiten. Das Strömen und

Wühlen ist sein uraltes Gesetz. Und die Seen liegen, wo sie seit langer, langer Zeit liegen. Sie springen nicht zur Sonne hinauf und spielen nicht Ball wie Kinder. Sie sind manchmal empört und schlagen ihre Wasser
25 und Wellen zornig zischend zusammen; aber sie verwandeln sich weder eines Tages in Wolken, noch eines Nachts in wilde Pferde. Alles in und auf der Erde gehorcht schönen, strengen Gesetzen, wie die Menschen.

10 Aller Anfang ist schwer

Mit einer Mappe und Zubehör versehen, lief ich bereits unter den grünen Hallen des Bergwaldes hin, jeden Baum betrachtend, aber nirgends eigentlich einen Gegenstand sehend, weil der stolze Wald eng verschlungen, Arm in Arm stand und mir keinen seiner Söhne einzeln preisgab; die
5 Sträucher und Steine, die Kräuter und Blumen, die Formen des Bodens schmiegten und duckten sich unter den Schutz der Bäume und verbanden sich überall mit dem großen Ganzen, welches mir lächelnd nachsah und meiner Ratlosigkeit zu spotten schien. Endlich trat ein gewaltiger Buchbaum mit reichem Stamme und prächtigem Mantel und Krone heraus-
10 fordernd vor die verschränkten Reihen, wie ein König aus alter Zeit, der den Feind zum Einzelkampfe aufruft. Dieser Recke war in jedem Aste und jeder Laubmasse so fest und klar, so lebens- und gottesfreudig, daß seine Sicherheit mich blendete und ich mit leichter Mühe seine Gestalt bezwingen zu können wähnte. Schon saß ich vor ihm und meine Hand lag mit
15 dem Stifte auf dem weißen Papiere, indessen eine geraume Weile verging, eh' ich mich zu dem ersten Strich entschließen konnte; denn je mehr ich den Riesen an einer bestimmten Stelle genauer ansah, desto unnahbarer schien mir dieselbe, und mit jeder Minute verlor ich mehr meine Unbefangenheit. Endlich wagte ich, von unten anfangend, einige Striche und suchte
20 den schön gegliederten Fuß des mächtigen Stammes festzuhalten; aber was ich machte, war leben- und bedeutungslos ... Hastig und blindlings zeichnete ich weiter, mich selbst betrügend ... Die Gestalt auf meinem Papiere wuchs ins Ungeheuerliche, besonders in die Breite, und als ich an die Krone kam, fand ich keinen Raum mehr für sie und mußte sie, breit
25 gezogen und niedrig, wie die Stirne eines Lumpen, auf den unförmlichen Klumpen zwingen, daß der Rand des Bogens dicht am letzten Blatte stand, während der Fuß unten im Leeren taumelte. Wie ich aufsah und endlich das Ganze überflog, grinste ein lächerliches Zerrbild mich an, wie ein Zwerg aus einem Hohlspiegel; die lebendige Buche aber strahlte noch
30 einen Augenblick in noch größerer Majestät als vorher, wie um meine Ohnmacht zu verspotten.

11 Kalaurea

Endlich, da er mir die stillen Gipfel in der Ferne wies und sagte, daß wir bald in Kalaurea wären, merkt' ich mehr auf, und mein ganzes Wesen öffnete sich der wunderbaren Gewalt, die auf einmal süß und still und unerklärlich mit mir spielte. Mit großem Auge, staunend und freudig, sah ich hinaus in die Geheimnisse der Ferne, leicht zitterte mein Herz, und die Hand entwischte mir und faßte freundlichhastig meinen Schiffer an – „So?" rief ich, „das ist Kalaurea?" Und wie er mich drum ansah, wußt' ich selbst nicht, was ich aus mir machen sollte. Ich grüßte meinen Freund mit wunderbarer Zärtlichkeit. Voll süßer Unruhe war all mein Wesen. 5

Den Nachmittag wollt' ich gleich einen Teil der Insel durchstreifen. 10 Die Wälder und geheimen Tale[1] reizten mich unbeschreiblich, und der freundliche Tag lockte alles hinaus.

Es war so sichtbar, wie alles Lebendige mehr, denn tägliche Speise, begehrt, wie auch der Vogel sein Fest hat und das Tier.

Es war entzückend anzusehn! Wie, wenn die Mutter schmeichelnd 15 frägt,[2] wo um sie her ihr Liebstes sei, und alle Kinder in den Schoß ihr stürzen, und das Kleinste noch die Arme aus der Wiege streckt, so flog und sprang und strebte jedes Leben in die göttliche Luft hinaus, und Käfer und Schwalben und Tauben und Störche tummelten sich in frohlockender Verwirrung untereinander in den Tiefen und Höhn, und was die Erde 20 festhielt, dem ward zum Fluge der Schritt, über die Gräben brauste das Roß und über die Zäune das Reh, und aus dem Meergrund kamen die Fische herauf und hüpften über die Fläche. Allen drang die mütterliche Luft ans Herz, und hob sie und zog sie zu sich.

Und die Menschen gingen aus ihren Türen heraus, und fühlten wunder- 25 bar das geistige Wehen, wie es leise die zarten Haare über der Stirne bewegte, wie es den Lichtstrahl kühlte, und lösten freundlich ihre Gewänder, um es aufzunehmen an ihre Brust, atmeten süßer, berührten zärtlicher das leichte klare schmeichelnde Meer, in dem sie lebten und webten.

O Schwester des Geistes, der feurigmächtig in uns waltet und lebt, 30 heilige Luft! wie schön ists, daß du, wohin ich wandre, mich geleitest, Allgegenwärtige, Unsterbliche!

12 Unterbrochene Stille

Er hatte seine Arbeit beendet und lehnte jetzt wartend an der schwarz-weißen Sperrstange.

Die Strecke schnitt rechts und links gradlinig in den unabsehbaren grünen Forst hinein; zu ihren beiden Seiten stauten die Nadelmassen gleichsam zurück, zwischen sich eine Gasse frei lassend, die der rötlich- 5 braune, kiesbestreute Bahndamm ausfüllte. Die schwarzen, parallellaufenden Geleise darauf glichen in ihrer Gesamtheit einer ungeheuren eisernen Netzmasche, deren schmale Strähne sich im äußersten Süden und Norden in einem Punkte des Horizontes zusammenzogen.

Der Wind hatte sich erhoben und trieb leise Wellen den Waldrand 10 hinunter und in die Ferne hinein. Aus den Telegraphenstangen, die die

---

[1] Veraltet. Jetzt *Täler* [2] Veraltet. Jetzt *fragt*

Strecke begleiteten, tönten summende Akkorde. Auf den Drähten, die sich wie das Gewebe einer Riesenspinne von Stange zu Stange fortrankten, klebten in dichten Reihen Scharen zwitschernder Vögel. Ein Specht flog
15 lachend über Thiels Kopf weg, ohne daß er eines Blickes gewürdigt wurde.

Die Sonne, welche soeben unter dem Rande mächtiger Wolken herabhing, um in das schwarzgrüne Wipfelmeer zu versinken, goß Ströme von Purpur über den Forst. Die Säulenarkaden der Kiefernstämme jenseits des Dammes entzündeten sich gleichsam von innen heraus und glühten wie
20 Eisen.

Auch die Geleise begannen zu glühen, feurigen Schlangen gleich, aber sie erloschen zuerst; und nun stieg die Glut langsam vom Erdboden in die Höhe, erst die Schäfte der Kiefern, weiter den größten Teil ihrer Kronen in kaltem Verwesungslichte zurücklassend, zuletzt nur noch den äußersten
25 Rand der Wipfel mit einem rötlichen Schimmer streifend. Lautlos und feierlich vollzog sich das erhabene Schauspiel. Der Wärter stand noch immer regungslos an der Barriere. Endlich trat er einen Schritt vor. Ein dunkler Punkt am Horizonte, da wo die Geleise sich trafen, vergrößerte sich. Von Sekunde zu Sekunde wachsend, schien er doch auf einer Stelle zu
30 stehen. Plötzlich bekam er Bewegung und näherte sich. Durch die Geleise ging ein Vibrieren und Summen, ein rhythmisches Geklirr, ein dumpfes Getöse, das, lauter und lauter werdend, zuletzt den Hufschlägen eines heranbrausenden Reitergeschwaders nicht unähnlich war.

Ein Keuchen und Brausen schwoll stoßweise fernher durch die Luft.
35 Dann plötzlich zerriß die Stille. Ein rasendes Tosen und Toben erfüllte den Raum, die Geleise bogen sich, die Erde zitterte – ein starker Luftdruck – eine Wolke von Staub, Dampf und Qualm, und das schwarze, schnaubende Ungetüm war vorüber. So wie sie anwuchsen, starben nach und nach die Geräusche. Der Dunst verzog sich. Zum Punkte ein-
40 geschrumpft, schwand der Zug in der Ferne, und das alte heil'ge Schweigen schlug über dem Waldwinkel zusammen.

13 Die Sonnenfinsternis

Seltsam war. es, daß dies unheimliche klumpenhafte tiefschwarze vorrük-kende Ding, das langsam die Sonne wegfraß, unser Mond sein sollte, der schöne sanfte Mond, der sonst die Nächte so florig silbern beglänzte; aber doch war er es, und im Sternenrohr erschienen auch seine Ränder mit
5 Zacken und Wulsten besetzt, den furchtbaren Bergen, die sich auf dem uns so freundlich lächelnden Runde türmen.

Endlich wurden auch auf Erden die Wirkungen sichtbar, und immer mehr, je schmäler die am Himmel glühende Sichel wurde; der Fluß schimmerte nicht mehr, sondern war ein taftgraues Band, matte Schatten
10 lagen umher, die Schwalben wurden unruhig, der schöne sanfte Glanz des Himmels erlosch, als liefe er von einem Hauche matt an, ein kühles Lüftchen hob sich und stieß gegen uns, über den Auen starrte ein unbeschreib-

lich seltsames, aber bleischweres Licht, über den Wäldern war mit dem
Lichterspiele die Beweglichkeit verschwunden, und Ruhe lag auf ihnen,
aber nicht die des Schlummers, sondern die der Ohnmacht – und immer 15
fahler goß sichs über die Landschaft, und diese wurde immer starrer –
die Schatten unserer Gestalten legten sich leer und inhaltslos gegen das
Gemäuer, die Gesichter wurden aschgrau – – erschütternd war dieses
allmähliche Sterben mitten in der noch vor wenigen Minuten herrschenden
Frische des Morgens. Wir hatten uns das Eindämmern wie etwa ein 20
Abendwerden vorgestellt, nur ohne Abendröte; wie geisterhaft aber ein
Abendwerden ohne Abendröte sei, hatten wir uns nicht vorgestellt, aber
auch außerdem war dies Dämmern ein ganz anderes, es war ein lastend
unheimliches Entfremden unserer Natur; gegen Südost lag eine fremde
gelbrote Finsternis, und die Berge und selbst das Belvedere wurden von 25
ihr eingetrunken – die Stadt sank zu unseren Füßen immer tiefer wie ein
wesenloses Schattenspiel hinab, das Fahren und Gehen und Reiten über
die Brücke geschah, als sähe man es in einem schwarzen Spiegel – die
Spannung stieg aufs höchste – einen Blick tat ich noch in das Sternrohr, er
war der letzte; so schmal, wie mit der Schneide eines Federmessers in das 30
Dunkel geritzt, stand nur mehr die glühende Sichel da, jeden Augenblick
zum Erlöschen, und wie ich das freie Auge hob, sah ich auch, daß bereits
alle andern die Sonnengläser weggetan und bloßen Auges hinaufschauten –
sie hatten auch keines mehr nötig; denn nicht anders, als wie der letzte
Funke eines erlöschenden Dochtes, schmolz eben auch der letzte Sonnen- 35
funken weg, wahrscheinlich durch die Schlucht zwischen zwei Mond-
bergen zurück – es war ein ordentlich trauriger Augenblick – deckend stand
nun Scheibe auf Scheibe – und dieser Moment war es eigentlich, der
wahrhaft herzzermalmend wirkte – das hatte keiner geahnt – ein ein-
stimmiges „Ah" aus aller Munde, und dann Totenstille, es war der 40
Moment, da Gott redete, und die Menschen horchten.

II Narrative

14 Der Unfall

Auch die Dame und ihr Begleiter waren herangetreten und hatten, über
Köpfe und gebeugte Rücken hinweg, den Daliegenden betrachtet. Dann
traten sie zurück und zögerten. Die Dame fühlte etwas Unangenehmes in
der Herz-Magengrube, das sie berechtigt war für Mitleid zu halten; es war
ein unentschlossenes, lähmendes Gefühl. Der Herr sagte nach einigem 5
Schweigen zu ihr: „Diese schweren Kraftwagen, wie sie hier verwendet
werden, haben einen zu langen Bremsweg." Die Dame fühlte sich dadurch
erleichtert und dankte mit einem aufmerksamen Blick. Sie hatte dieses
Wort wohl schon manchmal gehört, aber sie wußte nicht, was ein Bremsweg sei, und wollte es auch nicht wissen; es genügte ihr, daß damit dieser 10
gräßliche Vorfall in irgend eine Ordnung zu bringen war und zu einem

technischen Problem wurde, das sie nicht mehr unmittelbar anging. Man
hörte jetzt auch schon die Pfeife eines Rettungswagens schrillen, und die
Schnelligkeit seines Eintreffens erfüllte alle Wartenden mit Genugtuung.
15 Bewundernswert sind diese sozialen Einrichtungen. Man hob den Verun-
glückten auf eine Tragbahre und schob ihn mit dieser in den Wagen.
Männer in einer Art Uniform waren um ihn bemüht, und das Innere des
Fuhrwerks, das der Blick erhaschte, sah so sauber und regelmäßig wie ein
Krankensaal aus. Man ging fast mit dem berechtigten Eindruck davon, daß
20 sich ein gesetzliches und ordnungsmäßiges Ereignis vollzogen habe. „Nach
den amerikanischen Statistiken", so bemerkte der Herr, „werden dort
jährlich durch Autos 190.000 Personen getötet und 450.000 verletzt."

„Meinen Sie, daß er tot ist?" fragte seine Begleiterin und hatte noch
immer das unberechtigte Gefühl, etwas Besonderes erlebt zu haben.
25 „Ich hoffe, er lebt", erwiderte der Herr. „Als man ihn in den Wagen
hob, sah er ganz so aus."

15 Die Schlange

An einem heißen Sommertage kam ich schon gegen Mittag nach Hause,
stieg im Brunnen[1] aus und ging den Rest des Weges zu Fuß. Es war wind-
still, und als ich durch die Felder ging, stieg die erhitzte Luft flimmernd
und wirbelnd über dem Korn auf. Den Sommer, die heißen Tage, den
5 hohen Mittag liebte ich sehr, und ich entsinne mich dieses Tages überaus
deutlich. Es gibt Erinnerungen, deren Kraft bis zur Symmetrie geht;
alles ordnet sich in ihnen, bis sie eine Figur bilden, deren Proportionen
überraschen. Ich schmeckte die Süßigkeit des Lebens, ein außerordentliches
Glücksgefühl durchdrang mich, und ledig aller Pflichten tanzte ich den
10 Weg mehr entlang, als ich ihn ging. Auf einem Raine zwischen den Feldern
sah ich eine Natter liegen; mir schien, daß ich nie ein größeres Tier dieser
Art gesehen hatte. Sogleich ging ich auf die schöne Schlange zu. Ich
beschloß sie mitzunehmen und wie schon manche andere in der Nähe
unseres Hauses wieder auszusetzen. So neckte ich sie einige Zeit, indem ich
15 um sie herumging und sie vergeblich zu greifen suchte, da sie mir in halb-
erhobener Stellung, den Kopf hoch aufgerichtet, zischend folgte und nach
meiner Hand stieß. Sie war sehr gereizt und in der Hitze voller Lebens-
kraft. Ich pflegte die Nattern mit einem schnellen Griff am Schwanz zu
fassen und sie hochzuhalten, so daß sie, mit ihrem Gewicht nach unten
20 hängend, sich nicht mehr bis zu meiner Hand aufrichten konnten. Und
auch diese wollte ich so fangen. Immer schneller lief ich in engem Kreise
um sie herum, und unermüdlich folgte sie mir mit den wiegenden Bewegungen ihres Kopfes, so daß ihre Ausdauer mich verwunderte. Plötzlich
aber ergriff mich in der lautlosen Stille des Mittags ein Gefühl, das ich nie
25 zuvor hatte . . . Ich ließ von der Schlange ab und eilte halb laufend über die
Hügel, um nach Hause zu kommen.

[1] Proper name.

16 Nachhilfestunden

Als ich auf die Straße trat, fiel mir das grobe gütige Gesicht des Mädchens ein, und ich dachte, daß ich sie hätte um Geld fragen können – ich zögerte, nur einen Augenblick, klappte meinen Mantelkragen hoch, weil es immer noch regnete, und lief zur Bushaltestelle, die an der Kirche zu den Sieben Schmerzen Mariä ist. 5
Zehn Minuten später saß ich in einem südlichen Stadtteil in einer Küche, die nach Essig roch, und ein blasses Mädchen mit großen, fast gelben Augen sagte lateinische Vokabeln auf, und einmal öffnete sich die Tür zum Nebenzimmer, und ein mageres Frauengesicht erschien in der Tür, ein Gesicht mit großen, fast gelben Augen, und sagte: ,,Gib dir Mühe, Kind, 10 du weißt, wie schwer es mir wird, dich zur Schule zu schicken – und die Stunden kosten Geld.''
Das Kind gab sich Mühe, ich gab mir Mühe, und die ganze Stunde lang flüsterten wir uns lateinische Vokabeln zu, Sätze und Syntaxregeln, und ich wußte, daß es zwecklos war. Und als es punkt zehn nach drei war, kam die 15 magere Frau aus dem Nebenzimmer, brachte heftigen Essiggeruch mit, strich dem Kind übers Haar, blickte mich an und fragte: ,,Glauben Sie, daß sie es schaffen wird? Die letzte Arbeit hatte sie eine Drei. Morgen machen sie wieder eine.''
Ich knöpfte meinen Mantel zu, zog meine nasse Mütze aus der Tasche 20 und sagte leise: ,,Sie wird es wohl schaffen.'' Und ich legte meine Hand auf das stumpfe Blondhaar des Kindes, und die Frau sagte: ,,Sie muß es schaffen, sie ist meine Einzige, mein Mann ist in Winiza gefallen.'' Ich sah für einen Augenblick den schmutzigen Bahnhof von Winiza vor mir, voller rostiger Traktoren – blickte die Frau an, und sie nahm sich plötzlich 25 ein Herz und sagte das, was sie schon lange hatte sagen wollen: ,,Darf ich Sie bitten, zu warten mit dem Geld, bis …'', und ich sagte ja, noch bevor sie den Satz beendet hatte.

17 Das Kind und die Schlangen

Bei dieser Spende hielt Lampusa schon früh den kleinen Erio auf dem Arm, der ihren Ruf mit seinem Stimmchen begleitete. Wie sehr erstaunte ich indessen, als ich eines Abends, kaum daß es laufen konnte, das Kind das Kesselchen ins Freie schleppen sah. Dort schlug es seinen Rand mit einem Birnholzlöffel, und leuchtend glitten die roten Schlangen aus den Klüften 5 der Marmorklippen vor. Und wie im Helltraum hörte ich den kleinen Erio lachen, als er zwischen ihnen auf dem gestampften Lehm des Küchenvorhofs stand. Die Tiere umspielten ihn halb aufgerichtet und wiegten über seinem Scheitel in schnellem Pendelschlage die schweren Dreiecksköpfe hin und her. Ich stand auf dem Altan und wagte meinen 10 Erio nicht anzurufen, wie jemand, den man schlafend auf steilen Firsten wandeln sieht. Doch da erblickte ich die Alte vor der Felsenküche – Lampusa, die mit gekreuzten Armen stand und lächelte. Bei ihrem Anblick erfaßte mich das herrliche Gefühl der Sicherheit in flammender Gefahr.

15 Seit jenem Abend war es Erio, der uns so das Vesperglöcklein läutete. Wenn wir den Klang des Kesselchens vernahmen, legten wir die Arbeit nieder, um uns am Anblick seiner Spende zu erfreuen. Bruder Otho eilte aus seiner Bibliothek und ich aus dem Herbarium auf den inneren Altan, und auch Lampusa trat vom Herd hinzu und lauschte dem Kinde mit

20 stolzem, zärtlichem Gesicht. Wir pflegten uns dann an seinem Eifer zu ergötzen, mit dem es die Tiere in Ordnung hielt. Bald konnte Erio ein jedes bei Namen nennen und trippelte mit seinem Röckchen aus blauem, goldgefaßtem Sammet in ihrem Kreis umher. Auch achtete er sehr darauf, daß alle von der Milch bekamen, und schaffte für die Nachzüglerinnen

25 Raum am Kesselchen. Dann pochte er diese oder jene der Trinkerinnen mit seinem Birnholzlöffel auf den Kopf, oder er packte sie, wenn sie nicht schnell genug den Platz verließ, am Nackenansatz und zerrte sie mit aller Kraft hinweg. Wie derb er sie indes auch fassen mochte, immer blieben die Tiere gegen ihn ganz sanft und zahm, selbst in der Häutung, während deren

30 sie sehr empfindlich sind. So lassen während dieser Zeit die Hirten ihr Vieh nicht bei den Marmorklippen auf die Weide gehen, denn ein gezielter Biß fällt selbst den stärksten Stier mit Blitzes Kraft.

18 Auf der Galerie

Wenn irgendeine hinfällige, lungensüchtige Kunstreiterin in der Manege auf schwankendem Pferd vor einem unermüdlichen Publikum vom peitschenschwingenden erbarmungslosen Chef monatelang ohne Unterbrechung im Kreise rundum getrieben würde, auf dem Pferde schwirrend,

5 Küsse werfend, in der Taille sich wiegend, und wenn dieses Spiel unter dem nichtaussetzenden Brausen des Orchesters und der Ventilatoren in die immerfort weiter sich öffnende graue Zukunft sich fortsetzte, begleitet vom vergehenden und neu anschwellenden Beifallsklatschen der Hände, die eigentlich Dampfhämmer sind – vielleicht eilte dann ein junger Galerie-

10 besucher die lange Treppe durch alle Ränge hinab, stürzte in die Manege, riefe das: Halt! durch die Fanfaren des immer sich anpassenden Orchesters.

Da es aber nicht so ist; eine schöne Dame, weiß und rot, hereinfliegt, zwischen den Vorhängen, welche die stolzen Livrierten vor ihr öffnen; der Direktor, hingebungsvoll ihre Augen suchend, in Tierhaltung ihr

15 entgegenatmet; vorsorglich sie auf den Apfelschimmel hebt, als wäre sie seine über alles geliebte Enkelin, die sich auf gefährliche Fahrt begibt; sich nicht entschließen kann, das Peitschenzeichen zu geben; schließlich in Selbstüberwindung es knallend gibt; neben dem Pferde mit offenem Munde einherläuft; die Sprünge der Reiterin scharfen Blickes verfolgt; ihre

20 Kunstfertigkeit kaum begreifen kann; mit englischen Ausrufen zu warnen versucht; die reifenhaltenden Reitknechte wütend zu peinlichster Acht-

samkeit ermahnt; vor dem großen Saltomortale das Orchester mit aufgehobenen Händen beschwört, es möge schweigen; schließlich die Kleine vom zitternden Pferde hebt, auf beide Backen küßt und keine Huldigung des Publikums für genügend erachtet; während sie selbst, von ihm gestützt, 25 hoch auf den Fußspitzen, vom Staub umweht, mit ausgebreiteten Armen, zurückgelehntem Köpfchen ihr Glück mit dem ganzen Zirkus teilen will – da dies so ist, legt der Galeriebesucher das Gesicht auf die Brüstung und, im Schlußmarsch wie in einem schweren Traum versinkend, weint er, ohne es zu wissen. 30

III Portraits and Characters

19 Ein häßliches Gesicht

Er gehörte zu jenen Leuten, deren Sein etwas Konkaves, Hohlspiegelartiges an sich hat. Man ist da immer geneigt, Brennpunkte des Geistes zu vermuten, bis nicht das Gegenteil evident wird. Wer viel schweigt, hört und sieht viel, ohne Zweifel. Aber daß solche Zurückhaltung einfach einem erstaunlichen Mangel an Feuer entspringen könne, nimmt zunächst niemand an. Daß stille Wasser tief sind, ist eine Grundüberzeugung, die jeder hat; und mindestens sind diese Wasser unheimlich. Aber man hat sich auch schon aufmerksam über welche gebeugt, die in kaum Handtiefe nur gewöhnliche Kiesel am Grunde sehen ließen. Das Gesicht des Mannes, der sich eben hier am Teetisch niedergelassen hat, gehört einer seltenen Art 10 an, die aber bei jüdischen Männern eher noch gefunden werden kann als bei anderen, wenngleich solch ein Antlitz eine ganz allgemeine physiognomische Möglichkeit verwirklicht. Es ist ein nicht ganz zustande gekommenes Gesicht, oder wenn man so lieber will, der Schau- und Bauplatz höchst unverträglicher Materialien, die sich schon in den Ahnen nicht 15 haben einigen lassen, jetzt aber in Zerknall und Zerfall geraten sind, wie nach einer Explosion. Hiedurch entsteht eine außerordentliche Häßlichkeit, die um so profunder ist als sie nicht an einem Nasenerker, einer Kinnlade, einem verkniffenen Aug' oder sonst an einzelnen Bauteilen sich verhaftet zeigt, sondern demgegenüber sozusagen in zwischendinglicher 20 Schwebe bleibt, ein in der Luft hängendes Band (denn das ist es eben doch!), welches das Disparate nicht bindet und die Dissonanz immerfort stehen läßt. Solch ein Gesicht sieht aus, als trüge dieser Mensch an einer auferlegten Buße für ihm unbekannte Schuld.

20 Ein Mann von vierzig Jahren

Es war ein Mann von vierzig Jahren. Kurzgliedrig und beleibt, trug er einen weit offenstehenden Rock aus braunem Loden, eine helle und geblümte Weste, die in weicher Wölbung seinen Bauch bedeckte und auf der

eine goldene Uhrkette mit einem wahren Bukett, einer ganzen Sammlung
5 von Anhängseln aus Horn, Knochen, Silber und Korallen prangte – ein
Beinkleid ferner von unbestimmter graugrüner Farbe, welches zu kurz war
und aus ungewöhnlich steifem Stoff gearbeitet schien, denn seine Ränder
umstanden unten kreisförmig und faltenlos die Schäfte der kurzen und
breiten Stiefel. – Der hellblonde, spärliche, fransenartig den Mund über-
10 hängende Schnurrbart gab dem kugelrunden Kopfe mit seiner gedrungenen
Nase und seinem ziemlich dünnen und unfrisierten Haar etwas Seehund-
artiges. Die „Fliege", die der fremde Herr zwischen Kinn und Unterlippe
trug, stand im Gegensatz zum Schnurrbart ein wenig borstig empor. Die
Wangen waren außerordentlich dick, fett, aufgetrieben und gleichsam
15 hinaufgeschoben zu den Augen, die sie zu zwei ganz schmalen, hellblauen
Ritzen zusammenpreßten und in deren Winkeln sie Fältchen bildeten.
Dies gab dem solcherart verquollenen Gesicht einen Mischausdruck von
Ergrimmtheit und biederer, unbeholfener, rührender Gutmütigkeit. Unterhalb des kleinen Kinnes lief eine steile Linie in die schmale weiße Hals-
20 binde hinein ... die Linie eines kropfartigen Halses, der keine Vatermörder
geduldet haben würde. Untergesicht und Hals, Hinterkopf und Nacken,
Wangen und Nase, alles ging ein wenig formlos und gepolstert ineinander
über ... Die ganze Gesichtshaut war infolge aller dieser Schwellungen
über die Gebühr straff gespannt und zeigte an einzelnen Stellen, wie am
25 Ansatz der Ohrläppchen und zu beiden Seiten der Nase, eine spröde
Rötung ... In der einen seiner kurzen, weißen und fetten Hände hielt der
Herr seinen Stock, in der anderen ein grünes Tirolerhütchen, geschmückt
mit einem Gemsbart.

21 Der Geigenspieler

Endlich – und er zog meine ganze Aufmerksamkeit auf sich – ein alter,
leicht siebzigjähriger Mann in einem fadenscheinigen aber nicht unrein-
lichen Molltonüberrock mit lächelnder, sich selbst Beifall gebender Miene.
Barhäuptig und kahlköpfig stand er da, nach Art dieser Leute, den Hut als
5 Sammelbüchse vor sich auf dem Boden, und so bearbeitete er eine alte
vielzersprungene Violine, wobei er den Takt nicht nur durch Aufheben
und Niedersetzen des Fußes, sondern zugleich durch übereinstimmende
Bewegung des ganzen gebückten Körpers markierte. Aber all diese
Bemühung, Einheit in seine Leistung zu bringen, war fruchtlos, denn was
10 er spielte, schien eine unzusammenhängende Folge von Tönen ohne
Zeitmaß und Melodie. Dabei war er ganz in sein Werk vertieft; die Lippen
zuckten, die Augen waren starr auf das vor ihm befindliche Notenblatt
gerichtet – ja wahrhaftig Notenblatt! Denn indes alle andern, ungleich
mehr zu Dank spielenden Musiker sich auf ihr Gedächtnis verließen,
15 hatte der alte Mann mitten in dem Gewühle ein kleines, leicht tragbares
Pult vor sich hingestellt mit schmutzigen, zergriffenen Noten, die das in
schönster Ordnung enthalten mochten, was er so außer allem Zusammen-

hange zu hören gab. Gerade das Ungewöhnliche dieser Ausrüstung hatte
meine Aufmerksamkeit auf ihn gezogen, so wie es auch die Heiterkeit des
vorüberwogenden Haufens erregte, der ihn auslachte und den zum Sam- 20
meln hingestellten Hut des alten Mannes leer ließ, indes das übrige
Orchester ganze Kupferminen einsackte. Ich war, um das Original
ungestört zu betrachten, in einiger Entfernung auf den Seitenabhang
des Dammes getreten. Er spielte noch eine Weile fort. Endlich hielt er
ein, blickte, wie aus einer langen Abwesenheit zu sich gekommen, nach 25
dem Firmament, das schon die Spuren des nahenden Abends zu zeigen
anfing; darauf abwärts in seinen Hut, fand ihn leer, setzte ihn mit un-
getrübter Heiterkeit auf, steckte den Geigenbogen zwischen die Saiten;
„*Sunt certi denique fines*,"[1] sagte er, ergriff sein Notenpult und arbeitete
sich mühsam durch die dem Feste zuströmende Menge in entgegenge- 30
setzter Richtung, als einer, der heimkehrt.

22 Der Landgeistliche

Ich setzte mich also nieder, und was der Pfarrer vorausgesagt hatte,
geschah. Ich wurde mit manchem Anwesenden bekannt, von manchem
erfuhr ich Namen und Verhältnisse, und da die Gerichte sich ablöseten,
und der Wein die Zungen öffnete, war manche junge Bekanntschaft schon
wie eine alte. Nur ein einziger Gast war nicht zu erkennen. Lächelnd und 5
freundlich saß er da, er hörte aufmerksam alles an, er wandte immer das
Angesicht der Gegend, wo eifrig gesprochen wurde, zu, als ob ihn eine
Pflicht dazu antriebe, seine Mienen gaben allen Redenden recht, und wenn
an einem andern Orte das Gespräch wieder lebhafter wurde, wandte er
sich dorthin und hörte zu. Selber aber sprach er kein Wort. Er saß ziemlich 10
weit unten, und seine schwarze Gestalt ragte über das weiße Linnengedecke
der Tafel empor, und obwohl er nicht groß war, so richtete er sich nie
vollends auf, als hielte er das für unschicklich. Er hatte den Anzug eines
armen Landgeistlichen. Sein Rock war sehr abgetragen, die Fäden waren
daran sichtbar, er glänzte an manchen Stellen, und an andern hatte er die 15
schwarze Farbe verloren und war rötlich oder fahl. Die Knöpfe daran
waren von starkem Bein. Die schwarze Weste war sehr lang und hatte
ebenfalls beinerne Knöpfe. Die zwei winzig kleinen Läppchen von weißer
Farbe – das einzige Weiße, das er an sich hatte –, die über sein schwarzes
Halstuch herabgingen, bezeugten seine Würde. Bei den Ärmeln gingen, 20
wie er so saß, manchmal ein ganz klein wenig eine Art Handkrausen hervor,
die er immer bemüht war, wieder heimlich zurückzuschieben. Vielleicht
waren sie in einem Zustande, daß er sich ihrer ein wenig hätte schämen
müssen. Ich sah, daß er von keiner Speise viel nahm und dem Aufwärter,
der sie darreichte, immer höflich dankte. Als der Nachtisch kam, nippte er 25
kaum von dem besseren Weine, nahm von dem Zuckerwerk nur kleine

[1] 'There are, after all, definite limits' (Horace)

Stückchen und legte nichts auf seinen Teller heraus, wie doch die andern taten, um nach der Sitte ihren Angehörigen eine kleine Erinnerung zu bringen.

23 Martin Luther

Luther war und blieb zeitlebens eine kämpferische Natur, ein geborener Raufbold mit Gott, Mensch und Teufel. Kampf war für ihn nicht nur Lust und Entladungsform seiner Kraft, sondern geradezu Rettung für seine überfüllte Natur. Dreinschlagen, Zanken, Schimpfen, Streiten bedeutete
5 für ihn eine Art Aderlaß, denn erst im Aus-sich-Herausfahren, im Losdreschen spürt und erfüllt er sein ganzes menschliches Maß; mit einer leidenschaftlichen Lust stürzt er sich darum in jede gerechte oder ungerechte Sache hinein. „Fast tödlich durchschauerts mich", schreibt Bucer, sein Freund, „wenn ich an die Wut denke, die in dem Manne
10 kocht, sobald er mit einem Gegner zu schaffen hat." Denn unleugbar, Luther kämpft wie ein Besessener, wenn er kämpft, und immer nur mit ganzem Leib, mit entzündeter Galle, mit blutunterlaufenen Augen, mit schäumender Lippe; es ist, als ob er mit diesem furor teutonicus gleichsam ein fieberndes Gift aus dem Körper hetzte. Und tatsächlich, immer erst,
15 wenn er so recht blindwütig zugeschlagen und seinen Zorn entladen, wird ihm leicht, „da erfrischt sich mir das ganze Geblüt, das ingenium wird hell und die Anfechtungen weichen." Auf dem Kampfplatz wird der hochgebildete Doctor theologiae sofort zum Landsknecht: „Wenn ich komm, schlage ich mit Keulen drein", ein rasender Grobianismus, eine berser-
20 kerische Besessenheit erfaßt ihn, er greift rücksichtslos zu jeder Waffe, die ihm zur Hand kommt, zum feinfunkelnden dialektischen Schwert ebenso wie zur Mistgabel voll Schimpf und Dreck; rücksichtslos schaltet er jede Hemmung aus und schreckt auch notfalls vor Unwahrheit und Verleumdung zur Austilgung des Gegners nicht zurück. „Um des Besseren und der
25 Kirche willen muß man auch eine gute, starke Lüge nicht scheuen."

24 Stein

Ein unvergeßlicher Anblick, wie über den Großen dieser Größte erschien und, an den Grenzen Rußlands, in aller Todesnot, das innerste Leben dieses geschlagenen Staates mit dem Feuerstrome seines Genius durchflutete. Das alte Preußen war bankrott, der Wille der Erneuerung war jetzt da, und
5 dieser Wille wurde in ihm Person. Alles an ihm war gewaltig, fest und knorrig die Gestalt, über mächtigem Nacken ein mächtiger Kopf von großen Zügen, starker gebogener Nase, funkelnden kleinen Augen; ein Hauch von Kraft und Mut, von Wahrhaftigkeit und von Zorn ging von ihm aus, von Furchtlosigkeit und Strenge. Er suchte nie sich selbst und schlug
10 sich immer ganz in die Schanze; aus tiefer sittlicher Leidenschaft kam sein

Wollen und sein Handeln. Er gehört zu den Großen, in denen sich dem
Deutschen die reinste Gestalt unserer Volksart enthüllt, erdennah, derb
und zart, unsystematisch zugleich und einheitlich, vulkanisch und gütig
und im Innersten fromm, er steht unter ihnen bei Martin Luther und Otto
von Bismarck, bei den echtesten Söhnen des deutschen Bodens, dem 15
Bauernenkel und dem Landedelmann, ein Edelmann ganz und gar auch
er, unabhängig und stolz, großartig wie jene in der Ungebrochenheit des
Gefühls und in der Entladung seines Grimmes, verheerend und auf-
bauend, der Mann der schöpferischen Tat, der dämonisch mit sich reißen-
den Gewalt einer ursprünglichen Natur. Er war ungleich weniger als 20
Bismarck der Mann der Macht, und Diplomat war er gar nicht, die Klugheit des Tages ließ ihn so manches Mal schädlich im Stiche; ihn erfüllte
der ethische Idealismus seiner Zeiten und beherrschte mehr der allgemeine Gedanke seines Volkes als der greifbare des preußischen Staates,
der sittliche Inhalt der Dinge lag ihm näher als die Unbarmherzigkeit des 25
Ringens um die Wirklichkeit: ihr gegenüber blieb er gebunden, und seine
äußerlichen Siege sind unvollkommen. Jedoch die innerlichen wirkten
über die Zukunft hin.

25 Marie Curie

Dort sitzt sie, die Polin war von Herkunft und sich stolz dazu bekannte –
die feine, fühlsame Hand an der Skala eines Meßinstrumentes, in ihrem
Laboratorium. Das zarte Profil mit dem hochgekämmten, aschblonden
Haar ist nach oben gewandt; der einfache Laboratoriumkittel, aus dem
der blumenhaft leichte Hals steigt, verbirgt fast ihr Geschlecht. Die 5
Atmosphäre um diese Frau ist geladen mit Intensität. Eine nahezu uner-
trägliche Stille, ein offenes Geheimnis strahlt wie das Leuchten des
Radiums in tiefer Dunkelheit von ihr aus. Und dann dieser Blick: emporge-
hoben, weit aufgeschlagen, bedingungslos hingegeben, doch ohne Zucht-
losigkeit. Wo haben wir diesen Blick schon gesehen? Diese kristallene 10
Reinheit und tiefe Kontemplation? Bald wird die andere Hand ein Notizblatt in ihre Nähe ziehen und es mit nüchternen, klaren, aber geheimnisvollen
Kurven und Zeichen bedecken – ein Notizblatt, das in der Mitte gefaltet
und auf der anderen Seite mit der Schrift ihres Mannes bezeichnet ist:
genialen, eigenwilligen Formeln von vertikaler Tendenz, während ihr 15
eigenes Schriftbild in horizontaler Prägung verläuft, und beide zusammen
die Kathedrale der Wissenschaft erbauen; die Kathedrale der namenlosen,
asketischen Diener am Werk ihrer Gottheit: der reinen Wissenschaft. Daß
sie später, diese geduldige Nonne, um ihrer Wissenschaft willen, zur
„Wohltäterin der Menschheit" wurde, im Weltkrieg das Röntgenam- 20
bulatorium nicht nur ins Leben rief, sondern auch selbst mit eigener Hand
bediente und späterhin durch die Begründung unzähliger Forschungs-
stätten gegen die Geißel der Menschheit, den Krebs, einer mindestens
ebenso großen Zahl von Menschen das Leben erhielt und zurückgab, war

25 gleichsam nur ein Nebenprodukt ihrer Besessenheit, die nichts als Werk-
treue hieß. Diese Treue am Werk ist ihr tiefstes Geheimnis, der Schlüssel
zu ihrer Einsamkeit, die Erklärung ihres heroischen Lebens, jener fast
schmerzhaften Flamme, die jeden Menschen in ihrer Umgebung erbar-
mungslos verbrannte.

26 Wallenstein

Er war kein Freund von Zeremonien; wie oft unterbrach er lange von
Äußerungen der Untertänigkeit angeschwellte Anreden deutscher
Gesandten; er spottete der tiefen Reverenzen, wie sie damals am römischen
Hofe gang und gäbe wurden; – aber er liebte von Anfang an den Pomp
5 einer prächtigen Umgebung. Seine Pagen, die er gern aus den vornehmsten
Geschlechtern nahm, erschienen in blauem Samt, wie mit Rot und Gold auf
das prächtigste angetan; so war seine Dienerschaft glänzend ausgestattet;
seine Leibwache bestand aus ausgesuchten Leuten von hoher und schöner
Gestalt; er wollte besonders, seit er Herzog von Mecklenburg geworden
10 war, durch die Äußerlichkeit eines fürstlichen Hofhaltes imponieren. Er
lebte mäßig; aber seine Tafel sollte auf das trefflichste bedient sein. Es
gehörte zu seinem Ehrgeiz, wenn er sagen konnte, daß einer und der
andere seiner Kämmerer in kaiserlichen Diensten gestanden. Niemand
bezahlte reichlicher.
15 Er hatte sich in Italien die Sitte und Art der gebildeten Welt angeeignet.
Unter anderem weiß man, wie sehr er die Damen des Hofes zu Berlin, als
er einst daselbst erschien, einzunehmen wußte; von den Anmaßungen, die
einige seiner Obersten vor sich hertrugen, war bei ihm nicht die Rede.
Aber wehe dem, der ihn in Zorn versetzte! Wie in seiner Jugend, so in
20 seinem Alter, war er dann seiner selbst nicht mächtig; er war wie mit Wut
erfüllt und schlug um sich – man ließ ihn toben, bis es vorüber war …
Jedermann, der in seine Nähe kam, litt von seiner Launenhaftigkeit,
seinem zurückstoßenden Wesen, seinem gewaltsamen, rücksichtslosen
Gebaren. Sein Ruf schwankte zwischen zwei Extremen: daß er das wildeste
25 Untier sei, welches Böhmen hervorgebracht habe, oder der größte Kriegs-
kapitän, dessengleichen die Welt noch nicht gesehen.
Sein Antlitz erscheint, wie es die bestbeglaubigten Bilder darstellen,
zugleich männlich und klug; man könnte nicht sagen groß und imposant.
Er war mager, von blasser, ins Gelbe fallender Gesichtsfarbe, mit kleinen,
30 hellen, schlauen Augen. Auf seiner hohen Stirn bemerkte man die Signatur
der Gedanken, nicht der Sorgen: starke Linien, keine Runzeln; früh ward
er alt; schon in den vierziger Lebensjahren erbleichte sein Haar. Fast immer
litt er am Podagra. In den letzten Jahren konnte er nur mit Mühe an seinem
spanischen Rohre einherschreiten; bei jedem Schritt sah er um sich.
35 Aber in ihm lebte ein feuriger Impuls zu unaufhörlicher Bewegung,
Unternehmung, Erwerbung; durch seinen Gesundheitszustand nicht

allein nicht erstickt, sondern eher angereizt, der ehrgeizige Trieb, sich nach allen Seiten geltend zu machen, seine Macht und die Bedeutung seines Hauses zu gründen und die alten Feinde zu seinen Füßen zu sehen.

IV Philosophical and Reflective

27 Subjekt und Objekt

Die Grenzen zwischen Subjekt und Objekt beginnen zu fallen. Die äußerste Entfremdung zwischen beiden führt zur äußersten Identität. Nicht mehr stehen sich wie in der älteren Poesie ein empfindendes Ich und eine geschilderte Objektwelt beziehungsvoll und doch klar geschieden einander gegenüber, so daß sich das Subjekt im Medium der Natur und der 5 sozialen Umwelt unmittelbar ausdrücken kann, ohne doch die Grenzen zwischen beiden zu verwischen, wodurch eine vertraute und innige Wechselbeziehung zwischen beiden entsteht, die zugleich jede Sphäre in sich beläßt; nicht mehr also sind die poetischen Bilder Metaphern, Gleichnisse, Symbole für das vom Subjekt Empfundene, Gelebte, Ge- 10 meinte. Vielmehr werden Subjekt und Objekt im wörtlichen Sinne identisch, woraus sich zugleich ihre Undeutbarkeit ergibt. Denn nicht kann mehr dieses oder jenes poetische Bild auf eine bestimmte seelische Verfassung oder eine objektive Gegebenheit bezogen oder reduziert werden. Vielmehr sind alle poetischen Bilder bei Kafka subjektiv und objek- 15 tiv zugleich, Ausdrucksformen eines Gesamtzustandes von Welt, der auf nichts mehr außer sich selbst bezogen und daher auch nicht mehr gedeutet, auf einen sogenannten tieferen Sinn, auf ein anderes, eigentlich Gemeintes hin angedeutet werden kann, es sei denn ..., man erschließt in diesen Bildern eben diesen Gesamtzustand von Welt. 20

28 Probleme der Geschichtsschreibung

Viele Geschichtsforscher haben daher ihre Ansprüche noch mehr herabgesetzt und vom Historiker bloß verlangt, daß er den jeweiligen Stand unserer Geschichtskenntnisse völlig objektiv widerspiegle, indem er sich zwar der allgemeinen historischen Wertmaßstäbe notgedrungen bediene, aber aller persönlichen Urteile enthalten solle. Aber selbst diese niedrige 5 Forderung ist unerfüllbar. Denn es stellt sich leider heraus, daß der Mensch ein unheilbar urteilendes Wesen ist. Er ist nicht bloß genötigt, sich gewisser „allgemeiner" Maßstäbe zu bedienen, die gleich schlechten Zollstöcken sich bei jeder Veränderung der öffentlichen Temperatur vergrößern oder verkleinern, sondern er fühlt außerdem den Drang in sich, alle 10 Tatsachen, die in seinen Gesichtskreis treten, zu interpretieren, zu beschönigen, zu verleumden, kurz, durch sein ganz individuelles Urteil zu fälschen und umzulügen, wobei er sich allerdings in der exkulpierenden

Lage des unwiderstehlichen Zwanges befindet. Nur durch solche ganz
15 persönliche einseitige gefärbte Urteile nämlich ist er imstande, sich in der
moralischen Welt, und das ist die Welt der Geschichte, zurechtzufinden.
Nur sein ganz subjektiver „Standpunkt" ermöglicht es ihm, in der Gegenwart festzustehen und von da aus einen sichtenden und gliedernden Blick
über die Unendlichkeit der Vergangenheit und der Zukunft zu gewinnen.
20 Tatsächlich gibt es auch bis zum heutigen Tage kein einziges Geschichts-
werk, das in dem geforderten Sinne objektiv wäre. Sollte aber einmal ein
Sterblicher die Kraft finden, etwas so Unparteiisches zu schreiben, so
würde die Konstatierung dieser Tatsache immer noch große Schwierigkeiten machen: denn dazu gehörte ein zweiter Sterblicher, der die Kraft
25 fände, etwas so Langweiliges zu lesen.

29 Das künstlerische Schaffen

Wenn eine künstlerische Arbeit ins Stocken kommt und nicht vorwärts-
gehen will, so hat das jeweils seinen guten Grund. Zwar ist der Autor dann
meist überzeugt, daß ihm die rechte Stimmung fehle oder daß der von ihm
gewählte Stoff bockig sei und eigensinnigen Widerstand leiste. Mich
5 aber hat die Erfahrung belehrt, daß es niemals an der Stimmung liegt und
niemals am Stoff. Wenn die Stimmung fehlt, so stimmt etwas nicht. Und
nicht der Stoff bockt, sondern die an irgendeinem Punkte verletzte Wahrheit.
Ein einziger falscher Einschlag stellt das ganze Gewebe in Frage. In
keiner anderen menschlichen Betätigung ist das formale Gelingen so un-
10 löslich verknüpft mit Logik und Ethik wie im künstlerischen Schaffen,
dieser sogenannten „Welt des schönen Scheins". Ein alter, viel erfahrener
Dichter sagte einst zu mir: „Gott darf unlogisch sein, das heißt ohne
erkennbare Folgerichtigkeit, der Schriftsteller nicht." Der Mann hatte
Recht. Nur wenn bei einer Erzählung alle Grade der Wahrheit in Ord-
15 nung sind, von der niedrigen Wahrscheinlichkeit angefangen, über die
feinere Richtigkeit und Aufrichtigkeit hinaus bis zu den letzten Überein-
stimmungen, nur dann erlebt ein Verfasser das seltene Wunder, daß
gleichnisweise die Quellen des erfundenen Lebens wie von selbst zusam-
menströmen und einen epischen Wasserspiegel bilden, der ihn wie einen
20 glücklichen Schwimmer hochhebt und trägt. Sein Eigengewicht scheint
sich dann zu vermindern, und die elementare Wonne des Schöpfertums
durchströmt ihn. In solchen Ausnahmefällen ist er Spieler und Zuschauer
zugleich, und die Mühe des Schreibens besteht in einem atemlos raschen
Ablesen dessen, was in ihm und um ihn schon fertig aufgezeichnet steht.

30 Das Rationale und Irrationale im Seelenleben

Alles kommt beim Menschen der modernen Kultur und Zivilisation auf
ein gesundes, natürliches und harmonisches Verhältnis zwischen den

rationalen und irrationalen Kräften des Seelenlebens an. Denn eben diese moderne Kultur und Zivilisation bedroht durch ihre Eigenart dieses Gleichgewicht. Verstand und Vernunft heißen – sehr summarisch, aber 5 für unsere Zwecke ausreichend betrachtet –, die Kräfte der einen, Gemüt, Phantasie, Begehren und Wollen die Kräfte der anderen Sphäre. Letzten Endes soll die Vernunft, also eine rationale Kraft, das ganze wogende Spiel der Seele beherrschen. Aber diese Vernunft muß selbst schon, um ihr Höchstes und Bestes zu leisten, auch von den irrationalen Kräften sich 10 nähren. Das Gemüt muß ihr den Weg zum Guten, zur Zügelung der Selbstsucht, zu allen sittlichen und religiösen Zielen, die Phantasie den Weg zum Schönen und damit wieder zur Befreiung der Seele vom selbstisch-sinnlichen Begehren zeigen. Gemüt und Phantasie zusammen müssen ferner auch den Verstand in seiner Aufgabe, die Welt zu begreifen, 15 d.h. den Erkenntnis- und Wahrheitstrieb nähren und leiten, aber taktvoll, zurückhaltend, ohne Vergewaltigung. Der Wille aber, der auf allen Gebieten des Guten, Schönen und Wahren schließlich die Exekutive zu besorgen hat, schuldet Gehorsam der Königin Vernunft, jener aus der Totalität der Seelenkräfte emporsteigenden, sie alle verarbeitenden, ausgleichenden und 20 leitenden Herrscherin. Jede einseitige Entwicklung einzelner, sei es rationaler, sei es irrationaler Seelenkräfte droht das Ganze zu stören und kann schließlich, immer weiter gesteigert, zu Katastrophen führen, für den Einzelnen wie für Massen, für ganze Völker, wenn ein Sturm von Ereignissen sie in die gefährliche Richtung hineintreibt. 25

31 Lesen und Denken

Lesen ist ein bloßes Surrogat des eigenen Denkens. Man läßt dabei seine Gedanken von einem andern am Gängelbande führen ... Lesen soll man nur dann, wenn die Quelle der eigenen Gedanken stockt; was auch beim besten Kopfe oft genug der Fall sein wird. Hingegen die eigenen, urkräftigen Gedanken verscheuchen, um ein Buch zur Hand zu nehmen, ist 5 Sünde wider den heiligen Geist. Man gleicht alsdann dem, der aus der freien Natur flieht, um ein Herbarium zu besehen, oder um schöne Gegenden im Kupferstiche zu betrachten.

Wenn man auch bisweilen eine Wahrheit, eine Einsicht, die man mit vieler Mühe und langsam durch eigenes Denken und Kombinieren heraus- 10 gebracht hat, hätte mit Bequemlichkeit in einem Buche ganz fertig vorfinden können; so ist sie doch hundertmal mehr wert, wenn man sie durch eigenes Denken erlangt hat. Denn nur alsdann tritt sie als integrierender Teil, als lebendiges Glied, ein in das ganze System unserer Gedanken, steht mit demselben in vollkommenem und festem Zusammenhange, wird 15 mit allen ihren Gründen und Folgen verstanden, trägt die Farbe, den Farbenton, das Gepräge unserer ganzen Denkweise, ist eben zur rechten Zeit, als das Bedürfnis derselben rege war, gekommen, sitzt daher fest und

kann nicht wieder verschwinden ... Der Selbstdenker nämlich lernt die
20 Autoritäten für seine Meinungen erst hinterher kennen, wo sie ihm dann
bloß zur Bekräftigung derselben und zu eigener Stärkung dienen; während
der Bücherphilosoph von ihnen ausgeht, indem er aus fremden zusammen-
gelesenen Meinungen sich ein Ganzes konstruiert, welches alsdann einem
aus fremdem Stoff zusammengesetzten Automaten gleicht, jenes andere
25 hingegen einem lebenden erzeugten Menschen. Denn gleich diesem ist es
entstanden, indem die Außenwelt den denkenden Geist befruchtete, der
danach es austrug und gebar.

32 Das wissenschaftliche Weltbild

In der Tat gewährt das jetzige wissenschaftliche Weltbild, verglichen mit
dem ursprünglichen naiven Weltbild, einen seltsamen, geradezu fremdartig anmutenden Anblick. Die unmittelbar erlebten Sinneseindrücke,
von denen doch die wissenschaftliche Arbeit ihren Anfang nahm, sind
5 vollständig aus dem Weltbild verschwunden; vom Sehen, Hören, Tasten
ist darin nicht die Rede. Statt dessen gewahren wir, wenn wir einen Blick
in die Arbeitsstätten der Forschung werfen, eine Anhäufung von äußerst
komplizierten und unübersichtlichen, schwer zu handhabenden Meßgerä-
ten, erdacht und konstruiert zur Bearbeitung von Problemen, die nur mit
10 Hilfe von abstrakten Begriffen, von mathematischen und geometrischen
Symbolen, formuliert werden können und die dem Laien oft überhaupt
nicht verständlich sind. Man könnte an dem Sinn der exakten Wissenschaft irre werden, und es ist sogar in diesem Zusammenhang gegen sie der
Vorwurf erhoben worden, daß sie mit ihrer ursprünglichen Anschaulichkeit
15 auch ihren festen Halt verloren habe. Wer trotz aller angeführten Gründe
bei dieser Meinung verharrt, dem ist nicht zu helfen, es wird ihm aber
niemals gelingen, ebensowenig wie einem Experimentator, der grundsätzlich nur mit primitiven Apparaten arbeiten will, die exakte Wissenschaft wesentlich zu fördern. Denn um dies fertigzubringen, dazu genügt
20 nicht eine geniale Intuition und ein frisches Zupacken, sondern dazu gehört
auch sehr verwickelte, mühselige und entsagungsvolle Kleinarbeit, in der oft
zahlreiche Forscher zusammenwirken müssen, um für ihre Wissenschaft
den Aufstieg auf die nächst höhere Entwicklungsstufe schrittweise vorzu-
bereiten. Wohl bedarf der Pionier der Wissenschaft, wenn seine Gedanken
25 ihre tastenden Fühler ausstrecken, einer lebendigen Anschauung; denn
neue Ideen entspringen nicht dem rechnenden Verstand, sondern der
künstlerisch schaffenden Phantasie, aber für den Wert einer neuen Idee
maßgebend ist allemal nicht der Grad der Anschaulichkeit, die überdies zu
ihrem wesentlichen Teil Sache der Übung und der Gewohnheit ist,
30 sondern der Umfang und die Genauigkeit der einzelnen gesetzlichen
Zusammenhänge, zu deren Entdeckung sie führt.

33 Was ist Aufklärung?

Aufklärung ist der Ausgang des Menschen aus seiner selbst verschuldeten Unmündigkeit. Unmündigkeit ist das Unvermögen, sich seines Verstandes ohne Leitung eines andern zu bedienen. Selbstverschuldet ist diese Unmündigkeit, wenn die Ursache derselben nicht am Mangel des Verstandes, sondern der Entschließung und des Mutes liegt, sich seiner 5 ohne Leitung eines andern zu bedienen. Sapere aude! Habe Mut, dich deines eigenen Verstandes zu bedienen! ist also der Wahlspruch der Aufklärung. Faulheit und Feigheit sind die Ursachen, warum ein so großer Teil der Menschen, nachdem sie die Natur längst von fremder Leitung frei gesprochen, dennoch gerne zeitlebens unmündig bleiben; und 10 warum es Andern so leicht wird, sich zu deren Vormündern aufzuwerfen. Es ist so bequem, unmündig zu sein. Habe ich ein Buch, das für mich Verstand hat, einen Seelsorger, der für mich Gewissen hat, einen Arzt, der für mich Diät beurteilt, u.s.w., so brauche ich mich ja nicht selbst zu bemühen. Ich habe nicht nötig zu denken, wenn ich nur bezahlen kann; 15 andere werden das verdrießliche Geschäft schon für mich übernehmen. Daß der bei weitem größte Teil der Menschen (darunter das ganze schöne Geschlecht) den Schritt zur Mündigkeit, außer dem daß er beschwerlich ist, auch für sehr gefährlich halte: dafür sorgen schon jene Vormünder, die die Oberaufsicht über sie gütigst auf sich genommen haben ... Es ist also 20 für jeden einzelnen Menschen schwer, sich aus der ihm beinahe zur Natur gewordenen Unmündigkeit herauszuarbeiten. Er hat sie sogar lieb gewonnen und ist vor der Hand wirklich unfähig, sich seines eigenen Verstandes zu bedienen, weil man ihn niemals den Versuch davon machen ließ. Satzungen und Formeln, diese mechanischen Werkzeuge eines ver- 25 nünftigen Gebrauchs oder vielmehr Mißbrauchs seiner Naturgaben, sind die Fußschellen einer immerwährenden Unmündigkeit. Wer sie auch abwürfe, würde dennoch auch über den schmalsten Graben einen nur unsicheren Sprung tun, weil er zu dergleichen freier Bewegung nicht gewöhnt ist. 30

34 Die Dichtung des Expressionismus

Und immer wieder muß gesagt werden, daß die Qualität dieser Dichtung in ihrer Intensität beruht. Niemals in der Weltdichtung scholl so laut, zerreißend und aufrüttelnd Schrei, Sturz und Sehnsucht einer Zeit, wie aus dem wilden Zuge dieser Vorläufer und Märtyrer, deren Herzen nicht von den romantischen Pfeilen des Amor oder Eros, sondern von den 5 Peinigungen verdammter Jugend, verhaßter Gesellschaft, aufgezwungener Mordjahre durchbohrt wurden. Aus irdischer Qual griffen ihre Hände in den Himmel, dessen Blau sie nicht erreichten; sie warfen sich, sehnsuchtsvoll die Arme ausbreitend, auf die Erde, die unter ihnen auseinanderbarst; sie riefen zur Gemeinschaft auf und fanden doch nicht zueinander; sie 10 posaunten in die Tuben der Liebe, so daß diese Klänge den Himmel erbeben ließen, nicht aber durch das Getöse der Schlachten, Fabriken und Reden zu den Herzen der Menschen drangen. Freilich wird die Musik dieser Dichtung nicht ewig sein wie die Musik Gottes im Chaos. Aber was

15 wäre die Musik Gottes, wenn ihr nicht die Musik des Menschen antwortete, die sich ewig nach dem Paradies des Kosmos sehnt ... Von den vielen, vielen Dichtungen dieser Generation werden fast alle mit den verebbenden Stürmen ihrer Epoche untergegangen sein. Statt einiger großer leuchtender , wärmender Gestirne wird Nachlebenden ihre Menge wie die von unzähligen

20 kleinen Sternen erschimmernde Milchstraße erscheinen, die fahlklärenden Glanz in wogende Nacht gießt.

Keiner dieser Dichter kokettiert mit der Unsterblichkeit, keiner wirft sich den Triumphmantel mit distanzierend heroischer Gebärde um, keiner will als Olympier in edler Haltung entschweben; und wenn diese Dichter

25 in ausschweifender Weitschweifigkeit, und unmäßigem Fortissimo psalmodieren, stöhnen, klagen, schreien, fluchen, rufen, hymnen – so geschieht es niemals aus Hochmut, sondern aus Not und Demut. Denn nicht sklavisches Kriechen, untätiges Warten ist Demut; sondern es ist Demut, wenn einer hintritt und öffentlich aussagt, bekennt und fordert vor

30 Gott und den Menschen, und seine Waffen sind nur sein Herz, sein Geist und seine Stimme.

35 Eine neue Weltanschauung

Herders Gefühl des lebendigen Werdens und sein Sinn für die Individualität sind das fruchtbar Neue seines Geistes für die deutsche Bildung im allgemeinen und für Goethe im besondern. Dies gibt auch seinem Universalismus den besonderen Charakter neben dem Lessings, des anderen

5 großen damaligen Bildungsuniversalisten. Wenn für Lessing der Schlüssel zu allen Kammern der Welt das vernünftige Gesetz war, so wars für Herder die lebendige Kraft. Lessing suchte überall das Gültige, Herder überall das Wesenhafte, Lessing die Normen, d.h. das Allgemeinste, Herder die Gestalt und die Stimmung, d.h. das Besonderste, Lessing das

10 Gemeinsame, d.h. das Richtige, Herder das Unterscheidende, das So-und-nicht-anders-sein, das Individuelle – kurz Lessing das Sein im Raum, das Sinnbild und den Schauplatz vernünftiger und unabänderlicher Gesetzlichkeit, Herder das Werden in der Zeit, das Sinnbild beständiger Neuerung, Umgestaltung, das Zeichen der wirksamen Kraft. Ohne weiteres

15 ist klar was dem jungen Goethe gemäßer war: ein Universalismus des aktiven Gefühls, der Sympathie mit dem individuell Wirkenden und Werdenden, das „in schwankender Erscheinung lebt", das ihm verwirrend und lockend von allen Seiten her entgegendrang, das im eigenen Blut sich ahnungsvoll und frühlingshaft regte. Der Jüngling suchte und brauchte

20 einen Sinn, eine Sprache und Deutung der Kraft, des Gewühls, der drängenden Fülle und der strotzenden Freiheit, nicht ein neues – und sei

es das liberalste – Gesetz. An Gesetzen, an Vernunften stieß er sich ja bei jedem Schritt den er aus seiner Natur heraus der Natur draußen entgegen gehen wollte. Gefühl, Kraft, Ahnung hatte er in sich, aber diffus und vereinzelt, gehemmt durch die Zügel des Rationalismus und der Gesellschaft der er sich noch einbezogen sah ... Gesetze, Vernunft, Muster, Regeln, Konventionen sah er allerseits drau ßen, die er respektieren, beherrschen, erreichen, aber nicht mehr lieben und einverleiben konnte. Ihm fehlte noch Umfassung, Zusammenhang, Klarheit nicht der Vernunft, die nicht seine war, sondern der ihm gemäßen Kraft. So ward Herder sein Mann.

36 Der entzweite Mensch

Die Kultur selbst war es, welche der neuern Menschheit diese Wunde schlug. Sobald auf der einen Seite die erweiterte Erfahrung und das bestimmtere Denken eine schärfere Scheidung der Wissenschaften, auf der andern das verwickeltere Uhrwerk der Staaten eine strengere Absonderung der Stände und Geschäfte notwendig machte, so zerriß auch der innere Bund der menschlichen Natur, und ein verderblicher Streit entzweite ihre harmonischen Kräfte. Der intuitive und der spekulative Verstand verteilten sich jetzt feindlich gesinnt auf ihren verschiedenen Feldern, deren Grenzen sie jetzt anfingen mit Mißtrauen und Eifersucht zu bewachen, und mit der Sphäre, auf die man seine Wirksamkeit einschränkt, hat man sich auch in sich selbst einen Herrn gegeben, der nicht selten mit Unterdrückung der übrigen Anlagen zu endigen pflegt. Indem hier die luxurierende Einbildungskraft die mühsamen Pflanzungen des Verstandes verwüstet, verzehrt dort der Abstraktionsgeist das Feuer, an dem das Herz sich hätte wärmen und die Phantasie sich entzünden sollen.

Diese Zerrüttung, welche Kunst und Gelehrsamkeit in dem innern Menschen anfingen, machte der neue Geist der Regierung vollkommen und allgemein. Es war freilich nicht zu erwarten, daß die einfache Organisation der ersten Republiken die Einfalt der ersten Sitten und Verhältnisse überlebte; aber anstatt zu einem höhern animalischen Leben zu steigen, sank sie zu einer gemeinen und groben Mechanik herab ... Auseinandergerissen wurden jetzt der Staat und die Kirche, die Gesetze und die Sitten; der Genuß wurde von der Arbeit, das Mittel vom Zweck, die Anstrengung von der Belohnung geschieden. Ewig nur an ein einzelnes kleines Bruchstück des Ganzen gefesselt, bildet sich der Mensch selbst nur als Bruchstück aus; ewig nur das eintönige Geräusch des Rades, das er umtreibt, im Ohre, entwickelt er nie die Harmonie seines Wesens, und anstatt die Menschheit in seiner Natur auszuprägen, wird er bloß zu einem Abdruck eines Geschäfts, seiner Wissenschaft ...

Und so wird denn allmählich das einzelne konkrete Leben vertilgt, damit das Abstrakt des Ganzen sein dürftiges Dasein friste.

37 Der Reichtum

Was ist aber ... der Reichtum? Die Vorstellungen, die sich mit ihm verbinden, haben etwas Verworrenes, das aus einer Verwirrung und Vermischung der Begriffe hervorgeht. Der Reichtum ist seinem Begriffe nach entweder ein Sein oder ein Haben. Wenn ich den Reichtum als ein Sein
5 begreife, dann bin ich offenbar nicht deshalb reich, weil ich vieles habe, vielmehr hängt alles Haben von meinem reichen Sein ab. Der Reichtum ist dann nicht etwas, das den Menschen anfliegt und von ihm wegfliegt, er ist von Natur aus mitgegeben und unterliegt dem Willen und der Anstrengung nicht. Er ist ursprünglicher Reichtum, er ist ein Mehr an Freiheit,
10 das an gewissen Menschen aufschimmert. Denn Reichtum und Freiheit sind untrennbar miteinander verbunden, so eng, daß ich jede Art von Reichtum nach dem Grade der Freiheit abzuschätzen vermag, der ihm innewohnt. In diesem Sinn kann der Reichtum auch identisch mit der Armut sein, das heißt, ein reiches Sein ist vereinbar mit einem Nichthaben,
15 mit materieller Besitzlosigkeit. Homer denkt an nichts anderes, wenn er den Bettler einen König nennt. Und nur dieser Reichtum, der mir seinsmäßig zugeordnet ist, ist auch ein Reichtum, über den ich durchaus verfügen kann und den ich durchaus genießen kann. Denn solange der Reichtum in einem Haben besteht, ist die Fähigkeit zum Genusse dieses
20 Habens noch nicht mitgesetzt, sie kann also fehlen, ein häufiger Fall. Dort, wo der Reichtum Rang ist, hat er auch jene Festigkeit, die dem Wechsel und Zufall nicht unterworfen ist. Er ist so haltbar, so stabil, wie es die Schätze sind, deren Kennzeichen es ist, daß sie nicht angegriffen werden und dem Verzehr durch die Zeit nicht unterworfen sind. Wo er aber
25 auf einem bloßen Haben beruht, kann er mir jederzeit genommen werden. Die meisten glauben freilich, daß der Reichtum dadurch entstehe, daß man sich bereichere, ein Irrtum, den sie mit allem Pöbel dieser Welt gemein haben. Bereichern kann sich nur die Armut.

38 Die Pflicht des Schriftstellers

Wer den Menschen als verworfenes Wesen schildert, wer das Vertrauen auf seine Natur untergräbt, erschafft und vermehrt in den Herzen das Übel, vor dem er sich zu entrüsten vorgibt. Der Mensch ist nämlich keineswegs wie irgendein Gegenstand einfach da und mit festen Eigenschaften
5 behaftet. Sein Wesen ist Bereitschaft, unauslotbare schlummernde Möglichkeit. Wer ihn als Schurken ansieht, läuft Gefahr, den Schurken in ihm zu wecken. Wer einen Blick voll Liebe und Vertrauen auf ihn richtet, regt die höheren Kräfte auf und wird ihn des Vertrauens würdig finden ... Das Böse bedarf der Erklärung, wie bei Pelops, Atreus und Thyest, wie
10 auch bei Tantalus, dessen Vergehen Iphigenie „menschlich" nennt, verständlich aus der unangemessenen Lage, in die er hineingeriet, und das so fürchterlich nicht war, wie Dichter uns einreden wollen. Das Gute dagegen

276

versteht sich von selbst. So denke der Mensch zu seinem Heil. So zu denken, war Goethes kindlichem Sinn in der Jugend gemäß und in reiferen
Jahren Bedürfnis und Pflicht. 15

Wir freilich sind heute kaum mehr imstande, seine Überzeugung nach-
zufühlen, geschweige denn zu teilen. Wir haben Schopenhauer, Kierke-
gaard, Nietzsche und seine Jünger gehört. Wir sind von Dichtern der
Gegenwart so furchtbar erschreckt und gedemütigt worden wie kaum ein
Geschlecht vergangener Zeit. Und wir blicken in unsere Welt hinaus und 20
müssen bekennen: sie ist beherrscht vom Willen um Leben um jeden Preis,
vom Willen zur Macht und barbarischer Gier. Doch niemand darf sich
unterfangen, in dieser Wirklichkeit den Zettel säuberlich aus dem Einschlag zu lösen und Grund und Folge zu unterscheiden. Nietzsche
genießt die Ehre eines Propheten, dessen Weissagungen der Gang der 25
Geschichte bestätigt hat. Es ist unmöglich, zu widersprechen. Wohl aber
ist die Vermutung erlaubt, er habe selbst durch seine Lehre den Gang der
Ereignisse mitbestimmt. Das wäre im Sinne Goethes gesprochen. Aus
Sorge um die Menschheit wachte er über die Äußerungen der Dichter, und
je gewaltiger sich das Ungeheure und Entsetzliche meldete, desto ent- 30
schiedener lehnte er ab, so Schillers „Räuber" und „Fiesko", so die
„Penthesilea" Kleists.

39 Das Massenlesen

Die allgemeine Verwahrlosung des Lesens in unserer Zeit, das ober-
flächliche Massenlesen, ist eine oft beklagte Tatsache. Sie hat mancherlei
Gründe, die zum Teil im riesigen Angebot des bedruckten Papiers, zum
Teil in den Lesern zu finden sind. Die Menge der Nachrichten und Auf-
sätze in den Zeitungen zwingt den Leser, das auszuwählen, was ihm 5
wissenswert zu sein dünkt. Oft genügt der Titel oder die Schlagzeile, und
man läßt den betreffenden Schriftsatz ungelesen, oft muß man ihn anlesen
oder überfliegen, um festzustellen, ob er einem etwas zu sagen hat ... An
der Vernichtung der Lesekultur sind ferner die massenweise erscheinenden
Neuheiten des Buchhandels beteiligt, und zwar besonders die Romane. 10
Der merkwürdige Aberglaube, daß das Neue zugleich das Gute und Lesens-
werte sei, ist so stark, daß die meisten Menschen ihm erliegen. Ferner
wirkt mit das eitle Begehren, „auf der Höhe" zu sein und nicht als rück-
ständig zu gelten. Wenn in einer Gesellschaft über literarische Neuer-
scheinungen geplaudert wird, da will man doch mitreden können, nicht 15
wahr? Man kann doch nicht gut erzählen, man habe letzthin Homers
„Ilias" wieder einmal vorgenommen und an Stellen Entdeckungen
gemacht, an denen man als Schüler ahnungslos vorübergegangen sei; oder
man sei gerade bei der Lesung von Stifters Roman „Nachsommer", den
man früher als junger Mensch wohl einmal begonnen, aber aufgegeben 20
habe; oder man habe auf dem Nachttisch Goethes „West-östlichen Divan"

liegen und beschließe zur Zeit jeden Abend mit einem oder zwei Gedichten
daraus und kenne bereits einige auswendig.

25 Oh, man könnte schon davon sprechen, man würde vielleicht sogar
Aufsehen damit erregen – wenn es darauf ankäme ! – aber man traut sich
nicht. Lieber geht man zur Leihbücherei und holt sich für ein paar Tage
den Roman, den die andern „fabelhaft" und „phantastisch" und „ganz
groß" gefunden haben, während man selber beschämt gestehen mußte,
daß man ihn noch nicht kenne. Und dann liest man sich hurtig hindurch,
30 nimmt ihn auf zu den tausend andern, deren Erinnerungstrümmer im
Gedächtnis durcheinander liegen, und kann nun selber sagen, daß er
„flüssig geschrieben" und „kolossal interessant" sei, und dann ist er
erledigt und abgetan, und in den nächsten Tagen ist ein neuer an der
Reihe. Solchen Lesern ergeht es wie gewissen Reisenden, die in den
35 Städten, die sie besuchen, alles gesehen haben wollen und die großen
Museen in mäßigem Trab durcheilen, von keinem Gemälde und keinem
Standbild innerlich berührt, schließlich verwirrt und verdummt, aber mit
dem tröstenden Bewußtsein einer erfüllten Bildungspflicht.

40 Technik und Sport

In welcher Weise die Technik Einfluß auf den Menschen übt, wird uns
nicht nur deutlich, wenn wir ihn bei seiner Arbeit betrachten, wir sehen es
auch an den Vergnügungen, an den Sports, denen er huldigt. Der Sport
setzt die technisch organisierte Großstadt voraus und ist ohne sie nicht zu
5 denken. Die *termini technici* des Sports sind zu einem großen Teil engli-
scher Herkunft. Es hängt das mit dem Vorsprung in der Industrialisierung
zusammen, den die Engländer insbesondere in der ersten Hälfte des 19.
Jahrhunderts behaupten. Die Ingenieure und Maschinentechniker jener
Zeit reisten nach England, um ihr technisches Wissen zu vervollständigen.
10 Später, mit der Technisierung Amerikas, amerikanisiert sich auch der
Sport, während er von technisch rückständigen Ländern wie Rußland
oder Spanien wenig Förderung erfährt, gar keine aber von jenen weiten
Gebieten, die abseits von aller technischen Entfaltung liegen. Der Sport ist
also eine Reaktion auf die Bedingungen, in denen der Mensch in den großen
15 Städten lebt. Und diese Reaktion ist abhängig von der zunehmenden
Mechanik der Bewegung. Der „Wilde" treibt keinen Sport. Er übt seine
körperlichen Fähigkeiten, er spielt, tanzt, singt, aber an dieser Beschäftigung ist nichts Sportmäßiges, selbst wenn sie virtuos geübt wird. Unsere
besten Sportsleute kommen aus den Arbeitsgegenden, in denen die
20 Mechanisierung am weitesten fortgeschritten ist, vor allem also aus den
Städten. Bauern, Förster, Jäger, Fischer, deren Bewegung frei von
mechanischem Zwang ist, treiben wenig Sport ... Der Mensch, der aus
Lust am Laufen und Springen zu laufen und zu springen anfängt und
damit aufhört, wenn diese Lust in ihm erlischt, ist ein ganz anderer als
25 der Läufer und Springer, der sich zu einer Sportveranstaltung begibt und

unter Wahrung technischer Regeln, unter Verwendung von Zeituhren und Meßapparaten einen Rekord zu erspringen und zu erlaufen versucht. Der hohe Genuß, den uns das Schwimmen und Tauchen verschafft, entspringt der Berührung mit dem Element, seiner kristallischen Frische, Kühle, Reinheit, Durchsichtigkeit und Nachgiebigkeit. Offenbar spielt 30 dieser Genuß bei einer Sportveranstaltung, in der Schwimmer auftreten, gar keine Rolle, denn der Zweck solcher Veranstaltungen liegt in der Feststellung, welcher der Schwimmer sich technisch richtig im Wasser bewegt und am schnellsten von allen ans Ziel kommt. Das Training, das diesem Zwecke dient, läuft auf eine Anspannung des Willens hinaus, dem 35 sich der Körper auf mechanische Weise zu fügen hat. Eine solche Anspannung kann durchaus ersprießlich und fruchtbar sein. Das Training des Sportlers und seine sportliche Betätigung werden aber um so steriler, je mehr sie Selbstzweck werden.

Part Seven

German Poems and Verse Passages for Comment and Appreciation and/or Translation

The principles that apply to the literary analysis of prose (see pp. 240) apply also to that of verse; but clearly a student confronted by the task of writing a commentary on a German poem needs to have some knowledge of the basic principles of German versification. We therefore give first a brief account of German versification. It should, however, be realised that there is no universal agreement on many points of German versification, and a summary account like the one that follows cannot hope to do justice to the various theories that have been put forward. We refer the student interested in German versification to the select book-list on p. xiii for further information on this subject.

German Versification *(die Metrik)*

German, like English, is a strongly accented language. Its poetry is, therefore, like English poetry in that in every line of verse (except in 'free rhythms') there are more or less accented syllables occurring at more or less regular intervals.

The Foot

In most cases an accented syllable *(die Hebung)* preceded or followed by one or two, or very occasionally three, unaccented syllables *(die Senkung)* constitutes a foot *(der Versfuß)*. The number of feet in a line of German verse can vary from one to eight.

The commonest metrical feet are the following:

(a) Iamb(us) *(der Jambus)*: getán (× ∕)

Nimm beide fest und schick' sie mir hierher. (SCHILLER)

(b) Anapaest *(der Anapäst)*: instinktiv (× × ∕)

Wieder will ich wie du in den Ursprung zurück. (WEINHEBER)

(c) Trochee *(der Trochäus)*: Ausgang (∕ ×)

Sagt es niemand, nur den Weisen (GOETHE)

(d) Dactyl (*der Daktylus*): dáuerhaft (/××)

Álles Vergängliche

Íst nur ein Gleíchnis (GOETHE)

(e) Amphibrach (*der Amphibrachys*): Charákter (×/×)

Sie líndert geschäftig geheúchelte Leíden. (GOETHE)

(f) Spondee (*der Spondeus*), which comes normally only at the end of a line:

Weltschmérz (//)

Kómm, sagt die Mútter, zur Welt, Kínd. (KASCHNITZ)

(g) Cretic (*der Kretikus*), which is used only in conjunction with other feet:

aúfgebrácht (/×/)

Und diese Tótenklage, sie ruht nicht aus. (HÖLDERLIN)

(h) Choriamb (*der Choriambus*), which is used mainly in conjunction with other feet: Hándlungsmotív (/××/)

Schwánkend erscheint kaum noch das Bíld (GOETHE)

NOTE. By analogy with music verse *can* be scanned by taking the accented syllable always first (as in a musical bar) and considering the first unaccented syllable or syllables as the anacrusis (*der Auftakt*). This has the effect of reducing the possible types of metrical feet, if one excludes the rather rare spondee, cretic and choriamb, to two, i.e. trochee and dactyl. Thus

Nimm beíde fest und schick' sie mir hierher.

Wíeder will ich wie du in den Úrsprung zurück.

Sie líndert geschäftig geheúchelte Leíden.

(i) Feet that are incomplete at the end of a line or, as in the pentameter, before the caesura as well, are said to be catalectic (*katalektisch*):

Síehe! Da weínen die Götter, es weínen die Göttinen *álle*,

Dáß das Schöne vergéht, daß das Vollkommene *stírbt*. (SCHILLER)

The Line of Verse (*der Vers, die Verszeile*)

Lines of verse composed of more than one type of metrical foot are said to be mixed. Iambs are commonly mixed with anapaests, trochees with dactyls, but any 'mixture' is possible.

A line composed of iambs and/or anapaests is said to be in rising rhythm, one of trochees and/or dactyls in falling rhythm.

Lines can be masculine (*männlich, stumpf*), i.e. ending with an accented syllable (cf. (a), (b) above) or feminine (*weiblich, klingend*), i.e. ending with one or two unaccented syllables (cf. (c), (d), (e) above) or end-stopped, i.e. ending with an accented syllable where the sense ends (cf. (b) above).

Lines, especially longer ones, are sometimes broken by a caesura (*die Zäsur, der Einschnitt*) or caesuras, which is a pause dictated by the sense, coming either after a stressed syllable, when it is known as a masculine caesura, or after an unstressed syllable, when it is known as a feminine caesura (cf. (i) above). When the caesura comes in the middle of a line, as in the alexandrine and in the pentameter, the line is thereby broken up into two halves known as hemistichs (*das Hemistichion*) (cf. (i) above).

When lines run on there is said to be enjambement (*das Enjambement, der Zeilensprung*) (cf. (d) above). Within the line there may be reversal of feet, e.g.

$$\times \quad / \quad | \quad \times \quad / \quad | \quad / \quad \times \quad | \quad \times \quad /$$
Der Teich, von Goldfischen durchflammt. (CAROSSA)

The commonest **iambic** lines (*jambische Verszeilen*) are:

i the five-foot iambic (*der fünfhebige Jambus*) with masculine or feminine endings, with or without masculine or feminine caesuras, which when unrhymed is known as blank verse (*der Blankvers*):

Sein Blick ist vom Vorübergehn der Stäbe
so müd geworden, daß er nichts mehr hält.
Ihm ist, als ob es tausend Stäbe gäbe
und hinter tausend Stäben keine Welt.   (RILKE)

Nur in Entwürfen bist du tapfer, feig
In Taten? Gut! Gib deinen Feinden Recht!
Da eben ist es, wo sie dich erwarten.   (SCHILLER)

ii the five-foot iambic of eleven syllables and therefore with feminine endings, usually with a masculine caesura after the fourth syllable. It is known as the hendecasyllable (*der Endecasillabo*) and is often used in the sonnet and in terza rima and, together with alternating ten-syllabled iambics, particularly in ottava rima, as well as in terza rima and the sonnet:

Die Welle sprüht, und staunt zurück und weichet,
   Und schwillt bergan, sich immer selbst zu trinken;
   Gehemmt ist nun zum Vater hin das Streben. (GOETHE)

Und immer weht der Wind, und immer wieder
Vernehmen wir und reden viele Worte
Und spüren Lust und Müdigkeit der Glieder.   (HOFMANNSTHAL)

So wandelst du, dein Ebenbild zu schauen,
Das majestätisch uns von oben blickt,
Der Mütter Urbild, Königin der Frauen,
Ein Wunderpinsel hat sie ausgedrückt.

Ihr beugt ein Mann, mit liebevollem Grauen,
Ein Weib die Knie, in Demut still entzückt;
Du aber kommst, ihr deine Hand zu reichen,
Als wärest du zu Haus bei deinesgleichen.   (GOETHE)

ii   The six-foot iambic with masculine or feminine endings and a fixed
masculine caesura after the sixth syllable, commonly known as the
alexandrine (*der Alexandriner*):

Der schnelle Tag ist hin, die Nacht schwingt ihre Fahn'
Und führt die Sternen auf. Der Menschen müde Scharen ...
                                                    (GRYPHIUS)

v   the six-foot iambic with masculine endings, without a fixed caesura in
the middle of the line, known as the iambic trimeter (*der iambische
Trimeter*). It normally has a feminine caesura after the fifth or seventh
syllable and freely admits an admixture of anapaests:

Komm ich als Gattin? Komm ich eine Königin?
Komm ich ein Opfer für des Fürsten bittern Schmerz
Und für der Griechen langerduldetes Mißgeschick? (GOETHE)

The commonest **trochaic** lines (*trochäische Verszeilen*) are:

i   the four foot trochee (*der vierhebige Trochäus*), sometimes known as the
Spanish trochee, either rhyming or rhymeless, with or without catalectic lines. It has been used in the epic, the mock-epic and also in drama:

Eines Abends trat die Fürstin
Auf ihn zu mit raschen Worten:
,,Deinen Namen will ich wissen,
Deine Heimat, deine Sippschaft!''   (HEINE)

Wo wird einst des Wandermüden
Letzte Ruhestätte sein?
Unter Palmen in dem Süden?
Unter Linden an dem Rhein?   (HEINE)

Wie so schal dünkt mich dies Leben,
Wie so schal und jämmerlich!
Stets das Heute nur des Gestern
Und des Morgen flaches Bild;   (GRILLPARZER)

ii   the five-foot trochee, known sometimes as the Serbian trochee,
originally with feminine ending:

Melde mir die Nachtgeräusche, Muse,
Die ans Ohr des Schlummerlosen fluten!   (MEYER)

iii the shorter trochaic lines of two or three feet, often in combination with one another, lines much in favour with the 'Anacreontic' poets:

Trinke, küsse! Sieh, es ist
Heut Gelegenheit;
Weißt du, wo du morgen bist?
Flüchtig ist die Zeit!   (GLEIM)

The only **anapaestic** line (*anapästische Verszeile*) used with any frequency, and then with an admixture usually of iambic feet, is the four-foot anapaest (*der vierhebige Anapäst*):

In das Dunkel flog Wolke auf Wolke dahin.   (HEYM)

Im Frühlingsgefolge trat herrlich sie aus.   (GOETHE)

Lines of pure **dactylic** feet are not very frequent, and then usually with the last foot catalectic, e.g.

Ännchen von Tharau ist, die mir gefällt;
Sie ist mein Leben, mein Gut und mein Geld. (DACH)

Dactyls together with trochees are most commonly used:

i in the **hexameter** (*der Hexameter*), whose underlying rhythm is dactylic, though the first four dactyls (but never the fifth) may be replaced by trochees; the final foot is normally a trochee, occasionally a spondee. The caesura, which always falls within the foot, occurs most commonly near, but not actually at, the middle of the line; if it falls very near the beginning or the end of the line, a second caesura will often occur nearer the middle of the line:

Mancherlei Dinge bedarf der Mensch und alles wird täglich
Teurer: da seh' er sich vor, des Geldes mehr zu erreichen. (GOETHE)

ii in the **pentameter** (*der Pentameter*), which is used only in conjunction with the hexameter. Despite its name it has six feet, the third and sixth being for the most part monosyllables. The caesura comes regularly after the third foot, the fourth and fifth foot must be dactyls, the first and second may, however, be trochees:

Wie? Leichtsinniger Gott, missest du doppelt die Zeit? (GOETHE)

Gab sie mit reichlicher Hand alles der Einzigen, ihr. (GOETHE)

A great deal of German poetry is written in what is sometimes called non-syllabic verse. Its characteristic feature is the varying number of unaccented syllables between the accented (*die Füllungsfreiheit*). This feature is most marked in the so-called *Knittelvers*, which is a four-stressed line (*der Vierheber*), often with anacrusis, in which the number of syllables may vary from none to four:

i Wie herrlich leuchtet

   Mir die Natur.   (GOETHE)

   Mein Sohn, mein Sohn, ich seh' es genau:

   Es scheinen die alten Weiden so grau.   (GOETHE)

ii (*der freie Knittelvers*)

    Habe nun, ach! Philosophie,

    Juristerei und Medizin

    Und leider auch Theologie

    Durchaus studiert, mit heißem Bemühn.   (GOETHE)

    Wie machen wir's, daß wir kommen in Abrahams Schoß?

                                                    (SCHILLER)

Free Verse

The characteristic feature of free verse is the combination of lines of different length. These have, however, recognisable metrical feet, regular or mixed; and though there is no fixed strophic arrangement there is usually rhyme:

> ... Aus der Wolke
> Quillt der Segen,
> Strömt der Regen;
> Aus der Wolke, ohne Wahl,
> Zuckt der Strahl.
> Hört ihr's wimmern hoch vom Turm?
> Das ist Sturm!   (SCHILLER)

Free Rhythms

Free rhythms, on the other hand, have unrhymed lines of no fixed number of syllables and no fixed strophic form. Their essential characteristic is freedom within the line, and thus, generally, no recognisable metrical feet.

However, it is possible sometimes to sense something of the rhythm of the hexameter and/or pentameter:

> Da ich ein Knabe war,
> Rettet' ein Gott mich oft
> Vom Geschrei und der Rute der Menschen,
> Da spielt ich sicher und gut
> Mit den Blumen des Hains,
> Und die Lüftchen des Himmels
> Spielten mit mir. (HÖLDERLIN)

Rhyme

By rhyme is now normally meant end-rhyme (*der Endreim*), but older German poetry knew only head-rhyme or alliteration (*der Stabreim*).

(a) End-rhyme is the identity of sound between the last accented vowel of two or more words and all the subsequent consonants and vowels: *singen* – verbr*ingen*

(b) It is said to be a rich rhyme (*reicher Reim*) when the consonant (or consonants) preceding the accented vowel is (or are) also identical: ver*schlossen* – um*schlossen*.

(c) It is said to be an extended rhyme (*erweiterter Reim*) when it contains two accented syllables: gebúnden bíst – überwúnden bíst.

(d) It is said to be an identical rhyme (*rührender Reim*) when the rhyming words have identical spelling, though not necessarily the same meaning: Weise – weise.

(e) It is said to be impure rhyme (*unreiner Reim*) when the vowels or consonants are only similar, not identical: Luft – ruft; schla*fen* – Schlußoktaven.

(f) Rhyme may be

i   monosyllabic (masculine, *stumpf* or *männlich*): Wind – Kind
ii disyllabic (feminine, *klingend* or *weiblich*): singen – springen
iii trisyllabic (gliding, *gleitend*): sammelten – stammelten

(g) Rhyme occurs either

i   at the end of lines of verse – the most common practice – or at the beginning (*der Anfangsreim*), which is rare:

> Das Leben ist
> *Ein Laub*, das grünt und falbt *geschwind*
> *Ein Staub*, den leicht vertreibt der *Wind* (HARSDÖRFFER)

ii within the same line (*der Binnenreim*):

> Eine *starke* schwarze *Barke* (HEINE)

286

iii within the same line as consecutive words (*der Schlagreim*):

Sonne, Wonne, himmlisch Leben

iv at the end of one line and within the following line (*der Kettenreim*):

Wenn langsam Welle sich an Welle *schließet*,
Im breiten Bette *fließet* still das *Leben*,
Wird jeder Wunsch *verschweben* in den einen. (FR. SCHLEGEL)

(h) Rhymes can be grouped either

i in couplets (*der Paarreim*): aa bb cc ...
ii in cross rhyme (*der Kreuzreim*): abab cdcd ...
iii in enclosed rhyme (*umarmender Reim*): abba cddc
iv in interlaced rhyme (*verschränkter Reim*): abcabc; abcbac
v in tail rhyme (*der Schweifreim*): aabccb; aabaab
vi in chain rhyme (*der Kettenreim*): aba bcb cdc ...

(i) Refrain (*der Kehrreim*) is the repetition in two or more stanzas of a phrase or line(s) of verse. Such refrains usually come at the end of each stanza:

Röslein, Röslein, Röslein rot
Röslein auf der Heiden.

(j) Assonance (*die Assonanz, der Stammreim*) is the identity in two or more words of the vowel sound(s) but not of the consonants:

Andere wohnen bei dem Steuer droben (HOFMANNSTHAL)

(k) Alliteration (*die Alliteration, der Stabreim*) is the identity in two or more words of the initial sounds (consonants or vowels):

und unsre Rosse rauschen wie ein Regen. (RILKE)

The Stanza (*die Strophe*)

1 The elegiac couplet (*das Distichon*):

Im Hexameter steigt des Springquells flüssige Säule,
Im Pentameter drauf fällt sie melodisch herab. (SCHILLER)

2(a) Terza rima (*die Terzine*): rhyme scheme – aba bcb ... yzy/z:

Noch spür ich ihren Atem auf den Wangen:
Wie kann das sein, daß diese nahen Tage
Fort sind, für immer fort, und ganz vergangen? (HOFMANNSTHAL)

2(b) The ritornelle (*das Ritornell*): rhyme scheme – aba cdc etc.:

Blühende Myrte –
Ich hoffte süße Frucht von dir zu pflücken;
Die Blüte fiel; nun sah ich, daß ich irrte. (STORM)

3(a) Folk-song stanza (*die Volksliedstrophe*): rhyme schemes – abcb or abab or aabb:

i   Meine Ruh' ist hin,
Mein Herz ist schwer;
Ich finde sie nimmer
Und nimmermehr.   (GOETHE)

ii   Es war ein König in Thule,
Gar treu bis an das Grab,
Dem sterbend seine Buhle
Einen goldnen Becher gab.   (GOETHE)

iii   Wer reitet so spät durch Nacht und Wind?
Es ist der Vater mit seinem Kind;
Er hat den Knaben wohl in dem Arm,
Er faßt ihn sicher, er hält ihn warm.   (GOETHE)

3(b) The new Nibelungen stanza (*die neue Nibelungenstrophe*): a four-line stanza with six-stressed lines rhyming aa bb, with a feminine caesura after the third foot. If it had caesura-rhyme it would be indistinguishable for the ear from 3(a) (ii) above:

Es stand in alten Zeiten ein Schloß so hoch und hehr,
Weit glänzt' es über die Lande bis an das blaue Meer;
Und rings von duft'gen Gärten ein blütenreicher Kranz,
Drin sprangen frische Brunnen im Regenbogenglanz.

(UHLAND)

3(c) Chevy-Chase stanza (*die Chevy-Chase-Strophe*): a four-line stanza with alternating four-stressed and three-stressed lines, generally rhyming abab or abcb:

i   Nach Frankreich zogen zwei Grenadier',
Die waren in Rußland gefangen;
Und als sie kamen ins deutsche Quartier,
Sie ließen die Köpfe hangen.   (HEINE)

ii   Soll Spott und Hohn getragen sein,
Trag ich allein den Hohn.
Ich kenn ihn wohl, er kennt mich wohl,
Und Gott weiß auch davon.   (GOETHE)

3(d) The Alcaic stanza (*die alkäische Strophe*), which has the following metrical pattern:

```
                                      (⁄)
×  ⦙  ⁄ ×    ⁄ ⁄ ×    ⁄ × × ⁄ × ×
×  ⦙  ⁄ ×    ⁄ ⁄ ×    ⁄ × × ⁄ × ⁄
×  ⦙  ⁄ ×    ⁄ ⁄ ×    ⁄ × × ⁄ ×
      ⁄ × ×  ⁄ × × ⁄   ⁄ × ⁄   ⁄ ×
```

Du waltest hoch am Tag' und es blühet dein
Gesetz, du hältst die Wage, Saturnus Sohn!
   Und teilst die Los' und ruhest froh im
     Ruhm der unsterblichen Herrscherkünste. (HÖLDERLIN)

3(e) The Fourth Asclepiad (*die asklepiadeische Strophe*), which has the following metrical pattern:

```
/ × | / × × / | / × × / | × /
/ × | / × × / | / × × / | × /
/ × | / × ×    | / ×
/ × | / × ×    | / × /
```

Trennen wollten wir uns? wähnten es gut und klug?
Da wirs taten, warum schröckte, wie Mord, die Tat?
   Ach! wir kennen uns wenig,
     Denn es waltet ein Gott in uns. (HÖLDERLIN)

3(f) The Sapphic stanza (*die sapphische Strophe*), which has the following metrical pattern:

```
/ ×   | / × | / × × | / × | / ×
/ ×   | / × | / × × | / × | / ×
/ ×   | / × | / × × | / × | / ×
/ × × | / ×
```

Tot ist alles Buch und das Wort der Schriften.
Und die Fracht ward leicht, ihr beschwingten, zarten
stillen Vögel, die ihr heraufzieht über
   purpurne Meerflut. (WEINHEBER)

4 The five-line stanza (*die fünfzeilige Strophe*): rhyme scheme – ababa or abaab or aabba:

Am grauen Strand, am grauen Meer
Und seitab liegt die Stadt;
Der Nebel drückt die Dächer schwer,
Und durch die Stille braust das Meer
Eintönig um die Stadt. (STORM)

5 The six-line stanza (*die sechszeilige Strophe*): rhyme scheme – aabccb:

Komm, Trost der Welt, du stille Nacht!
Wie steigst du von den Bergen sacht!
Die Lüfte alle schlafen;
Ein Schiffer nur noch, wandermüd',
Singt übers Meer sein Abendlied
Zu Gottes Lob im Hafen. (EICHENDORFF)

6 The seven-line stanza (*die siebenzeilige Strophe*): rhyme scheme –
ababccd:

> Der Türmer, der schaut zumitten der Nacht
> Hinab auf die Gräber in Lage;
> Der Mond, der hat alles ins Helle gebracht,
> Der Kirchhof, er liegt wie am Tage.
> Da regt sich ein Grab und ein anderes dann:
> Sie kommen hervor, ein Weib da, ein Mann,
> In weißen und schleppenden Hemden.   (GOETHE)

7 Ottava rima (*die Stanze*): rhyme scheme – abababcc:

> Der Morgen kam; es scheuchten seine Tritte
> Den leisen Schlaf, der mich gelind umfing,
> Daß ich, erwacht, aus meiner stillen Hütte
> Den Berg hinauf mit frischer Seele ging;
> Ich freute mich bei einem jeden Schritte
> Der neuen Blume, die voll Tropfen hing;
> Der junge Tag erhob sich mit Entzücken,
> Und alles war erquickt, mich zu erquicken.   (GOETHE)

8 The sonnet (*das Sonett*)

The German sonnet is normally Petrarchan in form, the first two quatrains
rhyming abba abba or less strictly, abba cddc, and the sestet rhyming
variously, e.g. cde cde/efg efg or cdc cdc/efe efe, etc. In the seventeenth
century it was regularly written in alexandrines, but since the Romantics
it has usually been written in iambics. Rilke treated the form boldly in his
Sonette an Orpheus, often using a trochaic or a predominantly dactylic
metre.

It should be noted that not every fourteen-line poem is a sonnet! A
sonnet must have the characteristic structure of two quatrains and a sestet
which may or may not be divided into tercets.

DAS SONETT

> Sich in erneutem Kunstgebrauch zu üben,
>   Ist heilge Pflicht, die wir dir auferlegen:
>   Du kannst dich auch, wie wir, bestimmt bewegen
>   Nach Tritt und Schritt, wie es dir vorgeschrieben.
>
> Denn eben die Beschränkung läßt sich lieben,
>   Wenn sich die Geister gar gewaltig regen;
>   Und wie sie sich denn auch gebärden mögen,
>   Das Werk zuletzt ist doch vollendet blieben.

So möcht ich selbst in künstlichen Sonetten,
 In sprachgewandter Maße kühnem Stolze,
 Das Beste, was Gefühl mir gäbe, reimen;

Nur weiß ich hier mich nicht bequem zu betten,
 Ich schneide sonst so gern aus ganzem Holze,
 Und müßte nun doch auch mitunter leimen. (GOETHE)

Rhythm (*der Rhythmus*)

All speech has rhythm, and thus all poetry will be rhythmical; but rhythm
is not the same thing as metre. Poems written in the same metre will
rarely be rhythmically identical with one another; and a poem whose
rhythm does in fact correspond very closely with the metrical pattern will
strike the reader as monotonous, wooden and lifeless.

It is, however, undeniable that rhythm in poetry often keeps quite close
to the metrical pattern, that is to say, the rhythm of a poem is often dictated
primarily by the regular fall of the accented syllables in the lines. But other
factors do come into play, and sometimes so much so that the metrical
pattern is only barely sensed in the background while quite different
rhythms assert themselves, not infrequently with powerful contrapuntal
effect. Variation of rhythm in poetry is not to be thought of as an arbitrary
decision by the poet, but is appropriate to changes in thought and imagery,
in tone and feeling.

These other factors that play their part in establishing rhythms that
modify the metrical pattern are:

(a) the varying weight given to the *Hebungen* or 'lifts'. Conventional signs
can only hint at the great variety that is possible. The lifts may, however,
be roughly graded as heavily stressed (⫽), normally stressed (′), lightly
stressed (⌝) and virtually unstressed (ˣ). Compare:

Denkt Ihr, er habe sein bedeutend Leben

In kriegerischer Arbeit aufgewendet

Jedwedem stillen Erdenglück entsagt,

Den Schlaf von seinem Lager weggebannt,

Sein edles Haupt der Sorge hingegeben,

Nur um ein glücklich Paar aus euch zu machen? (SCHILLER)

(b) the varying length of time or duration given to words. This may, and
often does, correspond with the length of vowels, but not necessarily.
Compare:

In der ungeheuern Weite
Reget keine Welle sich.   (GOETHE)

which is somewhat slower than, though with vowels of much the same
length as

> Die Verändrung, ach, wie groß!
> Liebe! Liebe! Laß mich los! (GOETHE)

Compare the following lines of which the first two move far more slowly
than the last two:

> Das Dunkeln war wie Reichtum in dem Raum,
> darin der Knabe, sehr verheimlicht, saß.
> Und als die Mutter eintrat wie im Traum,
> erzitterte im stillen Schrank ein Glas. (RILKE)

(c) the varying degree of correspondence of the word-group with the
metrical pattern. Punctuation is something of a guide here, though not an
infallible one. Enjambement, unexpected caesuras, reversal of feet are some
of the ways in which such rhythms impose themselves over the metrical
pattern without destroying it:

> Und seine Sinne waren wie entzweit:
> indes der Blick ihm wie ein Hund vorauslief,
> umkehrte, kam und immer wieder weit
> und wartend an der nächsten Wendung stand, –
> blieb sein Gehör wie ein Geruch zurück. (RILKE)

> Die schönen Tage in Aranjuez
> Sind nun zu Ende. Eure königliche Hoheit
> Verlassen es nicht heiterer. Wir sind
> Vergebens hier gewesen. Brechen Sie
> Dies rätselhafte Schweigen. Öffnen Sie
> Ihr Herz dem Vaterherzen, Prinz. Zu teuer
> Kann der Monarch die Ruhe seines Sohns –
> Des einz'gen Sohns – zu teuer nie erkaufen. (SCHILLER)

> Dích sah ich, und die milde Freude
> Floß von dem süßen Blick auf mich. (GOETHE)

Rhythms tend to be of different, but recognisable kinds, either smoothly
flowing, or advancing steadily step by step, or struggling forward against
obstacles that seem to hold up progress, or sweeping powerfully forward.
Some poems are characterised throughout by one dominant type of
rhythm; in others there is a great variety of rhythms. Where the rhythm
is in perfect accord with the sense and feeling genuine poetry is not far
away.

'Rhythm and metre are dangerous branches of learning. Some poets and lovers of poetry refuse to think of them, and consequently live more comfortable lives, and give less anxiety to their friends.' (W. P. KER)

Examples of Literary Analysis of Verse

Needless to say, the technical terms that are used in any account of German versification are not substitutes for critical analysis. No purpose is served by *merely* observing (and stating) that the poem is, e.g. written in iambic pentameters or has, e.g. the rhyme scheme abba cddc, etc. Any such observation is only the starting-point for further analysis and the technical terms are merely useful and convenient 'shorthand'.

Since verse has peculiar problems of its own we have thought it might be of some interest and help to students to see our attempts at the literary analysis of two very different kinds of poetry. We have deliberately chosen poetry of a type that we have found in our experience gives considerable difficulty to students; and, though we are clearly not in the position of examination candidates who are generally asked to write a critical commentary on a poem by an unknown author, we have as far as possible, or as far as was sensible, approached our task as though the only important evidence we had was that given by the texts.

(a) NÄNIE

> Auch das Schöne muß sterben! Das Menschen und Götter bezwinget,
>   Nicht die eherne Brust rührt es des stygischen Zeus.
> Einmal nur erweichte die Liebe den Schattenbeherrscher,
>   Und an der Schwelle noch, streng, rief er zurück sein Geschenk.
> 5 Nicht stillt Aphrodite dem schönen Knaben die Wunde,
>   Die in den zierlichen Leib grausam der Eber geritzt.
> Nicht errettet den göttlichen Held die unsterbliche Mutter,
>   Wann er, am skäischen Tor fallend, sein Schicksal erfüllt.
> Aber sie steigt aus dem Meer mit allen Töchtern des Nereus,
> 10   Und die Klage hebt an um den verherrlichten Sohn.
> Siehe! Da weinen die Götter, es weinen die Göttinnen alle,
>   Daß das Schöne vergeht, daß das Vollkommene stirbt.
> Auch ein Klaglied zu sein im Mund der Geliebten, ist herrlich,
>   Denn das Gemeine geht klanglos zum Orkus hinab.
>
>   SCHILLER

To a modern reader this poem is likely to present certain difficulties that would not have been experienced by an educated contemporary of the poet. In Schiller's lifetime and indeed right up to the early years of this century higher education in schools was dominated by the 'classics' and

293

the classical allusions on which the poem largely depends would have been immediately perceived.

The title of this poem is a Germanicised form of a Greek word meaning *Klagelied* or elegy. Its theme is not altogether an original one, since it laments, as poets have done through the ages, the transience of the beautiful. The more original twist given to this theme is the idea that the beautiful, being different from and altogether nobler than other things – for Schiller meant by '*das Schöne*' not only physical beauty but excellence of all kinds – might have been expected to have been spared the general fate, and this, in a sense, is true, for when beauty and perfection die they give rise to lament, which enshrined in beautiful form has the eternity of art and lives on in men s memories.

The poem begins with the word '*auch*' (even). This has the effect of widening the poem's reference, of including in it by implication the death of all other living things, and to hint already at the world of difference between '*das Schöne*' and '*das Gemeine*', a term which the poet holds back until the last line. The theme, thus qualified by '*auch*' is stated in the first half of the first line. Then follow (lines 1–6) three examples of the death of beauty. In each case beauty is struck down in youth and dies, despite the, literally, superhuman efforts of a husband, a lover and a mother.

In the first example Orpheus, who by his music could compel all other things, momentarily and conditionally overcame Pluto's inexorable rule that none entering his domain, the abode of the dead, might ever leave it. This, the only example in the whole of Greek mythology of death overcome, was fated to be but a temporary reprieve; for Orpheus' love was too great for him to fulfil Pluto's condition that he should not look back at his wife till they had reached the earth again, and Pluto, the Stygian Zeus, the Lord of the Underworld, recalled his gift, and Eurydice had perforce to retrace her steps to Hades.

In the second example Aphrodite, the goddess of love, could not save her own beloved and beautiful Adonis from the cruel death of being torn to pieces by a wild boar.

In the third example the immortal Nereid Thetis, the mother of Achilles, was likewise unable to make her own son completely invulnerable and thus defeat death. He too died, illustrious hero though he was, his heel, the only vulnerable part of his body, pierced by an arrow outside one of the gates of Troy.

Thus the love of a husband endowed with such powers as Orpheus, the love of the goddess of love herself, the love of a mother using all the wiles of an immortal availed nothing against death, against the death of what was beautiful and perfect; and if such as these have failed, who can avert the fate that is meted out to all, mortals and heroes alike, however much they may excel all others?

On learning of Achilles' death Thetis and all the other daughters of Nereus, the god of the sea, broke out into loud lamentation in which all the other gods and goddesses joined; and though in the poem they lament Achilles it is by implication also Adonis and Eurydice and all others in whom beauty and perfection are embodied that are being mourned; and this is their immortal distinction.

Throughout the poem antithesis and repetition are used with great effect to help convey on the one hand the harshness and inexorability of the law that thus condemns beauty to extinction and on the other the vast distinction between the beautiful and the base. We have the adjectives and adverbs '*schön*', '*zierlich*', '*göttlich*' and '*herrlich*' contrasting with '*ehern*', '*streng*', '*grausam*' and '*klanglos*'; '*das Schöne*' and '*das Vollkommene*' are contrasted on the one hand with '*das Schicksal*' and on the other with '*das Gemeine*'. The threefold beginning of the main clause with the powerfully stressed word '*nicht*' (lines 2, 5 and 7) emphasises the triple frustration, a frustration mitigated momentarily by the similar inversion of '*einmal nur*' in line 3. The repetition of '*Daß das … daß das ….*' in the twelfth line corresponds to the repetition of '*Da weinen die Götter*' '*es weinen die Göttinnen*' in the preceding hexameter and adds to the poignancy of the grief; and the repetition of '*auch*', occurring at the beginning of the first and of the last hexameter of the poem pinpoints the radical change of mood from '*Auch das Schöne muß sterben!*' to '*Auch ein Klaglied zu sein im Munde der Geliebten ist herrlich*'.

For an elegy whose exemplification is in terms of classical mythology Schiller has fittingly chosen elegiacs. It is true that elegiacs can be, and have most successfully been, used in poetry not at all elegiac in tone, notably in Goethe's *Römische Elegien*; but they have also traditionally been associated with the elegy proper, and there is always about them a certain dignity. The marked difference between the component lines of a distich, the predominantly flowing hexameter followed by the twice abruptly checked pentameter, tends to encourage antithetical statements; and in *Nänie* the antithesis between the claims of beauty to immortality and its inexorable destruction is made with powerful effect four times in the first four distichs. It is as though waves were coming in again and again landwards from the sea only to be thrust back by adamantine rocks; and yet, as with the incoming tide, the continual assault is not entirely in vain. After eight such rebuffs (at the caesura and end of each pentameter) the '*aber*' at the beginning of the fifth hexameter suggests the beginning of a change of mood, the hint that death is not quite absolute; and this is confirmed by the majestic sweep of the next hexameter, the only one in the poem with five dactylic feet, when all the gods and goddesses are united in one chorus of lament that beauty, that perfection dies and perishes. (It should be noticed how the use of the present tense at this point universalises this fate.) Yet, in the very act of their lament, they give magnificent, and thus immortal, utterance to their grief; and the final pentameter marks the stark contrast between this splendid utterance and the irremediable blotting out of '*das Gemeine*' which is conveyed with masterly economy in the second hemistich: '*klanglos zum Orkus hinab*', with the stress on the last syllable of '*hinab*' underlining the irrevocability of it all.

By the forthright use of the rhetorical devices of repetition and antithesis, by the subtle changes in word order and metrical rhythm, by the employment of formal but nevertheless forceful epithets, by the austerity and economy of the language Schiller has built up a powerful structure tier by tier, corresponding to each distich; and though each distich is self-contained there is nevertheless continuity of thought throughout so that the seven couplets are fused into one whole. The language of the poem is elevated and generalised. What particularity the poem has comes through the examples given, and even here only one is actually named. There is no suggestion that this is an elegy inspired by the death of a particular person, like Milton's *Lycidas* or Shelley's *Adonais*. Rather is it a meditation on 'das Los des Schönen auf der Erde', expressed with remarkable economy in seven elegiac couplets whose poignancy is conveyed all the more forcibly by their classical restraint. Schiller accepts unflinchingly though sadly man's inexorable fate; but not all are condemned to utter extinction. Those in whom '*das Schöne*' has been embodied shall not be forgotten. 'Oblivion as they rose shrank like a thing reproved' (Shelley).

(b)

> Drum ist ein Jauchzen sein Wort.
> Nicht liebt er, wie andere Kinder,
> In Wickelbanden zu weinen.
> Denn, wo die Ufer zuerst
> 5 An die Seit ihm schleichen, die krummen,
> Und durstig umwindend ihn,
> Den Unbedachten, zu ziehn
> Und wohl zu behüten begehren
> Im eigenen Zahne, lachend
> 10 Zerreißt er die Schlangen und stürzt
> Mit der Beut und wenn in der Eil'
> Ein Größerer ihn nicht zähmt,
> Ihn wachsen läßt, wie der Blitz, muß er
> Die Erde spalten, und wie Bezauberte fliehn
> Die Wälder ihm nach und zusammensinkend die Berge.

HÖLDERLIN

The theme of this stanza, the fifth of a long poem in 'free rhythms', is the early upbringing of an exceptional 'child', the enormous difference between a philosophy of education that insists on imposing a predetermined pattern on a child, irrespective of its nature, and one that, though believing in firmness, allows a child to reach its full natural growth.

The stanza consists of three sentences. The first is very short, in form the hemistich of a pentameter. It is a statement, summing up an argument that has preceded it, as the word '*drum*' with which it begins implies. The line is end-stopped, firm and categorical. The second sentence (lines 2–3) is also short and, apart from the first syllable, which could be looked upon as the anacrusis or *Auftakt*, is a perfect hexameter. Its movement is pre-monitory of the rhythm of the rest of the stanza, pressing on and yet checked, though mostly ineffectually, at the caesuras and at the change from dactyl to trochee at the significant word *'Wickelbanden'* ('swaddling-clothes'). The second sentence is a further statement that this 'child', unlike other children, neither 'weeps' (which follows as a necessary consequence from the first sentence) nor is 'swaddled', which is a new idea. The remainder of the stanza consists of one long sentence of twelve lines of considerable grammatical complexity, yet vivid and clear. This third sentence is introduced by the conjunction *'denn'* ('for'), i.e. it is a justification of the assertions made in the first two sentences, giving reasons supporting them. The reasons which in prose one would have expected straight away are held back by two intervening relative clauses, which give important information about the opposing force, the would-be 'swaddling-clothes', and are themselves followed by an elaborate conditional sentence, expressed graphically in the present tense, whose apodoses (main clauses) are additional, though hypothetical, reasons, still dependent on *'denn'*.

It is clear that the *'Kind'* is no ordinary child, in two senses no ordinary child; for it does not behave like other children, nor is it a child at all in the proper sense of the word. Even when we read the stanza in isolation we realise by the time we reach the word *'Ufer'* that this child is perhaps after all a river, called a 'child' because it is here seen at the beginning of its course. At the same time it soon becomes obvious that this is no ordinary river and we rightly suspect that the river is a symbol. The imagery, which is throughout in the form of consistent metaphors with the occasional simile, has the effect of endowing the whole scene with life. The banks 'creep' to the child's side, they 'thirstily entwine it', they are its would-be mentors, longing to 'train' and 'guard' it 'within their teeth'. Thus by a natural development of the imagery the banks have become serpents. At the same time, by the use of the word *'umwindend'*, we are reminded of the *'Wickelbande'* referred to in line 3, the serpentine banks not only being the swaddling clothes but also attempting to swaddle the child. But this emphatically *is* no ordinary child. Like Hercules who strangled the serpents that Hera had placed in his cradle – and the poet seems to be alluding to this myth – the young river makes short work of the *'Schlangen'*, tears them to pieces and dashes off with the booty. In contrast to ordinary weeping children in swaddling clothes this child laughingly rejects all attempts to swaddle it, and but for some greater power, who, unlike the banks that merely wish unimaginatively to constrict and hem it in, tames the 'child' so that it shall grow to full stature, it could not but be a destructive force. Here the simile *'wie der Blitz'* conveys the idea not only of great speed but also of destructive and wanton power and the other simile *'wie Bezauberte'* ('as though bewitched') suggests that the dragging down after it of forests and mountains, sweeping them along in the same mad rush after it, can only be accounted for by some supernatural force innate in the 'child'.

But not only by the imagery, evocative and apt as this is, has the scene been endowed with life. The uneven struggle that can be felt taking place between the river-banks and the river is given the quality of movement in large measure through the thrust, check and counter-thrust of the rhythm. The bold post-positioning of the attributive adjective (die Ufer ..., die krummen; ihn, den Unbedachten) and the participial phrase (durstig umwindend ihn) as well as the post-positioned '*im eigenen Zahne*' check, or would check if they could, the river's headlong course. These would-be obstacles are laughingly brushed aside and the rhythm surges forward; and but for the real obstacle, likewise shown in the speech rhythm (zähmt, ihn wachsen läßt), nothing could stand in the way of the sweeping flow of the final lines (14–16).

The movement is given even greater force by the falling rhythm of the stanza as a whole, which though in 'free rhythms', is, as 'free rhythms' in German so often are, dominated by dactyls checked at strategic points by trochees (umwínden íhn, den Únbedáchten; zíehn und wóhl; Záhne, láchend; Béut, und wénn; íhn nicht záhmt, ihn wáchsen läßt).

Thus by its grammatical structure, by its speech-rhythms and metrical patterning as well as by its bold, original and apt imagery this stanza not merely describes the scene but succeeds in conveying to the reader an intensely imagined *Seelenzustand*. That it should be a river (a river, however, of no ordinary kind, as we would learn from an earlier stanza, for it is there spoken of as the child of Zeus and Mother Earth) that symbolises this *Seelenzustand* implies an attitude to Nature which is in stark contrast to the scientific attitude to it that was beginning to prevail in the early years of the nineteenth century and is an instance of a particular kind of Romantic revolt against the demythologising of Nature.

Poems for Literary Analysis

1 FENSTER, WO ICH EINST MIT DIR

> Fenster, wo ich einst mit dir
> Abends in die Landschaft sah,
> Sind nun hell mit fremdem Licht.
>
> Pfad noch läuft vom Tor, wo du
> 5 Standest ohne umzuschaun,
> Dann ins Tal hinunterbogst.
>
> Bei der Kehr warf nochmals auf
> Mond dein bleiches Angesicht ...
> Doch es war zu spät zum Ruf.

10 Dunkel – Schweigen – starre Luft
Sinkt wie damals um das Haus.
Alle Freude nahmst du mit.

2 NÄCHTLICHE STUNDE

Nächtliche Stunde, die mir vergeht,
da ich's ersinne, bedenke und wende,
und diese Nacht geht schon zu Ende.
Draußen ein Vogel sagt: es ist Tag.

5 Nächtliche Stunde, die mir vergeht,
da ich's ersinne, bedenke und wende,
und dieser Winter geht schon zu Ende.
Draußen ein Vogel sagt: es ist Frühling.

Nächtliche Stunde, die mir vergeht,
10 da ich's ersinne, bedenke und wende,
und dieses Leben geht schon zu Ende.
Draußen ein Vogel sagt: es ist Tod.

3 DANN –

Wenn ein Gesicht, das man als junges kannte
und dem man Glanz und Tränen fortgeküßt,
sich in den ersten Zug des Alters wandte,
den frühen Zauber lebend eingebüßt.

5 Der Bogen einst, dem jeder Pfeil gelungen,
purpurgefiedert lag das Rohr im Blau,
die Cymbel auch, die jedes Lied gesungen:
– „Funkelnde Schale" – „Wiesen im Dämmergrau" –

Dem ersten Zug der zweite schon im Bunde,
10 ach, an der Stirne hält sie schon die Wacht,
die einsame, die letzte Stunde –
das ganze liebe Antlitz dann in Nacht.

4 DIE WÄCHTER

Die Wächter, die man unsrer Haft gestellt,
sind brave Burschen. Bäuerliches Blut.
Herausgerissen aus der Dörfer Hut
in eine fremde, nicht verstandne Welt.

5 Sie sprechen kaum. Nur ihre Augen fragen
zuweilen stumm, als ob sie wissen wollten,
was ihre Herzen nie erfahren sollten,
die schwer an ihrer Heimat Schicksal tragen.

Sie kommen aus den östlichen Bereichen
10 der Donau, die der Krieg schon ausgezehrt.
Ihr Stamm ist tot. Ihr Hab und Gut verheert.

Noch warten sie vielleicht auf Lebenszeichen.
Sie dienen still. Gefangen – sind auch sie.
Ob sie's begreifen? Morgen? Später? Nie?

5 IN DER STADT

Wo sich drei Gassen kreuzen, krumm und enge,
Drei Züge wallen plötzlich sich entgegen
Und schlingen sich, gehemmt auf ihren Wegen,
Zu einem Knäu'l und lärmenden Gedränge.

5 Die Wachtparad' mit gellen Trommelschlägen,
Ein Brautzug kommt mit Geigen und Gepränge,
Ein Leichenzug klagt seine Grabgesänge;
Das alles stockt, es kann kein Glied sich regen.

Verstummt sind Geiger, Pfaff' und Trommelschläger;
10 Der dicke Hauptmann flucht, daß niemand weiche,
Gelächter schallet aus dem Freudenzug.

Doch oben, auf den Schultern schwarzer Träger
Starrt in der Mitte kalt und still die Leiche
Mit blinden Augen in den Wolkenflug.

6 AN DIE WELT

Mein oft bestürmtes Schiff, der grimmen Winde Spiel,
Der frechen Wellen Ball, das schier die Flut getrennet,
Das wie ein schneller Pfeil nach seinem Ziele rennet,
Kommt vor der Zeit an Port, den meine Seele will.

5 Oft wenn uns schwarze Nacht im Mittag überfiel,
Hat der geschwinde Blitz die Segel schier verbrennet.
Wie oft hab ich den Wind und Nord und Süd verkennet!
Wie schadhaft ist der Mast, Steur, Ruder, Schwert[1] und Kiel!

[1] 'centre-board'

Steig aus, du müder Geist! steig aus! wir sind am Lande.
10 Was graut dir für[1] dem Port! Itzt[2] wirst du aller Bande
Und Angst und herber Pein und schwerer Schmerzen los.

Ade, verfluchte Welt! du See voll rauher Stürme!
Glück zu, mein Vaterland! das stete Ruh im Schirme
Und Schutz und Frieden hält, du ewig lichtes Schloß!

7 DIE EWIGKEIT

Sie sagen, daß wir uns im Tode nicht vermissen
Und nicht begehren. Daß wir, hingegeben
Der Ewigkeit, mit andern Sinnen leben
Und also nicht mehr voneinander wissen.

5 Und Lust und Angst und Sehnsucht nicht verstehen,
Die zwischen uns ein Leben lang gebrannt,
Und so wie Fremde uns vorübergehen,
Gleichgültig Aug dem Auge, Hand der Hand.

Wie rührt mich schon das kleine Licht der Sphären,
10 Das wir ermessen können, eisig an
Und treibt mich dir ans Herz in wilder Klage.

O halt uns Welt im süßen Licht der Tage,
Und laß solang ein Leben währen kann
Die Liebe währen.

8 EIN LIED CHASTELARDS

Sehnsucht ist Qual!
Der Herrin wag ichs nicht zu sagen,
Ich wills den dunkeln Eichen klagen
Im grünen Tal:
5 Sehnsucht ist Qual.

Mein Leib vergeht
Wie schmelzend Eis in bleichen Farben,
Sie sieht mich dursten, lechzen, darben,
Bleibt unerfleht –
10 Mein Leib vergeht.

Doch mag es sein,
Daß sie an ihrer Macht sich weide!

_____
[1] = vor   [2] = jetzt

Ergetzt sie grausam sich an meinem Leide,
So denkt sie mein –
15 Drum mag es sein.

Sehnsucht ist Qual!
Dem Kühnsten macht die Folter bange,
Ein Grab, darin ich nichts verlange,
Gib mir, o Tal!
20 Sehnsucht ist Qual.

9 AN DEN ANTIKEN VERS

Bogen, groß gespannt über Meer und Inseln,
Herzschrein, holder, adlig Gefäß des Lichts, ge-
geben jener lieblichsten Stimme, die dem
Abendland vorsang:

5 Der du, unversehrt im Verfall der Zeiten,
Und im Ausgang Richte dem Sänger, fernher
bliebest, was du warst: der verwaisten Größe
Wappen und Zuflucht –

Der du in den Urgrund zurück und über
10 vieler Völker Sprachen hinaus, hinan das
Wort in letzte Heiligkeit hebst, bis an die
Lippen der Götter –

Der du ruhig führst durch den Schrecken, durch das
Übermaß der Welt, wie den Blinden eine
15 sichre Hand; nach deinem Gesetz, und keinen
Schritt ohne jenes:

Komm auch mir! Komm heut und erlös mich Armen
aus der Drangsal! Füll mir die Brust mit jener
Fülle Heimat, die sie begehrt. Sei wieder
20 Bruder im Kampf mir!

10 VEREINSAMT

Die Krähen schrein
und ziehen schwirren Flugs zur Stadt:
bald wird es schnein, –
wohl dem, der jetzt noch – Heimat hat!

5   Nun stehst du starr,
schaust rückwärts, ach! wie lange schon!
   Was bist du Narr
vor Winters in die Welt entflohn?

   Die Welt – ein Tor
10 zu tausend Wüsten stumm und kalt!
   Wer das verlor,
was du verlorst, macht nirgends Halt.

   Nun stehst du bleich,
zur Winter-Wanderschaft verflucht,
15   dem Rauche gleich,
der stets nach kältern Himmeln sucht.

   Flieg, Vogel, schnarr
dein Lied im Wüstenvogel-Ton! –
   Versteck, du Narr,
20 dein blutend Herz in Eis und Hohn!

   Die Krähen schrein
und ziehen schwirren Flugs zur Stadt:
   bald wird es schnein, –
weh dem, der keine Heimat hat!

11 ÜBER EINER TODESNACHRICHT

   Fühlt es das Weltherz denn nicht,
     Wenn so viel Liebeskraft stirbt?
   Wiegt ihm ein Leben so leicht,
     Weiß es so eilig Ersatz?
5 Wir, ach, wissen ihn nicht,
     Und heißen wohl unersetzlich,
   Was unsrem Herzen entreißt
     Der großmächtige Tod.
   Wege, ihr oftmals begangnen,
10   Wie endet ihr plötzlich im Dickicht!
   Stimme, du zwiesprachvertraute,
     Einsame, fürchtest du dich?

   Sie freilich, die er uns nahm,
     Der geheime Verwandler,
15 Schweigen sie dunklen Schlaf,
     Lauschen sie fernem Gesang?

Oder wärs, daß sie wirklich,
   Leicht nur ans Gitter gelehnt,
Nachbar noch hießen und Freund
20   Jeglichem Lassen und Tun?
Wärs, daß wir rufen und sie
   Kommen, die selig Befreiten,
Wärs – und sie blieben für immer
   Liebend auf unserer Bahn?

12 DER HAHN

Zornkamm, Gockel, Körnerschlinger,
Federnschwinger, roter Ritter,
Blaugeschwänzter Sporenträger,
Eitles, prunkendes Gewitter
5 Steht er funkelnd auf dem Mist,
Der erfahrne Würmerjäger,
Sausend schneller Schnabelschläger,
Königlich noch im Vergeuden,
Wenn er lässig-stolz verschenkt
10 Den Wurm, den er emporgeschwenkt.

Und nun spannt er seine Kehle,
Schwellt die Brust im Zorn:
Schallend tönt sein Räuberhorn.
Daß er keinen Ton verfehle,
15 Übt er noch einmal von vorn.

Hühnervolk, das ihn umwandelt,
Wenn er es auch schlecht behandelt,
Lauscht verzaubert seinem Wort.
Wenn sein Feuerblick rot blendet,
20 Keines wendet sich dann fort,
Denn er ist der Herr und Mann,
Der an ihnen sich verschwendet
Und die Lust vergeben kann.

Und, sie haben's oft erfahren,
25 Die um ihn versammelt waren:
Goldner Brust, der Liedersinger,
Ist der mächtige Morgenbringer,
Der selbst dem Gestirn befiehlt.
Wenn er seine Mähne schüttelt
30 Und schreit seinen Schrei hinaus,
Der am Nachtgewölbe rüttelt,
Steigt die Sonne übers Haus.

Ein Irrsal kam in die Mondscheingärten
Einer einst heiligen Liebe.
Schaudernd entdeckt' ich verjährten Betrug.
Und mit weinendem Blick, doch grausam,
5 Hieß ich das schlanke,
Zauberhafte Mädchen
Ferne gehen von mir.
Ach, ihre hohe Stirn
War gesenkt, denn sie liebte mich;
10 Aber sie zog mit Schweigen
Fort in die graue
Welt hinaus.

Krank seitdem,
Wund ist und wehe mein Herz.
15 Nimmer wird es genesen!

Als ginge, luftgesponnen, ein Zauberfaden
Von ihr zu mir, ein ängstig Band,
So zieht es, zieht mich schmachtend ihr nach!
– Wie? wenn ich eines Tags auf meiner Schwelle
20 Sie sitzen fände, wie einst, im Morgen-Zwielicht,
Das Wanderbündel neben ihr,
Und ihr Auge, treuherzig zu mir aufschauend,
Sagte, da bin ich wieder
Hergekommen aus weiter Welt!

14 HOCHBILD

Die Sonne, Helios der Griechen,
Fährt prächtig auf der Himmelsbahn,
Gewiß, das Weltall zu besiegen,
Blickt er umher, hinab, hinan.

5 Er sieht die schönste Göttin weinen,
Die Wolkentochter, Himmelskind,
Ihr scheint er nur allein zu scheinen;
Für alle heitre Räume blind

Versenkt er sich in Schmerz und Schauer
10 Und häufger quillt ihr Tränenguß:
Er sendet Lust in ihre Trauer
Und jeder Perle Kuß auf Kuß.

Nun fühlt sie tief des Blicks Gewalten
Und unverwandt schaut sie hinauf;
15 Die Perlen wollen sich gestalten:
Denn jede nahm sein Bildnis auf.

Und so, umkränzt von Farb und Bogen,
Erheitert leuchtet ihr Gesicht,
Entgegen kommt er ihr gezogen;
20 Doch er, doch ach! erreicht sie nicht.

So, nach des Schicksals hartem Lose,
Weichst du mir, Lieblichste, davon;
Und wär ich Helios der Große,
Was nützte mir der Wagenthron?

15 VORSTADT IM FÖHN

Am Abend liegt die Stätte öd und braun,
Die Luft von gräulichem Gestank durchzogen.
Das Donnern eines Zuges vom Brückenbogen –
Und Spatzen flattern über Busch und Zaun.

5 Geduckte Hütten, Pfade wirr verstreut,
In Gärten Durcheinander und Bewegung,
Bisweilen schwillt Geheul aus dumpfer Regung,
In einer Kinderschar fliegt rot ein Kleid.

Am Kehricht pfeift verliebt ein Rattenchor.
10 In Körben tragen Frauen Eingeweide,
Ein ekelhafter Zug voll Schmutz und Räude,
Kommen sie aus der Dämmerung hervor.

Und ein Kanal speit plötzlich feistes Blut
Vom Schlachthaus in den stillen Fluß hinunter.
15 Die Föhne färben karge Stauden bunter
Und langsam kriecht die Röte durch die Flut.

Ein Flüstern, das in trübem Schlaf ertrinkt.
Gebilde gaukeln auf aus Wassergräben,
Vielleicht Erinnerung an ein früheres Leben,
20 Die mit den warmen Winden steigt und sinkt.

Aus Wolken tauchen schimmernde Alleen,
Erfüllt von schönen Wägen, kühnen Reitern.
Dann sieht man auch ein Schiff auf Klippen scheitern
Und manchmal rosenfarbene Moscheen.

Großer Bär, komm herab, zottige Nacht,
Wolkenpelztier mit den alten Augen,
Sternenaugen,
durch das Dickicht brechen schimmernd
5 deine Pfoten mit den Krallen,
Sternenkrallen,
wachsam halten wir die Herden,
doch gebannt von dir, und mißtrauen
deinen müden Flanken und den scharfen
10 halbentblößten Zähnen,
alter Bär.

Ein Zapfen: eure Welt.
Ihr: die Schuppen dran.
Ich treib sie, roll sie,
5 von den Tannen im Anfang
zu den Tannen am Ende,
schnaub sie an, prüf sie im Maul
und pack zu mit den Tatzen.

Fürchtet euch oder fürchtet euch nicht!
20 Zahlt in den Klingelbeutel und gebt
dem blinden Mann ein gutes Wort,
daß er den Bären an der Leine hält.
Und würzt die Lämmer gut.
's könnt sein, daß dieser Bär
25 sich losreißt, nicht mehr droht
und alle Zapfen jagt, die von den Tannen
gefallen sind, den großen, geflügelten,
die aus dem Paradiese stürzten.

17 BALLADE DES ÄUSSEREN LEBENS

Und Kinder wachsen auf mit tiefen Augen,
Die von nichts wissen, wachsen auf und sterben
Und alle Menschen gehen ihre Wege.

Und süße Früchte werden aus den herben
5 Und fallen nachts wie tote Vögel nieder
Und liegen wenig Tage und verderben.

Und immer weht der Wind, und immer wieder
Vernehmen wir und reden viele Worte
Und spüren Lust und Müdigkeit der Glieder.

10 Und Straßen laufen durch das Gras, und Orte
Sind da und dort, voll Fackeln, Bäumen, Teichen,
Und drohende, und totenhaft verdorrte ...

Wozu sind diese aufgebaut? und gleichen
Einander nie? und sind unzählig viele?
15 Was wechselt Leben, Weinen und Erbleichen?

Was frommt das alles uns und diese Spiele,
Die wir doch groß und ewig einsam sind
Und wandernd nimmer suchen irgend Ziele?

Was frommts, dergleichen viel gesehen haben?
20 Und dennoch sagt der viel, der „Abend" sagt,
Ein Wort, daraus Tiefsinn und Trauer rinnt

Wie schwerer Honig aus den hohlen Waben.

18 CORRIDA

Seit er, klein beinah, aus dem Toril[1]
ausbrach, aufgescheuchten Augs und Ohrs,
und den Eigensinn des Picadors
und die Bänderhaken[2] wie im Spiel

5 hinnahm, ist die stürmische Gestalt
angewachsen – sieh: zu welcher Masse,
aufgehäuft aus altem schwarzen Hasse,
und das Haupt zu einer Faust geballt,

nicht mehr spielend gegen irgendwen,
10 nein: die blutigen Nackenhaken hissend
hinter den gefällten Hörnern, wissend
und von Ewigkeit her gegen Den,

der in Gold und mauver Rosaseide
plötzlich umkehrt und, wie einen Schwarm
15 Bienen und als ob ers eben leide,
den Bestürzten unter seinem Arm

durchläßt, – während seine Blicke heiß
sich noch einmal heben, leichtgelenkt,
und als schlüge draußen jener Kreis
20 sich aus ihrem Glanz und Dunkel nieder
und aus jedem Schlagen seiner Lider,

[1] Span. = Stall für die zu den Stiergefechten bestimmten Tiere
[2] 'banderillas'

ehe er gleichmütig, ungehässig,
an sich selbst gelehnt, gelassen, lässig
in die wiederhergerollte große
25 Woge über dem verlornen Stoße
seinen Degen beinah sanft versenkt.

19 AN LEVIN SCHÜCKING

Kein Wort, und wär' es scharf wie Stahles Klinge,
Soll trennen, was in tausend Fäden Eins,
So mächtig kein Gedanke, daß er dringe
Vergällend in den Becher reinen Weins;
5 Das Leben ist so kurz, das Glück so selten,
So großes Kleinod, einmal sein statt gelten!

Hat das Geschick uns, wie in frevlem Witze,
Auf feindlich starre Pole gleich erhöht,
So wisse, dort, dort auf der Scheidung Spitze
10 Herrscht, König über alle, der Magnet,
Nicht fragt er, ob ihn Fels und Strom gefährde,
Ein Strahl fährt mitten er durchs Herz der Erde.

Blick' in mein Auge, – ist es nicht das deine,
Ist nicht mein Zürnen selber deinem gleich?
15 Du lächelst – und dein Lächeln ist das meine,
An gleicher Lust und gleichem Sinnen reich;
Worüber alle Lippen freundlich scherzen,
Wir fühlen heil'ger es im eignen Herzen.

Pollux und Kastor, – wechselnd Glühn und Bleichen,
20 Des einen Licht geraubt dem andern nur,
Und doch der allerfrömmsten Treue Zeichen. –
So reiche mir die Hand, mein Dioskur!
Und mag erneuern sich die holde Mythe,
Wo überm Helm die Zwillingsflamme glühte.

20 KRIEGSLIED

's ist Krieg! 's ist Krieg! O Gottes Engel, wehre
Und rede du darein!
's ist leider Krieg – und ich begehre
Nicht schuld daran zu sein!

5 Was sollt ich machen, wenn im Schlaf mit Grämen
Und blutig, bleich und blaß
Die Geister der Erschlagnen zu mir kämen
Und vor mir weinten, was?

Wenn wackre Männer, die sich Ehre suchten,
10   Verstümmelt und halb tot
Im Staub sich vor mir wälzten und mir fluchten
   In ihrer Todesnot?

Wenn tausend tausend Väter, Mütter, Bräute,
   So glücklich vor dem Krieg,
15 Nun alle elend, alle arme Leute,
   Wehklagten über mich?

Wenn Hunger, böse Seuch' und ihre Nöten
   Freund, Freund und Feind ins Grab
Versammleten und mir zu Ehren krähten
20   Von einer Leich' herab?

Was hülf mir Kron und Land und Gold und Ehre?
   Die könnten mich nicht freun!
's ist leider Krieg – und ich begehre
   Nicht schuld daran zu sein!

21   WELTGEHEIMNIS

Der tiefe Brunnen weiß es wohl,
Einst waren alle tief und stumm,
Und alle wußten drum.

Wie Zauberworte, nachgelallt
5 Und nicht begriffen in den Grund,
So geht es jetzt von Mund zu Mund.

Der tiefe Brunnen weiß es wohl;
In den gebückt, begriffs ein Mann,
Begriff es und verlor es dann.

10 Und redet' irr und sang ein Lied –
Auf dessen dunklen Spiegel bückt
Sich einst ein Kind und wird entrückt.

Und wächst und weiß nichts von sich selbst
Und wird ein Weib, das einer liebt
15 Und – wunderbar wie Liebe gibt!

Wie Liebe tiefe Kunde gibt! –
Da wird an Dinge, dumpf geahnt,
In ihren Küssen tief gemahnt ...

In unsern Worten liegt es drin,
20 So tritt des Bettlers Fuß den Kies,
Der eines Edelsteins Verlies.

Der tiefe Brunnen weiß es wohl,
Einst aber wußten alle drum,
Nun zuckt im Kreis ein Traum herum.

22 DER GEFESSELTE STROM

Was schläfst und träumst du, Jüngling, gehüllt in dich,
Und säumst am kalten Ufer, Geduldiger,
    Und achtest nicht des Ursprungs, du, des
        Ozeans Sohn, des Titanenfreundes!

5 Die Liebesboten, welche der Vater schickt,
Kennst du die lebenatmenden Lüfte nicht?
    Und trifft das Wort dich nicht, das hell von
        Oben der wachende Gott dir sendet?

Schon tönt, schon tönt es ihm in der Brust, es quillt,
10 Wie, da er noch im Schoße der Felsen spielt',
    Ihm auf, und nun gedenkt er seiner
        Kraft, der Gewaltige, nun, nun eilt er,

Der Zauderer, er spottet der Fesseln nun,
Und nimmt und bricht und wirft die Zerbrochenen
15   Im Zorne, spielend, da und dort zum
        Schallenden Ufer und an der Stimme

Des Göttersohns erwachen die Berge rings,
Es regen sich die Wälder, es hört die Kluft
    Den Herold fern und schaudernd regt im
20   Busen der Erde sich Freude wieder.

Der Frühling kommt; es dämmert das neue Grün;
Er aber wandelt hin zu Unsterblichen;
    Denn nirgend darf er bleiben, als wo
        Ihn in die Arme der Vater aufnimmt.

23 PARZENLIED

Es fürchte die Götter
Das Menschengeschlecht!
Sie halten die Herrschaft

In ewigen Händen,
5 Und können sie brauchen,
Wie's ihnen gefällt.

Der fürchte sie doppelt,
Den je sie erheben!
Auf Klippen und Wolken
10 Sind Stühle bereitet
Um goldene Tische.

Erhebet ein Zwist sich,
So stürzen die Gäste,
Geschmäht und geschändet,
15 In nächtliche Tiefen,
Und harren vergebens,
Im Finstern gebunden,
Gerechten Gerichtes.

Sie aber, sie bleiben
20 In ewigen Festen
An goldenen Tischen.
Sie schreiten vom Berge
Zu Bergen hinüber:
Aus Schlünden der Tiefe
25 Dampft ihnen der Atem
Erstickter Titanen,
Gleich Opfergerüchen,
Ein leichtes Gewölke.

Es wenden die Herrscher
30 Ihr segnendes Auge
Von ganzen Geschlechtern
Und meiden, im Enkel
Die ehmals geliebten,
Still redenden Züge
35 Des Ahnherrn zu sehn.

So sangen die Parzen;
Es horcht der Verbannte
In nächtlichen Höhlen,
Der Alte, die Lieder,
40 Denkt Kinder und Enkel
Und schüttelt das Haupt.

312

Jardin du Luxembourg

Mit einem Dach und seinem Schatten dreht
sich eine kleine Weile der Bestand
von bunten Pferden, alle aus dem Land,
das lange zögert, eh es untergeht.
5 Zwar manche sind an Wagen angespannt,
doch alle haben Mut in ihren Mienen;
ein böser roter Löwe geht mit ihnen
und dann und wann ein weißer Elefant.

Sogar ein Hirsch ist da, ganz wie im Wald,
10 nur daß er einen Sattel trägt und drüber
ein kleines blaues Mädchen aufgeschnallt.

Und auf dem Löwen reitet weiß ein Junge
und hält sich mit der kleinen heißen Hand,
dieweil der Löwe Zähne zeigt und Zunge.

15 Und dann und wann ein weißer Elefant.

Und auf den Pferden kommen sie vorüber,
auch Mädchen, helle, diesem Pferdesprunge
fast schon entwachsen; mitten in dem Schwunge
schauen sie auf, irgendwohin, herüber –

20 Und dann und wann ein weißer Elefant.

Und das geht hin und eilt sich, daß es endet,
und kreist und dreht sich nur und hat kein Ziel.
Ein Rot, ein Grün, ein Grau vorbeigesendet,
ein kleines kaum begonnenes Profil –.
25 Und manchesmal ein Lächeln, hergewendet,
ein seliges, das blendet und verschwendet
an dieses atemlose blinde Spiel ...

25 MIT DEN FAHRENDEN SCHIFFEN

Mit den fahrenden Schiffen
Sind wir vorübergeschweift,
Die wir ewig herunter
Durch glänzende Winter gestreift.

5 Ferner kamen wir immer
Und tanzten im insligen Meer,
Weit ging die Flut uns vorbei,
Und der Himmel war schallend und leer.

Sage die Stadt,
10 Wo ich nicht saß im Tor,
Ging dein Fuß da hindurch,
Der die Locke ich schor?
Unter dem sterbenden Abend
Das suchende Licht
15 Hielt ich, wer kam da hinab,
Ach, ewig in fremdes Gesicht.

Bei den Toten ich rief,
Im abgeschiedenen Ort,
Wo die Begrabenen wohnen;
20 Du, ach, warest nicht dort.
Und ich ging über Feld,
Und die wehenden Bäume zu Haupt
Standen im frierenden Himmel
Und waren im Winter entlaubt.

25 Raben und Krähen
Habe ich ausgesandt,
Und sie stoben im Grauen
Über das ziehende Land.
Aber sie fielen wie Steine
30 Zur Nacht mit traurigem Laut
Und hielten im eisernen Schnabel
Die Kränze von Stroh und Kraut.

Manchmal ist deine Stimme,
Die im Winde verstreicht,
35 Deine Hand, die im Traume
Rühret die Schläfe mir leicht;
Alles war schon vorzeiten
Und kehret wieder sich um.
Gehet in Trauer gehüllet,
40 Streuet Asche herum.

26 DIE SCHÖNE BUCHE

Ganz verborgen im Wald kenn' ich ein Plätzchen, da stehet
 Eine Buche, man sieht schöner im Bilde sie nicht.
Rein und glatt, in gediegenem Wuchs erhebt sie sich einzeln,
 Keiner der Nachbarn rührt ihr an den seidenen Schmuck.

5 Rings, so weit sein Gezweig' der stattliche Baum ausbreitet,
  Grünet der Rasen, das Aug' still zu erquicken, umher;
  Gleich nach allen Seiten umzirkt er den Stamm in der Mitte;
  Kunstlos schuf die Natur selber dies liebliche Rund.
  Zartes Gebüsch umkränzet es erst; hochstämmige Bäume,
10 Folgend in dichtem Gedräng', wehren dem himmlischen Blau.
  Neben der dunkleren Fülle des Eichbaums wieget die Birke
  Ihr jungfräuliches Haupt schüchtern im goldenen Licht.
  Nur wo, verdeckt vom Felsen, der Fußsteig jäh sich hinabschlingt,
  Lässet die Hellung mich ahnen das offene Feld.
15 – Als ich unlängst einsam, von neuen Gestalten des Sommers
  Ab dem Pfade gelockt, dort im Gebüsch mich verlor,
  Führt' ein freundlicher Geist, des Hains auflauschende Gottheit,
  Hier mich zum erstenmal, plötzlich, den Staunenden, ein.
  Welch Entzücken! Es war um die hohe Stunde des Mittags,
20 Lautlos alles, es schwieg selber der Vogel im Laub.
  Und ich zauderte noch, auf den zierlichen Teppich zu treten;
  Festlich empfing er den Fuß, leise beschritt ich ihn nur.
  Jetzo, gelehnt an den Stamm (er trägt sein breites Gewölbe
  Nicht zu hoch), ließ ich rundum die Augen ergehn,
25 Wo den beschatteten Kreis die feurig strahlende Sonne,
  Fast gleich messend umher, säumte mit blendendem Rand.
  Aber ich stand und rührte mich nicht; dämonischer Stille,
  Unergründlicher Ruh' lauschte mein innerer Sinn.
  Eingeschlossen mit dir in diesem sonnigen Zauber-
30 Gürtel, o Einsamkeit, fühlt' ich und dachte nur dich!

27 HEIDELBERG

Lange lieb ich dich schon, möchte dich, mir zur Lust,
  Mutter nennen und dir schenken ein kunstlos Lied,
    Du, der Vaterlandsstädte
    Ländlichschönste, so viel ich sah.

5 Wie der Vogel des Walds über die Gipfel fliegt,
  Schwingt sich über den Strom, wo er vorbei dir glänzt,
    Leicht und kräftig die Brücke,
    Die von Wagen und Menschen tönt.

Wie von Göttern gesandt, fesselt' ein Zauber einst
10 Auf der Brücke mich an, da ich vorüber ging
    Und herein in die Berge
    Mir die reizende Ferne schien,

Und der Jüngling, der Strom, fort in die Ebne zog,
  Traurigfroh, wie das Herz, wenn es, sich selbst zu schön,
15   Liebend unterzugehen,
    In die Fluten der Zeit sich wirft.

Quellen hattest du ihm, hattest dem Flüchtigen
   Kühle Schatten geschenkt, und die Gestade sahn
      All ihm nach, und es bebte
20   Aus den Wellen ihr lieblich Bild.

   Aber schwer in das Tal hing die gigantische,
      Schicksalskundige Burg, nieder bis auf den Grund
         Von den Wettern zerrissen;
            Doch die ewige Sonne goß

25 Ihr verjüngendes Licht über das alternde
      Riesenbild, und umher grünte lebendiger
         Efeu; freundliche Bilder
            Rauschten über die Burg herab.

   Sträuche blühten herab, bis wo im heitern Tal,
30   An den Hügel gelehnt, oder dem Ufer hold,
         Deine fröhlichen Gassen
            Unter duftenden Gärten ruhn.

28 LOKOMOTIVE

Da liegt das zwanzigmeterlange Tier,
die Dampfmaschine,
auf blankgeschliffener Schiene
voll heißer Wut und sprungbereiter Gier –
5 da lauert, liegt das langgestreckte Eisen-Biest –

Sieh da: wie Öl- und Wasserschweiß
wie Lebensblut, gefährlich heiß,
ihm aus den Radgestängen: den offenen Weichen fließt.
Es liegt auf sechzehn roten Räder-Pranken,
10 wie fiebernd, langgeduckt zum Sprunge,
und Fieberdampf stößt röchelnd aus den Flanken.
Es kocht und kocht die Röhrenlunge –
den ganzen Rumpf die Feuerkraft durchzittert,
er ächzt und siedet, zischt und hackt
15 im hastigen Dampf- und Eisentakt –
dein Menschenwort wie nichts im Qualm zerflittert.

Das Schnauben wächst und wächst –
du stummer Mensch erschreckst –
du siehst die Wut aus allen Ritzen gären –

20 Der Kesselröhren-Atemdampf
ist hochgewühlt auf sechzehn Atmosphären:
Gewalt hat jetzt der heiße Krampf.

Das Biest, es brüllt, das Biest, es brüllt,
der Führer ist in Dampf gehüllt –
25 der Regulatorhebel steigt nach links:
der Eisen-Stier harrt dieses Winks!:

Nun bafft vom Rauchrohr Kraftgeschnauf:
nun springt es auf! Nun springt es auf!

Doch:

30 Ruhig gleiten und kreisen auf endloser Schiene
die treibenden Räder hinaus auf dem blänkernden[1] Band,
gemessen und massig die kraftangefüllte Maschine,
der schleppende, stampfende Rumpf hinterher –
dahinter – ein dunkler – verschwimmender Punkt –
35 darüber – zerflatternder – Qualm –

29 DAS IDEAL

Ja, das möchste:

Eine Villa im Grünen mit großer Terrasse,
Vorn die Ostsee, hinten die Friedrichstraße;
Mit schöner Aussicht, ländlich-mondän,
5 Vom Badezimmer ist die Zugspitze zu sehn –
Aber abends zum Kino hast du's nicht weit.

Das Ganze schlicht, voller Bescheidenheit:

Neun Zimmer – nein, doch lieber zehn!
Ein Dachgarten, wo die Eichen drauf stehn,
10 Radio, Zentralheizung, Vakuum,
Eine Dienerschaft, gut gezogen und stumm,
Eine süße Frau voller Rasse und Verve
(Und eine fürs Wochenend, zur Reserve) –
Eine Bibliothek und drumherum
15 Einsamkeit und Hummelgesumm.

Im Stall: zwei Ponys, vier Vollbluthengste,
Acht Autos, Motorrad – alles lenkste
Natürlich selber – das wär ja gelacht!
Und zwischendurch gehst du auf Hochwildjagd.

[1] = blank werdenden

20 Ja, und das hab ich ganz vergessen:
Prima Küche – erstes Essen –
Alle Weine aus schönem Pokal –
Und egalweg bleibst du dünn wie ein Aal.
Und Geld. Und an Schmuck eine richtige Portion.
25 Und noch 'ne Million und noch 'ne Million.
Und Reisen. Und fröhliche Lebensbuntheit.
Und famose Kinder. Und ewige Gesundheit.
Ja, das möchste!

Aber, wie das so ist hienieden:
30 Manchmal scheint's so, als sei es beschieden,
Nur pöapö,[1] das irdische Glück.
Immer fehlt dir irgendein Stück.
Hast du Geld, dann hast du nicht Käten;[2]
Hast du die Frau, dann fehl'n dir Moneten.
35 Hast du die Geisha, dann stört dich der Fächer;
Bald fehlt uns der Wein, bald fehlt uns der Becher.
Etwas ist immer. Tröste dich.
Jedes Glück hat einen kleinen Stich.
Wir möchten so viel: Haben. Sein. Und gelten.
40 Daß einer alles hat: das ist selten.

30 ERKLÄR MIR, LIEBE

Dein Hut lüftet sich leis, grüßt, schwebt im Wind,
dein unbedeckter Kopf hat's Wolken angetan,
dein Herz hat anderswo zu tun,
dein Mund verleibt sich neue Sprachen ein,
5 das Zittergras im Land nimmt überhand,
Sternblumen bläst der Sommer an und aus,
von Flocken blind erhebst du dein Gesicht,
du lachst und weinst und gehst an dir zugrund,
was soll dir noch geschehen –

10 Erklär mir, Liebe!

Der Pfau, in feierlichem Staunen, schlägt sein Rad,
die Taube stellt den Federkragen hoch,
vom Gurren überfüllt, dehnt sich die Luft,
der Entrich schreit, vom wilden Honig nimmt
15 das ganze Land, auch im gesetzten Park
hat jedes Beet ein goldner Staub umsäumt.

[1] = peu à peu   [2] Kurzform von Katharina

Der Fisch errötet, überholt den Schwarm
und stürzt durch Grotten ins Korallenbett.
Zur Silbersandmusik tanzt scheu der Skorpion.
20 Der Käfer riecht die Herrlichste von weit;
hätt ich nur seinen Sinn, ich fühlte auch,
daß Flügel unter ihrem Panzer schimmern,
und nähm den Weg zum fernen Erdbeerstrauch!

Erklär mir, Liebe!

25 Wasser weiß zu reden,
die Welle nimmt die Welle an der Hand,
im Weinberg schwillt die Traube, springt und fällt.
So arglos tritt die Schnecke aus dem Haus!

Ein Stein weiß einen andern zu erweichen!

30 Erklär mir, Liebe, was ich nicht erklären kann:
sollt ich die kurze schauerliche Zeit
nur mit Gedanken Umgang haben und allein
nichts Liebes kennen und nichts Liebes tun?
Muß einer denken? Wird er nicht vermißt?

35 Du sagst: es zählt ein andrer Geist auf ihn ...
Erklär mir nichts. Ich seh den Salamander
durch jedes Feuer gehen.
Kein Schauer jagt ihn, und es schmerzt ihn nichts.

31 DAS IDEAL UND DAS LEBEN

Schnell fertig ist die Jugend mit dem Wort,
Das schwer sich handhabt, wie des Messers Schneide;
Aus ihrem heißen Kopfe nimmt sie keck
Der Dinge Maß, die nur sich selber richten.
5 Gleich heißt ihr alles schändlich oder würdig,
Bös oder gut – und was die Einbildung
Phantastisch schleppt in diesen dunkeln Namen,
Das bürdet sie den Sachen auf und Wesen.
Eng ist die Welt, und das Gehirn ist weit.
10 Leicht bei einander wohnen die Gedanken,
Doch hart im Raume stoßen sich die Sachen;
Wo eines Platz nimmt, muß das andre rücken;
Wer nicht vertrieben sein will, muß vertreiben;
Da herrscht der Streit, und nur die Stärke siegt.

15 – Ja, wer durchs Leben gehet ohne Wunsch,
Sich jeden Zweck versagen kann, der wohnt
Im leichten Feuer mit dem Salamander
Und hält sich rein im reinen Element.
Mich schuf aus gröberm Stoffe die Natur,
20 Und zu der Erde zieht mich die Begierde.
Dem bösen Geist gehört die Erde, nicht
Dem guten. Was die Göttlichen uns senden
Von oben, sind nur allgemeine Güter;
Ihr Licht erfreut, doch macht es keinen reich,
25 In ihrem Staat erringt sich kein Besitz.
Den Edelstein, das allgeschätzte Gold
Muß man den falschen Mächten abgewinnen,
Die unterm Tage schlimmgeartet hausen.
Nicht ohne Opfer macht man sie geneigt,
30 Und keiner lebt, der aus ihrem Dienst
Die Seele hätte rein zurückgezogen.

32 DAS OBERSTE GESETZ

Herr, das Gesetz, das höchste, oberste,
Das wirken soll, in deiner Feldherrn Brust,
Das ist der Buchstab deines Willens nicht;
Das ist das Vaterland, das ist die Krone,
5 Das bist du selber, dessen Haupt sie trägt.
Was kümmert dich, ich bitte dich, die *Regel*,
Nach der der Feind sich schlägt: wenn er nur nieder
Vor dir, mit allen seinen Fahnen, sinkt?
Die Regel, die ihn *schlägt*, das ist die höchste!
10 Willst du das Heer, das glühend an dir hängt,
Zu einem Werkzeug machen, gleich dem Schwerte,
Das tot in deinem goldnen Gürtel ruht?
Der ärmste Geist, der, in den Sternen fremd,
Zuerst solch eine Lehre gab! Die schlechte,
15 Kurzsicht'ge Staatskunst, die, um eines Falles,
Da die Empfindung sich verderblich zeigt,
Zehn andere vergißt, im Lauf der Dinge,
Da die Empfindung einzig retten kann!
Schütt ich mein Blut dir, an dem Tag der Schlacht,
20 Für Sold, seis Geld, seis Ehre, in den Staub?
Behüte Gott, dazu ist es zu gut!
Was! Meine Lust hab, meine Freude ich,
Frei und für mich, im Stillen, unabhängig,
An deiner Trefflichkeit und Herrlichkeit,
25 Am Ruhm und Wachstum deines großen Namens!

Das ist der Lohn, dem sich mein Herz verkauft!
Gesetzt, um dieses unberufnen Sieges,
Brächst du dem Prinzen jetzt den Stab; und ich,
Ich träfe morgen, gleichfalls unberufen,
30 Den Sieg wo irgend zwischen Wald und Felsen,
Mit den Schwadronen, wie ein Schäfer, an;
Bei Gott, ein Schelm müßt ich doch sein, wenn ich
Des Prinzen Tat nicht munter wiederholte.
Und sprächst du, das Gesetzbuch in der Hand:
35 „Kottwitz, du hast den Kopf verwirkt!" so sagt ich:
Das wußt ich, Herr; da nimm ihn hin, hier ist er:
Als mich ein Eid an deine Krone band,
Mit Haut und Haar, nahm ich den Kopf nicht aus,
Und nichts dir gäb ich, was nicht dein gehörte!

33 DIE ZEIT IST AUS DEN FUGEN

Die Macht ist's, was sie wollen.
Mag sein, daß diese Spaltung im Beginn
Nur mißverstandne Satzungen des Glaubens,
Jetzt hat sie gierig in sich eingesogen,
5 Was Unerlaubtes sonst die Welt bewegt.
Der Reichsfürst will sich lösen von dem Reich,
Dann kommt der Adel und bekämpft die Fürsten;
Den gibt die Not, die Tochter der Verschwendung,
Drauf in des Bürgers Hand, des Krämers, Mäklers,
10 Der allen Wert abwägt nach Goldgewicht.
Der dehnt sich breit und hört mit Spotteslächeln
Von Toren reden, die man Helden nennt,
Von Weisen, die nicht klug für eignen Säckel,
Von allem, was nicht nützt und Zinsen trägt.
15 Bis endlich aus der untersten der Tiefen
Ein Scheusal aufsteigt, gräßlich anzusehn,
Mit breiten Schultern, weitgespaltnem Mund,
Nach allem lüstern und durch nichts zu füllen.
Das ist die Hefe, die den Tag gewinnt,
20 Nur um den Tag am Abend zu verlieren,
Angrenzend an das Geist- und Willenlose.
Der ruft: „Auch mir mein Teil, vielmehr das Ganze!
Sind wir die Mehrzahl doch, die Stärkern doch,
Sind Menschen so wie ihr, uns unser Recht!"
25   Des Menschen Recht heißt hungern, Freund, und leiden,
Eh noch ein Acker war, der frommer Pflege
Die Frucht vereint, den Vorrat für das Jahr;
Als noch das wilde Tier, ein Brudermörder,

Den Menschen schlachtete, der waffenlos,
30 Als noch der Winter und des Hungers Zahn
Alljährlich Ernte hielt von Menschenleben.
Begehrst ein Recht du als ursprünglich erstes,
So kehr zum Zustand wieder, der der erste.
Gott aber hat die Ordnung eingesetzt,
35 Von da an ward es licht, das Tier ward Mensch.
    Ich sage dir: nicht Scythen und Chazaren,
Die einst den Glanz getilgt der alten Welt,
Bedrohen unsre Zeit, nicht fremde Völker:
Aus eignem Schoß ringt los sich der Barbar,
40 Der, wenn erst ohne Zügel, alles Große,
Die Kunst, die Wissenschaft, den Staat, die Kirche
Herabstürzt von der Höhe, die sie schützt,
Zur Oberfläche eigener Gemeinheit.
Bis alles gleich, ei ja, weil alles niedrig.

34 DIE WELT

Was ist die Welt und ihr berühmtes Glänzen?
Was ist die Welt und ihre ganze Pracht?
Ein schnöder Schein in kurzgefaßten Grenzen,
Ein schneller Blitz bei schwarzgewölkter Nacht,
5 Ein buntes Feld, da Kummerdisteln grünen,
Ein schön Spital, so voller Krankheit steckt,
Ein Sklavenhaus, da alle Menschen dienen,
Ein faules Grab, so Alabaster deckt.
Das ist der Grund, darauf wir Menschen bauen,
10 Und was das Fleisch für einen Abgott hält.
Komm, Seele, komm, und lerne weiter schauen,
Als sich erstreckt der Zirkel dieser Welt.
Streich ab von dir derselben kurzes Prangen,
Halt ihre Lust für eine schwere Last;
15 So wirst du leicht in diesen Port gelangen,
Da Ewigkeit und Schönheit sich umfaßt.

WAS IST DIE WELT?

Was ist die Welt? Ein ewiges Gedicht,
Daraus der Geist der Gottheit strahlt und glüht,
Daraus der Wein der Weisheit schäumt und sprüht,
Daraus der Laut der Liebe zu uns spricht.

5 Und jedes Menschen wechselndes Gemüt,
Ein Strahl ists, der aus dieser Sonne bricht,
Ein Vers, der sich an tausend andre flicht,
Der unbemerkt verhallt, verlischt, verblüht.

Und doch auch eine Welt für sich allein,
10 Voll süß-geheimer, nievernommner Töne,
Begabt mit eigner, unentweihter Schöne,

Und keines Andern Nachhall, Widerschein.
Und wenn du gar zu lesen drin verstündest,
Ein Buch, das du im Leben nicht ergründest.

Compare these two poems, commenting on the similarities and differences
of theme, style and versification which you consider significant.

35   GESANG DER GEISTER ÜBER DEN WASSERN

Des Menschen Seele
Gleicht dem Wasser:
Vom Himmel kommt es,
Zum Himmel steigt es,
5 Und wieder nieder
Zur Erde muß es,
Ewig wechselnd.

Strömt von der hohen,
Steilen Felswand
10 Der reine Strahl,
Dann stäubt er lieblich
In Wolkenwellen
Zum glatten Fels,
Und leicht empfangen
15 Wallt er verschleiernd,
Leisrauschend
Zur Tiefe nieder.

Ragen Klippen
Dem Sturz entgegen,
20 Schäumt er unmutig
Stufenweise
Zum Abgrund.

Im flachen Bette
Schleicht er das Wiesental hin,
25 Und in dem glatten See
Weiden ihr Antlitz
Alle Gestirne.

Wind ist der Welle
Lieblicher Buhler;
30 Wind mischt vom Grund aus
Schäumende Wogen.

Seele des Menschen,
Wie gleichst du dem Wasser!
Schicksal des Menschen,
35 Wie gleichst du dem Wind!

HYPERIONS SCHICKSALSLIED

Ihr wandelt droben im Licht
Auf weichem Boden, selige Genien!
Glänzende Götterlüfte
Rühren euch leicht,
5 Wie die Finger der Künstlerin
Heilige Seiten.

Schicksallos, wie der schlafende
Säugling, atmen die Himmlischen;
Keusch bewahrt
10 In bescheidener Knospe
Blühet ewig
Ihnen der Geist,
Und die seligen Augen
Blicken in stiller
15 Ewiger Klarheit.

Doch uns ist gegeben,
Auf keiner Stätte zu ruhn,
Es schwinden, es fallen
Die leidenden Menschen
20 Blindlings von einer
Stunde zur andern,
Wie Wasser von Klippe
Zu Klippe geworfen,
Jahrlang ins Ungewisse hinab.

Compare these two poems, commenting on the similarities and differences
of theme, style and versification which you consider significant.

36 WELTENDE

Es ist ein Weinen in der Welt,
Als ob der liebe Gott gestorben wär,
Und der bleierne Schatten, der niederfällt,
Lastet grabesschwer.

5 Komm, wir wollen uns näher verbergen ...
Das Leben liegt in aller Herzen
Wie in Särgen.

Du! wir wollen uns tief küssen –
Es pocht eine Sehnsucht an die Welt,
10 An der wir sterben müssen.

WELTENDE

Dem Bürger fliegt vom spitzen Kopf der Hut,
In allen Lüften hallt es wie Geschrei,
Dachdecker stürzen ab und gehn entzwei
Und an den Küsten – liest man – steigt die Flut.

5 Der Sturm ist da, die wilden Meere hupfen
An Land, um dicke Dämme zu zerdrücken.
Die meisten Menschen haben einen Schnupfen.
Die Eisenbahnen fallen von den Brücken.

Write a critical analysis of these two poems – which were written about the
same time – bringing out clearly the attitude shown by the two poets to
their contemporary world.

37 DER RÖMISCHE BRUNNEN

(a) In einem römischen Garten
Verborgen ist ein Bronne,
Behütet von dem harten
Geleucht der Mittagssonne,
5 Er steigt in schlankem Strahle
In dunkle Laubesnacht
Und sinkt in eine Schale
Und übergießt sie sacht.

Die Wasser steigen nieder
10 In zweiter Schale Mitte,
Und voll ist diese wieder,
Sie flutet in die dritte:
Ein Nehmen und ein Geben,
Und alle bleiben reich,
15 Und alle Fluten leben
Und ruhen doch zugleich.

(b) Der Springquell plätschert und ergießt
Sich in der Marmorschale Grund,
Die, sich verschleiernd, überfließt,
In einer zweiten Schale Rund;

5 Und diese gibt, sie wird zu reich,
    Der dritten wallend ihre Flut,
    Und jede nimmt und gibt zugleich
    Und alles strömt und alles ruht.

(c) Aufsteigt der Strahl und fallend gießt
    Er voll der Marmorschale Rund,
    Die, sich verschleiernd, überfließt
    In einer zweiten Schale Grund;
5 Die zweite gibt, sie wird zu reich,
    Der dritten wallend ihre Flut,
    Und jede nimmt und gibt zugleich
        Und strömt und ruht.

These are three versions of the same poem, printed in the order of their composition. Show by a careful analysis of the means employed how changes in the tone and feeling and general poetic meaning have been effected. Which version do you prefer?

38 aus MENONS KLAGEN UM DIOTIMA

Aber wir, zufrieden gesellt, wie die liebenden Schwäne,
    Wenn sie ruhen am See, oder, auf Wellen gewiegt,
Niedersehn in die Wasser, wo silberne Wolken sich spiegeln,
    Und ätherisches Blau unter den Schiffenden wallt,
5 So auf Erden wandelten wir. Und drohte der Nord auch,
    Er, der Liebenden Feind, klagenbereitend, und fiel
Von den Ästen das Laub, und flog im Winde der Regen,
    Ruhig lächelten wir, fühlten den eigenen Gott
Unter trautem Gespräch; in Einem Seelengesange,
10   Ganz in Frieden mit uns kindlich und freudig allein.
Aber das Haus ist öde mir nun, und sie haben mein Auge
    Mir genommen, auch mich hab' ich verloren mit ihr.
Darum irr' ich umher, und wohl, wie die Schatten, so muß ich
    Leben, und sinnlos dünkt lange das Übrige mir.

WUNDER DER LIEBE

Oft will das Leben nicht mehr weitergehn,
Bleibt schwarz und zögernd stehn –
O schauerlich verwirrte Tage,
Da alles Lebende in uns sich selber haßt,
5 Sich selbst an der verhaßten Gurgel faßt,
Anklagend sich und Gott in frevelhafter Frage!

O Wunder, wenn uns dann die Liebe naht
Und unsern finstern Pfad
Mit ihrer stillen Flamme lichtet!
10 Wär diese Gnade nicht, längst hätten wir
Uns ganz verirrt ins teuflische Revier
Und Licht und Gott in uns vernichtet.

In the above two poems examine the imagery, rhythm, diction, effects of
sound, etc., describing their contribution to the tone, feeling and general
poetic meaning of each. Which poem seems to you to be the more successful? Give your reasons.

39 DER MENSCH IST STUMM

Ich habe dir den Abschiedskuß gegeben
Und klammre mich nervös an deine Hand.
Schon mahn ich dich, auf dies und jenes Acht zu geben.
Der Mensch ist stumm.

5 Will denn der Zug, der Zug nicht endlich pfeifen?
Mir ist, als dürfte ich dich nie mehr wiedersehn.
Ich rede runde Sätze, ohne zu begreifen ...
Der Mensch ist stumm.

Ich weiß, wenn ich dich nicht mehr hätte,
10 Das wär' der Tod, der Tod, der Tod!
Und dennoch möcht ich fliehn. Gott, eine Zigarette!
Der Mensch ist stumm.

Dahin! Jetzt auf der Straße würgt mich Weinen.
Verwundert blicke ich mich um.
15 Denn auch das Weinen sagt nicht, was wir meinen.
Der Mensch ist stumm.

ABSCHIED

Wie hab ich das gefühlt was Abschied heißt.
Wie weiß ichs noch: ein dunkles unverwundnes
grausames Etwas, das ein Schönverbundnes
noch einmal zeigt und hinhält und zerreißt.

5 Wie war ich ohne Wehr, dem zuzuschauen,
das, da es mich, mich rufend, gehen ließ,
zurückblieb, so als wärens alle Frauen
und dennoch klein und weiß und nichts als dies:

Ein Winken, schon nicht mehr auf mich bezogen,
10 ein leise Weiterwinkendes –, schon kaum
erklärbar mehr: vielleicht ein Pflaumenbaum,
von dem ein Kuckuck hastig abgeflogen.

Analyse carefully the means that are employed to evoke the mood and
feeling experienced on leave-taking in the above two poems, paying special
attention to the diction, rhythm, imagery and effects of sound. Which poem
seems to you to be the more successful?

Vocabulary

German-English

NOTES 1 The plural ending -(e)n of feminine nouns is not indicated.
2 Figures refer to the paragraphs of Part One.
3 Verbal nouns whose meanings are evident from the infinitive of verbs already listed are not given.
4 The commonest words are omitted, as are also those words whose meanings can easily be guessed.

a

abbeißer., s., bite off
abdrängen, thrust away
das **Abenteuer (-),** adventure
abermals, (once) again, another
abfahren, s., start
das **Abfallstück (-e),** reject
die **Abgeblühtheit,** faded flower
abgehen, s., pass the whole length of
abgeschlossen, concluded, finalized
abgesehen: – haben auf, be after, have designs on; – **davon, daß,** apart from the fact that
abgesessen, dismounted
abgesetzt, set down
abgewinnen, s., extract
der **Abgrund (¨e),** abyss
abhalten, s., check
abhängen, s., (**von**), depend (on)
sich **abheben,** s., (**von**), stand out (from)
abholen, fetch, meet
das **Abi (-tur),** school leaving examination
der **Ablauf (¨e),** course, sequence
ablehnen, decline, turn down
ableugnen, deny
åblösen, take off, over
abnehmen, s., take from, relieve of; lose weight
abraten, s., advise against
der **Abschaum,** scum (of the earth)
der **Abschied (-e),** parting
der **Abschluß (¨(ss)e),** conclusion
abschrecken, put off, deter
abschreiben, s., crib

der **Abschuß (¨(ss)e),** (gun) discharge
absehen, s., be likely outcome
abseits, at a distance from
die **Absicht,** purpose, intention
absolut, absolute(ly); – **nicht,** simply . . . not
der **Absolvent (-en, -en),** school-leaver; graduate
der **Abstand (¨e),** interval, distance (away)
abstehend, prominent
der **Abtransport,** carrying away
der **Abtrieb (-e),** driving down
abtrünnig, rebellious
abwarten, wait (till)
das **Abwasser (¨),** effluent
die **Abwechslung,** change
abwesend, absent-mindedly
sich **abzeichnen,** stand out
achtgeben, s., pay attention
der **Adler (-),** eagle
der **Affekt (-e),** emotion, emotional use
ähneln, resemble
ähnlich, like, similar
die **Ähnlichkeit,** similarity
die **Ahnung,** presentiment
ahnungslos, unsuspecting(ly)
die **Ahnungslosigkeit,** unawareness
der **Akademiker (-),** graduate
die **Akkuratesse,** care
die **Aktion,** operation
der **Aktionär (-e),** shareholder
der **Akzent (-e),** stress
die **Alkoholika** (pl.), alcoholic drinks
all, all; **vor -em,** above all; **-es,** everything
das **All,** universe
allenfalls, at all events
allerdings, to be sure
allerwärts, everywhere

329

allgemein, general,
universal(ly); im -en, in
general
die Allgemeinheit, general
public, community at large
alltäglich, everyday
alsbald, immediately
also, that is to say,
consequently, so
das Alter, (old) age
der Altersgenosse (-n, -n),
contemporary
die Altersgrenze, age-limit,
retirement age
altertümlich, ancient
altmodisch, old-fashioned
die Ameise, ant
der Amoklauf, running amok
anbieten, s., offer; sich –,
offer o.s.
der Anblick, sight
anblicken, look at
die Andacht, prayers
ander, other, different;
-es, other things; etwas -es,
something different; -s,
otherwise; unter -m,
among other things
ändern, change; sich –,
change (intr.), change one's
attitude
aneinander, against one
another
anerkennen, irr., acknowledge
der Anerkennungszuschlag (ᵉe),
supplement in recognition
anfangen, s., begin; do
anfangs, to begin with
der Anflug (ᵉe), copse
die Anforderung (an), demand
(on)
angeben, s., specify
angeblich, allegedly
angeboren, innate
angehen, s., concern
angehören, belong to
der Angehörige (see 29), member
der Angeklagte (see 29), accused
person
angemessen, in conformity/
harmony with
angstvoll, fear-ridden
anhaltend, continuous(ly)
der Anhänger (-), adherent
ankämpfen, struggle
ankommen, s. arrive;

darauf kommt es an, that
is what matters, that is the
point
sich ankündigen, announce o.s.
die Ankunft (ᵉe), arrival
anlegen, apply (e.g.
standards); plan, design
anmerken, see by s.b.'s
appearance
anmutig, graceful, charmingly
der Annäherungsversuch (-e),
tentative approximation
die Annahme, acceptance
annehmen, s., accept, assume
anno, in the year
anpacken, tackle
die Anpassung (an), adaptation
(to), conformity (with)
anpassungsfähig, adaptable
anregen, prompt, stimulate
die Anregung, prompting,
stimulation
der Anreiz (-e), inducement
anrichten, cause, do
anrüchig, disreputable
der Anrufer (-), caller
anschaffen, acquire
anschaulich, vividly; –
machen, illustrate
anscheinend, apparently
sich anschicken, prepare (to do
sth.)
die Anschrift, address
ansehen, s., look at; – als,
look upon as
das Ansehen, appearance; von –,
by sight
die Ansicht, view, opinion
ansichtig: – werden (G),
catch sight of
die Ansiedlung, settlement
der Ansporn, spur, incentive
die Ansprechzeit, operating time
der Anspruch (ᵉe), claim, right
anständig, respectable;
decently
ansteckend, infectious
die Ansteckungsweise, mode of
infection
anstrengend, arduous,
exacting
die Anstrengung, effort
der Anteil (-e): – nehmen an, be
concerned about
antihumanistisch, inimical
to man

das Antikglas, old glass
antreffen, *s.,* find
anvertrauen, entrust (with);
 sich –, entrust o.s. (to)
anwachsen, *s.,* increase, rise
anwenden, *irr.,* apply
die Anzahl, number
anziehen, *s.,* fold back
 (wings)
der Anzug (ːe), suit
anzünden, light
der Apparat (-e), (piece of)
 apparatus
die Apparatur, set of apparatus,
 equipment
appellieren (an), appeal (to)
die Arbeit, labour; **in – nehmen,**
 start work on
der Arbeitsbereich (-e), sphere of
 activity
der Arbeitslose *(see 29),*
 unemployed man
die Arbeitslosigkeit,
 unemployment
**der Arbeits-mann (-männer &
 -leute),** workman
der Arbeitsplatz (ːe), job
das Archiv (-e), film library
arg, bad, serious
der Ärger, vexation
ärgerlich, irascible
ärgern, annoy
das Ärgernis (-se), cause of
 offence
die Armut, poverty
die Artikulation, articulation, way
 of speaking
die Artistik, artistry
ästelos, branchless
die Atomrakete, nuclear rocket
die Atomwaffe, nuclear weapon
auch, *see (83a)*
der Aufbau, building up, creation
aufbrausen, swirl up
der Aufbruch, departure; **im –
 sein,** be starting
der Aufenthalt (-e), stay
auffahren, *s., – auf,* run into
 (vehicle in front); **zu dicht
 –,** tailgate
der Auffahrunfall (ːe), accident
 incurred through tailgating
auffällig, striking
aufflattern, flutter up
die Aufgabe, task, job; duty
aufgeben, *s.,* give up; set

(questions)
aufgehen, *s.,* become clear
aufgeschlagen, open
aufgestapelt, piled up
aufgrund (G), on the basis of,
 on account of
aufhängen, *s.,* hang up
aufheben, *s.,* capture *(archaic)*;
 sich –, rise up, lift o.s. up
aufhorchen, listen attentively
aufklären, enlighten
die Aufklärung, Enlightenment
auflösen, dissolve; **sich –,**
 dissolve
die Auflösung, disintegration
aufmerksam, attentive; **–
 machen auf,** call attention
 to
die Aufmerksamkeit, attention
die Aufnahme, admission;
 photograph
aufnehmen, *s.,* receive
aufopfernd, self-sacrificing,
 unselfish
aufrecht, upright
aufrechterhalten, *s.,*
 maintain
aufreißen, *s.,* tear open
aufsammeln, collect up
der Aufsichtsrat (ːe), board of
 directors
aufsitzen, *s.,* mount
das Aufstampfen, stamping of
 feet
aufsteigen, *s.,* rise
der Aufstieg (-e), rise
auftauchen, emerge
der Auftrag (ːe), order
der Auftraggeber (-), employer
sich auftun, *s.,* open (up)
aufwachen, wake up *(intr.)*
der Aufwand, expenditure, cost
aufwecken, wake up *(tr.)*
aufwenden, *irr.,* use (up)
die Aufzeichnung, note,
 record(ing), diagram
das Augenblinzeln, blinking of
 eyes
das Augenrollen, rolling of eyes
der Augenwinkel (-), corner of
 the eye
sich ausbilden in, acquire a
 knowledge of
die Ausbildung, development,
 training
ausbleiben, *s.,* be no longer

heard
ausbleichen, s., fade
ausbrechen, s., break
ausbreiten, spread out
die **Ausdehnung,** extent
der **Ausdruck** (ᵉe), expression
ausdrücklich, expressly
die **Ausdrucksmöglichkeit,**
  possibility of expressing o.s.
auseinandergehen, s.,
  disperse, separate
ausführen, make
ausführlich, in detail
der **Ausgang** (ᵉe), exit, way out
der **Ausgangspunkt** (-e),
  starting-point
ausgebleicht, bleached
ausgebreitet, spread out
ausgehen, s., go (doing sth.)
ausgelierfert: – sein, be at
  the mercy of
ausgeprägt, pronounced,
  strongly marked
ausgesetzt, exposed
ausgezeichnet, excellent
die **Ausgleichsmaßnahme,**
  compensating measure
das **Ausgleichstor** (-e), equalizing
  goal
die **Auskunft** (ᵉe), information
ausmachen, constitute,
  amount to
das **Ausmaß,** measure
die **Ausnahme,** exception
ausnehmen, s., take out,
  except; **sich –,** look
auspfeifen, s., boo
ausraufen, pull out
ausreichen, suffice
ausreichend, sufficient,
  enough
ausrotten, stamp out
die **Aussage,** stated view
aussagen, state
das **Aussagevermögen,**
  expressiveness
ausschalten, eliminate
ausschöpfen, exhaust, deal
  completely with
aussehen, s., look; **wie sieht's
aus?** how are things really?
das **Aussehen,** appearance
außen: nach –, outwards;
  von –, from outside
der **Außenseiter** (-), outsider
außer, external

außerdem, moreover
außergewöhnlich,
  remarkable, exceptional
äußern, utter; **sich –,** express
  o.s.; **sich – in,** betray o.s. in
außerordentlich,
  extraordin-ary (-arily)
äußerst, outermost
die **Äußerung,** remark
aussprechen, s., express;
  sich –, express o.s.
ausstrecken, stretch out
ausströmen, flow out
ausüben, exert
die **Auswahl,** choice
der **Ausweg** (-e), way out
auswendig, by heart
sich auswirken, have a
  (good, bad, etc.) effect
die **Auswirkung,** consequence
die **Autobahn,** motorway
der **Autofahrer** (-), car-driver

b

babylonisch, babel-like
der **Bach** (ᵉe), brook, little river
sich baden, bathe
die **Bahn,** railway; path
bald, soon; – . . . –, now . . . now
Bälde: in –, in a short time
der **Balken** (-), beam
das **Band** (ᵉer), band, ribbon
der **Band** (ᵉe), volume
bang(e), alarmed,
  apprehensively
bar, lacking, devoid of
der **Barbar** (-en, -en), barbarian
der **Batist** (-e), cambric
der **Bau** (-ten), building
bauen, build, construct
bäuerlich, rustic
das **Bauerntuch** (ᵉer), peasant's
  shawl
der **Baumgarten** (ᵛ), tree-nursery
das **Bauwerk** (-e), building
beabsichtigen, intend
die **Bearbeitung,** handling
beben, quiver
der **Becher** (-), calyx
der **Bedarf,** demand
bedauern, regret
bedenken, irr., reflect on; –
  mit, provide with, shower on
bedeutend, important
bedeutungsvoll, significant
sich bedienen (G), use

die Bedienung, service
die Bedingung, condition
das Bedürfnis (-se), need
sich beeilen, hurry
beeindrucken, impress
befallen, s., assail
der Befehl (-e), command
befehlen, s., order
sich befinden, s., find o.s., be
befördern, transport
sich begeben, s., proceed; – in,
    take refuge in
das Begebnis (-se), occurrence
die Begegnung, meeting
begleiten, accompany
beglückend, heart-warming
begreifen, s., understand,
    realize
begrenzt, within limitations
die Begrenzung, delimitation
der Begriff (-e), concept, idea
der Begriffsinhalt (-e),
    connotation
begrüßen, greet
begünstigen, favour
behäbig, stodgily
behalten, s., keep, retain
der Behälterwagen (-),
    container-waggon
beharrend, inert
behauchen, blow on
die Behauptung, assertion
beheben, s., repair
beherbergen, give shelter to
beherrschen, rule over,
    dominate
beherzt, brave, bold
die Behörde, authorities
behüten, watch over
beieinander, next to one
    another
beiläufig, incidentally
das Bein (-e), leg; bone
beispielsweise, for example
beisteuern, contribute
beitragen, s., contribute
bejubeln, acclaim
bekämpfen, combat
die Bekämpfung, fight (against)
bekannt, known
bekümmert, worried,
    concerned
belegen, cover
die Belehrung, instruction
das Belieben: nach –, according
    to choice

beliebt, liked
bemerkbar, noticeable
sich bemühen (um), try hard (to
    achieve, obtain sth.)
benachrichtigen, inform
sich benehmen, s., behave
benutzen, use
benützen, use
bequem, easy
die Bequemlichkeit, convenience,
    comfort
sich berauben (G), rob o.s. of
berauschen, intoxicate
berechtigt, justified
die Berechtigung, justification
beredt, eloquent
die Bereitschaft, preparedness,
    readiness
bergen, s., shelter, contain
der Berg-mann (-leute), miner
der Bericht (-e), report
berichtigen, correct
der Beruf (-e), profession, calling
der Berufskraftfahrer (-),
    professional driver
beruhen, be based
beruhigend, reassuring
besagen, say
beschäftigen, occupy, keep
    busy
beschäftigt, preoccupied, busy
die Beschimpfung, abuse
beschleunigen, accelerate
beschneiden, s., reduce
die Beschreibung, description
beschwören, swear
    (allegiance) to
beseitigen, destroy
besetzen, man, garrison
besetzt, occupied, taken
das Besinnen, reflection
sich besinnen, s., remember
der Besitz (-e), possession
der Besitzer (-), owner
besorgniserregend,
    disturbing(ly)
besorgt (um), worried (about)
besprechen, s., discuss
bestanden (mit), planted,
    covered (with)
beständig, steadfast,
    constantly
bestätigen, confirm
bestechen, s., captivate
bestehen, s., exist; – aus,
    consist of; – in, consist in

bestehend, existent
die Bestie, beast
bestimmen, intend, influence, appoint, determine
bestimmt, definite(ly), decided
die Bestimmung, decree
bestrafen, punish
bestreichen, *s.*, spread
bestreiten, *s.*, deny, challenge
die Beteiligung, participation
beten, pray
betrachten, examine, gaze at; **– als,** regard as
beträchtlich, consider-able (-ably)
betreffen, *s.*, concern
der Betrieb (-e), industrial concern, running (of business, etc.), industry
betrüblich, sadly, depressingly
der Betrug, humbug
betrügen, *s.*, deceive
betrüglich, deceptive, false
das Bettuch (¨er), sheet
beugen, bow; **sich –,** bend down
beunruhigen, disquiet
beunruhigend, alarming(ly)
die Beute, quarry
der Beutel (-), purse
beuteln, shake up
bevölkern, populate
bevölkert, (densely) populated
die Bevölkerung, population
bevormunden, keep in tutelage
bevorzugen, give preference to
bevorzugt, specially
der Bewacher (-), overseer
bewachsen, covered
die Bewältigung, overcoming, accomplishment
bewegen, move; **sich –,** move (*intr.*)
die Bewegung, movement
die Beweisaufnahme, (hearing/ giving of) evidence
beweisen, *s.*, prove
der Bewerber (-), applicant
bewirten, entertain
bewohnbar, (in)habitable
bewohnen, inhabit
der Bewohner (-), inhabitant
bewußt, aware, conscious(ly),

known (to), deliberate(ly)
bewußtlos, unconscious(ly)
das Bewußtsein, consciousness
die Bewußtseinsspaltung, divided consciousness
bezeichnen, indicate, describe, designate; **sich –,** describe, call o.s.
die Bezeichnung, title, name
sich beziehen, *s.*, **(auf),** refer, relate (to), be concerned (with)
bezug: in – auf, as regards
bieten, *s.*, offer
das Bild (-er), picture, reflection, exposure, shot; **ins – bringen,** explain
bilden, form; **sich –,** be formed
bildlich, figurative
die Bildung, culture, education
bisherig, former
ein bißchen, a bit
der Bissen (-), morsel
bisweilen, occasionally
bitten, *s.*, **(um),** ask (for)
bleiben, *s.*, remain; **– bei,** stick to
bleich, pale
bleiern, leaden
der Blick (-e), glance, gaze, eye(s)
blicken, look, glance
der Blitz (-e), flash of lightning, thunderbolt
blitzen, flash
der Block (¨e), boulder
blühen, bloom
blühend, in blossom, blooming
bluten, bleed
blutjung, very young
die Blutrunst, bloodthirstiness
der Boden (¨), earth, soil, ground, floor, boards
böse, bad
das Böse (*see 29*), evil
die Botschaft, message
der Brand (¨e), conflagration: **in – stecken,** set on fire
der Brandenburger (-), native of Brandenburg
brandenburgisch, Brandenburg (*adj.*)
brausen, roar; dash
die Breite, breadth; latitude
breiten, spread
breitschultrig, broad-

shouldered
die Bremse, brake
  bremsen, brake
das Bremsmanöver (-), braking
  operation
  bringen, *irr*. bring, take; **mit**
  sich –, entail; **dazu –,** make
  s.o. do sth.
der Bruch (¨e), fracture
  bruchlos, without a break
das Brummen, growl
das Brünnlein (-), tiny spring
  Brüssel, Brussels
der Buchhalter (-), bookkeeper
die Büchse, gun
das Bündel (-), bundle
  bundesdeutsch, of the
  German Federal Republic
die Bundestagswahl, election to
  the Lower House of
  Parliament
  bunt, gay, many-coloured
die Burg, castle
der Bürger (-), (solid middle-class)
  citizen; bourgeois
der Busen (-), bosom
der Bussard (-e), buzzard
der Bußmönch (-e), Penitentiary
  byzantinisch, Byzantine

c
die Charakteristik,
  characterization
der Chef (-s), boss
der Chock (-s), shock

d
  da, there, then
  dabei, (yet) at the same time,
  in doing so, in this
  connexion; in that case
  daher, therefore, consequently
  dahin, there, thither; **– sein,**
  be no more, be over
  damit, thereby, by that
der Damm (¨e), dam; roadway
  (*rly*.)
der Dämmer, dusk
  dämmern, glimmer, emit
  faint light, be dim, grow dusk
das Dämmernde (*see 29*), the
  inchoate
die Dämmerung, dawn
der Dampf (¨e), vapour
  danach, afterwards
  daneben, alongside

dankbar, grateful(ly)
die Dankbarkeit, gratitude
  darauf, whereupon, thereupon
  darin, in which
  darstellen, represent
  darüber, above them; –
  hinaus, beyond
  darum, therefore, for that
  reason
  darunter, among them
die Dauer, duration
  dauern, last
  davon, from them
  davorstehen, *s.*, have in front
  of one
  dazwischen, interspersed, in
  between
  dazu, for that purpose
  definierbar, definable
  denkbar, conceivable
das Denken, thought, thinking
der Denker (-), thinker
das Denkmal (¨er), monument;
  (*pl.*) relics, heritage
  denn, *see 83(b)*
  dennoch, nevertheless
  derart, such
  derjenige, he (who)
  derweil, while
  deshalb, so; **– daß,** because
  desto, all the (+comparative)
  deutlich, clear(ly)
  dicht, thick(ly), closely, close
  by
  dichten, write poetry
der Dichter (-), poet, creative
  writer
die Dichtung, poetry
das Dickicht (-e), thicket
der Dieb (-e), thief
die Diebsgilde, thieving
  fraternity
der Diebstahl (¨e), theft
der Dienst (-e), service
  diesmal, this time
  differieren, differ
  diplomiert, (armed) with a
  diploma
  direkt, directly, really
  doch, *see 83(c)*
  donnern, crash
  doppelt, double, doubly
der Draht (¨e), wire, string (of
  puppet)
der Drahtkorb (¨e), wire basket
  drängen (auf), press (for),

urge
draußen, outside
der Dreckeffekt (-e), spurious/
  bogus result
drehen, turn; sich –, revolve,
  turn, wind
drin, within
dringen, s., force one's way
dringend, pressingly
drinnen, inside
droben, up there
drohen, threaten
die Drohgebärde, threatening
  gesture
die Drohne, drone
drüben, over there; in E.
  Germany (when said by
  W. Germans)
drüber, over it
der Druck (¨e), pressure
drucken, print
drücken, press, oppress
drum, therefore
der Duckmäuser (-), yes-man,
  'goody-goody'
der Duft (¨e), scent
duftend, fragrant
duftig, fragrant
dulden, tolerate
duldend, patient
die Düne, dune, sandhill
dunkel, dark, obscure,
  mysterious
das Dunkel, darkness
die Dunkelheit, darkness
dünnhäutig, thin-skinned
der Dunst (¨e), haze
durchaus, thoroughly,
  altogether
durchbrochen, open-work
  (adj.)
durchfallen, s., fail (exam)
durchführen, execute, carry
  out
der Durchgang (¨e), thoroughfare
durchkommen, s., pass
  (exam)
der Durchschnitt (-e), average
  (mark)
das Durchschnittsmaß (-e),
  average (measure)
sich durchsetzen, assert o.s., win
  through
durchziehen, s., pervade
dürfen, irr., see 67(b)
dürftig, poor, wretched

dürr(e), dry
düster, gloomy, mournfully

e
eben, just, precisely, rather;
  – noch, a moment before
die Ebene, plain; plane
ebenfalls, likewise
ebenso, just as
ebensowenig, just as little
echt, real, genuine
edel, noble
der Edel-mann (-leute),
  nobleman
der Effekt (-e), result
egal, all the same
das Ehepaar (-e), married couple
die Ehre, honour
ehren, honour
ehrenhaft, honourable
die Ehrenrechte (pl.):
  bürgerliche –, civil rights
ehrlich, honest
die Eibe, yew
die Eiche, oak
die Eifersucht, jealousy
eigenartig, peculiar
die Eigenschaft, quality,
  capability
eigentlich, really, as a matter
  of fact, actual, real
der Eigentümer (-), owner
die Eigentümlichkeit, peculiarity
eilen, hurry
der Einbrecher (-), burglar
einbringen, irr., bring in
der Einbruch (¨e), burglary;
  intrusion, incursion
der Eindruck (¨e), impression
die Einfachheit, simplicity
der Einfall (¨e), incidence (of
  light); sudden idea
einfallen, s., occur to
der Einfluß (¨(ss)e), influence
die Einführung, introduction
der Eingang (¨e), entrance
eingeschmiegt, nestling
einig, united
die Einkommenssteigerung,
  rising incomes
der Einkommensunterschied
  (-e), difference of income
der Einkommensvorteil (-e),
  income advantage
einlassen, s., show in; sich –
  auf, let o.s. get involved in

einläuten, ring in, begin
einmal, once, in the first
place; **nicht –,** not even;
nun –, now (in fact); **auf –,**
all at once; **noch –,** once
again
einmalig, single
einnehmen, s., take in good
part
einpferchen, cram, crowd
together
einrichten, arrange; **sich –
auf,** organize o.s. for
einsam, lonely, solitary
die **Einsamkeit,** loneliness
der **Einsatz** (ⁿe), employment
einschlafen, s., fall asleep
einseitig, one-sided(ly)
einsetzen, risk, substitute
die **Einsicht,** insight
einst, once (upon a time)
einstig, former
einstmals, formerly
eintreffen, s., arrive
eintreten, s., come into
der **Einwand** (ⁿe), objection
einwandfrei, incontestably
einweisen, s. (in), assign (to)
der **Einwohner** (-), inhabitant
die **Einzelleistung,** individual
achievement
einzeln, separate(ly), single,
isolated, detached,
individual; **der -e,**
individual
einziehen, s., move in
einzig, only, single
eklatant, striking
die **Elendsnahrung,** wretched
food
das **Elendsquartier** (-e), squalid
dwelling, hovel
das **Elternhaus,** (one's parents')
home
elternlos, orphaned
das **Elternpaar,** parents
der **Empfang** (ⁿe), reception
empfangbereit, receptive
empfangen, s., receive
empfehlen, s., recommend
empfinden, s., perceive, feel
das **Empfinden,** feeling
empfindlich, sensitive; –
über, touchy about
die **Empfindsamkeit,** sensitivity
empor, up

das **Emporblicken,** looking up
emporstecken, raise
emportreiben, s., thrust up
emporwachsen, s., shoot up
emsig, assiduous
das **Ende** (-n), end; **zum –,** to the
bitter end
endgültig, once and for all
endlos, endless
die **Energie,** vigour, energy
eng, narrow, confined,
constricted; closely
die **Enge,** tightness
der **Enkel** (-), grandchild
entbehrlich, unnecessary
entdecken, discover
der **Entdecker** (-), discoverer
entfernen, remove, alienate;
sich –, become more distant,
go away
entfernt, distant
die **Entfernung,** distance
die **Entfesselung,** unleashing,
violence
entfliehen, s., escape
entgegenblicken, look
forward to
entgegengesetzt, opposite
entgegensetzen, oppose
entgegnen, say in reply, retort
enthalten, s., contain
enthüllen, reveal
entlarven, unmask
die **Entlarvung,** unmasking
entmutigen, discourage
entrüstet, indignant
entscheiden, s., decide
entscheidend, decisive
die **Entscheidung,** decision
entschieden, decidedly,
unhesitatingly
sich **entschließen** (zu), s., decide,
resolve upon
sich **entschuldigen,** apologize,
excuse
die **Entschuldigung; um –
bitten,** apologize
entsetzlich, terrible
entsetzt, horrified
die **Entspannung,** relaxation
entsprechend, corresponding,
tallying; consistent
entspringen, s., originate,
start (up)
entstehen, s., arise, be
produced

das **Entstehen**, genesis, birth
die **Entstehung**, origin
enttäuschen, disappoint
die **Enttäuschung**,
  disappointment
entweihen, desecrate
sich **entwickeln**, develop (*intr.*)
die **Entwicklung**, growth,
  development, evolution
das **Entwicklungsland** (-er),
  developing country
entzücken, delight
entzünden, light
eo ipso, ipso facto
erahnen, (vaguely) imagine
erbauen, erect
das **Erbe**, inheritance, legacy
erben, inherit
erbittert, incensed
erblinden, grow blind
die **Erde**, earth, ground
erdulden, put up with, suffer
erfahren, *s.*, experience
die **Erfahrung**, experience
erfassen, seize upon
erfinden, *s.*, invent
die **Erfindung**, invention
der **Erfolg** (-e), success
erfolgen, happen
erfüllen, fill
der **Erfüllungsgehilfe** (*see 29*),
  cat's-paw
ergeben, *s.*, show, prove;
  sich –, emerge
das **Ergebnis** (-se), outcome,
  result, conclusion
die **Ergebung**, resignation,
  submission
ergreifen, *s.*, seize
erhaben, sublime
erhalten, *s.*, get; **sich** –,
  preserve o.s; – **bleiben**, ⁴
  remain available
sich **erheben**, *s.*, spring up
sich **erhellen**, light up, brighten
erhöhen, heighten, raise
sich **erholen**, recover
die **Erholung**, recovery
erinnern, remind; **sich** –,
  remember
die **Erinnerung**, memory
erkalten, grow cold
erkennbar, recognizable
erkennen, *irr.*, recognize,
  realize
die **Erkenntnis** (-se), knowledge,

realization
erklären, explain; declare
der **Erklärer** (-), explainer,
  commentator
sich **erkühnen**, dare
erlangen, attain
erlauben, allow; **sich** –, take
  the liberty
erleben, experience, have had
das **Erlebnis** (-se), experience
erleiden, *s.*, suffer
erleuchtet, lit up
erlösen, free, release
die **Ermahnung**, exhortation
ermitteln, establish, discover
ermöglichen, make possible
ernst, solemn
der **Ernst**, gravity
der **Eroberer** (-), conqueror
erobern, conquer
eröffnen, open
erregen, excite
erreichen, reach
erröten, blush
erscheinen, *s.*, appear, seem;
  come out
erschlagen, *s.*, kill, strike dead
erschließen, *s.*, unlock, open
  up
erschöpft, exhausted
erschrecken, frighten
erschrecken, *s.*, be frightened
erschreckend, terrifying(ly)
erschrocken, terror-stricken
die **Erschütterung**, emotional
  impact
ersparen, save (expense of)
erst, first (of all); only
das **Erstaunen**, amazement,
  astonishment
erstaunlich, astonishing(ly)
zum erstenmal, for the first time
erteilen, give
ertragen, *s.*, put up with
erübrigen, spare
erwachsen, grown up
der **Erwachsene** (*see 29*), adult
die **Erwähnung**, mention
erwarten, expect, await
erwecken, arouse, awaken
erweisen, *s.*, do, render;
  sich – **als**, prove to be
erweitern, enlarge
erwirtschaften, make
  (e.g. profits)
erwischen, catch

erzählen, tell, talk
erzamerikanisch, American through and through
erzeugen, breed, produce
die **Erzeugung**, generation, creation
erzogen, (well) brought up
erzwingen, *s.*, force (on one)
der **Esser** (-), eater
etwa, *see 83(d)*
etwas, something, somewhat
die **Eule**, owl
eventuell, if necessary
ewig, eternal(ly)

f

die **Fabrik**, factory
die **Fächerkrone**, fan-shaped crown
fade, insipid, spent, listless
fähig (**zu**), capable (of)
fahl, pale
die **Fahne**, flag
fahren, *s.*, go, travel, issue
der **Fahrer** (-), driver
die **Fahrstraße**, highway
die **Fahrt**, journey
der **Fahrzeuglenker** (-), car-driver
der **Fall** (ˑe), case
fallen, *s.*, fall, come down
fälschen, fake
die **Falte**, undulation, ripple
der **Falter** (-), moth; (F.) butterfly
faltig, wrinkled
der **Fang** (ˑe), talon, claw
die **Farbe**, colour, paint, hue
farbig, colourful
die **Färbung**, colouring, (right) shade, colouration
fassen, seize, grasp
die **Fassung**, version
fatal, disastrous
fegen, sweep across
fehlen, be lacking/missing, miss
der **Fehler** (-), blunder, mistake
die **Feierlichkeit**, solemnity
die **Feigheit**, cowardice
feindlich, enemy (*adj.*)
feindselig, hostile
das **Feld** (-er), field; **ins** – **führen**, put forward (idea)
der **Feldbecher** (-), army mug, cup
der **Feldzug** (ˑe), campaign
der **Felsen** (-), rock

fernöstlich, far eastern
das **Fernsehen**, television
der **Fernsprecher** (-), telephone
fertigwerden, *irr.* (**mit**), cope, deal (with)
fest, firm(ly), fixed
festhalten, *s.*, hang on to
das **Festhalten**, keeping together
die **Festnacht** (ˑe), night of revelry
feststellen, see, perceive (fact)
die **Feststellung**, finding
fett, fertile
feucht, moist, wet
die **Fichte**, spruce fir
die **Figur**, form, figure
finden, *s.*, find; **sich** –, be
der **Fingerhut**, foxglove
die **Fingerspitze**, fingertip
finster, ominous, threatening; dark
die **Finsternis** (-se), darkness
die **Fläche**, expanse
die **Flamme**, flame
die **Flasche**, bottle
flattern, stream, flutter
der **Flecken** (-), speck
fleischfarben, flesh-coloured
fleischig, fleshy
der **Fleiß**, diligence
die **Fliege**, fly
die **Fliese**, paving-stone
der **Fluch** (ˑe), curse
flüchten, flee
der **Flug** (ˑe), flight
der **Flügel** (-), wing
das **Flugzeug** (-e), aeroplane
die **Flur**, field
flüstern, whisper
die **Flut**, flood, torrent
fluten, surge
die **Folge**, consequence
folgenschwer, portentous
folgern, conclude
die **Folter**, torture; **auf die** – **spannen**, put on the rack, torture
förderlich, beneficial
fördern, encourage
die **Forderung**, demand
die **Form**, form, shape
formen, shape
das **Formular** (-e), form (to fill up)
der **Forscher** (-), researcher
die **Forschung**, research
fort, away

die **Fortdauer**, continuance,
survival
sich **forternähren**, go on living
fortgehen, *s.*, proceed; go
away
fortleuchten, go on shining
der **Fortschritt (-e)**, progress
fortsetzen, continue
forttragen, *s.*, bear away
der **Fraß**, eating away (of foliage)
frech, cheekily
frei, free(ly), open, exposed
freilich, to be sure, admittedly
der **Freiraum**, scope
freiwillig, voluntary
fremd, dissimilar, foreign,
unfamiliar, alien
die **Fremde**, abroad
fressen, *s.*, eat (of animals)
die **Freude**, joy
sich **freuen**, rejoice (at)
freundlich, good-natured,
affably
der **Friede (-ns)**, peace
friedlich, peaceful
frieren, *s.*, freeze
frisch, anew, freshly
froh, joyful(ly), glad
fromm, godly
der **Frosch (¨e)**, frog
fröstelnd, shivering
frostig, frosty
die **Frucht (¨e)**, fruit
fruchtbar, fertile
fruchtbarkeitbewirkend,
inducing fertility
der **Frühaufsteher (-)**, early-riser
die **Frühe**, early morning; **in aller
–**, very early in the morning
früher, before, formerly
führen, take, conduct, lead
der **Führer (-)**, leader, guide; the
Führer (in Nazi Germany)
die **Fülle**, profusion
der **Funke (-ns, -n)**, spark
das **Funkeln**, sparkle, coruscation
funkelnd, gleaming
die **Furche**, furrow
furchen, furrow
fürchterlich, terrible
furchtsam, timorous
der **Fürst (-en, -en)**, sovereign,
prince

g

die **Gabe**, gift, talent, endowment
das **Gähnduett (-e)**, duet of
yawning
gähnen, yawn
der **Gang (¨e)**, corridor; course;
walk
ganz, quite, whole, entirely,
completely
gänzlich, entirely
gar, quite, even; – **nicht**, not at
all; – **nichts**, nothing at all
die **Gardine**, curtain;
schwedische -n, prison
bars
die **Gattin, (-nen)**, wife
das **Geäst**, branches
das **Gebäude (-)**, building
gebeugt, bowed
das **Gebiet (-e)**, area, territory,
sphere, domain, field
gebieten, *s.*, command
gebildet, cultivated
das **Gebirg(e) (-)**, mountains
gebogen, curved
der **Gebrauch (¨e)**, custom,
practice, use
der **Geburtstag (-e)**, birthday
das **Gebüsch (-e)**, bushes
das **Gedächtnis (-se)**, memory
der **Gedächtnisschwund**,
amnesia
der **Gedanke (-ns, -n)**, thought,
idea
der **Gedankensprung (¨e)**, jump
from one idea to another
gedeihen, *s.*, prosper
gedenken, *irr.*, propose
das **Gedicht (-e)**, poem
gedrungen, compact, squat
die **Geduld**, patience
geduldig, patient(ly)
die **Gefahr**, danger
gefährden, endanger
gefährlich, dangerous
gefallen, *s.*, (D), please
der **Gefallen (-)**, favour
der **Gefangene** (*see 29*), prisoner
die **Gefangenschaft**, captivity
gefeiert, celebrated
das **Gefüge**, structure, system
das **Gefühl (-e)**, feeling
die **Gefühlsanteilnahme**,
emotional sympathy
die **Gegenregung**, reaction

das **Gegenrezept** (-e), counter-
reply, answer (to it)
gegenseitig, mutually
der **Gegenstand** (̈e), (physical)
object
das **Gegenteil** (-e), opposite;
im –, on the contrary
gegenüber, opposite; (as)
compared with; vis-à-vis
gegenüberstehen, s., confront
die **Gegenwart**, present
gegenwärtig, present, extant,
actual, around us
der **Gegner** (-), adversary
das **Gehäuse** (-), box, receptacle,
space; shell
das **Gehege** (-), preserve
geheim, secret; **im -en**,
secretly
das **Geheimnis** (-se), mystery
geheimnisvoll, mysterious
gehen, s., go, work; **– um**, be
a matter, question of, be at
stake; **vor sich –**, occur,
happen; **sich –**, see 61(d)
das **Gehirn** (-e), brain
die **Gehirnwäsche**, brainwashing
das **Gehör**, hearing, ear
gehorchen (D), obey
gehören (D), belong to; **– zu**,
be part/one of, be among; be
entailed, required
gehörig, due
geifernd, foaming at the
mouth
der **Geist** (-er), spirit, mind, ghost
geistesabwesend, absent-
minded(ly)
geistig, intellectual(ly)
der **Geiz**, niggardliness
gekleidet, dressed
das **Geklingel**, ringing (of
telephone)
das **Geklippe**, rocks
das **Gelände** (-), building-site
das **Geländer** (-), banister
gelangen, attain to
der **Geldschrank** (̈e), safe
gelegen, situated
der **Gelehrte** (see 29), man of
learning, savant
geleiten, escort
geliebt, beloved
der **Geliebte** (see 29), loved one
gellend, piercing
gelten, s., be essential,

imperative to + inf.; **– als**,
count as
das **Gelüste** (-), lust
das **Gemälde** (-), picture
die **Gemeinschaft**, community
das **Gemüse** (-), vegetable
das **Gemüt** (-er), spirit, heart
gemütlich, agreeable,
comfortable
der **Gemütswechsel**, change of
spirit
genau, exact(ly), accurate(ly),
scrupulously
geneigt, inclined
genialisch, cleverly
genießen, s., enjoy
genügen, suffice
die **Genugtuung**, satisfaction
der **Genuß** (̈(ss)e), partaking,
enjoyment
das **Gepäcknetz** (-e), luggage-rack
das **Gepräge**, stamp
gerade, straight; forthright;
just, exactly, directly,
precisely
geradezu, almost, really
geraten, s., get (into)
das **Geräusch** (-e), noise
geräuschlos, silently
gering, slight, unimportant,
short, little
geringschätzen, think little of
gesamt, all, entire
der **Gesang** (̈e), song
das **Geschäft** (-e), business
der **Geschäftsladen** (̈), shop
die **Geschichte**, story, history
das **Geschick** (-e), fate, destiny;
skill
geschickt, skilled
das **Geschirr**, dishes
das **Geschlecht** (-er), sex
der **Geschmack** (̈e), taste
das **Geschmetter**, blare
das **Geschütz** (-e), gun
die **Geschwindigkeit**, rapidity
die **Geselligkeit**, social life
die **Gesellschaft**, society
gesellschaftlich, social
der **Gesellschaftsvertrag** (̈e),
social contract
das **Gesetz** (-e), law
die **Gesetzmäßigkeit**, conformity
to law
das **Gesicht** (-er), face; (sense of)
sight

das **Gesims** (-e), sill
das **Gesindel**, rabble
gespannt, stretched out; tense, intent
das **Gespenst** (-er), ghost, spectre
das **Gespräch** (-e), conversation, talk, call; **ein – führen**, have a conversation
der **Gesprächsteilnehmer** (-), person one can talk to
die **Gestalt**, shape, figure
gestalten, make, fashion, shape
der **Gestank**, stench
gestatten, allow
die **Geste**, gesture
gestehen, s., confess
das **Gestirn** (-e), star(s), constellation
getrost, confidently
gewahr: – werden, perceive
die **Gewähr**, guarantee
die **Gewalt**, power, (use of) force
das **Gewässer** (-), stretch of water; (pl.) water bodies
das **Gewehr** (-e), rifle
die **Gewerbefreiheit**, freedom to exercise any trade
das **Gewesene** (see 29), past
der **Gewinn** (-e), profit, gain
gewinnbringend, profitable
gewinnen, s., gain, win
das **Gewitter** (-), thunderstorm
die **Gewogenheit**, affection
gewöhnlich, customary, ordinary
gewohnt, used to
das **Gewölk**, clouds
gezielt, directly aimed
gezwungen, willy-nilly
der **Giebel** (-), gable
das **Gift** (-e), poison
giftig, poisonous
das **Giftkraut** (⸚er), poisonous plant
das **Gitter** (-), bars
der **Glanz**, gleam, radiance, lustre
glänzen, gleam
glänzend, lustrous, gleaming, brilliant
gläsern, glassy
glatt, smooth(ly), sleek; – **rasiert**, clean shaven
der **Glaube** (-ns), faith, belief
glauben, think, believe
der **Gläubige** (see 29), believer
gleich, like, similar, same;

equally, just as, immediately; **ins -e**, in order; **ganz –**, all the same
gleichermaßen, in like manner, equally
gleichfalls, likewise
das **Gleichgewicht**, equilibrium
gleichgültig, indifferent(ly)
die **Gleichgültigkeit**, indifference
gleichmäßig, equally
gleichrangig, of equal rank
gleichsam, as it were
das **Glied** (⸚er), limb
der **Gliedermann** (-er), lay figure, jointed doll
glitzern, glitter
der **Glockenschlag** (⸚e), stroke (of the hour)
das **Glück**, happiness; (a matter of) luck; **zum –**, fortunately
glücklich, happy
glückverheißend, auspicious
der **Glückwunsch** (⸚e), congratulation
die **Glühbirne**, electric bulb
glühend, glowing
das **Glykosid** (-e), glycoside
die **Glyzinie**, wisteria
der **Goldfink** (-en, -en), goldfinch
graben, s., bury, dig
gradlinig, in a straight line
die **Granate**, shell
gräßlich, ghastly
grauenhaft, dreadful
greifen, s., seize, grasp; – **nach**, clutch at, reach out for; – **zu**, take up
die **Grenze**, limit
grenzenlos, unlimited
griechisch, Greek
der **Griff** (-e), handle
grinsen, smirk
grob, rude
grollen, rumble
großangelegt, large-scale
großartig, grand
die **Größe**, magnitude, greatness
großflächig, broad (of features)
die **Großstadt** (⸚e), metropolis
die **Grubenlaterne**, miner's safety-lamp
der **Grund** (⸚e), reason; base, basis; floor; depths; background; soil; **im -e**, basically

der **Grundboden**, family estate
gründen, found
die **Grundfrage**, basic question
der **Grundgedanke (-ns, -n)**,
  fundamental idea
grundlegend, fundamental,
  basic
die **Gründlichkeit**, thoroughness
der **Grundsatz (ˎe)**, principle
grundsätzlich, on principle,
  really
das **Grundstück (-e)**, landed
  property
der **Gruß (ˎe)**, greeting
grüßen, greet
gucken, peep
der **Guß: aus einem –**, a perfect
  whole, all of a piece; **in
  einem –**, in one go, sitting
gut, good, kind; well
das **Gut**, good
die **Güte**, goodness; quality
gütig, kind(ly)
die **Gütigkeit**, kindness
der **Gutshof (ˎe)**, farm
der **Gymnasiast (-en, -en)**,
  grammar school pupil
das **Gymnas-ium (-ien)**, grammar
  school
der **Gynäkologe (-n, -n)**,
  gynaecologist

h

haarsträubend, hair-raising
der **Habenichts (-e)**, have-not
die **Habgier**, cupidity
der **Hafen (ˎ)**, harbour, haven
haften, adhere, cling
der **Haken (-)**, hook
halbbewußt, half conscious
der **Halbhandschuh (-e)**, mitten
halbwegs, fairly, reasonably
die **Hälfte**, half
der **Halt (-e)**, support
halt, just, simply, I'm afraid
halten, s., hold, keep, sustain,
  stop; **es –**, be; **auf sich –**,
  have a proper self-respect;
  – für, consider
haltmachen, stop, call a halt
die **Hand (ˎe)**, hand; **zur – haben**,
  have at one's command
das **Handbuch (ˎer)**, manual
sich **handeln (um)**, be a question,
  matter (of)
das **Handeln**, action, behaviour

handelnd, active
die **Handelsabkürzung**,
  abbreviation used in
  commerce
der **Händler (-)**, dealer
handlich, handy
die **Handlung**, action
die **Handlungsweise**, behaviour,
  conduct
der **Hang (ˎe)**, slope
hängen, s., hang, droop
hassen, hate
häßlich, ugly
hastig, hasty, hurried
sich **häufen**, accumulate, amass
häufig frequently
das **Haupt (ˎer)**, head
Haupt- (in compounds), main,
  chief
das **Hauptquartier (-e)**,
  headquarters
die **Hausaufgaben** (f. pl.), school
  homework
der **Hausgenosse (-n, -n)**, member
  of the family
häuslich, domestic, of their
  own homes
das **Heck (-e or -s)**, stern (of ship),
  tail (of car)
das **Heer (-e)**, army
heftig, fiercely, violently
heilen, heal
heillos, calamitous
der **Heilschlaf**, therapeutic sleep
heimlich, secret(ly)
heimsuchen, descend (up)on
heiraten, marry
heißen, be called; **es heißt**, is
  meant, asserted; is what is
  said; **das heißt**, that is;
  was heißt das? what do you
  mean (by that)?
der **Heizkörper (-)**, radiator
der **Held (-en, -en)**, hero
der **Heldenvater (ˎ)**, heroic father
helfen, s., help, be of avail
hell, light (-coloured),
  bright(ly), lucid, pellucid,
  clear
die **Helle**, brightness, bright light
hemmen, slow up, delay,
  impede
der **Henker (-)**, hangman
herab, down
heran, up
herantragen, s., bring (to,

upon)

der Heranwachsende (*see 29*), youngster growing up

herauf, up

heraufranken, climb up, creep up

heraus, out

herausfinden, *s.*, discover

herausheben, *s.*, emphasize

sich herausstellen, turn out to be

heraustreten, *s.*, emerge

herbeizwingen, *s.*, produce by force

die Herbstzeitlose, autumn crocus

der Herd (-e), hearth

der Herdsitz (-e), seat by the hearth

herkommen, *s.*, come along

der Herr (-n, en), master

herrisch, imperiously

herrlich, magnificent, glorious(ly), delicious

die Herrschaft, dominion, domination

herrschen, reign, prevail

herüber, (coming) across

herum, around, about

herumschnüffeln, pry around

sich herumschweifen, curve round

herunter, down

hervorbringen, *irr.*, bring about

hervorgehen, *s.*, go forth

hervorkommen, *s.*, peep out

hervorspringen, *s.*, project

hervortreten, *s.*, emerge

das Herzgift (-e), cardiac poison

der Herzinfarkt (-e), cardiac infarction

herzlich, cordial, hearty

der Herzschlag (¨e), heart-beat

die Herzstromkurve, electro-cardiogram

die Hetze, (mad) rush

das Heu, hay

heutig, present

der Himmel (-), sky, heaven; **aus allen -n (gefallen),** bitterly disappointed

die Himmelsrichtung, direction

hie: hie..., dort..., on this side, ... on the other side

hin, thither, there, **- und wieder,** every now and

again; ... **hin,** ... **her,** blow! never mind!

hinab, down

hinauf, up

hinaus, out, outside

hinauslaufen, *s.* **(auf),** amount to

das Hindernis (-se), obstacle

hindurch, through

hineinführen, lead (in)

hineinschlingen, *s.* **(in),** cram (into)

hineinstoßen, *s.*, thrust into

hineintragen, *s.* **(in),** bring (into)

die Hingabe, devotion

sich hingeben, *s.*, surrender o.s.

die Hinnahme, acceptance

hinnehmen, *s.*, accept

hinreichen, be sufficient

hinschauen, look (at)

die Hinsicht, respect

sich hinstellen (als), set o.s. up (as)

hintenrum (F. = **hintenherum**), in a round-about way

der Hintergrund (¨e), background

hinter ... her, along behind

der Hinterherfahrer (-), the man driving along behind

der Hinterkopf, back of the head

der Hintermann (¨er), brain behind the scenes

das Hintertreffen: ins – geraten, be left behind, be neglected

hinunterfallen, *s.*, fall away

hinweg, away; gone

der Hinweis (-e), hint

hinweisen, *s.* **(auf, nach),** point (to, towards)

hinzukommen, *s.*, be added; **hinzu kommt,** added to which

das Hirn (-e), brain

der Hirsch (-e), stag

der Hirt (-en, -en), drover

die Hitze, heat

hitzig, hot, glowing

hochachten, esteem

hochaufliegend, standing up high

hochentwickelt, highly developed

hochgestimmt, exalted

das Hochhaus (¨er), multi-storied building, skyscraper

344

der **Hochmut**, arrogance
der **Hochschulabsolvent** (-en, -en), graduate
die **Hochschule**, university
höchst, ultimate
höchstens, at (the) most
das **Hochwasser** (-), flood
die **Hochzeit**, wedding
der **Hof** (⸚e), farm(yard), courtyard
die **Hoffnung**, hope
höflich, courteous(ly)
die **Höhe**, top, height
hohl, hollow; **-er Muskel**, smooth muscle
höhnend, derisive(ly)
hohnlachen, deride
holen, bring, take
die **Hölle**, hell
die **Hol(l)underbeere**, elderberry
die **Holzfuhre**, cartload of wood
der **Holzschuh** (-e), clog
der **Horst** (-e), eyrie
der **Huf** (-e), hoof
die **Hülle**, envelope, cover, shroud
hüllen, wrap
humanistisch, classical
hurtig, swift
der **Hustenanfall** (⸚e), fit of coughing

i

der **Ideenkreis**, range of ideas
sich **identifizieren**, identity o.s.
die **Ilias**, Iliad
immer, see *83(e)*
immerhin, nevertheless
die **Impfvorschriften** (*f. pl.*), inoculation regulations
imponieren, impress
indem, since, while
indessen, while
indirekt, indirectly
individuell, individual, in individual fashion
infolgedessen, consequently
der **Informant** (-en, -en), person supplying information
der **Inhalt** (-e), content(s)
innehalten, *s.*, maintain
innen, within, on the inside
das **Innere** (*see 29*), inside
innerlich, internally
die **Innerlichkeit**, inwardness
der **Innungszwang**, compulsory membership of guilds

insgesamt, all together
der **Intendant** (-en, -en), director (of theatre)
das **Interesse** (-n), interest
inzwischen, meantime
irgendwas, anything
irren, be mistaken

j

ja, after all, indeed; – **eben**, just
jagen, drive, hunt
das **Jahr** (-e), year; **das** – **über**, throughout the year
das **Jahrhundert** (-e), century
das **Jahrtausend** (-e), a thousand years, millennium
je, ever; – **nach**, according to; – **nachdem**, according as
jedenfalls, at any rate, in any case, at least
jedesmal, every time
jedoch, however, nevertheless
jenseitig, opposite
jeweils, at any given time
der **Judasbaum** (⸚e), Judas-tree
der **Jude** (-n, -n), Jew
die **Jugend**, youth
der **Jugendliche** (*see 29*), young person
der **Junge** (-n, -n), lad, boy

k

kahl, bald, bare
der **Kajütplatz** (⸚e), berth
der **Kakadu** (-s), cockatoo
die **Kamelie**, camellia
kämmen, comb
die **Kampagne**, campaign
der **Kampf** (⸚e), struggle, fight
kämpfen, fight, struggle
der **Kanzelredner** (-), preacher, pulpiteer
kapieren, understand
der **Karabiner** (-), carbine
die **Karre**, wheelbarrow
die **Karte**, map, ticket
die **Kastanie**, chestnut (-tree)
der **Kasten** (⸚), box; rickety building
der **Kauf** (⸚e), purchase
der **Käufer** (-), purchaser
das **Kaufhaus** (⸚er), (departmental) store
der **Kaufhof** (⸚e), (departmental) store

der **Keim** (-e), origin, germ
keineswegs, by no means
der **Keller** (-), cellar
der **Kenner** (-), judge, student
die **Kenntnis** (-se), knowledge;
  zur – nehmen, note
der **Kerl** (-e), chap
die **Kerze**, candle, taper
die **Kette**, chain
kettenweise, one after the
  other
die **Kiefer**, Scots pine
das **Kindbettfieber**, puerperal
  fever
die **Kinderei**, childishness
das **Kissen** (-), cushion, pillow
der **Kitsch**, trash
klagen, bewail, say deploringly
der **Klang** (-̈e), timbre
klangvoll, sonorous
klar, clear, lucid, limpid,
  clearly-marked
der **Klassenkamerad** (-en, en),
  classmate
das **Klassenklima**, climate,
  atmosphere in the classroom
klatschen, gossip
die **Klavierstunde**, piano lesson
kleben, stick
der **Klebstoff** (-e), glue, gum
die **Kleinigkeit**, trifle, a mere
  fraction
kleinmütig, faint-hearted
sich **klemmen**, get jammed
die **Klingel**, bell
der **Klingelknopf**, bell-push
klingeln, ring, sound
das **Klingeln**, jingling, ringing
klingen, s., ring, clank
das **Klirren**, jingling
klopfen, tap
das **Kloster** (-̈), monastery
klug, intelligent
der **Knabe** (-n, -n), boy
knallen, slam; **sie werden
  auf den Tisch des Hauses
  geknallt**, they are being
  foisted, slapped down on us
knapp, barely, a bare ...
knarren, creak
der **Knicks** (-e), curtsy
knirschen, gnash
knistern, crackle
knochig, bony
der **Knopf** (-̈e), button
der **Koch** (-̈e), cook

der **Kollege** (-n, -n), colleague
die **Kolonne**, column
der **Kommissari-us** (-en),
  commissary
die **Kommode**, chest of drawers
die **Komponente**, element,
  component
komponieren, compose
die **Konditorei**, café
können, irr., see 67(c)
der **Kopf** (-̈e), head; person
das **Kopfballtor** (-e), headed goal
das **Korn** (-̈er), grain
der **Kornett** (-e), cornet,
  standard-bearer
körperlich, physical
kraftlos, powerless
kramen, rummage
krankhaft, diseased, morbid
kränklich, sickly
die **Krause**, frill
sich **kräuseln**, curl
das **Kraut** (-̈er), plant, herb
kreisrund, circular
kriegerisch, warlike
der **Kuchen** (-), cake
der **Kuckuck** (-s), cuckoo
kugelsicher, bullet-proof
kühn, bold(ly)
die **Kultur**, civilization
künftig, future, in (the) future
der **Künstler** (-), artist
künstlerisch, artistic
künstlich, artificial
der **Kunststein** (-e), artificial stone
die **Kuppel**, dome
kurz, short, brief, in a word
kurzärmelig, short-sleeved
kurzgestielt, short-handled

l
lächerlich, ridiculous
laden, s., invite
der **Laderaum** (-̈e), hold (of ship)
das **Lager** (-), bed, couch
das **Land** (-̈er), land, country,
  region
die **Landschaft**, landscape, piece
  of scenery
die **Landzerstörung**, destruction
  of the countryside
langbefreundet, friends of
  long standing
langfristig, over a long period
langgestreckt, extensive
längst, long since, long ago

346

langweilen, bore
der Lärm, noise
lassen, s., let, leave, see 68; look
lässig, indolent
das Lastauto (-s), lorry
das Lastgefährt (-e), goods
waggon
das Laub, foliage, leaves
der Lauf (¨e), course
die Laufbahn, career
die Laune, mood
der Laut (-e), sound
läuten, ring
die Lautgebung, utterance
lebendig, alive; vividly
lebhaft, lively
das Leder, leather
lediglich, merely
legen, lay, put; sich -, lie
down; sich - um, coil round
lehnen, lean
der Leib(-er), body
leicht, light(ly), slight; easy,
easily; delicately
leid: einem - tun, be sorry
for s.o.
das Leid, sorrow
leiden, s., suffer
das Leiden (-), suffering, pain;
disease, disorder
die Leidenschaft, passion
leidenschaftlich,
passionate(ly)
leider, unfortunately; alas
sich leihen, s., borrow
leise, soft, quietly; slightly
leisten, achieve, accomplish;
sich -, afford
die Leistung, achievement,
performance
der Leistungsdruck, pressure to
produce results
die Lektüre, reading
lenken, control, govern, drive
der Lenker (-), ruler
der Lernstoff, learning matter,
things to learn
der Lesezirkel, magazine rental
service
leuchten, shine
das Leuchten, scintillation
leuchtend, luminous
der Leuchter (-), candlestick
das Licht (-er), light, candle
der Lidschlag (¨e), batting of
eyelids

der Liebling (-e), favourite
liefern, supply
die Lieferung, making
der Lieferwagen (-), delivery van
liegen, s., lie, be; woran liegt
es, daß..., how does it
come that...
lila, lilac
links, on the left
die Linse, camera-lens
der Lippenstift (-e), lipstick
die List, cunning
loben, praise
das Loch (¨er), hole
locken, curl; entice
loh, blazing
der Lohn (¨e), reward, wages
die Lore, truck
das Los (-e), lot; das Große -,
first prize
losbrechen, s., break away
lose, loose
lösen, untie; sich -, be solved;
sich - von, leave
losschießen, s., fire away, go
ahead
die Lösung, solution
loswerden, irr., get rid of
lotrecht, perpendicular
der Löwenanteil (-e), lion's share
die Luft (¨e), air, atmosphere
der Luftraum, air space
lugen, peer
die Lust (¨e), joy
lustig, gaily
die Lyrik, lyric, poetry

m
machen, make; give (joy);
take (exam)
mächtig, mighty
die Machtlosigkeit, powerlessness
die Machtausübung, exercise of
power
mager, thin
die Mahnung, exhortation
mal, just
malen, paint
der Maler (-), painter
manch, many a;-es, quite a
lot of things
manchmal, sometimes,
occasionally
der Mangel (¨), lack
die Mangelhaftigkeit,
defectiveness

347

mangeln, lack, be missing
mannigfach, manifold, diverse
die Mannigfaltigkeit, variety
die Mannschaft, team
das Märchen (-), fairy-tale
märchenhaft, fabulous, fairy-tale *(adj.)*, enchanted
die Marionette, puppet
die Marktordnung, market system
marschieren, march
maschinell, mechanical, machine-like
das Maschinenschreiben, typing
das Maß (-e), extent, measure
mäßigen, temper
maßlos, outrageously
die Maßnahme, measure
der Maßstab (ᵒe), standard, yardstick, gauge
mästen, fatten
matt, feeble
der Mauerstein (-e), brick
das Maul (ᵒer), mouth
die Maxime, precept
mehrere, several; **zu -en,** several together; **-s,** several things
mehrmals, several times
der Mehr-Wisser (-), person who knows better
die Meile, league, German mile (=7,500 m.)
meinen, think, mean
meinetwegen, I've no objection
meistern, master
• **melden,** report
die Menge, crowd; **eine -,** a lot of
der Menschenmord, murder
der Menschenverstand:
  gesunder -, common sense
menschenwürdig, humane
der Menschenzug (ᵒe), procession of people
menschlich, human(e)
merken, notice
das Merkmal (-e), feature
merkwürdig, remarkable
messen, *s.,* measure
der Messinghaken (-), brass hook
die Messung, measurement
das Mieder (-), bodice
die Miene, mien, face
mies, wretched, 'lousy'
mieten, let (=hire)

mild, mild, tenderly
der Militär (-s), officer
die Mimik, miming
mindern, lessen
das Ministeri-um (-en), ministry
das Minus (-): **um 2 im -,** minus 2
die Mischung, mixture
die Misere, wretched business
die Mißachtung, disdain
mißbrauchen, take unfair advantage of
das Mißfallen, displeasure
mißgelaunt, bad-tempered
mißmutig, disgruntled
mißtrauisch, mistrustful
der Mist, dung(-heap)
mitarbeiten, collaborate
die Mitbestimmung, co-determination, participation
mitbringen, *irr.,* bring along with
das Mitglied (-er), member
mitschwingen, *s.,* be also present; (there is) a note, echo of
das Mittel (-), means
mittelbar, indirectly
der Mittelpunkt (-e), centre
mittlerweile, meanwhile, in the meantime
mitunter, occasionally
mitziehen, *s.,* take with one
das Möbel (-), piece of furniture
moderat, avoiding extremes
mögen, *irr., see 67(d)*
möglichst, as . . . as possible
monatweise, a month at a time
der Mönch (-e), monk
das Mondscheingespräch, late-night call
der Mondscheintarif (-e), late-night call charges
die Montur, uniform
das Moor (-e), moorland
das Moos (-e), moss
moralbefreit, amoral
der Mord (-e), murder
der Mörder (-), murderer
der Motor, driving-force
die Möwe, seagull
mühsam, laborious, arduous
mühselig, difficult
die Mulde, trough, basin, mould
der Mund (ᵒer), mouth; **einem nach dem - reden,** say

what s.b. likes to hear
munkeln, whisper (furtively)
die Münze, coin
der Musiker (-), musician
die Muße, leisure
müssen, *irr.*, *see 67(e)*
müßig, idle
der Musterschüler (-), model
schoolboy
der Mut, courage

n
na (*F.*), well; – **ja,** oh well
nach, according to, judging by
nachahmen, imitate
der Nachahmer (-), imitator
die Nachahmung, imitation
nachblicken, gaze after
der Nachdruck, force
die Nachfolge, succession
nachfolgen, follow
die Nachfrage, inquiry
nachgehen, *s.*, go into, pursue
nachgiebig, indulgent(ly)
nachhaltig, lasting, sustained
nachlassend, slowing up
die Nachrichten, (*f. pl.*), news,
information
nachschenken, fill up
glass(es) again
die Nachsicht, indulgence
nachsichtig, indulgent
nachsprechen, *s.*, repeat
der Nachteil (-e), disadvantage
nächtens (*Lit.*), by, at night
die Nachteule, night-bird
nächtigen, spend the night
nächtlich, nocturnal
der Nacken (-), (back of) neck;
im –, threatening (one)
nackt, naked, bare
der Nagel (⸚), nail
nah(e), near (by), close (to);
– **kommen,** get, come close
to
die Nähe, proximity; **in der** –,
near by; imminence
nahebei, near by
näher, more closely
nahrhaft, nutritious
die Nahrung, food(-stuffs)
die Naht (⸚e), seam
nahtlos, seamless, without a
hiatus, break
namens, named

namentlich, especially
die Narbe, scar
narkotisieren, anaesthetize,
drug
der Naturforscher (-), scientist,
naturalist
der Naturwissenschaftler (-),
scientist
naturwissenschaftlich,
scientific
der Nebel (-), mist
der Nebengedanke (-ns, -n),
other thought
nehmen, *s.*, take (up), get
neigen, incline, tilt, bend
nennen, *irr.*, call; **sich** –, call
o.s.
nervös, nervous, tense
neu, new; **aufs -e,** once more,
anew; **von -em,** anew
neuerlich, once again
die Neugier, curiosity
die Neuigkeit, item of news; (*pl.*),
news
Nicht- (*in compounds*), non-
das Nichts, nothingness
nichtsnutzig, useless
nieder, down
niederschreiben, *s.*, write
down
die Niederung, low ground
nikotingefärbt, nicotine-
stained
noch, *see 83(i)*; **auch** –,
besides, in addition
nochmalig, further
nochmals, (once) again
die Not (⸚e), need, privation
der Notbehelf (-e), makeshift,
expedient
die Note, mark (in school); (*pl.*),
music
das Notengerangel, wrestling for
marks
die Notwendigkeit, necessity
der Numerus clausus, restricted
admission to university
nun, *see 83(j)*
nur, *see 83(k)*
nützlich, useful

o
ob, (I wonder) whether
oben, up (here); **nach** –,
upwards; **von** – **her,** coming

from above; **mir steht's
bis –**, I'm fed up to the teeth
obendrein: noch –, into the
bargain
ober, upper; **-er Teil**, top
die Oberfläche, surface
der Oberkörper (-), torso
der Oberschüler (-), grammar
school pupil
obig, above
das Objekt (-e), article
die Öde, desolation
offenbar, obviously
offensichtlich, obvious
öffentlich, public(ly)
ökonomisch, economic(al);
– gesehen, from an
economic point of view
das Opfer (-), victim; sacrifice;
– bringen, make sacrifices
die Opferbereitschaft, willingness
to make sacrifices
opfern, offer as a sacrifice
optimal, best possible
ordentlich, tidy
ordinär, common, vulgar
die Ordnung, order
orientieren, orientate
der Ort (-e), place
die Ortschaft, country-town
das Ortsgespräch (-e), local call
der Ortswechsel (-), change of
place/scene

p

das Päckchen (-), little parcel
pädagogisch, educational
das Pärchen (-), loving couple
die Partei, (political) party
die Partnerschaftlichkeit, spirit
of partnership
die Pauke, kettle-drum
pauken (*F.*), swot, learn up
die Pause, interruption
der Pelz (-e), fur
perlmutterfarben, mother-of-
pearl colour
die Person, character
der Personalleiter (-), personnel
manager
der Personenwagen (-), private
car
persönlich, personal,
individual
die Persönlichkeit, (man of)
personality, real person

pervers, perversely,
unnaturally
der Pfad (-e), path
pfeifen, *s.*, whistle
pflegen, look after, take care
of; be used to
die Pflicht, duty
pflichtgemäß, as in duty
bound
die Phantasie, imagination
die Physiognomie, physiognomy,
features
piepen, chirp
der Pinsel (-), brush
die Platane, plane-tree
die Platte, (gramophone) record
platzen, burst
pochen, knock, tap
die Pointe, joke
das Pokalspiel (-e), cup-match
der Pole (-n, -n), Pole
die Politik, policy, politics
die Polizei, police
die Polyglottie, polyglottism
popanzhaft, buffoon-like
die Portion, amount
das Postauto (-s), bus
die Postgebühren (*pl.*), postal
rates
prächtig, splendid
prägen, mint
das Predigerhafte, preacher-like
manner
preisgeben, *s.*, reveal
preisgekrönt, prize-winning
preiswürdig, good value for
money
pro, per
promoviert, (armed) with a
doctorate
das Prozent (-e), per cent
die Prozentzahl, percentage
prüfen, try, test
die Prüfung, test; tribulation
publizieren, publicize, make
public knowledge
pulsieren, pulsate, pulse
das Pult (-e), (teacher's) desk
die Puppe, doll; puppet
putzen, clean

q
quälend, torturing
der Qualitätsanspruch (ᵘe),
qualitative claim/demand
das Quartier (-e), quarters

die Quelle, spring
quer, oblique(ly)
die Querele, petty complaint;
(pl.) wrangles

r

sich rächen, avenge o.s.
der Räderkasten (- & ⁔), box on
wheels
der Rahmen (-), frame; im –,
within the limits, in the
framework
rammen, ram
der Rand (⁔er), edge, rim
rasch, swift(ly), quick(ly)
der Rasen (-), grass, lawn
rasieren, shave
rasseln, rattle, patter
ratlos, at a loss, helplessly
rätselhaft, enigmatic, puzzling
der Rattenfänger (-), Pied Piper
der Raubzug (⁔e), (predatory) raid
der Raum (⁔e), room, space
raunen, whisper
die Raupe, caterpillar
rauschen, rustle, murmur
reagieren, react
die Realisierung, realizing,
implementation
der Rechenpfennig (-e), counter
rechnen, reckon, count;
– mit, be prepared for
das Rechnungswesen, accounting
system
recht, quite; right
das Recht (-e), right
die Rechte (see 29), right hand
rechts, on the right
der Rechtsstaat (-en), state based
on law
rechtzeitig, in time,
punctually
die Rede, speech, conversation
die Regel, rule; in der –, as a rule
die Regelmäßigkeit, regularity
regeln, regulate
der Regierende (see 29), ruler
die Regierung, reign, government
der Regisseur (-e), producer (of
plays)
das Reh (-e), deer
reich, rich; – an, full of
das Reich (-e), realm, empire; das
dritte –, the Third/Nazi
Reich
reichen, be enough, suffice

reichlich, abundant
der Reichtum (⁔er), riches
reif (zu), mature enough (for)
reifen, ripen
die Reifeprüfung, school leaving
exam
die Reihe, rank, row, series
rein, pure, sheer
die Reinheit, purity
reinigen, clean; sich –, purge
o.s.
der Reiter (-), trooper
die Reiterei, cavalry
die Reizbarkeit, susceptibility
der Reklamationsbrief (-e),
letter of complaint
die Reklamewand (⁔e),
(advertisement) hoarding
rennen, irr., run
rentabel, profitable
Ressort- (in compounds),
departmental
der Rest (-e), remains, rest
retten, rescue, secure
der Retter (-), deliverer, saviour
reuen, regret
richten, turn (one's eye); –
auf, aim at, direct towards
die Richtung, direction, line
riechen, s. (nach), smell (of)
der Riemen (-), strap
riesig, enormous
die Rille, rill, furrow, groove
das Rind (-er), ox, cow; (pl.) cattle
das Rindfleisch, beef
rings, all round; -um, all
round
die Rinne, groove
riskant, risky
der Riß (-(ss)e), cleft
der Rock (⁔e), tunic
der Rohstoff (-e), raw material
rollen, roll, go (of car)
rollenförmig, cylindrical
rosa, pink
der Rosenkranz (⁔e), rosary
die Rosenterrasse, rose-terrace
das Rosmarinkräutlein,
rosemary herb
rötlich, reddish
das Rückchen (-), little jerk
der Rücken (-), back
rücken, move (on)
die Rückkehr, return
die Rücksicht (auf), regard,
consideration (for); –

nehmen auf, take into consideration, take account of
der Rückzug (⁻e), retreat
der Ruf (-e), reputation
rufen, s., call, summon
die Ruhe, calm, peace and quiet, peace (of mind)
der Ruhm, fame
sich rühren, stir
rumänisch, Rumanian
die Runde, circle
rütteln, shake

S

der Saal (Säle), room, hall
die Sache, thing, matter
die Sachkenntnis, expertise
sachlich, matter-of-fact, objective
sächsisch, Saxon
der Sachverhalt (-e), facts of the case
der Sachverstand, expertise
die Sage, legend
der Sammler (-), collector
der Samt (-e), velvet
samten, velvet
sämtlich, all, every single
sanft, gentle, gently, softly
die Sänfte, sedan-chair
die Sanftmut, gentleness
der Saphir (-e), sapphire (stylus)
satt (G), sick of; full (up); – **haben,** be fed up with
der Sattel (⁻), saddle
der Satz (⁻e), sentence
sauber, clean, impeccable, clear-cut
die Sauberkeit, impeccability
die Sauerstoffversorgung, provision of oxygen
die Säule, column
der Saum (⁻e), hem, fringe
säumen, border
die Schachtel, box
schade, it's a pity
der Schädel (-), skull
der Schaden (⁻), damage
schadenstiftend, causing damage
schädlich, harmful, noxious
schaffen, bring, convey, achieve, do
schaffen, s., create
die Schaffenskraft, creative power
der Schall (-e & ⁻e), sound

die Schallplatte, (gramophone) record
die Schar, crowd, host
die Schattenseite, dark (shady) side
schattig, shady
schätzen, appreciate
die Schätzung, estimation
schauen, look
schauerlich, ghastly
schaukeln (F.), 'fix'
der Schaum (⁻e), foam
der Schauplatz (⁻e), scene
das Schauspiel (-e), play
der Schauspieler (-), actor
das Scheibchen (-), little circle
scheiden, s., leave, depart
der Schein (-e), light
schenken, give
scheren, s., clip
das Scherenfernrohr (-e), stereo-telescope
die Schicht, class
schichten, stack
schieben, s., push, shift
das Schielen, squint
schießen, s., shoot; rush
schildern, describe, depict
schimmeln, moulder
der Schimmer, shimmer, glint
das Schimpfwort (-e & ⁻er), term of abuse
das Schindeldach (⁻er), shingle roof
die Schlacht, battle
die Schläfe, temple
schlagen, s., strike, beat, slam
das Schlaginstrument (-e), percussion instrument
der Schlamm (-e), mud
schlank, slender
der Schleimer (-) (F.), 'sucker-up'
schleppend, dragging
schleudern, hurl
schlicht, plain
schließen, s., shut, conclude; **sich –,** knit together
schließlich, after all, eventually, in the end, finally
der Schlittschuh (-e), skate
die Schlucht, gorge
schmähen, scorn
schmal, narrow, tight-lipped
schmausend, feasting
schmecken (nach), taste (of)
der Schmetterling (-e), butterfly

der **Schmutz**, dirt
die **Schnecke**, snail
schneiden, *s*., cut; chisel
der **Schneidbrenner** (-), cutting
  torch
schnellen, jerk
die **Schnellverkehrsstraße**, fast
  traffic road
schon, *see 83(m)*
der **Schoß** (÷e), lap, bosom (*fig.*)
der **Schoßrock** (÷e), tail-coat
die **Schränker-Arbeit** (*F.*), safe-
  breaking
die **Schraube**, screw
die **Schreckspanne**, period of
  fright
der **Schrei** (-e), call
schreien, *s*., cry out, shout
schreiten, *s*., walk
die **Schrift**, handwriting
schriftlich, written
der **Schriftsteller** (-), writer
der **Schritt** (-e), step
das **Schrittempo**, walking-pace
schüchtern, shy
der **Schuft** (-e), blackguard
der **Schulbetrieb**, school activity/
  industry
schuldig, guilty
schultern, shoulder
die **Schurkerei**, villainy
der **Schutt**, rubble
schütteln, shake
der **Schutz**, protection; – **für**,
  care of
schützen, protect
schwanken, shake, falter
schwankend, unsteady
der **Schwarm** (÷e), swarm
die **Schwarzföhre**, Austrian pine
schweben, hover, hang, float,
  move
schwedisch, Swedish
die **Schweigsamkeit**, stillness
die **Schweinerei**, disgusting
  behaviour/language
der **Schweiß**, sweat
Schweizer, Swiss (*adj.*)
schwerfällig, heavily
schwerlich, scarcely
schwierig, difficult,
  complicated
die **Schwierigkeit**, difficulty
die **Schwinge** (*Lit.*), wing, pinion
schwingen, *s*., swing,
  brandish; **sich** –, swing along

die **Seele**, soul, mind
das **Segel** (-), sail
segensreich, prosperous
die **Segnung**, blessing
die **Sehnsucht** (÷e), yearning
  (desire)
sehnsüchtig, yearningly
sei: – ... – (*or* **oder**), whether
  ... or
das **Seidenpapier**, tissue-paper
seinerseits, in its turn
selbst, itself; even; **wir** –, we
  ourselves; **von** –, of its own
  accord; **-geschaffen**, created/
  made by o.s.
selbstanklägerisch, self-
  accusatory
das **Selbstbewußtsein**, self-
  assurance
selbstgerecht, self-righteous
seltsam, strange
senken, sink
die **Senkung**, reduction
sicher, certain; safe
die **Sicherheit**, safety
sicherlich, certainly
sichern, ensure
sichtbar, visible
sichtlich, evidently
der **Sieg** (-e), victory
silberig, silvery
silbern, silver (*adj.*)
der **Singvogel** (÷), song-bird
der **Sinn** (-e), sense
sinngemäß, appropriately
sinnlich, sensuous
sinnschwer, pregnant
sinnvoll, sensible
die **Skal-a** (-en & -s), scale
so, so, thus, in such a way; – ?
  have you?; – **etwas**, that
  sort of thing; – ... **als**,
  both ... and
der **Sog** (-e), strong pull, influence
sogar, even
sogenannt, so-called
sollen, *see 67(f)*
sommerlich, summery
somit, consequently, thus
sonst, otherwise, at other times
sonstig, other
die **Sophistik**, sophistry
die **Sorge**, concern, anxiety
sorgen (**für**), see (to)
die **Sorgfalt**, care
sorgfältig, carefully

sortieren, arrange
soviel, so much
soweit, thus far
der Spalt (-e), crack
die Spaltung, cleavage
der Spanier (-), Spaniard
sparsam, economical, sparsely
der Spaß: – machen, be fun
spazieren: -gehen, go for a
walk; -fahren, go for a drive
der Spaziergang (¨e), walk
der Specht (-e), woodpecker
speichern, store up
sich sperren, struggle (against)
der Spiegel (-), mirror
spiegeln, mirror, reflect
das Spiel (-e), game, playing
spielen, play; – auf, play for
(e.g. time)
der Spieler (-), player
der Spießer (-), narrow-minded
person
der Spitzenverdiener (-), top-
earner
der Sportverein (-e), sports club
die Sprachbildung, formation of
language(?); language
education(?)
sprachlich, linguistic
sprachlos, speechless
die Sprachübung, language
practice
die Sprechstunde, consulting
hour
springen, s., leap, jump about
der Spruch (¨e), dictum; spell
die Spur, trace
spüren, feel
staatlich, state (adj.)
der Staatsbürger (-), citizen,
subject
das Stadi-on (-en), stadium
das Stadi-um (-en), stage, phase
die Stadtlandschaft, landscape of
towns
die Staffel, section, group
die Staffelei, easel
der Stamm (¨e), trunk
stammen, spring, originate
der Stand (¨e), profession
ständig, constantly, ever
stark, strong, loudly
starr, rigid
die Stätte, place, scene
der Staub, dust
stechen, s., prick

stecken, stick
das Stehen: zum – kommen, stop
stehlen, s., steal
steif, stiff(ly)
steifbeinig, stiff-legged
steigen, s., climb, rise; increase
steigern, increase (tr.)
steil, steep(ly)
der Steinhaufen (-), heap of stones
die Stelle, job, post
stellen, place, put; provide;
einen Anspruch –, make a
demand; eine Frage –, ask
a question; sich –, put o.s.
die Stellung, position; – zu,
position vis-à-vis
die Stellungnahme, attitude
der Stengel (-), stem
die Stenographie, shorthand
stets, always
der Stich: im – lassen, leave in the
lurch
stickig, close, stifling
der Stiefel (-), boot
der Stier (-e), bull
der Stil (-e), style
still, silent(ly), quiet, hushed
die Stille, stillness
stimmen, make sense
die Stimmung, mood
die Stirn, forehead, brow
der Stoff (-e), substance, material
stolpern, stumble
stören, disturb; sich –, get/
become out of order
der Störfaktor (¨en), disturbing
factor
der Stoß (¨e), knock, kick, blow
stoßen, s., knock, swoop;
sich –, knock against each
other
der Stoßseufzer (-), deep sigh
die Strafe, punishment
strahlend, radiant
der Strang (¨e), track
der Stratege (-n, -n), strategist
streben, strive, aspire
strebsam, ambitious, aspiring
streifen, streak
streiten, s., argue
streng, severe
das Stoh, straw
der Strom (¨e), broad river
strömen, stream, flow
die Strömung, current
der Strumpf (¨e), stocking

354

das Stück (-e), piece
die Stückzahl, number of articles, quantity of goods
der Student (-en, -en), under-graduate, student
die Stufe, step, stage
stumm, mute(ly)
der Stumme (*see* 29), dumb man
der Sturm (¨e), storm, gale
stürmen, storm
stürmisch, stormy
der Sturm-und-Drang, Storm and Stress (movement)
der Sturz (¨e), dive, collapse
stürzen, dash, hurry, plunge
stützen, support, prop up
suchen, try, seek, try and find
der Sumpf (¨e), swamp, bog
synthetisieren, synthesize

t
der Tagebuch (¨er), diary
der Tagelöhner (-), day-labourer
täglich, daily
der Takt: im –, in step
die Tanne, (silver) fir
tapezieren, paper (wall)
die Tarnung, camouflage, mask
das Taschenbuch, 'paper-back'
das Taschengeld, pocket-money
tasten, grope
tastend, gropingly
tätig, active
tatsächlich, in fact
taufen, baptize
tausendpfadig, with thousands of paths
die Technik, technology, technique, skill
der Techniker (-), technologist
technisch, technological, technical
die Teilung, division
telegraphisch, by telegraph
das Tempo (-s & Tempi), pace, tempo
die Terz (-en), third (music)
der Test (-e & -s), check, scrutiny, examination
das Them-a (-ata & -en), theme
der Tick (-s), tic, twitch
die Tiefe, depth
tiefleuchtend, bright, lustrous
tiefschürfend, profound, probing
das Toben, raging

der Tod (-esfälle), death
der Ton (¨e), (musical) note; intonation
das Tor (-e), gate; goal
töricht, foolish
tot, dead, lifeless
der Tote (*see* 29), dead man
töten, kill
die Tracht, costume, garb
trachten, endeavour
träg(e), indolent
die Trägheit, inertia
der Tragiker (-), tragedian
der Trainsoldat (-en, -en), soldier of service-unit
die Träne, tear
trauen, trust
das Trauerspiel (-e), tragedy
treffen, *s.*, strike, hit
treiben, *s.*, go in for, study, drive, burst forth
trennen, separate
der Tresor (-s), safe
der Tresorknacker (-), safe-breaker
treten, *s.*, (vor), come, appear (before)
treu, loyal; retentive, faithful
die Treue, loyalty
das Trockene (*see* 29), dry land
trocknen, dry
die Trommel, drum
trommeln, beat drum
das Tröpfchen (-), little drop
trösten, console
trotzdem, nevertheless
trotzen, defy, withstand
trübe, melancholy, dimly, sadly
trübsinnig, gloomily
die Trübung, cloudiness
der Trunk (¨e), drink
die Truppensammlung, troop concentration
tüchtig, sound, capable
tückisch, malicious
die Tugend, virtue
der Tupfen (-), dot, spot

u
übel, bad
üben, practise
über, concerning, throughout, beyond; over, across; because of; – ... hinaus, beyond

überbieten, s., surpass
die Übereinstimmung, harmony
überempfindlish, hyper-
sensitive
die Übergewalt, excessive force
der Übergriff (-e), encroachment
überhaupt, at all
überhüllt, overgrown
überklettert, grown over
überkommen, s., come over
überleben, survive
übermitteln, transmit, convey
die Überprüfung, scrutiny of
examination
überraschend, surprising
die Überraschung, surprise
überreden, persuade
überrinnen, s., flow over,
bathe
die Überschwemmung,
flood(ing)
übersehen, s., overlook
überstehen, s., get through,
weather
übersteigen, s., exceed
übertreiben, s., exaggerate
überwinden, s., overcome
überwölbt, arched over
überzeugen, convince
die Überzeugung, conviction
üblich, customary
übrig, other
übrigbleiben, s., remain, be
left
die Ulme, elm
die Umbildung, change
sich umblicken, look round
sich umdrehen, turn round
umfangen, s., embrace,
encompass
umfassen, clasp, comprise
die Umfrage, inquiry
der Umgang (ⁿe), relations
die Umgebung, surroundings
umgehen mit, s., handle, deal
with
umher, around
umhergehen, s., walk about
umkränzen, wreathe
umnebeln, confuse, fog
der Umriß (-(ss)e), outline
der Umsatz (ⁿe), turnover
sich umsehen, s., look round
sich umsetzen, be transformed
der Umstand (ⁿe), fact;
circumstance

umstellen (auf), change over
die Umwelt, social surroundings
unabänderlich, inexorably
unabhängig, independent
unablässig, uninterrupted,
incessant
unabsehlich, immeasurably
unabweisbar, inescapable
unangekündigt, unannounced
unangemessen, incongruous
unauffällig, unobtrusive,
inconspicuously
unaufhörlich, incessantly
unaufhaltsam, uncheckable
unaussprechlich,
inexpressible
unbedingt, unconditional;
whatever happened; wir
müssen –, we simply must
die Unbefangenheit, unself-
consciousness
unbegrenzt, unlimited
unbeschreiblich,
indescribable
unbesieglich, invincibly
unbestimmt, indefinite
unbrauchbar, unusable
undankbar, ungrateful
undenkbar, unthinkable
uneins, in two minds
unendlich, infinite
die Unendlichkeit, infinity
unentbehrlich, indispensable
unentwickelt, undeveloped
unerhört, shocking
unermeßlich, immeasurable
unermüdlich, indefatigable,
untiringly
unerreichbar, unattainable
unerträglich, unbearable
unerwartet, unexpected(ly)
der Unfall (ⁿe), accident
unfreundlich, unkind
die Ungeduld, impatience
ungehemmt, unchecked
ungeheuer, huge
ungelegen, unwelcome
ungenießbar, uneatable
ungerecht, unjust
ungerufen, unbidden
ungeschickt, clumsily
ungestört, undisturbed
ungetrübt, unruffled, serene
ungewöhnlich, unusual(ly)
ungiftig, non-toxic
das Unglück, misfortune, accident

der **Unglücksfall** (̈e), accident
ungreifbar, elusive
unheimlich, uncanny
unmerklich, unnoticeably
unmittelbar, immediate(ly), directly
die **Unordnung**, disorder
das **Unrecht**, wrong
unregelmäßig, irregular
die **Unruhe**, anxiety, nervousness
unsagbar, ineffably
unscheinbar, plain
die **Unschlüssigkeit**, irresolution
unschmackhaft, unpalatable
unschön, plain
die **Unsitte**, abuse, bad habit
unsterblich, undying
der **Unstern** (-e), unlucky star
unstreitig, indisputable
unten, down below
unterbrechen, s., interrupt
die **Unterbrechung**, interruption
unterdrücken, suppress
untereinander, among one another
die **Unterhaltung**, conservation
der **Unternehmer** (-), entrepreneur
die **Unterordnung**, subordination
der **Unterrichtsvormittag**, morning lessons
untersetzt, thick-set
untersuchen, examine
die **Untersuchung**, inquiry, investigation
unterwegs, out (e.g. walking); on the way (there)
unterwühlen, undermine
ununterbrochen, uninterruptedly
unverdientermaßen, unmeritedly, undeservedly
unverkennbar, unmistak-able (-ably)
unverwandt, steadfast, unaverted
unwiderstehlich, irresistible
unwirklich, unreal
unwissend, ignorant
unzählig, countless
unzureichend, inadequate
die **Ursache**, cause
der **Ursprung** (̈e), origin
ursprünglich, originally; primal
der **Urstamm** (̈e), primeval trunk

das **Urteil** (-e), judgment
der **Urwald** (̈er), virgin forest

V
die **Vaterlandsliebe**, patriotism
der **Verachtete** (see 29), despised man
die **Verachtung**, contempt
veraltet, obsolete
verändern, alter; **sich** –, change
verantworten, justify
verantwortlich, responsible
die **Verantwortung**, responsibility
die **Verarbeitung**, elaboration
verbergen, s., conceal, hide
verbieten, s., forbid
verbinden, s., connect, unite; associate
verbittert, embittered
verbleiben, s., remain
verblüffend, staggering
verboten, forbidden
der **Verbraucher** (-), consumer
verbreiten, spread
verbringen, irr., spend (time)
der **Verdacht**, suspicion
verdanken, owe
verderben, s., spoil
die **Verderbnis** (-se), corruption
verdienen, earn; deserve
die **Verdrängung**, repression
verdreht, distorted
verdrossen, peevish
die **Vereinigung**, fusion
verenden, die
das **Verfahren** (-), procedure, method
verfallen, s., come under the sway of
die **Verfassung**, constitution
der **Verfassungsstaat** (-en), constitutional state
verfechten, s., advocate
verfehlen, miss, fail to make
die **Verfügung**, disposal; **zur** – **stellen**, make available
verführen, seduce
der **Verführer** (-), tempter
die **Verführung**, seduction
vergangen, past (adj.)
die **Vergangenheit**, past
vergebens, in vain
vergeblich, in vain; vain
vergehen, s., pass, perish; **mir vergeht**, I lose

das Vergehen, dissolution, death
der Vergleich (-e), comparison
vergrößert, enlarged
der Verhack (-e), tangle of dead
 branches
sich verhalten, s., behave; be the
 case
das Verhalten, attitude
das Verhältnis (-se), relation(ship)
verhältnismäßig, relatively
verhängnisvoll, disastrous
verharscht, cicatrized
verhelfen, s. (zu), procure,
 help to acquire
verhindern, prevent
sich verirren, lose one's way
verkaufen, sell
der Verkehr, traffic, stream
die Verkehrsmittel (n.pl.), means
 of communication
verkleinern, belittle
verkommen, s., become
 demoralized, destitute
verkörpern, personify
verlangen (nach), wish for,
 ask, demand; mich
 verlangt nach, I wish for
verlangsamen, slow down
verlassen, s., leave, abandon,
 desert
der Verlauf, course
sich verlaufen, s., lose one's way
verletzen, offend
die Verletzung, injury
verlieren, s., lose; sich –,
 disappear
das Verließ (-e), dungeon
sich vermählen, marry
die Vermehrung, increase
der Vermietungszettel (-),
 notice to let
vermischt, mixed
vermissen, feel the lack of
vermögen, irr., be able
das Vermögen (-), ability; wealth
vernachlässigen, neglect
die Vernunft, reason
vernünftig, sensible
die Verpackung, wrapping,
 packing
verpassen, miss
die Verpestung, pollution
verpflichtet, obliged
verraten, s., betray
verrückt, crazy
das Versagen, failure

sich versammeln, assemble
die Verschändelung, disfiguring
verschieden, varying, various,
 different
verschlafen, sleepy
verschlechtern, spoil,
 worsen, make worse; sich –,
 grow worse
verschlossen, barred
die Verschmelzung, fusion,
 melting
verschmiert, smeared
die Verschmutzung, fouling
verschränken, fold
die Verschuldung, indebtedness,
 debt
verschütten, bury
verschwinden, s., disappear
versetzen, place apart; in
 Schrecken –, terrify
versichert, assured
versinken, s., sink
versorgen (mit), provide
 (with)
versprengt, dispersed,
 scattered
der Verstand, sense,
 understanding
verständig, sensible
das Verständnis, understanding
verständnislos,
 uncomprehending
verstärken, increase
verstehen, s., understand,
 know how to; sich –, get on
 with one another
die Verstimmung, ill-feeling
verstört, confused, disturbed,
 troubled
verstoßen, s., reject, repudiate
verstreichen, s., elapse
verstrickt, involved
verstummen, become silent
der Versuch (-e), attempt
die Versuchung, temptation
verteidigen, defend
der Verteidiger (-), defender
die Vertiefung, depression,
 indentation
vertragen, s., tolerate; sich –,
 get on (well) with
das Vertrauen, trust
vertrauenswürdig, trust-
 worthy, reliable
der Verunglückte (see 29), victim
 (of accident)

veruntreuen, embezzle
verursachen, cause
vervielfachen, duplicate
die Verwaltung, administration
verwandeln, transform;
   sich –in, turn into
der Verwandte (see 29), relative
verwaschen, vague, 'wishy-
   washy'
verwechseln, confuse
verwehren, hinder
verwenden, irr., employ,
   apply
die Verwendung, use, application
die Verwirklichung, realization
verwirren, confuse
die Verwirrung, confusion
verwunderlich, astonishing
verzaubern, bewitch
verzichten (auf), forgo
verzieren, adorn, decorate
verzogen, distorted, twisted
   out of shape
verzögern, delay
die Verzögerung, delay
die Verzweiflung, despair
das Vieh, cattle
vielbedeutend, very significant
vielerlei, diverse, various
vielfach, frequently
vielmehr, rather
die Vielseitigkeit, many-sidedness
vielversprechend, very
   promising
vierstöckig, four-storied
der Volksgenosse (-n, -n), citizen
voll, full (of); thick
vollauf, fully
vollenden, complete,
   accomplish
vollgelaufen, filled to the brim
vollgültig, unexceptionable,
   perfect
völlig, complete(ly)
vollkleben, stick on all over,
   cover
vollkommen, completely
die Vollkommenheit, perfection
vollpfropfen, cram
vollschenken, fill up
das Vollzugsorgan (-e), executive
   organ
   von: – wegen (F.), because of
   vonstatten: – gehen, proceed
der Vorausfahrende (see 29),
   driver in front

voraussichtlich, probably
vorbereiten, prepare
vordem, previously
der Vordermann (¨er), driver in
   front
vorenthalten, s., withhold
vorerst, for the time being
vorfinden, s., come upon, find
der Vorgang (¨e), process
das Vorhandensein, presence
der Vorhang (¨e), curtain
vorher, before, previously
vorhergehend, preceding
vorhin, a short time ago
vorkommen, s., seem
vorleben, offer as an example
vorlegen, submit sth. to s.o.
der Vormann (¨er), man in front
vorne, in front
vornherein: von –, from the
   outset
das Vorrecht (-e), privilege
vorschieben, s., push in front
vorschlagen, s., suggest
vorsichtig, cautious(ly)
die Vorstadt (¨e), suburb
sich vorstellen, imagine
die Vorstellung, mental image,
   idea
der Vorteil (-e), advantage
der Vortrag (¨e), lecture
die Vortrefflichkeit, excellence
vorüber, past
der Vorübergehende (see 29),
   passer-by
die Vorverlegung, lowering
vorwärts, forwards
das Vorwärtskommen, advance
vorwerfen, s., reproach
vorwiegend, predominantly
die Vorzüge (m. pl.), good
   qualities
vorzüglich, excellent
vulkanisch, volcanic

W

die Waage, weighing-machine
waagerecht, horizontal(ly)
wach, awake
wachen, be on guard
wachsen, s., grow
wächsern, waxen
das Wachslichtchen (-), tiny wax
   candle, taper
das Wachstum, growth
der Wächter (-), watchman, guard

der **Waffengefährte** (-n, -n),
comrade in arms
wagen, risk, dare
das **Wagnis** (-se), risk
wählen, choose
die **Wählscheibe,** telephone-dial;
die **- bewegen,** dial
der **Wahnbegriff** (-e), delusion
wähnen, think, imagine;
sich -, fancy o.s.
wahnsinnig, mad
die **Wahrhaftigkeit,** truthfulness
die **Wahrheit,** truth; **in -,**
actually
wahrlich, truly
wahrnehmen, *s.,* perceive,
observe
die **Walderdbeere,** wild
strawberry
walten: - lassen, give free
rein to
wandern, go walk
die **Wanderung,** walk
die **Wandlung,** transformation
die **Wange,** cheek
das **Wappenschild** (-er),
escutcheon
die **Warnfarbe,** warning colour/
signal
die **Warnfärbung,** warning
colouration
was, what; something; how;
why; **- alles,** all the things
that
die **Wäsche,** laundry, washing
das **Waschmittel** (-), detergent
die **Wasserblase,** (water-) bubble
das **Wasserstoff,** hydrogen
webend, active, astir
der **Wechsel** (-), change
wechseln, exchange, change;
- über, move across
wecken, wake, awake
sich wegkehren, turn away
weh: - um, alas for; **- tun,**
hurt
sich wehren (gegen), resist
das **Weib** (-er), woman
weiblich, womanly
weichen, *s.,* give way to; leave
die **Weichheit,** mellowness
weilen, sojourn, stay, linger
der **Weise** (*see 29*), sage,
philosopher
die **Weise,** way(s)
weißleuchtend, gleaming

white
weit, far, wide
weiter, further, on; **immer -,**
on and on; **- bringen,**
advance
weiterarbeiten, go on working
weitergeben, *s.,* pass on
weiterhin, furthermore
das **Weiterleben,** survival
welk, languid
die **Welle,** wave, ripple
das **Wellenband** (¨er), band of
waves
die **Welt,** world
das **Weltall,** universe
weltentrückt, secluded
weltpolitisch: - informiert,
well up in world politics
wenden, *irr.,* turn; **sich -,**
turn (*intr.*)
der **Wendepunkt** (-e), turning-
point
ein wenig, for a bit
wer, he who
das **Werk** (-e), job; workshop
die **Werkstatt** (¨en), workshop
der **Wermut,** wormwood; (*fig.*)
gall
wert, esteemed
der **Wert** (-e), worth
wertlos, worthless
die **Wertskala,** scale of values
wertvoll, valuable
das **Wesen** (-), essence, nature,
character; being, creature
wesentlich, substantially
die **Weste,** waistcoat
der **Widder** (-), ram
die **Widerstandskraft,** power of
resistance
widerstreben (D), resist
sich widmen, devote o.s.; mark
(opponent)
wie, like, as though; **wie ...**
auch, however (much)
wieder, again; **immer -,**
again and again
sich wiederfinden, *s.,* regain
die **Wiedergabe,** reproduction
wiederum, in (their) turn
die **Wiese,** meadow
die **Wildgans** (¨e), wild goose
die **Willkür,** arbitrariness
sich winden, *s.,* writhe, wind
die **Windstille,** lull
winken, beckon

der Wipfel (-), treetop
das Wirbeltier (-e), vertebrate
animal
wirken (auf), have an effect
(on), affect
die Wirksamkeit, effectiveness
die Wirkung, effect
wirkungsvoll, effective
die Wirtschaft, (the) economy,
business world; industry and
commerce
wirtschaftlich, economic,
economical(ly)
wirtschaftswissenschaftlich,
economic
das Wissen, knowledge
der Wissenschaftler (-), scholar,
scientist
wissenschaftlich, scholarly,
scientific
der Witz (-e), witticism
witzig, witty, wittily,
clever(ly)
wogegen, whereas
wohl, certainly, probably; –
oder übel, willy-nilly
die Wohlfahrt, welfare, weal
der Wohlklang, euphony
die Wohnung, house; (pl.)
accommodation
wollen, irr., want, demand;
see 67(g)
das Wort (-e & ⁼er), word,
language
der Wortausdruck (⁼e), verbal
expression
wozu, to/for what purpose
die Wunde, wound
das Wunder (-), miracle, wonder
wunderlich, strange, queer
sich wundern, imp., be surprised
der Wunsch (⁼e), wish
die Würde, dignity
die Wurst (⁼e), sausage
wurstig, apathetic

Z
die Zahl, figure, number
zählen (zu), count (among)
zahllos, countless
zahm, tame
zähmen, curb
zart, tender, delicate
zärtlich, fondly
die Zauberei, witchcraft
der Zauberer (-), sorcerer

das Zeichen (-), sign
zeigen, show, point; sich –,
show o.s.
der Zeiger (-), (hour-)hand
die Zeile, line, row
der Zeisig (-e), siskin
die Zeit, time, age; zur –, at the
moment
das Zeitalter (-), age
die Zelle, cell
die Zensur, mark(s); school report
zerbrechen, s., break, shatter
zerfetzt, lacerated
zersplittern, break up
zerstören, destroy
die Zerstörung, destruction
zerstreuen, dispel
zeugen (von), be evidence
(of), show
das Zeugnis (-se), testimonial
ziehen, s., draw, move; an der
Nase –, lead by the nose
das Ziel (-e), goal, aim
zielen, take aim
ziemlich, fairly
zierlich, dainty
der Zigarettenstummel (-),
cigarette-end, stub
zimmerrein, house-trained
das Zitat (-e), quotation
zittern, tremble
zögernd, hesitatingly
der Zoll (-), inch
der Zoll (⁼e), duty, tariff
der Zorn, anger
züchten, cultivate; arouse,
generate
das Zückchen (-), little twitch
zucken, flash
zücken, pull out
zudem, moreover
zufällig, by chance
das Zufällige (see 29), the
contingent
die Zuflucht, refuge
zufrieden, satisfied
der Zug (⁼e), feature, trait,
characteristic; stroke
der Zugang (⁼e), access
zugeben, s., admit
zugehen, s., come about
zugekehrt, turned to(wards)
zugewandt, turned to(wards)
zugleich, at the same time
zugrundeliegend, underlying
zuhören, listen to

die Zukunft, future
zuletzt, in the end
zumuten, expect of
zunächst, at first
zünden, set alight
zunehmen, *s.* **(um),** increase (by)
zunehmend, increasing
zupacken, take effect
zurück, behind; back
zurückbleiben, *s.*, be left
zurückführen (auf), trace back (to), attribute (to)
zurückgestaut, pent up, dammed up
zurückkehren, return
zurückprallen, recoil
zurückstehen, *s.*, **(hinter),** be below (in standard)
zurücktreten, *s.*, recede
der Zusammenhalt, cohesion
das Zusammenleben, living together
das Zusammensein, gathering
der Zustand (¨-e), state
zutreffen, *s.* **(für),** be true (of)
die Zuverlässigkeit, certainty
der Zuwachs, growth
zuweilen, occasional(ly)
zuweisen, *s.*, assign
der Zwang, compulsion
zwar, it is true; **und –,** and in fact
der Zweck (-e), purpose
die Zweckmäßigkeit, functionalism, conformity with ends
der Zweifel (-), doubt
zweifelhaft, uncertain
der Zweig (-e), branch; side, department (of school)
das Zwielicht, half-light

Vocabulary

English–German

NOTES 1 The plural ending -(e)n of feminine nouns is not indicated.
2 Figures refer to the paragraphs of Part One.
3 Proper nouns not listed will be found in Part One, paragraph 17.

a

aback: taken —, verdutzt
abandoned, stehengelassen, im Stich gelassen
ability, Fähigkeit, f.
able, fähig; to be — to, vermögen, irr., können, irr.
about, ungefähr, etwa
above, oberhalb; — all, vor allem; — all things, mehr noch als alles andere; from —, von oben her
abreast, längsseits
abroad, im Ausland, n.
to abrogate, kündigen
absence, Abwesenheit, f., Fehlen, n.
absent, abwesend; (= absent-minded), zerstreut
absolute, absolut
absolutism, Absolutismus, m.
abstraction, Zerstreutheit, f.
to abuse, beleidigen
accent, Akzent (-e), m.
to accept, see 84
acceptance, Annahme, f.
accident: by —, aus Versehen, n.
to accompany, begleiten
to accomplish, erfüllen
accordance: in — with, in Übereinstimmung mit
accurately, mit großer Genauigkeit
to accuse, an-klagen
accustomed (to), gewöhnt (an) (A)
ache: -s and pains, Leiden und Schmerzen
to achieve, erreichen
acquaintance, Bekanntschaft, f.
acquainted, bekannt; become — with, kennen-lernen
to acquiesce (in), sich ab-finden, s. (mit)

to acquire, erwerben, s.
across, über; right —, quer über
to act, handeln
action, Handlung, f.; Handeln, n.
active(ly), tätig
activity, Tätigkeit, f.
actual (= real), wirklich; (= strictly speaking), eigentlich
to add, hinzu-fügen; (= include), auf-nehmen, s. (in) (A)
to adhere (to), beharren (auf) (D)
adjunct, Begleiterscheinung, f.
to administer to, fördern
admiration, Bewunderung, f.
admirer, Verehrer (-), m.
to admit, zu-geben, s.
to adopt, an-nehmen, s.
to adore, vergöttern
to advance, *vorwärts-gehen, s.
advancement, Förderung, f.
advancing, herandringend
advantage, Vorteil (-e), m.
adventure, Abenteuer (-), n.
adversary, Gegner (-), m.
advertisement, Werbeanzeige, f.; recruiting —, militärische Werbeanzeige
advertising, Reklame, f., Werbung, f.
advice, Rat, m., Ratschlag (-e), m.
to advise, beraten, s., raten (AD)
aeroplane, Flugzeug (-e), n.
affair, Angelegenheit, f.
to affect, stark beeinflussen
affected, erheuchelt
affection, Zuneigung, f.; —s, Zärtlichkeitsgefühl, n.
afflicted, belastet
to afford, liefern; (s.th. expensive), sich (D) leisten
afraid: be — of, sich fürchten vor (D), Angst haben vor (D)
afresh, aufs neue
afternoon, Nachmittag (-e), m.
again, wieder

363

age, Alter, *n.*; Zeitalter, *n.*, for
untold **—s,** seit undenklichen
Zeiten
agitated, aufgeregt
ago, vor (D)
to agree, bei-stimmen (D), zu-stimmen
agriculture, Landwirtschaft, *f.*
aim, Ziel (-e), *n.*
air, Luft (ːe), *f.*
alas, leider
alien, fremd
alike, wie
alive: **— with,** mit . . . Leben
erfüllt; **newly —,** neubelebt
all, ganz, alles
to allay, beschwichtigen
alleviation, Linderung, *f.*
alliance, Bündnis (-se), *n.*
to allow, lassen, *s.*
allowance: **make — for,** Nachsicht haben mit
alloy, Zusatz (ːe), *m.*
almost, beinahe; ja
alone, allein
along, an
already, schon; schon früher einmal
also, auch
to alter, ändern
alternately, abwechselnd
always, immer, stets
amazed, erstaunt
amazing(ly), erstaunlich
ambitious, ehrgeizig
amiss: take **—,** übel-nehmen, *s.*
among, inmitten (G)
to amount (to), *hinaus-laufen, *s.*
(auf) (A); (= **tantamount to),**
*gleich-kommen, *s.* (D)
amphitheatre, Amphitheater (-), *n.*
amusement, Unterhaltung, *f.*
amusing, amüsant
anarchist, Anarchist (-en, -en), *m.*
anchored, (fest-) verankert
ancient, antik
angry, wütend, zornig
animal, Tier (-e), *n.*
ankle, Fußknöchel (-), *m.*
to annoy, ärgern
another, noch einer; **to one —,**
zueinander
answer, Antwort, *f.*
to answer, antworten, *see 74, 79(d)*
antiquated, veraltet
antiquities, Altertümer, *n. pl.*
anxious, bekümmert

any, irgendein, jeder, jedweder,
welcher; **— one,** jemand
anyhow, ohnehin
anything, etwas; **if —,** eher
anywhere, irgendwo; **— else,**
woanders
apart: **— from,** abgesehen von
aphorism, Aphoris-mus (-men), *m.*
to apologise, sich entschuldigen
apparently, anscheinend
apparition, Gespenst (-er), *n.*
to appear, *erscheinen, *s.*; (= **seem),**
scheinen, *s.*
appearance, *see 84*
to applaud, Beifall klatschen
applicable to, anwendbar auf (A)
applied, angewandt
appointment, Verabredung, *f.*
to apprehend, erfassen
to approach, sich nähern (D); (a
matter), an-gehen, *s.*
appropriate to, gemäß
to approve, gut-heißen, *s.*; **— of,**
durchaus für . . . *sein; **not — of,**
entschieden gegen . . . *sein
aquatic, *see race*
arch, Bogen (ː), *m.*
architecture: **style of —,** Baustil
(-e), *m.*
argument, Auseinandersetzung, *f.*;
Meinungsverschiedenheit, *f.*;
Argument (-e), *n.*
to arise, *entspringen, *s.*; *entstehen
arm, *see 84*
Armada, die Armada
armaments, Waffen, *f. pl.*
armchair, Sessel (-), *m.*
army, Heer (-e), *n.*, Armee, *f.*
to arrange, ein-richten, wollen;
(= **put in order),** ordnen
to arrest, verhaften
arrival, Ankunft (ːe), *f.*
to arrive, *an-kommen, *s.*
art, Kunst (ːe), *f.*
article, Artikel (-), *m.*
artificial, künstlich
artist, Künstler (-), *m.*
as: **— for (me),** was (mich) (an)be-
trifft; **— if,** als ob; **— it were,**
gleichsam; *see 9(a)*
to ascend, *auf-steigen, *s.*
ashes, Asche, *f. sing.*
aside, zur Seite
to ask, *see 84*
asphalt, Asphalt (-e), *m.*; *(adj.)*
asphaltiert

aspiring, aufstrebend
assertion, Behauptung, f.
assiduity, Beharrlichkeit, f.
assistant, Gehilfe (-n, -n), m.;
—s, Hilfskräfte, f. pl.
associated, verbunden
association, Verbindung, f.
to assume, an-nehmen, s.
assurance, Zuversicht, f.
to assure, versichern
astern, achtern
astonished, erstaunt
atmosphere, Luft (¨e), f., Atmosphäre, f.
atom, Atom (-e), n.
attempt, Versuch (-e), m.
attention, Aufmerksamkeit, f.
attentively, aufmerksam
attitude, Haltung, f.
attractive, anziehend
audience, Zuhörerschaft, f.
to augment, vermehren
august, erhaben
author, Autor (-en), m., Schriftsteller (-), m.
automatically, automatisch
to avail: not —, zu nichts nütze *sein
available, vorhanden
to avoid, vermeiden, s.
to awake, erwecken
aware: be — of, sich (D) bewußt
*sein (G)
away, weg, fort; (= distant), entfernt; (= absent), abwesend
awe, Ehrfurcht, f.
to awe, ein-schüchtern
awfully, schrecklich
awhile, eine Weile

b

baby, Baby (-s), n.
back, zurück; be —, *zurück-
kommen, s.
back, Rücken (-), m.; (of chair),
Rückenlehne, f.; (of house),
Rückseite, f.
background, Hintergrund (¨e), m.
bad(ly), schlecht
baggage, Gepäck, n.
balcony, Balkon (-e & -s), m.
bamboo, Bambus, m.
to bandage, verbinden, s.
to bang: — up at, tosend entgegen-
schlagen, s.; — shut, zu-werfen, s.
bank (of river), Ufer (-), n.; (of
flowers), Terrasse, f.

barbarism, Barbarei, f.
barefooted, barfüßig
bargain, ein guter Handel
barrier, Schranke, f.
based: be — on, beruhen auf (D)
bath, Bad (¨er), n.; Badewanne, f.
to bathe, waschen, s.; baden
bathing costume, Badeanzug (¨e),
m.
bathroom, Badezimmer (-), n.
battle (of), Schlacht (bei), f.
battlement, Zinne, f.
to be, see 84
to bear, in sich bergen, s.; ertragen, s.
bearable, erträglich
beard, Bart (¨e), m.
bearded, bärtig
beast, Tier (-e), n.
to beat, schlagen, s.; — the air,
Streiche in die Luft tun, s.
beautiful(ly), schön, wunderschön,
herrlich
beauty, Schönheit, f.
to beckon, winken, zu-winken (D)
to become, *werden, irr.
bed, Bett (-en), n.
beechwood, Buchenwald (¨er), m.
beekeeping, Bienenzucht, f.
beg: I — your pardon, es tut mir
leid
beggar, Bettler (-), m.
to begin, beginnen, s.
beginning, Beginn (-e), m., Anfang
(¨e), m.; at the —, zu Anbeginn
on behalf of, zugunsten (G)
to behave, see 84
behaviour, see 84
to behold, zu sehen bekommen, s.,
sehen, s.
being, Wesen (-), n.
to believe, glauben
bell, Glocke, f.
to belong, see 84
belt, Gürtel (-), m.
bend, Biegung, f.
to bend (over), sich beugen (über)
benediction, Segensspruch (¨e), m.
benevolent, wohlwollend
bent, gebeugt
besides, außerdem
better, lieber; — off, besser dran
between: in —, dazwischenliegend
beyond, darüber hinaus; (= behind it), dahinter; (= behind),
hinter
bigoted, fanatisch, bigott

big town, Großstadt (∺e), *f.*
biguns, Erwachsene, *pl. (see 29)*
bill, Rechnung, *f.*
to bind, fesseln, binden, *s.*
biography, Biographie, *f.*
bird, Vogel (∺), *m.*
birth, Geburtswehen, *f. pl.*
birthday, Geburtstag (-e), *m.*
birthplace, Geburtsort (-e), *m.*
bitter, bitter
bivouac, Biwak (-e), *n.*
black, schwarz
blackguard, Schurke (-n, -n), *m.*,
    Halunke (-n, -n), *m.*
blade: — of grass, Grashalm (-e),
    m.
to blame, einem den Vorwurf machen
bland, sanft
blended, verschmolzen
blessing, Segen (-, *or* Segnungen),
    m.
blind, blind
blindness, Blindheit, *f.*
blood, Blut, *n.*; — -red, blutrot
blow, Schlag (∺e), *m.*
to blow, blasen, *s.*; — up, sprengen
    (*tr.*); *hoch-gehen (*intr.*)
blue, blau; Blau, *n.*
blunt, stumpf
to blush, *erröten
boarder, Pensionär (-e), *m.*
boarding house, Pension, *f.*; —
    system, Internatssystem, *n.*
to boast, sich rühmen, stolz *sein
boat, Boot (-e), *n.*
boat-house, Bootshaus (∺er), *n.*
body, Körper (-), *m.*; — of men,
    Gruppe, *f.*; — of persons,
    Menge Leute, *pl.*
bold(ly), kühn
bolt, Riegel (-), *m.*
bomb, Bombe, *f.*
bond, Pakt (-e), *m.*
bone, Knochen (-), *m.*
book, Buch (∺er), *n.*
bookie, Buchmacher (-), *m.*
bookseller, Buchhändler (-), *m.*
boot, Stiefel (-), *m.*
bore, lästiger Kerl
bored, gelangweilt
boring, langweilig
born, geboren
to borrow, borgen
botanising, Botanisieren, *n.*
both, beide; — . . . and, sowohl . . .
    wie/als (auch)

bottle, Flasche, *f.*
bottom (of stairs), Fuß (∺e), *m.*;
    valley —, Talgrund (∺e), *m.*
bough, Ast (∺e), *m.*
boulder, Geröllblock (∺e), *m.*
to bounce up, *zurück-springen, *s.*
bound, Satz (∺e), *m.*
boundary, Grenze, *f.*
bounds, Grenzen, *f. pl.*
to bow, sich verbeugen
bowl, Schale, *f.*
boy, Junge (-n, -n), *m.*; old —! alter
    Knabe!
boyish, jungenhaft
brace, Paar (-e), *n.*
brains, Kopf (∺e), *m.*; (= clever-
    ness), Verstand, *m.*; (= clever
    people), Intellektuelle, *pl. (see 29)*
brass, Messing, *n.*
brawl, Schlägerei, *f.*
bread, Brot (-e), *n.*
to break, brechen, *s*, zerbrechen;
    (= interrupt), unterbrechen; —
    into (laughter), *aus-brechen
breakfast, Frühstück (-e), *n.*
to breakfast, das Frühstück essen, *s.*,
    frühstücken
breast, Brust (∺e), *f.*
breath, Atemzug (∺e), *m.*
breathless, atemberaubend
breeding animals, Tierzucht, *f.*
brick, Backstein (-e), *m.*
to brick in, vermauern
bridge, Brücke, *f.*; (= captain's
    —), Kommandobrücke, *f.*
to bring, bringen, *irr.*, führen, mit-
    bringen, mit-nehmen, *s.*; — to
    bear on, zu-wenden, *irr.* (D)
brioche, Brioche (-s), *f.*
brisk: become —, sich beleben
broadly, weit
broken, gebrochen; — English,
    gebrochen Englisch
brother, Bruder (∺), *m.*
brow (of hill), Vorsprung (∺e), *m.*
brown, braun
to brush, streifen
buckle, Schnalle, *f.*
to build, bauen
building, Gebäude (-), *n.*
bulk, Massiv (-e), *n.*
bullet, Kugel, *f.*
to bully, tyrannisieren
bunk, Schwindel, *m.*
bush, Gebüsch (-e), *n.*
busy, beschäftigt

butler, Diener (-), *m.*
to buy, kaufen, erkaufen

C

cab, Droschke, *f.*
cake, Kuchen (-), *m.*
to call (= term, name), nennen, *irr.*;
  (= summon), an-rufen, *s.*; —
  on, besuchen
calm, ruhig
to calm, beruhigen
calmly, friedlich, ruhig
camel, Kamel (-e), *n.*
capable, fähig
cape, Cape (-s), *n.*, Pelerine, *f.*
capital, Hauptstadt (⸚e), *f.*
captain, Kapitän (-e), *m.*
car, Auto (-s), *n.*, Wagen (-), *m.*
card, Karte, *f.*
cardboard box, Pappschachtel, *f.*
care (=precaution), Vorsorge, *f.*
to care (for s.th.), Lust zu etwas
  haben
career, Karriere, *f.*
careful, vorsichtig; (= thrifty),
  sparsam
carefully, sorgfältig
carriage, Abteil (-e), *n.*
to carry, tragen, *s.*; — down, hinun-
  ter-schiffen; — with it, mit sich
  bringen, *irr.*; — through, hinweg-
  tragen über
cart, Fuhrwerk (-e), *n.*
to carve, zerlegen
case, see *84*
to cast, werfen, *s.*; (in Greek costume), kleiden in (A)
caste, Kastenwesen, *n.*
castle, Schloß (⸚(ss)er), *n.*
casual, zufällig
cat, Katze, *f.*; — -call, Auspfeifen,
  n.
to catch, see *84*
cathedral, Dom (-e), *m.*
Catholic, katholisch
cause: the good —, die gute
  Sache
cautious, vorsichtig
cavernous, höhlenartig
to cease, auf-hören
to celebrate, feiern
celebration, Feier, *f.*
centre, Mitte, *f.*
to centre, sich konzentrieren
century, Jahrhundert (-e), *n.*

cereals, Getreide, *n. sing.*
ceremony, Feier, *f.*
certain, gewiß
certainly, sicherlich; ganz sicher;
  bestimmt
chair, Stuhl (⸚e), *m.*; arm—,
  Sessel (-), *m.*
to champion, sich ein-setzen für
chance, Zufall (⸚e), *m.*; by —,
  zufällig
change, Veränderung, *f.*; — of
  site, Ortswechsel (-), *m.*
to change, wechseln; (= alter),
  ändern; (clothes), sich um-
  ziehen, *s.*
chapter, Kapitel (-), *n.*
character, Charakter (-e), *m.*
characteristic, Hauptmerkmal (-e),
  n., Eigentümlichkeit, *f.*
charm, Reiz (-e), *m.*
charming, entzückend
charred, verkohlt
chasm, Abgrund (⸚e), *m.*, Kluft
  (⸚e), *f.*
to chatter, schwatzen; — on, weiter
  schwatzen
cheap, billig
check, Kontrolle, *f.*
to check, im Zaume halten, *s.*; —
  mate, matt-setzen
cheerfully, heiter
cheery, freundlich
cheese, Käse (-), *m.*
cheque, Scheck (-s), *m.*; — book,
  Scheckbuch (⸚er), *n.*
chess, Schach, *n.*; — board,
  Schachbrett (-er), *n.*
chief, Haupt-
child, Kind (-er), *n.*; —'s play, ein
  Kinderspiel, *n.*
childhood, Kindheit, *f.*
chilly, kalt
chime of bells, Glockengeläute, *n.*
chimney, Schornstein (-e), *m.*
chocolate: block —, Tafelschoko-
  lade, *f.*
choice, auserlesen
choice, Wahl, *f.*
to choose, wählen; (= want), wollen
Christmas : — carol, Weihnachtslied (-er), *n.*; —tree, Weihnachts-
  baum (⸚e), *m.*
church, Kirche, *f.*
churl, Flegel (-), *m.*
cigar, Zigarre, *f.*
cigarette, Zigarette, *f.*

cinders, verkohlte Reste, *m. pl.*
cinema, Kino (-s), *n.*
circle, Kreis (-e), *m.*; — of light,
Lichtkreis; Lichtkegel (-), *m.*
to circle, sich drehen
circumstance, Umstand (¨e), *m.*
citizen, Bürger (-), *m.*, Staatsbürger
city, Stadt (¨e), *f.*; great —,
Großstadt
civil, höflich; — service, Staats-
dienst, *m.*
civilisation, Kultur, *f.*; Zivilisation, *f.*
claim, Anspruch (¨e), *m.*
clash, Aufeinanderprallen, *n.*
class, Klasse, *f.*
classical, klassisch
clean, rein, sauber
clear, klar; —ly, ganz augenscheinlich
to clear, sich auf-heitern
clearing, Lichtung, *f.*
clearing-house, Abrechnungshaus
(¨er), *n.*
clerk, der Angestellte (*see* 29)
clever, klug
cleverness, Klugheit, *f.*
cliff, Klippe, *f.*, Steilhang (¨e),
m., Felswand (¨e), *f.*; — plinth,
Felsenfußplatte, *f.*
to cling, sich klammern, sich an-
klammern
cloak, Mantel (¨), *m.*
clock, Uhr, *f.*
close, dicht, dicht neben; — to it,
dicht daneben; — to, nahe an
to close, schließen, *s.*
closely, eng
cloth, Tuch (¨er), *n.*
to clothe, kleiden
clothes, Kleider, *n. pl.*
cloud, Wolke, *f.*
clown, Clown (-s), *m.*
to cluster: — round, umdrängen
coal, Kohle, *f.*
coat, Mantel (¨), *m.*
cock! altes Haus!
coffee, Kaffee, *m.*
coin, Münze, *f.*
to coincide, identisch *sein, irr.*
cold, kalt
cold, Kälte, *f.*
collar-bone, Schlüsselbein (-e), *n.*
to collect, sammeln
collection, Sammlung, *f.*
collective, Kollektiv-

college, College (-s), *n.*
colonist, Kolonist (-en, -en), *m.*
colour, Farbe, *f.*
combined, zusammengefaßt
to come, *kommen, *s.*; (of night),
*herein-brechen, *s.*; — across,
kennen-lernen; — at *s.b.*, auf
einen zugestürzt *kommen;
back, *zurück-kommen; —
down, *herunter-kommen; —
from, *entspringen (*s.*) aus; —
in, *herein-kommen; (of train),
ein-fahren, *s.*; — off it, damit
auf-hören; — one's way, einem
über den Weg *laufen, *s.*; — to
(do *s.th.*), an-fangen, *s.*; — to
doing *s.th.*, dazu *kommen,
etwas zu tun; — up (close),
*herauf-kommen, *heran-kom-
men; — upon (= meet), treffen,
s., (= run into), *stoßen (*s.*)
auf (A); (of night), *herein-
brechen (*s.*) über (A)
comedian, Komiker (-), *m.*
comfort, Trost, *m.*
comfortable, beruhigend
coming, Kommen, *n.*
command, *see* 84
to command, *see* 84
to commence, beginnen, *s.*
to commit (a crime), begehen, *s.*;
— (to one's charge), übergeben
commode, Kommode, *f.*
common: have in — with,
(etwas) gemein haben mit
commonplace, gewöhnlich, banal
communion, enge Verbindung, *f.*
community, Gesellschaft, *f.*, Gemeinschaft, *f.*, Staatsgemeinschaft
companion, Begleiter (-), *m.*
comparative, vergleichend
to compare, vergleichen, *s.*
compared: — with, im Vergleich
zu
comparison: in — with, im
Vergleich zu
compartment (railway), Abteil
(-e), *n.*
to compel, zwingen, *s.*
to compete, konkurrieren
to complain, sich beklagen
complete(ly), vollständig, völlig
complicated, verwickelt, kompliziert
to compose, ab-fassen
composer, Komponist (-en, -en), *m.*

composition, Zusammensetzung, *f.*
to compound, zusammen-setzen
comprehension, Auffassungsvermögen, *n.*
compromise, Kompromiß (-(ss)e), *m.*
compulsory: — education, allgemeine Schulpflicht, *f.*
to conceive, auf-fassen, sich (D) vorstellen
to concentrate (on), sich konzentrieren (auf) (A)
to concern: it does not — me, es geht mich nichts an
concerned: — with, bedacht auf (A); be — with, sich befassen mit
concerning, über (A)
concert, Konzert (-e), *n.*; — -hall, Konzertsaal (-säle), *m.*
conciliation, Versöhnung, *f.*
to conclude, schließen, *s.*
conclusion, Schlußfolgerung, *f.*
concourse, Zudrang, *m.*
to condemn, verurteilen
condition (= stipulation), Bedingung, *f.*; (= state), Zustand (-̈e), *m.*; (= circumstance), Umstand (-̈e), *m.*; (= prerequisite), Vorbedingung, *f.*
to conduct, führen, leisten
confederation, Staatenbund (-̈e), *m.*
to confess, ein-gestehen, *s.*, gestehen
confidence, Vertrauen, *n.*
confident, zuversichtlich
to confine, ein-schließen, *s.*
conflicting, gegensätzlich
to confront, gegenüber-stehen, *s.*, sich gegenüber-sehen, *s.*
confused, verworren
confusion, Verwirrung, *f.*
congested, überfüllt
congregation, Gemeinde, *f.*
to connect, verbinden, *s.*
to conquer, erobern
conqueror, Eroberer (-), *m.*
conscientious, gewissenhaft
conscious, bewußt; be — of, sich (D) bewußt *sein (G)
consent, Zustimmung, *f.*
to consent, ein-willigen
consequence, Folge, *f.*
consider, in Betracht ziehen, *s.*; erwägen, *s.*; betrachten
considerable, beträchtlich

consistent, konsequent; (= compatible), miteinander verträglich
consolation, Trost, *m.*
to consolidate, sicher-stellen
consonant, Konsonant (-en, -en) *m.*
conspirator, Verschwörer (-), *m.*
constitutionally, verfassungsmäßig
contact: be in —, in Berührung stehen, *s.*
to contain, enthalten, *s.*
contempt, Verachtung, *f.*
content, zufrieden
to continue, fort-fahren, *s.*; fortsetzen (*tr.*)
continuously, ununterbrochen
contrary: to the —, gegensätzlich; — to, entgegen (D)
to contribute, bei-tragen, *s.*
contusion, Quetschung, *f.*
convention, Konvention, *f.*
conviction, Überzeugung, *f.*
convinced, überzeugt
cook, Köchin (-nen), *f.*
cool, kühl; keep —, einen kühlen Kopf behalten, *s.*
to co-operate, zusammen-arbeiten
to cope (with), fertig *werden (mit)
copper, Kupfer, *n.*
copy, Nummer, *f.*
corner, Ecke, *f.*
correctness, Richtigkeit, *f.*
to correspond, entsprechen, *s.*
cost: to our —, zu unserem Schaden
to cost, kosten
costume, Gewand (-̈er), *n.*
countenance, Gesicht (-er), *n.*; Gesichtsausdruck (-̈e), *m.*
countless, unzählig
country, Land (-̈er), *n.*; (= motherland), Vaterland, *n.*; (= countryside), Landschaft, *f.*; — house, Landsitz (-e), *m.*
countryman, Landmann (-leute), *m.*; (= fellow —), Landsmann
couple, Paar (-e), *n.*
courage, Mut, *m.*
of course, natürlich
courtesy, Höflichkeit, *f.*
cousin, Kusine, *f.*, Vetter (-n), *m.*; first —, Kusine
to cover, bedecken; — o.s., sich zu-decken
covering, Decke, *f.*
to covet, begehren

cow, Kuh (⸚e), *f.*; — bell, Kuhglocke, *f.*
craftsman, Handwerker (-), *m.*
cranny, Riß (-(ss)e), *m.*, Ritze, *f.*
crash, Krachen, *n.*
to crash down, *ab-stürzen
to crave for, dringend verlangen nach
creation, Schöpfung, *f.*
creative, schöpferisch; — power,
Schöpfungskraft, *f.*
crew, Mannschaft, *f.*
cricketer, Kricketspieler (-), *m.*
crime, Verbrechen (-), *n.*
crippled, verkrüppelt
criterion, Kriteri-um (-en), *n.*
critic, Kritiker (-), *m.*
criticism, Kritik, *f.*
crookedly, krumme Wege (*gehen)
to cross, *hinüber-gehen, *s.*; über-
schreiten, *s.*; (a place) to —,
zum Übergang
crowbar, Brecheisen (-), *n.*
crowd, Menge, *f.*
crowded, zusammengepfercht
crude, plump
cruel, grausam
to crumble, *zerbröckeln
cry, Ruf (-e), *m.*, Schrei (-e), *m.*
cultivated, bebaut
culture, Kultur, *f.*, Bildung, *f.*
cultured, gebildet
cunning, schlau
cup, Tasse, *f.*; (coffee-) —, Täß-
chen (-), *n.*
curable, heilbar
cure, Kur, *f.*
curious(ly), sonderbar
to curse, verfluchen
curtain, Vorhang (⸚e), *m.*; final —,
Schlußvorhang
to curve, sich wölben
cut, schneiden, *s.*; — off, ab-
schneiden; — down to,
beschränken auf (A)

d

daily, alltäglich
damp, feucht
dance, Tanz (⸚e), *m.*
to dance, tanzen
danger, Gefahr, *f.*
dangerous, gefährlich
to dare, wagen
dark, dunkel; Dunkel, *n.*
darkness, Dunkelheit, *f.*, Dunkel, *n.*

dart, Pfeil (-e), *m.*
to dart; *flitzen
daughter, Tochter (⸚), *f.*
day, Tag (-e), *m.*; some —,
(ein)mal; — -dream, Wach-
traum (⸚e), *m.*; — long, tagsüber;
one —, eines Tages
daybreak, Tagesanbruch, *m.*
daylight, Tagesanbruch, *m.*
dead, tot, erstorben; völlig
deadened, abgestumpft
deal: a great —, sehr viel; a good
—, eine ganze Menge
to deal with, sich befassen mit
dear, lieb, geliebt
death, Tod (-esfälle), *m.*
decay, Verfall, *m.*
to deceive, täuschen
decent, anständig
to decide, entscheiden, *s.* (über),
beschließen, *s.*
decided, bestimmt
decision, Entschluß (⸚(ss)e), *m.*;
make a —, einen Entschluß
fassen
decisive, entscheidend
to declare, erklären
to decline, ab-lehnen
to decorate, schmücken
decoratively, dekorativ
decorum, Anstand, *m.*
to deem, halten (*s.*) für
deep(ly), tief
defeat, Niederlage, *f.*
defective, fehlerhaft
to defend, verteidigen
defensive, Verteidigung, *f.*, Defensive, *f.*; (adj.) defensiv
deference, Hochachtung, *f.*
definitely, bestimmt
degree, Grad (-e), *m.*
deliberation: with —, langsam
delicate, zart
delight, Entzücken, *n.*; —s, Vergnügen, *n.*
to delight, entzücken
delightful, entzückend, reizend
delirium, Deliri-um (-en), *n.*
demand, Forderung, *f.*
to demand, fordern, verlangen; zu
wissen verlangen
democracy, Demokratie, *f.*
democratically, demokratisch
to demoralise, entmutigen
denial, Verneinung; (= rejection),
Ablehnung, *f.*

to denounce, öffentlich an-klagen
dense, dicht
to deny, leugnen; — s.b. s.th., einem
etwas versagen
departing (of sun), untergehend
to depend (on), ab-hängen, s. (von);
it all —s, es kommt darauf an
dependent on, angewiesen auf
(A)
depressed, deprimiert aussehend
depth, Tiefe, f.
derivative, nachschaffend
to derive, ab-leiten
to descend, *hinunter-steigen, s.
descendant, Nachkomme (-n, -n),
m.
descent, Hang (-̈e), m.
desert, Wüste, f.
design, Plan (-̈e), m.
desire, Wunsch (-̈e); — to know,
Wissensdrang, m.
to desire, sich (D) wünschen
desolate, trostlos, öde
despair, Verzweiflung, f.
to despair of, verzweifeln an (D)
despatch: — case, Aktentasche, f.
desperately, verzweifelt
despite: — that, trotzdem; — the
fact that, obwohl
to destine, bestimmen
to destroy, zerstören
detail, Einzelheit, f.
determined, (fest) entschlossen
to develop, sich entwickeln
development, Entwicklung, f.
devil, Teufel (-), m.
devoid of, ohne (A)
to devote, widmen (AD)
devoted, hingebungsvoll
dialogue, Dialog (-e), m.
diary, Tagebuch (-̈er), n.
to dictate, diktieren
dictionary, Wörterbuch (-̈er), n.
to die, *sterben, s.; (of light), *ver-
löschen, s.
to differ, sich unterscheiden, s.
difference, Unterschied (-e), m.;
(= quarrel), Wortstreit (-e), m.
different, verschieden, ander
difficult, schwer, schwierig
difficulty, Schwierigkeit, f.
diggings, Bude, f.
dignity, Würde, f.
dilapidated, verfallen
diligently, fleißig
dim, undeutlich

to diminish, vermindern
dinner, Abendessen (-), n.; —
party, Abendgesellschaft, f.
diplomacy, Diplomatie, f.
direction, Richtung, f.; —s, Aus-
künfte, f. pl., Anweisungen, f. pl.
directly, unmittelbar
dirty, schmutzig
disadvantage: place at a —,
benachteiligen
to disappear, *verschwinden, s.
disappointed (in), enttäuscht
(über) (A)
disapprobation, Mißbilligung, f.
disc, Scheibe, f.
to discharge, erfüllen
discipline, disziplinarische Maßnahmen, f. pl.
discontented, unzufrieden
discordant, unmelodisch
discourse, Rede, f.
to discover, entdecken, heraus-finden
discussion, Diskussion, f.
disembodied, körperlos
to disguise, verkleiden; (= conceal),
verhehlen
disinclination, Abneigung, f.
disinterested, unparteiisch, unei-
gennützig
dismal, trostlos
to dispel, zerstreuen
display (of), Entfaltung, f. (von)
to display, zeigen, zur Schau tragen, s.
to dispose, lenken
disruptive, zersetzend
distance, Ferne, f., Entfernung, f.;
(= interval), Abstand (-̈e), m.
distant, fern; — view, Fernsicht, f.
distaste: have no — for, nicht
verachten
distinction, Vornehmheit, f.
to distinguish, unterscheiden, s.
to distort, entstellen
distress, Kummer, m.; (=
wretchedness), Elend, n.
be distressed, sehr/tief bedauern
distressingly, auf beklemmende
• Weise
distrust, Mißtrauen, n.
to distrust, mißtrauen (D)
disturbance, see wave
to divide, trennen
divine, göttlich
to divine, ahnen
to do, machen, tun, s.; — without,
verzichten auf (A)

doctor, Arzt (ᵛe), *m.*; Doktor (-en), *m.*
doctrine, Lehre, *f.*
dog, Hund (-e), *m.*
doing: from their own —, aus eigener Schuld
doll, Puppe, *f.*
domain, Herrschaftsgebiet (-e), *n.*
dominant, vorherrschend
to dominate, beherrschen
door, Tür, *f.*; out of —s, im Freien
double: — rupture, Doppelbruch (ᵛe), *m.*; — sails, Doppelsegel, *n. sing.*
doubt: no —, zweifellos, ohne Zweifel
down, herab, herunter, hinunter; — below, dort unten
downfall, Sturz (ᵛe), *m.*
dozen, Dutzend (-e), *n.*
drama, Dram-a (-en), *n.*
dramatic, dramatisch
dramatist, Dramatiker (-), *m.*
draught, Zugluft (ᵛe), *f.*
to draw (= pull), ziehen, *s.*; (picture), zeichnen; (salary), beziehen, *s.*; — (admiration), erregen; — near, näher *kommen, *s.*; — (attention) to, lenken auf (A)
drawing-room, Salon (-s), *m.*
dread, Grauen, *n.*
dream, Traum (ᵛe), *m.*
dreary, öde; (of person), griesgrämig
dress, Kleid (-er), *n.*
to dress, sich an-ziehen, *s.*
dressed, angezogen, gekleidet; (hair), frisiert
dressing-gown, Schlafrock (ᵛe), *m.*
drift of hail, Hagelschauer (-), *m.*
to drift, *treiben, *s.*
drink, trinken, *s.*; — in, ein-saugen, *s. (or weak)*
to drive, *fahren, *s.*, treiben, *s.*; — off, *ab-fahren; — past, *vorbeifahren
driver, Autofahrer (-), *m.*
drop of water, Wassertropfen, (-), *m.*
to drop down, *herunter-fallen, *s.*
to drown, ertränken, *tr.*
drunk, betrunken
dry, ausgetrocknet
to dry, trocknen

due: give s.b. his —, einem Gerechtigkeit widerfahren lassen, *s.*; be — to s.b., einem gebühren
dull, langweilig
to dwell on, immer wieder betonen
dynastic, dynastisch

e

each, jeder; — other, einander
eager(ly), eifrig
early, früh — rising, Frühaufstehen, *n.*
to earn, verdienen
earth, Erde, *f.*
earthenware, Steingut, *n.*
earthly, irdisch
earthy, erdig
ease, Ungezwungenheit, *f.*
easier, müheloser
east, Osten, *m.*
easy, leicht
to eat, essen, *s.*
eaves, Dachrand, *m. sing.*
eccentricity, Ausgefallenheit, *f.*
echo, Echo (-s), *n.*; Widerhall (-e), *m.*
to echo, hallen
edge, Rand (ᵛer), *m.*; at the very —, hart am Rande
to educate, erziehen, *s.*
educated, gebildet
education, Erziehung, *f.*, Bildung, *f.*, Ausbildung, *f.*
educational, Erziehungs-
to efface, verwischen
effect, Wirkung, *f.*; have an enigmatic —, rätselhaft wirken
effective, wirkungsvoll
efficacy, Wirksamkeit, *f.*
efficiency, Tüchtigkeit, *f.*
effort, Anstrengung, *f.*, Bemühung, *f.*
egoism, Egois-mus (-men), *m.*
either . . . or, entweder . . . oder
elaborate, kompliziert
elder, älter
electron, Elektron (-en), *n.*
elegant, elegant
element, *see* primary
elementary (truth), einfach
elm, Ulme, *f.*; — tree, Ulme, *f.*
else, außerdem
embarrassment, Verlegenheit, *f.*
embodiment, Verkörperung, *f.*
to emerge, *heraus-treten, *s.*

emotion, Gemütsregung, *f.*
emotional, gespannt
empire, Reich (-e), *n.*
employment, Beschäftigung, *f.*
empty, leer
to enact, spielen
enchantment, Verzauberung, *f.*
to encourage, ermutigen
end, Ende (-n), *n.*; Endzweck (-e),
   m., Zweck (-e), *m.*
to end, enden
to endeavour, versuchen
ending, Ausgang (⸚e), *m.*
to endorse, es halten (*s.*) mit
to endow, aus-statten
endowment, Begabung, *f.*
to endure, ertragen, *s.*
enduring, beständig
enemy, Feind (-e), *m.*
energy, Energie, *f.*
to engage, an-stellen
engagement, Verlobung, *f.*
engine, Maschine, *f.*
enigmatic, rätselhaft
to enjoy, genießen, *s.*; — o.s., sich
   amüsieren
enjoyment, Genuß (⸚(ss)e), *m.*
to enlarge, vergrößern
enlargement, Übersichhinauser-
   hobenwerden, *n.*
Enlightenment, Aufklärung, *f.*
enormous, ungeheuer
enough, genug; recht, sehr
to enquire, sich erkundigen
to enrich (soil), an-reichern; (*fig.*)
   bereichern
to enter, *ein-treten, *s.*; ·(= pene-
   trate), *ein-dringen, *s.*
to enthuse, schwärmen (für)
enthusiasm, Begeisterung, *f.*
enthusiastically, begeistert
entirely, ganz, ganz und gar
entrance, Eingang (⸚e), *m.*
entry, Eingang (⸚e), *m.*
to envisage, betrachten
envy, Neid, *m.*
epigram, Epigramm (-e), *n.*
epoch, Epoche, *f.*, Zeit, *f.*
equal, gleich; to be — to, gewachsen *sein, irr.* (D)
equally, in gleichem Maße
escape: make one's —, *entkommen, *s.*
to escape (pain), *entgehen, *s.*
escort, Begleiter (-), *m.*
esoteric, esoterisch

especially, besonders
established, eingeführt; get —,
   sich ein-richten
estate, Gut (⸚er), *n.*; entailed —,
   Erbgut, *n.*
to estimate, ab-schätzen
eternal, ewig; (= constant), ständig
ethical, ethisch
ethics, Ethik, *f.*
even, selbst, sogar; — if, auch
   wenn
even, gleichmäßig
evening, Abend (-e), *m.*
event, Ereignis (-se), *n.* Begeben-
   heit, *f.*
ever, je
every, jeder
everybody, jeder
everything, alles
everywhere, überall
evidence, Beweise, *m. pl.*
evident, offensichtlich, klar
evidently, augenscheinlich
evil, Übel, *n.*; (contrasted with
   good), das Böse (*see 29*)
to evoke, hervor-rufen, *s.*
exactly, genau
examination, Prüfung, *f.*
to examine, prüfen
example: for —, zum Beispiel
excellent, ausgezeichnet
except, ausgenommen; — for,
   abgesehen von; — with, außer
   mit
exception, Ausnahme, *f.*
exceptional, außerordentlich
excess, Übermaß (-e), *n.*
to exchange, tauschen; um-tauschen
excited, aufgeregt; grow —, sich
   auf-regen
excitement, Aufregung, *f.*, Erre-
   gung, *f.*
exciting, aufregend, spannend
to exclaim, rufen, *s.*, aus-rufen
exclusively, ausschließlich
excursion, Ausflug (⸚e), *m.*
excuse (justification), Berechtigung, *f.*; (pretext), Vorwand
   (⸚e), *m.*
to execute, aus-führen
exemplary, musterhaft
exercise (*e.g.* of imagination),
   Gebrauch, *m.*
to exert o.s., sich an-strengen
to exhaust, erschöpfen

373

to **exhibit,** zur Schau stellen, vor-zeigen
exhibition, Vorzeigen, *n.*
exhilarated, erheitert
to **exist,** bestehen, *s.*
existence, Existenz, *f.*
exit, Ausgang (:̈e), *m.*
expanse, Ausdehnung, *f.*
to **expatiate (on),** sich ausführlich aus-lassen, *s.* (über)
to **expect,** erwarten; — **back,** zurück-erwarten
experience, Erfahrung, *f.*, Erlebnis (-se), *n.*
to **experiment,** experimentieren; —**ing with radio,** Radiobasteln, *n.*
expert, Fach-mann (-leute), *m.*
expert, fachmännisch
to **explain,** erklären
explanation, Erklärung, *f.*
to **exploit,** aus-nutzen
exploiting, Ausnutzung, *f.*
exploration, Entdeckungen, *f. pl.*
to **explore,** erforschen
explosion: — **of laughter,** Lach-salve, *f.*
exponent, Verfechter (-), *m.*
to **express,** aus-drücken; — **(grati-tude),** Ausdruck geben, *s.* (D)
expression, Ausdruck (:̈e), *m.*; **wear the** —, aus-sehen, *s.*
exquisite, ausgezeichnet
to **extend,** sich aus-breiten
extension, Erweiterung, *f.*
external, äußerlich
to **extract,** heraus-ziehen, *s.*
extraordinary, außerordentlich
extreme, extrem
extremely, äußerst
eye, Auge (-n), *n.*
eyebrow, (Augen-) braue, *f.*

f

fabric, Stoff (-e), *m.*
face, Gesicht (-er), *n.*; (**of house**), Fassade, *f.*; (= **features**), Gesichtszüge, *m. pl.*
to **face,** entgegen-blicken (D); (**of house**), *gehen, *s.* (auf) (A)
fact, Tatsache, *f.*
factory, Fabrik, *f.*
faculty, Fähigkeit, *f.*, Gabe, *f.*
to **fail,** *scheitern; (**in exam**), *durch-fallen, *s.*; — **to,** nicht *gelingen

failure, Fehlschlagen *n.*; (= **in-ability**), Unfähigkeit, *f.*
fain, gern
fair, Messe, *f.*
fair, fair; **it was all — play,** es ging alles mit rechten Dingen zu
fairly, ziemlich
faith (in), Glaube (-ns), *m.* (an) (A)
to **fall,** *fallen, *s.*; *stürzen; — **asleep,** *ein-schlafen, *s.*; — **short of,** hinter . . . *zurück-bleiben, *s.*; — **to one's lot,** einem zuteil *werden
false, nicht richtig; falsch
familiar, vertraut
family, Familie, *f.*
famous, berühmt
fanatic, Fanatiker (-), *m.*
to **fancy,** sich (D) vor-stellen
far, weit; — **easier,** viel leichter
farm, Bauernhof (:̈e), *m.*
farther, weiter darüber hinaus
fashion: be in —, mit der Mode *gehen, *s.*
to **fashion,** gestalten
fashionable, tonangebend
fashioning, Formung, *f.*
fast, schnell
to **fasten,** befestigen
fat, Fettleibigkeit, *f.*
fatal, verhängnisvoll
father, Vater (:̈), *m.*
fault, Schuld, *f.*; (= **misde-meanour**), Fehltritt (-e), *m.*, Fehler (-), *m.*
fear, Furcht, *f.*
to **fear,** sich fürchten vor (D), fürchten
fearfully, fürchterlich
feature, Gesichtszug (:̈e), *m.*; **-s,** Züge, *m. pl.*
feeble, schwach
to **feed,** ernähren
to **feel,** fühlen, empfinden, *s.*; (= **trace**), spüren; (+ *adjective*), sich fühlen
feeling, Gefühl (-e), *n.*; Empfinden, *n.*; **without —,** gefühllos
feint, Finte, *f.*
feline: — element, das Katzen-artige (*see 29*)
fellow, Kerl (-e), *m.*; (= **school-mate**), Mitschüler (-), *m.*; — **Junkers,** andere Junker, *m. pl.*
ferment, Gärung, *f.*; **alive with — of genius,** von gärendem genialem Leben erfüllt
ferry, Fähre, *f.*

374

be **fervent,** glühen
fervently, voll Inbrunst, *f.*
to **fête,** feiern
few, wenige; **a —,** einige, ein paar
fewer: the —, weniger
to **fidget,** kribblig *werden, irr.
field, Feld (-er), *n.*; Gebiet (-e), *n.*
fiercely, wütend; **(of flames),**
lichterloh
fiery, feurig
fight, Schlägerei, *f.*
to **fight,** kämpfen (gegen); sich schlagen, *s.* (mit)
fighting, kampflustig
figure, Gestalt, *f.*; Menschengestalt;
Form, *f.*; **(= statue),** Standbild
(-er), *n.*
to **fill,** erfüllen; aus-füllen; **(time),**
tot-schlagen, *s.*
filled (= steeped), durchdrungen
Film, Film (-e), *m.*
final, Schluß-
finally, endlich, schließlich
finances, Finanzen, *f. pl.*
financial, finanziell
to **find,** finden, *s.*; **(= notice),** merken; **— back,** zurück-finden, *s.*
finding, Entdeckung, *f.*
fine, schön, fein, vorzüglich
finely, fein, vornehm
finer, besser
finger, Finger (-), *m.*
to **finger,** zupfen
to **finish,** beenden; fertig-schreiben, *s.*
fire, Feuer (-), *n.*
fire-eater, Hitzkopf (·:e), *m.*
fireplace, Kamin (-e), *m.*
fireside, Kamin (-e), *m.*
firmly, fest; standhaft ·
first, zuerst, zunächst; **at —,** zuerst
first-rate, erstklassig
fish, Fisch (-e), *m.*
to **fish (for),** angeln (nach)
fishing-boat, Fischerboot (-e), *n.*
fitted, geeignet
fix, an-setzen
flame, Flamme, *f.*
flanked, flankiert
flashing, funkelnd
flat, flach
flat, Ebene, *f.*
flattery, Schmeichelei, *f.*
flicker, Funke (-ns, -n), *m.*
flickering, flackernd
flight: — of steps, Treppe, *f.*
to **float,** *schwimmen, *s.*

to **flood,** überfluten
floor, Boden (- & ·:), *m.*
to **flourish,** in Blüte stehen, *s.*;
*gedeihen, *s.*
to **flow: — out,** *entspringen, *s.*
flower, Blume, *f.*; **(on tree),**
Blüte, *f.*; **— -pot,** Blumentopf
(·:e), *m.*
fluently, fließend
flushed, glühend
to **flutter,** flattern
to **fly,** *fliegen, *s.*; **— past,** *vorbei-
fliegen; **(of sparks),** *stieben, *s.*
foam, Schaum, *m.*; **—s,** Schaum-
kronen, *f. pl.*
fog, Nebel (-), *m.*
to **follow,** *folgen (D)
following, folgend
food, Essen, *n.*
fool, Tor (-en -en), *m.*; **I felt a —,**
ich kam mir idiotisch vor
foolish, töricht
foot, Fuß (·:e), *m.*; **on —,** zu Fuß
football, Fußball (·:e), *m.*
forbidding, abstoßend, abschrek-
kend
force, Kraft (·:e), *f.*; Gewalt, *f.*
forced, gezwungen
foreboding, Vorahnung, *f.*
forehead, Stirn, *f.*
foreign, ausländisch; **— parts,**
Ausland, *n.*
foreigner, Ausländer (-), *m.*
foresight, Voraussicht, *f.*
forest, Wald (·:er), *m.*
to **forget,** vergessen, *s.*
to **forgive,** vergeben, *s.*
forlorn, einsam
form (= genre), Gattung, *f.*; **(of
art),** Form, *f.*
to **form,** bilden; **(= order),** ordnen
former, früher
fortress, Festung, *f.*
fortunate, der Glück hat
fortune, Vermögen (-), *n.*; **(=
fate),** Schicksal (-e), *n.*
forward, vorwärts
to **found,** gründen; **be —ed on,** sich
auf-bauen auf (A)
fountain pen, Füllfederhalter (-),
m.
fracas, 'fracas' **(*Fr.*)**
fragment, Stückchen (-), *n.*
frankness, Offenheit, *f.*
frantic: — quality, das Wahnsinnige **(*see* 29)**

375

free, frei
to free, befreien; be — to, einem
frei-stehen (s.) zu
freely, freiwillig
in French, auf französisch
frequently, oft; häufig
friend, Freund (-e), *m.*
friendliness, Freundlichkeit, *f.*
friendly, freundlich
friendship, Freundschaft, *f.*
front, Front, *f.*; — door, Vordertür,
f.; (of house), Fassade, *f.*; in —
of, vor
frontier, Grenze, *f.*
frozen, erstarrt
to frustrate, (Pläne) vereiteln
full, voll; (of train), voll besetzt;
— of, voll von; voller; (= com-
prehensive), umfassend
fully, ausführlich
function, Aufgabe, *f.*, Funktion, *f.*
fundamental, Grund-
funeral pile, Scheiterhaufen (-), *m.*
fur, Pelz (-e), *m.*
furiously, heftig; wild
furnished, möbliert
further, weiter; weiterhin; (=
opposite), gegenüberliegend
future, später

g

gain, Gewinn (-e), *m.*
gale, Sturm (⁀e), *m.*
game, Spiel (-e), *n.*
garden, Garten (⁀), *m.*; —ing,
Gärtnern, *n.*, Gartenarbeit, *f.*
gate, Gartentür, *f.*; (of town), Tor
(-e), *n.*
gauze, Schleier (-), *m.*
to gaze, vor sich hin sehen, *s.*
general, General (⁀e), *m.*
general, allgemein; —ly, gewöhnlich
generation, Generation, *f.*
generosity, Großzügigkeit, *f.*
genial, freundlich
genius, Genie (-s), *n.*; of —, genial
genteel, vornehm
gentle, sanft
gentleman, Herr (-n, -en), *m.*
gently, sanft
gesture, Geste, *f.*
to get, see *84*
ghost, Gespenst (-er), *n.*, Seele, *f.*
ghostly, gespensterhaft

gift, Talent (-e), *n.*; Begabung, *f.*;
(= present), Gabe, *f.*
to giggle, kichern
gipsy, Zigeunerin (-nen), *f.*
girl, Mädchen (-), *n.*; old —!,
Mädel!
to give, geben, *s.*; — as a present,
schenken; — up, auf-geben; —
(a cry), aus-stoßen, *s.*; — (an
impression), erwecken; — o.s.
up to, sich hin-geben (D); be —n
(power) to, betraut *sein mit; —
(advice, orders), erteilen
glacier, Gletscher (-), *m.*
glad, froh
glamour, Zauber (-), *m.*
glance, Blick (-e), *m.*
glare, Glanz, *m.*; Grelle, *f.*
glass, Glas (⁀er), *n.*; (= mirror),
Spiegel (-), *m.*
gleam, Lichtschimmer (-), *m.*;
Lichtstrahl (-en), *m.*
glimmering, flüchtiger Blick (-e)
glimpse, Blick (-e), *m.*
glitter, Glitzern, *n.*
to glitter, glitzern
glittering, glitzernd
gloomy, düster
glorious, glorreich
glove, Handschuh (-e), *m.*
glow, Glut, *f.*; (faint light),
Schimmer (-), *m.*
glowing, glühend
to go (on foot), *gehen, *s.*; (not on
foot), *fahren, *s.*; (of water),
*fließen, *s.*; — ahead, man zu!;
— away, *fortgehen; — back,
*zurück-kommen, *s.*; (= return),
*zurück-kehren; — down (of
ground), *ab-fallen, *s.*; — for a
walk, *spazieren-gehen; — off,
*fort-gehen; (= die, *vulg.*), *ab-
kratzen; — off into, *aus-platzen;
— on, *weiter-gehen; (= continue), fort-fahren; (= happen),
vor sich *gehen; — on to, *über-
gehen zu; — up, *hinauf-gehen,
*hinauf-steigen, *s.*; *auf-gehen;
— up to, *zu-gehen auf (A); —
to the bad, auf den Hund
*kommen
goal, Ziel (-e), *n.*
goat, Ziege, *f.*
God, Gott (⁀er), *m.*
going, Gehen, *n.*
gold, Gold, *n.*

golden, golden
gone, weg, fort; **all —** (= **spent**), alle, verbraucht; nicht mehr
good, gut; lieb; **—bye,** auf Wiedersehen!
good-fellowship, (gute) Kameradschaft, *f.*
goodness, Güte, *f.*; **my —!,** du liebe Zeit!
goods, Waren, *f. pl.*
good-tempered, gutgelaunt
goose, Gans (¨e), *f.*
gorgeous, prächtig
grace, Anmut, *f.*; (= **mercy**), Gnade, *f.*
graceful, anmutig
gracious: good — me!, um Gottes willen!
grammar, Grammatik, *f.*
grammatical, grammatisch
grand, groß
grandchild, Enkelkind (-er), *n.*
grandfather, Großvater (¨), *m.*
to **grasp,** ergreifen, *s.*
grasping, geizig
grass, Gras (¨er), *n.*; **— path,** Rasenweg (-e), *m.*
grateful, dankbar
to **gratify,** einem seinen Willen lassen, *s.*; (= **satisfy**), befriedigen
gratitude, Dankbarkeit, *f.*
great, groß; hervorragend
greatness, Größe, *f.*
greedy, habgierig
green, grün
green, Grün, *n.*; (**village**) **—,** Anger (-), *m.*
grey, grau; Grau, *n.*
to **grin: — at,** an-grinsen
grind, Plackerei, *f.*
to **grip,** ergreifen, *s.*
grizzled, ergraut, grau
grotto, Grotte, *f.*
ground, Boden (¨), *m.*
group, Gruppe, *f.*
to **grow,** *wachsen, *s.*; *werden, *irr.*; **— out,** *heraus-wachsen; **— up,** *auf-wachsen; **— up among,** *kommen (*s.*) zu; **— (*tr.*),** ziehen
growing, wachsend
guardsman, Gardegrenadier (-e), *m.*
guest, Gast (¨e), *m.*
guile, Arglist, *f.*
guitar, Gitarre, *f.*
gulf, Kluft (¨e), *f.*

gull, Möwe, *f.*
gully, Gießbachbett (-en), *n.*
gulp, großer Schluck (-e), *m.*
gun, Kanone, *f.*
gust: — of air, Windstoß (¨e), *m.*
gusto, Behagen, *n.*
gutter, Dachrinne, *f.*, Regenrinne, *f.*

h

habit of mind, Geisteshaltung, *f.*
habitation, Behausung, *f.*
to **hail,** an-rufen, *s.*
hailstones, Hagelkörner, *n. pl.*
hair, Haar (-e), *n.*
hale, rüstig
half, halb; **—boots,** Halbstiefel, *m. pl.*; **—born,** halbgeboren; **— dead,** halbtot; **— fainting,** halbohnmächtig; **— way down,** auf halbem Weg
hall, Diele, *f.*, Flur (-e), *m.*
hand, Hand (¨e), *f.*; **— -lamp,** Handlaterne, *f.*
to **handle,** fertig *werden, *s.*; (= **concern o.s. with**), sich befassen mit
handleless, henkellos
handsome, schön, hübsch
handwriting, Handschrift, *f.*
to **hang,** hängen, *s.*; **— over,** tief über (D) . . . gebeugt sitzen, *s.*
to **happen (to),** *geschehen, *s.*, (mit)
happiness, Glückseligkeit, *f.*; Glück, *n.*
happy, glücklich
hard, hart; heftig; schwer, fleißig
hard-bitten, zäh
hardly, kaum
hardship, Strapaze, *f.*
hardworking, fleißig
harm: no — meant, nichts für ungut
to **harm,** ein Leid zu-fügen (D)
harmful, schädlich
harsh, barsch
haste, Eile, *f.*
hat, Hut (¨e), *m.*
to **hate,** hassen
hatred, Haß, *m.*
to **have,** haben *irr.*; **— on,** tragen, *s.*
hawker, Hausierer (-), *m.*
haystack, Heuschober (-), *m.*
haze, Dunst (¨e), *m.*
hazel, nußbraun
head, Kopf (¨e), *m.*
headache, Kopfschmerzen, *m. pl.*

headless, kopflos
headway, Fortschritte, *m. pl.*
health: — **insurance**, Krankenversicherung, *f.*
to **hear**, hören
heart, Herz (-ens, -en), *n.*; **in his** —, innerlich; **by** —, auswendig
hearth, Herd (-e), *m.*
heartily, herzlich
heat, Hitze, *f.*
heating, Heizung, *f.*
heaven, Himmel (-), *m.*
heavy, schwer; **(face)**, aufgeschwemmt
hedge, Hecke, *f.*
height, Höhe, *f.*; **(of person)**, Größe, *f.*
heir, Erbe (-n, -n), *m.*
hell, Hölle, *f.*
help, Hilfe, *f.*
to **help**, helfen, *s.*; verhelfen, *s.*; — **o.s.**, sich bedienen
here, hier
hereafter, im Jenseits, *n.*
heretofore, zuvor
heroic, heroisch
to **hesitate**, zögern
hesitation: **without** —, unbedenklich
hidden, verborgen
to **hide**, verbergen, *s.*, verstecken
hideous, gräßlich
hierarchical, hierarchisch
high, hoch; —**ly** (= **well**), gut
highmindedness, Hochherzigkeit, *f.*
Highness, Hoheit, *f.*
high-shouldered, hochschultrig
high treason, Hochverrat, *m.*
hill, Anhöhe, *f.*; Berg (-e), *m.*; Hügel (-), *m.*
hint, Wink (-e), *m.*; **very strong** —, Wink mit dem Zaunpfahl
history, Geschichte, *f.*; **(of a person)**, Lebensgeschichte, *f.*
to **hit**, einem einen Schlag versetzen; — **on**, *kommen (s.) auf (A)
hitherto, bisher
to **hold**, halten, *s.*; umschließen, *s.*; — **on**, sachte!; — **one's tongue**, schweigen, *s.*; — **out**, aus-strecken
holiday, Urlaub (-e), *m.*; —**s**, Ferien, *pl.*
home, Heimat, *f.*; Haus (-̈er), *n.*; Zuhause, *n.*; **at** —, zu Hause; **from** —, abwesend; **go** —, nach Hause *gehen, s.*

honest, ehrlich
honorary: — **citizen**, Ehrenbürger (-), *m.*
honour, Ehre, *f.*
to **honour**, ehren
honourable, ehrenwert
hope, Hoffnung, *f.*
to **hope**, hoffen
hoping, in der Hoffnung
horizon, Horizont (-e), *m.*
horrible, entsetzlich
horrified, entsetzt
horror, Entsetzen, *n*
horse, Pferd (-e), *n.*
hospitable, gastfreundlich
hospital, Krankenhaus (-̈er), *n.*
host, Gastgeber (-), *m.*
hostility, Feindseligkeit, *f.*
hot, heiß
hotel, Hotel (-s), *n.*
hour, Stunde, *f.*; Zeit, *f.*
hourly, stündlich
house, Haus (-̈er), *n.*; — **of Commons**, Unterhaus; —**hold**, Haushalt (-e), *m.*; —**keeper**, Haushälterin, *f.*; — **surgeon**, Anstaltschirurg (-en, -en), *m.*
how, wie; — **many**, wieviel
however, jedoch
huddled, in sich zusammengezogen; — **forward**, vornübergekauert
human, menschlich; — **being**, Mensch (-en, -en), *m.*
humanity, Menschheit, *f.*
humble, demütig, bescheiden
humdrum, eintönig
hunger, Hunger, *m.*
hurdle, Hürde, *f.*
to **hurl**, schleudern
to **hurry**, schnell machen, *eilen
to **hurt**, weh tun, *s.*, verletzen
husband, Mann (-̈er), *m.*
hypocrisy, Heuchelei, *f.*

i
idea, Idee, *f.*
ideal, Ideal (-e), *n.*
identical, identisch
idle, faul
idler, Faulenzer (-), *m.*
idly, lässig
i.e., d.h. (= das heißt)
ignorance, Unkenntnis, *f.*; Unwissenheit, *f.*

ill, krank; (= **badly**), schlecht
illness, Krankheit, *f.*
to **illuminate**, zum Aufleuchten bringen, *irr.*
illuminated, beleuchtet
illustrated, illustriert
imagination, Einbildungskraft, *f.*;
Vorstellungskraft; Fantasie, *f.*
to **imagine**, sich (D) vor-stellen
imbecile, Idiot (-en, en), *m.*
immediacy, Unmittelbarkeit, *f.*
immediate, sofortig; —**ly**, sofort,
unmittelbar
immense, riesig
immensely, ungeheuer
impact, Aufprall, *m.*
to **impart**, berichten über (A)
impatient, ungeduldig
imperial, kaiserlich
imploringly, beschwörend
to **import**, übertragen, *s.*
importance, Wichtigkeit, *f.*
important, wichtig
to **impose**, auf-erlegen (AD)
imposing, eindrucksvoll
to **impress**, beeindrucken
impression, Eindruck (-̈e), *m.*;
Gefühl (-e), *n.*
impressive, eindrucksvoll
imputation, imputative Rechtfertigung, *f.*
incandescent: — **quality**, Glut, *f.*
inch, Zoll (-), *m.*
incidentally, nebenbei gesagt
to **incite**, an-regen
incompetent, unfähig
incomprehension, Nichtverstehen, *n.*
inconvenient, unbequem
to **increase**, vermehren
indeed, zweifelsohne, in Wirklichkeit
indefinite, unbegrenzt
independence, Unabhängigkeit, *f.*
independent, unabhängig
indestructible, unzerstörbar
to **indicate**, an-deuten; (= **allude**
to), an-geben, *s.*
indication, Spur, *f.*
indifference, Gleichgültigkeit, *f.*
indifferent (**to**), gleichgültig (gegen)
indiscriminate, unterschiedslos
indispensable, unentbehrlich
individual, Individu-um (-en), *n.*
to **induce**, bewegen, *s.*

indulgence, Ablaß (-̈(ss)e), *m.*
industrious, fleißig
industry, Industrie, *f.*
inert, abgestanden
inevitable, unvermeidlich
infallibly, unfehlbar
infected, verseucht
infinite(ly), unendlich
influence, Einfluß (-̈(ss)e), *m.*
information, Kenntnis, *f.*, Information, *f.*, Mitteilungen, *f. pl.*
infringement, Verletzung, *f.*
inhabitant, Bewohner (-), *m.*
inheritance, Erbschaft, *f.*
initial, Anfangsbuchstabe (-ns, -n),
m.
initiative, Initiative, *f.*
to **injure**, Schaden zu-fügen (D)
injury, Schaden (-̈), *m.*; **do o.s.** —,
sich (D) einen Schaden zu-fügen
ink, Tinte, *f.*
inn, Gasthaus (-̈er), *n*; —**keeper**,
Wirt (-e), *m.*
to **inquire**, fragen
inquiring, tiefschürfend
inquiry, Forschung, *f.*
inquisitive, neugierig
insect, Insekt (-en), *n.*
insincerity, Unaufrichtigkeit, *f.*
to **insist on**, bestehen (*s.*) auf (D)
insolent, frech
to **inspire**, ein-flößen (AD); begeistern
instance: for —, zum Beispiel
instantly, sofort
instead, statt dessen
instinct, Instinkt (-e), *m.*
instinctively, instinktiv; von Natur
aus
instrument, Werkzeug (-e), *n.*;
(**musical**), Instrument (-e), *n.*
insult, Beleidigung, *f.*
to **insult**, beleidigen
intellectual, geistig, intellektuell
intelligence, Intelligenz, *f.*, Verstand, *m.*
intelligent, intelligent
intelligible, verständlich
to **intend**, die Absicht haben; beabsichtigen
intensity, Stärke, *f.*
intent (**on**), bedacht (auf) (A);
to all —**s and purposes**, praktisch
intention, Absicht, *f.*
intentionally, absichtlich

379

intently, aufmerksam
to interact, gegenseitig aufeinander
ein-wirken
interchange (= exchange of
ideas), Gedankenaustausch, *m.*
interest, Interesse (-n), *n.*; Teilnahme, *f.*
to interest, interessieren
interested in, interessiert an (D)
interestedly, teilnahmsvoll
interesting, interessant
interior, das Innere (*see 29*)
to interject, ein-werfen, *s.*
intermediate, Zwischen-
internal, innenpolitisch
international, international
interrupt, unterbrechen, *s.*
intersected, durchzogen
intersection, Schnittpunkt (-e), *m.*
interstellar, interstellar
introduction, Vorstellung, *f.*
invasion, Einfall (⁻e), *m.*
to invent, ersinnen, *s.*
invention, Erfindung, *f.*
invisible, unsichtbar
invitation, Einladung, *f.*
to invite, ein-laden, *s.*
involuntarily, unwillkürlich
to involve, verwickeln; mit sich bringen, *irr.*
involved, dazugehörig; (= complicated), zu kompliziert
inward, inner
irksome, lästig
iron, Eisen, *n.*; (for ironing),
Bügeleisen (-), *n.*
iron, eisern
to iron, plätten, bügeln
irony, Ironie, *f.*
irregular, unregelmäßig
irreligious, irreligiös
irritation: with —, gereizt
island, Insel, *f.*
isolated, vereinzelt, einzeln
to issue (of sound), *erschallen, *s.*
iteration, Wiederholung, *f.*

j

jacket, Jacke, *f.*
jaded, ermattet
jazz, Jazz, *m.*
jealous, eifersüchtig
jealousy, Eifersucht, *f.*
jettison, über Bord werfen, *s.*
jewelled, mit Edelsteinen besetzt

job, Stelle, *f.*
to join, verknüpfen
jolly: too — (hot), barbarisch (heiß)
to jostle, sich drängen
journey, Reise, *f.*
journeying, Reisen, *n.*
joy, Freude, *f.*
judgement, Urteil (-e), *n.*
Judo-expert, geübter Judo-Kämp-
fer (-); Judo-Experte (-n, -n), *m.*
jump, Sprung (⁻e), *m.*
Junker, Junker (-), *m.*; (*adj.*) jun-
kerisch
just, gerade; halt; gerecht; — as,
ebenso; — as well, gerade so gut

k

to keep, halten, *s.*; bewahren; —
ready, bereit-halten; — in
check, im Zaum halten; — appointments, Verabredungen ein-
halten
keeping, Obhut, *f.*
key: — of house, Hausschlüssel
(-), *m.*
kind, Art, *f.*
kind, freundlich
kindle, entzünden
king, König (-e), *m.*
kingfisher, Eisvogel (⁻), *m.*
kitchen, Küche, *f.*
kitten, Kätzchen (-), *n.*; ein Junges
(*see 29*)
knee, Knie (-), *n.*
knight, Ritter (-) *m.*; (chess),
Springer (-), *m.*
to knock, klopfen
to knot together, zusammen-knoten
to know, *see 84*
knowledge, *see 84*
known, bekannt
knuckleduster, Schlagring (-e), *m.*

l

label, Etikett (-e), *n.*
laborious, mühselig
labour, Tätigkeit, *f.*
to labour, sich durch-arbeiten
lack, Mangel (⁻), *m.*
to lack, fehlen (D); be —ing, fehlen
ladder, Leiter, *f.*
lady, Dame, *f.*
lake, See (-n), *m.*
lamp, Lampe, *f.*

land, Land (¨er), n.; —lord,
Gutsherr (-n, -en), m.; —owner,
Gutsbesitzer (-), m.; —scape,
Landschaft, f.
landingstage, Landungsplatz (¨e),
m.
language, Sprache, f.
large, groß; (= wide), weit; —ly,
zum großen Teil, zu einem großen Teil
last: at —, endlich, schließlich; —
night, gestern abend
to last, dauern
lasting, von Dauer
late, spät; (= deceased), verstor-
ben; be —, zu spät *kommen, s.
to laugh, lachen
laughter, Gelächter (-), n.; a roar
of —, schallendes Gelächter
law, Gesetz (-e), n.
lawyer: —'s clerk, Aktenschreiber
(-), m.
to lay, legen; — (table), decken; —
down (conditions), stellen;
(= prescribe), vor-schreiben, s.;
— out, her-richten
to lead, führen, an-führen; (s.b. to),
bringen (irr.) zu
leadership, Führung, f.
leaf, Blatt (¨er), n.
leafy: — tree, Laubbaum (¨e), m.
lean, hager
to lean, sich beugen; — back(ward),
sich zurück-lehnen
leap, Sprung (¨e), m.
learn, lernen; (= discover), erfahren, s.
least: at —, wenigstens
leather, Leder, n.
to leave, see 84
ledge, Felsband (¨er), n. Vorsprung
(¨e), m.
left: be left, *übrig-bleiben, s.;
— of, *bleiben
left, link
leg, Bein (-e), n.; pull s.o.'s —, auf-
ziehen, s.
legend, Legende, f.
leisure, Freizeit, f.
to lend, leihen, s.
lesson, Unterricht, m.; German
—s, Deutschunterricht, m.,
Deutschstunden, f. pl.
to let, lassen, s.; (house), vermieten
let down, ernüchtert
letter, Brief (-e), m.

level, Stufe, f., Stand (¨e), m.
level, eben
liberator, Befreier (-), m.
liberty, Freiheit, f.
library, Bibliothek, f.
lie, Lüge, f.
to lie, liegen, s.; — around, herumliegen; — down, sich hin-legen
lifetime: in our —, zu unseren
Lebzeiten
life, Leben; (of a country), Weiterleben, n.
light, Licht (-er), n.; —house,
Leuchtturm (¨e), m.; —s, Licht-
reklame, f.
to light, beleuchten
light, hell; —ly, zart
to like, gefallen, s.; lieben; gern tun,
s.; gern haben; mögen, irr.
be like (= resemble), gleichen, s.,
(D); (= look like), aus-sehen, s.
like, wie; gleich; ähnlich; a snake
— that, so eine Schlange, f;
(= as if), als ob; — that, so
likeness, Ähnlichkeit, f.
limb, Glied (-er), n.
limit, Grenze, f.
to limit, begrenzen
line, Linie; —s of hills, Bergkon-
turen, f. pl.
lip, Lippe, f.
to listen, zu-hören (D)
listless, teilnahmslos
literal, buchstäblich
literature, Literatur, f.
littered, bestreut, überall unordentlich bedeckt
little, klein; wenig; a —, ein wenig
to live, wohnen; leben
liveliness, Lebendigkeit, f.
living, lebendig
to lock, verschließen, s.
lodge, wohnen
logically, logisch; logischerweise
lonely, einsam
to long, sich sehnen
long, lang; lange; — drawn, lang-
gezogen; a — time, lange
to look, see 84; — down, die Augen
nieder-schlagen, s.
looking-glass, Spiegel (-), m.
lord, Herr (-n, -en), m.
lordly, erhaben
to lose, verlieren, s.
loss: at a —, ratlos; at a — for,
verlegen um (A)

lost, verlorengegangen
lot, Geschick (-e), *n.*; a — (of),
viel(e)
lotion: have a —, trinken Sie eins!
loud: out —, laut
love (of), Liebe, *f.* (zu); be in —,
einander lieben
to love, lieben
lovely, wunderschön
low, niedrig
lower, unter-
luck, Glück, *n.*; with —, wenn man
Glück hat
luggage, Gepäck (-stücke), *n.*
lunch, Mittagessen (-), *n.*; eat —,
zu Mittag essen, *s.*
lust: — of power, Machtgier, *f.*
lyric: — poetry, Lyrik, *f.*
lyrical, lyrisch

m
machine: —s, Maschinerie, *f.*
mad: go —, verrückt *werden, *irr.*
madness, Wahnsinn, *m.*, Verrückt-
heit, *f.*
magazine, Zeitschrift, *f.*
magic, Zauber, *m.*
magnificent, herrlich
main, Haupt-
to maintain, behaupten
majority, Mehrheit, *f.*
to make, machen; — out, heraus-
bekommen, *s.*; (= build, construct), bauen; — sacrifice,
Opfer bringen, *irr.*; — a speech,
eine Rede halten, *s.*; — a decision, einen Entschluß fassen; —
headway, *vorwärts- kommen, *s.*
malice, Bosheit, *f.*
malicious, boshaft
man, *see 84*
to manage, *gelingen, *s.*
manifestation: — of interest,
Interessenbezeigung, *f.*
manipulatory, fingerfertig
mankind, Menschheit, *f.*
manner, Art und Weise, *f.*;
(= conduct), Betragen, *n.*
manoeuvre, Bewegung, *f.*
manual, manuell
manure, Dünger, *m.*
marble: — top, Marmorplatte, *f.*
mark, Ziel (-e), *n.*; Note, *f.*; Mark
(-), *f.*
to mark, bezeichnen

marked, deutlich umrissen
market, Markt (-e), *m.*
marking, Fältchen (-), *n.*
married, verheiratet; — life, das
eheliche Leben
to marry, heiraten
masonry, Mauerwerk (-e), *n.*;
Gemäuer (-), *n.*
mass, Menge, *f.*; Masse, *f.*
massacre, Blutbad, *n.*; —s,
Gemetzel (-), *n.*
massive, massiv
massiveness: no —, nichts Ge-
waltiges
mast, Mast (-en), *m.*
to master, bewältigen, beherrschen
master, Herr (-n, -en), *m.*; — of
the house, Hausherr; (= teacher), Lehrer (-), *m.*
mat, Matte, *f.*
match, Streichholz (-er), *n.*
to match, passen zu
materialism, Materialismus, *m.*
materials, Material, *n. sing.*; Stoffe,
m. pl.
mathematical, mathematisch
mathematics, Mathematik, *f.*
matter, *see 84*
maxime, Maxime, *f.*; Grundsatz
(-e), *m.*
maximum, größt-
may, *see 67(d)*
meagre, kümmerlich
meal, Mahlzeit, *f.*
to mean, meinen; im Sinn haben;
(= intend), wollen, *irr.*
meaning, Bedeutung, *f.*
means, Mittel (-), *n.*; by no —,
unter keinen Umständen, keineswegs
measure, Maßstab (-e), *m.*
medieval, mittelalterlich
to meet, sich treffen, *s.*; *begegnen;
*zusammen-kommen, *s.*; (= get
to know), kennen-lernen; — half
way, *entgegen-kommen, *s.*
meeting, Begegnung, *f.*
melancholy: with —, schwermütig
to melt, *verschmelzen, *s.*
member, das Mitglied (-er), *n.*;
(of state), Bürger (-), *m.*
mental: — defective, der geistig
Minderwertige (*see 29*)
mention, erwähnen; don't — it,
schon gut

merchant, Kauf-mann (-leute), m.
merciful, barmherzig
mere, bloß; —ly, nur
merit, Verdienst (-e), n.
merrily, fröhlich
mesh, Masche, f.
message, Botschaft, f.
metal, Metall (-e), n.
metal (adj.), aus Metall, n.
metaphysical, metaphysisch
method, Methode, f.; Methodik, f.
methylated: — spirits, Spiritus, m.
middle, Mitte, f.; in — life, in (seinem) mittleren Alter; — size, Mittelgröße, f.; — age, mittleres Alter
midnight, Mitternacht, f.
midst: in the — of, inmitten (G)
mile, Meile, f.; for —s, meilenweit
milk, Milch, f.
mill, Mühle, f.
millennium, das Tausendjährige Reich, das Millennium
million, Million, f.
mind, Geist (-er), m.; keep in —, im Auge behalten, s.; have in — (to), im Sinne haben
to mind: he did not —, es machte ihm nichts aus
mine, Mine, f.
minister, Minister (-), m.
minster, Münster (-), n.
minute, Minute, f.; at the last —, im letzten Augenblick
miracle play, Mirakelspiel (-e), n.
mirage, Luftspiegelung, f.
to misbehave, sich ungehörig benehmen, s.
miscellaneous, verschiedenartig
misfit, Außenseiter (-), m.; der nicht in die Gesellschaft Hereinpassende (see 29)
misfortune, Unglück, n.
misgiving, Zweifel (-), m.
mishap, Unglück, n.
to misinterpret, mißdeuten
misplaced, unangebracht
miss, Fräulein (- & -s), n.
to miss, versäumen; verpassen; — mark, verfehlen
mission, Aufgabe, f.
missionary, Missionar (-e), m.
mist, Nebel (-), m.
mistake, Fehler (-), m.; by —, aus Versehen, n.

to misunderstand, mißverstehen, s., falsch verstehen
misuse, Mißbrauch (¨e), m.
to mix o.s. up (in), sich ein-mischen (in) (A)
mixture, Mischung, f.
mob, Gedränge, n.
to mobilise, mobilisieren
mocking, spöttisch
model, Vorbild (-er), n.
modern, modern
to modernise, modernisieren
modest, bescheiden
molecule, Molekül (-e), n.
moment, Augenblick (-e), m.; Weile, f.; of the —, augenblicklich
momentarily, einen Augenblick lang
momentary, vorübergehend
monarch, Monarch (-en, -en), m.
monastic, klösterlich
money, Geld; make — (from), Geld verdienen (mit)
monstrous, ungeheuer groß
monstrously, ungeheuer
month, Monat (-e), m.; for —s, monatelang; for 10 —s, 10 Monate lang
mood, Stimmung, f.; Laune, f.
moonlight, Mondschein, m.
moonlit, mondbeschienen
moored, angelegt
moral, sittlich
more, mehr
moreover, außerdem
morning, Morgen (-), m.; this —, heute morgen
mortal, sterblich
most, die meisten; —ly, meistens
mother, Mutter (¨)
motherless, mutterlos
mound, Hügel (-), m.
mountain, Berg (-e), m.; —side, Bergabhang (¨e), m.
mournful, traurig
mouth, Mund (¨er), m.
to move, rühren; sich bewegen; — house, *um-ziehen, s.
moved, bewegt; be —, gerührt *sein, irr.
movement, Bewegung, f.
moving, packend, anregend
Mr., Herr (-n, -en), m.
Mrs., Frau, f.

mud, Straßenschmutz, *m.*
muddy, schlammig; trübe
municipal, Stadt-
murder, Mord (-e), *m.*
to murder, morden
to murmur, murmeln
muscular, muskulös
muse, Muse, *f.*
museum, Museum (Museen), *n.*
music, Musik, *f.*
must, *see 67(e)*
mutual, wechselseitig
my, my!, nein, so was!
mystery, Myster-ium (-ien), *n.*;
Geheimnis (-se), *n.*, Rätsel (-),
n.
myth, Myth-os (-en), *m.*
mythology, Mythologie, *f.*

n
nail, Nagel (∵), *m.*
name, Name (-ns, -n), *m.*; **what is
your —?** wie heißen Sie?
narrator, Erzähler (-), *m.*
narrow, schmal, eng
national, national; **— state,** Na-
tionalstaat (-en), *m.*
native, heimatlich; **— land,** Hei-
matland, *n.*
native, der Einheimische (*see 29*)
natural, natürlich
nature, Natur, *f.*
near, in der Nähe; nahe
nearly, fast
neat, ordentlich
neatness, Ordentlichkeit, *f.*
necessary, nötig
necessity, Notwendigkeit, *f.*; **of —,**
notgedrungen; **see no —,** es nicht
nötig haben
neck, Hals (∵e), *m.*
to need, *see 84*
needed, *see 84*
negligible, gering (-fügig)
neighbour, Nachbar (-n), *m.*;
(Biblical sense), der Nächste
(*see 29*)
neither . . . nor, weder . . . noch
nerve, Nerv (-en), *m.*
nervously, nervös
nest, Nest (-er), *n.*
network, Netz (-e), *n.*
never, nie, niemals
nevertheless, dennoch
new, neu

news, Nachricht, *f.*
newspaper, Zeitung, *f.*
next, nächst; **— door,** nebenan
nice, hübsch
night, Nacht (∵e), *f.*; **last —,**
gestern abend, heute nacht; **—
-class,** Abendklasse, *f.*
nightmare, Alpdruck (∵e), *m.*
nimbleness, Leichtigkeit, *f.*
noble, edel; **— (lord),** erlaucht
to nod, nicken
noise, Geräusch (-e), *n.*; Lärm, *m.*
nominal, nominell
nonsense, Unsinn, *m.*
noonday, Mittagsstunde, *f.*
no one, niemand
normal, normal
north, Norden, *m.*
nose, Nase, *f.*
no(t), nicht; **— at all,** überhaupt
nicht; überhaupt kein, gar kein;
— till, erst dann . . . wenn; **— yet,**
noch nicht
nothing, nichts; **— at all,** gar
nichts
nothingness, Nichts, *n.*
to notice, *auf-fallen, s.*, bemerken
notion, Begriff (-e), *m.*; Idee, *f.*
novel, Roman (-e), *m.*
now, nun; **by —,** nun; jetzt; **— and
again,** hin und wieder; **— and
then,** ab und zu
nowadays, heutzutage
number, Anzahl, *f.*
numerous, zahlreich
nurse, Krankenschwester, *f.*
nutshell: in a **—,** in aller Kürze,
in nuce

o
obduracy, Unnachgiebigkeit, *f.*
obdurate, unnachgiebig
obedience, Gehorsam, *m.*
to obey, gehorchen (D)
object, Objekt (-e), *n.*; Gegenstand (∵e), *m.*
to object, ein-wenden, *irr.*
objection: **have no —,** nichts dagegen haben
obliged, gezwungen
obscure, unklar
to observe (= **remark),** bemerken
observing, beobachtend
obstinate, hartnäckig
obvious(ly), offensichtlich

occasion, Gelegenheit. *f.*
occasional, vereinzelt; —ly, gele-
gentlich
occupation, Beschäftigung, *f.*
to occupy, bewohnen
to occur, statt-finden, *s.*; *geschehen,
s.; — to, *ein-fallen, *s.*
ocean, Ozean (-e), *m.*
o'clock, Uhr, *f.*
October, Oktober, *m.*
odd, sonderbar; komisch; wunderlich
ode, Ode, *f.*
odious, verhaßt
odour, Geruch (∺e), *m.*
to offend, beleidigen
offensive, Angriff (-e), *m.*, Offensive, *f.*; (*adj.*) offensiv
offer, Angebot (-e), *n.*
to offer, an-bieten, *s.*
office, Amt (∺er), *n.*; Büro (-s), *n.*
officer, Offizier (-e), *m.*; — class,
Offiziersklasse, *f.*
oil, Öl (-e), *n.*
old, alt; — man, Greis (-e), *m.*
old-fashioned, altmodisch
omen, Vorzeichen (-), *n.*
ominous, unheilverkündend; verhängnisvoll
on, weiter
once, einst, einmal; at —, sofort,
auf der Stelle; — more, wieder
one, man
oneself, sich
only, nur, lediglich, bloß; einzig;
erst
open, offen; in the — air, im
Freien
to open, öffnen, auf-tun, *s.*; be —ed
sich eröffnen
opening, Öffnung, *f.*
openly, offen
opera, Oper, *f.*
opinion, Meinung, *f.*, Ansicht, *f.*
opponent, Gegenspieler (-), *m.*
opportunity, Gelegenheit, *f.*
opposite, gegenüber; entgegengesetzt, gegensätzlich
oppressor, Bedrücker (-), *m.*
opulent, üppig
oracle, Orakel (-), *n.*
oratory, Redekunst, *f.*
to ordain, weihen
order, Befehl (-e), *m.*; Ordnung, *f.*;
give —s, Befehle erteilen; have
—s, Befehl haben

to order, befehlen, *s.*; (= arrange in
order), ordnen
ordinance, Fügung, *f.*
ordinary, gewöhlich
to organise, organisieren, ein-richten
oriental, orientalisch
origin, Ursprung (∺e), *m.*
original, ursprünglich; — world,
Urwelt, *f.*
ornamented, ausgeschmückt
other, ander; each —, einander
ought, *see* 67(*f*)
out, aus; — here, hier draußen;
— of doors, im Freien
outbreak, Ausbruch (∺e), *m.*
outcome: be — of, *entspringen
(*s.*) aus
outline, Umriß (-(ss)e), *m.*
outlying, abgelegen
out-of-date, veraltet
outside, draußen·
outsider, Außenseiter (-), *m.*
outstretched, ausgestreckt
outward, äußer
outwardly, nach außen hin
outwards, nach außen
over: — there, (da) drüben
overflowing, überfließend
overhead, über (ihm)
overladen, überladen
to overlook, übersehen, *s.*
to overshadow, überschatten, in den
Schatten stellen
to overwhelm, überschütten
overwhelming(ly), überwältigend
to owe, verdanken (AD)
own, eigen

p
pace, Schritt (-e), *m*,
to pad (away), *stapfen, *trotten
page, Seite, *f.*
pain, Schmerz (-en), *m.*; aches and
—s, Leiden und Schmerzen
painful, schmerzvoll
to paint, malen
pair, Paar (-e), *n.*
palace, Palast (∺e), *m.*
pale, blaß, fahl; — red, blaßrot
palm, Handfläche, *f.*
palpable, greifbar
pane, Fensterscheibe, *f.*; Scheibe
to panel (in), täfeln (mit)
paper, Papier (-e), *n.*; Zeitung, *f.*
parchment, pergamenten

parliament, (Prussian) Landtag, *m.*; (English), Parlament (-e), *n.*
parlour, Wohnzimmer (-), *n.*
part, Rolle, *f.*; (= members), Mitglieder, *n. pl.*; for the most —, zum größten Teil, *m.*
to part, sich trennen
to partake (of), teil-nehmen, *s.* (an) (D)
to participate (in), teil-nehmen, *s.* (an) (D)
particular, besonder; in —, besonders
particularly, besonders
partly, teilweise
party, Partei, *f.*
pass: make —es, in der Luft herum-fuchteln
to pass, reichen; (exam), bestehen, *s.*
passably, leidlich
passage, Durchreise, *f.*, (= career), Laufbahn, *f.*
passionate, leidenschaftlich
passive, passiv
past, Vergangenheit, *f.*
pastor, Pastor (-en), *m.*
pasture, Weidewiese, *f.*
to pat, tätscheln
path, Pfad (-e), *m.*; Weg (-e), *m.*
pathetic, kläglich
patience, Geduld, *f.*
patient, Patient (-en, -en), *m.*
patient, geduldig
patriotic, patriotisch
pattern, Muster (-), *n.*
pause, Pause, *f.*
pavement, Bürgersteig (-e), *m.*
pawn, Bauer (-n, -n), *m.*
pay, Lohn (⸚e), *m.*
to pay, bezahlen; zahlen; — out, auszahlen; — attention, auf-passen
peace, Friede, *m.*; make—, Frieden schließen, *s.*; at —, im Frieden befindlich
peace-making, Friedenmachen, *n.*
peal: — of laughter, Lachsalve, *f.*
peasant, Bauer (-n, -n), *m.*
peculiarity, etwas Besonderes (see 29)
pen, Feder, *f.*, Federhalter (-), *m.*
penalty: pay the — for, etwas (schwer) büßen
pencil, Bleistift (-e), *m.*
to pencil, hin-zeichnen
people, see 84 ('man')
to perceive, wahr-nehmen, *s.*

perception, Wahrnehmung, *f.*
perfect, vollkommen
perfectly, vollkommen, völlig; (of language), perfekt
to perform, machen
performer, Schauspieler (-), *m.*
perhaps, vielleicht
period, Zeit, *f.*
permanent, von Dauer; dauernd
permission, Erlaubnis (-se), *f.*
to persist, an-halten, *s.*; (= insist), bestehen, *s.* (auf) (D)
person, Person, *f.*; English —, Engländer; see 84 ('man')
personage, Person, *f.*
personal, persönlich
personality, Persönlichkeit, *f.*
persuasion, Überredung, *f.*
to pertain (to), gehören (zu)
perusal, Durchsicht, *f.*
perversity, Eigensinn, *m.*
pet, Lieblings-
petrol, Benzin, *n.*
phantasmal, gespensterhaft
pheasant, Fasan (-e), *m.*
phenomenon, see 29(*f*); — of nature, Naturphänomen (-e), *n.*, Erscheinung, *f.*
philosopher, Philosoph (-en, -en), *m.*
philosophy, Philosophie, *f.*; Weltanschauung, *f.*
photograph, Fotografie, *f.*; coloured —, Farbfotografie; —y, Fotografieren, *n.*
phrase, Wendung, *f.*; Schlagwort (-e & ⸚er), *n.*
physical, physikalisch; (= bodily), körperlich
physics, Physik, *f.*
physiognomy, Gesichtsausdruck, *m.*
piano, Klavier (-e), *n.*
picture, Bild (-er), *n.*
picturesque, malerisch
piece, Stück (-e), *n.*; (chess), Figur, *f.*
to pierce, stechen, *s.*
pig, Schwein (-e), *n.*
pile: —s of masonry, aufgeschichtetes Mauerwerk
piled, aufgehäuft
pine, Kiefer, *f.*; — plantations, Kiefernpflanzungen, *f. pl.*; — wall, Kiefernholzwand (⸚e), *f.*; — wood, Kiefernholz (⸚er), *n.*; — woods, Kiefernwälder, *m. pl.*

pipe, Pfeife, *f.*
pit, Talmulde, *f.*
pitiful, mitleiderregend, erbärmlich
pity, Mitleid, *n.*
to pity, bedauern, bemitleiden
place, Stelle, *f.*; Ort (-e), *m.*; Platz (ːe), *m.*
to place, stellen
plain, Ebene, *f.*
plain, einfach; (truth), nackt
plan, Plan (ːe), *m.*
to plan, sich (D) vor-nehmen, *s.*
planning, Planung, *f.*
to plant, pflanzen
plaster, Mörtel, *m.*
plastic, bildend
play, Stück (-e), *n.*; Theaterstück; in —, im Scherz; it was all fair —, es ging alles mit rechten Dingen zu; (= playing), Spielen, *n.*
to play, spielen
player, Spieler (-), *m.*
playground, Schulhof (ːe), *m.*
pleadingly, beschwörend
pleasant, angenehm
please, bitte
pleased, zufrieden; — with himself, selbstgefällig
pleasure, Vergnügen, *n.*; Freude, *f.*; —s, Vergnügungen, *f. pl.*
plot, Fabel, *f.*, Handlung, *f.*
to plough, pflügen
to plug in, ein-schalten
pocket, Tasche, *f.*
poem, Gedicht (-e), *n.*
poet, Dichter (-), *m.*
poetry, Dichtung, *f.*; Gedichte, *n. pl.*
point, Punkt (-e), *m.*; Stelle, *f.*; — of time, Zeitpunkt; — of view, Gesichtspunkt
to point (at), zeigen (auf) (A); hin-weisen, *s.* (auf) (A)
police, Polizei, *f.*
policeman, Schutz-mann (-leute), *m.*; Polizist (-en, -en), *m.*
policy, Politik, *f.*
polite, höflich
political, politisch
politics, Politik, *f.*
poor, arm; (of opinion), geringschätzig
popular, beliebt
population, Bevölkerung, *f.*
pore, Pore, *f.*

portion, Teil (-e), *m.*
position, Haltung, *f.*; Lage, *f.*
to possess, besitzen, *s.*
possession, Besitztum (ːer), *n.*
possible, möglich
possibly, überhaupt
post, Stelle, *f.*
to post, ein-stecken
postcard, Postkarte, *f.*
posterity, Nachwelt, *f.*
potent, wirkungsvoll
pound, Pfund (-e), *n.* (see *41*)
to pour (*intr.*), strömen
power, Macht (ːe), *f.*; — of mind, Geisteskraft, *f.*
practical, praktisch; praktisch veranlagt
practice: put into —, in die Tat um-setzen
to practise, aus-üben
to prattle, prasseln
precarious, bedenklich, prekär
precariously, gefährlich, prekär
to precede, *voraus-gehen, *s.* (D)
precious, kostbar
precipitous, abschüssig
precision, Genauigkeit, *f.*
predestination, Prädestination, *f.*
pre-eminence, Vorherrschaft, *f.*
prefect, Aufsichtsschüler (-), *m.*
to prefer, vor-ziehen, *s.* (AD)
to prejudge, im Voraus entscheiden, *s.*
prejudice, Vorurteil, *n.*
premise, Prämisse, *f.*
to prepare (for), sich vor-bereiten (auf) (A)
preparedness: — for war, Kriegsbereitschaft, *f.*
to prescribe, vor-schreiben, *s.*; (medicine), verschreiben, *s.*
presence, Gegenwart, *f.*; — of imagination, Einbildungskraft, *f.*; an invisible —, ein unsichtbar Gegenwärtiges (see *29*)
present, Geschenk (-e), *n.*; Gegenwart, *f.*; at —, augenblicklich
present, zugegen; (of today), gegenwärtig
to present, überreichen; — o.s. as, sich geben (*s.*) als; — (difficulty), bereiten; — (problem), stellen
presently, bald
preserved, erhalten

387

president, Präsident (-en, -en), *m.*

to press, drücken; (= **iron**), bügeln; — (**advantage**), aus-nützen

presumably, vermutlich

presumption, Anmaßung, *f.*

presumptuous, anmaßend

to pretend, Anspruch machen auf (A); vor-geben, *s.*; tun, als ob; (= **imagine wrongly**), sich (D) ein-bilden

pretension, Anspruch (¨e), *m.*

pretty, reizend

to prevent, ab-halten (*s.*) von; verhindern

prevention, Vorbeugung, *f.*

previously, vorher

to prick, durchstechen, *s.*

pride, Stolz, *m.*

priest, Priester (-), *m.*

priesthood, Priestertum, *n.*

primary: — **element,** Grundelement (-e), *n.*

prime minister, Premierminister (-), *m.*

prince, Prinz (-en, -en), *m.*

principal, Direktor (-en), *m.*

principality, Fürstentum (¨er), *n.*

principle, Grundsatz (¨e), *m.*; Prinzip (-ien), *n.*

print, Druck (-e), *m.*

prison, Gefängnis (-se), *n.*

private, privat

probably, wahrscheinlich

problem, Problem (-e), *n.*

to proceed, daran *gehen, *s.*; anfangen, *s.*; sich daran machen

process, Vorgang (¨e), *m.*

proclamation, Verkündigung, *f.*

prodigious, erstaunlich groß

to produce (**money**), hervor-ziehen, *s.*; (**impression**), hervor-rufen, *s.*; — **a surprising impression,** überraschend wirken

profession, Beruf (-e), *m.*

professor, Professor (-en), *m.*

profit, Gewinn (-e), *m.*

profusion, Fülle, *f.*

programme, Programm (-e), *n.*

progress, Fortschritt (-e), *m.*; **make** —, Fortschritte machen

prominent, ausgeprägt

promise, Verheißung, *f.*, Versprechung, *f.*, Versprechen (-), *n.*

to promise, versprechen, *s.*

prompt, sofortig

to pronounce, aus-sprechen, *s.*

proof, Beweis (-e), *m.*

to propagate (**news**), verbreiten; **be** —**d,** sich fort-pflanzen

properly, ordentlich

to propose, vor-schlagen, *s.*

to propound, vor-legen

prosperous-looking, wohlhabend aussehend

to protect, schützen

protest, Protest (-e), *m.*

protestant, protestantisch

Protestant, Protestant (-en, -en), *m.*

proudly, stolz

to prove, beweisen, *s.*; — **to be** sich erweisen als

to provide, versehen, *s.*, versorgen

psychology, Psychologie, *f.*

public, Publikum, *n.*

public, öffentlich; — **schoolboy,** Internatsschüler, (-), *m.*

puddle, Pfütze, *f.*

to puff, paffen

pulsation, Pulsieren, *n.*

to punish, bestrafen

pupil, Schüler (-), *m.*

pure, rein

purely, ganz allein

purity, Lauterkeit, *f.*

purple, purpurrot; purpurn

purpose (= **God's**), Wille (-ns), *m.*

to pursue, *nach-gehen, *s.*; (**leisure**), verwenden, *irr.*

pursuits, Beschäftigungen, *f. pl.*

to push, stoßen, *s.*; — **open,** auf-stoßen, *s.*

to put, see *84*

to puzzle, stutzig machen

pyjamas, Schlafanzug (¨e), *m.*

q

quaint, seltsam, absonderlich

qualifications, Fähigkeiten, *f. pl.*

quarrel, Wortwechsel (-), *m.*

quarter of a mile, Viertelmeile, *f.*

quavering, zitternd

queen, Königin (-nen), *f.*

question, Frage, *f.*

quick, schnell; schnellströmend; — **as a flash,** blitzschnell; **be** —, schnell machen

quickly, schnell

quiet, ruhig

quietly, gelassen
quite, ganz

r

race, Rasse, *f.*; **aquatic —,** Art von Wassertieren; (= **competition**), Wettlauf (⁓e), *m.*; **— course,** Rennplatz (⁓e), *m.*
rack, Gepäcknetz (-e), *n.*
radiance, Glanz, *m.*
radiator, Heizkörper (-), *m.*
radically, durch und durch
railway, Eisenbahn, *f.*, **— terminus,** Eisenbahnendstation, *f.*
rain, Regen, *m.*; **—bow,** Regenbogen (-), *m.*
to rain, regnen
to raise, erheben, *s.*
range, Bergkette, *f.*; **— of mountains,** Bergkette, *f.*
rapacious, habgierig
rapid, schnell
rare, selten
rash, vorschnell
rather, *see 84*
to rattle, rattern
ravenous, gierig
reach, Reichweite, *f.*; **put within our —,** in unsere Reichweite bringen, *irr.*
to reach, erreichen
reactionary, reaktionär
to read lesen, *s.*; **— aloud,** vorlesen
reader, Leser (-), *m.*
readiness, Bereitwilligkeit, *f.*
reading, Lektüre, *f.*, Lesen, *n.*
ready, fertig; bereit; bereitwillig; **be — with,** bereit halten, *s.*; **— for war,** zum Krieg ausgerüstet *or* kriegsbereit; **— for,** gefaßt auf (A); **— to his hand,** fertig zur Hand
real, wirklich; (= **in its strict sense**), eigentlich
to realise, *see 84*
really, *see 84*
reason, Vernunft, *f.*; Grund (⁓e), *m.*; **for this —,** aus diesem Grund, deswegen; **by — of,** wegen (G)
to reassure (*o.s.*), (sich) beruhigen
rebellious, aufrührerisch
to rebuild, wieder auf-bauen
receding (**of forehead**), fliehend

to receive (**person**), empfangen, *s.*; (**ideas**), auf-nehmen, *s.*
recently, erst kürzlich
recess, Parlamentsferien, *pl.*
to recognise (**by**), erkennen, *irr.*, (an) (D); (= **establish**), fest-stellen
recognition, Erkennen, *n.*
record, Chronik, *f.*
to recover (**health**), sich erholen; (**get back**), zurück-gewinnen, *s.*
to recur, immer wieder *kommen
red, rot
redder, röter
reddish, rötlich
to redouble, verdoppeln
redoubled, doppelt
to refill, wieder füllen
to refine, sich verfeinern
to reflect, nach-denken, *irr.*; (**of light**), reflektieren, wider-spiegeln; (= **occur to**), *ein-fallen, *s.*
Reformation, Reformation, *f.*; **— Tract,** Reformationstraktat (-e), *n.*
refuge, Zuflucht, *f.*; **find a —,** Zuflucht finden, *s.*
refusal, Weigerung, *f.*
to refuse, sich weigern; (= **reject**), ab-lehnen
to regain, zurück-gewinnen, *s.*
to regard (**as**), betrachten (als)
regard: with — to, im Hinblick auf (A)
region, Gegend, *f.*, Region, *f.*
to regret, bedauern
reign, Regierung, *f.*
reigning, regierend
reinforcement, Verstärkung, *f.*
rejection, Ablehnung, *f.*
to rejoice, sich freuen
to relate, in Beziehung bringen, *irr.*
relation (= **connection**), Beziehung, *f.*; (= **relationship**), Verhältnis (-se), *n.*
relatively, verhältnismäßig
to release, frei-lassen, *s.*
relics, Überreste, *m. pl.*
relief, Ablösung, *f.*; (= **deliverance**), Erlösung, *f.*; **with infinite —,** unendlich erleichtert
relieved, erleichtert
religious, religiös
to remain, *bleiben, *s.*
remaining, übriggeblieben
remark, Bemerkung, *f.*
to remark, bemerken

remedy, Heilmittel (-), *n.*
to remember, sich erinnern an (A);
nicht vergessen, *s.*
to remind, erinnern an (A)
remorse, Reue, *f.*; (= mercy,
pity), Barmherzigkeit, *f.*
remote, weit entfernt
remoteness, Entrücktheit, *f.*
to remove, beseitigen, entfernen
Renaissance, Renaissance, *f.*
renewed: be —, sich erneuern
rent, Miete, *f.*
to reorganise o.s., sich wieder fassen
to repay, wieder-geben, *s.*
to repeat, wiederholen
to repent, bereuen
repertory, Repertoire-
reply, Antwort, *f.*
to reply, antworten, erwidern
to report, berichten
republican, republikanisch
required, notwendig, erforderlich;
be —, bedürfen (G); be — of,
gefordert/benötigt *werden von
to rescue, retten
residence, Aufenthalt (-e), *m.*
resolved, entschlossen
resource, Hilfsmittel (-), *n.*; Hilfs-
quelle, *f.*
rest, Rast, *f.*; all the — of it,
solches Zeug; the —, die anderen
to rest, ruhen (auf) (D); sich aus-ruhen
restaurant, Restaurant (-s), *n.*
resting-place, Ruheplatz (ᵘe), *m.*
to restore, wiederher-stellen
result, Ergebnis (-se), *n.*
resultant, daraus resultierend
to resume, wieder beginnen, *s.*
retainer, der Bediente (*see* 29)
reticent, zurückhaltend
to retire, sich pensionieren lassen, *s.*;
in den Ruhestand *treten, *s.*
return (= income), Einkünfte,
f. pl.; — home, Heimkehr, *f.*;
— journey, Rückreise, *f.*
to return, erwidern; *zurück-kommen, *s.*; zurück-geben, *s.*
to reveal, enthüllen
revenge, Rache, *f.*; thoughts of —,
Rachegedanken, *m. pl.*
reverberation, Echo (-s), *n.*
reverence, Ehrfurcht, *f.*
reverie, Träumerei, *f.*
to revise, verbessern
revolution, Revolution, *f.*
revolutionary, revolutionär

revulsion, Umschwung (*m.*) in der
Stimmung
reward, Belohnung, *f.*
rib, Rippe, *f.*
rich, reich
richness, Reichtum (ᵘer), *m.*
rickety, wacklig
ricocheting, abprallend
ridiculous, lächerlich
rift, Spalte, *f.*
right, Recht (-e), *n.*
right, recht; gerecht; richtig; be —,
recht haben; — across, quer über
righteous, rechtschaffen
rightly, von Rechts wegen; mit
Recht, *n.*
rigid, unabänderlich
rim, Rand (ᵘer), *m.*
ring, Ring (-e), *m.*
to ring, klingeln; — off, ein-hängen,
s.; — up, an-rufen, *s.*
to rise, sich heben, *s.*; sich erheben;
— from, *heraus-treten (*s.*) aus;
(dusk), *auf-steigen, *s.*; — up
from, *hervor-steigen (*s.*) aus
risk, Gefahr, *f.*
river, Fluß (ᵘ(ss)e), *m.*; — bank,
Ufer (-), *n.*
road, Straße, *f.*; Landstraße; (*fig.*)
Weg (-e), *m.*
robber, Räuber (-), *m.*
robbery, Räuberei, *f.*
rock, Fels (-ens, -en), *m.*; cranny of
the —, Felsriß (-(ss)e), *m.*
rocky fabric, Felsengefüge (-), *n.*
rogue, Lump (-en, -en), *m.*
roll, sich wälzen; — down, *herun-
ter-rollen
rolls, Ehrenliste, *f.*
romance, Romantik, *f.*
romantic, romantisch
roof: — ridge, Dachfirst (-e), *m.*;
red-tiled —, rotes Ziegeldach
(ᵘer), *n.*
room, Zimmer (-), *n.*; Raum (ᵘe),
m.
rose (= colour), Rosa, *n.*;
(= flower), Rose, *f.*
rough (of feature), derb
round (= passage of arms),
Waffengang (ᵘe), *m.*
round, rund
to round, um . . . herum *sein
to rouse, auf-rütteln
routine, Routine, *f.*
row, Reihe, *f.*

390

royal, königlich
ruby, Rubin (-e), *m.*; **pale — red,**
blasses Rubinrot
ruin, Ruine, *f.*; Untergang (⁻e), *m.*
rule, Regel, *f.*; **—s of the game,**
Spielregeln, *f. pl.*
ruler, Herrscher (-), *m.*
ruling, herrschend
to run, *laufen, *s.*; **— away,** *fort-
laufen; **— into,** *ein-laufen in
(A); **— over,** überfahren, *s.*;
— round, *herum-laufen; **— up,**
*heran-laufen; **— up to,** *zulaufen auf (A); **—ning with,**
überflutend mit
rush, Schwall, *m.*
rusty: **— gold,** Rostgold, *n.*
ruthless, unbarmherzig

S

sacrament, Sakrament (-e), *n.*
sacred, heilig
sacrifice, Opfer (-), *n.*
to sacrifice, auf-opfern
sad(ly), traurig
sail, Segel (-), *n.*
salary, Gehalt (⁻er), *n.*
salon, Salon (-s), *m.*
salt, Salz (-e), *n.*
salt, gesalzen
same: the **—,** dasselbe; das gleiche
sand, Sand, *m.*
sandstone, Sandstein (-e), *m.*
sandy, sandig
sane, vernünftig
satisfied, zufrieden
to satisfy, befriedigen
savage, der Wilde (*see 29*)
to save (money, time), sparen;
— o.s. s.th., sich (D) etwas
ersparen
save, ausgenommen (A)
to say, sagen
scarcely, kaum
scene, Szene, *f.*; Landschaft, *f.*
scenery, Landschaft, *f.*
scheme, Programm (-e), *n.*
scholastic, akademisch
school, Schule, *f.*; **— of learning,**
Bildungsanstalt, *f.*; **— life,** Schul-
leben, *n.*; **— master,** Lehrer (-),
m.; **— room,** Schulzimmer (-),
n., Klassenzimmer (-), *n.*; **—
work,** Schularbeit, *f.*
science, Naturwissenschaft, *f.*;
Naturforschung, *f.*

scientific, wissenschaftlich
scientist, Naturforscher (-), *m.*;
Naturwissenschaftler (-), *m.*
scope, freier Spielraum
to scorch, verbrennen, *irr.*
scorn, Verachtung, *f.*
scrawl, Gekritzel (-), *n.*
to scream, schreien, *s.*
scroll, Schnörkel (-), *m.*; **— of**
smoke, Rauchschnörkel (-), *m.*,
Rauchfahne, *f.*
to sculpture, meißeln
sea, Meer (-e), *n.*; **— poppies,**
Seemohn, *m. sing.*
seashore, Strand (-e), *m.*
seat, Sitz (-e), *m.*, Platz (⁻e), *m.*
second, Sekunde, *f.*; Moment (-e),
m.
second-rate, zweitklassig
secret, Geheimnis (-se), *n.*
secret, geheim
secular, säkularisiert
secularised, säkularisiert
to secure, sichern
sedge, Schilfgras (⁻er), *n.*
to see, betrachten; **— ahead,** voraus-
sehen; **you —,** weißt du; siehst
du; *see 84*
seed-horn, Samenhorn (⁻er), *n.*
to seek, suchen
to seem, scheinen, *s.*; *vor-kommen, *s.*
to seep down, *herunter-sickern
to seize, ergreifen, *s.*
seizure, Besitzergreifung, *f.*
selection, Auswahl, *f.*
self-control, Selbstbeherrschung, *f.*
self-deception, Selbstbetrug, *m.*
self-discipline, Selbstzucht, *f.*
selfish, egoistisch
to sell, verkaufen
to send, senden, *irr.*; **— away,** fort-
schicken
sensation: **— of sight,** Sehemp-
findung, *f.*
sense, Sinn (-e), *m.*
sensible, vernünftig
sensuous, sinnlich
sentence, Satz (⁻e), *m.*
sentiment, Empfinden, *n.*; Gefühl
(-e), *n.*
to separate, sich trennen
separately, jeder für sich; getrennt
serene, klar
series, Reihe, *f*
serious(ly), ernst, ernsthaft
sermon, Predigt, *f.*

servant, Diener (-), *m.*
serve, dienen (D); — its turn, seinen Zweck erfüllen; — as, dienen als
to set (of sun), *unter-gehen, *s.*; — apart, voneinander ab-sondern; — in, ein-setzen; have s.b. set, in der Klemme haben; (jewels), besetzen
setting, Milieu (-s), *n.*
to settle, bestimmen; (boundary), fest-legen
several, mehrere
severe, schwer, ernsthaft
to sew, nähen
shabby, schäbig
shadow, Schatten (-)', *m.*
shaggy, zottelhaarig
to shake, schütteln; — s.b.'s hand, einem die Hand schütteln/geben
shaky, ungewiß
shallow, schmal
shanty, Bretterbude, *f.*
shape, Gestalt, *f.*
share (of), Anteil (-e), *m.* (an) (D)
sharp, scharf; (jagged), gezackt; (stars), scharf *or* hart glänzend
to shed (blood), vergießen, *s.*
sheepish: sound —, blöde wirken
shelf, Bücherbord (-e), *n.*
shell (= skeleton), Gerippe (-), *n.*
to shift, gleiten lassen, *s.*
shilling, Schilling (-e), *m.* (see *41*)
to shine, scheinen, *s.*
shingle, kiesiger Strand
shining, blank
ship, Schiff (-e), *n.*
to ship, verfrachten
to shirk, aus dem Weg *gehen
to shiver: he —s, es überläuft ihn kalt
shock, Schock (-e & -s), *m.*
shocking, schockierend
shoddy, minderwertig
shoe, Schuh (-e), *m.*
shooting party, Jagdgesellschaft, *f.*
shop, Laden (⁖), *m.*
shore, Ufer (-), *n.*; Küste, *f.*
short, kurz; (of stature), klein; in —, kurz
shot (play of colour), schillernd
should, *see* 67(*f*)
shoulder, Schulter, *f.*; shrug one's —s, die Achseln zucken
to shout, schreien, *s.*
to show, zeigen, erweisen *s.*; be —n,

sich heraus-stellen; (= look), aussehen, *s.*; (give expression to), Ausdruck verleihen, *s.* (D)
shrub(s), Buschwerk, *n.*
to shrug, zucken
to shuffle (away), *schlurfen
to shut, schließen, *s.*; — in, einschließen; — up! halt's Maul!
sick, krank
side, Seite, *f.*; —s of chest, Brustkorb, *m.*; (of mountain), Hang (⁖e), *m.*; on the other —, auf der anderen Seite; at his —, an seiner Seite; on the Protestant —, von seiten der Protestanten
sight, Anblick, *m.*; be in —, zu sehen *sein; hidden from my —, meinen Augen verborgen
sign, Zeichen (-), *n.*
to signal, übermitteln
signature, Unterschrift, *f.*
silence, Schweigen, *n.*; Stille, *f.*; in —, schweigend
silent, schweigend
be silhouetted (against), sich abheben, *s.* (von)
silk, Seide, *f.*
silver, Silber, *n.*; — piece, Silberstück (-e), *n.*
silver(y), silbrig
similar, ähnlich
simple, einfach
simply, einfach
simultaneously, gleichzeitig
sin, Sünde, *f.*
since, da; seit (D)
to sing, singen, *s.*
single, einzig, einzeln; einmalig
singly, einzeln
singular, eigenartig
singularly, ungemein
sinister, unheilvoll
sink, *sinken, *s.*; (= set), *untergehen, *s.*, *versinken; — back, *zurück-sinken
sir, mein Herr; my dear —, mein Herr
sister, Schwester, *f.*; (in hospital), Oberschwester, *f.*
to sit, sitzen, *s.*; — down, sich setzen, sich hin-setzen; — up, sich aufrichten
sitting-room, Wohnzimmer (-), *n.*
situation, Lage, *f.*; Zustand (⁖e), *m.*
sketch, Skizze, *f.*
skiing, Skilaufen, *n.*

skill, Geschicklichkeit, *f.*; (=**know-how**), Können, *n.*
to skim, streifen
skin, Haut (ʺe), *f.*
skirt, Rock (ʺe), *m.*
sky, Himmel (-), *m.*
skyscraper, Wolkenkratzer (-), *m.*; Hochhaus (ʺer), *n.*
slap, Klaps (-e), *m.*
slate, Schiefertafel, *f.*; — **roof,** Schieferdach (ʺer), *n.*
to sleep, schlafen, *s.*
sleepy, schläfrig
slender, schlank; (*fig.*), dürftig
slight, leicht
slightly, ein wenig; leicht
slim, schlank
slowly, langsam
small, klein; (**of feature**), schmal; (= **slight**), leise
smart: **is — to,** es gehört dazu, zu…
to smell (of), riechen, *s.* (nach)
smile, Lächeln, *n.*
to smile, lächeln; **make —,** zum Lächeln bringen, *irr.*
smoke, Rauch, *m.*
to smoke, rauchen
snack, Imbiß (-(ss)e), *m.*
snake, Schlange, *f.*
snob, Snob (-s), *m.*
snow-streaked, schneegestreift
snowy, schneebedeckt
so, so; — **much the (more),** um so (mehr)
to soak (into), *ein-sickern (in)
social, sozial, gesellschaftlich
society, Gesellschaft, *f.*
sofa, Sofa (-s), *n.*
to soften (into), sich erweichen (zu)
softly, sanft
soil, Boden (ʺ), *m.*
soldier, Soldat (-en, -en), *m.*
sole(ly), einzig
solid, dicht
solitary, einzig
solution, Lösung, *f.*
some, einige
somehow, irgendwie
something, etwas
sometimes, manchmal
somewhat, etwas; ein bißchen
son, Sohn (ʺe), *m.*
song, Lied (-er), *n.*
sonnet, Sonett (-e), *n.*
soon, bald; — **afterwards,** bald darauf

soot, Ruß, *m.*
sorrow, Gram, *m.*
sort, Art, *f.*; *see 40(d), 51(b)*
sound, Schall (-e *or* ʺe), *m.*
to sound, klingen, *s.*
soup, Suppe *f.*
source, Quelle, *f.*
sourly, säuerlich
space, Raum (ʺe), *m.*
spare, hager
spark, Funke (-ns, -n), *m.*
to speak, sprechen, *s.*
specs, Brille, *f. sing.*
spectator, Zuschauer (-), *m.*
speech, Rede, *f.*; **make a —,** eine Rede halten, *s.*
speedily, schnell, geschwind
to spend (**money**), aus-geben, *s.*; (**time**), verbringen, zu-bringen, *irr.*; tätig *sein
sphere, Bereich (-e), *m.*
spice, Gewürz (-e), *n.*
spine, scharfe Nadel, *f.*
spirit, Geist (-er), *m.*; (= **prevailing mood**), Stimmung, *f.*; **on my —s,** in meiner Seele; **in a judicious —,** mit Überlegung, *f.*
spiteful, gehässig
to splash, platschend *gehen
splendour, Herrlichkeit, *f.*; **—s,** Pracht, *f.*
spoilt, verwöhnt
spokesman, Wortführer (-), *m.*
sport, Sport, *m.*
spot, Stelle, *f.*; Winkel (-), *m.*
sprawling, schlaksig
to spread, sich aus-breiten (*intr.*); — **out,** aus-breiten
spring, Quelle, *f.*
spring: **early —,** Vorfrühling, *m.*
to spring out, *entspringen, *s.*
to squander, verschwenden
square, Platz (ʺe), *m.*
square yard, Quadratmeter, *n.*
squarely, viereckig
staff, Personal, *n.*
stage, Bühne, *f.*
stained (**glass**), bunt
staircase, Treppe, *f.*
stakes, Gewinne, *m. pl.*
stall, Bude, *f.*
to stammer, stammeln
stand, *see 84* ('take')
to stand, stehen, *s.*; sich stellen; — **up,** empor-ragen
star, Stern (-e), *m.*

393

to stare, starren; — at, an-starren
to start, *ab-reisen; sich in Bewegung
setzen; an-fangen, s.; — a row
with, mit einem an-binden, s.
startle, auf-scheuchen
startling, alarmierend
starveling, kümmerlich
state, Staat (-en), m.
stately, stattlich
statement, Erklärung, f.
station, Bahnhof (⸗e), m.
stay, Aufenthalt (-e), m.
to stay, *bleiben, s.; sitzen *bleiben;
stehen *bleiben; — away, *fort-
bleiben; (= spend), verbringen
steady, beständig
to steal, stehlen, s.; — away, sich
fort-stehlen
stealthy, hinterhältig
steam-engine, Dampfmaschine, f.
steamer, Dampfer (-), m.
steeply, steil
step, Schritt (-e), m.; take —s,
Maßnahmen treffen, s.
to step, *treten, s.; — back, *zurücktreten
steppe, Steppe, f.
stick, Stock (⸗e), m.
stiffly, steif
still, still; (adv.) trotzdem
to stimulate, an-regen
to stir, auf-rütteln; (= stimulate),
an-regen
stirring, ergreifend
stocking, Strumpf (⸗e), m.
stone, steinern
stone, Stein, m.; — wall, Stein-
mauer, f.
to stop, an-halten, s.; *stehen-bleiben,
s.; ein Ende machen; (cease),
auf-hören
store, Vorrat (⸗e), m.
storm, Gewitter (-), n.; (= gale),
Sturm (⸗e), m.
stormy, stürmisch
story, Geschichte, f.
stove, Kocher (-), m.
straight, gerade; — away, sofort
to straighten: — one's back, sich
auf-richten
straightway, sofort
strain, Anstrengung, f.
strained, im Zustand der Spannung
stranded (in), verschlagen (nach)
strange, seltsam; fremdartig

strangely, sonderbarerweise
stranger, der Fremde (see 29)
streak (of hair), Strähne, f.; — of
wind, Windhauch, m.
stream, Strom (⸗e), m.
to stream, fluten; — down, *herab-
strömen; — out, *hinaus-
strömen; — through, durch-
fluten
street, Straße, f.; — lamp,
Straßenlaterne, f.
strength, Kraft (⸗e), f., Stärke, f.;
— of purpose, Willenskraft, f.
strenuous, anstrengend
to stress, betonen
stretch, Stück (-e), n.; — of time,
Zeitspanne, f.
to stride along, mit langen Schritten
*gehen, s.
to strike, schlagen, s.; — upon their
backs, sie im Rücken treffen, s.
striking, schlagend
string, Saite, f.
to strip, nackt aus-ziehen, s.
strong, stark, kräftig
struggle, Kampf (⸗e), m.
to struggle, kämpfen
to strum, klimpern
be stuck, stecken
student, Student (-en, -en), m.
study, Studi-um (-en), n.
to study, studieren
stuff (= nonsense), Unsinn, m.
stupid, dumm
style, Art, f.
subject, Them-a (-en), n.; Gegenstand (⸗e), m.; (school), Fach
(⸗er), n.; (political), Untertan
(-en), m.
sublimity, Erhabenheit, f.
to submerge, ein-tauchen
submission (to), Unterwerfung, f.
(unter) (A)
subordinate, der Untergebene (see
29)
subsequent(ly), nachträglich
substance, Gegenständlichkeit, f.
to succeed, *gelingen, s.; erfolgreich
*sein; Erfolg haben
succeeding, nachfolgend
success, Erfolg (-e), m.
successful, erfolgreich
succinctness, Gedrängtheit, f.
such, solch, derartig, ähnlich
sudden(ly), plötzlich
to suffer, leiden, s., erdulden

suffering, Leid, *n.*
sufficient(ly), genügend
suffrage, Wahlrecht (-e), *n.*
to suffuse, überfluten
sugar, Zucker, *m.*; — refinery, Zuckerraffinerie, *f.*
to suggest, vor-schlagen, *s.*
suggestion, der Vorschlag (-̈e), *m.*; (vague), Ahnung, *f.*
to suit, passen (D); (correspond to), entsprechen, *s.* (D)
suitable, angemessen
suit-case, Koffer (-), *m.*
summer, Sommer (-), *m.*; — house, Sommervill-a (-en), *f.*
summit, Spitze, *f.*
sun, Sonne, *f.*
sun-dial, Sonnenuhr, *f.*
sunset, Sonnenuntergang (-̈e), *m.*
superfluous, unnötig; überflüssig
superiority, Überlegenheit, *f.*
superman, Übermensch (-en, -en), *m.*
to supervene, *hinzu-kommen, *s.*
supper, Abendbrot (-e), *n.*
to supplant, verdrängen
supply, Vorrat (-̈e), *m.*
to suppose, an-nehmen, *s.*
to suppress, unterdrücken
supreme, oberst
sure, sicher; (= convinced), überzeugt; — enough, tatsächlich; why, I am —, ja freilich; I'm sure, wirklich, wohl
surely, sicher
surface, Oberfläche, *f.*
to surge, branden
surprise, Erstaunen, *n.*
to surprise, überraschen
surprising, erstaunlich
surrender, Aufgeben, *n.*
to surrender, auf-geben, *s.*
to surround, umgeben, *s.*
surroundings, Umgebung, *f. sing.*
survey, Überblick (-e), *m.*
to survey, betrachten
survival, Weiterleben, *n.*
to survive, überleben
to suspect, im/in Verdacht haben; (= surmise), vermuten; (= half believe), halb glauben
suspense, bange Erwartung, *f.*
suspicion, Verdacht, *m.*
to sway, schwingen, *s.*
to sweep, fegen; — away, sich weithin erstrecken

sweet, entzückend, liebenswürdig
swift(ly), schnell; (of wind), heftig
to swim, (*)schwimmen, *s.*
swimming-pool, Schwimmbad (-̈er), *n.*
to swing, sich wiegen
swol(le)n, geschwollen
to swoop down, sich stürzen auf (A)
sycophant, Speichellecker (-), *m.*
syllable, Silbe, *f.*
to symbolise, versinnbildlichen
sympathy, Mitleid, *n.*
system, System (-e), *n.*

t

table, Tisch (-e), *m.*; at —, bei Tisch
tacitly, stillschweigend
tactful, taktvoll
tail, Schwanz (-̈e), *m.*
to take, *see 84*; — up, greifen (*s.*) nach
tale, Geschichte, *f.*
talk, Gespräch (-e), *n.*
to talk, sprechen, *s.*
tall, hoch; (of person), groß
tap, leichter Schlag (-̈e), *m.*
task, Aufgabe, *f.*
tax, Steuer, *f.*
taxi, Taxi (-s), *n.*
tea, Tee, *m.*; — -time, Teezeit; before — -time, vor dem Tee
to teach, bei-bringen, *irr.*; unterrichten; Unterricht geben, *s.*; lehren
teacher, Lehrer (-), *m.*
teaching (= doctrine), Lehre, *f.*; — pupil, Lehrschülerin (-nen), *f.*
tear, Träne, *f.*
technical, technisch
telegram, Telegramm (-e), *n.*
to tell, sagen; (= order), befehlen, *s.*; (= narrate), erzählen
temperament, Temperament, *n.*
temple, Tempel (-), *m.*
be tempted, in Versuchung *geraten, *s.*
tenant, Pächter (-), *m.*
to tend, neigen
tendency, Neigung, *f.*
term, Ausdruck (-̈e), *m.*
terrace, Terrasse, *f.*
terrible, schrecklich
territory, Landesgebiet (-e), *n.*; Gebiet (-e), *n.*
terror, Grauen, *n.*
test, Probe, *f.*
theatre, Theater (-), *n.*

then (= at that time), damals;
(= at that moment), dann
thence, von dort aus
theological, theologisch
theology, Theologie, f.
theory, Theorie, f.
there, dort, da; dahin, nach dort
thereafter, nachher
therefore, daher, also
thick(ly), dicht; nebeldicht
thickly-built, untersetzt
thief, Dieb (-e), m.
thigh, Schenkel (-), m.
thin, dünn
thing, Ding (-e), n.; —s for tea,
alles zum Tee
to think, see 84; (be of opinion),
meinen
third-rate, drittklassig
thoroughly, gründlich; (= perfectly), vollkommen
those, diejenigen
thought, Gedanke (-ns, -n), m.;
Denken, n.
thoughtful(ly), nachdenklich
thousand, Tausend (-e), n.
thread, Faden (¨), m.
threat, Bedrohung, f.
to threaten, drohen (D)
threatening, drohend
three-legged, dreibeinig
throne, Thron (-e), m.
to throw, werfen, s.; (of light), aus-
strahlen; — aside, weg-werfen
to thud, dumpf hämmern
thumb, Daumen (-), m.
thump, Herzschlag (¨e), m.
thunderbolt, Donnerkeil (-e), m.
thus, so
ticket, Fahrkarte, f., Karte
tide, Flut, f.
tight, fest
time, Zeit, f.; Mal (-e), n.; Weile,
f.; the first —, das erstemal;
what is the —? wie spät ist es?;
at what —? um wieviel Uhr ;
in — (= in course of —), mit
der Zeit; in — (= punctually),
zur rechten Zeit; for some —,
eine Weile (lang); for the —
being, vorläufig; behind the —s,
hinter der Zeit zurückgeblieben
time-absorbing, zeitraubend
timidly, schüchtern
tinge, Tönung, f.
tint, Farbton (¨e), m.

tired, müde
toad, Kröte, f.
together, zusammen; miteinander
to-morrow, morgen
tone, Ton (¨e), m.; Tonfall (¨e),
m.
tongue, Zunge, f.
too, zu; allzu; (= also), auch;
(= simply), einfach
tooth, Zahn (¨e), m.
top (of head), Scheitel (-), m.
to top, krönen
topic, Gesprächsstoff (-e), m.
torment, Höllenqual, f.
touch, Beiklang (¨e), m.
to touch, an-rühren; — on, berühren
touching, rührend
tough: — customer, gefährlicher
Bursche (-n, -n)
to tower, sich auf-türmen
town, Stadt (¨e), f.; small —,
Kleinstadt
tracery, Maßwerk, n.
tract, Traktat (-e), n. or m.
trader, Händler (-), m.
tradition, Tradition, f.
traditional, traditionell
traffic, Verkehr, m.; — jam, Ver-
kehrsstockung, f.
tragedy, Tragödie, f.
train, Zug (¨e), m.
trained, geschult
tranquil, ruhig
tranquillity, Ruhezustand (¨e), m.
transcending, erhaben über (A)
to transform, verwandeln
to translate, übersetzen
to transpose, um-stellen
travel: on her —s, auf ihren Reisen
to travel, *reisen; auf Reisen *gehen,
s.; — out, *heraus-reisen
traveller, der Reisende (see 29)
tread, Tritt (-e), m.
to treat, behandeln
tree, Baum (¨e), m.
tremendous, ungeheuer
trifle, Kleinigkeit, f.
to trim, stutzen
trip, Reise, f.; go on a — abroad,
eine Auslandsreise machen
triumph, Triumph (-e), m.
to triumph, triumphieren
triumphant, glorreich
triviality, Trivialität, f.
troops, Truppen, f. pl.
trotting, mittrottend

trouble, Mühe, *f.*; it costs —, es macht Mühe
troubled, unruhig
truck, Lastauto (-s), *n.*
true, richtig; wahr
truly, wirklich; wahrhaft
trunk, Reisekoffer (-), *m.*
to trust, vertrauen auf (A)
truth, Wahrheit, *f.*
to try, versuchen
turmoil, Wirbeln, *n.*
turn, Reihe, *f.*; be one's —, an der Reihe *sein; — about, abwechselnd
to turn, drehen, sich um-wenden, *irr.*; — away, (sich) ab-wenden; — into, (sich) verwandeln in (A); — off, ab-stellen; — one's back on, den Rücken zu-drehen (D); — one's hand to, in Angriff nehmen, *s.*; — out, hinaus-werfen, *s.*; — out of doors, vor die Tür setzen; — over (leaves), um-wenden, um-blättern
turquoise, Türkis (-e), *m.*; (colour), Türkis, *n.*
turquoise-blue, türkisblau
TV set, Fernsehapparat (-e), *m.*
tweed-suit, Tweedanzug (⸚e), *m.*
twin, geschwisterlich
typist: lady —, Stenotypistin (-nen), *f.*
tyrannicide, Tyrannenmörder (-), *m.*
to tyrannise over, tyrannisieren
tyranny, Tyrannei, *f.*
tyrant, Tyrann (-en, -en), *m.*

U
ultimate, letzt
umbrella, Regenschirm (-e), *m.*
unavoidable, unvermeidlich
unbearable, unerträglich
unbounded, unbeschränkt
uncertain, unsicher
uncertainty, Unsicherheit, *f.*
uncle, Onkel (-), *m.*
uncontrolled, unbeherrscht
uncritical, wahllos
underneath: from —, von unten her
to understand, verstehen, *s.*
understanding, Verständigung, *f.*
undertake, unternehmen, *s.*; (problem), in Angriff nehmen

undiscoverable, unauffindbar
to undress, sich aus-ziehen, *s.*
unearthly, überirdisch
uneducated, der keine Bildung genossen hat
unembarrassed, nicht verlegen
unemployment: — insurance, Arbeitslosenversicherung, *f.*
unexpected, unerwartet
unexpressed, unausgesprochen
unfinished, unvollendet
to unfold (a tale), erzählen
unforgiven, unvergeben
unfortunate, vom Unglück verfolgt
unfriendliness, Unfreundlichkeit *f.*
unfriendly, unfreundlich
unfruitful, fruchtlos
unhappy, unglücklich
unimportant, unwichtig
uninhabited, unbewohnt
uninterested, uninteressiert
unit, Einheit, *f.*
to unite, vereinigen
united, einheitlich
universal, allgemein, universell; — (love), allumfassend; — state, Universalstaat, *m.*
universally, allgemein
universe, Weltall, *n.*
university, Universität, *f.*; — teacher, Dozent (-en, -en), *m.*
unkindness, Unfreundlichkeit, *f.*
unlike, im Gegensatz zu
unlimited, unbeschränkt
unmusical, unmusikalisch
to unpack, aus-packen
unpatriotic, unpatriotisch
unpleasant, unangenehm
unpopularity, Unbeliebtheit, *f.*
unprecedented, beispiellos
unprepossessing, wenig anziehend
unreal, unwirklich
unregarded, unbeachtet
unruly, unbändig
unshakable, unerschütterlich
unsheltered, ungeschützt
unsubstantial, unwirklich
untidy, unordentlich
untold, see ages
untouched, unberührt
unusual, ungewöhnlich
unwell, nicht wohl
up, herauf; — and down, auf und ab; — to, bis zu

upright, aufrecht; sich aufrecht
haltend
upstream, stromaufwärts
up-to-date, zeitgemäß
upwards, nach oben
use, Gebrauch (⸚e), m.; — be little —
to, wenig von Nutzen *sein
to use, gebrauchen; (time), an-wen-
den, irr.; — as, benutzen als
useful, nützlich, brauchbar
useless, nutzlos
usual, üblich
usually, gewöhnlich

V

vague, vage, unbestimmt
vainly, umsonst
valley, Tal (⸚er), n.; up the —,
talaufwärts
value, Wert (-e), m.; set — on,
Wert legen auf (A)
vanity, Eitelkeit, f.
varied, abwechslungsreich; (of
hair), variiert
variety, Mannigfaltigkeit, f.
vast, ungeheuer, unermeßlich
vegetable-matter, Pflanzenstoffe,
m. pl.
to veil, verschleiern
venture: at a —, aufs Geratewohl
veranda, Verand-a (-en), f.
verge, Rand (⸚er), m.; (threshold),
Schwelle, f.
vertical, senkrecht
very, schon; genau; — greatest,
allergrößt
viands, Speisen, f. pl.
victim, Opfer (-), n.
victory, Sieg (-e), m.
view, Aussicht, f.; Ansicht, f.; with
a — to, mit der Absicht, zu
vigilance, Wachsamkeit, f.
vigilant, wachsam
vigorous, kerngesund
village, Dorf (⸚er), n.
vine, Weinstock (⸚e), m.
vineyard, Weinberg (-e), m.; Wein-
garten (⸚), m.
violent, heftig
violet, violett
virtue, Tugend, f.
virtuous, tugendhaft
visit, Besuch (-e), m.
to visit, besuchen
visitor, Besucher (-), m.

voice, Stimme, f.
to voice, äußern
voluntarily, freiwillig
vote, Stimme, f.
vowel, Vokal (-e), m.

W

wages, Lohn (⸚e), m.
to wait, warten; — on s.b., bedienen
to wake up, *auf-wachen; wecken, tr.
walk, Spaziergang (⸚e), m.
to walk, zu Fuß *gehen, s.; *laufen,
s.; — back, *zurück-laufen; —
beside, an etwas *entlang-gehen;
down, *hinunter-gehen, *entlang-gehen; — in, *hinein-gehen
wall, Mauer, f.; Felswand (⸚e), f.;
Bergwand, f.; — paper, Tapete, f.
to want, see 67(g); (= be lacking)
fehlen (D)
war, Krieg (-e), m.; at — with o.s.,
mit sich selbst auf dem Kriegsfuß;
at —, im Kriegszustand befindlich
warm(ly), warm
to warm, wärmen
to warn, warnen
warship, Kriegsschiff (-e), n.
to wash, (sich) waschen, s.; — out,
vergessen, s.
waste, Verschwendung, f.
to waste, verschwenden
wasteful, verschwenderisch
watch, Taschenuhr, f.
to watch, beobachten, zu-sehen, s.
(D); — over, bewachen
watchful, wachsam
watchmaker, Uhrmacher (-), m.
water, Wasser (-), n.
to water, tränken
watery, wässerig
wave, Welle, f.; — of disturbance,
Störungswelle, f.; — of light,
Lichtwelle, f.
way, Weg (-e), m. (= manner),
Art, f.; — back, Rückweg; —
out, Ausweg; the only —, die
einzige Art und Weise; only one
—, der einzige Weg; in any —,
auf irgendeine Weise; make
one's —, sich durch-schlagen, s.
weak, schwach
weakness, Schwäche, f.
weapon, Waffe, f.
to wear, tragen, s.

weariness, Müdigkeit, *f.*
weary, ermattet; (hours), mühsam
weather, Wetter, *n.*
to weather, aus-halten, *s.*
to weave, weben
weeds, Unkraut (–er), *n.*
week, Woche, *f.*
weekend, Wochenende (-n), *n.*
weekly, wöchentlich
to weep, weinen
weight: no —, nichts Wuchtiges
welcome, willkommen
to welcome, willkommen heißen, *s.*,
  begrüßen
well, Brunnen (-), *m.*
well, *see 84*; as — as, wie auch
well-behaved, wohlerzogen
well-lit, gut beleuchtet
western, westlich
wet, naß; (= raining), regnerisch
when, wann
where, wo
whereby, wobei
which, welcher
while, Weile, *f.*
whirl, Wirbel (-), *m.*
whiskey, Whisky, *m.*
white, weiß; — hot, weißglühend
white, Weiß, *n.*
whole, ganz; the — , das Ganze
  (*see 29*)
wholly, völlig
why, warum; that is —, deswegen
wide, breit
to widen, sich erweitern
widowed, verwitwet
widower, Witwer (-), *m.*
wife, Frau, *f.*
will, Wille (-ns), *m.*; free —,
  Willensfreiheit, *f.*
willing, bereit
willingly, gern
willingness, Bereitwilligkeit, *f.*
to win, gewinnen, *s.*; (victory), errin-
  gen, *s.*
wind, Wind (-e), *m.*; —shaken,
  windgerüttelt
window, Fenster (-), *n.*
wine, Wein (-e), *m.*
wing, Türflügel (-), *m.*; (theatre),
  Seitenkulisse, *f.*
winter, Winter (-), *m.*
wisdom, Weisheit, *f.*
wise, weise, klug
wish, Wunsch (–e), *m.*
to wish, wünschen; wollen (*see 67(g)*)

wisp of straw, Strohhalm (-e), *m.*
with (= by means of), mittels (G)
to withdraw, hinweg-nehmen, *s.*;
  (*intr.*), sich zurück-ziehen, *s.*
wobbly, wack(e)lig
woe, weh(e)
woman, Frau, *f.*
wonder, Wunder (-), *n.*
to wonder, überlegen; (= ask o.s.),
  sich fragen
wonderful, wundervoll
wood, Wald (–er), *m.*; Holz (–er), *n.*
wooded, bewaldet
woodwork, Holzwerk, *n.*
wool, Wolle, *f.*
word, Wort (-e & –er), *n.*
work, Arbeit, *f.*; Werk (-e), *n.*
to work, arbeiten; — out, aus-arbeiten
world, Welt, *f.*; not for the —, um
  alles in der Welt nicht; in the
  other —, im Jenseits, *n.*
worried, bekümmert
worse, schlimmer
to worsen, sich verschlechtern
worth, Wert (-e), *m.*; prove one's
  —, sich bewähren
worth, wert
worthless, wertlos
wound, Wunde, *f.*
to wound, verwunden
to wrap (round), ziehen, *s.* (um)
wrinkle, Fältchen (-), *n.*
to write, schreiben, *s.*
writer, Verfasser (-), *m.*; (author),
  Schriftsteller (-), *m.*
writing, Schrift, *f.*
be wrong, sich irren

y
yard, Schritt (-e), *m.*
year, Jahr (-e), *n.*
yellow, gelb
yesterday, gestern
yet, doch; jedoch; as —, bis dahin;
  and — (= at the same time),
  zugleich
young, jung
youth, junger Mann (–er *or* Leute);
  Jugend, *f.*

z
zest, Eifer (-), *m.*
to zigzag up, im Zickzack hinauf-
  führen

Index to Grammar and Syntax